Y0-ARW-759

HETERICK MEMORIAL LIBRARY
OHIO NORTHERN UNIVERSITY
ADA, OHIO 45810

KARL MARX
FREDERICK ENGELS

COLLECTED WORKS

VOLUME

49

KARL MARX
FREDERICK ENGELS

COLLECTED WORKS

INTERNATIONAL PUBLISHERS
NEW YORK

KARL MARX
FREDERICK ENGELS

Volume
49

ENGELS: 1890-92

INTERNATIONAL PUBLISHERS
NEW YORK

This volume has been prepared jointly by Lawrence & Wishart Ltd., London, International Publishers Co. Inc., New York, and Progress Publishing Group Corporation, Moscow, in collaboration with the Russian Independent Institute of Social and National Problems (former Institute of Marxism-Leninism), Moscow.

Editorial commissions:
GREAT BRITAIN: Eric Hobsbawm, John Hoffman, Nicholas Jacobs, Monty Johnstone, Jeff Skelley, Ernst Wangermann, Ben Fowkes.
USA: James E. Jackson, Victor Perlo, Betty Smith, Dirk J. Struik.
RUSSIA: for Progress Publishing Group Corporation— Yu. V. Semyonov, Ye. N. Vladimirova: for the Russian Independent Institute of Social and National Problems—L. I. Golman, M.P. Mchedlov, V. N. Pospelova, G. L. Smirnov.

Copyright © Progress Publishing Group Corporation, Moscow, 2001
© Lawrence & Wishart, London, 2001
© International Publishers, New York, 2001

All rights reserved. Apart from any fair dealing for the purpose of private study, research, criticism or review, no part of this publication may be reproduced, stored in a retrieval system, or transmitted, in any form or by any means, electronical, electrical, chemical, mechanical, optical, photocopying, recording or otherwise, without the prior permission of the copyright owner.

Library of Congress Cataloging in Publication Data

Marx, Karl, 1818-1883
    Karl Marx, Frederick Engels: collected works.
1. Socialism—Collected works. 2. Economics—
Collected works. I. Engels, Friedrich, 1820-1895.
Works. English. 1975. II. Title
HX 39.5. A 16 1975 335.4 73-84671
ISBN 0-7178-0549-2 (v. 49)

Printed in the USA

335.4
M39E
1975 -
v. 49

Contents

FREDERICK ENGELS
LETTERS

1890

APPENDICES

NOTES AND INDEXES

ILLUSTRATIONS

TRANSLATORS:

K. M. COOK: Letters 13, 20
PETER and BETTY ROSS: Letters 1-12, 14-17, 22, 24-28,
        30-33, 34-40, 42-51, 53-69, 71-80, 82-88, 90-103, 105-
        09, 111-16, 118, 121-23, 126-31, 133-35, 137, 139-41,
        143, 145, 146, 148, 150-52, 154, 156-58, 160-64, 167,
        168, 170-73, 175, 176, 178, 179, 181-83, 185-88, 191-
        95, 197, 198, 200-04, 206, 208-17, 219, 220, 222, 223,
        225-34, 236, 238, 239, 240-45, 247-55, 257-63, 265-69,
        271-76
VICTOR SCHNITTKE: Letter 177
BARRY SELMAN: Letter 205

Wir deutschen Sozialisten sind stolz darauf, abzustammen nicht nur von Saint-Simon, Owen und Fourier, sondern auch von Kant, Fichte und Hegel. Die deutsche Arbeiterbewegung ist die Erbin der deutschen klassischen Philosophie.

London 4. Januar 1891.

Friedrich Engels

Preface

Volume 49 of the *Collected Works* of Karl Marx and Frederick Engels contains Engels' letters from August 1890 to September 1892.

As is clear from a number of events, including the May Day demonstrations that swept over nearly the whole of Europe, the successes of the German Social-Democrats in the elections to the Reichstag and the repeal of the Anti-Socialist Law, and the foundation of new trades unions in England, the working-class and socialist movement gained considerable ground in these years. The letters in this volume give a vivid picture of the still unflagging scholarly and political activity of Engels, seventy years of age on 28 November 1890, during this period. They reflect the many problems facing the working-class movement in the early 1890s after the foundation and consolidation of the socialist parties and the formation of a new international association, the Second International. They also reflect the complications facing the spread and confirmation of Marxist ideas.

Of particular importance during the 1890s were the propagation of Marxism, the explanation of its fundamental theoretical propositions, and the safeguarding of those propositions from oversimplification and contemporary misinterpretation.

Engels gave much of his time to preparing new editions for the press and editing translations of Marx's works and of his own writings, including those that had become virtually unobtainable by that time. Engels bore in mind the theoretical significance and potential import of the work being republished and, in editing the translations, the peculiarities of the respective country. All these publications were brought out with his direct participation: he worked on the texts, wrote notes when necessary and read the proofs. As a rule, Engels wrote special introductions for them which were, in effect small-scale studies in their own right. The editions prepared by Engels influenced the views and practical activities of the Marxists and the development of the working-class parties.

During these years, Engels still regarded it as his 'urgent duty' (see this volume, p. 396) to prepare for publication Marx's economic manuscripts, above all those comprising Volume III of *Capital* (see pp. 329, 331, 334, 379, 385, 390, 440, 450, etc.). Because of the many tasks in hand and his state of health, however, Engels was not able to begin this work until November 1891. He wrote to Karl Kautsky on 3 December 1891: 'I have just got to the most difficult part, i. e. the last chapters (six to eight or thereabouts) on money capital, banks, credit, etc., and, once having started, I shall have to keep at it without a break and work through the relevant literature again, in short make myself completely *au fait*, if only so that I may — as is probable — eventually leave most of it as it stands, yet at the same time feel quite sure that I have committed no blunders either in the positive or the negative sense' (pp. 314-15). At the beginning of 1892, he was again compelled to break off work on Volume III and was not able to resume it until September.

Of considerable interest are Engels' letters dealing with theoretical problems and the development and deepening of certain propositions of Marxist theory that had become particularly important in the early 1890s. As the ideas of Marx and Engels spread further, they were taken up by representatives of the most diverse ideological trends. Many propositions of the theory were being digested by the members of the working-class movement in a one-sided and oversimplified manner as various slogans, and were sometimes grossly distorted. Certain members of the socialist movement, as Engels noted in his letter to Conrad Schmidt of 12 April 1890, tended to impose their own personal conjectures on the works of Marx and Engels instead of reading what they actually contained (see present edition, Vol. 48).

Particularly widespread in the early 1890s was a perverse interpretation of the materialist understanding of history in the spirit of 'economic materialism', according to which economics was the sole active factor in the historical process. These views were especially typical of a number of young socialists in Germany. Some of them asked Engels directly to explain certain points about the materialist interpretation of history.

In this respect, Engels' famous letters to Conrad Schmidt of 5 August and 27 October and to Joseph Bloch of 21-22 September 1890 deserve attention. They give not only a compressed exposition of the Marxist analysis of the historical process, but take an important step forward in elaborating certain vital problems of the materialist interpretation of history (see also Engels' letters to Paul Ernst of 5 June 1890, to Franz Mehring of 14 July 1893, and to W. Borgius of 25 January 1894 — present edition, vols 48 and 50).

In his letters to Schmidt and Bloch, Engels examines the interaction of basis and superstructure, economics and politics, the dialectics of the objective and the subjective factors of social development, and the role of the conscious activity of the masses. In his letter to Schmidt of 5 August 1890, Engels used the term 'historical materialism' for the first time (p. 8). In doing so, he wanted to indicate that the economic factor, definitive in the final analysis, is itself subject to feedback from the superstructure (pp. 34-35 and 59-63).

Worried about the prospects for revolution and the nature of the future society, many socialists turned to Engels for clarification. Engels considered that the level of socio-economic development in the main European capitalist countries was creating the conditions for revolutionary transformations in the relatively near future. Consciously avoiding detailed predictions about the future society, he confined himself to the most general terms.

In his letters to Conrad Schmidt of 5 August and 1 July 1890, Otto Boenigk of 21 August 1890, and Max Oppenheim of 24 March 1891, Engels expressed himself decisively against the idea of the communist society as something 'fixed for all time' (p. 8) and emphasised that, like any other social structure, the new society would not arise straightaway, but only by a process of gradual formation; it would develop uninterruptedly by 'constant change and transformation' (p. 18). He described the decisive feature of the new society as 'the organisation of production on the basis of common ownership, initially by the nation, of all means of production' (ibid.). In his letter to Otto Boenigk, he expressed the idea of the definite sequence of transformation of private property into public, and marked out ways for the transformation of agriculture on collective principles (pp. 18-19). An important condition for the organisation of life in the new society was the attraction of specialists in engineering, agriculture, medicine and also lawyers, teachers, etc. (pp. 19, 272).

In his letter to Schmidt of 5 August 1890, Engels gave his view on distribution in communist society. The 'method of distribution depends almost entirely upon *how much* there is to distribute ... since this is likely to change as advances are made in production and social organisation' (p. 8).

At the same time, Engels repeatedly stressed the impossibility of determining in full detail how precisely the communist transformation of society was going to develop. This 'must depend on local conditions at the time, nor can anything of a general nature be said about them beforehand,' he wrote to Max Oppenheim on 24 March 1891 (p. 153). The problem of stages in the development of the communist society and the specific measures which the workers must take when they have taken over state power is 'the most difficult subject on earth' (p. 212).

The letters in this volume show the many-sidedness of Engels' activity in co-ordinating the international working-class and socialist movement. Correspondence was an important source of information for him about the state of the working-class movement in various countries, and it was also his principal means of passing on revolutionary experience and of exerting an ideological influence on the activities of the members of the socialist parties and organisations.

The organisation of the working-class movement, the efforts of the socialist parties to consolidate their ranks and opposition to dogmatism and sectarian trends have an important place in Engels' letters. Since they were not intended for publication, his assessments of reformist and 'left-wing' sectarian elements in the working-class movement were often very harsh. He emphasised that the 'class-conscious continental proletariat has no intention of placing itself under the leadership of people who regard the wage system as an eternal and immutable universal institution' (p. 524). On the other hand, those who, 'more or less, have the correct theory *as to the dogmatic side of it*, become a mere sect because they cannot conceive that living theory of action, of working with the working class at every possible stage of its development, otherwise than as a collection of dogmas to be learnt by

heart and recited like a conjurer's formula or a Catholic prayer'
(p. 186). Advocating independence from the bourgeois influences of
the class policy of the workers' parties and considering that unity of
views and party discipline should be based on the high awareness and
activity of its members and on the participation of each one in working
out party policy and tactics, Engels nevertheless admitted: 'That
...doesn't preclude our failure to agree on many points. But these
again are points where in course of time agreement is automatically
reached as a result of discussion or of new events' (p. 158). Engels
considered the development of broad party democracy and the free
exchange of opinions as an indispensable condition, with the reminder that 'discipline in a big party cannot be anything like as strict as it
is in a small sect' (p. 182), but that the criticism must be made within
the framework of the programme and with the strict observance of
party ethics. Engels drew attention to the inalienable right of the rank-
and-file members to influence the activity of their leaders and prevent them from breaking away from the grass roots of the party. In
his letter to Karl Kautsky on 11 February 1891 Engels wrote: 'It is
also imperative that the chaps should at long last throw off the habit
of handling the party officials — their servants — with kid gloves and
kow-towing to them as infallible bureaucrats, instead of confronting
them critically' (p. 131).

It can be seen from the letters how much Engels did to widen and
strengthen international ties, including personal contacts between socialists of various countries, to arrange for the exchange of information between the socialist parties about their activities and to encour-
age co-operation in the press. Engels considered it highly important
for the information to be comprehensive and fully objective.

From Engels' letters, and also from those of Eleanor Marx-Aveling
printed in the Appendices to this volume, it is clear that he himself
initiated a number of international meetings between the socialists.
He used his seventieth birthday celebrations for the organisation of
a meeting of socialists from the leading European countries and for
the discussion of problems in common (see pp. 76-77). It was also at
Engels' suggestion that an international conference of socialists was
held during the Congress of German Social-Democrats at Halle in
the autumn of 1890 to prepare the Congress of the Second International in Brussels in 1891 (see pp. 24, 29 and 42).

Engels devoted much attention to the recently formed new international socialist association — the Second International. The letters

published in the present volume make it possible to reconstruct the
entire course of preparations for the Second and Third congresses of
the Second International and Engels' own part in their convocation.
He endeavoured to widen as much as possible the number of the congresses' participants, especially such mass working-class organisations
as the British trades unions (pp. 24, 28, 29, 42-43, 46, 74, 229, 238,
520-21, 523-24, 533-34, 545-46, 548).

A number of letters contain fundamental ideas on the stand the socialists took because of the threat, intensified in the early 1890s, of an
all-European war. Engels continued developing the idea, expressed
many times in the preceding years, of the profound interest of the
working class in the preservation of peace, stressing this as one of the
most important conditions for the future success of the workers' movement. From his letters to Sorge, Bebel and others, it is clear that the
rapidly growing influence of Social-Democracy, especially in Germany, had given him hope that the proletariat might gain political
power in that country in a relatively short historical period. Engels
wrote to Bebel on 24-26 October 1891: 'I ... hope and pray that this
splendid, unerring progress of ours, evolving with the impassivity and
inexorability of a natural process, will continue along its appointed
course' (p. 272).

Should war break out (at that time, this meant the possibility of
France, in alliance with Tsarist Russia, waging war on Germany),
the socialist parties should proceed from the interests of the workers'
struggle for emancipation. But since a victory by Russian Tsarism in
such a war would mean not only a threat to Germany's national unity, but the total destruction of German Social-Democracy, at that
time the vanguard of the European working-class movement, Engels
considered that the German socialists must endeavour to fight the
war by 'revolutionary means' (p. 271). These ideas of Engels were
stated in great detail in his letters to Bebel and Sorge (pp. 242-46,
258, 266-67, 270-72, 327) and were finally formulated in his article
'Socialism in Germany' (present edition, Vol. 27).

Of particular importance in Engels' correspondence during these,
as in the preceding years, are the letters to the leaders of German Social-Democrats—August Bebel, Wilhelm Liebknecht, Karl Kautsky,
Franz Mehring and others. Many problems associated with the German working-class movement were also reflected in Engels' letters to

other active members of the international working-class movement, particularly to Friedrich Adolph Sorge and to Paul and Laura Lafargue.

The early 1890s in the German working-class movement were conspicuous for many important events associated above all with the repeal of the Anti-Socialist Law. The party, which at that time was 'the paramount party in Europe' (p. 47), now had considerably wider scope for all its activities. It was now essential for its tactics and organisation to be changed and for a new programme to be drawn up. Engels followed very closely the sharp struggle that developed in the party in the summer of 1890 during preparations for the Halle Congress. Much of his correspondence is concerned with the opposition group of the Jungen (Young Ones), which attacked legal forms of struggle, deplored the parliamentary activities of the party and, exploiting the opportunist blunders of some leaders, demagogically accused the entire leadership of renouncing its revolutionary goals, violating party democracy, and of corruption. The Jungen harshly criticised the draft of the new Party Rules, published at the beginning of August 1890.

Engels supported the Marxist section of the party leadership, although this did not prevent him, in a number of letters, from talking about the validity of certain criticisms directed at it.

He considered, not without justification, that the pseudo-revolutionary jargon of the Jungen could easily influence those party members who did not yet have sufficient theoretical training and experience of practical struggle, and find in them definite support. 'Herein lies a danger which should not be underestimated,' he warned Wilhelm Liebknecht (p. 14). At the same time, in his letters to the leaders of German Social-Democracy, Engels cautioned them against hasty organisational measures against the Jungen, advising flexibility in the controversy with them and tolerance about the different opinions within the party. He wrote to Liebknecht on 10 August 1890: 'Do not make martyrs unnecessarily, show that there is freedom of criticism, and *if* you have to throw anyone out, do so in cases where the *facts* — overt acts of turpitude and betrayal — are quite blatant and completely demonstrable!' (pp. 14-17).

Particularly interesting and valuable for an understanding of Engels' attitude to the Jungen are his letters to Friedrich Adolph Sorge, in which he gave a frank assessment of the party leadership, noting in particular the excessive harshness and irritation which Bebel and

Liebknecht permitted themselves in the struggle with the opposition. 'The biggest party in the empire,' Engels wrote to Sorge on 9 August 1890, 'cannot remain in existence unless every shade of opinion is allowed complete freedom of expression, while even the *semblance* of dictatorship ... must be avoided...' (p. 11).

Engels did a great deal to help the leaders of the German Social-Democrats in their restructuring of the organisation after the repeal of the Anti-Socialist Law. He analysed the completely new conditions that had come into being and under which the party must act in future. In his letter to Liebknecht of 10 August 1890, he critically examined the draft Party Rules, which had to be discussed at the next congress, and noted the points violating, in his opinion, democratic principles. He considered it most unacceptable that, according to the draft, the Social-Democratic group of the Reichstag was virtually being placed over the Party Executive elected by the Congress. Engels also criticised the points on the election to the Congress of an equal number of representatives from all the electoral districts irrespective of the number of party members in them, and also the allocation to the Executive of more responsible functions than those carried out by the Congress (p. 14). In the Rules' final version, as accepted by the Halle Congress, these points were removed.

Many of Engels' letters are concerned with preparations for the party congress in Erfurt, which accepted a new programme of the German Social-Democratic Party. Much attention is given in them to the publication, early in 1891, of Marx's *Critique of the Gotha Programme* written back in 1875 (see present edition, Vol. 24). With this publication, Engels endeavoured not to allow a repetition in the new programme of the erroneous propositions of the Gotha Programme and to inflict a blow on the Lassalle cult, widespread amongst the German Social-Democrats. '...It was *my duty* to publish the thing the moment the programme came up for discussion,' he wrote to Kautsky (p. 134). His letters to Kautsky of 7 and 15 January, 3, 11 and 23 February 1891, to Bebel of 1-2 May 1891, to Paul and Laura Lafargue of 1-2 May 1891, and to Sorge of 24 October 1891, show what a principled significance Engels attributed to the publication of this document, and with what patience and tact Engels prevailed over the opposition of certain party leaders to the publication of Marx's critical comments.

Engels had faith in the ideological strength and maturity of the party itself. 'And I knew that the party was amply strong enough to stand it and I reckoned that today it would even *tolerate* the forth-right language used 15 years ago,' wrote Engels to Kautsky on 23 February 1891 (p. 133). In the same letter, he gave a general apprecia-tion of the personality and activities of Ferdinand Lassalle, stressing the duality of his role in the German working-class movement (pp. 134-35).

That the publication of *Critique of the Gotha Programme* had been well timed was confirmed when, in the summer of 1891, the Opportunists, represented by Vollmar, leader of the Bavarian party organisation, spoke out on pragmatic grounds for co-operation with the Junker-bourgeois monarchist state. Observing with satisfaction Vollmar's defeat at the Erfurt Congress (pp. 266, 273, 282), Engels gave Bebel practical advice on the tactics in the struggle with opportunism (p. 480).

In Engels' letters, mainly those to Paul and Laura Lafargue, much space is given to the problems of the working-class movement in France. Analysing France's internal situation, he noted the increas-ing political reaction, the existence of revanchist moods and the deepening of a political crisis.

Observing the growth of political activity among the French work-ers, the struggle for the right to strike and the development of the trade union movement, Engels repeatedly spoke of the need for unity of action in the Workers' Party and other socialist groups and the winning of the broad working masses over to its own side. He considered that the main task of the French socialists was to overcome the split in the country's working-class movement. Unity, however, must be achieved by meticulous daily work. Observing, on the one hand, the strengthening of the Workers' Party and, on the other, the crisis of the Possibilists, who had split into two factions in the autumn of 1890, Engels warned against the forcing of events, drawing an analo-gy with the unification of the two trends in the German working-class movement in 1875 (p. 97). He thought that the tactics of the French Workers' Party should be the conclusion of an agreement on practical co-operation with other socialist groups and the rejection of any attempt at unification at that time (p. 117).

Engels attributed great importance to the parliamentary activities of the French socialists. He paid special attention to the election cam-paign in the autumn of 1891. Informing Bebel that Lafargue had been elected at the second ballot to the Chamber of Deputies, he wrote that it would have a considerable influence on France, since 'on this occasion literally *all* the socialist parliamentary groups, including the Possibilists ... pulled together' (p. 291). He looked with great hope on the prospects for the development of the socialist movement in France and stated with satisfaction that the Workers' Party was not 'a riotous force liable to act on the spur of the moment, but ... a regular, organised, *political* force' (p. 424).

The letters in this volume show how Engels, as a witness of the development of the working-class and socialist movement in Great Britain, noted entirely new factors in this process. He took a keen interest in the spectacular rise of the working-class movement during those years — the appearance of new trades unions, the impressive May Day demonstrations in 1890 and 1891, and the successful strikes testifying to the entry into the struggle of new and, until recently, oppressed and disorganised strata of the proletariat.

With great sympathy, Engels followed the struggle of the new trades unions, with many of whose leaders — William Thorne, Benjamin Tillet, John Burns, Tom Mann and others — he kept in personal contact. He welcomed the results of the Liverpool Trades Union Congress of 1890, at which, for the first time, the representatives of the new trades unions achieved the passing of a resolution on the struggle for the legal eight-hour working day. He considered that 'with its acceptance came the collapse of the empire of the old, conservative labour movement...' (p. 26), which had previously been opposing any kind of state regulation of relations between workers and capitalists.

Engels' letters also contain a description of the British socialist organisations. He thought that, in spite of definite progress, they were still 'far removed from the genuine English movement' (p. 167). The sectarianism of the Social Democratic Federation was revealed, he thought, by the fact that, although its platform was in the main theoretically right, it did not take the real demands of the people into consideration (ibid.). 'It has ossified Marxism into a hard and fast dogma and, by repudiating *any* labour movement that isn't orthodox Marxist (and, what's more, Marxist in a very wrong-headed way) ... has put itself in such a position that it can never become anything other than a sect' (pp. 493-94).

At the same time, Engels noted that the participants of the new trades union movement, members of the Social Democratic Federation among them, showed interest in socialism (p. 167).

Engels wrote with satisfaction that Edward Aveling and Eleanor Marx-Aveling had authority in the left wing of the Social Democratic Federation and among the members of the new trades unions (ibid.). Particularly creditable, he thought, was their organisation of the May Day demonstrations carried out under the leadership of the Legal Eight Hours and Internationl Labour League, which was formed in the summer of 1890 out of the Central Committee for the preparations for the May Day demonstration of 1890 and played a considerable part in the socialist propaganda and formation of the Independent Labour Party in 1893. Describing, in a letter to Laura Lafargue, the May Day demonstration of 1891, Engels stressed that 'it has been almost exclusively Edward's and Tussy's work and they had to fight it through from beginning to end' (p. 185).

Some of Engels' letters contain his evaluation of another socialist organisation, the Fabian Society, which represented the democratic intellectuals and part of the workers. He disapproved of the Fabian thesis on the transition from capitalism to socialism through the education of the working class (p. 75). He criticised the Fabian Society because 'it preached and practised *the affiliation of the workers to the Liberals*' (p. 515). The grounds for this criticism were, in part, a letter from George Bernard Shaw to Bebel of 29 May 1892, which the latter forwarded to Engels. Outlining the pre-election tactics of the Fabians, Shaw wrote: '...Our only chance where the workers are not completely organized is to force the Liberals to accept our men as their party candidates' (see p. 563). Engels wrote about this to Kautsky: 'As regards our tactics we have one firm rule for all modern countries and for all times and that is to prevail upon the workers to form their own independent party in opposition to all bourgeois parties' (p. 515).

In a number of letters, Engels reacted to the problems of the working-class movement in the USA. His chief correspondents during those years were Sorge and Schlüter. The latter, having emigrated to the USA in 1889, ran the *New Yorker Volkszeiting*, a German-language newspaper of the Socialist Labor Party. It was from their letters that Engels drew much of his information about the condition of the working-class movement.

Engels could see the complexity and contradictoriness of the working-class and socialist movement in the USA. On the one hand, a fairly powerful trade union movement represented by the American Federation of Labor, an organisation of the skilled workers, mainly native-born Americans; on the other hand, contingents of immigrant workers, some of whom were outside the ranks of the organised working-class movement. The largest of these contingents consisted of emigrants from Germany who had brought their own traditions to the American working-class movement and were the core of the Socialist Labor Party. Its isolation in the working-class movement and its consequent failure to become a mass party resulted from its underestimation of work in the mass organisations, especially those representing the trades, and from its lack of contact with the native-born American and the Black working men who were beginning to join in the struggle.

Engels did not approve of the standpoint taken by the Socialist Labor Party at the end of 1890 and the beginning of 1891, when its leaders refused to work in the biggest American workers' organisation, the American Federation of Labor, rejecting the terms, as proposed by Gompers, for entry to the organisation in individual order. In his letter to Schlüter of 29 January 1891, Engels put the question directly: 'Where do you propose to find a recruiting-ground if not amongst the trades unions?' (p. 114).

In answer to Sorge on 24 October 1891, Engels agreed with him that an 'ebb-tide had begun' in the working-class movement in the USA, considering this to be a characteristic sign of the movement, which was developing spasmodically. He thought that one of the causes of such ebbs was that 'the standard of living of the native American working-man is notably higher even than that of his English counterpart and this alone is enough to put him out of the running for some time to come' (p. 265).

At the same time, Engels hoped that 'when the time comes over there, things will move with tremendous speed and dynamism, but that may not be for some while yet. Miracles never happen' (ibid.).

In the early 1890s, Engels continued to take a lively interest in the state of affairs in Russia. He kept in personal contact with young Russian Marxists, revolutionary Narodniks (Populists) and progressive scholars. His main Russian correspondent during those years was the economist Nikolai Danielson, the translator of Marx's *Capital* into Russian. Danielson's letters, devoted chiefly to economic problems and the position of the Russian peasantry, like the Russian books which he sent regularly, were an important source of information for Engels about the situation in the country and about the views of the Narodnik-oriented section of the Russian intelligentsia, who still had hopes of the non-capitalist way of development for Russia. Engels disputed these views in his replies, stating and substantiating his own viewpoint on Russia's present and on its immediate future.

As is very clear from these letters, Engels was definitively convinced that Russia had decisively taken the road of capitalist development, and that the peasant commune, despite of isolated indications of its relative vitality, was unable 'to resist the incessant blows dealt to it ... by rampant capitalism' (p. 443). This idea was expressed with precision in his letter of 15 March 1892. Recalling what Marx had said at the end of the 1870s to the effect that the development of capitalism in Russia would inevitably lead the peasant commune to its destruction, Engels wrote: 'That seems to me to be in course of fulfilment just now.... I am afraid we shall have to treat the община [commune] as a dream of the past, and reckon, in future, with a capitalist Russia' (p. 384). Objecting to Danielson, who affirmed that capitalism in Russia was developing artificially, and solely because of the government's protectionist policy, Engels proved the historical inevitability of capitalist production in Russia with all its consequences. He wrote on 22 September 1892: '...If Russia required after the Crimean war a *grande industrie* of her own, she could have it in one form only: the *capitalistic form*' (p. 536). Engels also convinced his correspondent that whatever might or might not be the forms of this process, its essence and the contradictions inherent in it were, on the whole, the same as those in other countries.

In connection with the terrible famine that swept Russia in 1891 and which, Engels supposed, could lead to an acute internal political crisis, he analysed, in a letter to Bebel of 29 September-1 October 1891, the correlation of the class forces in the country that were capable of taking charge of a coup. 'In Russia three classes suffer — the landowning aristocracy, the peasantry, the emergent proletariat. The latter is still, and the first is already, too weak for revolution, while all the peasantry could achieve would be local insurrections which would be fruitless unless given the necessary cohesion and moral support by a successful insurrection in urban centres,' i. e. unless the workers were strong enough to play the leading role in overthrowing the autocracy. The bourgeoisie, which owed its position exclusively to the state, would hardly be able to head the struggle against Tsarism, although objectively it was the bourgeoisie alone that could assume power in the event of a coup (p. 243).

*　*　*

Volume 49 contains 276 letters by Engels, of which 173 are published in English for the first time, and 103 were published in this language earlier, 40 of them in part only. The details of the earlier English publications are given in the notes.

Obvious slips of the pen have been silently corrected. Proper and place names, and separate words abbreviated by the author are given in full. Defects in the manuscript are indicated in the footnotes, while passages of lost or illegible texts are indicated by omission points. Where restoration seems possible, it is given in square brackets. Passages deleted by the author are reproduced in footnotes only where they substantially affect the meaning.

Foreign words and expressions are retained in the form in which they were used by the author with a translation where necessary in the footnotes, and are italicised (if underlined by the author, they are given in spaced italics). English words and expressions used by Engels in text written in German and French are printed in small caps. Longer passages written in English in the original are placed in asterisks.

The number of notes relating to the same facts and events given in the texts of different letters, are duplicated.

The texts of the letters and notes were prepared by Alexander Vatutin (letters from August 1890 to October 1891) and by Yuri Vasin (letters from November 1891 to September 1892). The preface was written by Alexander Vatutin and Yuri Vasin. The volume was edited by Boris Tartakovsky. The name index and the indexes of quoted and mentioned literature and periodicals were prepared by Alexander Panfilov (Russian Independent Institute of Social and National Problems).

The translations were made by Peter and Betty Ross, Barry Selman (Lawrence & Wishart), K. M. Cook, Victor Schnittke (Progress Publishing Group Corporation) and edited by Nicholas Jacobs (Lawrence & Wishart), Yelena Kalinina and Natalia Karmanova (Progress Publishing Group Corporation) and Norire Ter-Akopyan (Russian Academy of Sciences).

The volume was prepared for the press by the editors Yelena Kalinina and Margarita Lopukhina (Progress Publishing Group Corporation).

FREDERICK ENGELS

LETTERS

August 1890-September 1892

1890

1

ENGELS TO WILHELM LIEBKNECHT [1]

IN LEIPZIG

[London, 1 August 1890]

Dear Liebknecht,

Unfortunately I shan't be able to remain here until 15 August —
we are probably going to the seaside at the end of next week; I shall
write and let you know where as soon as this has been settled to the
satisfaction of all concerned. Your statement has appeared in *The
People's Press*,[a] but it won't put a stop to the sniping in *Justice*.[2] Those
chaps are incorrigible; they want to force you people and myself to
knuckle under to them and the Possibilists,[3] but in that case they
have a long wait ahead of them. They now possess an ally in the great
Gilles — congratulations!

Your
F. E.

First published in: Marx and Engels,
Works, First Russian Edition, Vol.
XXVIII, Moscow, 1940

Printed according to the original

Published in English for the first
time

---

[a] W. Liebknecht, 'To the Editor of *The People's Press*', *The People's Press*, No. 22,
2 August 1890.

2

ENGELS TO JOHANN HEINRICH WILHELM DIETZ

IN STUTTGART

London, 5 August 1890

Dear Mr Dietz,

Fischer has raised further objections to the *immediate* re-issue of the *Origin*.[a] *Au fond*[b] this is quite acceptable to me, since I still have to go to the seaside where there can be no question of work, nor do I yet find work in any way conducive to my well-being. So I shall wait until the whole business has been settled to the satisfaction of all concerned.

Will you kindly take a look at the enclosed note for K. Kautsky[c] before sending it on and, if necessary, do what is required.

Kindest regards.

Yours,
F. E.

First published in: Marx and Engels, *Works*, First Russian Edition, Vol. XXVIII, Moscow, 1940

Printed according to the original

Published in English for the first time

---

[a] F. Engels, *The Origin of the Family, Private Property and the State*. - [b] Lit.: at bottom - [c] See next letter.

3

ENGELS TO KARL KAUTSKY

IN STUTTGART

London, 5 August 1890

Dear Kautsky,

.   Your letter of 3 July lay here neglected while Schorlemmer and I were away gallivanting in Norway — much to the benefit of our health, be it said.

Since I don't know where to write to, I am sending this to Dietz without sealing it, so that the prospectus for the *Neue Zeit*,[4] which Ede [a] showed me on Sunday,[b] can be altered accordingly, should it be thought desirable.

You may promise yourself an article by me entitled *Von den letzten Dingen* and I in turn promise that you shall have it. I also intend to keep my promise — indeed I have partially done so already, since a good half of the article is finished. As to when it will be completely finished, however, that could be either very soon or not for a long time to come, depending on circumstances — let's say in time for the first of next year's issues.[5]

If Bebel's review of the week is as well done as his articles to date in Victor's [c] *Arbeiter-Zeitung*, you may certainly congratulate yourselves. Here, of course, I am thinking first and foremost of *Germany*.

Sorge's address is: F. A. Sorge, Hoboken, N. J. (i. e. New Jersey), U. S. America. He's the best man for you people. I shall also write to him about it.[d] Obviously you must pay him *exceptionally well* — otherwise he'd prefer to give music lessons. He is also unlikely to submit *regular* reports and indeed it is better that he should not. Sometimes months may go by without anything of real importance happening, sometimes he may send you a crucial piece of news every week.

During our voyage of discovery we pressed on as far as North Cape where we ate COD caught by ourselves. For five days on end there was no night, or rather only dusk; to make up for it we saw all kinds of Laplanders, funny little chaps, obviously of very mixed RACE, with brown, black or even very fair hair — features Mongoloid on the

---

[a] Eduard Bernstein - [b] 3 August - [c] Victor Adler - [d] See this volume, p. 20.

whole but with variations ranging from the American Indian (except that it would take six of them to make one Indian) to the Teuton. These little chaps, who are still three-quarters in the Stone Age, are most interesting.

Many regards.

Your

F. E.

First published in *Aus der Frühzeit des Marxismus. Engels Briefwechsel mit Kautsky*, Prag, 1935

Printed according to the original

Published in English for the first time

4

ENGELS TO CONRAD SCHMIDT [6]

IN BERLIN

London, 5 August 1890

Dear Schmidt,

Your letter travelled with me in my pocket up to North Cape and in and out of half a dozen Norwegian fjords; I had intended to answer it during the journey, but the writing facilities aboard the ship in which Schorlemmer and I made the whole trip were too frightful. So I am making up for it now.

Many thanks for the news about your doings which are always of great interest to me. You should really try and do the article on Knapp,[a] the subject being one of such importance. What we are concerned with is the destruction of Prussian tradition in one of its strongholds and with showing up the old braggadocio for the humbug it really is.[7]

Summarising the English Blue Books[8] for the 'archives'[b] could hardly be done by anyone not resident in London and therefore not *himself* in a position to assess the theoretical or practical importance

---

[a] The reference is to G. F. Knapp, *Die Bauern-Befreiung und der Ursprung der Landarbeiter in den älteren Theilen Preußens*. - [b] *Archiv für soziale Gesetzgebung und Statistik*

of the various publications. The number of parliamentary publications is so great as to require a separate monthly catalogue — and thus you might find yourself in the position of having to search for a needle in a haystack, only to lay your hands on an occasional pin. If, however, you would nevertheless care to do some work in this field from time to time — as a rule it's a terrible sweat if one wants to produce anything worthwhile — I shall be glad to let you have any information you may require. If, incidentally, Braun wants a regular man for it, he could do no better than to ask E. Bernstein, 4 Corinne Road, Tufnell Park, N. For it so happens that Ede Bernstein *wishes* to study conditions in England as soon as he can get away from the *Sozialdemokrat* and so this would suit him very well. But he leaves for a few weeks at the seaside either today or tomorrow, so I shall not be able to put the matter to him, it having only just occurred to me.

I saw a notice of Paul Barth's book [a] in the Vienna *Deutsche Worte* written by that bird of ill-omen Moritz Wirth [b] and *this* review made an unfavourable impression on me which also extended to the book itself. I shall take a look at it, but if little Moritz is right when he quotes Barth as saying that, in all Marx's writings, he can find only one example of the dependence of philosophy, etc., upon the material conditions of existence and that Descartes declares animals to be machines, I can only say I feel sorry for a man capable of writing such things. And if that man has not yet found out that, if the material mode of existence is the *primum agens*, [c] this does not preclude the ideal fields from in turn exerting a reciprocal but secondary influence upon it, then he cannot possibly have understood the subject he is writing about. But as I have said, this is all at second hand and little Moritz is a friend one can well do without. Nor, today, has the materialist view of history any lack of such friends to whom it serves as a pretext for *not* studying history. As Marx said of the French Marxists in the late seventies: '*Tout ce que je sais, c'est que je ne suis pas Marxiste.*' [d9]

There has also been a discussion in the *Volks-Tribüne* [e] about the distribution of products in the society of the future — whether this should be made in accordance with the amount of work performed or in some other way. [10] A very 'materialist' view was taken of the matter, in opposition to certain idealist jargon about justice. But oddly

---

[a] P. Barth, *Die Geschichtsphilosophie Hegel's und der Hegelianer bis auf Marx und Hartmann. Ein kritischer Versuch.* - [b] M. Wirth, 'Hegelunfug und Hegelaustreibung im modernen Deutschland', *Deutsche Worte*, No. 5, 1890. - [c] prime mover - [d] 'All I know is that I'm not a Marxist.' - [e] *Berliner Volks-Tribüne*

enough it occurred to no one that the method of distribution depends almost entirely upon *how much* there is to distribute and that, since this is likely to change as advances are made in production and social organisation, similar changes might also take place in the method of distribution. But in every case the participants in the debate saw 'socialist society', not as something that is constantly changing and progressing, but as something stable and fixed for all time and which must therefore also have a method of distribution that is fixed for all time. Yet surely, if one is to be rational, all one can do is 1. discover what method of distribution should be used *to start off with*, 2. find *what the general trend* of future developments is likely to be. But not a word of that have I found in the whole of the debate.

In general the word 'materialist' is used by many of the younger writers in Germany as a mere cliché with which to label anything and everything without bothering to study it any further; in other words, having once attached the label, they imagine they have sorted things out. Our view of history, however, is first and foremost a guide to study, not a tool for constructing objects after the Hegelian model. The whole of history must be studied anew, and the existential conditions of the various social formations individually investigated before an attempt is made to deduce therefrom the political, legal, aesthetic, philosophical, religious, etc., standpoints that correspond to them. Little has been done along these lines hitherto because very few people have seriously set their minds to it. Here we could do with any amount of help; it is a truly immense field and anyone who is prepared to apply himself to it seriously could achieve much and make a name for himself. Instead, the only use to which the cliché (*anything* can be turned into a cliché) of historical materialism has been put by all too many younger Germans is hastily to run up a jerry-built system out of their own relatively inadequate historical knowledge — for economic history is as yet in its infancy — thus becoming great prodigies in their own eyes. And then a Barth can come along and attack the thing itself which has, of course, been debased to a mere cliché in his own milieu.

However, all this will presumably sort itself out. We are now strong enough in Germany to withstand a great deal. One of the great services the Anti-Socialist Law [11] has done us is to rid us of the importunities of German academics of vaguely socialist complexion. We are now strong enough to be able to digest even your German academic who has once again started to give himself great airs. You, who have really achieved something, must yourself have noticed how few of the young men of letters who attach themselves to the party take the trouble to go in for political economy, the history of political economy, the history of trade, of industry, of agriculture, of social formations. How many know anything about Maurer except his name? A journalist's competence must suffice for everything, and the result is what you might expect. Sometimes it seems these gentry think anything is good enough for the worker. If only these gentry knew how Marx used to regard even his best stuff as not nearly good enough for the workers, how he thought it a crime to offer the workers anything less than the very best!

After the way they have so brilliantly stood the test since 1878, I have implicit faith in our workers and in them alone. They, like every big party, will make mistakes over particular aspects of their development, perhaps big mistakes. For it is only from the consequences of their own mistakes and by experiments on their own persons that the masses will learn. But all that will be overcome, and far more easily in Germany than anywhere else because the soundness of our lads is proof against anything, and again because Berlin, which is unlikely at an early date to shake off its specifically Berlin-like character is, for us, a centre only in the formal sense, like London is, not as Paris is for France. The French and English workers—despite my being able to see the reasons for their blunders—have often given me cause for vexation, but never, since 1870, the Germans, save perhaps for certain individuals who spoke in their name—but never the masses who have always brought things back onto the right lines again. And I wouldn't mind betting that they never will give me cause for vexation.

Yours,

F. Engels

I am addressing this to the *Volks-Tribüne*, not knowing whether 'Pankow'[a] still holds good.

First published in full in *Sozialistische Monatshefte*, Nr. 18-19, Berlin, 1920

Printed according to the original

Published in English in full for the first time

---

[a] Part of Berlin where Conrad Schmidt lived.

5

ENGELS TO FRIEDRICH ADOLPH SORGE

IN MOUNT DESERT

London, 9 August 1890

Dear Sorge,

A week ago on Wednesday I sent you a postcard[a] gratefully acknowledging receipt of Morgan.[b] Today, a few lines in so far as time allows before the post goes.

The trip to North Cape did us both[c] a great deal of good and, after another 3 or 4 weeks of extra recuperation at the seaside, whither we shall be going next week (I have been held up here by sundry domestic business), I think I shall be absolutely fit again. On the face of it I look very well. Aboard our ship (a steam yacht of 2,200 tons), upon which we spent all our time going in and out of all the Norwegian fjords, there were 3 doctors who refused to believe that I'm going to be 70 this year. In fact, I am able to sleep without sulphonal, but how long will it last?

Tussy and Aveling likewise went to Norway on Wednesday. Considering what Ibsen enthusiasts they are, I'm surprised they should have waited so long before seeing the new promised land. I wonder if they are in for another disappointment, as in America? At any rate, Norway is by nature, just as America is socially, a pillar of what the philistines call 'individualism'. At intervals of 2 or 3 miles there are pockets of light soil among the rocks upon which a family *might* just be able to subsist—and, sure enough, it does, cut off from all the rest of the world. The people are handsome, strong, honest, bigoted and— fanatically religious, i. e. in the country. The towns are just like those on the Dutch or German coast. In Bergen there is a Social Democratic association which, to the horror of the reigning teetotallers, is de-

---

[a] See Engels' letter to Sorge of 30 July 1890 (present edition, Vol. 48).- [b] L. H. Morgan, *Houses and House-Life of the American Aborigines*. - [c] Engels and Carl Schorlemmer

manding the right to serve beer in its club. I read an indignant article about it in the *Bergensposten*.

In Germany there's a minor row in store for the congress.[12] Mr Schippel — a protégé of Liebknecht's — and other men of letters propose to attack the party leadership and form an opposition.[13] Well, after the abolition of the Anti-Socialist Law,[11] there would be no real objection to that. The party is so big that complete freedom of discussion within its ranks is imperative. Otherwise the many new elements who have joined it during the past 3 years and who are in some cases still exceedingly green and unpolished, could not be assimilated and trained. An accretion of 700,000 in 3 years (only counting the voters) isn't like a bunch of schoolboys into whom you can drum things; discussion and a certain amount of dissension is necessary and will help them over the first hurdle. There's not the slightest danger of a split; the press, now 12 years old, will take care of that. But these insolent literary men, bent on satisfying their colossal vanity, are intriguing and forming cliques for all they are worth, thereby arousing far more wrath than they warrant among the party leaders for whom they create a great deal of unaccustomed trouble and vexation. Hence the latter's conduct of the battle has been anything but skilful; Liebknecht is constantly on the warpath with his 'expulsions' and even Bebel, usually so tactful, has been stung by anger into publishing a somewhat foolish letter.[14] Which is why our literary gents are now screaming about the silencing of the free expression of opinion, etc. The chief organs of the new opposition are the *Berliner Volks-Tribüne* (Schippel), *Sächsische Arbeiter-Zeitung* (Dresden) and the Magdeburg *Volksstimme*. They have gained a certain following in Berlin, Magdeburg, etc., particularly among the new recruits who are still susceptible to the lure of stock-phrases. I shall probably be seeing Bebel and Liebknecht over here before the congress, and shall do my utmost to convince them of the imprudence of any expulsion that rests not on convincing proof of *activities* harmful to the party, but solely on charges of opposition-mongering. The biggest party in the empire cannot remain in existence unless every shade of opinion is allowed complete freedom of expression, while even the *semblance* of dictatorship *à la* Schweitzer must be avoided. I shall have no difficulty so far as Bebel is concerned, but Liebknecht is so subject to the mood of the moment that he is capable of breaking all his promises and doing so, as always, for the best of reasons.

Here the peace of summer reigns save that, in his answer in *Justice* to my May article in the Vienna *Arbeiter-Zeitung*,[a] Hyndman has again sent me to kingdom come as the 'grand lama of Regent's Park Road'.[15]

Lafargue writes [16] to say that in France all the generals in the government, the Senate and the Chamber are definitely opposed to any war. And rightly so. For if there were war, it would be 3 to 1 against that Russia and Prussia would fight a couple of battles and then make it up at the expense of Austria and France, so that each of the latter would lose an ally.

Lafargue's article on the French movement[b] in the *Neue Zeit* is very good and is charmingly written, but I wish Ede Bernstein had translated it instead of Kautsky, who is too heavy-handed.

I have just received copies of the new German edition of the *Manifesto*[c] and enclose one herewith.

Many regards from myself and Schorlemmer to your wife and yourself and also to the Schlüters,

Your
F. Engels

First published abridged in *Briefe und Auszüge aus Briefen von Joh. Phil. Becker, Jos. Dietzgen, Friedrich Engels, Karl Marx u. A. an F. A. Sorge und Andere*, Stuttgart, 1906 and in full in: Marx and Engels, *Works*, First Russian Edition, Vol. XXVIII, Moscow, 1940

Printed according to the original

Published in English for the first time

---

[a] F. Engels, 'May 4 in London.' - [b] P. Lafargue, 'Die sozialistische Bewegung in Frankreich von 1876-1890', *Die Neue Zeit*, No. 8, August 1890. - [c] K. Marx and F. Engels, *Manifesto of the Communist Party*, 4th authorised German edition.

6

ENGELS TO WILHELM LIEBKNECHT

IN LEIPZIG

London, 10 August 1890

Dear Liebknecht,

I am still held up here because my house is in the process of changing owners. So far as I can see, we shall not be leaving until Thursday, when we shall probably go to Folkestone. I shall leave our address at the OFFICE[a] here in Kentish Town and shall also send it to you in Leipzig. I hope that, as soon as you arrive, you will come and join us at the seaside. As you write and say that you cannot come *before* the 15th of this month, I would venture to suppose that you won't be able to get away immediately *after* the 15th either — to judge by recent delays, at any rate. So if you were to come on about 1 September or soon after, you would still be able to spend some time with us, and then return to London *in our company* (about 11 September), where you would be assured of a place to stay with us.

During our absence the house is being decorated; this year the carpets have got to be taken up, and there is also the papering and whitewashing to be done. Moreover, owing to some unfortunate experiences *in puncto*[b] of expenditure, I shall be obliged while we're away to put the housemaid on BOARD WAGES, i. e. give her so much a week in return for which she has to keep herself — an arrangement that is awkward, in that it precludes, not only hospitality, but also to some extent the very possibility of my spending a night in the house during that particular period. So if you were to arrive earlier, it would probably mean your accepting Motteler's invitation. However, I dare say you will be able to fall in with the above suggestions.

At all events I hope to see you before the congress. Your draft [17] has its weaker sides, the weakest, and one which to my mind provides quite unnecessary occasion for perpetual recrimination, being the proposal that the Executive should *itself* — albeit with the consent of the parliamentary group — determine its own rates of pay. I have today received the *Sächsische Arbeiter-Zeitung* in which the literary gents

---

[a] editorial office of the *Sozialdemokrat* - [b] in the matter

criticise the draft. Much of their criticism is utterly puerile, but they have instinctively smelt out isolated weaknesses. For instance, that *every* constituency may send up to 3 representatives. Any old Bahlmann or Höchberg, provided he is prepared to stake his money on it, could thus send 3 representatives from a constituency in which we had polled barely a thousand votes. Needless to say, money as regulator of the number of delegates sent will, generally speaking, play only an *indirect* role. However, I think it unwise that the proportion of delegates to the number of party comrades they represent should be made to depend on that alone.

Again, according to § 2 — *to go by the wording* — any three nonentities may combine to expel *you* from the party until such time as you are rehabilitated by the party Executive. The party conference, on the other hand, may not expel anyone but only act as a court of appeal.

In *any* active party having parliamentary representatives, the parliamentary group is a power of great importance. It has that power, whether or not it is expressly recognised in the rules. It may therefore be asked whether it is wise that the rules should accord it the additional status whereby it has absolute authority over the Executive, as is done in §§ 15-18. Supervision of the Executive, ALL RIGHT, but maybe it would be preferable for an indictment to come up before an independent committee which would be responsible for the verdict.

During the past 3 years your party has seen a massive increase of one million. The existence of the Anti-Socialist Law [11] has meant that these new recruits have not had sufficient opportunity for reading or for agitation to place them on a par with the older party members. Many of them have only the good will and good intentions with which the road to hell is notoriously paved. It would be a miracle if they were not burning with zeal like all neophytes. Thus they constitute material that positively invites appropriation and exploitation by the thrustful literati and academics who oppose you. As, indeed, has transpired in, for instance, Magdeburg. Herein lies a danger which should not be underestimated. Obviously at *this* congress, you will easily be able to cope with it. But you must take care that no seeds of *future* difficulties are sown. Do not make martyrs unnecessarily, show

Sozialdemokratische Bibliothek.

XXXIII.

Das
Kommunistische Manifest.

Vierte autorisirte deutsche Ausgabe.

Mit einem neuen Vorwort von Friedrich Engels.

Louise Laura Lafargue
F. Engels
London 9/8/90.

London.
German Cooperative Publishing Co.
114 Kentish Town Road NW
1890.

Title page of the fourth German edition
of the *Manifesto of the Communist Party*
with Engels' dedication to Laura Lafargue

that there is freedom of criticism, and *if* you have to throw anyone out, do so in cases where the *facts* — OVERT ACTS of turpitude and betrayal — are quite blatant and completely demonstrable. That is what I think. More when we meet.

Your
F. E.

Many regards to your wife and to Theodor.[a]

First published in: Marx and Engels, *Works*, First Russian Edition, Vol. XXVIII, Moscow, 1940

Printed according to the original

Published in English for the first time

7

ENGELS TO WILHELM LIEBKNECHT [1]

IN LEIPZIG

Folkestone, 15 August 1890

Dear Liebknecht,

We are temporarily installed here in the Bellevue Hotel, St John's Road, Folkestone and are awaiting word from you or, better still, you yourself.

We shall probably find more suitable lodgings within the next week or fortnight at the most. In any case we shall be here until next Thursday, the 21st, and, as soon as I'm certain of another address, I shall write to you. Should you arrive in the meantime, the people in Kentish Town[b] are kept constantly informed of my WHEREABOUTS.

---

[a] Wilhelm Liebknecht's son -[b] at the editorial office of the *Sozialdemokrat*

So let's hope we see you soon. Warm regards to you and your wife from Nim, Pumps and

Your
F. E.

First published in: Marx and Engels, *Works*, First Russian Edition, Vol. XXVIII, Moscow, 1940

Printed according to the original Published in English for the first time

8

ENGELS TO OTTO VON BOENIGK [18]

IN BRESLAU[a]

Folkestone near Dover, 21 August 1890

Otto von Boenigk, Esq.,
Breslau

Dear Sir,

I can only reply to your inquiries [19] briefly and in general terms, for otherwise I should have to write a dissertation on the first one.

Ad I. So-called 'socialist society' is not, in my view, to be regarded as something that remains crystallised for all time, but rather as being in process of constant change and transformation like all other social conditions. The crucial difference between that society and conditions today consists, of course, in the organisation of production on the basis of common ownership, initially by the nation, of all means of production. I see absolutely no difficulty in carrying out this revolution over a period, i. e. gradually. The fact that our working men are up to it is borne out by their many productive and distributive associations which, wherever they have not been deliberately wrecked by

---

[a] Wrocław

the police, are managed no worse and far more honestly than the joint-stock companies of the middle classes. I fail to see how you can talk of inadequate education among the masses in Germany, now that our workers have given such striking proof of political maturity in their victorious struggle against the Anti-Socialist Law.[11] The arrogant, pontifical presumption of our so-called educated men seems to me a far greater obstacle. Admittedly we are still short of technicians, agronomists, engineers, chemists, architects, etc., but if the worst comes to the worst we can buy them, just as the capitalists do, and if a stern example is made of a traitor or two — of whom there will assuredly be some in such company —, they will find it in their interest to cease robbing us. But apart from specialists like these, among whom I also count school-teachers, we shall manage very well without the rest of the 'educated' men; e. g. the present heavy influx of literati and students into the party will be attended by all manner of mischief unless those gentry are kept within bounds.

With proper technical management there would be no difficulty in leasing the large Junker estates east of the Elbe to the present day labourers and/or farm servants for communal cultivation. If there are excesses, it will be the Junkers' own fault, since it was they who, heedless of all existing educational legislation, were the cause of the people's becoming so brutalised.

The biggest obstacle is presented by the small farmers and the importunate, educated smart-Alecks whose superior knowledge of a subject is always in inverse proportion to their understanding of it.

Assuming, therefore, that we have an adequate number of supporters among the masses, the socialisation of large-scale industry and of the farms on the big estates can be carried out very quickly, once we have gained political supremacy. The rest will soon follow at a faster or slower pace. And when the large sources of production are ours, we shall be masters of the situation.

You speak of the absence of a uniform opinion. This does exist — but it is to be found among the educated men who come from aristocratic and bourgeois circles and who have absolutely no idea of how much they still have to learn from the working man.

Ad II. Mrs Marx was the daughter of Regierungsrat von Westphalen of Trier and the younger sister of the von Westphalen who was minister of reaction in Manteuffel's government.

Yours faithfully,

F. Engels

First published in *Beiträge zur Geschichte der deutschen Arbeiterbewegung*, Nr. 2, Berlin, 1964

Printed according to the original

Published in English in full for the first time

9

ENGELS TO FRIEDRICH ADOLPH SORGE

IN HOBOKEN

Folkestone, 27 August 1890

Have received postcards of 9 and 13 August. There was so much to be seen to at the time of our departure[a] that a great deal had to be shoved to one side. Moreover I had to keep pretty quiet about my destination, since young William[b] was also over there and I didn't want my pleasure marred by police chicanery.

Who is the present editor-in-chief of the *Volkszeitung*[c]? Tussy ran into Schewitsch at a meeting in London and he told her he had heard in New York that I had spoken about him in very spiteful terms. That, however, is absolutely untrue. Might it have originated from A. Jonas?

The little students' revolt in Germany[13] was quickly broken up by Bebel. One *very good* thing about it was that it showed what we have to expect from literati and Berliners.

Your

F. E.

---

[a] to Norway - [b] William II - [c] *New Yorker Volkszeitung*

The *Neue Zeit* will be asking you to report on America and will pay well.[a]

First published abridged in *Briefe und Auszüge aus Briefen von Joh. Phil. Becker, Jos. Dietzgen, Friedrich Engels, Karl Marx u. A. an F. A. Sorge und Andere*, Stuttgart, 1906 and in full in: Marx and Engels, *Works*, First Russian Edition, Vol. XXVIII, Moscow, 1940

Printed according to the original

Published in English for the first time

10

ENGELS TO PAUL LAFARGUE [20]

AT LE PERREUX

Bellevue Hotel, Folkestone, 27 August 1890

My dear Lafargue,

Yes, we're at the SEASIDE and what's more, until your letter of the 4th inst. reached me, no one had suggested my going to Le Perreux, which, by the way, I should have done with much pleasure had it not been for the perfectly good reasons which I mentioned to Laura and which she evidently found acceptable at the time. We have been here for the past fortnight in a small PUBLIC HOUSE; the landlady, a most handsome woman, looks after us very well, but the place is a long way from the sea and not FIRST CLASS. We have our fourth bed in the parlour.

As I am somewhat uncertain about my balance at the bank, being unable to compare my books, I can only send you a cheque for *ten pounds*, which I enclose.

There has been a students' revolt in the German party.[13] During 2 or 3 years a crowd of students, literati and other young déclassé bourgeois invaded the party, arriving just in time to take most of the editorial posts in the new papers that were then proliferating. In their usual fashion they regarded their bourgeois universities as socialist Saint-Cyrs [21] entitling them to enter the party in the rank of officer, if

---

[a] See this volume, p. 5.

not of general. These gentry all dabble in Marxism, albeit of the kind you were acquainted with in France ten years ago and of which Marx said: 'All I know is that I'm not a Marxist.' [9] And he would doubtless say of these gentry what Heine said of his imitators: 'I sowed dragons and I reaped fleas.'

These worthies, whose impotence is equalled only by their arrogance, found support in the new recruits to the party in Berlin—a peculiar Berlinism, combining impudence, cowardice, rodomontade and GIFT OF THE GAB, would seem to have temporarily come to the surface. The young university gents now had a chorus.

They attacked the deputies [a] for no reason at all and no one could explain this sudden recrudescence. The truth is that the deputies, or most of them, didn't take sufficient notice of the little wretches. Admittedly Liebknecht conducted the polemic on behalf of the deputies and the Central Committee with a rare lack of finesse. But then along came Bebel, their main target, who, at two meetings in Dresden and Magdeburg, proceeded to demolish two of their newspapers. [b] The Berlin meeting was guarded by the police who surreptitiously egged on the opposition or else got others to do so. [22] But it's all over nevertheless and the congress [12] is unlikely to have to concern itself further with the matter. This little stunt has done us good inasmuch as it has demonstrated the impossibility of allotting a LEADERS' role to the Berliners. All very well, perhaps, if they'd been Parisians—but we have had enough and more of your Parisians.

The revelations about Boulanger in *Figaro* [23] must be astounding. Could you let me have them? It is sad for the 247,000 or, rather 274,000 nincompoops, who in January 1889 allowed themselves to be taken in by that bogus panjandrum. [24]

In Kovalevsky's book [c] there is an important bit in which he assigns a place between the matriarchate and the mark (or *mir* [d]) community to the patriarchal family group of the kind that existed in France (Franche-Comté and Nivernais) up till 1789 and still exists today amongst the Serbs and Bulgars under the name of *Zádruga*. He tells me that in Russia this is the generally accepted view. If the thing were to be confirmed, it would clear up a number of difficulties in Tacitus et al., while at the same time raising others. The chief fault of Kova-

---

[a] of the Social-Democratic group in the German Reichstag - [b] *Sächsische Arbeiter-Zeitung* and *Volksstimme* - [c] M. Kovalevsky, *Tableau des origines et de l'évolution de la famille et de la propriété*. - [d] rural community in Russia ('мiръ')

levsky's book lies in the *illusion of legality*. I shall be discussing this in the new edition of my book.[a] Another fault (not uncommon amongst Russians who dabble in science) is an exaggerated faith in *recognised authorities*.

Nim and Pumps send their love.

Give Laura and Mémé a kiss from me.

Yours ever,

F. E.

First published in full, in German, in *Einheit*, Nr. 11, Berlin, 1955   Printed according to the original

Translated from the French

11

ENGELS TO PAUL LAFARGUE [25]

AT LE PERREUX

London, 15 September 1890

My dear Lafargue,

In great haste.

Bonnier has written to me about the 1891 congress and the convocation drawn up by the Belgians.[26] I have replied in a letter[b] which I asked him to send on to Guesde so that he can discuss it with you, Deville, etc., as well as with our Blanquist allies, and then inform me of everyone's views.

What has happened is that the Belgians have played a trick on us which places our entire congress in jeopardy. They have invited the Liverpool TRADES UNIONS [27] and the latter have accepted with alacrity. Needless to say, we weren't there to invite them ourselves! Why are we always conspicuous by our absence whenever there is something vital to be done! Why have we been so stupid as to leave the arrangements for the next congress to the Belgians and Swiss!

Tussy and Aveling tell me that the English will undoubtedly at-

---

[a] F. Engels, *The Origin of the Family, Private Property and the State*. - [b] F. Engels, *The International Workers' Congress of 1891*.

tend the Belgian, i. e. the Possibilist,[3] congress and that there isn't the remotest chance of getting it into their heads that there will be another and much better congress! I myself obviously share that opinion. The English will proceed *en masse*, with the enthusiasm of neophytes, to the first international congress they have been invited to.

There is only one way in which we can parry this, namely by proposing a merger. If it is to take place, the essential conditions must be: basis of complete equality, convocation by the mandatories of *both* 1889 congresses, the 1891 congress to have *complete* sovereignty in regard to its actions; method of representation to be determined jointly in advance — assuming these are met, we shall easily gain the upper hand. If it does not take place, the Possibilists will be to blame. We shall have shown the working-class world that they alone are the cause of splits and then there might be a chance of our successfully reopening the campaign here in England.

If the French approve this in principle, I propose that we take advantage of the Halle Congress of 12 October[12] to settle the preliminaries. One or two Frenchmen will be going, D. Nieuwenhuis, Adler[a] from Vienna, probably a Swiss, perhaps a Belgian. Tussy would attend so as to explain how things stand in England. It would be quite a conference![28] A plan of action could very well be roughed out and matters put in train.

The point is that here we have an outstanding chance, probably the last for the next five to ten years, of forming an alliance of Frenchmen, Germans and Englishmen. If we let it slip, don't be surprised if the movement over here sinks completely into the rut now occupied by the SOCIAL DEMOCRATIC Federation[29] and the Possibilists.

Our rivals are active and astute. They have always been our superiors in this respect. We, in our international dealings, have abused the right to be lazy.[b] That must stop. Let's get up and bestir ourselves!

As soon as I hear that you all approve, I shall write to the Germans.

I believe I did a stupid thing in writing to Bonnier, who is at Templeuve, instead of to you directly. But it was his letter which per-

---

[a] Victor Adler - [b] An allusion to Paul Lafargue's pamphlet *Le Droit à la Paresse. Réfutation du 'Droit au Travail' de 1848.*

suaded me to attend to this matter and, as I sat pen in hand, the subject simply expanded.

Give Laura a kiss.

Yours ever,
F. E.

First published in: F. Engels, P. et L. Lafargue, *Correspondance*, t. II, Paris, 1956

Printed according to the original

Translated from the French

12

ENGELS TO KARL KAUTSKY

IN STUTTGART

London, 18 September 1890

Dear Kautsky,

I have had your letters of 22 August and 8 September. I should really have answered the first from Folkestone where I spent a month. But I overlooked the bit about your leaving for Stuckart[a] on 25 August and so didn't know where to write to.

The little rumpus among the students[13] soon collapsed. C. Schmidt was able to keep out of it and Bebel writes to say he is ALL RIGHT. Apart from that I know no more about the silly business than you do.

The editor in you was certainly well to the fore when you tried to involve me in your critique of the programme.[30] But you know yourself that I have no time. *Ničego*[b]!

In view of the many plans that are of necessity being made in Germany these days, only to be replaced by others, no purpose would be served by my seeking to comment on the plans you told me about in your last other than to say that *I* know of nobody here whom I could recommend for the *Neue Zeit* and the *Schwäbische Tagwacht*. Schmidt would be unlikely to want to leave Berlin. Cannot Bebel get hold of anyone for you?[31]

A telling blow has been struck in Liverpool.[27] And by a quirk of history the noble Brentano happened to be present on the platform to

---

[a] Stuttgart - [b] Absolutely none (Russ.)

witness the collapse of his contention, which he had been disseminating with such tenacity and passion, that the English TRADES UNIONS were the best defence against socialism.[a]

The struggle is now in full swing. An eight hours' legal working-day — that was the critical turning point and with its acceptance came the collapse of the empire of the old, conservative labour movement that was based on capitalist relations of production. The socialisation of land, mines and transport was universally conceded, while that of the other means of production had the support of a large minority. In short, things are now moving and the events between 1 and 4 May have greatly contributed to this. The 4th of May was the *pronunziamento*,[b] the Liverpool congress the first skirmish.

The Belgians have taken advantage of the congress to invite the English to an international congress in Belgium, a most perfidious manoeuvre. In Liverpool the delegates from the new unions, which of late have been making impassioned calls for international action, accepted with alacrity. Since the Belgians have hitherto been able to do *nothing* off their own bat save issue an invitation to the Possibilist congress in Belgium, the above manoeuvre is intended to force our hand. *This time* the English are seriously committed, thanks to the idiotic nature of our resolutions in Paris concerning the place and the convocation of the next congress,[26] which condemn *us* to inactivity while the others act.

Something has got to be done about it. Having discussed the matter with the others over here, I wrote to France[c] and as soon as there is anything definite in the wind, you will doubtless hear from Ede or me. For the present, *absolute discretion* is called for, as well as a cautious approach to the Belgians' action (in the meantime it would be best simply to *record* it in the press), lest any unnecessary obstacles should arise. Will you be going to Halle on 12 October?[12]

There'll be an article by me[d] in the final No. of the *Sozialdemokrat* which will cause a good deal of annoyance over there. But I can't pitch into the literary gang without also taking a sideswipe at the philistine element in our party, which provided the former with a pretext for a row. Indirectly, of course — a valedictory number is not the place for attacks. For that reason I was glad that the

---

[a] An allusion to L. Brentano's *Die Arbeitergilden der Gegenwart.* - [b] See Engels' letters to August Bebel of 9 May and to Laura Lafargue of 10 May 1890 (present edition, Vol. 48). - [c] See previous letter. - [d] 'Farewell Letter to the Readers of the *Sozialdemokrat*'

literati forced me to square accounts with them *beforehand*.[a]
I continue to get good news from Sam Moore in Africa. Every 6 or
8 weeks he goes down with fever for 2 or 3 days, but the attacks are
very mild and leave no after-effects.

Schorlemmer is back here, having arrived from Manchester yesterday evening. Since his return from the Norwegian trip he has been
suffering from deafness and buzzing in the ears — a stubborn aural
catarrh; though it is improving somewhat, it has undone the good effects of his 6 weeks' holiday.

According to the English, young William [b] went to Norway simply
because he could play at sailors there without getting seasick. Indeed
you can sail from Skudenes in the south right up to North Cape without ever leaving perfectly calm water, and only in 2 or 3 places are
you likely to suffer 2 or 3 hours of seasickness. And as for the fjords!
They're so calm that the smallest lake in the Alps is a storm-tossed
ocean by comparison. A landlubber of an admiral can feel as safe
there as on a drive from Charlottenburg [c] to Potsdam. It so happened
that the young man sneaked past us in a torpedo boat while entering
the Sunelv Fjord from the Geiranger Fjord. When we landed in
Molde, Schorlemmer and I climbed the Moldehaj, a vantage point
approximately 1,300 feet above sea level (the same as the one that appears in Ibsen's *Fruen fra Havet* (*The Lady from the Sea*) which is set in
Molde). At the top we found half a dozen young lieutenants from the
fleet below, dressed in civilian clothes. I thought I was back in Potsdam. The same old haw-haw voices of the Prussian guards,[d] the
same old ensigns' jokes, the same old subalterns' swagger. By contrast
we later ran into a bunch of engineers who seemed quite nice, decent
fellows. And the sailors, who were to be seen all over the place, really
were splendid lads. But as for the admirals — what obesity!

First published in *Aus der Frühzeit des
Marxismus. Engels Briefwechsel mit Kautsky*,
Prag, 1935

Printed according to the original

Published in English for the first
time

---

[a] 'Reply to the Editors of the *Sächsische Arbeiter-Zeitung*' - [b] William II - [c] a suburb of
Berlin - [d] In the original: *janz die alte Jardesprache* (Berlin dialect).

13

ENGELS TO PAUL LAFARGUE

AT LE PERREUX

London, 19 September 1890

My dear Lafargue,

Thank you for your good news.[32] If that's how things are, it would be truly idiotic of us not to do everything in our power to attend a congress where the very fact of our presence would give us the upper hand.

So far as we are concerned, the following conditions are vital:

1) Convocation of the joint congress by the mandatories, and on the strength of the mandates, of the two 1889 congresses.[26] The Belgians and the Swiss would either sign one convocation only, or else the Belgians and the Swiss would convene on the strength of our mandate, and only the Belgians on the strength of the other mandate. This ought to be laid down in advance, as also the text of the convocation.

2) The absolute sovereignty of the congress, for which no preceding congress would have force of law.— Nor would it be bound in any respect whatever by any committee, whether nominated by one of the earlier congresses, or as the result of negotiations over a merger. It will establish its own rules and agenda and will alone determine the manner in which the verification of credentials is to be carried out.

3) The manner and the proportions in which the various associations are to be represented at the congress to be laid down in advance.

4) An international committee, appointed as soon as a merger has been decided upon, will prepare draft rules and agenda on which the congress will pronounce.

Ad 2): The complete freedom of the congress is vital to ourselves because, once in a position to haggle over the agenda, rules, etc., the Possibilists and the Belgians would diddle us; our negotiators have always been more naïve than theirs and the consequence would be an unending discussion of which everyone would lose the thread, thus making it impossible for us to lay the blame on the Possibilists. To the objection that the congress will be wasting valuable time, our rejoinder will be that it behoves us first to *create* a joint congress which of itself would be of vastly greater significance than any resolutions it might pass; that we do not have a mandate to constrain the future congress; that, once assembled, the congress may do away with restrictions previously imposed upon it, etc. And, eventually providing the conditions laid down are satisfactory, we might after all make some concessions to the Belgians on that score.

Now, if you Frenchmen would amend, complete and fill out the details of the above draft, you would be doing a worthwhile job.

This was the gist of my letter to Bonnier,[a] though I can assure you that I never try to settle anything with him. My chief aim in writing to him was to make the idea of a merger acceptable to you all; now I have had your letter the whole discussion has become otiose.

I therefore wrote at once to Bebel, suggesting that the question be discussed at an informal international gathering at Halle.[33] If, together with the official representatives of some of the smaller nationalities, we should then succeed in laying the foundations of a merger, it might be possible to approach the Belgians about it.[28] In fact, I asked Bebel to arrange, if possible, for a Belgian—preferably from Ghent—to be present.

Meanwhile I await your news on the opinion of Guesde, Deville, etc., and also the Blanquists.

The *Idée nouvelle* has sent me a list of subscriptions—what shall I do?

A Monsieur Ch. Caron, 8 rue du Croissant (thus evidently from the *Idée nouvelle*), has sent me a prospectus for the republication of socialist brochures and asks me for permission to publish my writings as well as those of Marx. Judging by these efforts, one might say that the French and particularly the Parisians are on the point of performing a miracle. But has this gentleman the wherewithal to publish even a single brochure? Please let me know, for I must reply within 4-5 days.[b]

Sonnenschein has sent me his account: £5.4—of which 1/5 for Laura = £1.-.9, 1/5 for the children,[c] 1/5 for Tussy and 2/5 for the translators.[d] Here is the cheque for Laura. Meissner's account will

---

[a] F. Engels, 'The International Workers' Congress of 1891'.- [b] See next letter.- [c] Longuet's children - [d] Samuel Moore and Edward Aveling

probably arrive soon, but if the expenses of the 4th edition[a] are already included in it, which I do not know, there will be little or nothing.

The Boulangist revelations could not be more edifying. Congratulate yourself on having been able to resist when the Boulangists tempted you. But what idea does that give you of the political capacity of the Parisian public! To have been duped, what am I saying, frenetically egged on by this simple ne'er-do-well who gives his word as a soldier to the royalists provided that they pay him the expenses of his good fortunes! Pfui Teufel![b] Fortunately the province is there to make amends for Parisian foolishness. It's incredible![34]

Hyndman celebrates the immortal Joffrin in *Justice,* and says that it is him and the Possibilists who have crushed Boulanger and saved the republic.[35] He ought to know that the case of the Possibilists is too desperate in Paris to come and lie so impudently.

Give Laura a kiss from Nim, myself and Schorlemmer who arrived the day before yesterday.

Yours ever,
F. E.

Will send you the last number of the *Sozialdemokrat* in a day or two. Ede Bernstein is staying here to send reports on England, particularly to the *Neue Zeit.* Fischer is going to Berlin to join the *Vorwärts,*[c] and will get a seat in the Reichstag as soon as occasion arises. Tauscher is going to Stuttgart. As for the great Julius Motteler, no one yet knows what is to be done with him. He is the party's greatest incubus — in his own eyes an unrecognised genius, in those of everybody else ineptitude personified.

See if you can arrange for Guesde and Vaillant to go to Halle[d]; Guesde will have to take Bonnier as interpreter.

First published in: Marx and Engels, *Works,* Second Russian Edition, Vol. 37, Moscow, 1965

Printed according to the original

Translated from the French

Published in English for the first time

---

[a] of the first volume of *Capital* - [b] Hang it all! - [c] *Berliner Volksblatt* - [d] to the congress of the German Social-Democratic Party

14

ENGELS TO CHARLES CARON

IN PARIS

[Draft]

[London, 20 September 1890]

Dear Citizen,

In reply to your letter of the 17th,[36] I cannot give you the authorisation you ask for until I receive clarification on a number of points.[a]

In the first place it seems to me that, if any pamphlets are to be reissued, they should appear as complete and separate pamphlets and not in the form of a revue, each number of which would contain a mixed assortment of disconnected fragments of works that would, as often as not, contradict one another. Hence I should like, first of all, to be in a position to weigh up the reasons that have led you to prefer this latter form.

Again, is it not the intention of the Workers' Party to republish a large part of these same works in its *Bibliothèque socialiste?* If so, the party undertaking ought to take precedence over the private undertaking.

Lastly, you have yourself a pretty expensive task. It would take you from 4 to 6 months merely to complete the publication of the six pamphlets advertised [b] as commencing in your first number. Were the revue to cease appearing for want of funds midway through the publication of a work I had authorised you to reprint, a heavy responsibility would fall on my shoulders.

So have you the necessary funds?

There are, in addition, further points to be considered.

So as to settle the matter I would ask you to get in touch with Citizen Lafargue, to whom I have sent a copy of this letter.

I should be obliged if you would refer to me in future before using

---

[a] See previous letter. - [b] Engels has in mind the advertisement of *L'Œuvre Socialiste. Revue politique et littéraire*, enclosed in Charles Caron's letter of 17 September 1890.

my name in public; indeed, as to the present instance, I reserve the right to have recourse, if I think fit, to measures of an equally public nature.

First published in: Marx and Engels, *Works*, First Russian Edition, Vol. XXVIII, Moscow, 1940

Printed according to the original

Translated from the French

Published in English for the first time

15

ENGELS TO PAUL LAFARGUE

AT LE PERREUX

London, 20 September 1890

My dear Lafargue,

Thank you for the information about Caron.[37] Herewith my reply[a] to this amiable fellow who 'is in no doubt that my reply will be in the affirmative'. Don't talk to me of 'LONDON ASSURANCE' or YANKEE journalists' cheek. The Germans and French outdo them by far and, what's more, with an elegant effrontery that suits them to a T. However I'm not sure that it isn't my own dear countrymen who don't carry off first prize.

Nothing new to report here. Aveling must have written to you about Lavigerie.[b] However it's very curious that this individual should have in his possession a document (copy) signed by Lafargue, Guesde, Deville, etc., announcing Guesde's impending arrival in London and a letter from Coulombeau inviting Aveling and Tussy to the Lille Congress[38] on behalf of the National Committee of the Workers' Party.[39] The originals of all the documents he purports to

___

[a] See previous letter. - [b] See Engels' letter to Laura Lafargue of 30 July 1890 (present edition, Vol. 48).

have must have been seen by Aveling last Monday — but I've heard nothing since Sunday.[a]

Herewith cheque for £20.

                                        Yours ever,
                                              F. E.

First published in: Marx and Engels, *Works*, Second Russian Edition, Vol. 37, Moscow, 1965

Printed according to the original

Translated from the French

Published in English for the first time

16

ENGELS TO JOSEPH BLOCH [40]

IN KÖNIGSBERG

London, 21[-22] September 1890

Dear Sir,

Your letter of the 3rd of this month was forwarded to me in Folkestone; but since I did not have the book in question [b] with me I was not able to reply to it. After arriving home on the 12th, I found such an accumulation of urgent work awaiting me that I have been unable until today to get round to writing you a line or two. This, merely by way of explanation for the delay which I trust you will be good enough to excuse.[41]

Ad I. First, on p. 19 of the *Origin* you will see that the process of growth of the punaluan family is shown as taking place so gradually that even in this century there have been marriages between brothers and sisters (*born of one mother*) in the Hawaian royal family. And throughout antiquity we find examples of intermarriage between siblings, e. g. amongst the Ptolemaeans. Here, however,— secondly — we must distinguish between siblings *by the same mother* and siblings merely *by the same father*; 'αδελφός, 'αδελφή [c] derive from δελφύς uterus, and hence originally denoted only siblings *by the same mother*. And

---

[a] 15 September - [b] F. Engels, *The Origin of the Family, Private Property and the State* (see present edition, Vol. 26). - [c] brother, sister

a feeling has long persisted from the period of mother right that the children of one mother, even if by different fathers, are more closely related than the children of one father but by different mothers. The punaluan form of family precludes marriage only between the former, but not at all between the latter who, according to the above conception, *are not related at all* (since mother right is in force). Now, so far as I know, cases of sibling marriage in Greek antiquity are confined to those in which the pair either have different mothers or at any rate to those in which this is not known and is therefore not ruled out; hence it is by no means inconsistent with punaluan custom. What you have overlooked is the fact that, between the punaluan period and Greek monogamy, the change-over from matriarchy to patriarchy took place, which puts quite a different complexion on the matter.

According to Wachsmuth's *Hellenische Alterthümer*,[a] there is, among the Greeks of the Heroic Period,

'no trace of reservations regarding unduly close kinship between married partners, aside from relations between parent and child' (III, p. 157). 'In Crete, marriage to a full sister was not considered an offence' (ibid., p. 170).

This last from Strabo, Book X[b]; however, I cannot find the passage at this moment because of the absence of proper chapter divisions.— *Full* sisters — failing proof to the contrary — I assume to be sisters by the same father.

Ad II. I would qualify the first of your main propositions as follows: According to the materialist view of history, the determining factor in history is, *in the final analysis*, the production and reproduction of actual life. More than that was never maintained either by Marx or myself. Now if someone distorts this by declaring the economic moment to be the *only* determining factor, he changes that proposition into a meaningless, abstract, ridiculous piece of jargon. The economic situation is the basis, but the various factors of the superstructure — political forms of the class struggle and its consequences, namely constitutions set up by the ruling class after a victorious battle, etc., forms of law and, the reflections of all these real struggles in the minds of the participants, i. e. political, philosophical and legal theories, religious views and the expansion of the same into dogmatic systems — all these factors also have a bearing on the course of the historical struggles of

---

[a] W. Wachsmuth, *Hellenische Alterthumskunde aus dem Geschichtspunkte des Staates.-*
[b] Strabo, *Geographica*.

which, in many cases, they largely determine the *form*. It is in the interaction of all these factors and amidst an unending multitude of fortuities (i. e. of things and events whose intrinsic interconnections are so remote or so incapable of proof that we can regard them as non-existent and ignore them) that the economic trend ultimately asserts itself as something inevitable. Otherwise the application of the theory to any particular period of history would, after all, be easier than solving a simple equation of the first degree.

We make our history ourselves but, in the first place, under very definite premises and conditions. Of these, the economic are ultimately decisive. But the political, etc., and even the traditions still lingering in people's minds, play some, if not a decisive, role. The Prussian state itself owes its origin and development to historical and, in the final analysis, economic circumstances. It could, however, hardly be maintained without pedantry that what caused Brandenburg, of all the many small principalities of North Germany, to become a great power, the embodiment of the economic, linguistic and — since the Reformation — also the religious, differences between North and South, was economic necessity irrespective of any other factors (above all its involvement, through its possession of Prussia, in Poland and hence in international political relations — which likewise played a decisive role in the formation of the Austrian dynasty). Without making oneself a laughing-stock, it would scarcely be possible to provide an economic explanation for the existence of every small German principality, past and present, or for the origin of the High German sound shift whereby the geographical partition formed by the mountains from the Sudetes to the Taunus became a veritable rift running right across Germany.

In the second place, however, history is made in such a way that the ultimate result is invariably produced by the clash of many individual wills of which each in turn has been made what it is by a wide variety of living conditions; there are thus innumerable conflicting forces, an infinite number of parallelograms of forces, productive of one result — the historical event which itself may be seen as the product of a power operating *unconsciously* and involuntarily as a whole. For what each individual wants is obstructed by every other individual and the outcome is something that no one wanted. Thus, the course of history up till now has been like a natural process and has, indeed, been subject to much the same laws of motion. But the fact that individual wills — each of which wants what it is driven to want by bodily constitution and extrinsic and, in the final analysis, economic (whether personal or general social) circumstances—do not attain what they want but merge into an overall mean, a common resultant—does not justify the conclusion that they are nonentities. On the contrary, each one contributes to the resultant and is, to that extent, part and parcel of it.

Another thing I would ask you to do is to study this theory in the original source books and not at second-hand; it is really far easier. While Marx wrote hardly anything in which it did not play some role, *The Eighteenth Brumaire of Louis Bonaparte* is a quite outstanding example of its application. There are also many allusions to the theory in *Capital*. I might further draw your attention to my works, *Herr Eugen Dühring's Revolution in Science* and *Ludwig Feuerbach and the End of Classical German Philosophy* in which the account I give of historical materialism is, so far as I know, the most exhaustive in existence.

If some younger writers attribute more importance to the economic aspect than is its due, Marx and I are to some extent to blame. We had to stress this leading principle in the face of opponents who denied it, and we did not always have the time, space or opportunity to do justice to the other factors that interacted upon each other. But it was a different matter when it came to depicting a section of history, i. e. to applying the theory in practice, and here there was no possibility of error. Unfortunately people all too frequently believe they have mastered a new theory and can do just what they like with it as soon as they have grasped—not always correctly—its main propositions. Nor can I exempt from this reproach many of the more recent 'Marxists' who have, indeed, been responsible for some pretty peculiar stuff.

Ad I, I yesterday discovered (I am writing this on 22 September) in Schoemann's *Griechische Alterthümer*, Berlin, 1855, I, p. 52, the following vital passage which fully substantiates what I have said above. It runs:

'It is known, however, that marriage between half-brothers and sisters born of *different mothers* was not subsequently regarded as incest in Greece.'

Trusting that you will not be too much put off by the appalling convolutions to which my pen has, for brevity's sake, succumbed, I remain

Yours faithfully,
F. Engels

First published in *Der sozialistische Akademiker*, Nr. 19, Berlin, 1895   Printed according to the journal

17

ENGELS TO HERMANN ENGELS

IN ENGELSKIRCHEN

[London,] 22 September 1890

Dear Hermann,

When your letter of 28 May arrived I was just expecting a visit from my Dublin wine merchant and so I decided to wait and discuss the matter with him in person. As it happened, however, the man didn't come until the end of June when I was wholly taken up with my impending departure[a] and so forgot about your sherry until reminded a few days ago by another look at your letter and again today by your second one. Not that you will have suffered as a result, since travelling during the hot weather would have done the wine no good and it will at any rate now travel more safely. I shall write to Dublin at once and see what can be done. Brett will certainly supply you with good wine; I have laid down another 50 or 60 dozen claret and port of the recent good years; I don't use much sherry, but in this respect, too, the chap is reliable. So more news very shortly. I have just

---

[a] to Norway

spent 4 weeks beside the Channel, at Folkestone, and feel extremely well and cheerful. Let's hope it lasts! Love to you and yours,

From your old
Friedrich

First published in *Deutsche Revue*, Jg. 46, Bd. 3, Stuttgart-Leipzig, 1921

Printed according to the original

Published in English for the first time

18

ENGELS TO JAKINS

IN LONDON

[Draft]

[London, 23 September 1890]

In pursuance of the conversation I had with you, I now beg to say that I am willing to take the house 122 Regent's Park Road on a three years agreement (similar to the one I previously had with the late Marquis de Rothwell) and at the rent of £60 a year on the condition that the landlord does for me what he would be required to do for a new tenant.

Besides smaller repairs, such as papering, etc., which might be necessary by next spring, there are two points which in my opinion come under that class, viz.

1) a new efficient kitchen range to replace the present one which is 20 years old and quite worn out;

2) efficient arrangements for a hot and cold water bath, the present bath having only cold water to turn on.

I hope these demands will not be found unreasonable and remain

Dear Sir
etc.

First published in: Marx and Engels, *Works*, Second Russian Edition, Vol. 37, Moscow, 1965

Reproduced from the original

Published in English for the first time

19

ENGELS TO STRUTT AND PARKER

IN LONDON

[Draft]

[London,] 23 September 1890

Dear Sirs,

In pursuance of a conversation I had yesterday with Mr Jakins, I wrote to him a letter stating what repairs and alterations I should expect to be made in the house occupied by me before signing a new three years agreement. This letter he promised to lay before you.

As this question cannot well be settled before the impending quarterday Mr Jakins found it quite natural that I should give you notice to quit, so as to protect myself. This notice I beg to enclose. It is however perfectly understood that I am willing to withdraw such notice again as soon as we shall have satisfactorily settled the conditions and terms of the new agreement.

Trusting that this will not be a matter of difficulty

I remain, etc.

Gentlemen,

I hereby give you notice that on the 25th day of March next (1891) I shall quit and deliver up possession of the house and premises I now hold on the Estate of the late Richard R. Rothwell Esq. and situated at 122 Regent's Park Road, N. W. in the Parish of St Pancras. Dated this 23rd day of September 1890.

First published in: Marx and Engels, *Works*, Second Russian Edition, Vol. 37, Moscow, 1965

Reproduced from the original

Published in English for the first time

20

ENGELS TO JULES GUESDE

IN PARIS

London, 25 September[a] 1890

My dear Guesde,

Thank you for your correction — I was indeed wrong concerning the congress resolution on the convocation.[42] But the resolution as it was adopted was enough to condemn us to inaction, while others would have acted.

I have written to Bebel about the Swiss. I suggested to him, since he agrees with us on the conference in Halle,[28] that everyone should be invited, included the English, so as to avoid the complaints which were produced after The Hague in 1889.[43] The Germans have the habit of dispensing with formalities, which in international affairs always leads to misunderstandings if not quarrels, and I have reminded them of this.[44]

If Vaillant could go with you to Halle, that would be very useful, particularly after what Bonnier writes to me, i. e., that he has to return to England immediately and probably will not be able to accompany you.

---

[a] The original has: June.

I hope that either the two Avelings, or at least Mrs Aveling, will be able to go.

Yours ever,

F. Engels

First published in: Marx and Engels, *Works*, Second Russian Edition, Vol. 37, Moscow, 1965

Printed according to the original

Translated from the French

Published in English for the first time

21

ENGELS TO LAURA LAFARGUE

AT LE PERREUX

London, 25 September 1890

My dear Laura,

Today being your birthday will be duly celebrated with a good bottle of wine and your health drunk with musical honors — and *such* musical honors! Nim, Schorlemmer and myself, three splendid musicians!

Many thanks for the pears which Nim is expecting with the utmost anxiety. That 'brown fellow' of yours shall be settled before he knows where he is; as for the rest, Nim will certainly take care that their

Lebenslauf
ist angefangen und beschlossen in
Der Santa Casa heiligen Registern.[a]

Today, the last number of the *Sozialdemokrat* is published. I shall miss that paper almost as much as the *Neue Rheinische Zeitung*. Ede is going to remain here, Tauscher left yesterday for Stuttgart; Fischer, the best of the lot after Ede, will settle in Berlin; the unspeakable muddler Motteler and his elegantly-bred missus nobody knows what

---

[a] births and deaths are registered in the annals of the Holy Inquisition.

to do with, so I suppose they will stay here for some time longer, though we could miss them very well—only unfortunately everybody else seems to be in that same position.

Bebel and Liebknecht have now both removed to Berlin. In case urgent communication with them might become necessary, I give you Bebel's address, the only one I have: A. B. Grossgörschenstraße, 22a, Berlin.

Fine scoundrels in Berlin amongst the nobility—one shot himself while quarreling with a *rat du ballet*,[a] another for debt and swindling, a third in prison for everlasting rows and delirium tremens, a chief officer—Major—of the Unteroffiziersschule [b] at Potsdam shot himself and even the *Kreuzzeitung*[c] telling the nobility that they are close upon the deluge which they expect only '*après nous*'! [45] Could not be better!

Ever yours
F. Engels

First published, in the language of the original (English), in: F. Engels, P. et L. Lafargue, *Correspondance*, t. II, Paris, 1956

Reproduced from the original

22

ENGELS TO PAUL LAFARGUE [25]

AT LE PERREUX

London, 25 September 1890

My dear Lafargue,

Bebel has written to say that he is in agreement with us as regards Belgium.[d] I have now suggested that he send out invitations to a preliminary congress 'to discuss means of preventing a repetition in 1891 of what happened in 1889, namely two rival and independent working men's congresses'; to invite everyone, Belgians, Swiss, the two Danish parties,[46] Swedes, Italians (have you any addresses?), Span-

---

[a] ballet dancer - [b] subalterns' school - [c] *Neue Preussische Zeitung* - [d] See this volume, pp. 28-29.

iards and English (the PARLIAMENTARY COMMITTEE,[47] the EIGHT HOURS LEAGUE,[48] the SOCIAL DEMOCRATIC Federation [29] and the SOCIALIST LEAGUE [49]).

As to your resolution to insist on the sovereignty of the congress in respect of only 3 questions, to wit verification of mandates, drawing up of the agenda, and method of voting, it seems to me that you are treading on distinctly dangerous ground. It means that, so far as all other questions are concerned, you accept the resolutions passed by former Possibilist congresses and that, when each case crops up, you call for a fresh debate in order to get rid of these obstacles. It means that you recognise the series of Belgian-Possibilist congresses, including the London caricature of 1888,[50] as the working men's only genuine means of international representation and that you debase ours of 1889 [51] to the status of an act of rebellion as groundless as it was fruitless.

So consider what you would be doing. You intend to propose, with no reservations other than those cited above, that there should be one man, one vote. And at the last Possibilist congress,[52] *three* delegates from each association were admitted. True, those three were allowed only one vote, but unless all the congress's time is to be wasted on roll-calls, how can this be verified? Whoever is going to stop the Belgians' sending three delegates from each of their little associations and lording it over the congress by courtesy of your own proposal? And how many times will you be able to extract a roll-call from a vociferously impatient congress?

It seems to me that you have been carried away by the Possibilist debacle.[53] Don't forget that from now until September 1891, when the congress will probably be held, many things can happen. Why abandon the important positions we hold today? Between now and then we may be in dire need of them. Remember that there are Possibilists pretty well everywhere, not least in Belgium.

I haven't had your paper.[a] Has it in fact come out?

Regards,

F. E.

First published in: F. Engels, P. et L. Lafargue, *Correspondance*, t. II, Paris, 1956

Printed according to the original

Translated from the French

---

[a] *Le Socialiste*

23

ENGELS TO LAURA LAFARGUE

AT LE PERREUX

London, 26 September 1890

My dear Löhr,

Yesterday we celebrated your impending birthday by a bottle of good claret, and to-day we shall drink, in honour of the real event, a bottle of champaign and wish you many happy returns of the day, hoping that you have only arrived

nel mezzo del cammin della tua vita.[a]

As a birthday present herewith your share in Meissner's remittance of £45, just to hand, in shape of a cheque for £15; it comes very appropriate!

The last No. of the *Sozialdemokrat* is creating a stir here — Edward yesterday had a long extract in *The Daily Chronicle*, and is to interview E. Bernstein for Monday's *Star* (with photograph).[54]

Meissner has not yet sent the account, only the remittance, so further particulars must be delayed.

Love from Nim, Schorlemmer and yours ever

F. Engels

Next time you come here you will be able to have a hot bath in the house. The old Marquis[b] died some time ago and the estate has gone into the hands of other agents, so I *posais la question du cabinet*[c] and gave notice unless a new kitchen range and a new bath with hot water arrangements was put in. To-day the people have been here to look at the premises and I am informed that these demands of mine will be complied with. Of course there may be some little difficulty yet, but from what I hear I believe that I have carried my point.

---

[a] in the middle of the journey of your life (Dante, *The Divine Comedy*, 'Inferno', I, paraphrased). - [b] de Rothwell - [c] raised the question of bathroom

The box of pears has not arrived yet, up to 3 p. m. to-day, but very likely it will be here before dinner.

First published, in the language of the orig-   Reproduced   from   the   original
inal (English), in: F. Engels, P. et L. La-
fargue, *Correspondance*, t. II, Paris, 1956

24

ENGELS TO FRIEDRICH ADOLPH SORGE

IN HOBOKEN

London, 27 September 1890

Dear Sorge,

Both your letters of the 10th of this month have arrived.

Today I am enclosing some copies of the last issue of the *Sozialdemokrat* with the usual newspapers. You might care to have some extra copies of this historic issue.

Your information about Schewitsch is probably correct.[a] When he passed through London, he ran into Tussy at a meeting and told her he had heard that I had expressed myself in very malicious terms about him, which was why he preferred not to call on me. I lay this at the door of the noble Jonas — though it may also have been due to the prickings of an uneasy conscience. It's the same old story as with so many Russians — *une jeunesse orageuse et une vieillesse blasée*,[b] as one of them has put it.

Grunzig is a belletrist. And the rebellious little undergraduates in Germany are also belletrists (more *triste* than *belle*[c]) who are out to revolutionise the whole of literature. This explains the whole business of the *Volkszeitung* article,[55] for the MUTUAL ASSURANCE Co. run by these gents also comprises Grunzig. Come to that, if a chap's called Grunzig or Greulich[d] he'd do best to vanish without trace.

---

[a] In two letters of 10 September 1890 Sorge informed Engels that Schewitsch had moved to Riga after the pardon by the Tsar. - [b] a stormy youth and a blasé old age - [c] more *sad* than *beautiful* - [d] Grunzig resembles *grunzen* (grunt), Greulich — greuel (horrid, dreadful).

I spent half of August and September in Folkestone near Dover, and this extra recuperation after the trip to North Cape has done me a power of good. I am refreshed and once more game for anything and, indeed, have an enormous amount to do—everybody looks to me now.

Much will now be clarified by the congresses—Lille, 9 October, French *parti ouvrier*[a][38] (ours); Calais, 13 October, ditto trades unions[56]; Halle, 12 October will be the most important.[12] I shall now tell you what is going on (*for your own information*—nothing whatever must get into the press about it):

The Brussels chaps, entrusted by the Possibilists with the convocation of *their* congress in Belgium,[26] invited the Liverpool TRADES UNION congress,[27] who accepted with alacrity. In this way the English are committed and we have been placed in something of a predicament. After consulting the people over here, therefore, I asked first the French and then the Germans[b] to pave the way for the amalgamation of both the 1891 congresses, always supposing it is possible to obtain acceptable terms, namely, sovereign powers for the congress—which the Possibilists refused to concede to us last time—, the convocation to be the responsibility of *both* mandatories of *both* the 1889 congresses, the procedure for the sending of delegates to be determined beforehand, and a few other details. The French and Germans have agreed. Since a number of representatives of foreign parties will in any case be going to Halle, I proposed that a preparatory conference be held there with a view to settling the preliminaries.[28] This, too, is well in hand. Well, I suppose that every kind of asininity will nevertheless be perpetrated there; Tussy will probably be present and put a stop to some of them but the chaps are SO GUSHING in international affairs, just when this attitude is least called for, that things may take a different course from the one I have set them on. At any rate I don't rule that out. But nevertheless I think it will turn out all right.

For a start, by holding our own congress in 1889,[51] we showed the smaller nations (the Belgians, Dutch, etc.) that we were not prepared to let them have it all their own way, and next time they'll mind their p's and q's.

Secondly, the Possibilists would appear to be in a state of complete disintegration.[53] Brousse, who controls the clique of Possibilist mu-

---

[a] Workers' Party - [b] See this volume, pp. 28 - 29 and 40.

nicipal councillors and, through them, the Labour Exchanges,[57] is openly at war with Allemane who controls the Paris trades unions and, more significantly still, is for peace with our people. Allemᵃne wants to get into the Chamber in place of Joffrin, now defunct; Brousse wants Lavy or Gély to get in. They are so much at daggers drawn that Brousse did not dare to appear at Joffrin's funeral where Allemane acted as master of ceremonies. They have also had a row with their few supporters in the provinces. And finally their coming out in opposition to the May Day demonstration [58] did them enormous harm in the eyes of the Belgians and Dutch. Brousse and Allemane are also warring quite publicly in their papers.[a]

So favourable are the circumstances—aside from the enormous moral invigoration derived by the Germans from their electoral victory [b] and its consequences, namely the overthrow of Bismarck and of the Anti-Socialist Law,[11] and which is directly responsible for making them the paramount party in Europe—that even with faulty tactics we can hope for victory. Either we shall succeed in obtaining fusion on a rational basis, in which case the congress will be dominated by the German and French Marxists, or the Possibilists and the few who support them will be so manifestly put in the wrong that the English (the new TRADES UNIONS) will desert them; for *in that case* we should again be able to conduct in this country a campaign as in the spring of 1889, and with even better success.

I am very glad that you intend to write for the *Neue Zeit*. If you find the conditions of payment unsatisfactory—needless to say, you must be paid at American rates—don't hesitate to tell them what you want, and refer the chaps to me. The *Neue Zeit* could become an organ of great importance. Bernstein will write from this country, Lafargue from Paris, and Bebel will do the weekly survey on Germany; that he can make a brilliant job of it has already been demonstrated in the Vienna *Arbeiter-Zeitung*. I never formed a definite opinion about events in Germany until I read Bebel's articles on them. The lucid, objective way in which he presented the facts without allowing himself to be swayed by his own preferences was unsurpassed.

The *Sozialdemokrat* leaves a very big gap. However, before two years are out we shall be quarrelling openly with little Willie[c] and then we may see some fun.

---

[a] *Le Prolétariat* and *Le Parti ouvrier* - [b] to the German Reichstag on 20 February 1890 - [c] William II

Regards from Schorlemmer who is here, and from myself to you and your wife.

Your
F. E.

I expect to get the 4th edition of *Capital*, Vol. I shortly, whereupon you shall instantly have a copy. The preface[a] might provide matter for the *Volkszeitung*.

First published abridged in *Briefe und Auszüge aus Briefen von Joh. Phil. Becker, Jos. Dietzgen, Friedrich Engels, Karl Marx u. A. an F. A. Sorge und Andere*, Stuttgart, 1906 and in full in: Marx and Engels, *Works*, First Russian Edition, Vol. XXVIII, Moscow, 1940

Printed according to the original

Published in English for the first time

25

ENGELS TO FRIEDRICH ADOLPH SORGE

IN HOBOKEN

[London,] 4 October 1890

In my last letter I forgot to mention the circumstance that I had given the Romm couple a letter of introduction to you, and you may have thought this improper.[b] It was sheer forgetfulness on my part. The Romms—I do not know him personally—frequented the best party circles in Berlin where they enjoyed everyone's confidence, and will in any case be able to tell you a great deal that is of interest about conditions there. As I have said, she is the sister-in-law of Ede Bernstein who, as editor of the *Sozialdemokrat*, has proved to be one of the best of the younger generation, and her literary work in introducing progressive Russian literature to the Germans deserves great praise.—They will have told you all about the personal side—the hows, whys and wherefores of their coming to America.

---

[a] F. Engels, 'Preface to the 4th German Edition of *Capital*, Vol. I'. - [b] The letter of introduction has not been found.

The *Socialiste* is appearing again—I wrote and told Lafargue to send it to you.

The matter of the congress is going swimmingly. Complete unanimity between Germans and French. Guesde, Nieuwenhuis, Tussy, a Belgian and a Swiss will be going to Halle [28] on the 12th and will doubtless settle everything. The Possibilists are quarrelling openly—next week they will probably have a show-down. [53]

Nim thanks you for the *Kalender*.[a] She, Schorlemmer and I send our kindest regards to you both.

Your
F. E.

We over here know nothing about blows received by Tussy—WHAT DOES IT MEAN? [59]

First published abridged in *Briefe und Auszüge aus Briefen von Joh. Phil. Becker, Jos. Dietzgen, Friedrich Engels, Karl Marx u. A. an F. A. Sorge und Andere*, Stuttgart, 1906 and in full in: Marx and Engels, *Works*, First Russian Edition, Vol. XXVIII, Moscow, 1940

Printed according to the original

Published in English for the first time

26

ENGELS TO KARL KAUTSKY

IN STUTTGART

[London,] 5 October 1890

Dear Kautsky,

Would you kindly arrange for me to be sent another copy of the *Neue Zeit*[b]? It's for our friend Sam[c]

'On the banks of the distant Niger
Where he hunts the lion and tiger'

---

[a] *Pionier. Illustrirter Volks-Kalender* - [b] *Die Neue Zeit*, 9. Jg. 1890/91, 1. Bd., Nr. 1. - [c] Samuel Moore

and if I get No. 1 *immediately* I shall be able to send it off next Friday. Dietz can deduct it from my fee.

Many regards — also from Jollymeier.[a]

Your

F. E.

First published in *Aus der Frühzeit des Marxismus. Engels Briefwechsel mit Kautsky,* Prag, 1935

Printed according to the original

Published in English for the first time

27

ENGELS TO WILHELM LIEBKNECHT

IN BERLIN

L[ondon,] 7 October 1890

Dear Liebknecht,

Volksblatt[b] 1-4, and 7 copies of 5,[c] received with thanks, also your letter.

I would gladly contribute to the *Volksblatt* if time permits and opportunity arises. But just now I shall have to desist from all journalistic activity for a while until I have at last completed the third volume.[d]

As in the case of the *Neue Zeit* and other papers, I have to lay down two conditions: 1. that in articles signed by me, nothing be altered without my consent, 2. that fees, IF ANY, are paid into the party funds as my contribution.

The first thing to be eliminated from the *Volksblatt* is the deadly boring tone which has now pervaded it. The *Hamburger Echo* is a cosmopolitan paper by comparison, though the leading articles may be dry; otherwise its tone is urbane and smacks of a big city. The *Volksblatt*, on the other hand, is largely written as though in

---

[a] Schorlemmer's jocular name - [b] *Berliner Volksblatt* - [c] with Engels' article 'Reply to Mr Paul Ernst' - [d] of *Capital*

a dream and Lenchen maintains that the *Sankt Johann-Saarbrücker Zei-tung* is more interesting. This impression of somnolence is what has always struck us about the paper. Them Berliners prides themselves on their wit, does they? Cor lummy!! So put a bit of life into the thing, otherwise our Political Advertiser will be competing altogether too unfairly against its Prusso-German counterpart [a] — and we can't after all take that for our model.

Besides the papers in question, I am sending you a *Daily Chronicle* containing the true story of the recent GAS SCARES when one or two officious generals wanted to send 700 troops to Becton (east of the EAST END, on the Thames).[60] This will show you what kind of paper it is.

I am glad that you should both be settling down so quickly in Berlin.

Tussy and Guesde will probably be coming from Lille to join you.

Your
F. E.

Warm regards to your wife and children.

First published in: Marx and Engels, *Works*, First Russian Edition, Vol. XXVIII, Moscow, 1940

Printed according to the original

Published in English for the first time

28

ENGELS TO FRIEDRICH ADOLPH SORGE

IN HOBOKEN

[London,] 18 October 1890

Dear Sorge,

The *Kalender* [b] has arrived — Lenchen sends her thanks!

Have today sent you a whole parcel of odds and ends — relating to the congresses. The Possibilists are done for; Allemane, Clément, Faillet, etc., and the majority of the Paris workers have expelled

---

[a] *Deutscher Reichs-Anzeiger und Königlich Preußischer Staats-Anzeiger* - [b] *Pionier. Illustrirter Volks-Kalender*

Brousse from the party and he, in turn, has expelled *them*. Hence a split.[53] All that remains to Brousse are the leaders who are dependent on him (because of documents about the dirty tricks perpetrated by each of them), i. e. the municipal councillors and the paid officials of the *bourse du travail*,[a] and — Mr Hyndman who, to my intense glee, declared his solidarity with Brousse in the last number of *Justice*.[b] At all events, *both* factions are now ruined and in process of total disintegration, a process we must hope will not be disturbed by intervention from our people. Our congresses, on the other hand, went off splendidly. First Lille — the French 'Marxists' as a party,[38] then Calais — the TRADES UNIONS, under their direction[56]; then Halle, the crowning of the whole.[12] Tussy was at Lille and Halle, Aveling at Lille and Calais. I have not yet heard how the international negotiations went at Halle.[28] At all events, throughout this week we have been *second to none* in the eyes of the world's press.

Best wishes

Your
F. E.

First published in *Briefe und Auszüge aus Briefen von Joh. Phil. Becker, Jos. Dietzgen, Friedrich Engels, Karl Marx u. A. an F. A. Sorge und Andere*, Stuttgart, 1906

Printed according to the original

Published in English for the first time

29

ENGELS TO LAURA LAFARGUE[61]

AT LE PERREUX

London, 19 October 1890

My dear Löhr,

At last! This week I have been, if not busy, at all events 'occupied' and 'engaged' over head and ears. I have sorted about 4 cubic feet of old letters of Mohr's (that is to say addressed mostly to him) of the

---

[a] Labour Exchange - [b] 'The Split in France', *Justice*, No. 353, 18 October 1890.

period 1836-64. All higgledy-piggledy in a big basket, which perhaps you may remember. Dusting, straightening, sorting — it took more than a week to put them into rough order. During all that time my room upset, covered with paperasses[a] in various degrees of order and disorder, so that I could neither go out nor do any other kind of work. That was No. 1. Then came the congresses[62] with — not work, but loss of time for me by callers, etc. And finally, Nim has been quite out of sorts all this week, went to bed on her own accord on Thursday morning and actually sent for the Doctor,— who however told her there was no reason for her to stick in bed, she might sit up at least a few hours which she does. He cannot as yet exactly make out what it is, there are symptoms (jaundice) of liver complaint, she has no appetite and is weak. However since last night she is better and in better spirits, and I hope will be well in a few days.

I hope Paul has got rid of his intimate friend inside. If he has not, it's his own fault, a dose of felix mas or cousso will soon put an end to that nuisance. It will poison the brute and do him no harm.

Our congresses have come off gloriously and when we compare them with the Possibilists,[53] they come out in still bolder relief. *That* nuisance now will soon put a stop to itself. Only I hope that our friends will give them every inch of rope they may require and not interfere in the least by approaches or otherwise. *Il faut qu'ils cuisent dans leur propre jus.*[b] Any attempt on our side to meddle with them would only arrest for a time the process of disintegration and *pourriture.*[c] The masses are sure to come round to us by and by. And the longer we allow the leaders to kill each other, the less of them shall we have to take over on the day of reunion. If Liebknecht had not been in such a hurry with regard to the Lassalleans coming over to us, he would not have had to take over Hasselmann and others who had to be kicked out six months afterwards.[63] And now in France, as then in Germany, the whole lot of the leaders are rotten to the core.

To my great surprise and relief in last *Justice* Hyndman declares for Brousse[d]! What a piece of good luck. I was beginning to be afraid I might get into a position where Hyndman would have to be taken on again as at least passively a friend, whereas I like him 10,000 times better as an enemy.

---

[a] wretched scraps of paper - [b] Let them stew in their own juice. - [c] decay - [d] 'The Split in France', *Justice*, No. 353, 18 October 1890.

Paul now *may* be right: the Possibilists *may* abstain again from their own Congress.[64] The date and place appear to have been fixed at Halle [28]: Brussels, 16 August 1891. This is all I know. To-morrow I shall hear it all from Tussy who left Halle yesterday, her return ticket to Cologne expiring on that day.[65]

I am glad Fischer has been put on the *Parteivorstand.*[a] You have seen him here. He is very intelligent, very active, revolutionary, *absolutely anti-philistine*, and more international in his ways and manners than most Germans. Tussy writes that after the Lille Congress,[38] the German Reichstag men, a great portion of them, at least, made a rather philistine impression upon her. I fully expected that. As our M. P. s are not paid, we cannot get always the best men, but must accept from those in a relatively bourgeois position the *least bad*. Therefore our masses are far better than the *fraction*. The latter may congratulate themselves that they had such asses and shady fellows (many of them probably *mouchards*[b]) for an opposition.[66] If they should rebel against Bebel, Singer and Fischer, they will have to be acted against — but I am sure Bebel will always be strong enough to cow them.

Paul *est bien naïf avec ses questions sur Bebel et le 'Gil Blas'. Il connaît Bebel et il connaît le 'Gil Blas'; est-ce qu'il ne se connaîtrait plus soi-même?*[c] At any rate I shall send the *'Gil Blas' fortement souligné*[d] to Bebel and tell him to disown. Such impudent lying exceeds all measure, even for *Gil Blas.*[67]

Tussy is quite in love with the Lille delegates, and indeed they seem to have been a regular élite, and shown the very qualities which it has been the fashion of late in France to cry down because the Germans showed them to a higher degree, though up to 1870 it had been the regular thing to claim discipline, *esprit d'organisation et action combinée* as *des qualités tout ce qu'il y a de plus françaises.*[e] I was very much interested in Paul's account of these delegates[68] and shall take care that it gets into the English and German Press. The great advantage of the French is that they are bred and born in a revolutionary medium. Both English and Germans lack that advantage and are moreover brought up in the religion of the bourgeoisie — protestantism. That

---

[a] Party Executive -[b] police spies -[c] Paul is very naive with his questions about Bebel and *Gil Blas*. He knows Bebel and also *Gil Blas*; is it that he does not know himself better? -[d] specially underlined -[e] this spirit of organisation and collective action as the qualities which are French to the extreme

gives to their habits, manners and customs a *spiessbürgerlichen An-strich*[a] which they have to shake off by going abroad, especially to France. Look at the redaction of the Lille and the Halle resolutions! That is the great progress: we cannot now do without any one of the three. Only the Belgians and the Swiss we could very well spare. Love from Nim and yours affectionately

F. E.

As Paul has said so much in the *Neue Zeit*[b] about the fleets constructed by Mohr for you girls when you were children, I enclose him the, probably, last specimen extant of Mohr's naval architecture.

First published, in German, in *Einheit*, Nr. 11, Berlin, 1955

Reproduced from the original

30

ENGELS TO EDUARD BERNSTEIN[c]

IN LONDON

[London,] 20 October [1890]

Tussy arrived home yesterday morning. Adler[d] had told her that Louise Kautsky had come back from Berchtesgaden in the best of spirits, was looking 10 years younger and proving a tremendous success. Tussy was very full of the congress[12]; the masses, she said, were first-rate but the parliamentary group for the most part still philistine— Bebel had been greatly alarmed upon hearing of the electoral victories of certain of their number and had at once written to say that, while the damage had already been done, it must not be allowed to

---

[a] philistine tinge - [b] P. Lafargue, 'Karl Marx. Persönliche Erinnerungen', *Die Neue Zeit*, 9. Jg. 1890/91, 1. Bd., Nr. 1-2. - [c] This letter is a postscript to Eleanor Marx-Aveling's letter to Engels of 16 October 1890 from Halle, which he sent to Bernstein. - [d] Victor Adler

happen again. Provided this gang follows Bebel's lead, things will still be all right.

Your

F. E.

I am sending what remains of the reports, amongst them a Hamburg paper, as I don't know whether you have already got the Berlin report about the 14th of October.[a]

First published in: Marx and Engels, *Works*, Second Russian Edition, Vol. 37, Moscow, 1965

Printed according to the original

Published in English for the first time

31

ENGELS TO WILHELM LIEBKNECHT [69]

IN BERLIN

L[ondon,] 25 October 1890

I am sending you, addressed to your office, today's *Justice* containing an article by A. S. Headingley (alias Adolphe Smith), in which the lot of you, and yourself in particular, are branded Possibilists.[b] The writer is an Englishman born in Paris, *literatus vulgarissimus*, who was in Paris at the time of the Commune and afterwards came to this country with a MOVING PANORAMA of Paris and the Commune; as a speculation this was a total flop, something for which he never forgave us, for he had believed that the General Council of the International would drum up a nightly audience for him. He therefore became an intimate of the *branche française* [70] in which all the *mouchards* [c] and scoundrels — Vésinier, Caria, etc., — foregathered to hatch plots and, with the help of French *fonds secrets*, published newspapers in which to attack the General Council — *des calomnies ordurières*.[d] For the past eight years or so he has been Brousse's principal agent here and the intermediary between him, the SOCIAL DEMOCRATIC Federation

---

[a] 'Der Partei-Kongreß', *Berliner Volksblatt*, No. 239, 14 October 1890. - [b] A. S. Headingley, 'French and German Possibilists', *Justice*, No. 354, 25 October 1890. - [c] police spies - [d] filthy calumnies

here,[29] and sundry Belgians (he is resident interpreter at the Possibilists' and miners' international congresses). The evil intent will be
obvious to you, as will the stupidity—these chaps have utterly failed
to understand the Halle resolution [28] and believe that the Possibilists,
who are killing themselves off in France, can be salvaged in Germany.
POOR FELLOWS!

Your
F. E.

First published in: Marx and Engels,
Works, First Russian Edition, Vol.
XXVIII, Moscow, 1940

Printed according to the original

Published in English for the first
time

32

ENGELS TO CONRAD SCHMIDT [71]

IN BERLIN

London, 27 October 1890

Dear Schmidt,

I am taking advantage of this, the first free time I have had, to answer you letter. I think you would be very well advised to accept the
post in Zurich.[72] At any rate you'll be able to learn a good deal about
economics there, especially if you bear in mind that Zurich is, after all,
only a third-rate financial and speculative market and hence that the
impressions to be gained there will be dulled, if not deliberately distorted, these being but reflections seen at second or third remove. But
you will learn how the machinery works in practice and will be obliged to follow at first hand the stock market reports from London,
New York, Paris, Berlin and Vienna, and thus the world market—in
its reflection as a money and stock market—will be revealed to you.
Economics, politics, etc., are reflected as objects are in the human
eye—they pass through a converging lens and are therefore seen the
wrong way up, standing on their heads. Except that there is no
nervous apparatus to set them on their feet again for the benefit of the

imagination. Your money market man sees the trend of industry and of the world market merely in the inverted reflection of the money and stock markets and thus for him effect becomes cause. I observed this back in the 40s in Manchester [73]; as a guide to industrial progress and its periodical peaks and troughs, the London stock market reports were absolutely useless, since the gentlemen sought to explain everything in terms of money market crises, though these were themselves for the most part little more than symptoms. At that time they were concerned to explain away industrial crises by attributing them to temporary overproduction and thus the thing also had a tendentious aspect which invited distortion. This is a point which has now ceased to apply — once and for all, at any rate so far as we are concerned, and it is, moreover, a fact that the money market may also have its own crises in which actual industrial disturbances play only a subordinate role, if any at all, and in this sphere there is much to be ascertained and investigated, particularly in regard to the history of the last 20 years.

Where there is division of labour on a social scale, the various sections become mutually independent. Production is, in the final analysis, the decisive factor. But as soon as trade in products becomes independent of actual production, the former follows a trend of its own which is, by and large, undoubtedly dictated by production but, in specific cases and within the framework of that general dependence, does in turn obey laws of its own, laws inherent in the nature of this new factor; it is a trend having its own phases and reacting in turn on the trend of production. The discovery of America was due to the gold famine which had already drived the Portuguese to Africa (cf. Soetbeer's *Edelmetall-Produktion*), because the vast expansion of European industry and the corresponding growth in trade in the 14th and 15th centuries called for more means of exchange than Germany — the main source of silver from 1450 to 1550 — was able to provide. The conquest of India by the Portuguese, Dutch and British between 1500 and 1800 had as its aim *import from* India and no one thought of sending *exports* there. And yet how tremendous were the repercussions upon industry of these discoveries and conquests carried out solely in the interests of trade — it was only the need to *export to* those countries which created and developed large-scale industry.

It is the same with the money market. Once trade in money becomes divorced from trade in commodities, it will — under certain circumstances determined by production and by the trade in commodities and within those limits — develop in its own way subject to the special laws and distinctive phases determined by its own nature. If, in addition and in the course of this further development, the trade in money expands to comprise trade in securities, the said securities being not simply government paper, but also the shares of industrial and commercial concerns, i. e. if the trade in money gains direct control of a section of the production by which it is largely dominated, then the reaction of the trade in money on production will be even stronger and more complex. The traders in money own railways, mines, foundries, etc. These means of production assume a twofold aspect: They must be run, now in accordance with the immediate interests of production, now in accordance with the needs of the shareholders in so far as these are traders in money. The most striking example of this is the North American railroads, the running of which is entirely dependent on the day-to-day stock market operations of a Jay Gould, Vanderbilt, etc., which have nothing whatever to do with any particular railroad or its interests *qua*[a] means of transport. And even here in England the railway companies have for decades been fighting over the boundary areas separating this concern or that — struggles in which a vast amount of money has been squandered, not in the interests of production and transport, but solely out of a rivalry which for the most part had but one purpose, namely to facilitate the stock market operations of the traders in money who held the shares.

With these few remarks about my view of the relationship of production to the trade in commodities and of both to the trade in money, I have already dealt in the main with your questions about historical materialism generally.[74] The subject is best approached from the standpoint of the division of labour. Society engenders certain common functions which it cannot do without. Those nominated for this purpose form a new branch of the division of labour *within society*. They thereby acquire interests of their own vis-à-vis, amongst others, their mandatories and become independent of them — and so you have the state. From then on the process is much the same as in the trade in commodities and, later, the trade in money — while the new independent power must, it is true, generally follow the trend of production, it will also, by virtue of its inherent independence, i. e. a relative independence formerly conferred upon it and which it has

---

[a] as

gradually enlarged, react in turn upon the conditions and the course of production. It is the interaction of two unequal forces, of the economic trend on the one hand and the new political power which is striving for the greatest possible independence and which, having once been installed, assumes a trend of its own, on the other. By and large, the economic trend will predominate but it must also be reacted upon by the political trend which it has itself induced and which has been endowed with relative independence — the trend of, on the one hand, state power and, on the other, of the simultaneously engendered opposition. Just as the trend of the industrial market is largely reflected in the money market, given the provisos set out above, but, of course, the *wrong way up*, the struggle between the already extant and warring classes is reflected in the struggle between government and opposition, and again the wrong way up; it is no longer reflected directly but indirectly, not as a class struggle but as a struggle over political principles, and in so distorted a form that it has taken us a thousand years to sort it out again.

The government may react to economic developments in three ways: it can take the same direction, in which case things go faster; it may take a contrary one, in which case, as conditions are today and in any of the larger nations, it will eventually come to grief, or it may block certain lines of economic development and lay down others — which will ultimately amount to the same as one of the two foregoing instances. But it is obvious that, in instances 2 and 3, political power can wreak havoc with economic development and cause energy and materials to be squandered on a vast scale.

Then again there is the instance of the seizure and brutal destruction of economic resources which, in earlier days and in certain circumstances, could ruin economic development both locally and nationally. Today, this would mostly have the opposite effect, at least where the larger nations are concerned. In the long run the vanquished may have more to gain economically, politically and morally than, on occasion, the victor.

It is much the same in the case of the law: As soon as the new division of labour becomes necessary and creates professional lawyers, yet another new, independent field is opened up which, for all its general dependence on production and trade, is nevertheless capable of reacting in its own way to those spheres. In a modern state not only must the law correspond to the general economic situation and be its expression, it must *of itself* constitute a *coherent* expression that does not, by reason of internal contradictions, give itself the lie. And to achieve this, the fidelity with which economic conditions are reflected is increasingly thrown to the winds. All the more so for the rarity with which a statute book is the harsh, unmitigated, unadulterated expression of the domination of one class: this of itself would be contrary to the 'concept of law'. The pure, logical concept of law of the revolutionary bourgeoisie of 1792-96 had already been adulterated in many respects even in the Code Napoléon [75] and, in so far as it was embodied therein, has had to be constantly subjected to all manner of modifications as a result of the growing power of the proletariat. Not that this has prevented the Code Napoléon from being the statute book on which all new codifications in every part of the world are based. Thus the course of the 'law's development' has largely consisted simply in this: Firstly, the attempt to eliminate the contradictions arising from the direct translation of economic conditions into legal principles and to establish an harmonious legal system and, secondly, the fact that the influence and pressure of further economic developments repeatedly disrupt that system, involving it in fresh contradictions (at this stage I am speaking only of civil law).

The reflection of economic conditions as legal principles is likewise necessarily one that presents the image the wrong way up; it does so without the beholder being aware of it; the lawyer imagines he is dealing in a priori principles whereas they are, in fact, no more than economic reflections — and thus the whole thing is the wrong way up. And it seems to me self-evident that this inversion which, in as much as it is not recognised, constitutes what we call an *ideological view*, reacts in its turn on the economic base and may, within certain limits, modify the same. The basis of the law of inheritance, assuming the family to have attained the same stage of development, is an economic one. Nevertheless, it would be difficult to prove that, for instance, absolute testamentary freedom in England and the strict limits imposed thereon in France are in every respect of economic origin. But both, in a very significant way, react on the economy in that they influence the distribution of wealth.

Now as regards the more rarefied ideological fields such as religion, philosophy, etc.; these have a prehistorical fund of what today would be termed rubbish which was taken over lock, stock and barrel by the historical period. In so far as these various false conceptions of nature, of the nature of man, of spirits, magic forces, etc., are economically based, it is only in a negative sense; false conceptions of nature are the corollary of the low level of economic development in the prehistorical period, but also on occasion its precondition if not its actual cause. And even if economic necessity may have provided the main incentive for progress in natural science and done so to an increasing extent, it would be pedantic to seek economic causes for all this primitive rubbish. The history of science is the history of the gradual elimination of that rubbish and/or its replacement by new, if progressively less ridiculous, rubbish. The people responsible for this in turn belong to special spheres of the division of labour and see themselves as working in an independent field. And to the extent that they constitute an independent group within the social division of labour, what they produce, including their errors, exerts a reciprocal influence on social development as a whole and even on economic development. But for all that, they are themselves in their turn subject to the dominant influence of economic development. In philosophy, for example, this is most easily demonstrated in respect of the bourgeois period. Hobbes was the first modern materialist (in the 18th-century sense), but an absolutist at a time when, throughout Europe, absolute monarchy was in its heyday and, in England, was embarking on a struggle with the populace. In religion as in politics, Locke was the product of the class compromise of 1688.[76] The English deists [77] and their more logical successors, the French materialists, were the true philosophers of the bourgeoisie — and, in the case of the French, even of the bourgeois revolution. German philosophy, from Kant to Hegel, is permeated by the German philistine — now in a positive, now in a negative, sense. But in every epoch philosophy, as a definite sphere of the division of labour, presupposes a definite fund of ideas inherited from its predecessors and from which it takes its departure. And that is why economically backward countries can nevertheless play first fiddle where philosophy is concerned — France in the 18th century as compared with England, upon whose philosophy the French based themselves and, later on, Germany as compared with both. But in France as in Germany, philosophy, like the general flowering of literature at that time, was also the result of growing economic prosperity. I am in no doubt about the ultimate supremacy of economic development over these fields also, but it will come about within the terms laid down by each individual field; in philosophy, for instance, by the operation of economic influences (which again for the most part operate only in their political, etc., guise) on extant philosophical material handed down by predecessors. Here, political economy creates nothing *a novo*,[a] but determines the way in which the existing fund of ideas changes and develops, and this too is done for the most part indirectly, since it is its political, legal and moral reflections which exert the greatest immediate influence on philosophy.

As for religion, I have said all that is necessary in the last chapter of Feuerbach.[b]

So if Barth opines that we deny that the political, etc., reflections of the economic trend have any effect whatsoever on that trend itself, he is simply tilting at windmills. After all, he only has to look at Marx's *Eighteenth Brumaire*[c] which is devoted almost exclusively to the *particular* role played by political struggles and events — needless to say within the framework of their *general* dependence on economic conditions. Or again at *Capital*, e. g. the section on the working day where legislation, which is, after all, a political act, appears in such an uncompromising light. Or at the section on the history of the bourgeoisie (Chapter 24).[78] Otherwise why should we be fighting for the political dictatorship of the proletariat if political power is economically powerless? Might (i. e. state power) is also an economic force!

But I have no time at present to criticise the book.[d] The third volume[e] has got to come out first and in any case I believe that e. g. Bernstein is also perfectly capable of attending to it.

What all these gentlemen lack is dialectics. All they ever see is cause on the one hand and effect on the other. But what they fail to see is that this is an empty abstraction, that in the real world such metaphysically polar opposites exist only in a crisis, that instead the whole great process takes place solely and entirely in the form of interplay — if of very unequal forces of which the economic trend is by far the strongest, the oldest and the most vital — and that here nothing is absolute and everything relative. So far as they are concerned, Hegel might never have existed.

As regards the rumpus in the party, I was forcibly dragged into it by the gentlemen of the opposition and thus had no choice. Mr Ernst's conduct vis-à-vis myself is quite indescribable unless I call it that of a schoolboy.[79] I am sorry if he's a sick man and forced to write for his

---

[a] from scratch - [b] F. Engels, *Ludwig Feuerbach and the End of Classical German Philosophy*. - [c] *The Eighteenth Brumaire of Louis Bonaparte* - [d] P. Barth, *Die Geschichtsphilosophie Hegel's und der Hegelianer bis auf Marx und Hartmann. Ein kritischer Versuch*. - [e] of *Capital*

living. But if someone has an imagination so vivid that he can't read
a line without inferring the opposite of what it says, he should apply
his imagination to spheres other than socialism which is no figment.
He should write novels, plays, art criticism and the like, when all he
will harm is bourgeois culture, benefiting us in the process. He might
then acquire sufficient maturity to be able to achieve something in
our field also. Never before have I seen such a rigmarole of half-baked
material and utter rubbish as has been dished out by the said opposition. And these callow lads, who are blind to everything but their
own boundless egotism, propose to dictate party tactics. I have learnt
more from a single one of Bebel's articles in the Vienna *Arbeiter-
Zeitung* [a] than from all the rigmarole these chaps have produced. And
they imagine they are worth more than that clear-sighted man who
has such an admirably correct grasp of circumstances and depicts
them so graphically and succinctly. They are all of them failed belletrists, and even a successful belletrist is a pretty obnoxious animal.

I should be sorry were the *Volks-Tribüne* to succumb. Under your
editorship it has shown that something might well be achieved by
a weekly which devotes more space to theory than to news—and
I am well aware what sort of contributors you have! But I must say
that, now that the *Neue Zeit* has become a weekly, it's somewhat
doubtful whether yours can be kept going. At all events, you will be
glad to cast off the joys and sorrows of editorship and have time for
something other than purely journalistic tasks. And even in Berlin the
immediate future will be dominated by all the various reverberations
of the late rumpus, and there'll be nothing to gain for anyone by being mixed up in it.

Your printing the passage from my letter did no harm, [80] but that
sort of thing is best avoided. In a letter, one writes from memory and
at speed, without looking anything up, etc., and is thus always liable
to let slip some expression which may well be seized on by one of those
people we Rhinelanders describe as a *Korinthenscheisser*, [b] and God
knows what rubbish might not come of it.

---

[a] [A. Bebel,] 'Berlin, 7. Oktober. Der 30. September bezeichnete den glorreichen
Abschluß einer geschichtlichen Epoche...', *Arbeiter-Zeitung*, No. 41, 10 October 1890.-
[b] i. e. someone who trivialises everything

Many thanks for your anticipatory congratulations on my 70th birthday which is still a month ahead. So far I am still very well except that I still have to spare my eyes and am not allowed to write by gaslight. Let's hope I remain so.

Now I must close.

With warm regards,

Yours,

F. Engels

First published in full in *Sozialistische Monatshefte*, Nr. 20-21, Berlin, 1920

Printed according to the original

Published in English in full for the first time

33

ENGELS TO PAUL LAFARGUE [25]

AT LE PERREUX

London, 2 November 1890

My dear Lafargue,

Poor Nim is very ill. For some time past it would seem that there has been a recurrence of menstruation, and three weeks ago she suffered an appreciable loss of blood. Dr Read, whom we consulted, thought her complexion very sallow, although he found no trace of bile in her urine — which led him to suspect the possibility of an uterine tumour, but he didn't examine her manually. She then began to feel pains in the left groin when her faeces passed through the colon towards the sigmoid flexure — these subsided again and I thought she was on the road to recovery until she began to suffer intense pain in her left foot. During all this time a total lack of appetite, severe thirst (she has been living on milk and beef-tea, no solid food). The pain in the left foot culminated in a thrombosis in a vein of the calf. It appeared to be taking its natural course, the pain diminished and this morning she woke up after a good night, somewhat refreshed in appearance, if not actually cheerful. However between 11 and midday a change came over her and Read found she had a temperature of 104°F. = 40°C., although the thermometer had been in her mouth for only a minute and a half. She has fallen, as it were, half asleep, her mental faculties are impaired and her pulse is rapid and feverish, consistent with her temperature. In fact Read suspects that, given the cachectic state of her blood (more or less indicated by the previous symptoms), the coagulated blood is decomposing and poisoning the live blood. He hopes to return here this afternoon with Heath of the Gower Street Hospital for a consultation.

That's all I can tell you just now. If Heath turns up, I shall let you know the result.

Give Laura a kiss from me.

Yours ever,
F. E.

Consultation with a Mr Packard, the only man who could be found. He thinks there has been a diffuse suppuration in the foot causing septicaemia. The method of fomentation has been changed and 4 grains = 4/15 gramme of quinine administered. The uterus was examined after a fashion, but at this stage nothing has been discovered save for a small slightly suspect spot by the orifice, to which, however, no importance is attached 'so far'. Naturally there is always the possibility of an embolism and with it the possibility of further complications, pulmonary and otherwise. But the chap takes a more 'HOPEFUL' view of the case than Read does.

If there is any change I shall write again tomorrow.

First published in: F. Engels, P. et L. Lafargue, *Correspondance*, t. II, Paris, 1956

Printed according to the original

Translated from the French

34

ENGELS TO FRIEDRICH ADOLPH SORGE [81]

IN HOBOKEN

[London,] 5 November 1890

Today I have some sad news to pass on to you. My good, dear, loyal Lenchen fell peacefully asleep yesterday afternoon after a short and for the most part painless illness. We had spent seven happy years together in this house. We were the only two left of the old guard of the days before 1848. Now here I am, once again on my own. If Marx was able to work in peace over a period of many years as I have during the past seven, it was largely thanks to her. How I shall manage now I do not know. Another thing I shall sorely miss is her marvellously tactful advice in party matters. Cordial regards to your wife; would you please pass on this news to the Schlüters.

Your
F. E.

First published in *Briefe und Auszüge aus Briefen von Joh. Phil. Becker, Jos. Dietzgen, Friedrich Engels, Karl Marx u. A. an F. A. Sorge und Andere*, Stuttgart, 1906

Printed according to the original

35

ENGELS TO KARL KAUTSKY

IN STUTTGART

[London,] 5 November 1890

Our dear, good Nimmy fell peacefully asleep yesterday afternoon at half past two. She had been ill for only a short time and suffered little pain — none towards the end.

Your
F. E.

First published in *Aus der Frühzeit des Marxismus. Engels Briefwechsel mit Kautsky,* Prag, 1935

Printed according to the original

Published in English for the first time

36

ENGELS TO LOUISE KAUTSKY [82]

IN VIENNA

[London, 9 November 1890]

...What I have been through these many days, how terribly bleak and desolate life has seemed and still seems to me, I need not tell you. And then came the question — what now? Whereupon, my dear Louise, an image, alive and comforting, appeared before my eyes, to remain there night and day, and that image was you. Then, like Nimmy, I said: 'Oh, if only I could have Louise here!' But I didn't dare to think that it might come true. ...No matter what happens, I should not have had a moment's peace had I not put this question to you first of all and straight away... Whoever keeps house for me will have to conform to local customs whereby a lady may not undertake any MANUAL SERVICES. This might even be forced upon me, and

I should most certainly be compelled to have recourse to someone who was not a member of our party... So all you would have to do is supervise things, and the rest of the time you'd be free to do anything you liked...

In that case we could talk over the whole matter here and either remain together as good friends or part company as good friends. Well, it's for you to decide. Think the matter over, discuss it with Adler.[a] If, as I fear, this day-dream of mine cannot be realised, or if you should think that the drawbacks and vexations would, so far as you are concerned, outweigh the advantages and pleasures, then let me know without beating about the bush. I am far too fond of you to want you to make sacrifices for my sake... And for that very reason I would beg you not to make any such sacrifice and would request Adler through you to advise you against so doing. You are young and have a splendid future in store. In three weeks' time I shall be seventy and have only a short while left to live. A young and hopeful existence ought not to be sacrificed to those few remaining years. For after all, I am still strong enough to make shift for myself...

With undying love

First published in: G, Mayer, *Friedrich Engels. Eine Biographie*, Bd. 2, Haag, 1934

Printed according to the book

Published in English for the first time

37

ENGELS TO ADOLF RIEFER [83]

IN SAARBURG, LORRAINE

London, 12 November 1890
122 Regent's Park Road, N. W.

To Mr Adolf Riefer in Saarburg, Lorraine

I write today to inform you of the sad news that your aunt, Miss Helene Demuth, my friend of many years who had lived in my house for the last seven, passed away peacefully and without pain on the 4th

---

[a] Victor Adler

of this month after a short illness. We had been friends since 1845 and when, after the death of my friend Karl Marx, she did me the honour and pleasure of taking charge of my household, it marked for me the beginning of many years of calm and contentment, indeed, of domestic happiness such as had not been vouchsafed me since the death of my wife in 1878. But all that has now gone and gone for ever. We laid her to rest on Friday, 7 November in the same grave as that in which Marx and Mrs Marx are buried. Together with myself and Marx's daughters, thousands of friends from every nation mourn her loss, in the prairies of America as in the political prisons of Siberia and in all the countries of Europe.

The deceased made a will in which she named as her sole heir Frederick Lewis, the son of a deceased friend, whom she had adopted when he was still quite small and whom she gradually brought up to be a good and industrious mechanic. The latter, out of gratitude and with her permission, assumed the name Demuth a long time ago and he is also so named in the will. This is in the hands of the solicitor who attended to the legal formalities and who has, in addition, declared it to be fully valid, so that towards the end of this week it will be my duty to hand over the entire estate to the heir. After deduction of all expenses it will amount in money to about forty pounds sterling, on top of which there are clothes etc. of comparatively little value. Should you or any other relatives wish to have a small memento, perhaps you would be so good as to inform me, whereupon I shall lose no time in attending to the matter.

Enclosed in translation is a copy of the will.

Yours very truly,
Fr. Engels

Copy of the will

* I Helen Demuth of 122 Regent's Park Road declare this to be my last will. I leave all my monies, effects and other property to Frederick Lewis Demuth of 25 Gransden Avenue, London Lane, Hackney, E., and being too weak bodily to affix my name have affixed hereto my mark in the presence of the undersigned witnesses. At 122

Regent's Park Road this fourth day of November 1890, the above having been read to me and perfectly understood by me

Helen Demuth

In the presence of Frederick Engels of 122 Regent's Park Road
Eleanor Marx Aveling, 65 Chancery Lane
Edward Aveling, 65 Chancery Lane* [a]

First published in *Wuppertaler Rundschau*, 8. November 1984

Printed according to the original

Published in English for the first time

38

ENGELS TO VICTOR ADLER

IN VIENNA

London, 15 November 1890
122 Regent's Park Road, N. W.

Dear Adler,

Many thanks for your letter. The Avelings have just arrived with a telegram — 'SEND MONEY' — from Louise who was proposing to leave Vienna today.[b] Aveling at once sent her a cheque for ten pounds. But since I fear that it won't be paid before it has been referred back, which takes time, I thought it safer to take out a money order for ten pounds over here, and to do this *in your name*, since Louise may already have left by the time it arrives; over here it has been taken out in the name of Edward Aveling. According to what the Post Office says, we are to retain the order itself over here, as the money will be paid to you at your home address which was the one we gave.

---

[a] In the original this is followed by the German translation of the will. - [b] See this volume, pp. 68-69.

Should Louise have already left, please keep the money at our disposal until further notice.

Your

F. Engels

Aveling has just come back — it's altogether too late, since orders are not issued after 4 o'clock on Saturdays!!

So we shall send it on Monday.

First published in *Victor Adlers Aufsätze, Reden und Briefe.* Erstes Heft: *Victor Adler und Friedrich Engels*, Wien, 1922

Printed according to the book

Published in English for the first time

39

ENGELS TO VICTOR ADLER

IN VIENNA

London, 17 November 1890

Dear Adler,

You will have had my letter written on Saturday.[a] Meanwhile the Avelings have had a telegram from Louise (last night at about 11 o'clock): 'THUSDAY MORNING VICTORIA.' Well, this might mean THURSDAY, but also TUESDAY. That is the least of our problems however. We know nothing whatever about the latest routes for through express trains from Vienna, but only that it's possible to come via Calais, Ostend or Flushing. On the journey via Calais or Ostend the trains arrive at about 5 a.m., and via Flushing at about 8 a.m. I therefore telegraphed you (being uncertain whether or not Louise had already left) shortly before four o'clock: 'Is Louise travelling via Flushing, Ostend or Calais, reply paid (12 words).' This is to explain what has happened, which might otherwise strike you as puzzling and odd.

Since Louise has now definitely announced her arrival here, no

---

[a] See previous letter.

purpose would be served by sending another ten pounds per money order and this has consequently not been done.

Your

F. Engels

First published in *Victor Adlers Aufsätze, Reden und Briefe.* Erstes Heft: *Victor Adler und Friedrich Engels*, Wien, 1922

Printed according to the book

Published in English for the first time

40

ENGELS TO FRIEDRICH ADOLPH SORGE

IN HOBOKEN

London, 26 November 1890

Dear Sorge,

Since the time I informed you of the death of my good Lenchen,[a] Louise Kautsky — the one who's divorced, not No. II — has come to live with me for a time and, with her, a little sunshine has returned. She is a quite marvellous woman and Kautsky must have been out of his senses when he divorced her.

Good wishes for my 70th birthday the day after tomorrow are already coming in and now Singer, Bebel and Liebknecht have announced their intention of visiting me. I wish the business was all over; I'm far from being in a birthday mood, and on top of that there's all the unnecessary FUSS which I cannot abide even at the best of times. And after all, I am, to a large extent, simply the chap who is reaping what Marx has sown in the way of fame.

The Halle Congress [12] went off brilliantly. Tussy was there and was quite delighted with the delegates but not so much with the parliamentary group,[b] which includes a fair number of philistines. But steps have been taken to ensure that this shouldn't happen again at the next elections. Meanwhile the chaps in the Reichstag are observ-

---

[a] See this volume, p. 67. - [b] the Social-Democratic group in the German Reichstag

ing better discipline than might have been hoped, and are keeping their mouths shut, otherwise they'd have been bound to make fools of themselves.

Our campaign for a joint congress in 1891 was wholly successful. You will have read about the resolutions passed at the international conference at Halle [28]—a congress to be held in Brussels, on the understanding that the congress has full sovereignty. That is all we wanted, and the Belgian Anseele himself proposed that the Swiss *and* the Belgians, the mandatories of *both* the 1889 congresses, [26] should jointly send out the convocation. Since, moreover, the Possibilists are hopelessly divided amongst themselves and openly engaged in inter-necine strife, [53] and since the collapse of Parisian Boulangism will mean that the socialist elements by whom it was previously favoured will accrue to *us* and not to the Possibilists, we shall, so to speak, WALK OVER THE COURSE. Hyndman has had the abysmal stupidity to join forces with the noble Brousse against Allemane,[a] which again will do him an enormous amount of harm.

The Germans would certainly be glad to get in touch with the AMERICAN FEDERATION OF LABOR [84]; I shall talk to the chaps over here and bring influence to bear on Fischer who's a member of the Party Executive. Fischer is one of our best men, highly intelligent, can read French and English, and is acquainted with the movement in both countries. He will counterbalance the one-sided influence exerted by Liebknecht in international affairs.

You have made an excellent début in the *Neue Zeit* [85]; just carry on as you are and you will soon get into the way of writing again. The fee is about twice what is paid to contributors over here (5 marks a page); once you've got back into your stride and are able to work faster, it won't seem so small to you. I'd like to see further evidence in support of what Schlüter told you. That I and others are paid 5 marks a page by the *Neue Zeit*, and that this is the customary fee in Germany, is a fact. I have myself written and told Kautsky[b] that you must be offered more. Schlüter is apt to trot out remarks without really thinking what he's saying. By American standards, of course, $2 a page isn't much and, if you think you ought to be paid American rates, you are quite right to ask for them. But Kautsky, who is certainly doing all he can for you, is also obliged to consider Dietz, who is paymaster,

---

[a] Engels has in mind the editorial 'The Split in France' in *Justice*, No. 353, 18 October 1890. - [b] See this volume, p. 5.

and I wouldn't like it if such considerations were to be responsible for one of the *Volkszeitung* or *Sozialist* people gaining admission to the *Neue Zeit*. Think the matter over again and, if you are intent on getting a rise, write and tell me and I'll approach Kautsky about it; that would leave all doors open.

Rosenberg & Co. had already pronounced a boycott against me and if the Nationalists now do the same,[86] it only serves me right. Why can't I give up the class struggle? In this country Marx and I are suffering just the same fate at the hands of the Fabians[87] who also wish to see the emancipation of the workers brought about by the 'heddicated'.[a]

I shall save up the articles about George in the *Labor Standard*[b] and read them at my leisure, of which I have so far had none.[88] You have no idea of the mass of papers, pamphlets, etc., that people send me.

Volume One of *Capital* has been brought out in Polish by Kasprowicz of Leipzig and has been sent me from Warsaw.[c]

Your
F. Engels

First published abridged in *Briefe und Auszüge aus Briefen von Joh. Phil. Becker, Jos. Dietzgen, Friedrich Engels, Karl Marx u. A. an F. A. Sorge und Andere*, Stuttgart, 1906 and in full in: Marx and Engels, *Works*, First Russian Edition, Vol. XXVIII, Moscow, 1940

Printed according to the original

Published in English for the first time

---

[a] In the original: *jebildeten* (Berlin dialect). - [b] *Paterson Labor Standard* - [c] *Kapitał. Krytyka ekonomii politycznej*. Tom I.

41

ENGELS TO LAURA LAFARGUE

AT LE PERREUX

London, 1 December 1890

My dear Laura,

Enfin! [a] I have got that 70th birthday behind me. On Thursday Bebel, Liebknecht, and Singer arrived. On Friday letters and telegrams *en masse*, the latter from Berlin (3), Vienna (3), Paris (Roumanian students and Frankel), Berne (*Russische Sozialdemokraten*), Leipzig *Stadt und Land*,[b] Bochum (*Klassenbewusste Bergleute*[c]—miners), Stuttgart (*Sozialdemokraten*, Württemberg's), Fürth, Höchst (Paulis), London (*Arbeiterverein*[d]),[89] Hamburg. The fraction[e] sent me a splendid album with their 35 portraits, Dietz a book of photos of some excellent Munich pictures, the Solingers a knife with inscription, etc., etc. *Enfin j'étais écrasé.*[f] Well, in the evening we had the whole lot here, embellished by and bye by little Oswald and four delegates from the *Arbeiterverein* (one of whom speechless drunk) and we kept it up till half past three in the morning and drank, besides claret, 16 bottles of champaign — the morning we had had 12 dozen oysters. So you see I did my best to show that I was still alive and kicking.

But it's a good job. One can celebrate one's 70th birthday only once. It will take me a devil of a time to reply to all those letters — even those I *must* reply to personally. That is the prose following upon the poetry of life, and to break my fall I begin by writing the only one I can write with true pleasure — this one to you.

Louise Kautsky came on the Tuesday after you left and has since then made me extremely comfortable. As to the future, we have not yet talked about it. I want her to see how things will settle down before asking her to come to a definite resolution. We are getting on very well with Pumps; my lecture and a few hints, repeated later on, that her position in my house depends very much upon her own behaviour, seem to have had some effect. We'll hope it may last.

Bebel looks rather delicate and a deal older than when I last saw him. Singer too is getting gray, and of course Liebknecht too, though

---

[a] At last! - [b] town and country - [c] class-conscious miners - [d] workers' society - [e] the Social-Democratic group in the German Reichstag - [f] In a word, I was overwhelmed.

he looks fat and *content de lui-même* [a]; he complains awfully about the few capacities among the younger generation, and the impossibility consequently of getting good men for his paper,[b] but otherwise he is very well satisfied with things in general and the Berliners in particular. To-morrow the Reichstag opens, and we had the greatest trouble to keep Singer and Bebel here to meet Burns, Cunninghame-Graham, Thorne and others at Tussy's. And now we *have* kept them here, a damnable fog is setting in (2 p. m.) which even prevents me from writing and may, if not dispersed in time, nullify the whole intended international conference.[90]

Interrupted by fog — forbidden to write by the gaslight — *donc,*[c] conclusion.

Ever yours,
F. Engels

Dites à Mémé que mon nase se porte parfaitement à l'extérieur mais qu'à l'intérieur il y a un rhume de cerveau.[d]

First published, in the language of the original (English), in: F. Engels, P. et L. Lafargue, *Correspondance*, t. II, Paris, 1956

Reproduced from the original

42

ENGELS TO FERDINAND DOMELA NIEUWENHUIS [91]

IN THE HAGUE

London, 3 December 1890

Dear Comrade,

My warmest thanks for the good wishes you sent me on my seventieth birthday, now happily surmounted. I welcome these as tendered both in your own name and in that of the Dutch Labour Party [92] and wish the latter the best possible progress and you yourself the health and strength that will enable you to fulfil the important role that has fallen to you. And I would request you to act as interpreter

---

[a] pleased with himself - [b] *Berliner Volksblatt* - [c] therefore - [d] Tell Mémé that outwardly my nose looks perfect, but there's a cold inside.

in conveying these my thanks and good wishes to the comrades over there.[a]

As regards your query about buying your son out of military service there would, I think, be nothing improper about this in principle. It is — generally speaking — just as permissible for us to make use of the advantages conceded by the present-day state to the privileged members of society, as it is for us to make use of the products[b] of others, to live indirectly on the exploitation of others, as indeed we *must* in so far as we are not ourselves economically productive. If the labour party benefits as a result, I would even regard it as a duty. Moreover, the class from which *remplaçants*[c] are recruited is not, as a rule, the working class proper, but that stratum which already overlaps to a large extent with the lumpenproletariat. And if one of the latter sells himself into the army for a few years, it does at least mean that an unemployed man has found himself a berth.

What calls for particular consideration, however, is the impression such a course of action on your part might make on your party comrades and, further, on the vast mass of workers who still remain outside the party — whether the matter would be one of indifference to working-class opinion or whether it would stir it up against Social-Democracy. That is a point that can only be determined on the spot by someone with a thorough knowledge of the circumstances, and I shall therefore refrain from voicing an opinion on it.

I am equally unfamiliar with the situation of the common soldier in the Dutch army, and upon that a great deal depends. In Germany it is our chaps who go to make the best soldiers.

Cordial regards from

Yours,
F. Engels

After your Bielefeld experience, you will not, I suppose, be in any particular hurry to return to the Holy German Empire of the Prussian Nation![d]

First published, in Russian, in *Istorik-marksist*, No. 6 (40), Moscow, 1934

Printed according to the original

Published in English for the first time

---

[a] This paragraph is missing from the draft. - [b] The draft contains the words 'of the labour'. - [c] replacements - [d] This sentence is missing from the draft.

Helene Demuth

Herr *Friedrich Engels*

wird von den Unterzeichneten eingeladen, dem

Parteitag

der

ungarländischen Sozialdemokratie

als **Gast** beizuwohnen.

Zeit: 7. und 8. Dezember 1890.

Ort: Budapest, alte bürgerl. Schiessstätte, VII. Schiessstätte-Platz.

Budapest, 24. November 1890.

Die Redaktion der „Arbeiter-Wochenchronik," Budapest.
Die Redaktion der „Népszava", Budapest.

To the Congress of the Hungarian Social-Democrats.
Invitation sent to Engels.[93]

43

ENGELS TO AMAND GOEGG

IN RENCHEN (BADEN)

London, 4 December 1890

Dear Goegg,

Many thanks for your kind good wishes. We old ones are beginning to be thin on the ground, a fact of which I have again been painfully reminded by the death of my beloved Lenchen. Well, I suppose there's bit of time left and I hope to make proper use of it.

Your old friend
F. Engels

First published in: Marx and Engels, *Works*, Second Russian Edition, Vol. 37, Moscow, 1965

Printed according to the original

Published in English for the first time

44

ENGELS TO LUDWIG SCHORLEMMER

IN DARMSTADT

London, 4 December 1890

Dear Mr Schorlemmer,

Not till today have I been able to get round to sending you my best thanks for your good wishes. My health is still pretty fair, if only my eyes permitted me to work at my desk; it's a wearisome and tedious business, but one has got to accept it. Again, smoking is something

I can seldom permit myself, and your beautiful pipes stand on the chimney piece and

> seem to say as they look at me:
> 'What, old chap, have they done to thee?'

Warmest regards to your mother, your brothers and sisters and their families, and to all party comrades from

Your old friend
F. Engels

First published in: Marx and Engels, *Works,* First Russian Edition, Vol. XXVIII, Moscow, 1940

Printed according to the original

Published in English for the first time

45

ENGELS TO ÉDOUARD VAILLANT [25]

IN PARIS

London, 5 December 1890
122 Regent's Park Road, N. W.

Dear Citizen Vaillant,

Very many thanks for your letter of the 28th ult. and your good wishes. On that day I was overwhelmed with honours by socialists of all countries. Fate has decreed that, in my capacity as survivor, I should glean the honours due to the works of my deceased contemporaries, above all those of Marx. Believe me, I harbour no illusions whatever about that, or about the tiny portion of all this homage that falls to me by right.

I am also grateful for the sympathy you express concerning the death of dear Helene, thanks to whose care I was able to work in peace for seven years. For me it is a very sad loss. But we are still right in the midst of the struggle and, with the enemy before us, looking back too often is forbidden. If I'm not mistaken the battle is approaching a crisis. In your country the collapse of Boulangism has, on the one hand, rid the opportunist government, [94] corrupted and corrupting, of all those enemies who might be immediately dangerous, and has reopened the market in which France is sold to the sharks of the Stock Exchange. On the other, however, that collapse has released elements of the revolutionary opposition who had gone astray and who, having regrouped — after the removal of the chief traitors —, should again take the field reunited in one way or another with the mass of revolutionaries who have remained faithful to their traditions. After the farce, the tragedy.

In Germany the rapid advance of the Socialist Party should quickly dispel young William's [a] illusions about the power of attraction he fondly imagines he exercises on the working class. That, too, should lead to a crisis; and the longer it is delayed, the more severe it will be.

Accordingly, in four or five years time at the most, we shall have the crisis which will, I trust, lead to victory. And I hope I shall live to see that *fin de siècle* [b]!

Please remember me kindly to Mrs Vaillant and your mother.

Yours affectionately,

F. Engels

First published in: F. Engles, P. et L. Lafargue, *Correspondance*, t. II, Paris, 1956

Printed according to the original

Translated from the French

---

[a] William II's - [b] end of the century

46

ENGELS TO PYOTR LAVROV [95]

IN PARIS

London, 5 December 1890
122 Regent's Park Road, N.W.

My dear friend Lavrov,

Many, many thanks for your kind letter of 27 November and your congratulations, as also those of your socialist compatriots on whose behalf you speak. But it's always the same. The lion's share of the honours that were showered upon me last Friday doesn't fall to me by right and no one knows that better than I do. So permit me to place on Marx's grave the lion's share of the flattering things you were good enough to say to me and which I accept, but only as his continuator. And as for the small portion which, without being presumptuous, I accept on my own account, I shall do my best to prove worthy of it.

After all, we are not so very old, you and I. And we have hopes of living and seeing. We have seen Bismarck's rise, heyday and decline, so why should we not also see, after its heyday, the decline (already in progress) and ultimate fall of Russian Tsarism, the great enemy of us all?

Yours affectionately,
F. Engels

First published, in Russian, in *Bolshevik*, No. 14, Moscow, 1935

Printed according to the original

Translated from the French

47

ENGELS TO WILHELM LIEBKNECHT

IN BERLIN

London, 8 December 1890

Dear Liebknecht,

There is more trouble in store for Brentano than he expects — just you wait and see! Thanks for the note about Gladstone, but I should point out that *I require the issues of the 'Deutsches Wochenblatt' containing the text of what Brentano and Gladstone actually said* — the short note would only mislead me, and I mustn't allow that to happen. If you haven't got time to obtain them for me, ask Fischer who will certainly do so at once.

Leave Brentano to me. You won't be disappointed. But without this *new* material I can't finish the thing off.[96]

Your
F. E.

Since Gladstone's letters were dated 22 and 28 November, there can be no doubt about *which* issues of the *Wochenblatt*[a] the stuff is in.

First published in: Marx and Engels, *Works*, First Russian Edition, Vol. XXVIII, Moscow, 1940

Printed according to the original

Published in English for the first time

---

[a] 'Mittheilung', signed: O. A., *Deutsches Wochenblatt*, No. 49, 4 December 1890.

48

ENGELS TO MOHRHENN

IN BARMEN

London, 9 December 1890
122 Regent's Park Road, N. W.

Dear Comrade Mohrhenn,

I really must thank you most warmly for the trouble you have taken over the photographs of my childhood home in the Bruch. They have given me enormous pleasure and have recalled many a youthful prank connected with the front doorstep and this or that room or window. Old Miss Demuth is right—the house in the Bruch, which in my time was No. 800, is the right one; behind it was our garden, between it and the Engels-Gang lay the bleachery and opposite that the houses belonging to my grandfather Caspar and his brother Benjamin Engels in which my uncles, Caspar and August, subsequently lived. I believe I can just remember Miss Demuth; I must have seen her once or twice at my cousin Caspar's house when we were both young. No doubt she can tell you about our original family home where my grandfather was born. It was up at the top of the Engels-Gang, where it joins the Bruch, opposite the path which leads up to the Böken and which was then nameless. It was a typical lower middle class, two-storied house; when I was young the ground floor was used for storage, while the upper floor was occupied by two of my grandparents' former maids, by then pensioned off, who were known as Drütschen and Mineken. They would often treat us children to spiced apples and bread. The house was demolished when the railway came.

Even in those days we used to say that the Bruch wasn't anything like as god-fearing as it used to be and not so many years ago my brother Rudolf was quite outspoken on the subject.[97] Pointing at the house opposite, where a man called Ottenbruch had once lived and which bore an inn sign, he said: 'See that place? Nowadays it's a favourite haunt for Social-Democrats!' Social-Democrats in the Bruch—that was, to be sure, a tremendous revolution as compared with 50 years before.

It would certainly be a far greater one, however, if our old house

were to become a Social-Democratic press. But you would have to go about it very artfully. Unless it's been resold, the house now belongs to my brother Hermann, and he wouldn't be likely to sell it if he knew what purpose you meant to put it to. Well, I don't suppose anything will come of that just yet—it would be altogether too good to be true. Well, good-bye. Soom day Ah'll coom to Barmen agean, an' then Ah'll coom an' see thi, an' then tha can tell me baht t'mucky tricks they played on thi wi' you Anti-Socialist Law o' theirn.[a]
Kindest regards,

Yours,

F. Engels

First published in *Vorwärts* (Abend-Ausgabe), Berlin, 24. November 1920

Printed according to the newspaper

Published in English for the first time

49

ENGELS TO VICTOR ADLER

IN VIENNA

London, 12 December 1890

Dear Adler,

I was on the point of writing to thank you and your wife for the telegram when I got your letter of the 9th with Aveling's dishonoured CHEQUE.[b] In its place I am sending you the enclosed cheque on the local branch of the same bank for £10 4/- to include expenses, and this CHEQUE will not be dishonoured.

It's the slapdash literary Bohemian in Aveling that leads to this kind of thing, especially when the said Bohemian insists on having a bank account. 'So young and already a Bohemian' might also be said of him. Incidentally the pair of them will soon be arriving to lunch with me, when I shall be able to give him a thorough dressing-down for this piece of carelessness and her for the frightful adulation

---

[a] This phrase is in the Rhenish dialect in the original. - [b] See this volume, p. 71.

she expended on me in the *Sozialdemokratische Monatsschrift*.[a] She's right in only one respect, namely my beard's being curiously lopsided—there are, incidentally, perfectly good reasons for this which, however, I shall spare you.

Many thanks for your hints about Louise. It is also my wish that she should remain with me and if this should fall through, I shall find it very hard to part with her. But I should have a constant feeling of uneasiness if I thought she had sacrificed other duties and other prospects on my account. Well, the matter will probably be decided in a week or two. If she stays, she will have to return to Vienna at least once this winter so as to get everything straightened out there.

As regards the danger of overwork, this was, I should say, very real in Vienna. Here, on the other hand, it is hardly likely to arise. She is not to do any actual house-work, indeed could not do so—if only on account of the maids who would not in that case regard her as a proper LADY. All she has to do is to direct and supervise. She is, besides, acting as my secretary; I dictate to her or give her things to copy out so that I can spare my eyes, and then there are various subjects I shall be studying with her—chemistry to begin with, then French; she also wants to do Latin and that presents no difficulty. After luncheon we sleep, and at night, to give my eyes a rest from reading, we play cards from 11 to 12; I also sleep better if my mind is empty. I know, by the way, what an urge she feels to sacrifice herself for others and it is *this*, in particular, that is preventing me from urging her to stay here. On the evening of the day before yesterday we discussed the matter at length when the chief obstacle seemed to be her mother to whom she only wrote yesterday about her intention to remain here. The answer to this will, of course, be of crucial importance. But imagine the state I'd be in if I had to tell myself that I had reft Louise away from a new, congenial and promising career, only to place her in a position in which she could not rid herself of the feeling of having done her mother an injury?

So, far from taking any kind of umbrage at your remarks on this subject, I am on the contrary most grateful for what you have said. For the only occasion on which Louise will depart from her instinctive candour is when she is intent on concealing her selflessness. And so it behoves us all to keep a close watch on her.

---

[a] E. Marx - Aveling, 'Friedrich Engels', *Die Sozialdemokratische Monatsschrift*, No. 10-11, 30 November 1890.

Warm regards to your wife and children about whom Louise tells me many amusing stories, and likewise to yourself from Louise and

Your
F. Engels

First published in *Victor Adlers Aufsätze, Reden und Briefe*. Erstes Heft: *Victor Adler und Friedrich Engels*, Wien, 1922

Printed according to the book

Published in English for the first time

50

ENGELS TO JOHANN HEINRICH WILHELM DIETZ

IN STUTTGART

London, 13 December 1890

Dear Mr Dietz,

I have yet to tender you my warmest thanks for the magnificent birthday present you sent me. I was particularly delighted with Reinicke's pictures; it's the first time I have seen German genre paintings depicting life in a big city that are altogether free of the stiffness and affectation which otherwise so obstinately dog German painters of genre and historical pieces. But here we have no poses—here we have life as it is lived.

That we tippled our way merrily through my 70th birthday you will have heard from the three Magi on their return to the Orient.[a] And that things are proceeding at a brisk pace in Germany I see and hear daily, and that is best of all.

With cordial regards

Yours,
F. Engels

First published in: Marx and Engels, *Works*, First Russian Edition, Vol. XXVIII, Moscow, 1940

Printed according to the original

Published in English for the first time

---

[a] Bebel, Liebknecht and Singer who came to celebrate Engels' 70th birthday.

51

ENGELS TO KARL KAUTSKY [98]

IN STUTTGART

London, 13 December 1890

Dear Kautsky,

Very many thanks for your two letters [99] and for the article devoted to me [a] which was, alas, all too flattering. I got through my birthday all right and, even though the outside air was clear of fog, my head wasn't when I went to bed at half past three in the morning. I fared almost as you did at my birthday in 1883, when the tippling took place round my sick-bed.

I enclose herewith a preliminary piece about Brentano and would be obliged if you could contrive to get it into the next number of the *Neue Zeit*, should this be feasible. I'll give the man something to remember me by. He'd like to keep Gladstone's letters up his sleeve until I have answered, but we'll soon put a stop to that. [96]

You will also shortly be getting a contribution from Marx's unpublished work, something quite new and extremely topical and to the point. [b] It has already been copied out but I shall have to look it over first and possibly write a few lines by way of an introduction. But please tell no one else about it yet; my hands are completely full, what with correspondence and replying to the many letters I get, and I can't say exactly *when*.

I cannot possibly entrust the remaining fascicles of Marx's Volume IV [100] to the post or any other intermediary. So when you've had the 2nd fascicle you won't be getting any more for a while. This is also because, in the later fascicles, there are all sorts of divagations and long deleted passages which may not have to be copied out and, since this will entail constant discussion, the work could only be done over here. Later on, if you come back to this country again, and I have been able to familiarise myself a bit more with the ms., we shall see what

---

[a] [K. Kautsky,] 'Friedrich Engels. Zu seinem siebzigsten Geburtstag', *Die Neue Zeit*, 9. Jg. 1890/91, 1. Bd., Nr. 8. - [b] *Critique of the Gotha Programme*

can be done. Needless to say, you are to finish what you have already got.

I should be obliged if you would send me another 6 copies of the 8th issue[a]; that will, I think, suffice.

Now, however, I must close; herewith a note to Dietz, which kindly pass on to him.

Your old friend
F. Engels

First published in full in *Aus der Frühzeit des Marxismus, Engels Briefwechsel mit Kautsky,* Prag, 1935

Printed according to the original

Published in English for the first time

52

ENGELS TO LAURA LAFARGUE

AT LE PERREUX

London, 17 December 1890

My dear Laura,

Two pieces of good news.

First. Your usual box of puddings, cake and sweets, for Mémé and brothers, has been sent off yesterday as usual and hope will reach by Friday[b] at latest. Otherwise please apply to the Bureau des Expéditions Grande Vitesse, Gare du Nord, or at 23 Rue Dunkerque, P. Bigeault or 18 Rue Bergère, *chez* E. D'Odiardi.

Second. Louise Kautsky remains here for good. So my troubles are settled. She seems to like it better after all than setting other people's children into this world.[c] And we get on capitally. She superintends the house and does my secretary's work which saves my eyes and enables me to make it worth her while to give up her profession, at least for the present. She wishes me to send you her kindest regards.

Padlewski deserves a monument and a life pension. Not so much

---

[a] of *Die Neue Zeit* containing Engels' *Outlines of a Critique of Political Economy* - [b] 19 December - [c] Louise Kautsky studied obstetrics in Vienna.

for polishing off that vile brute Seliverstov than for delivering Paris from the Russian incubus.[101] The change in the Paris press since that execution is indeed wonderful and if a *voyou*[a] like Labruyère finds it to pay him to get Padlewski out of the way, the revulsion of feeling generally must be very great indeed. Even the Boulangists and the *Intransigeant* have to follow suit.

But it's genuine Parisian. Argument and reason is no use against this chauvinistic enthusiasm for the Czar's[b] alliance. All at once a fact occurs, which lightens up the mental darkness like a flash of lightning. Now they see that they are making themselves accomplices of this Russian official infamy, and that, if they themselves have not the courage to get out of it, a Pole has, and can they assist in sending that Pole over to bourgeois 'justice'? The enthusiasm for the Czar is at once transferred to the Poles and Nihilists, and the Czar is in for it, for his trouble and his money spent.

All the same, the effect would hardly have been so great if our people had not so constantly and determinedly attacked the Czar.

Anyhow, *je m'en réjouis*.[c]

Pumps has all at once come round. Louise and I coaxed her a bit. After the talking to I had given her, Percy gave her another, and now she is friendliness all over, not only with Louise, but also Annie. Well, I hope it will last, and if it does not, it will be her own fault and then I shall be in a clear position and act accordingly. This time I *can* be master and I shall.

How is Paul's affair with Levraut getting on?[102]

Fortin writes to say that he and Paul wished to publish the *18 Brumaire* in the *Socialiste* but required my consent. That of course I gave him with pleasure.— He also said the *Revue Socialiste* wanted the same and also the *Misère de la philosophie* for republication. I said as to that, Marx would never forgive me if I entrusted any ms. of his to the hands of such people who were capable of making all sorts of changes in it; as to the *Misère*, after all the disappointments I had with that,[103] I should consent to its republication *in book-form only*, and only after having full guarantees for the execution of the promise.

What Paul writes about the part of the Rothschilds in the Krach[d] Baring seems not without foundation.[104] The Barings are rich enough to pay all losses and have plenty left. So that the guarantors will be perfectly safe. But the Barings cannot remain a first rate firm

---

[a] guttersnipe, hooligan - [b] Alexander III's - [c] I am glad. - [d] row

and cannot therefore continue to be financial agents of the Argentine Government. There the Rothschilds will naturally step into the Barings' shoes. And in order to squeeze the Argentine Government into compliance, the French and German Argentine committees must resist the very sensible (in the interest of *all parties*) proposals of the London Committee, and insist upon cash payment of the coupons which the Londoners are willing to suspend for 3 years and have the amount transformed into a new debt. And the *gobemouches*[a] of the Paris press, *payés comptant*,[b] work hard in the interest of the Rothschilds.

I am afraid this will be the last long letter you will have for some time. I am so overworked that correspondence will have to be confined to the necessary minimum. I have an urgent quarrel with Brentano on my hands (preface, 4th edition of *Capital*[96]) and those sort of things I cannot dictate.

Love to Mémé.

Ever yours,
F. Engels

Bien des choses à Paul.[c]

First published, in the language of the original (English), in: F. Engels, P. et L. Lafargue, *Correspondance*, t. II, Paris, 1956

Reproduced from the original

53

ENGELS TO WILHELM LIEBKNECHT

IN BERLIN

London, 18 December 1890

Dear Liebknecht,

You guessed the names aright.

I fail to see what point there would be in publishing this muddled correspondence, the Hegelian language of which would today be in-

---

[a] simpletons - [b] paid in cash - [c] Best regards to Paul.

comprehensible.[105] Either you intend to publish everything bearing Marx's name or — might this be the beginning of the *Collected Works* in pamphlet and/or serial form planned by you and Paul Ernst?

Against this I would protest here and now as, indeed, I shall continue to do.

I would gladly agree to the publication in pamphlet form of such individual pieces by Marx as are comprehensible today without notes or a commentary, but to *their publication only, without notes or a commentary of any description*. Should the plan you propose here be put into effect, however, I shall intervene forthwith.

I cannot write a preface. The most I could say about the correspondence is that Marx told me more than once that his part of it had been tinkered with by Ruge who had inserted all manner of nonsense.

If only you people would leave off pestering me so that I had time to finish the 3rd volume,[a] I could myself do something worthwhile along those lines. I have already told you that the time is past when I can do work to order for you. I shall take on absolutely nothing further, even though it may amount to no more than 3 lines, until I have dealt with the mountain of stuff I have already undertaken to do.

When a chap can only write by daylight and, what's more, at most 3, and quite often only 2, hours a day and with constant interruptions into the bargain, you will understand that every superfluous letter robs him of his most precious time. Besides which, there has been virtually no daylight for the past 12 days.

So will you at long last be kind enough to let me work in peace?

Despite a lengthy search I cannot immediately put my finger on the passage in Sybel.[b] It is so cunningly concealed that leafing through the book is no good. However, it would do you no harm, in view of your preoccupation with Bismarck, to go through this important source yourself, in which case you would yourself find the passage in the 4th or 5th volume.[106]

---

[a] of *Capital* - [b] H. von Sybel, *Die Begründung des Deutschen Reiches durch Wilhelm I*, vols I - V.

Kindest regards from my household to yours, and a happy holiday to you.

Your
F. E.

Today I have had another reminder from Dietz about the new edition of the *Origin*.[a] How can I possibly manage if I don't get a moment's peace?

First published in: Marx and Engels, *Works*, First Russian Edition, Vol. XXVIII, Moscow, 1940

Printed according to the original

Published in English for the first time

54

ENGELS TO FRIEDRICH ADOLPH SORGE

IN HOBOKEN

[London,] 20 December 1890

Dear Sorge,

Have had your letters up to the 9th of this month. Use my letters as you think fit.[107] I am glad that you consulted Schlüter about the question of the fee[b] and that all is now settled. As things go in *Germany*, what they offer is *very* respectable. Schoenlank, by the way, who wrote and told you this, is a most depraved fellow who in fact does not hesitate to seize on any and every opportunity to extort money from the party. Of this he again gave proof at the Halle Congress.[12]

I am greatly overworked, hence just a postcard today. I have taken on Mr Brentano who must now be disabled 'good and proper'.[96]

Louise Kautsky has decided to stay with me *for good*. I am, of course, absolutely delighted and deeply grateful to the sweet child. She is giving up a great deal for my sake, but luckily I am in a position to offer her in return much that would not be available to her in Vienna. Besides keeping house for me, she does a fair amount of secre-

---

[a] F. Engels, *The Origin of the Family, Private Property and the State*. - [b] See this volume, p. 74.

tarial work—just what I needed. So as you will see, I cannot for the present accept your kind invitation to move to Hoboken [108]; I am engaged in renewing my lease for another three years.[a]

I hope that, by the time this arrives, your wife will have completely recovered. Schorlemmer will again be unable to visit us this Christmas because of his persistent aural catarrh; otherwise he might go deaf. So more anon. A Happy Christmas to you.

Your old friend,

F. E.

First published abridged in *Briefe und Auszüge aus Briefen von Joh. Phil. Becker, Jos. Dietzgen, Friedrich Engels, Karl Marx u. A. an F.A. Sorge und Andere*, Stuttgart, 1906 and in full in: Marx and Engels, *Works*, First Russian Edition, Vol. XXVIII, Moscow, 1940

Printed according to the original

Published in English for the first time

55

ENGELS TO LEO FRANKEL [109]

IN PARIS

London, 25 December 1890

Dear Frankel,

Having just got a minute or two to spare—by no means usual during the daytime (the only time in which I am allowed to write)—I shall reply to you straight away.

Many thanks for your telegram and retrospective good wishes. You must excuse me for not having acknowledged receipt of the former. I have been swamped, in the truest sense of the word, with correspondence.

Well, let's have done with the formalities and get on to the main point of your letter. I was already aware of your attitude to the ructions in France [110]—an entirely understandable one in view of your

---

[a] See this volume, p. 5.

long absence from the movement there—as a result of reading your article in the *Sächsische Arbeiter-Zeitung*[a] which had been sent to me from Berlin. The ructions are just as regrettable and just as inevitable as were those in the past between the Lassalleans and the Eisenachers for the simple reason that in both cases cunning business men placed themselves at the head of one of the two parties and exploited that party for their own business interests for as long as the party would tolerate it; accordingly it is no more possible to co-operate with Brousse & Co., than with Schweitzer, Hasselmann and partners. If, like me, you had been engaged in the struggle from the beginning and in its every detail, you would see as clearly as I do that in this case unification would above all mean capitulating to a gang of schemers and place-seekers who are betraying to the ruling bourgeoisie the party's true basic principles and its well-tried fighting method ... the better to secure positions for themselves and small, insignificant advantages for the working men who support them. Unification would thus amount to the same thing as capitulating to these gentlemen outright, a point further borne out by the discussions at the Paris Congress of 1889.[51]

Unification will come, just as in Germany, but it can only last if the fight is fought to a finish, the contradictions are resolved and the rascals hounded out by their own supporters. When the Germans were drawing close to union, Liebknecht came out for union at all costs. We were against it on the grounds that, since the Lassalleans were near to collapse, we should await the completion of that process, when unification would come about of its own accord. Marx wrote a long critique of the so-called unification programme, which was distributed in manuscript form.[b]

They didn't listen to us, with the result that we had to bring Hasselmann into our ranks and rehabilitate him in the eyes of the world, only to chuck him out as a blackguard six months later.[111] And we had to incorporate Lassallean inanities into our programme, thereby destroying the programme for good. It was a double fiasco which, given a little more patience, could have been avoided.[63]

In France the Possibilists are going through just the same process of disintegration as did the Lassalleans in 1875. The leaders of *both* the

---

[a] L. F[rankel,] 'Zur französischen Arbeiterbewegung', *Sächsische Arbeiter-Zeitung*, Nos. 170 and 178, 3 and 12 December 1890. - [b] K. Marx, *Critique of the Gotha Programme*.

persuasions that emerged from the split[53] are, in my view, worthless. This process, in which the leaders devour one another and which nevertheless brings over to us the intrinsically sound majority of members, can, in my view, be interrupted or checked—if not actually brought to a complete halt—by only *one* error on our part—that is to say if we make a premature attempt at unification.

On the other hand we have already taken a decisive step which will in any case hasten the advent of unification and may, perhaps, achieve it straight away. For at my suggestion—after Tussy had discussed it with Aveling, Bernstein and Fischer (presently of the party leadership[28])—first the French (*our* Marxists) and then the Germans at Halle,[12] where they also had the support of the Swiss, Danes, Swedes and Austrians, resolved unanimously that, instead of holding a separate congress in 1891, they should attend the congress in Brussels convoked by the Possibilists in view of the fact that the Belgians had accepted the conditions laid down by us in 1889, conditions which, axiomatic though they were, were nevertheless rejected by the Possibilists. You will admit that this was a major concession on our part, since the overwhelming majority of the European parties were behind us. Yet we acted *as we did* because we knew we had to fight the Possibilists with like weapons and on like terms if the supremacy of Brousse on the one hand and of Allemane on the other was to be brought swiftly to an end. Not until the bulk of the Possibilist working men see that they are isolated in Europe, that they have no sure allies save Messrs Hyndman & Co. (who are in the same boat vis-à-vis their supporters as was Brousse) and that all the braggadocio has been solely for the benefit of the leaders, will the fuss die down. And that will clear the way for the congress.

So just be patient for another six months. Any attempt on our part to achieve a settlement sooner would be interpreted by Brousse as well as by Allemane as a sign of weakness and would hinder rather than help us. But when the time comes, and in my view, it is not far off, the Possibilist working men will join us just as the Lassalleans did and, what's more, without our having to offer leading positions to the schemers, traitors and ne'er-do-wells among them.

No one is more anxious than I am to see a strong socialist party in France. However I have to pay due regard to the facts as they are and I am anxious that it should come about only on a basis which holds out a promise of permanence, which is *real* and which won't result in a HUMBUG movement *à la* Brousse.

With warm regards.

Your old friend

F. Engels

Thank you also for the *Bataille* article.[112] Louise Kautsky, who is here and will be staying here, sends you her warm regards.

First published, in Hungarian, in *Népszava*, No. 130, Budapest, 3 June 1906

Printed according to the newspaper

Translated from the Hungarian

Published in English for the first time

56

ENGELS TO G. BLUME[113]

IN HAMBURG

London, 27 December 1890

Dear Comrade,

Mr Stinzleih has passed on to me the kind greetings conveyed by you on behalf of the delegates to the Congress, the representatives of 596,000 German working men. There is no need for me to tell you in so many words how glad I was to be remembered at that Congress. Unfortunately I am unable to thank those concerned, who will by now have dispersed to all parts of Germany, and can do no more than express my sincere thanks to you, Mr Chairman, while giving you my firm assurance that, so long as it remains in my power, I shall persevere in the struggle for the emancipation of the working class.

Yours very sincerely,

F. Engels

First published as a supplement to *Begründung der Beschlüsse des vom 8. bis 11. 12. in Berlin abgehaltenen Hilfskassenkongresses*, Hamburg, 1891

Printed according to the photocopy of the supplement

Published in English for the first time

57

ENGELS TO GEORG SCHUMACHER [114]

IN SOLINGEN

[London, December 1890]

My dear Schumacher,

Since you will now be at home, I am taking the opportunity of asking you to convey my warmest thanks to my friends in Solingen for the beautiful present they gave me on my 70th birthday. But at the same time, I wish to thank you, too, for your contribution to the parliamentary group's[a] magnificent present.

As a boy, whenever I saw a knife like this, I would gaze at it admiringly and envy the owner of a tool so suited to all manner of uses. Now, in my old age, one such has come into my possession, and in such a fashion to boot, and with so honourable an inscription.

As you know, since 1849 my attachment to Solingen has been of a very special kind, since the time, that is, when I, along with the Solingen volunteers, marched to Elberfeld where, confronted by a reactionary civic militia, unorganised Elberfelders and a highly reactionary security committee, I could not have remained unscathed for three days if it had not been for the Solingeners who, almost alone amongst those taking part, represented the revolutionary element.[115] And, since I am anxious that those ties attaching me to Solingen should not be allowed to slacken or break, it is a very special pleasure to note that in Solingen I, too, am still remembered.

With warm regards to you and to all the members of the party from your old friend,

F. Engels

First published in *Rheinische Zeitung*, Nr. 47, Köln, 24. Februar 1906

Printed according to the newspaper

Published in English for the first time

---

[a] the Social - Democratic group in the German Reichstag

1891

58

ENGELS TO FRIEDRICH ADOLPH SORGE

IN HOBOKEN

London, 3 January 1891 [a]

Dear Sorge,

Avant tout [b] a Happy New Year to you and your wife. [c]

Unfortunately I didn't make a note of the date of my last postcard in which I replied to the more urgent points in your letter. [116]

Many thanks for the excellent photograph of you and your wife. I should like to send you one of myself but the constant fog and snow we have had since 25 November have made it impossible to obtain either a photograph or a print from the negative plate. As soon as the light is suitable, I shall have my photograph taken again so as to see what I look like at the age of 70, and your requirements will then be promptly attended to.

Louise Kautsky is staying with me. I'm very very grateful to the good child for the sacrifice she is thereby making on my behalf. Once again I am able to work in tranquillity, indeed better than ever, as she will also be my secretary. I have enough for her to do but not for a man brought in from outside. So everything is proving unexpectedly pleasant and snug and there is sunshine in my house once more, even though the fog is as thick as ever outside.

---

[a] 1890 in the original. - [b] First of all - [c] Katharina Sorge

I think I have already told you that you may use my letters in any way you think fit. But after all it's *you* who are supposed to keep *us* informed about America!

Your complaint was promptly forwarded to Paris.[117] But will it do any good? BUSINESS IS NOT THEIR FORCE!

According to latest reports Sam Moore, Chief Justice at Asaba on the Niger, is in poor health. Having stood the climate so well, he has now been afflicted all of a sudden with diarrhoea, fever, and congestion of the spleen and liver—I am anxiously awaiting the next post the day after tomorrow. He will be back here in April on 6 months' furlough.

In Europe the most important event of the last 3 months has been the slaying of Seliverstov by Padlewski[101] and—which is what the government *wanted*—the latter's escape. Evidence that Paris was the headquarters of Russia's *mouchards*[a] abroad, that the French Republic was to carry out espionage and render ignoble services for the Tsar as the prior condition of an alliance with Russia and, finally, Padlewski's bold deed which evoked a powerful and sympathetic response from every fibre of the French tradition—all this proved the last straw. The Franco-Russian alliance was dead before it had reached its term and been born (Louise Kautsky is a midwife, hence the simile) and this, not only because the bourgeois Republicans would not have liked it, even today, but also because the people in Petersburg have realised that it would misfire at the crucial moment and hence isn't worth a damn. As far as world peace is concerned, that is a tremendous gain.

Fog, darkness—must stop.

Many regards to your wife and you yourself.

Your
F. E.

First published abridged in *Briefe und Auszüge aus Briefen von Joh. Phil. Becker, Jos. Dietzgen, Friedrich Engels, Karl Marx u. A. an F. A. Sorge und Andere*, Stuttgart, 1906 and in full in: Marx and Engels, *Works*, First Russian Edition, Vol. XXVIII, Moscow, 1940

Printed according to the original

Published in English for the first time

---

[a] police spies

59

ENGELS TO KARL KAUTSKY[98]

IN STUTTGART

London, 7 January 1891

Dear Kautsky,

Yesterday I sent to you by *registered* post Marx's ms. which will have given you much pleasure.[118] I doubt whether it will be able to appear in the Holy German Empire *as it stands*. Take a look at it and delete the objectionable bits wherever feasible, replacing them with dots. Where the context does not permit of this, however, kindly mark the passages for me in the proofs and, if possible, inform me in a couple of lines of the *reasons* for the objection and I shall then do what I can. I should then place the amended bits in brackets and point out in my introductory note that these are *amended* passages. So let me have your corrections on the galleys, please.

But there may well be other people, apart from the bigwigs in the police, who will be displeased when it appears. Should you feel it necessary to take this into account, I would ask you to send the ms. *registered* to Adler. In Vienna it will doubtless be possible to print it (with the exception, alas, of the splendid passage on religious needs) in its entirety *and printed it will be, whatever happens*. I should imagine, however, that this *very positive* intention of mine, of which I herewith notify you, will afford you complete protection against whatever lamentations may arise. For after all, since none of you can stop its being printed, it would be far better for it to appear in Germany itself and in the *Neue Zeit*, the party organ founded expressly for such purposes.

I have stopped work on the *Brentano*[96] so as to get this thing ready for you; for I want to make good use of the passages it contains on the iron law of wages[119] and it would have been pointless not to have got this thing ready for the press at the same time. I had intended to polish off *Brentano* this week but once again so many disturbances and so much correspondence have intervened that it will be virtually impossible to do so.

So if you come up against any snags, be so good as to let me know.

Over here it's still freezing hard. Poor Schorlemmer has a cold and is temporarily deaf; he was unable to come for Christmas. Sam Moore is seriously ill in Asaba and I am anxiously awaiting further news.

Your

F. Engels

Regards to Tauscher.

First published in full in *Aus der Frühzeit des Marxismus. Engels Briefwechsel mit Kautsky*, Prag, 1935

Printed according to the original

Published in English for the first time

60

ENGELS TO PASQUALE MARTIGNETTI

IN BENEVENTO

London, 9 January 1891

Dear Friend,

Your sister's misfortune has aroused my heartfelt sympathy. And I can imagine what an indescribable state of agitation it has put you into. But don't lose your head. What good would it do your sister if you were to kill the dirty dog? He would bear with him to the grave the satisfaction of having ruined not one family but two. I know that in societies such as those of southern Italy, where a good many memories from the time of the gens still live on, a brother is regarded as the natural protector and avenger of his sister. But this brother is also married, he has a wife and children, he has obligations towards them, and in today's society those obligations take precedence over everything else. In my view, therefore, you owe it to your family to refrain from any action that would inevitably condemn you to lifelong separation from them.

So far as I am concerned, your sister is still as pure and as deserving of respect as she always was.

But if you believe you must take your revenge, there is, after all, yet another way in which you can brand the seducer in the eyes of the public with the mark of disgrace.

Over here the brother would give the scoundrel a public thrashing.

In France or Germany a publicly administered box on the ears would suffice.

In Austrian Poland (Leopol[a]) a journalist had sold himself to the Russians. Some young Poles laid hold of him on the public promenade, placed him over a bench and gave him 25 of the best.

You in Italy will also have ways of publicly branding a scoundrel like this and of exposing him to universal scorn without taking his life or causing him permanent physical damage.

As I have said, far be it from me to advise you about this matter. But if you are firmly convinced that some sort of vengeance must be done, then it had best be vengeance affecting the seducer's *honour* rather than any other kind.

With warm regards,

Yours,

F. Engels

Very many thanks for your good wishes on my 70th birthday.

First published, in the language of the original (German), in *La corrispondenza di Marx e Engels con italiani. 1848-1895*, Milano, 1964

Printed according to the original

Published in English for the first time

---

[a] Lvov

61

ENGELS TO STANISŁAW MENDELSON

IN LONDON

[London,] Tuesday, 13 January 1891
122 Regent's Park Road, N. W.

Dear Citizen Mendelson,

Last Sunday,[a] when we discussed the day and time at which it would be convenient for you to do me the pleasure of dining here, we were in such a hurry that, in order to avoid any misunderstanding, I had better repeat what I meant to say to you.

I take it that I may expect you, that is to say you, Mrs Mendelson and Citizen Jodko on Thursday, the day after tomorrow, at six o'clock. It is possible that I didn't express myself clearly enough in regard to the last named. If so, I would ask you to be so good as to request him again on my behalf to do me the honour of coming.[b]

My compliments, as also those of Mrs Kautsky, to Mrs Mendelson.

Yours very sincerely,
F. Engels

First published in: Marx and Engels, *Works*, Second Russian Edition, Vol. 38, Moscow, 1965

Printed according to the original

Translated from the French

Published in English for the first time

---

[a] 11 January - [b] See this volume, p. 108.

62

ENGELS TO KARL KAUTSKY [98]

IN STUTTGART

London, 15 January 1891

Dear Baron,

You will see from the accompanying corrected proofs [a] that I am not inhuman and have even gone so far as to inject some soothing morphine and bromide into the introduction, [b] which no doubt will have a sufficiently anodyne effect on the melancholy mood of our friend Dietz. I shall only write to Bebel today. [120] I didn't mention the matter to him before since I had no desire to place him in a false position vis-à-vis Liebknecht. He would have been *honour bound* to speak to the latter about it and Liebknecht, who has made extracts from the ms., as is evident from his speech on the programme at Halle, [121] would have raised heaven and earth to prevent its being published.

If the passage 'to attend to his religious *as well as his bodily* [needs]' [c] cannot very well stand, delete the five words underlined and insert dots. The allusion will then gain in subtlety and still be sufficiently comprehensible. In which case it will not, I trust, give rise to misgivings.

For the rest I have obliged you and Dietz by doing everything you wanted and *more*, as you will see.

The Mendelsons have arrived here from Paris. On his release the magistrate *forbade* him to leave France. The Minister, *Constans*, on the other hand, *enjoined* him to leave voluntarily, failing which he would be expelled. [122] Constans entrusted Labruyère, who is notoriously hand in glove with the police, with the task of spiriting Padlewski away. Had Padlewski appeared before a jury, the intrigues with the

---

[a] K. Marx, *Critique of the Gotha Programme*. - [b] Preface to Karl Marx's *Critique of the Gotha Programme*. - [c] While preparing the ms. for the press Engels for reasons of censorship replaced the word *Notdurft* used by Marx by the word *Bedürfnisse* and put it in the square brackets (cf. present edition, Vol. 24, p. 98).

Russians would have come to a head. The activities of the Russian *mouchards*[a] in Paris could not have been concealed from the court and Padlewski might have been *acquitted*! Consequently he was an enormous embarrassment to the government and had to go. Ask Lafargue to write an article for you on the disruption by Padlewski of the Russo-French alliance.[b][101] Liebknecht has got hold of completely the wrong end of the stick, as he always does where foreign affairs are concerned.

The Mendelsons arrived here without any addresses and fell into the hands of Smith Headingley and Hyndman who took them to a meeting,[123] etc. Finally they came to my house and I gave them Ede's address; on my paying them a formal return visit for diplomatic reasons, who should come in at the door but Mr Smith Headingley. This gave me an opportunity to treat him with icy disdain in front of the Poles, which seemed to have the desired effect. They were here on Sunday,[c] and today they, the Edes and Avelings are coming to dine at my house. This will doubtless frustrate the intrigues set in train in the interests of Brousse, Hyndman & Co. Pity you won't be there. We start off with oysters.

Your

F. E.

First published in full in *Aus der Frühzeit des Marxismus. Engels Briefwechsel mit Kautsky*, Prag, 1935

Printed according to the original

Published in English for the first time

---

[a] police spies - [b] See this volume, pp. 123, 129. - [c] 11 January

63

ENGELS TO FRIEDRICH ADOLPH SORGE

IN HOBOKEN

[London,] 17 January 1891

Dear Sorge,

Herewith the 4th edition of *Capital*[a] (registered) and a parcel of newspapers. As Sam Moore is doubtless already on his way back to Europe from the Niger—6 months' furlough every 2 years—various things he has been getting hitherto will now become available for you, viz. the *Berliner Volks-Tribüne*, which was set on a pretty good course by little Conrad Schmidt and has not as yet been ruined by Paul Ernst, and the *Cri du Travailleur* which reprints the main items from *Le Socialiste*. Also a *Vorwärts*[124] with our revelations about Mr Reuß.

Constant snow and ice since 25 November. The water pipes under the street have been frozen for the past 5 days and we're having no end of trouble over our water. No. 17 of the *Neue Zeit* will contain a bombshell, to wit Marx's critique of the draft programme of 1875.[b] You'll be delighted, but it will cause rage and indignation among a good many people in Germany.

Regards to your wife[c] and to the Schlüters and Romms when you see them.

Your
F. E.

First published in *Briefe und Auszüge aus Briefen von Joh. Phil. Becker, Jos. Dietzgen, Friedrich Engels, Karl Marx u. A. an F. A. Sorge und Andere*, Stuttgart, 1906

Printed according to the original

Published in English for the first time

---

[a] the fourth German edition of the first volume of *Capital* - [b] K. Marx, *Critique of the Gotha Programme*. It was published in *Die Neue Zeit*, No. 18 and not No. 17 as had been planned. - [c] Katharina Sorge

64

ENGELS TO STANISŁAW MENDELSON

IN LONDON

[London,] Sunday, 18 January 1891

Dear Citizen Mendelson,

After my conversation with Mrs Mendelson yesterday evening I discovered an article in the Paris *Socialiste* [125] on the strength of which you could, I believe, write a letter to the English press regarding the matter Mrs Mendelson and Citizen Jodko spoke to me about.

I have discussed the matter with Aveling and his wife.[a] They will be dropping in on you tomorrow morning. If you and Aveling would then care to fix a time for the two of you to do me the pleasure of calling here, we could compose a letter and arrange for it to appear in the press.[126]

My compliments to Mrs Mendelson and Citizen Jodko.

Yours very sincerely,

F. Engels

First published in: Marx and Engels, *Works*, First Russian Edition, Vol. XXVIII, Moscow, 1940

Printed according to the original

Translated from the French

Published in English for the first time

---

[a] Eleanor Marx-Aveling

65

ENGELS TO CARL SCHORLEMMER [128]

IN MANCHESTER

London, 27 January 1891

Dear Jollymeier,

In my dictionary of modern Greek I find:

λουμπάρδα, ἡ *bombarde, canon*
λουμπαρδάρης, *bombardier*
λουμπαρδάρω, *bombarder*, etc.

The heavy gun reached the Byzantines from Italy and the earliest generic name for a gun of this kind is *bombarda*. Since the modern Greek ß = the Italian v, b is denoted by μπ (μπάγκα, *banc pour s'asseoir*,[a] μπαζάρι, *bazar, marché public*[b]). So as to avoid having this dreadful combination twice, the first b appears here as β.

According to the above, therefore, the fact that λουμπάρδος means bronze used for cannon cannot present any difficulties.

I trust you received Louise's letter and are feeling better. Something to cheer you up will be going off per book post. Regards from Louise and

Your
F. E.

First published in *Einheit*, Nr. 7, Berlin, 1958

Printed according to the original
Published in English for the first time

---

[a] bench - [b] market

66

ENGELS TO HEINRICH SCHEU

IN LONDON

[London,] 27 January 1891
122 Regent's Park Road, N. W.

Dear Mr Scheu,

Please forgive me for having kept you waiting so long for a reply to your kind note of the 10th.[129] But in the first place I have had an extremely urgent job to do, secondly, owing to appointments with doctors, the timing of which did not depend on me, I have virtually never been master of my own time and, thirdly, the weather has not, until quite recently, been propitious for photography.

I shall, I think, now be at your disposal — at any rate as from the day after tomorrow, especially if you are able to give me 12 or 24-hours' NOTICE. I thought I might again go to Debenham quite close by, but would go to anyone else you like (save for Mayall, who refused to take money from Marx, which makes it *gênant*ᵃ) and I should be very glad if you were also to attend and yourself explain to the man what you want and how you want it.

With kind regards,

Yours sincerely,
F. Engels

First published in: Marx and Engels, *Works*, Second Russian Edition, Vol. 38, Moscow, 1965

Printed according to the original

Published in English for the first time

ᵃ embarrassing

67

ENGELS TO HERMANN SCHLÜTER [130]

IN HOBOKEN

London, 29 January 1891

Dear Schlüter,

At last I can get round to answering your letter of 19 November. Many thanks for your and your wife's[a] kind wishes.[b] I wish you had been there. We tippled until half past three in the morning and, besides claret, downed 16 bottles of sparkling wine.

Unfortunately I cannot take advantage of Sorge's invitation.[108] I have put down so many roots here in Europe and have such a vast amount to do that I could never consider withdrawing to America unless absolutely compelled to do so. Moreover, now that Louise Kautsky is here, my domestic affairs are again in perfect order.

Many thanks for the *Kalender*.[131]

Some of the articles in the *Cyclopaedia*[c] are by Marx and some by me, all, or nearly all, being devoted to military subjects — biographies of military commanders, articles on ARTILLERY, CAVALRY, FORTIFICATION, etc. Pure hack-work, no more; may be safely consigned to oblivion.[132]

That the Socialist Labor Party [133] over there is going to rack and ruin I can see plainly enough from its fraternisation with the Nationalists [86] compared with whom our native Fabians [87] — likewise middle-class — are positively radical. I should have thought it scarcely possible that, by mating with the *Nationalist*, the *Sozialist* could have engendered further tedium. Sorge sends me the *Nationalist* but, try as I may, I cannot find anyone who is prepared to read it.

Another thing I don't understand is the row with Gompers.[134] So far as I know, his Federation [84] is an association of TRADES UNIONS and nothing but TRADES UNIONS. Thus the chaps are *formally entitled* to turn away anyone who comes as representative of a working men's association that is *not* a TRADES UNION, or to turn away the delegates of a society to which such associations are admitted. Whether it was advisable from the point of view of *propaganda* to court a rebuff of this kind,

---

[a] Anna Schlüter's - [b] on Engels' 70th birthday - [c] *The New American Cyclopaedia* (for articles by Marx and Engels see present edition, Vol. 18)

is, of course, impossible for me to judge from where I am. But that it was bound to happen was, after all, beyond doubt and I, for one, cannot hold Gompers responsible.

However, bearing in mind next international congress in Brussels,[135] I should have thought it might have been a good thing to keep in with Gompers who has at least got more working men behind him than the Socialist Labor Party, and thus ensure as large a representation as possible—including *his* people—from America. For while there the chaps would, after all, see much that would shake their faith in their blinkered TRADES UNION standpoint—and, quite apart from that, where do you propose to find a RECRUITING-GROUND if not amongst the TRADES UNIONS?

Many thanks for the stuff about silver.[136] If you can find me anything containing notes on *current silver production* in the UNITED STATES, I should be grateful. The bimetal currency [137] idiots in Europe are nothing but the DUPES of the American silver producers and are perfectly prepared to pull the latter's chestnuts out of the fire for them. Vainly, alas,—nothing will come of this shady affair. See my note on precious metals in the 4th edition of *Capital*.[138]

Do please let me have further details about the speech by Marx on protective tariffs which you mention.[139] All I can remember is that, when the discussion began to flag at the German Workers' Society in Brussels,[140] Marx and I arranged between ourselves to conduct a mock debate in which he advocated free trade and I protective tariffs; I can still see the chaps' astonished expressions when they suddenly saw us go at it hammer and tongs. The speech might have been printed in the *Deutsche-Brüsseler-Zeitung*. I cannot remember any other.

It's unlikely that you will be able to return to Germany within the next few years. True, Tauscher has been released, but only because nothing could be proved against him. On the other hand, it transpired on the same occasion that hitherto the statute of limitations has been regularly suspended so far as you people are concerned.

Cordial regards to yourself and your wife from Louise Kautsky and

Your

F. Engels

Motteler is still here, winding up the business at 114 Kentish Town Road [a]; how he will manage when the house is vacated on 25 March and he can only carry on with this job at home, I do not know. But he absolutely refuses to go back to Switzerland although we know it to be perfectly feasible. Ede is doing well; he works like a Trojan and is writing some very good stuff for the *Neue Zeit*.

First published abridged in *Briefe und Auszüge aus Briefen von Joh. Phil. Becker, Jos. Dietzgen, Friedrich Engels, Karl Marx u. A. an F. A. Sorge und Andere*, Stuttgart, 1906 and in full in: Marx and Engels, *Works*, First Russian Edition, Vol. XXVIII, Moscow, 1940

Printed according to the original

68

ENGELS TO PAUL LAFARGUE [141]

AT LE PERREUX

London, 31 January [b] 1891

My dear Lafargue,

Like nine-tenths of the news published in Paris about Germany, the item that has alarmed you [142] is nothing more than a canard.

The leading committee of the German party has not budged in regard to 1 May. The parliamentary *faction* (the socialist members of the Reichstag) has resolved (with one dissenting vote) that *in Germany* (but not elsewhere) it would be desirable to hold the celebrations on Sunday 3 May and not on 1 May. [143] That is all. Since the Party Rules do not confer any official function on the 'faction', it is simply the expression of a desire which, however, will probably meet with general approval.

As to the idea of suggesting to other nationalities that they make a similar change in the date of the demonstration, our newspapers say

---

[a] the premises of the *Sozialdemokrat* editorial office in 1888-90 - [b] 30 January in the original

not a word. However there is the possibility that *individually* one or other of the deputies might have thought of it. As Bebel is in Zurich for his daughter's [a] wedding, I shall write to Fischer [144] so that a stop can be put to this nonsense if, that is, anybody is entertaining it.

You and Bonnier, whose long letter on the subject I have in my pocket,[145] may say whatever you like. The English will probably do the same as the Germans and hold their celebrations on Sunday. As regards the Germans, they are virtually bound to act in this way. Last year you thought their conduct 'weak'. Well now, in Hamburg, the city where we are best organised and in greater strength relative to the rest of the population, and where we have the strongest finances (both party and trades unions) — in Hamburg they generally celebrate 1 May under the noses of the employers. But business being pretty bad, the latter took advantage of the one day's cessation to close their workshops and declare that they would reopen only to those workmen who left their unions and promised not to unionise in future. The struggle continued throughout the summer and into the autumn. Eventually the employers abandoned their demands; however our trades union organisation in Hamburg has been badly shaken, the coffers have been emptied, as indeed elsewhere, as a result of funds disbursed for the LOCKOUTS, and nobody has the slightest desire to repeat the performance this spring, conditions in industry having worsened still further.

It's all very well for you to talk of irresolution and weakness. You are in a republic and the bourgeois republicans, in order to defeat the royalists, have been obliged to accord you the political rights that we are far from possessing in Germany. Moreover, divided as you have been hitherto, with the Broussists in the tow of the government,[146] you are not particularly dangerous; on the contrary, Constans likes to see you 'demonstrate' and put the wind up the radicals.[147] In Germany our people are a real force, between one and a half and two million electors, the only disciplined and growing party. If the government wants the socialists to hold demonstrations, that is because it wants to get them involved in a riot when it would crush them and have done with them for the next ten years. For the German socialists their best form of demonstration is their very existence and their slow, steady, ineluctable advance. We are still a long way from being able to sustain an open struggle and it is our duty vis-à-vis the whole of

---

[a] Frieda Bebel

Europe and America not to suffer defeat but rather, when the time comes, to emerge victorious from the first great battle. It is to this consideration that I subordinate all others.

Needless to say, it would be very nice to see all socialist workmen in both worlds abstain from work on the same day, 1 May. But it would not be a simultaneous, uniform abstention. You in Paris would abstain from, say, 8 in the morning to 8 in the evening; when the New Yorkers began at 8, it would be 1 in the afternoon in Paris, while the Californians would begin 3 hours later. Last year the demonstration lost nothing by being spread over 2 days and this year it would lose even less. The Austrians are in an altogether different situation; regular agitation and organisation have been made so difficult that a 1 day cessation is their sole means of demonstrating, a procedure admirably developed by Adler.[148]

So console yourselves. The movement won't suffer as a result of this lack of 'unity'; and such purely formal unity is not worth the price we should have to pay for it in Germany and also perhaps in England.

Your behaviour towards the anti-Broussists[53] strikes me as unexceptional. Making a compact of practical co-operation, setting aside for the moment any attempt at a merger, trusting to the passage of time and, ultimately, to the International Congress — there could be no better way of exploiting the situation in which you find yourselves. It is what Marx suggested to Liebknecht at the time of the merger with the Lassalleans,[63] but our friend was in too much of a hurry.

Guesde has played a nice trick on him in his articles for the *Vorwärts*.[149] Liebknecht has always championed the bourgeois republic in order to annoy the Prussians; in his view Constans, Rouvier, etc., were virtually faultless. And along comes Guesde to shatter that illusion! Delightful and also good for Germany.

Give Laura a kiss from me. My congratulations to Doctor Z. on the article on the Toulon affair.[150] Louise is particularly grateful for it. She has happy memories of you and Laura.

Yours ever,

F. E.

First published in: F. Engels, P. et L. Lafargue, *Correspondance*, t. III, Paris, 1959

Printed according to the original

Translated from the French

69

ENGELS TO KARL KAUTSKY [98]

IN STUTTGART

London, 3 February 1891

Dear Kautsky,

You'd have thought that we over here would have been bombarded with letters about Marx's article[a] — on the contrary; not a sign nor a word have we had.

When the *Neue Zeit* failed to arrive on Saturday,[b] I thought something had gone wrong again. On Sunday Ede arrived and showed me your letter, whereupon I believed that the attempt at suppression had been successful. The issue finally arrived on Monday and, not long after, I found the piece had been reprinted in the *Vorwärts*.[151]

The disciplinary action *à la* Anti-Socialist Law having failed,[152] this daring move was the best thing the chaps could have done. But it was also good in another way, namely in going a fair way towards repairing the almost unbridgeable gulf alluded to by August[c] in the first moment of alarm. Not that that alarm was in any way unjustified, arising as it did out of concern for what their opponents might make of the thing. By printing it in the official organ, they forestalled hostile exploitation and put themselves in the position of being able to say: 'See how we criticise ourselves — we are the only party that can afford to do so; just you try and do the same!' This was, in fact, the correct attitude and one the chaps should have adopted from the start.

Another consequence is that it will be difficult to initiate disciplinary action against yourself. My request that the thing might be sent to Adler[d] was intended on the one hand to put pressure on Dietz and, on the other, to relieve you of responsibility by presenting you with Hobson's choice. I also wrote and told August that I was prepared to take full responsibility.[153]

If anyone else is to be held responsible, that person is Dietz. As he is

---

[a] *Critique of the Gotha Programme* - [b] 31 January - [c] August Bebel - [d] See this volume, p. 103.

aware, I have, where he is concerned, always shown myself very *coulant*[a] over such matters. I have not only complied with, but actually exceeded, every request he has made to tone things down. Had he side-lined anything else, that too would have received consideration. But if a thing met with no objection from Dietz, why should it not be passed by me?

Come to that, having once got over their initial alarm, almost everyone save Liebknecht will be grateful to me for having published the thing. It will eliminate all possibility of prevarication and phrase-mongering in the next programme and will provide irrefutable arguments such as the majority of them would hardly have had the courage to advance on their own initiative. Their failure to change a bad programme while the Anti-Socialist Law was in force because unable to do so is no cause for reproach. And they have after all now voluntarily relinquished that programme. Nor need they hesitate to admit today that, 15 years ago, they behaved like boobies over the matter of unification [63] and allowed themselves to be done in the eye by Hasselmann, etc. At all events, the programme's 3 ingredients — 1. specific Lassalleanism, 2. vulgar democracy à *la* People's Party [154] and 3. balderdash, have not improved as a result of 15 years' pickling qua official party programme, and if this can't be openly said today, when if ever can it be?

If you hear anything new, please let us know. Many regards,

Your

F. E.

First published in full in *Aus der Frühzeit des Marxismus. Engels Briefwechsel mit Kautsky,* Prag, 1935

Printed according to the original

Published in English for the first time

---

[a] co-operative

70

ENGELS TO LAURA LAFARGUE

AT LE PERREUX

London, 5 February 1891

My dear Laura,

Louise and I are going up to Highgate to take a copy of the inscription on the grave so as to be able to propose an additional one for Nimmy.[a] In the meantime will you please sign the enclosed, as *you and Tussy* are the joint owners registered and will both have to sign. We shall then let you know what we propose doing.

The socialists of Northampton have proposed to Edward[b] to stand in place of Bradlaugh deceased![c] Edward and Tussy went over to reconnoitre on Wednesday[d] but I have not heard since. I advised him to accept only in case all expenses were forthcoming. Today they say they want £100 to £150 before they can nominate him, and nomination is on Monday next[e] already!

Love from Louise and your

F. E.

First published, in the language of the original (English), in: F. Engels, P. et L. Lafargue, *Correspondance*, t. III, Paris, 1959

Reproduced from the original

---

[a] Helene Demuth, see also this volume, pp. 219-20. - [b] Aveling - [c] See this volume, pp. 123-24 and 126-27. - [d] 4 February - [e] 9 February

71

ENGELS TO PAUL LAFARGUE[141]

AT LE PERREUX

London, 6 February 1891

My dear Lafargue,

This from a letter I have had from Fischer on the subject of the alleged intervention of the Germans in favour of 3 May:

'You are perfectly right. None of us here would be so insane as to seek to impose anything at all on the parties of other countries. The parliamentary faction's resolution was addressed *exclusively* to the German working man. It arose simply out of recognition of the fact that in the present situation, and given the severe political and economic tension now prevailing, any celebration on Friday 1 May would be a sheer impossibility. Unfortunately there are only too many who, despite themselves, will abstain from work on 1 May. Our capitalists are furious over the turn of political events in Germany.* They would like nothing better than to find occasion to mount a general attack on us. The crisis that has recently gripped the iron, textile and building industries has presented them with that opportunity, thereby placing them in a position to deliver a general onslaught which at this moment we should be unable to fend off. Consider the case of the Hamburg cigar workers. That will show you who holds the trump cards today.** They represent our *corps d'élite*, not a BLACKLEG amongst them, and yet the battle was lost weeks ago. Ultimately it is the small manufacturers who will have to foot part of the bill. But it is costing our working men a hundred thousand marks from their own funds — not counting the contributions from other towns which are sending money to support the strike. Accordingly 1 May is out of the question, financially speaking.'

That, I think, ought to satisfy you. Nor should you be surprised if, as I have already pointed out to you, the English follow the Germans' example. Tussy believes it highly probable. You Frenchmen have a passion for uniformity, which is all very well, provided the cost is not too high. But to preserve uniformity by ruining our prospects in

---

* Fall of Bismarck, state socialism, fear that the prohibitive entry duties [155] introduced in 1878 may be abolished, etc., etc.
** LOCKOUT of workpeople as a means of compelling them to resign from their union.

Germany and putting paid to any real success in England would be pedantic indeed.

Yours ever,

F. E.

First published in: F. Engels, P. et L. Lafargue, *Correspondance*, t. III, Paris, 1959

Printed according to the original

Translated from the French

72

ENGELS TO PAUL LAFARGUE [141]

AT LE PERREUX

London, 10 February 1891

My dear Lafargue,

Herewith the cheque for £20. I hope it arrives before you leave for Allier. My mind was elsewhere when I wrote it, otherwise I should have made it out to Laura's order so as to facilitate its endorsement should you be away.

As to what has transpired at the congress on the subject of 1 May, I know nothing. You may say what you will,[156] but at this juncture it would be sheer madness for the Germans to persist in holding their celebrations on the 1st and not on Sunday the 3rd. For that matter the divergence of opinion is quite natural; it is the antagonism between north and south. You southerners sacrifice everything to form, whereas the northerners tend to underrate it, concentrating rather on the substance. You like a theatrical effect; they, perhaps, pay too little heed to it. But for them 1 May means a repetition throughout the country of last year's LOCKOUTS [a] in Hamburg and in much less favourable circumstances; it means an outlay of between 200,000 and 300,000 marks, the exhaustion of all the funds for which the party is directly or indirectly responsible, the disorganisation of all our trades unions and, as a result, general discouragement. You must admit

---

[a] See this volume, p. 116.

that if this is the price to be paid for the theatrical effect of a simultaneous demonstration, it is distinctly on the steep side.

The success of the *Socialiste* gives me much pleasure. It goes to show that your working men are beginning to read again and to acquire a taste for other things besides sensational and pornographic newspapers. You may be proud of this success; it augurs very well. Here, for the first time in many years, is a weekly that covers its expenses.[157] It is also very well produced. Do you send it to Sorge?

Marx's article[a] has aroused great wrath in the party's Central Committee and many encomiums in the party itself. They tried to suppress the whole edition of the *Neue Zeit* but it was too late, whereupon they put a good face on it and boldly reprinted the article in the official organ.[b] When they have calmed down, they will thank me for having prevented them from entrusting the preparation of yet another equally shameful programme to Liebknecht, who fathered the thing.[63] In the meanwhile I have heard nothing from them directly; they are boycotting me to some extent.

Your article on the Russian alliance is very good[c]; it will rectify Liebknecht's repeated assurances that no one in France has dreamt of a Russian alliance, that it is all pure invention on Bismarck's part, etc. The fellow believes it his duty to heap praise on whatever goes on in France (or to conceal discreditable facts) because it's *a Republic*!

I haven't yet been able to read your article on feudal property.[158]

In Northampton it was the *local section of the Social Democratic Federation*[29] which invited Aveling to stand[d] and duly notified Hyndman, who tried to prevent them from putting him up. However they *insisted*, with the result that, last Saturday,[e] Hyndman had to rally the faithful here in London in order to pass a resolution that they had had nothing to do with Aveling's candidature. Since no one was suggesting that they had, this was tantamount to a public admission of insubordination within the bosom of the *Federation*. Hyndman's star is on the wane, even in the eyes of his supporters. The impetus given to the movement 18 months ago brought the FEDERATION a significant number of recruits and it is now stronger than ever before. But the said recruits are totally ignorant of the scabrous antecedents of this

---

[a] *Critique of the Gotha Programme* - [b] *Vorwärts* - [c] P. Lafargue, 'Der Schuß Padlewsky's', *Die Neue Zeit*, 9. Jg. 1890/91, 1. Bd., Nr. 19 (see this volume, p. 108). - [d] See this volume, pp. 120 and 126-27. - [e] 7 February

gang and haven't the slightest intention of accepting responsibility for any of them. They leave the FEDERATION'S foreign policy to Hyndman & Co. because it is quite above their heads. But if Hyndman tried to revive old personal squabbles, or if he were forced to do so, he would no longer, as previously, have a submissive band of supporters to back him up. A fair number of GASWORKERS also belong to the Federation and, so far as they are concerned, any interference with Aveling and Tussy would spell war.

Moreover Aveling's candidature must be all the more galling to Hyndman in that Aveling, who did not possess the £100 DEPOSIT for the expenses of the POLL, roundly refused a TORY's offer to make him a present of it. At which loud panegyrics in the liberal press (see *The Daily News* which I shall send you).[a] In similar circumstances Hyndman and Champion *accepted* money from the TORIES, as you know.[159]

All it amounts to is a postponement. There can be no doubt that, come the General Election, the Northampton workmen will have the necessary money. They would have had it this time had they had a week in which to raise it. And they were counting on between 900 and 1,000 votes.

You have no maid. As for us, Annie gave notice yesterday as from 21 November; she is to marry her BLOKE at last.

What curious people the Roshers are! Percy's little boy has had to be circumcised because of some infantile disorder—and now his brother Howard's son is in similar case! Old Rosher is completely at a loss: is it divine vengeance for the 19 children (INCLUDING MISCARRIAGES) he has engendered? I myself submit that it is religious atavism. Hereditarily speaking they are so very Christian! Now, since Christianity is Judaism's natural child, what we have here is a reversion to the ORIGINAL ANCESTRAL TYPE, a foreskin so extravagant that it calls for an operation instituted as a sign of the bond between Jehovah and his chosen people.

Kovalevsky has published his Oxford lectures.[b] Prehistorical part, weak, historical, on Russia, interesting.

---

a 'Election News. Nomination at Northampton. Enthusiastic Liberal Meeting', *The Daily News*, 10 February 1891. - b M. Kovalevsky, *Modern Customs and Ancient Laws of Russia being the Ilchester Lectures for 1889-90.*

We are drafting an inscription for Helene's[a] grave to be submitted to Laura. Give her a kiss from me.

Yours ever,

F. E.

First published in: F. Engels, P. et L. Lafargue, *Correspondance*, t. III, Paris, 1959

Printed according to the original

Translated from the French

73

ENGELS TO FRIEDRICH ADOLPH SORGE [160]

IN HOBOKEN

London, 11 February 1891

Dear Sorge,

Letter of 16 January received.

I am *delighted* to hear that you propose to do away with the *Nationalist*. Over here I can find no one, not a solitary soul, who is prepared to read it, and I myself have not got the time to scrutinise the sagacious lucubrations of all the various RESPECTABLE panjandrums. I would have suggested such a course long since had I not thought that, if a chap like you sent me the thing, there was bound to be something in it *some time*.

The photograph is in the offing. Heinrich Scheu wishes to do a wood-cut of me, for which reason I recently had to position myself before the lens again.[b] Of the seven pictures, one will presumably turn out well.

I trust your wife[c] will have completely recovered by the time you get this; also you yourself.

I cannot tell you anything about the AMERICAN EDITION OF *Capital*, since I have never seen it and do not know what it contains. That the people over there *can* pirate our stuff, we are aware. That they *do* so

---

[a] Helene Demuth's, see also this volume, pp. 219-20. - [b] See this volume, p. 112. - [c] Katharina Sorge

proves that it's a good speculation and is gratifying, although detrimental to the heirs. But it was something we had to reckon with the moment sales assumed significant proportions over there.

By now you will presumably have had the fourth ed.[a]

You will have read Marx's article[b] in the *Neue Zeit*. To begin with it aroused great wrath in the socialist powers-that-be in Germany but now they appear to be simmering down a bit. In the party itself, on the other hand, there was great rejoicing, except among the old Lassalleans. The Berlin correspondent of the Vienna *Arbeiter-Zeitung*, which you will get by the *next* post, actually thanks me for the service I have rendered the party [161] (I believe it's Adolf Braun, Victor Adler's brother-in-law and Liebknecht's deputy editor on the *Vorwärts*). Liebknecht, of course, is furious, since all the criticism was aimed specifically at him and he was the progenitor, together with that bugger Hasselmann, of the rotten programme.[63] I can comprehend the initial dismay felt by the chaps, who have hitherto insisted that 'comrades' should approach them only with the utmost delicacy, on finding themselves being handled thus *sans façon*,[c] and their programme unmasked as pure rubbish. According to what I hear from K. Kautsky who has behaved very courageously throughout this affair, the parliamentary group intends to issue an edict [162] to the effect that publication took place without their knowledge and is deplored by them. They're welcome to that gratification. However, it may come to nothing if the party increasingly voices its assent and the fuss about 'placing a weapon against ourselves in the hands of our foes' is found to be without substance.

In the meantime I am being boycotted by the gentlemen, which suits me very well as it saves me quite a deal of time. Not that it's likely to last for long.

After Bradlaugh's death, Aveling was invited to stand in Northampton and by none other than the local BRANCH OF THE SOCIAL DEMOCRATIC FEDERATION,[29] i. e. nominally Hyndman's people. Because of the leap forward made by the movement generally in the past 18 months, the FEDERATION has acquired a large following. These people are glad to leave foreign policy (plotting with the Possibilists,[3] etc.), which is quite outside their ken, to Hyndman & Co., but are completely unaware of the said gentry's previous plotting and intriguing at home, and would certainly deny all responsibility for the same; — IN FACT, it

---

[a] of the first volume of *Capital* - [b] *Critique of the Gotha Programme* - [c] rudely

is only because Hyndman & Co. have, since that time, pretty well eluded attack at home that they have acquired the afore-mentioned following. Hence the move made by the Northampton people which seriously alarmed Hyndman, the more so since the BRANCH immediately informed the Executive Council of what they had done. A certain amount of plotting ensued, but to no avail. Aveling went down and was given a brilliant reception, but it was only 4 days until nomination day, and a £100 deposit had to be raised for election expenses. Twenty working men undertook to put up £5 each, and a man turned up who offered to provide the money against that undertaking. But upon closer investigation this man proved to be one of the Conservatives' principal agents, whereupon Aveling refused the money with a proper display of righteous indignation and withdrew. This must have been doubly vexatious for Hyndman in as much as, 5 years ago, he and Champion accepted £250 or £350 from the TORIES for electoral purposes.[159] At all events, Aveling is now the workers' nominee for Northampton and stands a good chance of obtaining an increasing number of votes. On this occasion he would have received between nine hundred and a thousand.

The young man I recommended to you[a] will already have come to see you. The Romms, by the by, know him personally, something of which I was unaware at the time.

The French are very angry because this year the Germans intend to celebrate May Day on the 3rd of May, and not the 1st. It's all nonsense; by celebrating on 1 May last year, the Hamburg chaps involved themselves in a LOCKOUT[b] (for which, having no contracts, the manufacturers yearn); it cost the workers there 100,000 marks — not counting outside contributions — broke the backs of their TRADES UNIONS, which were the best organised, and crippled them for a long time to come. In Germany today there is chronic overproduction in all branches of industry and, since a general celebration throughout Germany could not be held on 1 May without breach of contract and would thus bring about a general LOCKOUT, use up all our funds, disrupt all our TRADES UNIONS and engender discouragement rather than enthusiasm, it would be madness. However, at the Paris Congress, our people evinced such enthusiasm for the 1st of May,[51] that this now looks like a retreat. And again the parliamentary group's proclamation is a deplorably feeble affair.[163]

---

[a] Stanisław Padlewski - [b] See this volume, pp. 116 and 122-23.

Here in England the day is to be decided next Sunday. Realising what a mistake they had made last year, Hyndman and Co. are intent on somehow pushing themselves to the fore on this occasion, and 1 May will find many supporters. But since the capitalists in this country are ever eager to seize on any pretext for disrupting the two best hated TRADES UNIONS—the DOCKERS and more particularly that BOSSED by Tussy, the GASWORKERS AND GENERAL LABOURERS,[164] Tussy is going to do all she can to avoid providing them with the pretext of breach of contract and will propose 3 May as being a Sunday. The GASWORKERS are now the most powerful organisation in Ireland and, in the next elections, are going to put up their own candidates regardless of Parnell or M'Carthy. Parnell's demonstrative friendliness towards working men is the result of a meeting he had with these selfsame GASWORKERS who didn't hesitate to give him a piece of their mind. Even Michael Davitt, who used to call for independent Irish TRADES UNIONS, now knows better: The constitution they have got allows them HOME-RULE with no strings attached. It is to them that credit is due for having, for the first time, got the labour movement in Ireland going. Many of their BRANCHES consist of AGRICULTURAL LABOURERS.

Kindest regards to your wife,

Your
F. E.

First published abridged in *Briefe und Auszüge aus Briefen von Joh. Phil. Becker, Jos. Dietzgen, Friedrich Engels, Karl Marx u. A. an F. A. Sorge und Andere*, Stuttgart, 1906 and in full in: Marx and Engels, *Works*, First Russian Edition, Vol. XXVIII, Moscow, 1940

Printed according to the original

Published in English in full for the first time

74

ENGELS TO KARL KAUTSKY [98]

IN STUTTGART

London, 11 February 1891

Dear Kautsky,

Many thanks for your two letters.[165] I return herewith those of Bebel and Schippel.

The boycott imposed upon me by the Berliners has not yet been lifted; there's been no sign of a letter and it's obvious they haven't yet made up their minds. By contrast, the *Hamburger Echo* published a leading article that was very fair,[166] considering that the chaps are still strongly tainted with Lassalleanism and actually swear by the system of acquired rights.[167] From this, and from the *Frankfurter Zeitung*, I also gathered that the onslaught of the opposition press was already at its height, if not actually abating. Once they have survived that—and so far as I could see, it has so far been very mild—the chaps will recover from their initial alarm. By contrast, Adler's Berlin correspondent (A. Braun?) has actually thanked me for publishing the thing.[161] A few more such voices and the opposition will languish.

It became evident to me that the document had been deliberately suppressed and concealed from Bebel in May/June 1875 the moment he informed me that the date of his release from prison had been 1 April; indeed, I have written to him[153] saying that he was *bound* to have seen it unless 'something untoward' had happened. In due course I shall, if necessary, request him to reply to this point. For a long time the document was held by Liebknecht from whose clutches Bracke had some difficulty in retrieving it; Liebknecht wished to keep it entirely to himself in order to use it for the final version of the programme. How, needs no saying.

Send me Lafargue's article[168] by registered book post as a ms.; I'll smooth things out all right. Come to that, his article on Padlewski[a] was quite good and very useful, considering the way the *Vorwärts* misrepresents French politics. All in all, Wilhelm[b] would seem to be out of luck in this respect. *He* is always praising the French Republic to

---

[a] P. Lafargue, 'Der Schuß Padlewsky's', *Die Neue Zeit*, 9. Jg. 1890/91, 1. Bd., Nr. 19 (see also this volume, pp. 108, 123). - [b] Wilhelm Liebknecht

the skies while Guesde, the correspondent whom he himself appointed, is for ever tearing it to pieces.[149]

The parliamentary group's pronouncement,[162] heralded by Schippel, is a matter of complete indifference to me. Should they wish, I am prepared to confirm that I am not in the habit of asking their permission. Whether or not they approve of the fact of publication is all one to me. Nor do I begrudge them the right to express their disapproval of this and that. Unless the affair turns out in such a way as absolutely to compel me to take it up, it would not occur to me to reply. So we shall wait and see.

I shall not write to Bebel about it, for in the first place he himself must first let me know what view of the matter he has finally arrived at and, in the second, every resolution is signed by everybody in the parliamentary group whether or not they voted for it. By the way, Bebel is wrong in thinking I would allow myself to become embroiled in acrimonious dispute. For that to happen, they would first have to provoke me with falsehoods, etc., which I could not overlook. On the contrary, I am positively steeped in a spirit of conciliation, having after all no cause for anger, and am only too anxious to build that bridge—pontoon bridge, trestle bridge, iron, stone or even golden bridge—across the potential abyss or gulf which Bebel thought he saw yawning in the distance.

Odd! Schippel now writes of the many old Lassalleans who pride themselves on their Lassalleanism—yet when they were over here,[169] it was unanimously agreed that there were no Lassalleans left in Germany! Indeed, this was the main reason for my abandoning many of my reservations. And then Bebel also chimes in, saying that a large number of the best comrades are seriously offended. If [so],[a] they ought to have [described][a] things to me as they really were.

Come to that, if you cannot now, 15 years later, speak your mind about Lassalle's theoretical balderdash and his prophetic mission, when if ever will you be able to?

However, the party as such, the Executive, the parliamentary group and *tutti quanti*[b] are exempted by the Anti-Socialist Law[11] from all blame save that of having accepted such a programme (and there is no getting round this). So long as that law was in force there could be no question of any revision; no sooner was it suspended than revision was included in the agenda. So what more do they want?

---

[a] Manuscript damaged. - [b] all the rest

It is also imperative that the chaps should at long last throw off the habit of handling the party officials—their servants—with kid gloves and kow-towing to them as infallible bureaucrats, instead of confronting them critically.

Your
F. E.

You will no doubt have heard that Aveling is standing for Northampton in place of Bradlaugh.[a] The invitation came from the local BRANCHES OF THE SOCIAL DEMOCRATIC FEDERATION[29] and from the GASWORKERS. He went down there and his tub-thumping met with great applause. He was assured of 900-1,000 votes. But he hadn't got the deposit for the election expenses and, when offered this by a TORY agent, indignantly refused it. Thus he was not nominated, but from now on will stand as labour candidate for Northampton.

First published in full in *Aus der Frühzeit des Marxismus. Engels Briefwechsel mit Kautsky*, Prag, 1935

Printed according to the original

Published in English for the first time

75

ENGELS TO KARL KAUTSKY

IN STUTTGART

London, 21 February 1891

Dear Kautsky,

First of all my heartiest congratulations on the arrival of your infant.[b] I trust it keeps tippling away and that the confinement went off normally and easily. My heartiest congratulations to your wife[c] also. May the lad give you much joy.

Bebel's letter returned herewith.[170] Today I had to correct the proof

---

[a] See this volume, pp. 120, 123-24 and 126-27. - [b] Felix Kautsky - [c] Luise Kautsky, née Ronsperger

of sheet 1 of the *Anti-Brentano*,[a][96] otherwise I should have finished my letter to you. You'll therefore have to wait.

So my best wishes until tomorrow or the day after.

Your

F. E.

First published in *Aus der Frühzeit des Marxismus. Engels Briefwechsel mit Kautsky,* Prag, 1935

Printed according to the original

Published in English for the first time

76

ENGELS TO KARL KAUTSKY

IN STUTTGART

London, 23 February 1891

Confidential

Dear Kautsky,

Seeing that you have sent me Bebel's letter and that one good turn deserves another, I have worded the enclosed letter[b] in such a way that you can send it to Bebel *should you also consider it desirable in the interests of peace.* This I leave entirely to you.

Your notes on the *Vorwärts* article are *very* good.[171] Likewise your proposal to remind Bebel of the indifference with which Schramm's attacks on Marx were allowed to pass.

In great haste—the post goes in 5 minutes.

Your

F. E.

First published in *Die Gesellschaft,* Nr. 5, Berlin, 1932

Printed according to the original

Published in English for the first time

---

[a] F. Engels, *In the Case of Brentano Versus Marx.* - [b] See next letter.

77

ENGELS TO KARL KAUTSKY [172]

IN STUTTGART

London, 23 February 1891

Dear Kautsky,

You will have got my hasty congratulations of the day before yesterday.[a] So let us now return to the matter in hand, namely Marx's letter.[b]

The fear that it would place a weapon in the hands of our opponents was unfounded. Malicious insinuations are, of course, made about anything and everything, but by and large the impression gained by our opponents was nevertheless one of utter stupefaction at this ruthless self-criticism, stupefaction combined with the feeling that a party must be possessed of great inner strength if it could treat itself to that sort of thing. This much is apparent from the opposition newspapers I have been getting from you (very many thanks) and elsewhere. And I frankly admit that this was what I had in mind when I published the document. That it was bound at first to give grave offence in certain quarters I was aware, but it couldn't be helped and in my view this consideration was more than outweighed by its factual content. And I knew that the party was amply strong enough to stand it and I reckoned that today it would even *tolerate* the forthright language used 15 years ago, that it would point with justifiable pride to this test of its strength and say: Show us another party that would dare do the same. In the meantime this has been left to the Saxon and the Vienna *Arbeiter-Zeitung* and the *Züricher Post*.[173]

To have assumed, in No. 21 of the *Neue Zeit*, responsibility for its publication is most courageous of you,[171] but don't forget that it was I, after all, who first instigated the thing and, in addition, presented you, as it were, with Hobson's choice. Accordingly I consider the main responsibility to be mine. As to details, one can of course always

---

[a] See this volume, pp. 131-32. - [b] K. Marx, *Critique of the Gotha Programme*.

hold differing views about such things. I deleted or altered everything that you and Dietz took exception to and, even if Dietz had made more deletions, I should still have been *coulant*[a] wherever possible; at no time have I failed to give the two of you proof of this. As to the main issue, however, it was *my duty* to publish the thing the moment the programme came up for discussion. And especially after Liebknecht's speech at Halle,[121] in which he coolly quotes parts of it as though they were his own, while contesting others without naming their source, Marx would unquestionably have confronted this version with the original and in place of him I was duty bound to do the same. Unfortunately the document was not immediately to hand and I only found it much later after a long search.

You mention that Bebel has written to you saying that Marx's treatment of Lassalle has caused bad blood amongst the old Lassalleans. That may be. Those people don't, of course, know the true story and nobody seems to have done anything to enlighten them on the subject. If they don't know that Lassalle's reputation as a great man is solely attributable to the fact that for years Marx allowed him to flaunt as his own the fruits of Marx's research and, what's more, to distort them because of his inadequate grounding in political economy, that is no fault of mine. But I am Marx's literary executor and as such I also have my obligations.

For the past 26 years Lassalle has been part of history. If, while the Exceptional Law [11] was in force, he has been exempt from historical criticism, it is now high time that such criticism came into its own and that light be thrown on Lassalle's position in regard to Marx. The legend which veils the true image of Lassalle and deifies him cannot, after all, become an article of faith for the party. However highly one may rate Lassalle's services on behalf of the movement, his historical role inside it remains an equivocal one. Everywhere Lassalle the socialist goes hand in hand with Lassalle the demagogue. In Lassalle the agitator and organiser, the Lassalle who conducted the Hatzfeldt lawsuit [174] is everywhere apparent: the same cynicism in the choice of methods, the same predilection for consorting with corrupt and shady people who may be used simply as tools and then be discarded. Up till 1862 a specifically Prussian vulgar democrat in practice with marked Bonapartist tendencies (I have just been looking through his letters to Marx), he made a sudden volte-face for purely personal rea-

---

[a] compliant

sons and began to engage in agitation. And before 2 years had gone by he was demanding that the workers side with the monarchy against the bourgeoisie and had begun intriguing with his kindred spirit Bismarck in a manner that could only have led to the actual betrayal of the movement had he not, luckily for him, been shot in the nick of time. In his propagandist writings the correct arguments he borrowed from Marx are so interwoven with his own invariably false ones that it is virtually impossible to separate the two. Such workers as have been offended by Marx's judgment know nothing of Lassalle save for his 2 years of agitation and, furthermore, see the latter only through rose-tinted spectacles. But historical criticism cannot forever remain standing hat in hand before such prejudices. It was my duty to settle accounts once and for all between Marx and Lassalle. That has been done. With this I can content myself for the time being. Besides, I have other things to do. And the publication of Marx's ruthless judgment of Lassalle will undoubtedly prove effective on its own and put heart into others. But if I were forced to do so, there'd be no alternative: I should have to dispose of the Lassallean legend once and for all.

That voices should have been raised in the parliamentary group demanding that the *Neue Zeit* be subject to censorship is truly delectable. Is the spectre of the parliamentary group's dictatorship at the time of the Anti-Socialist Law (a dictatorship that was, of course, essential and excellently managed) still at large or is it a harking back to the sometime close-knit organisation of von Schweitzer? After the liberation of German socialist science from Bismarck's Anti-Socialist Law, what more brilliant idea than to subject it to a new Anti-Socialist Law to be thought up and implemented by the officials of the Social-Democratic Party. However, we've taken care that they don't get too big for their boots.

I have lost no sleep over the *Vorwärts* article.[162] I shall await Liebknecht's account of the affair and then reply to both in as amicable tones as possible. There are only a few inaccuracies to put right in the *Vorwärts* article (e. g. that we hadn't wanted unification, that events had given Marx the lie, etc.) and some obvious points to confirm. I intend that this reply should conclude the debate so far as I am concerned, provided I am not compelled to resume it as a result of fresh attacks or inaccurate statements.

Tell Dietz that I am revising the *Origin*.[a] However I have today also heard from Fischer who writes to say that he wants three new prefaces![175]

Your
F. E.

First published, in Russian, in *Bolshevik*, No. 22, Moscow, 1931   Printed according to the original

78

ENGELS TO ANTONIO LABRIOLA[176]

IN ROME

[Copy]

London, 27 February 1891

... Unfortunately I cannot place the old ms. on Stirner at Mr Mackay's disposal. If it is published it will be by me or my assigns. But to hand over to a third party for such use as he may think fit an unpublished ms. in which Marx had a hand is something I have no right to do, nor would I do so if I had. I have had some *highly* peculiar experiences in this respect. Never again shall I part with *unica*,[b] whatever the circumstances. And besides, the ms. is a tome which in print would be as thick as Stirner's *Einziger*[c] itself—it's very tattered and fragmentary—and is still in need of rearrangement...

(Frederick Engels)

First published in: Marx and Engels, *Works*, Second Russian Edition, Vol. 38, Moscow, 1965   Printed according to a manuscript copy of unknown origin

Published in English in full for the first time

---

[a] the fourth German edition of Engels' *The Origin of the Family, Private Property and the State* - [b] original texts - [c] M. Stirner, *Der Einzige und sein Eigenthum*.

79

ENGELS TO FRIEDRICH ADOLPH SORGE [177]

IN HOBOKEN

London, 4 March 1891

Dear Sorge,

Your letter of 19 February received. In the meantime you will doubtless have heard various things about the great indignation of the Social-Democratic parliamentary group at the publication in the *Neue Zeit* of Marx's article on the programme.[a] The matter is still taking its course. For the present I shall let the chaps make fools of themselves, an end towards which Liebknecht has materially contributed in the *Vorwärts*.[162] Obviously I shall reply in due course though without needless acrimony; without some gentle irony, however, I hardly think it can be done. All those who count for anything in the field of theory are, of course, on my side — I must except only Bebel who was, in fact, not altogether unjustified in feeling offended by my action — but that was inevitable. Owing to an excess of work I have not been able to look at the *Volkszeitung*[b] for the last 4 weeks, so I don't know whether any answering sparks have been struck in America — after all you have plenty of Lassallean left-overs where you are, — and in Europe these people are beside themselves with rage.

I now have three pamphlets to finish. The re-issue of 1. *The Civil War in France* — the General Council's address with regard to the Commune. I am arranging for this to be reprinted in a *revised* version[c] together with the 2 addresses of the General Council on the Franco-Prussian War which are more topical today than ever before. Also an introduction by me.— 2. *Wage Labour and Capital*[d] by Marx which I must bring up to the standard of *Capital*, for otherwise it will cause confusion in working-class circles — on account of the then still im-

---

[a] *Critique of the Gotha Programme* - [b] *New Yorker Volkszeitung* - [c] the third German edition of Marx's *The Civil War in France* - [d] the separate German edition of 1891

perfect terminology (e. g. sale of labour instead of labour *power*, etc.) for which reason an introduction is also needed.— 3. My *Entwicklung des Sozialismus*[a]; this will be popularised if possible, but no more. The party is publishing them, each in an edition of 10,000. This will ensure I get a bit of peace in *that* quarter. But I had to take the thing on because it was essential to counter the never-ending flow of rubbishy Lassallean reprints. Luckily a *new* edition of Lassalle with notes, etc. is to appear under *Bernstein*'s aegis [178] (*this between our-selves*).

In order that the person I recommended [b] should not lie fallow, I enclose herewith a CHEQUE for £ 10 out of which you can make him payments as you think fit, either with a view to his removal to one of the larger cities in the interior, which may be the best thing if he is to get on, or to enable him to keep his head above water where he is.

Hyndman is again inveighing against me [179]; it happens every 6 months, but he can talk till he's blue in the face and shout from every rooftop in London without eliciting a reply from me. He has also resumed his attacks upon Aveling and is again bringing up the American business. Now that Rosenberg has been chucked out,[180] do you think it might be possible to get a satisfactory statement from the party over there? All I want is your opinion; I'm not authorised to re-quest that any sort of steps be taken.

The French are furious because the Germans and English will be celebrating on Sunday the 3rd instead of Friday the 1st of May. But there was no alternative. Last year the 1st of May celebrations in Hamburg involved the party in a strike (or rather LOCKOUT) which cost the chaps in Hamburg 100,000 marks— and now that trade is more wretched than ever, the bourgeois are longing for a pretext to shut down. And over here the DOCKERS are gradually being brought to heel, nor dare they grumble, for otherwise their TRADES UNION would be completely disrupted — admittedly a partial consequence of their own blunders —, and only by dint of the utmost caution will the GAS-WORKERS be capable of saving themselves from a STRIKE which would disrupt them too.[164] At the outset the transformation of GAS WORKS into municipal undertakings will still mean an attempt by your phi-listine to extract as much profit as possible so as to bring down the rates in his municipality; the point of view that the municipality should

---

[a] the fourth German edition of *Socialism: Utopian and Scientific* - [b] Stanisław Pad-lewski

insist on the gasworkers' being well paid, precisely *because* they are workers, has yet to penetrate. The disruption of the GASWORKERS and DOCKERS, however, would bring with it the complete disruption of the new TRADES UNIONS which were introduced over here 2 years ago and the old conservative TRADES UNIONS, the ones that are *rich* and for that very reason cowardly, would then have the field to themselves.

The French are not wholly in the wrong. At the congress everyone enthusiastically supported the 1st of May.[51] But why should the French of all people, whose mighty words have so often been followed by insignificant deeds, now insist all of a sudden that no one else may pitch things a bit too high from time to time. The point is that, so far as we are concerned, the situation in France is remarkably favourable, especially now, as a result of the collapse of the Possibilists[53] and if, on this occasion, the 1st of May were to be celebrated successfully and simultaneously throughout the world it might well destroy the Possibilists completely. But that will happen either way.

So until my next.— My kind regards to your wife.[a] I hope she is now quite better.

Your
F. E.

Louise Kautsky sends you both her best wishes.

First published abridged in *Briefe und Auszüge aus Briefen von Joh. Phil. Becker, Jos. Dietzgen, Friedrich Engels, Karl Marx u. A. an F. A. Sorge und Andere*, Stuttgart, 1906 and in full in: Marx and Engels, *Works*, First Russian Edition, Vol. XXVIII, Moscow, 1940

Printed according to the original

Published in English in full for the first time

---

[a] Katharina Sorge

80

ENGELS TO PAUL LAFARGUE [141]

AT LE PERREUX

London, 6 March 1891

My dear Lafargue,

Old Mother Victoria has behaved like a perfect idiot.[181] She ought to have known that in France, where people have fought for the Republic for the past hundred years, her royal person would cut no ice and that in Paris they don't give a fig for her. But these personages cannot get it out of their heads that merely to appear in one place or another is to do it an honour for which all and sundry are obliged to render thanks.

Like the Broussists [3] in your country, the Social Democratic Federation [29] over here has had to give way over the May demonstration. They sent 3 delegates to the Eight Hours Committee, of which Aveling is chairman. This evening he will submit the *Justice* articles [179] to the delegates of that committee and thus force their hand. He wrote a letter to *Justice* in which he challenged Hyndman to confront him at a public meeting and the latter has refused, not only to publish the letter, but to respond to the challenge: he would invite comparison with Aveling the moment he began to canvass the working man's vote.

Meanwhile you have scored a great victory by forcing the Broussists to stick to 1 May.[182] To PUT IN THE THIN EDGE OF THE WEDGE you must treat those delegates as nicely and as obsequiously as you can. Just wait and see, the demonstration will lose little, if anything at all, by being spread over two days rather than one. Perhaps you were right to complain that the Germans in Paris were wholeheartedly in favour of the 1st [51] and that they now seem to be having second thoughts,[a] but apart from that (and Tussy says that in effect no one who saw them in Paris would have guessed at their attitude today) — apart from that, no one will persuade the Germanic nations to sacrifice or even endanger the whole future of their movement for the sake of a demonstration.

Now for something else. Kautsky wrote to me a few weeks ago to

---

[a] See this volume, pp. 123-24.

say that he had had an article from you on Marx and the bourgeois economists,[168] which he thought was not entirely suited to the German public. However he hesitated to return it to you. What was he to do? I asked him to send me the article, which he did. I read it and indeed I, too, share Kautsky's opinion that the article cannot be published in German and for the following reasons:

First of all, not one German economist has ever accused Marx of advancing theories that were not connected with those of Smith and Ricardo. On the contrary, what they do is reproach Smith and Ricardo with having produced Marx who, in their view, has merely drawn inferences from the theory, propounded by the aforesaid predecessors, of value, profit, rent and, lastly, the division of the product of labour. That is why they have become *vulgar* economists who don't give a damn for the classicals. You cite Brentano whose reply to you would be that all your shots are wide of the mark.

Next, everything and more you say about and quote from these two economists and other authors has been said and quoted by us in Germany:

1. Theory of value: In his *Critique of Political Economy*, 1859, Marx concludes each chapter with an outline of the history of the theory therein developed. After the theory of value you will find on p. 29 'historical notes on the analysis of commodities' in which, after Petty and Boisguillebert, Franklin and Steuart, the Physiocrats and Galiani and their ideas on value, he discusses A. Smith on p. 37 and Ricardo on pp. 38-39[183] — hence all of it familiar stuff to the Germans. I would mention further that the passage you quote from Smith is not one of his best; there are others in which he gets much closer to the truth. In your passage he fixes the value of a product in accordance, not with the labour *it contains*, but with what can be *bought* with that product. A definition which embraces the whole contradiction of the old system.

2. Surplus value. Everything you say about this subject has been said by me in my preface to Vol. II of *Capital* in the passages indicated to Laura who will translate them for you if you ask her nicely.

3. The man *Say* is no longer of any significance in Germany. What's more you rehabilitate him by discerning beneath the vulgarity a strain of classicism, which is more than he deserves.

The post is about to go — I am holding the article here at your disposal.

Yours ever,

F. E.

First published in: F. Engels, P. et L. Lafargue, *Correspondance*, t. III, Paris, 1959

Printed according to the original

Translated from the French

81

ENGELS TO HENRI RAVÉ [184]

IN POITIERS

[Notes]

[London,] 6 March [1891]

To send proof-sheet or two of his translation of Bebel.[a] Has he a publisher? No promise. Might indicate him the chapters[b] which will not be changed or not much so that he might begin. *No promise.*

First published in: Marx and Engels, *Works*, Second Russian Edition, Vol. 38, Moscow, 1965

Reproduced from the original

Published in English for the first time

82

ENGELS TO PASQUALE MARTIGNETTI [185]

IN BENEVENTO

London, 6 March 1891

Many thanks for *Critica Sociale*.[186] Sig. Avv.[c] Turati had already sent it to me direct and promises to send it regularly. Trust that your

---

[a] A. Bebel, *Die Frau in der Vergangenheit, Gegenwart und Zukunft* and *La Femme dans le passé, le présent & l'avenir.* - [b] of *The Origin of the Family, Private Property and the State* - [c] advocate

prospects are brighter. I am anxious to see the translation of the *Communist Manifesto*.

Warm regards from

Your

F. E.

First published in the language of the original (German), in *La corrispondenza di Marx e Engels con italiani. 1848-1895,* Milano, 1964

Printed according to the original

Published in English for the first time

83

ENGELS TO FILIPPO TURATI

IN MILAN

London, 7 March 1891

122 Regent's Park Road, N. W.

Dear Sir,

Very many thanks for your kind letter of 23 February,[187] the 3 numbers of the *Critica Sociale* and your offer to send it to me regularly in future. As former Secretary for Italy on the General Council of the International I naturally take a great interest in the progress of the socialist movement in your country and particularly in Lombardy where, as a young man, I spent three months,[188] of which I still retain happy memories.

I should like to thank you equally for the good wishes you were kind enough to send me on the occasion of the publication of the article by Marx[a] in the *Neue Zeit*. In publishing it I was merely carrying out my duty to the memory of Marx on the one hand and to the German party on the other.

You are quite right when you wonder whether I shall have time to contribute either to your revue or to the socialist library you are about to publish. Indeed the preparation of new editions of Marx's

---

[a] *Critique of the Gotha Programme*

works and of my own pamphlets will barely leave my time to finish the manuscript of Volume III of Marx's *Capital*. Just now I have *four* pamphlets *a* to revise, complete and furnish with new introductions, so how can I possibly find time for any other work? Nevertheless I wish you every success and shall be interested to see a good Italian translation of our 1847 *Manifesto* *b* and, were you to find that one or other of my articles might be of interest to the Italian public, I should be delighted to re-read my work in your *bella e ricchissima lingua.* *c*

E con distinta stima La saluto, *d*

F. Engels

Il di Lei amico Stepniak viaggia in questo momento nell'America. *e*

First published, in Italian, in *Critica Sociale*, No. 6, Milano, 10 March 1891

Printed according to the original

Translated from the French

Published in English for the first time

84

ENGELS TO HENRI RAVÉ [189]

IN POITIERS

[Notes]

[London, mid-March 1891]

1. Translate pp. 121-25 and 140-45 as a sample. [190]
2. Ten copies of the translation, otherwise no conditions.
3. Lafargue to send him *Socialisme: utopique et scientifique.* *f*

First published in: Marx and Engels, *Works*, Second Russian Edition, Vol. 38, Moscow, 1965

Printed according to the original

Published in English for the first time

---

a See this volume, pp. 136, 137, 145. - *b* K. Marx, F. Engels, 'Il Manifesto del Partito Comunista (1848)', *Lotta di Classe*, Nos. 8, 10, 12, 13, 15-17, 19-22; 17-18 September, 1-2, 15-16, 22-23 October, 5-6, 12-13, 19-20 November, 3-4, 10-11, 17-18, 24-25 December 1892. - *c* rich and beautiful language - *d* With my best compliments and greetings - *e* Your friend Stepniak is at present on his way to America. - *f* the French edition of Engels' book

85

ENGELS TO KARL KAUTSKY [191]

IN STUTTGART

London, 17 March 1891

Dear Kautsky,

Thank you for your letter of the 9th.— The 6 Dahn fascicles [a] went off to you yesterday by parcel post. I should have been hard at work on the *Origin* [b] if Fischer hadn't come up with a demand for a new edition *of 10,000 copies* of 1. *The Civil War in France,* [c] 2. Marx, *Wage Labour and Capital,* [d] 3. *Entwicklung des Sozialismus,* etc. [c] So I had to write an introduction to the *Civil War,* which went off on Saturday, [f] and at the same time thoroughly revise the thing and append thereto the General Council's 2 addresses on the Franco-Prussian War; fortunately Louise undertook to translate the latter. Nevertheless it has consumed a great deal of time. For *Wage Labour and Capital* was written in pre-surplus value terminology which cannot possibly be allowed to stand today in a propaganda piece running to 10,000 copies. So I shall have to translate it into present-day language and preface it with an apology. Finally, the *Socialism* also needs to be revised and, if possible, a little more popularised — 10,000 copies is no trifling matter—, so how can I find time for anything else? And of all times I ought not to withdraw from the field, leaving it free for Lassallean pamphlets. But as soon as I have rid myself of this task, I shall tackle the *Origin.* I have pretty well completed the preliminary studies. And now along comes a Frenchman, H. Ravé, who wishes to translate the thing—he has translated Bebel's *Frau* [g]—not all that marvellously—and wants me if possible to send him revises or clean proofsheets. But the matter has not yet been agreed.

---

[a] F. Dahn, *Urgeschichte der germanischen und romanischen Völker,* vols 1-4. - [b] F. Engels, *The Origin of the Family, Private Property and the State.* - [c] the third German edition - [d] the separate German edition of 1891 - [c] the fourth German edition of *Socialism: Utopian and Scientific* - [f] 14 March - [g] A. Bebel, *Die Frau in der Vergangenheit, Gegenwart und Zukunft* and *La Femme dans le passé, le présent & l'avenir.*

I congratulate Peschel on his translator.[192] Hope I shan't suffer the same fate.

The Anti-Brentano[a96] is being [pub]lished[b] by Meissner, $4^1/_2$ sheets — I am getting him to print *all* documents, including Sedley Taylor and my preface to the 4th edition.[c] Printing almost complete. Apropos, has the *Neue Zeit* had a review copy of the (*Capital*) 4th edition? If not, *write and let me know at once* (postcard) — I had made *a particular point of this*. If it has I should be glad if you would publish a brief notice in which, in connection with my preface,[d] you might also make a discreet allusion to Brentano.

For want of time I have not been able to have my introduction to the *Civil War* — about 9 or 10 pages of the *Neue Zeit* — copied out for you; this house is a hive of activity; Annie is getting married and Louise is having to see about a new girl, etc., added to which there have been the promptings of the Berliners. But I have asked Fischer to send me 3 clean proof-sheets; alternatively, if the revise turns out well I shall send it to you so that you may use it beforehand should you wish. If, for one reason or another, it doesn't suit you, nothing will have been lost.

Not a word from August[e] — there's no hurry. Sorge thinks I should take no notice of the mighty *Vorwärts* article.[193] What do you think? I am beginning to incline towards his view.

The bit in my letter to you about responsibility[f] was *solely for August's consumption*; if I had thought it would hurt your feelings in any way, I would have omitted it — such a thing had never even crossed my mind. And I *certainly wasn't* thinking of your note[171] on the parliamentary group's ukase.[162] I simply regarded it as my duty, in the event of your forwarding the letter to the Berliners, to relieve you of as much responsibility as possible in their eyes and to take it upon myself. *Voilà tout.*[g]

Thank you for the *Volkszeitung*[h] and *Critica Sociale*. The first was sent me by Sorge, the second by Turati (at the behest of that braggart Loria); he now sends it regularly. Since then a still more forceful article, inspired by Sorge, and written by Schlüter, has appeared in the *Volkszeitung*.[194]

---

[a] F. Engels, *In the Case of Brentano Versus Marx.* - [b] Manuscript damaged. - [c] of the first volume of *Capital* - [d] to the first volume of *Capital* - [e] August Bebel - [f] See this volume, p. 133. - [g] That's all. - [h] *New Yorker Volkszeitung*

I too am coming increasingly to believe that the affair has aroused no indignation whatever in the party as such and that, for one reason or another, it has only hurt the feelings of the gentry in Berlin. And even the latter seem to have realised that the provocations in the *Vorwärts* proved abortive as soon as they were uttered and produced no effect at all — *tombés à plat*,[a] as the French say. Otherwise I should have certainly had word from them.

Your complaints about *the Vorwärts* (since when has the thing acquired the masculine gender?) find a sympathetic echo over here. Never has such a paper been seen before. I can only wonder how long people will stand for it.

Percy and his family are shortly going to Ryde, Isle of Wight, where Percy is to set up and manage an agency for his brothers.

Kindest regards from
Your
F. E.

First published in *Aus der Frühzeit des Marxismus. Engels Briefwechsel mit Kautsky*, Prag, 1935

Printed according to the original

Published in English in full for the first time

86

ENGELS TO FRIEDRICH ADOLPH SORGE

IN HOBOKEN

London, 21 March 1891

Dear Sorge,

Have shown your letter re Miss Anna [b] to our friends and promptly complied with your instructions. Enclosed you will find a brief note to the same in which she is hauled over the coals and notified that the letters she has written hitherto, with their repeated requests for money, have fallen on stony ground. I have been asked to tell you

---

[a] fell flat - [b] Stanisław Padlewski

that people in this country are of the opinion that enough has now been done for her both over here and out there, that she must now arrange for her own advancement and that this could best be achieved out in the country, doing agricultural work such as she is used to. To this I replied that that sort of thing would be possible only in a district where she could get along without any English, but that since such districts did exist out there, the thing was not impossible. At all events, New York and sea-ports generally would not appear to be at all the right terrain for a female of her ilk and if she is to achieve anything, she must go so far away as to make it very difficult for her to come back again.

In the meantime you will also have had my letter [a] with a money order for ten pounds and will, under the circumstances, have been able to put it to good use. Between ourselves, I believe that, should need arise, I could again raise a like amount, but that would probably be that. I have also been asked to request you people to be *strict* in regard to money matters so that the person concerned may finally realise that this idling can't go on for ever.

Besides the Vienna *Arbeiter-Zeitung* I am also sending you today a *Volks-Tribüne* and *Figaro* (Paris MEETING), and an Italian translation of the *Manifesto*.[b] The *People's Press* and *Commonweal* have both gone phut.

I do not yet know whether or not I shall reply to the *Vorwärts* article,[162] but I am beginning to incline towards your view.[193] There are a few points I really *ought to* touch on; however, it might be possible to do so in some other way.

I am having to arrange for new editions and/or new introductions to 1. *The Civil War in France*,[c] 2. Marx's *Wage Labour and Capital*[d] and 3. *Entwicklung des Sozialismus*[e]; the German party is to bring them out in editions of 10,000 copies.

My reply to Brentano[f][96] will be published by Meissner in about 8 or 10 days' time. You shall have it straight away.

Then I have a new edition of *The Origin of the Family, etc.*[g] to see to

---

[a] See this volume, pp. 137-39. - [b] *Il Manifesto del Partito Comunista 1847*, Milan, 1891. - [c] the third German edition - [d] the first separate German edition - [e] the fourth German edition of *Socialism: Utopian and Scientific* - [f] F. Engels, *In the Case of Brentano Versus Marx*. - [g] the fourth German edition of *The Origin of the Family, Private Property and the State*

(5,000 sold!), after which, however, I shall apply myself inexorably and unremittingly to Volume III.[a]

Sam Moore arrived in Liverpool the day before yesterday and will probably be here in about a week's time. At Christmas he caught some horrible disease from which, however, he has completely recovered.

I trust your wife[b] is her old self once more. Warmest regards to her and to you.

Your

F. E.

First published abridged in *Briefe und Auszüge aus Briefen von Joh. Phil. Becker, Jos. Dietzgen, Friedrich Engels, Karl Marx u. A. an F. A. Sorge und Andere*, Stuttgart, 1906 and in full in: Marx and Engels, *Works*, First Russian Edition, Vol. XXVIII, Moscow, 1940

Printed according to the original

Published in English for the first time

87

ENGELS TO HERMANN SCHLÜTER

IN HOBOKEN

London, 21 March 1891

Dear Schlüter,

Your letter of the 10th arrived day before yesterday.[c] Many thanks' for the information about conditions out there,[195] which is all the more welcome in that, journalistic methods being what they are in America, one knows that one cannot believe the papers and is, as a result, completely at sea.

Likewise many thanks for the books on silver and MINERAL RESOURCES. The one on silver and gold for 1890 will also be of interest to me when it appears. But more important to me than anything else, following last year's census, would be the *Compendium of the (eleventh) Census*

---

[a] of *Capital* - [b] Katharina Sorge - [c] 19 March

1890 when this comes out; I inherited from Marx the COMPENDIUM of the 10th CENSUS 1880 in 2 volumes, but it wasn't published until 1883 [a]; not that that matters—this time it's unlikely to take so long.

I have no recollection at all of Marx's second speech, nor can I imagine what it might be.[139] If the few pages seem worth bothering about, it might be best if you were to print them in the *Volkszeitung* [b] and let me have a few copies.

You are quite right; Marx's critique of the programme [c] will achieve its object all right, and it was with this in mind that I published it. It seems, however, that the rage it has aroused in 'influential circles' in the party is terrible to behold; save for Fischer, who was pleased about the thing, no one has written to me—something, I'm glad to say, I can quite well put up with.

If your wife [d] should come to Europe, we shall, I trust, have a chance to see her here in London, when she may convince herself that we are still going strong.

The Roshers are shortly moving to the Isle of Wight where Percy is to manage an agency for his brothers. They left their house the day before yesterday and for the time being are staying with his parents, a few doors away from me.

You would oblige me by forwarding the enclosed to Sorge straight away.

Predictably, Julius [e] has not yet completed the removal from 114 Kentish Town Road [f] (due on the 25th); they have taken it on for another six weeks. Ede is busy writing for the *Vorwärts* and the *Neue Zeit* and is coming on tremendously. The Avelings are doing well; now that *The People's Press* has gone phut, you ought to read *The Daily Chronicle*; though the paper is UNIONIST LIBERAL and as such an ally of the TORIES, it provides the best news concerning the labour movement over here, and is prepared to accept all reports. The Eight Hours movement is going splendidly (cf. Ede's articles in the *Vorwärts* [g] and ditto in the *Neue Zeit*).[h] The TRADES COUNCIL [196] has given way; this time the demonstration is going to be enormous and, what's more, *of*

---

[a] Engels has in mind two censuses: *Department of the Interior, Census Office. Compendium of the Tenth Census (June 1, 1880)*..., Parts I-II, Washington, 1883 and *Department of the Interior, Census Office. Compendium of the Eleventh Census: 1890*, Parts I-III, Washington, D. C., 1892-1897. - [b] *New Yorker Volkszeitung* - [c] K. Marx, *Critique of the Gotha Programme*. - [d] Anna Schlüter - [e] Julius Motteler - [f] the premises of the *Sozialdemokrat* office - [g] E. Bernstein, 'Arbeiterschutz - Gesetz - Reformen in England', *Vorwärts*, Nos. 56, 64 and 67; 7, 17 and 20 March 1891. - [h] E. Bernstein, 'Briefe aus England', *Die Neue Zeit*, 9. Jg. 1890/91, 2. Bd., Nr. 25.

one mind. For the English, the LEGAL 8 HOURS AGITATION is the gateway to the socialist movement; once they have swallowed the 8 hours BILL for *everyone*, including men (and they are well on the way to doing so), they will stick at nothing — they'll have broken with the old middle-class FREE-TRADE viewpoint.

Warm regards to your wife and yourself from Louise and

Your
F. E.

First published in: Marx and Engels, *Works*, First Russian Edition, Vol. XXVIII, Moscow, 1940

Printed according to the original

Published in English for the first time

88

ENGELS TO MAX OPPENHEIM [197]

IN DRESDEN

London, 24 March 1891
122 Regent's Park Road, N. W.

Dear Mr Oppenheim,

First of all I must crave your forgiveness for not having answered your esteemed letter of 26 November until now — almost four months later to the day! But if you knew what an unending mass of work and correspondence of all kinds I have had during that time and that, moreover, I am not allowed to wield my pen for more than 3 hours daily because of my weak eyes — and by daylight at that! — you would, I am sure, excuse me.

My heartfelt thanks then for your kind good wishes which would appear to be coming true in as much as I am on the whole very well, all things considered, and everyone alleges that I do not look my age. Let us hope that I so continue.

You further touch on a few difficult themes which cannot be dealt with anything like exhaustively in a short letter. Certainly, it would spell progress if workers' unions could negotiate wage settlements with the entrepreneurs direct and on everyone's behalf. Indeed, here in England this has been the aim for the past 50 years, though the capitalists know too well where their interests lie to swallow the bait save under duress. That aim was achieved in the big DOCK STRIKE of 1889 [198] as it has been sporadically both before and since; but at the first opportunity the masters emancipate themselves from this, the unions' 'intolerable tyranny', and declare it inadmissible for such third parties, interlopers, to meddle in the patriarchal relations between them and their working men. It's the old story—when business is good, demand compels the masters to be accommodating, when it is bad, they exploit the excessive supply of labour to contest all these concessions again. On the whole, however, the resistance of the workers increases as they become better organised,—so much so, in fact, that the general situation—on average—improves slightly and no crisis can lastingly drag the workers *down to* or *below* zero, the *nadir* of the previous crisis. But it would be difficult to say what would happen if at any time we were to experience a prolonged, chronic, *general* industrial crisis of 5 or 6 years' duration.

The employment of surplus workers by the state or the municipalities and the nationalisation of the trade in foodstuffs are matters which, in my view, need to be seen in a wider context than occurs in your letter. It is not the *trade* alone, but also the *production of* all foodstuffs a country can itself supply, that must be taken into account here. For how else do you propose to employ the surplus workers? If they are surplus, it is precisely because there is no market for their products. This, however, brings us to the expropriation of the landowners, i. e. considerably further than the present German or Austrian state would be prepared to go. Nor, for that matter, is it the kind of task we could entrust to either of them. How it would be done and what the result would be if Junkers were ordered to expropriate Junkers may be seen here in England where, despite all the medieval trappings, the general run of political life is far more modern than on either side of the Erzgebirge. Therein precisely lies the rub; for, so long as the propertied classes remain at the helm, nationalisation never abolishes exploitation but merely changes its form—in the French, American or Swiss republics no less than in monarchist Central, and despotic Eastern, Europe. And to dislodge the propertied classes from the helm we first need a revolution in the minds of the working masses—as, indeed, is now taking place, if relatively slowly; and in order to bring this about, we need an even more rapid revolution in production methods, more machinery, more displacement of labour, the ruin of more peasants and petty bourgeois, more tangible evidence on a vaster scale of the inevitable results of modern large-scale industry.

The more quickly and irrevocably this economic revolution takes place, the more imperative will measures impose themselves which, apparently intended to cure evils that have suddenly assumed vast and intolerable proportions, will eventually result in undermining the foundations of the existing mode of production; and the more rapidly, too, will the working masses obtain a hearing thanks to universal suffrage. *What* those initial measures will be must depend on local conditions at the time, nor can anything of a general nature be said about them beforehand. But as I see it, steps of a truly liberating nature will not be possible until the economic revolution has made the great majority of the workers alive to their situation and thus paved the way for their political rule. The other classes can only patch up or palliate. And this process of clarifying the workers' minds is daily gaining momentum and in 5 or 10 years' time the various parliaments will look very different from what they do today.

Work on Volume III[a] will begin as soon as the confounded little ancillary jobs and the endless correspondence with people here, there and everywhere leave time enough. Then, however, I shall rebel, shut up shop and refuse to be disturbed. I hope to get it finished this year; I am itching to do it and have *got* to get it over and done with.

Shall you be visiting England again? Tussy is very well and cheerful, very happily married and has grown quite plump.

Yours sincerely,
F. Engels

First published in full in: Marx and Engels, *Works*, First Russian Edition, Vol. XXVIII, Moscow, 1940

Printed according to the original

Published in English in full for the first time

---

[a] of *Capital*

89

ENGELS TO LAURA LAFARGUE

AT LE PERREUX

London, 30 March 1891

My dear Laura,

Very many thanks for your kind offer to revise Ravé [199] *qui en sera ravi*[a] — but I am afraid *you* will not be *ravie.*[b] I have made him do me a sample — two passages from the last chapter, pp. 121 and 140, [190] — which I have looked over and now submit to you with my notes and suggested alterations. Please look it over and then decide for yourself, whether you will undertake the job. Like all professional translators he is the slave of his original and forgets that a phrase to be done from French into German and vice versa, has to be turned topsy-turvy. Moreover he does not understand the synonymic *nuance* expressed by many German words; he knows what genus it belongs to, but not what species, much less what variety. But that, I am afraid, most translators will fail in.

I shall write to Ravé that I have sent the manuscript to Monsieur Lafargue (whom he suggests as revisor) and that I cannot give him a definite answer until I hear from him. As he mentioned Paul, I thought it best not to mix *you* up with the matter at the present stage.

Jollymeier is coming to-night at last. At Christmas he had a cold and seems to have kept it until now. He intended coming last Thursday[c] but his cold got worse, and as the weather was bad, delayed from day to day. Yesterday it was nice and warm, but he did not turn up, today at last he writes announcing his arrival to-night *aber sicher.*[d] His deafness seems to bother him awfully.

Sam arrived at Liverpool last Thursday week, and is with his parents at Bumford, will be here about end of this or beginning of next week. Had himself thoroughly examined on arrival by Gumpert who reports him perfectly sound, with only a small enlargement of the spleen, which is expected to be soon curable.

Pumps and Percy are now staying at the old Roshers', they have given up their house and stored the furniture until their removal to

---

[a] who will be delighted - [b] delighted - [c] 26 March - [d] for sure

Ryde, Isle of Wight, whither Percy will go this week with his brothers to make the commercial arrangements for the new agency for Roshers' cement, artificial stone, and builders' and gardeners' materials generally. After that, he will take Pumps to select a house and then the transfer will take place. I do hope Percy will at last learn how to earn his own living, it's a pretty penny they have cost me and the worst of it is there is no return in the shape of benefit to the party. Of course I shall have to go on subsidising for a year or two until the new business can be expected to begin paying.

Annie has left us and is going to be married this week. We have taken two girls as I want Louise to help me in my work and not waste her time in the kitchen. The devil's trouble it was to get girls but I believe we have been lucky — so far — that is the first week — we are satisfied. They are two girls who have been together and prefer to be again at one and the same place.

The May demonstration will be a severe letting down to the Social Democratic Federation [29] and Hyndman. Their over-cleverness, in trying to play off the Trades Council [196] against the Legal Eight Hours League, [200] has landed them between two stools. They quite forgot that this year the Trades Council has a quite different majority to that of last year. They wanted again two platforms for themselves, but will not get them, as they are represented neither on the Trades Council nor on the Legal 8 Hours Committee (they sent three delegates but these soon stayed away and their names were consequently struck off the roll). Moreover, Edward, in return for the slanderous attacks of Hyndman, [179] now takes the offensive and will have the matter brought before the East End branch of the Social Democratic Federation. Indeed, Hyndman seems already to show the white feather.

Bernstein says he saw in *La Justice* that on the 1 May Committee in Paris the Broussists [3] applied for admission, that the Blanquists and Allemanists [53] were against, but that on Guesde's motion they were admitted by a majority of 5. Can you give me any details? as contradiction or confirmation? [201] I hear nothing at all about Brousse and Co. now, are they merely lying in wait, or are they so completely down that they dare not stir? I should like to be well *au courant* of these matters, as the Brussels Congress [135] will very likely bring about a change in the relations of the Social Democratic Federation and the Possibilists with the Germans. If these two sets of intriguers go to Brussels and thereby publicly renounce their pretensions of being the only to be acknowledged parties in England and France, then the Germans will not be able to refuse entering into communication with them. And from Liebknecht's way of acting at present, I should not wonder if he were to try to play the Possibilists off against you, and the Social Democratic Federation against us here, as a means of making you and us more pliant towards himself. I do not know if you read the *Vorwärts*, but here we are all disgusted with it. Never had a large party such a miserable organ. Anyhow, to be able to guard against possibilities, I have a particular interest just now in the doings, sayings and position of Brousse and Co.

Kind regards from Louise.

Ever yours,

F. E.

Will Paul hop over the water while at Calais?

First published, in the language of the original (English), in: F. Engels, P. et L. Lafargue, *Correspondance*, t. III, Paris, 1959

Reproduced from the original

90

ENGELS TO STANISŁAW MENDELSON

IN LONDON

[Draft]

[London,] 31 March 1891

Dear Citizen Mendelson,

I have just received the letter a copy of which is enclosed herewith. [202] I have absolutely no knowledge of how things stand between you and Wróblewski. It is a matter that does not concern me in the slightest. [a] But in view of the delicate situation in which this letter has placed me, I have no choice — and I think you will agree with me

---

[a] In the ms., the first, deleted version of this sentence reads: 'I have neither the intention nor the slightest desire to meddle in private matters or things which concern no one but the Poles amongst themselves.'

here — other than to inform you of the above and to advise Wróblewski of your address. Please, therefore, come to an understanding with him direct.

I trust you have almost finished moving house. I know only too well how disagreeable these things are. Mrs Mendelson, to whom kindly remember me, must have had quite enough of it.

Yours ever,
F. E.

Mrs Kautsky sends her regards both to you and to Mrs Mendelson.

First published in: Marx and Engels, *Works*, Second Russian Edition, Vol. 38, Moscow, 1965

Printed according to the original

Translated from the French

Published in English for the first time

91

ENGELS TO AUGUST BEBEL

IN BERLIN

[Draft]

[London, beginning of April 1891]

Dear Bebel,

I shall not get round today to answering your letter of the 30th — that will be done shortly [a] as soon as the present mass of work allows me a free moment; instead I wish to send you and your wife [b] my heartiest congratulations on your silver wedding. I trust that the two of you will still be there to celebrate your golden wedding on 6 April 1916 and, come that day, will drain a glass in memory of the old boy now writing these words, who by then will have long since gone up in smoke and ashes.

One thing I can tell you: there are few people alive today whom I could congratulate with the same sincerity and warmth on the occa-

---

[a] See this volume, pp. 175-84. - [b] Julie Bebel

sion of such an anniversary. Ever since we started corresponding and subsequently struck up a personal acquaintanceship, [203] I have noticed time and again how our lines and mode of thought have coincided to an extent that is literally miraculous between people whose processes of development have been so different. That — I'm glad to say — doesn't preclude our failure to agree on many points. But these again are points where in course of time agreement is automatically reached as a result of discussion or of new events, or else where such agreement eventually ceases to signify. And so I hope it will always remain. I don't believe that a case will ever again arise in which one of us had to take a step immediately affecting the other without first having consulted him.[a] [204] And I, for one, still bless the day when you entered into regular correspondence with me.

First published in: Marx and Engels, *Works*, First Russian Edition, Vol. XXVIII, Moscow, 1940

Printed according to the original

Published in English for the first time

92

ENGELS TO KARL KAUTSKY

IN STUTTGART

London, 2 April 1891

Dear Kautsky,

In great haste on the most urgent matters. At last a letter from Bebel, quite amiable, though with sundry reservations, but the tone is as warm as ever and he expresses the wish to let bygones be bygones. [205]

I have written Meissner a most peremptory letter about the 4th edition[b] and again asked him to send it to you. Also about the clean proofs for you of my concoction on Brentano[c] [96] — if I don't get them

---

[a] In the ms., the first, deleted version of this sentence reads: 'I don't believe that I shall ever again find myself in the position of taking a step immediately affecting the German party without first having consulted you.' - [b] of the first volume of *Capital* - [c] F. Engels, *In the Case of Brentano Versus Marx*.

soon I shall send you — *enfin*,[a] I'd better do it straight away — I shall send you the master proof corrected by me so that you'll at least be able to see what the thing is like in the raw.

No doubt you will have got the introduction to the *Civil War*; it went off a few days ago. Perhaps you would be so good as to write the introductory note.[206]

Everything has been straightened out with Lafargue. I pointed out to him[b] that his arguments from Ricardo and A. Smith had been anticipated long before in the *Critique*[c] and my preface to the 2nd volume,[d] whereupon he seems to have promptly calmed down.[168]

Schorlemmer is here and sends you his best wishes. It's now time for our meal and Aveling is coming — he is a grass widower, as Tussy is in Norwich drumming up support — so *adieu*.

Your
F. E.

First published in *Aus der Frühzeit des Marxismus. Engels Briefwechsel mit Kautsky*, Prag, 1935

Printed according to the original

Published in English for the first time

93

ENGELS TO PASQUALE MARTIGNETTI

IN BENEVENTO

London, 2 April 1891

Dear Friend,

It will be perfectly acceptable to me if Fantuzzi publishes the *Socialismo utopistico*,[e] though I shall write and tell him[f] not to inflict on me prefaces by unknown quantities *à la* Gori.[207] The biographical sketch from *Lo Sviluppo* can also be used.[208] I have just had my

---

[a] in short - [b] See this volume, pp. 140-42. - [c] K. Marx, *A Contribution to the Critique of Political Economy*. - [d] of *Capital* - [e] the Italian edition of Engels' *Socialism: Utopian and Scientific* - [f] See next letter.

photograph taken again and shall send you one as soon as I myself receive the prints.

So as to assist you in your English studies I have sent you the English edition of the *Communist Manifesto*[a] and shall get hold of a copy of the English edition of *Capital*[b] for you. Just now there is no English socialist periodical worth reading. From time to time, however, I shall send you a copy of a—if possible interesting—bourgeois newspaper for you to study. With an English grammar and a dictionary you will then make good progress. Admittedly you won't learn the pronunciation unless you have a good teacher. However the language is very easy, since it has virtually no grammar.

If you would like to have a copy of the *Manifesto* in *German*, let me know by postcard.

With most cordial regards,

Yours,

F. Engels

First published, in the language of the original (German), in *La corrispondenza di Marx e Engels con italiani. 1848-1895,* Milano, 1964

Printed according to the original

Published in English for the first time

94

ENGELS TO ROMUALDO FANTUZZI [209]

IN MILAN

[Draft]

[London,] 2 April [1891]

I shall be glad to give you permission to reprint and republish the Italian translation (by P. Martignetti) of my *Socialism: Utopian and Scientific* provided that it is published not later than 3 months from to-

---

[a] K. Marx and F. Engels, *Manifesto of the Communist Party.* Authorized English translation. Edited and annotated by Frederick Engels. London, 1888.- [b] K. Marx, *Capital: a critical analysis of capitalist production.* Translated from the third German edition by Samuel Moore and Edward Aveling and edited by Frederick Engels, Vol. I, London, 1887.

day and that no one whosoever is allowed to write a preface to it or make alterations, still less alterations made without my express and written consent.

(May reprint the biography from [a] *Origine della famiglia.* [b])

As to the reprinting of the latter pamphlet, it is a question of knowing when the new edition can appear; if this could be managed in the course of the year, we should be able to come to an understanding.

It goes without saying that I shall expect you to send me 12 *free* copies of each of my works you publish.

First published in: Marx and Engels, *Works*, First Russian Edition, Vol. XXVIII, Moscow, 1940

Printed according to the original

Translated from the French

Published in English for the first time

95

ENGELS TO PAUL LAFARGUE [141]

AT LE PERREUX

London, 3 April 1891

My dear Lafargue,

Thank you for your letter, which is of great interest, [210] firstly because we must be *au courant* with things of this kind if we are to be adequately armed vis-à-vis Hyndman; next because the tactics you have adopted are precisely those recommended by Marx to the Germans in 1875 vis-à-vis the Lassalleans [63] and I shall be able to make good use of this, should need arise, to show that in 1875 the Germans could have pursued a line of conduct different from the one they then followed; and thirdly for the reason given to Laura. [c] But this last you have misunderstood. If you care to re-read my letter, you will see that I only discuss the prospects for an acceptable future *after* the Brussels Congress. [135] Never mind the letters Liebknecht is writing to you just now; you ought to know him well enough to realise that he can face

---

[a] The beginning of the sentence is in German. - [b] F. Engels, *The Origin of the Family, Private Property and the State.* - [c] See this volume, pp. 155-56.

one way and then another in the twinkling of an eye. For the past twenty years his policy abroad has been to maintain connections independent of those that Marx and I were able to secure for him. Abroad, as at home, he likes to form his own personal party of people whom he has placed under an obligation. Nor is he overparticular. Cast your mind back to the Buffenoir affair. [211] He will behave no differently the moment new connections become available to him. And since, at Brussels, his last remaining reasons for keeping aloof from the Possibilists [3] and Hyndman will doubtless disappear, it should come as no surprise to you if he approaches those gentlemen in order to use one lot as a counterweight to yourselves and the other to hold the scales against us over here. Were that to happen, it could well be of vital importance that I should intervene at an appropriate moment and for that I should have to be prepared in advance. If it doesn't happen, so much the better.

The £50 from the Calais net-makers have made a deep impression but, as you know, the English are a MATTER OF FACT people and if international cordiality is to be maintained, it would be better not to restrict the generosity of the French working man to the foregoing. What would create an excellent impression over here would be if a sum of money were to be sent by a French trades union which *has yet to receive a contribution from England*. That would be an example of French initiative which would be much appreciated here.

Sam Moore has arrived in good health; he has had himself examined by Gumpert who declared him PERFECTLY SOUND apart from a slight swelling of the spleen, which he hopes to cure before long. Unfortunately Sam arrived at his parents' place in the Derbyshire Peak District just in time for the snow, which is none too good for a man arriving from the tropics. He will be here next week.

The assassination in Sofia [212] was undoubtedly a Russian exploit, but, since they missed Stambulov, who was the real target, it probably won't lead to anything much. Otherwise we might have seen a bit of EXCITEMENT and I'm very glad that that hasn't happened. For I have grave doubts about the Paris public's powers of resistance to a chauvinist outcry at a time of crisis, just as I have doubts about my Berliners in similar circumstances. Neither Bismarck nor Boulanger are so dead as to be incapable of resuscitation by the virtual inevitability of war.

Your tactics towards the two Possibilist sections are the best you can adopt in the circumstances. Since you are in a minority in Paris, you must set one lot off against the other and gradually attract the masses. Besides, there are divergencies of principle which entitle you to refuse a merger pure and simple.

Where on earth in the *Socialiste* is the letter from Rouen of which you speak? I have searched through every number from 11 February to 1 April and found nothing. [213]

Louise and Schorlemmer send their best wishes to you and Laura, as does

Yours,

F. E.

Schorlemmer has nearly recovered from his cold, though he looks somewhat tired.

We expect you next week so that Sam can retail to you all manner of things about your Negro relations.

First published in: F. Engels, P. et L. Lafargue, *Correspondance*, t. III, Paris, 1959

Printed according to the original

Translated from the French

96

ENGELS TO KARL KAUTSKY

IN STUTTGART

London, 7 April 1891

Dear Kautsky,

Your letter has just arrived. Pity you weren't able to induce Schmidt [214] to join you there; he'd have been just the man for you. Meissner writes to say that he has *only now* sent off the review copies of the 4th edition[a] *along with* the *Anti-Brentano*[b] [96] and that both have gone to the *Neue Zeit*. So you can begin *forthwith*; at all events you should have both of them before your article is printed. [215] If not, write to O. Meissner, *citing me* and this communication.

An Alsatian, Henri Ravé, presently in jug, who translated Bebel's

---

[a] of the first volume of *Capital* - [b] F. Engels, *In the Case of Brentano Versus Marx*.

Frau [a] and is now translating my *Origin* [b] under Laura Lafargue's supervision, wants to know whether your *Thomas Morus* [c] is worth translating. I have recommended the book to him but at the same time written to say that I would ask you to send him a copy so he can make up his own mind about it. Address: H. Ravé, *détenu à la prison*, [d] Poitiers (Vienne, France).

Just now the French are fully occupied with their own affairs, namely May Day and the attendant negotiations with the Possibilists of both Allemanist [53] and Broussist [3] persuasion—in which our own chaps are acting as arbitrators!!—etc., and also with their *Socialiste*, which explains why Paul Lafargue has done no work for the *Neue Zeit*. [216] Odd that the French should be adopting exactly the same policy towards the crumbling ranks of the Possibilists as that recommended by Marx in his accompanying letter of 1875 for adoption towards the Lassalleans. [63] And, indeed, they have done so successfully up till now—a success that will doubtless be sealed by the Brussels Congress. [135]

Many regards.

Your
F. E.

First published in *Aus der Frühzeit des Marxismus. Engels Briefwechsel mit Kautsky*, Prag, 1935

Printed according to the original

Published in English for the first time

---

[a] A. Bebel, *Die Frau in der Vergangenheit, Gegenwart und Zukunft* and *La Femme dans le passé, le présent & l'avenir*. Traduction française par Henri Ravé. Paris, 1891. - [b] F. Engels, *L'Origine de la famille, de la propriété privée et de l'état*. Traduction française par Henri Ravé. Paris, 1893. - [c] K. Kautsky, *Thomas More und seine Utopie*. - [d] kept in prison

97

ENGELS TO HENRI RAVÉ [217]

AT POITIERS

[Draft]

[London,] 7 April [1891]

If you were to set to work about the 15th of this month, you would be able to send Lafargue the first chapter about the beginning of May and so on, chapter by chapter, as and when you complete them.[a] You will have finished the whole lot by about the end of June and in July you should, I hope, have the proofs of the new edition [b]; but that does not depend upon me alone. Thus we should probably be able to bring it out in September.[c]

First published in: Marx and Engels, *Works*, First Russian Edition, Vol. XXVIII, Moscow, 1940

Printed according to the original

Translated from the French

Published in English for the first time

98

ENGELS TO FRIEDRICH ADOLPH SORGE [218]

IN HOBOKEN

London, 8 April 1891

Dear Sorge,

Today I am able to send you at long last a few new photographs; 2 small ones are enclosed herewith and a larger one (a so-called PANEL) is going off registered as a BOOK PACKET. They were taken this February and hence give a pretty accurate picture of the present state of affairs.

---

[a] See this volume, p. 154. - [b] the fourth German edition of *The Origin of the Family, Private Property and the State* - [c] See previous letter.

As to your course of Banting, gout is a perfectly normal consequence of an increased consumption of meat, eggs and other nitrogenous foodstuffs. In fact the sole function of these is to renew muscular flesh and other nitrogenous parts of the body (fibrin, in short all
albuminous substances) and replace what has been wasted. If, however, you take more than is necessary for this purpose, they will be
burned up in the body as normal nourishment for the replacement of
body heat; the residue from the burning process consists largely of so-
called uric acid which may appear in the body in greater quantities
than can be excreted through the kidneys. In which case the surplus
either lingers in the muscles or else forms crystals in the joints, and
this is what is termed rheumatism and gout. You must either get
more exercise or else change your diet and eat more bread, etc., and
less meat and eggs. Beer you should certainly shun.

Thank you for your answer concerning the Avelings. The affair
was at one time tentatively brought up over here, I no longer know
by whom, and, lest anything precipitate should be done, I took it
upon myself to consult you about it.[a]

Singer and Bebel have written to me in most affable terms.[219] Your
German can never get accustomed to the fact that someone in office
cannot lay claim to being handled more gently than anyone else.
That, at bottom, is the main reason why offence was taken. Since
I failed to respond to Liebknecht's pompous drivel [162] and took no
notice whatever of any provocations, Liebknecht may imagine that
he has won a great victory over me. He is welcome to that pleasure.
In any case he will edit the *Vorwärts* out of existence for them soon
enough and everyone is grumbling about it. Liebknecht is incorrigible and will remain so, to judge by the way he still seems to be conniving with Rosenberg in America. The decisive role in the party is de-
volving more and more upon Bebel and that is an excellent thing. Bebel is a calm, clear-headed thinker, and as a theoretician, too, he is in
a quite different class from Liebknecht. But one can't just cast Liebknecht aside; moreover he still wields a good deal of influence, thanks
to his expenditure of hot air and the vehemence of his tone at popular
meetings, hence all these compromises.

Things are going well over here. Hyndman's attacks on Aveling
may cost him very dear. Hyndman is incapable of assessing accurately his powers relative to what he aims to achieve. He thought he'd

---

[a] See this volume, p. 138.

be able to do Aveling down and now he himself has landed in the cart. As a result of the last TRADES UNION Congress in Liverpool [27] the majority of the London TRADES COUNCIL [196] has come round in favour of the LEGAL 8 HOURS DAY. Hyndman sought to play it off against the LEGAL 8 HOURS LEAGUE [200] but his plan miscarried; his Federation was represented on the LEGAL 8 HOURS COMMITTEE but he withdrew his delegates and wrote to the TRADES COUNCIL demanding 2 separate speakers' platforms for the Federation at the demonstration in the PARK.[a] But the TRADES COUNCIL will probably turn this down flat, as has already been done by the 8 HOURS COMMITTEE, in which case Hyndman will find himself between two stools.[b] Aveling is being accorded votes of confidence from all the associations he works with, since Hyndman refuses to voice his accusations in public debate and will, after May Day, doubtless have to change his tactics. Over here he is the only troublemaker who stands in the way. He has shown how useless a programme is — however right it may be theoretically — if it fails to relate to the real needs of the people. Though in this instance such people are Englishmen, they are almost as far removed from the genuine English movement as is the Socialist Labor Party in America.[133] The movement over here has come into its own by virtue of the new TRADES UNIONS, especially the GASWORKERS,[164] and of the agitation in support of a LEGAL 8 HOURS (Eight Hours Bill), the Avelings being in the forefront of both. There are, in both these spheres of agitation, many people who also belong to the SOCIAL DEMOCRATIC Federation. But they are the very ones who are wriggling out of Hyndman's clutches and who regard the SOCIAL DEMOCRATIC Federation as a negligible quantity. And, if Hyndman oversteps the mark in his squabble with Aveling, these are the very people he may have to reckon with.

In France, thanks to the split among the Possibilists,[3] our people also have the whip-hand in Paris just now. First the Allemanists [53] (according to Lafargue they're in the majority in Paris, but I doubt it) and then, eventually, also the Broussists, sent delegates to the May Day demonstration committee — i.e. they deigned to comply with a Marxist resolution. And, since the Allemanists want to chuck out the Broussists, our people find themselves in the position of acting as advocates of equal rights for the Broussists!! Best of all, our Frenchmen are employing exactly the same tactics vis-à-vis the Possibilists as

---

[a] Hyde Park - [b] See this volume, pp. 185-86.

those recommended by Marx to the Eisenachers for use vis-à-vis the Lassalleans[63]! And so far with success.

The Paris miners' congress all but broke down over the Belgians' tomfoolery with regard to a GENERAL STRIKE.[220] So as to avoid this the English called for a vote on the basis of the number of working men represented. That would have given the English all but an absolute majority and here the others rebelled. I almost hoped that the Walloon colliers, who on this occasion were at the bottom of all the nonsense about a GENERAL STRIKE, might succeed in bringing about a GENERAL STRIKE in Belgium in favour of universal suffrage; they would be hopelessly trounced and that would put an end to the nonsense. But the others in Germany and France would have to take the consequences.

Schorlemmer was here for a week; he has grown very susceptible to changes in the weather, is contending with bouts of deafness brought on by a cold, and ought sometime to spend a winter in a warm climate. Sam is in Derbyshire and I expect him any day. But I doubt if he'll do any work while over here, as he must recoup his strength for another eighteen months on the Niger. Apparently he finds the climate out there very pleasant and grumbles about ours.

Warm regards to your wife.[a]

Your
F. E.

The *duplicate* portrait is for Schlüter, to whom please convey my regards.

First published abridged in *Briefe und Auszüge aus Briefen von Joh. Phil. Becker, Jos. Dietzgen, Friedrich Engels, Karl Marx u. A. an F. A. Sorge und Andere*, Stuttgart, 1906 and in full in: Marx and Engels, *Works*, First Russian Edition, Vol. XXVIII, Moscow, 1940

Printed according to the original

Published in English in full for the first time

---

[a] Katharina Sorge

99

ENGELS TO WALERY WRÓBLEWSKI

IN LONDON

[Draft]

[London,] 9 April 1891

My dear Wróblewski,

You must forgive me if I ask you not to insist on my carrying out the commission entrusted to me in your letter of the 5th. I have no right to meddle either in the Polish party's internal affairs, of which I have virtually no knowledge, or in the private affairs of Citizen Mendelson.[a] In the circumstances it seems to me that further intervention on my part could only be detrimental to the effect you hope to achieve. In your own interest it would, I believe, be preferable for you to come to an understanding with Mendelson direct. You can do so without the slightest fear that letters addressed to 1 Hyde Park Mansions, N.W. will fail to reach him, for I know that he is now installed there.

Hoping that you will be successful and that you will soon be able to let me have better news,

I remain,
Yours sincerely

First published in: Marx and Engels, *Works*, Second Russian Edition, Vol. 38, Moscow, 1965

Printed according to the original

Translated from the French

Published in English for the first time

---

[a] See this volume, pp. 156-57.

100

ENGELS TO HEINRICH SCHEU

IN LONDON

London, 10 April 1891
122 Regent's Park Road, N. W.

Dear Mr Scheu,

Thanks to the diligence of Mrs Kautsky who over the past weeks has sorted out a whole pile of Marx's letters, I am today able to send you 2 signatures of Marx's.[221]

The one at the foot of the English draft of the letter is the clearest. On the other hand you might perhaps consider reproducing the four lines in the German draft from 'I need, etc.' to 'available' including all deletions and alterations so as to give an example of his handwriting (and at the same time of the way in which he worked). At any rate I can't supply you with anything better, that is to say without corrections and, as it were, tailored to your requirements. This I leave to you, as also to whether you include the words 'Yours very truly' and 'Dear Sir' and/or the date.

I should be grateful if you would return the letters.

It will always be a pleasure to see you here. In any case I should like to see you again before you start on my new portrait, for a peculiar snag has cropped up as regards the photographs by Debenham, and this in the quite literal sense.

With best wishes from Mrs Kautsky and

Yours respectfully,
F. Engels

First published in: Marx and Engels, *Works*, Second Russian Edition, Vol. 38, Moscow, 1965

Printed according to the original

Published in English for the first time

101

ENGELS TO LEO FRANKEL

IN PARIS

London, 24 April 1891

Dear Frankel,

I owe you a reply to your letters of 27 December and the 16th of this month. As regards the first I am well aware of the disagreeable feeling that comes over one on returning to a country after many years of absence to find what was formerly a group of good friends locked together in violent fratricidal strife. Still—*à la guerre comme à la guerre*.[a] That is a necessary condition of progress and there's nothing one can do about it.[b] The moment will come when you will be able to intervene in the interests of them all, but I don't believe that that time has yet come. Brussels will throw light on many matters, if indeed Brussels ever takes place,[135] since it is threatened by the Belgians' ill-considered general strike.[220]

What has recently been happening among the various factions in connection with the 1st of May has, in my view, demonstrated once and for all that, so far as we are concerned, the first commandment must be self-restraint. Self-restraint is what I too must impose upon myself in regard to your request concerning the May Day number of the *Bataille*,[222] even if there were no other reasons for my doing so. In the first place I have not seen a single copy of the *Bataille* since June 1889 and all I know about it, and this purely from hearsay, is that it sided with the Rue Cadet[223] in the anti-Boulangist struggle; secondly, I have for the past two months been so snowed under with requests of a similar nature that I have had to make up my mind once and for all to turn these down—one such letter is going off to Vienna today.

It's high time Volume III of *Capital* came out. Before I set to work on it I have got to get some new editions[c] ready and *this I cannot possibly refuse to do*. But so long as Volume III remains unfinished I shall

---

[a] war is war -[b] See this volume, pp. 96-97. -[c] Ibid., pp. 148-49.

take nothing on and, what's more, shall actually have to cut down on much of my correspondence.

With best wishes from myself and also from Louise Kautsky.

Your

F. Engels

First published, in Hungarian, in *Népszava*, No. 130, Budapest, 3 June 1906

Printed according to the newspaper

Translated from the Hungarian

Published in English for the first time

102

ENGELS TO KARL KAUTSKY

IN STUTTGART

London, 30 April 1891

Dear Baron,

I have before me your letters of the 5th and 25th. *Ad vocem* [a] *Brentano* [b] [96]—Herkner, to whom I sent a copy, has replied to the effect that, while the allegation of deliberate falsification could not be substantiated, Marx had nevertheless, if no doubt unintentionally, used quotations in *Capital* of such a kind that no clear idea could be obtained of Gladstone's real views, etc.—on the whole, everything you'd expect of so 'ardent' a disciple of Brentano's.

You will have got my postcard about Ravé.[c] Laura Lafargue is going to read over and correct his translation of the *Origin*,[d] otherwise I could hardly have entrusted him with the thing. He will probably take some time over your *Morus*[e] which he wishes to translate; he spoke of having to do 'more rewarding, i. e. better paid' work.

I cannot begrudge Schmidt the lectureship—something he and his parents have dreamed of for years. And in present-day Switzerland

---

[a] As regards - [b] F. Engels, *In the Case of Brentano Versus Marx*. - [c] See this volume, pp. 163-64. - [d] F. Engels, *L'Origine de la famille, de la propriété privée et de l'état*. Traduction française par Henri Ravé. - [e] K. Kautsky, *Thomas More und seine Utopie*.

even a Marxian stands some chance. True, you have thereby lost a most reliable — if not most tractable — fellow editor; however, someone will doubtless turn up to whom you can entrust much of the mechanical stuff, at any rate.

If Liebknecht were to leave Berlin for Leipzig many people besides yourself would be *instantly* overjoyed. But I don't believe it will happen. It would mean his abdicating. In Leipzig — what historical irony! — he would be the Social-Democratic Bismarck of Friedrichsruh[a] which would eventually lead to a rumpus. Whether things will go on much longer without there being one is in any case questionable.

The Peruvian affair interests me very much; I should be glad if you could send me the *Ausland* articles.[224] But tell me *when* you have got to have them back, and I can regulate my reading accordingly.

I wrote to Ravé about your *Morus* as follows[225]:

'*Le "Thomas Morus" de Kautsky contient un aperçu général juste, et sous beaucoup d'aspects original, de la période de la renaissance dans les pays de réforme protestante, et surtout l'Angleterre. C'est de cet aperçu général des conditions historiques de la période que se dégage la personnalité de T. More, comme enfant de son temps. La renaissance italienne et française, par conséquent, ne figurent dans le livre qu'à l'arrière-plan. J'écrirai à Kautsky un de ces jours, et je le prierai de vous envoyer son livre, je crois que vous trouverez, qu'il vaut bien la peine d'être traduit.*'[b]

I have no recollection whatever of Marx's Geneva memorandum.[226] We are now engaged in sorting out the old letters and newspapers and I shall see if I can find it. But just now I haven't got much time to look, let alone do notes, etc., on it. I have got to make sure of getting back to Volume III[c] and have firmly resolved to be ruthless about refusing *any more work* — were it only 3 lines — unless of the *utmost urgency*, and likewise to restrict my correspondence to *bare essentials*, until I have done with Volume III. First, of course, there's the *Origin*[d] which I shall, I think, get round to next week. Meanwhile Louise will search for the Geneva document. However, it may take

---

[a] Bismarck's estate where he lived after his resignation. - [b] 'Kautsky's *Thomas Morus* contains a survey, by and large correct and in many respects original, of the Renaissance period in the countries of the Protestant Reformation, notably England. It is from that general survey of the historical conditions of the period that T. More's personality emerges as the child of his times. In this book, therefore, the Italian and French Renaissance figures only in the background. One of these days I shall write to Kautsky and ask him to send you his book. I believe you will find it well worth translating.' - [c] of *Capital* - [d] the fourth German edition of *The Origin of the Family, Private Property and the State*

some time; the quantity of stuff is tremendous and the disorder even more so.

As you will have seen, the *Vorwärts* has altered course somewhat [227] in regard to the miners' strike.[228] Liebknecht is hopeless in such matters. The man has only two colours on his palette, black and white, with no nuances in between, so what can one do? Our chaps in Berlin see everything solely from their *own* standpoint. Thus they sometimes forget that, unlike the party *veterans*, the miners cannot be expected to have the kind of discipline that would have been drilled into them by the Anti-Socialist Law [11]; they also forget *that every* new group of workers *accrues to us* as the result of injudicious and necessarily unsuccessful wild-cat strikes which, however, are inevitable in the circumstances. I shall write to Bebel about this. [a] You can't just enjoy what is pleasing in a movement; you also have to put up with its momentary unpleasantnesses. Come to that, the strict discipline of a *sect* cannot be maintained in the case of a *big party*, nor is this altogether a bad thing.

As for Lafargue, don't let yourself be confused. Lafargue is a bit of an *enfant gâte* [b] and is enamoured of his prehistoric theories which do not by any means always hold water. Hence his Adam and Eve [c] are dear to his heart and seem to him far more important than Zola, for whom he's just the right sort of chap.[229] And the delay over the paradisal Platonists—who only learnt what's what when chucked out by old Jahweh—coming as it does so hard on the heels of the affair of his other, economic, article,[168] is to him a personal affront. Now, all of a sudden, he expects the *Neue Zeit* to carry nothing but Adam and Eve articles, as though it had been in the habit of doing so before. Now he looks for a contrast, which is non-existent, between the old and the new *Neue Zeit*, and behaves as though the paper had never before contained any *articles d'actualité*. [d] I find the *Neue Zeit* far better than it used to be—no one, surely, can expect me to read the serials; it has at last succeeded in getting Schippel to write really good articles that are a pleasure to read. That a weekly must give *more* space than a monthly to *actualités* goes without saying. If you could find a niche for Adam and Eve before too long, then all would be well.

The American militia system is *in practice* nothing but a kind of *na-*

---

[a] See this volume, pp. 182-83. - [b] spoilt child - [c] P. Lafargue, 'Der Mythus von Adam und Eva. Ein Beitrag zur vergleichenden Mythologie', *Die Neue Zeit*, 9. Jg. 1890/91, 2. Bd., Nr. 34, 35. - [d] topical articles

tional guard of middle-class volunteers, and as much as 10 years ago Hyndman wrote to Marx from America saying that the middle classes there did a vast amount of drill so as to protect themselves against the workers. Proof of how utterly useless this is against an *external* enemy may be found in all the wars the United States has ever fought using newly formed regiments of volunteers (enlisted men) — on the largest scale of all in the Civil War when the militia melted away completely. Even when I was in America I heard of the militia regiments' ARMORIES which were said to be veritable fortresses in the heart of New York. Until such time as every working man has a rifle and a hundred live rounds at home, the whole thing will remain an absurdity.[230]

Your old friend
F. E.

As you know, Mother Besant has now joined Grandmother Blovatsky's (Blamatsky's?) [a] Theosophists. Now, writ large in gold on her garden gate at 19 Avenue Road, is the legend: THEOSOPHICAL HEADQUARTERS. Such is the result of Herbert Burrows' love.

First published in *Aus der Frühzeit des Marxismus. Engels Briefwechsel mit Kautsky*, Prag, 1935

Printed according to the original

Published in English for the first time

103

ENGELS TO AUGUST BEBEL[231]

IN BERLIN

London, 1 May 1891

Dear Bebel,

Today I shall reply to your two letters of 30 March and 25 April.[232] I was delighted to hear that your silver wedding went off so well and has whetted your appetite for the next, your golden one. I sincerely hope that you will both live to see it. We shall need you

---

[a] Helena Blavatsky

long after the devil has come for me — as the old man of Dessau [a] used to say.

I must — I hope for the last time — revert to Marx's critique of the programme.[b] That '*no one* would have raised any objection to its publication' I feel bound to contest. Liebknecht would *never* have willingly consented and would have done everything in his power to prevent it. So greatly has the critique rankled since 1875 that he recalls it the moment the word 'programme' is mentioned. The whole of his Halle speech turns upon it.[121] His pompous *Vorwärts* article [162] is, throughout, nothing but an expression of his bad conscience in regard to this self-same critique. And it was, in fact, primarily aimed at him. We regarded, and I still regard him, as the progenitor of the unification programme[63] or the *shoddier* aspects thereof. And it was this point that led me to act off my own bat. Had I been able to discuss the thing with you alone and then send it straight on to K. Kautsky for publication, a couple of hours would have sufficed for us to agree. But as it was, I considered you were under an obligation — both from the personal and the party viewpoint — to consult Liebknecht as well. And I knew what the result would be if I went ahead regardless. Either suppression or an open row — a temporary one at any rate — even with yourself. That I wasn't wrong is evident from what follows: Now, since you came out of quod on 1 April [1875], and the document is dated 5 May, it is obvious — until some other explanation is forthcoming — that the thing was *deliberately withheld* from you and that this could, in fact, *only* have been done *by Liebknecht*. But just for the sake of peace and quiet you have allowed him to disseminate the lie that, because you were under lock and key, you had not been able to see the thing.[233] Hence I take it that, even before publication, you could have spared his feelings in order to avoid a rumpus in the Executive. Indeed I find this explicable, as I trust you will likewise find my having allowed for the fact that this, in all probability, was how you acted.

I have just taken another look at the thing. It's possible that some of it could have been left out without impairing the whole. But certainly not *very much*. What was the position? We knew as well as you did and, for instance, the *Frankfurter Zeitung* of 9 March 1875,[c] which

---

[a] Leopold, Prince of Anhalt-Dessau - [b] K. Marx, *Critique of the Gotha Programme*. - [c] 'Frankfurt, 8. März', *Frankfurter Zeitung und Handelsblatt*, No. 68, morning edition, 9 March 1875.

Frederick Engels. 1891.

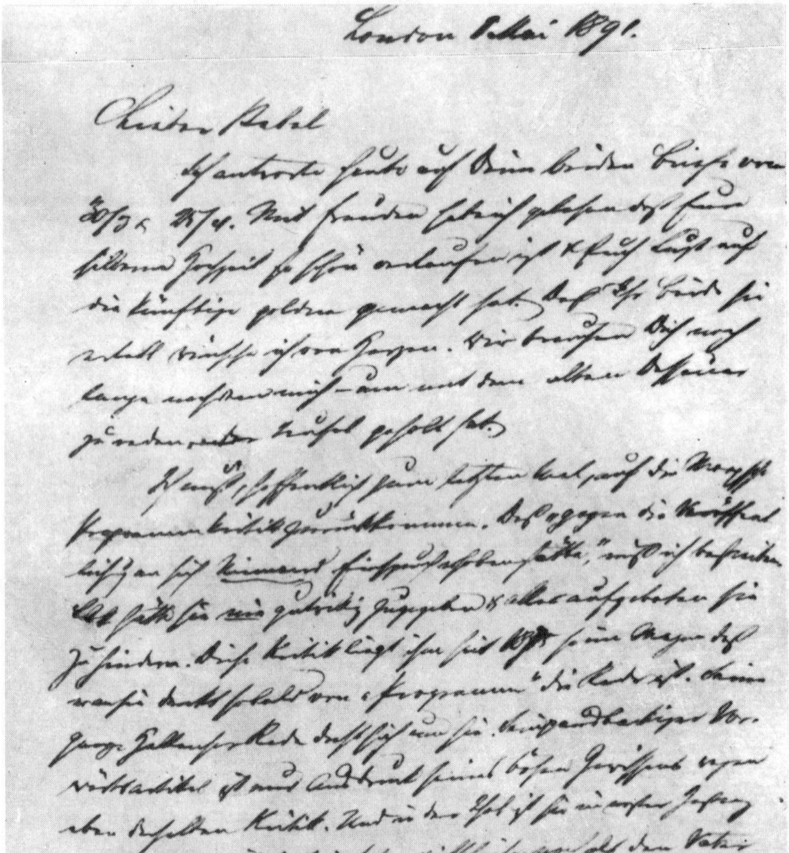

First page of Engels' letter to August Bebel of 1-2 May 1891

I found, that the *matter was decided* when your accredited representatives accepted the draft. Hence Marx wrote the thing merely to salve his conscience, as is testified by the words he appended—*dixi et salvavi animam meam*[a]—and not with any hope of success. Hence Liebknecht's big talk about the 'categorical no'[234] is mere braggadocio and he knows it. Well, if you blundered in choosing your representatives and were then forced to swallow the programme lest the whole business of unification came to naught, you surely cannot object to the publication, *fifteen years later*, of the warning that was sent you before you finally made up your minds. It does not brand you either fools or traitors unless, of course, you lay claim to infallibility so far as your official actions are concerned.

You, however, did not see that warning. Indeed this fact has been made public and you are thus in an exceptionally favourable position as compared with the others who, though they had seen it, nevertheless fell in with the draft.

I consider the accompanying letter to be most important.[63] For it propounds what would have been the only correct policy. Parallel action for a trial period—that was the one thing that could have saved you from trafficking in principles. But, come what may, Liebknecht was determined not to forego the glory of having effected unification and, in the circumstances, it is a miracle that he didn't make even more concessions than he did. From bourgeois democracy he brought with him and has retained ever since a positive mania for unification.

The fact that the Lassalleans came over because they *had to*, because their entire party was disintegrating and because their leaders were scoundrels or jackasses whom the masses would no longer follow, is something that can be said today in tastefully moderate form. Their 'tightly knit organisation' naturally ended in total dissolution. Hence it is absurd when Liebknecht excuses the wholesale acceptance of the Lassallean articles of faith on the grounds that the Lassalleans had sacrificed their tightly knit organisation—there was nothing left of it to sacrifice!

You wonder about the provenance of the muddle-headed and convoluted clichés in the programme. But all these are surely quintessential Liebknecht; they have been a bone of contention between us for years and the chap's besotted with them. Theoretically he has always been muddle-headed and our clear-cut style is still an abomination to

---

[a] I have spoken and saved my soul.

him today. As a sometime member of the People's Party [154] he, on the other hand, still loves resounding phrases which leave one free to think what one will or, for that matter, not think at all. The mere fact that, long ago and out of ignorance, some muddle-headed Frenchman, Englishman or American spoke of the 'emancipation of labour' rather than of the working *class*, and that, even in the documents of the International one sometimes had to use the language of the people one was addressing, was, to Liebknecht, reason enough for forcibly making the phraseology of the German party conform to this same outmoded point of view. Nor can he possibly be said to have done this 'despite his knowing better' for he really didn't know better and I am not sure whether this is not still the case today. At all events, he is still as susceptible as he ever was to the old, woolly phraseology which, rhetorically, is certainly easier to use. And since he undoubtedly attached at least as much importance to basic democratic demands, which he thought he understood, as to economic principles, of which he had no clear understanding, he was undoubtedly sincere in believing he had pulled off a splendid deal in bartering democratic staples for Lassallean dogmas.

So far as the attacks on Lassalle are concerned, these seemed to me, as I have already said, more important than anything else. By accepting *all* the essential Lassallean economic catchwords and demands, the Eisenachers had *in fact turned into Lassalleans* — at least if the programme is anything to go by.[63] The Lassalleans had sacrificed nothing, nothing whatever that was capable of preservation. And so as to make the latter's victory more complete you people adopted for your party anthem the rhymed, moralising prose in which Mr Audorf celebrates Lassalle.[a][235] During the 13 years in which the Anti-Socialist Law was in force [11] there was, of course, no possibility of combatting the Lassalle cult within the party. This had got to be quashed and I set about doing so. I shall no longer permit Lassalle's bogus reputation to be maintained and revived *at Marx's expense*. Those who knew and revered Lassalle personally are thin on the ground; in the case of all the rest, the Lassallean cult is *purely factitious*, the result of our having tacitly tolerated it against our better judgment; hence it has not even the justification of personal attachment. We showed ample consideration for the feelings of inexperienced and new recruits by publishing the thing in the *Neue Zeit*. But

---

[a] J. Audorf, *Lied der deutschen Arbeiter.*

I am in no way prepared to concede that in such circumstances historical truth — after 15 years of meek forbearance — should give way to expediency and the fear of causing offence within the party. That deserving people should have their feelings hurt on such occasions is unavoidable and their grumbling after the event no less so. And if they then proceed to say that Marx was envious of Lassalle, and the German press, including even (!!) the Chicago *Vorbote* (which writes for more self-confessed Lassalleans — in Chicago — than exist in the whole of Germany) chimes in, it affects me no more than a flea-bite. We have had far worse things cast in our teeth and none the less carried on with the business in hand. The example has been set; Marx has laid rough hands on the sacrosanct Ferdinand Lassalle and that for the time being is enough.

And now just one more thing. In view of the attempt made by you people forcibly to prevent publication of the article, and your warnings to the *Neue Zeit* that, in the event of a recurrence, it, too, might be taken over and subjected to censorship by the party, the latter's appropriation of your entire press cannot but appear to me in a singular light. In what respect do you differ from Puttkamer if you introduce an Anti-Socialist Law into your own ranks? So far as I myself am concerned, it doesn't signify; no party in any country can impose silence upon me once I have made up my mind to speak. But all the same I would suggest you consider whether you would not do well to show yourselves slightly less touchy and, in your actions, slightly less — Prussian. You — the party — *need* socialist science and this cannot exist without freedom to develop. Hence one has to put up with the unpleasantnesses and to do so for preference with good grace and without flinching. Tension, however slight, let alone a rift, between the German party and German socialist science would be an unprecedented misfortune and disgrace. That the Executive and/or you yourself still have and must retain considerable *moral* sway over the *Neue Zeit* and everything else that is published, goes without saying. But with that you must and can rest content. Inalienable freedom of discussion is constantly being vaunted in the *Vorwärts* but is not greatly in evidence. You have absolutely no idea how odd an impression this proclivity for forcible measures makes upon one who lives abroad and is accustomed to see the most venerable party leaders being well and truly taken to task within their own party (e. g. the TORY government by Lord Randolph Churchill). And again, you should not forget that discipline in a big party cannot be anything like as strict as it is in a small sect, and that the Anti-Socialist Law, which forged the Eisenachers and Lassalleans into a single whole (though Liebknecht avers this was the work of his magnificent programme) and necessitated such close cohesion, no longer exists.

Ouf! So much for that old affair, and now for something else. There would seem to be some high jinks going on in the upper regions over there.[236] But it's all to the good. That the state machine should be thrown out of gear in this way suits us very well. Always providing peace is maintained by the universal fear of what the outcome of a war might be! For Moltke's death has removed the last obstacle to the disorganisation of the army by the arbitrary appointment of new commanders, and every year must contribute towards making victory more uncertain and defeat more probable. And little though I would wish for another Sedan, I am no more anxious to see the Russians and their allies victorious, even if they are republicans and otherwise have cause for complaint about the Peace of Frankfurt.[237]

The trouble you expended on the revision of trade regulations has not been in vain. Better propaganda would be difficult to imagine. We over here followed the business with considerable interest and were delighted by the pertinence of the speeches.[238] In this connection I recalled the words of old Fritz: 'For the rest, our soldiers' genius lies in the attack, as is, indeed, right and proper.'[a] And what party, given the same number of deputies, could boast so many confident and forceful speakers? Bravo me lads!

No doubt you deplore the pit strike in the Ruhr,[228] but what can you do? After all, it is usually via the unpremeditated wild-cat strike that we acquire large new categories of workers. In my view, insufficient account was taken of *this* fact in discussing the matter in the *Vorwärts*.[227] Liebknecht ignores all nuances; to him everything is either black or white and if he feels it incumbent on him to prove to the world that our party did not stir up this strike but actually poured oil on troubled waters, then God help the poor strikers; they're getting

---

[a] Friedrich II, 'Instruktion für die General-Majors von der Cavallerie (14. August 1748)'. In: Friedrich der Große, *Militärische Schriften erläutert und mit Anmerkungen versehen durch v. Taysen, Oberstlieutenant und Abtheilungschef im Neben-Etat des Großen Generalstabes.*

less consideration than they ought if they are to come over to us in the near future. But come they will in any case. By the way, what's wrong with the *Vorwärts*? Not a cheep out of my Liebknecht for 2 days; no doubt he's on his travels. Today, 2 May, he is back again, live and kicking.

2 May. Come to that, the pit strike will doubtless soon fizzle out; it would seem to be only a very partial one and in no way to accord with the assertions and assurances at the delegates' meeting. It's all to the good. Not for one moment do I doubt that there's a powerful urge to resort to the sword and the musket.

The *first* [of May] went off very well. Vienna again takes pride of place. In Paris it fell more or less flat thanks to the bickering which is as yet by no means a thing of the past. Mistakes have been made there on every side. Our people in Lille and Calais had committed themselves to a specific type of demonstration — the sending of delegates to the Chamber.[239] The Blanquists were not asked. The Allemanists[53] did not join the demonstration *comité* until later. This suited neither the Blanquists nor the Allemanists; in the Chamber, the Blanquists had apostates who had been elected under Boulanger's aegis, the Allemanists had a Broussist opponent[3] there, and neither party wanted to appear as petitioners before these men. The same applied to the deputations which our chaps suggested sending to the 20 Paris *mairies*[a] to which it was also proposed to summon the municipal councillors so that they might there hear 'the will of the people'. Thus a split ensued, our chaps withdrew and the demonstration split up into 3 or 4 partial demonstrations. Lafargue sent me word yesterday afternoon; under the circumstances he is fairly satisfied with what happened, but maintains that Paris will come off badly by comparison with the provinces. Of one thing we may be certain; the countries which chose the 3rd [of May] — Germany and England — will muster the most impressive crowds, providing the weather's not too bad. It's wretched here today, heavy, drenching showers, a strong wind and only an occasional ray of sunshine.

Fischer will have received what he wanted for *Wage Labour and Capital*.[b] *Entwicklung*[c] will follow in a few days' time. But then there

---

[a] town halls - [b] F. Engels, 'Introduction to Karl Marx's *Wage Labour and Capital* (1891 Edition)'. - [c] F. Engels, 'Preface to the Fourth Edition of *Socialism: Utopian and Scientific*'.

must be no more requests. I have been promising a new edition of the *Origin*[a] for a year now, and that has got to go off, after which I shall undertake *nothing further whatsoever* until the 3rd volume of *Capital* is ready in ms. That has *got* to be completed. So if over there you hear rumours of fresh demands to be made on my time, I would beg you to back me up. I shall also reduce my correspondence to a minimum, with only one exception, namely yourself. It is through you that I can most easily remain in touch with the German party and again, to be honest, I enjoy this correspondence far more than any other. Once Volume III is in print I can get cracking again, starting with the revision of the *Peasant War*.[b] And if I have nothing else to do, I shall probably complete Volume III this year.

Well, kindest regards to your wife,[c] Paul,[d] Fischer, Liebknecht and *tutti quanti*[e] from

Your

F. E.

[From Louise Kautsky]

Dear August,

Many thanks for your kind letter; I shall answer it as soon as possible and let you have the information you ask for. Did you know that we, i. e. the United International Social-Democrats, namely: Tussy (representing France, England), Ede[f] (Ireland), Ede[g] (Berlin), Gine[h] (Posen[i]) and I, Austria and Italy, proposed to move a vote of no confidence when *The Daily News* praised you so exceedingly? Fie upon you, August! You are the last person I should have expected this from. Warm regards to you and your wife.

Your

Mummy

More anon.

First published, in Russian, in *Proletar-skaya Revolyutsia*, Moscow, No. 2, 1939

Printed according to the original

Published in English in full for the first time

---

[a] F. Engels, *The Origin of the Family, Private Property and the State.* - [b] F. Engels, *The Peasant War in Germany.* - [c] Julie Bebel - [d] Paul Singer - [e] all the rest - [f] Edward Aveling - [g] Eduard Bernstein - [h] Regina Bernstein - [i] Polish name: Poznan

104

ENGELS TO LAURA LAFARGUE

AT LE PERREUX

London, 4 May 1891

My dear Löhr,

Yesterday was glorious, both as to weather and demonstration. Louise, Sam Moore and I went there at 2,[240] the platforms extended in an immense arc across the Park,[a] the procession began to march in at 2.30 and had not done by 4.15, indeed fresh processions came in up to 5 o'clock. I was on Edward's platform with Sam, Louise on Tussy's. The crowd was immense, about the same or more even than last year.

Now a little gossip about the history of the affair. It has been almost exclusively Edward's and Tussy's work, and they had to fight it through from beginning to end. There was of course a deal of friction, but the Trades' Congress last September at Liverpool[27] and the changed majority (in favour of *legal* 8 hours) had considerably smoothed the way. Shipton was awfully polite to Edward, but obstructive in many small matters, and threatened to throw up everything if his right (divine?) to be Marshal in command of the procession should be ever questioned. Well, they let him, it will probably be the last time he will appear *hoch zu Ross*.[b]

The principal thing was that the resolution was passed in the form proposed by our people, and that they carried in the joint committee (5 from the Trades Council,[196] 5 from the Demonstration Committee).

Now for the fun — the Social Democratic Federation.[29] At first they sent 3 delegates to the Demonstration Committee where Edward was Chairman. But after a few meetings they remained absent, and were struck off the rolls. Then the Social Democratic Federation applied to the Trades Council for 2 platforms for themselves, as they had last year. But Shipton himself suggested to the Joint Committee that this would never do, and it was rejected, as in the same way every Trades Union might have asked for 2 platforms. Then the Social Democratic Federation announced in their Moniteur[c] that they

---

[a] Hyde Park - [b] on horseback - [c] official newspaper

would hold a meeting of their own with four platforms and red flags.[a] Unfortunately they had to join our procession from the Embankment in order to get into the Park in an orderly and showy manner, and once there, marched off about 100 yards and held there their promised meetings — without proper platforms, we had big carts, they only chairs. They were just near enough to reckon upon some stragglers from our overflow, and just far enough to show how few of them they were able to attract.

The decisive thing had been, for them, the resolution of the Demonstration Committee: that every association affiliated to them should pay 5/- *for every branch* towards general expenses. Thus, the Social Democratic Federation would have had either to pay 5/- for the many bogus branches they exhibit in their Moniteur, or else own they were bogus. And that decided their final retreat.

They have been made to feel their real position, and that is: the same position which the Germans of the Socialistic Labor Party in America [133] hold there, that of a *sect*. And that is their position, though they are real live Englishmen. It is very characteristic of the Anglo-Saxon race and their peculiar mode of development, that both here and in America the people who, more or less, have the correct theory *as to the dogmatic side of it*, become a mere sect because they cannot conceive that living theory of action, of working with the working class at every possible stage of its development, otherwise than as a collection of dogmas to be learnt by heart and recited like a conjurer's formula or a Catholic prayer. Thus the real movement is going on outside the sect, and leaving it more and more. The Canning Town Branch of the Federation sticks to Edward and Tussy in spite of Hyndman and marches with our people, and that is their strongest branch. Since the Dockstrike [198] the Social Democratic Federation had for a time profited by the general socialist revival, but that is over now, they are fast for cash for their new Hall in the Strand, and the decline has set in again. And as their friends and allies the Possibilists [3] are eating each other up as fast as they can, they cannot even brag with their grand foreign connexions.

Sam Moore was very much struck with the immense progress made here during the 2 years of his absence. He, by the bye, is very well, likes the climate and easy life amazingly and will, I am almost sure, be homesick for Africa after a while.

[a] 'Eight Hours' Demonstration, Sunday May 3rd, 1891', *Justice*, No. 381, 2 May 1891.

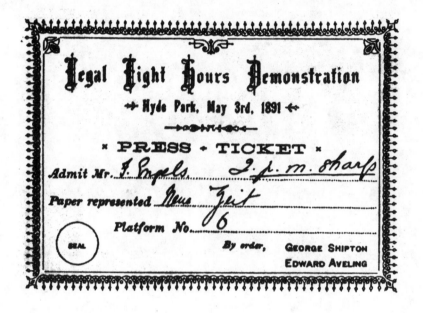

Engels' press ticket to the platform in Hyde Park
during the demonstration on 3 May 1891

I saw Cunninghame Graham on our platform (No. 6, Edward's, see *Chronicle*[a]) but he could not tell me much more about Paris than was said in Paul's letter Friday afternoon.[b] After all I hope the Committee's demonstration in the evening was *not* a failure, as, Graham says, was that of the Broussists. If we cannot work together, we have all an interest in having as much of a demonstration as possible.

It's no use crying over spilt milk, but I cannot help thinking that our friends made a slight mistake, thanks to the usual French inclination of miscalculating the strength of the relative forces. A very heroic disposition sometimes, '*mais ce n'est pas la guerre*'.[c][241] After all we intended to work as usual with the Blanquists, and *they* were not bound by the resolutions of Calais and Lille.[239] These resolutions could only bind our people; the Blanquists too might have passed resolutions as to the 1st of May and then said they were bound by them. Why then determine beforehand by our own selves and without our only allies, how the demonstration was to be arranged *in Paris* where we are in an, at present, decided minority? Why thus *froisser*[d] our only allies? *Froisser* them still more by the plan of delegations to the *mairies*[e] and summonses to all the *élus*[f] to meet the delegates there? a plan which on the face of it they were sure to repudiate? I am not at all astonished that they fell into the arms of the Allemanists[53] after this. At least that is the view I came to from the information I possess, there may be another side to the case but I do not know it.

We have very little news from Germany to-day. Hamburg had a splendid procession, 80,000 according to *Daily Telegraph*. From Berlin very little news; the Havas of Berlin, Wolff, has orders from Government to suppress everything, and the London correspondents are all under the influence of the Freisinnigen,[242] and do exactly the same.

When we came home last night, we wound up with a *Maibowle*[g] the *Maikraut*[h] of which Percy had sent us from Ryde. We put in 4 bottles Moselle, 2 claret, 1 Champagne, and finished it — we, Bernsteins and the Tussy's.[i] Late in the evening Cunninghame Graham came in and actually had two or three glasses of it — he seems to have left his teetotalism at Tangiers. There is a slight but rather agreeable Kater,[j] kept in proper bounds this morning by a bottle of Pilsener.

---

[a] 'Eight Hours Day.—Demonstration in Hyde Park.—Enormous Gathering', *The Daily Chronicle*, No. 9092, 4 May 1891.- [b] 1 May- [c] but this is not war- [d] offend- [e] town halls- [f] municipal councillors- [g] punch- [h] woodruff (a plant used for making punch)- [i] Eleanor and Edward Aveling- [j] hangover

Why did not Paul turn up? Graham says he was too tired — his name figures as a speaker on platform 8, with Jack Burns.[a]
Viele Grüsse von Louise.

Dein alter[b]
F. E.

First published in *Labour Monthly*, No. 9, London, 1955   Reproduced from the original

105

ENGELS TO PAUL LAFARGUE[141]

AT LE PERREUX

London, 19 May 1891

My dear Lafargue,

First of all I did not suggest what tactics you should adopt; I merely said the following: if, at your congresses, you, the Workers' Party, decide in advance how you intend to celebrate 1 May *in Paris* without regard for the convenience or the wishes of your allies the Blanquists, you must not be surprised if you find them deserting you.[c] If your hand was forced by the provincial gentry, the blame is theirs. In either case you have miscalculated the respective forces at work *in Paris* and you have been forced out of the committee created by yourselves. That's not what you would call a victory and neither would I.

It remains to be seen what becomes of the Blanquists and, in particular, the Allemanists,[53] to whom you have given the opportunity of once again setting themselves up as the true representatives of the Paris proletariat and at the same time of acquiring A NEW LEASE OF LIFE. And you complain that the English are too slow for you, although they have forced our own Possibilists,[3] the SOCIAL DEMOCRATIC FEDERATION[29] to exclude themselves from the great demonstration, and you also say that over there it spread like wildfire.

---

[a] John Burns - [b] Best regards from Louise. Your old friend - [c] See this volume, p. 189.

Maybe, but it is Possibilist fire and will eventually flare up in your faces.

There have been demonstrations in the provinces over here, but as I haven't kept the newspapers, I haven't got a list of them.

If you seriously believe Reuters' reports with their estimate of 60,000 people in the Park, do you want us to do likewise with regard to the Havas reports in which your demonstration hardly figures at all? What would you say to that? There were at least 500,000 in Hyde Park.

I see in the German papers that at Fourmies, when the command was given to open fire,[243] the only soldiers to do so were those of the 145th, whereas the detachment of the 84th remained with their arms at the order. And that is why neither the Government nor the Chamber will consent to an inquiry that would establish the fact *officially*. If this is true, it is a good sign. The Prussian system requires that soldiers be allotted to regiments garrisoned in the region from which the whole of the army corps draws its recruits. Accordingly in the event of mobilisation it is no longer possible, without creating enormous difficulties, to despatch Gascons to the north and Flemings, Walloons and natives of Picardy to the south. This is yet another danger of the system and one that will make itself felt earlier in France than in Germany.

You are right to protest against the ultra-foolish follies attributed to you.[244] That is the danger with countries possessing a revolutionary past, inasmuch as any new region invaded by socialism is tempted to have its revolution within 24 hours. There is no need whatsoever to urge them on; on the contrary they should be reined back. All that the Walloons, in particular, comprehend is rioting and in this they are nearly always the losers. Consider the struggles of the Belgian miners[245]; organisation nil or virtually nil, irrepressibly impatient, hence doomed to defeat.

Clemenceau has had what he wanted: his day of brilliant opposition,[246] a reminder of the good old times when he made and unmade ministries. On the morrow he remembered that he was now a nobody and that it was Constans who, after all, was the paragon in the eyes of the bourgeoisie. *He out-ferries Ferry.*

Tussy and Aveling are in Dublin for a congress of the GASWORKERS AND GENERAL LABOURERS.[247] Bernstein's entire family is ill with influenza, Percy and Pumps are disporting themselves in the Isle of Wight, seeing that Percy hasn't yet very much to do because the price list he will have to use is still at the printers. It is snowing here and when it isn't snowing it's raining and feels as chilly as November and we have had fires. For the past week our BASEMENT has been in utter disorder as a result of repairs to the DRAINS, which stink horribly; we shall have at least another week of it. Old Harney is in Richmond and very ill; he suffers from chronic bronchitis and is afraid, or so he tells me in his letter today, that he will get pleurisy on top of it. Weak as he is, that could be very serious at 75.

Tomorrow I shall at last be able to turn my attention to my *Origin of the Family* [a] — if nothing crops up!

After Cunninghame-Graham's expulsion and with your Constans in a temper ugly enough to match that of any Père Duchesne, what foreign socialist could feel safe in France [248]? And supposing that, in retaliation against the Japanese attempt on the life of the Tsarevitch [249] (who had committed improprieties and caused scuffles in a TEA-GARDEN, to wit a brothel, whereupon the police arrived) a number of minor outrages or coups d'état were to be inflicted upon the Russians in France?

Here comes another squall and it's raining cats and dogs. Dinner in ten minutes. So I shall close this *olla podrida* [b] of an epistle or, as the Milanese have it, *arlecchino*.

I believe you get the Vienna *Arbeiter-Zeitung*. This week it has a letter from Louise on the MEETING in Hyde Park. [c]

I spend my evenings studying Louise's books on the physiology of birth and related matters. It's really wonderful — since the *process* is such an *excessively* ugly one. I am discovering things of the utmost importance from the philosophical viewpoint.

Give Laura a kiss from me. Regards from Louise.

Yours ever,

F. E.

Herewith Ravé [d] and cheque for £20.

First published in: F. Engels; P. et L. Lafargue, *Correspondance*, t. III, Paris, 1959

Printed according to the original

Translated from the French

---

[a] the fourth German edition of *The Origin of the Family, Private Property and the State* -
[b] hotch-potch -
[c] L. K[autsky], 'London den 4. Mai. Die Arbeit von zwölf langen Monaten fand gestern eine Belohnung...', *Arbeiter-Zeitung*, No. 20, 15 May 1891. -
[d] Ravé's letter to Lafargue

106

ENGELS TO PAUL LAFARGUE [141]

AT LE PERREUX

London, 29 May 1891

My dear Lafargue,

Thank you for the information contained in your letter of the 21st.[250] I have passed it on to Aveling for submission to the London press.

Whatever you may say, the fact remains that the Possibilists [3] have ousted you from your own committee and that Vaillant and Allemane and Dumay acted in concert and spoke at the Mur des Fédérés, whereas not a word is said about speeches made by you or Guesde.[251] In the provinces you are in a majority, but it is now openly asserted that in Paris you are, for the time being, IN A HOPELESS MINORITY. And that is an assertion for which you yourselves are accountable.

Now for another matter. To help me in the preparation of the new edition [a] of the *Origin of the Family* I have had in front of me *Les Origines du mariage et de la famille* by Giraud Teulon, Paris and Geneva, 1884. It is a new, entirely revised edition of his work, *Les Origines de la famille*, 1874 (Geneva). In his later work, dated 1884, he advances some claim to having anticipated, in the edition of 1874, the discoveries made by Morgan. Unfortunately the 1874 edition is out of print. But Lavrov or Létourneau will be bound to possess one. As it is essential for me to clear up this point, could you not procure me one of these copies *for a few days only* and send it to me 'REGISTERED' (the 1874 book, the *Origines de la famille*)? If, by chance, neither of them has it, could you get a copy for me from a second-hand bookseller? And if that will take too much time (for the thing has brought me up short), would you be good enough to make a few inquiries at the Bibliothèque nationale (I would do this here at the British Museum but 1. I haven't a ticket, 2. Louise doesn't know enough

---

[a] the fourth German edition

French, 3. Tussy isn't sufficiently up in such matters). The problem is this.

McLennan is, as you know, the proponent of *exogamous tribes* who are obliged to obtain their wives from outside either by abduction or by purchase.[a] In *Ancient Society*,[b] as you also know, Morgan (who in his *Systems of Consanguinity*[c] still describes the exogamous *gens* as 'tribe') has proved that the exogamous tribe does not exist, that exogamy is an attribute of one *fraction* or subdivision of the tribe, i. e. of the *gens*, and that within the tribe there are no restrictions on marriage provided it takes place outside of the *gens*.

Now here is what Giraud Teulon has to say on p. 104, footnote:

'Morgan, in his later works, while recognising the necessity of not confusing *tribe* with *clan*' (in Giraud Teulon *clan* is the equivalent of Morgan's *gens*), 'has abandoned his definition of tribe without, however, seeking to provide a new one.'

And he then proceeds to give a description of the tribe divided into *clans* (*gentes*) exactly as Morgan does, but as though this had been arrived at quite independently of Morgan and was attributable to him, Giraud Teulon.

The manner in which he presents his claims is so equivocal that it doesn't inspire me with much confidence. But since this concerns a discovery that has entirely revolutionised the science of prehistory, perhaps you would be good enough (should occasion arise) to compare the 1874 edition and tell me

1. What alternative he suggests to McLennan's *exogamous tribe*.

2. If in 1874 he has already discovered that the tribe was subdivided into *exogamous clans* equivalent to Morgan's *gentes*.

3. (Briefly, names only), if he really did discover this, what examples does he cite? Does he acknowledge that his *clan* is identical with the Greek or Roman *gens*?

As to 1. and 2., the relevant passages in his own words if that is possible.

Old Harney is pretty ill; he is suffering from chronic bronchitis — at 75! He intends to move from Richmond to Ventnor. I trust he arrives there safe and sound and that it will do him good.

Your article on Adam and Eve[d] is very witty. There is evidently

---

[a] J. F. McLennan, *Primitive Marriage. An Inquiry into the Origin of the Form of Capture in Marriage Ceremonies.* - [b] L. H. Morgan, *Ancient Society or Researches in the Lines of Human Progress from Savagery, through Barbarism to Civilisation.* - [c] L. H. Morgan, *Systems of Consanguinity and Affinity of the Human Family.* - [d] P. Lafargue, 'Der Mythus von Adam und Eva. Ein Beitrag zur vergleichenden Mythologie', *Die Neue Zeit*, 9. Jg. 1890/91, 2. Bd., Nr. 34, 35.

some truth in it, but perhaps you go too far in your interpretation, especially in your catalogue of Noah's ancestors. Although in the case of Noah's descendants there can be no doubt whatever that they constitute a catalogue of tribes. *Elōăh* = the Arabic *Allah* both etymologically and lexically. The 'ă' (*patách furtivum*) [a] is obligatory in Hebrew if the end of the word has an 'o' or 'u' before 'h' or 'ch' (*rūăch Elohîm*, the Spirit of Elohim in the 2nd verse of the 1st chapter of Genesis). In the plural *Elôhîm* the 'ă' disappears.

I am sending you *The Workman's Times*, a *non-political* working-class paper which calls for the formation of *a working men's party*!! The best of the working men's or so-called working men's papers over here. As regards facts it is admirable. The paper was founded by Yorkshire and Lancashire workmen and originally appeared in Huddersfield before being transplanted to London.

Give Laura a kiss from me. LOUISE SENDS HER KINDEST REGARDS.

Yours ever,
F. E.

First published in: F. Engels, P. et L. Lafargue, *Correspondance*, t. III, Paris, 1959

Printed according to the original
Translated from the French

107

ENGELS TO FRANZ MEHRING [b]

IN BERLIN

London, 5 June 1891

Kapital und Presse [c] received with thanks. I wish it every success. I didn't know your address, hence belated reply.

First published in: Marx and Engels, *Works*, First Russian Edition, Vol. XXVIII, Moscow, 1940

Printed according to the original
Published in English for the first time

---

[a] The original has '*furtirena*'. - [b] Engels wrote this note on his visiting card. - [c] F. Mehring, *Kapital und Presse. Ein Nachspiel zum Falle Lindau.*

108

ENGELS TO FRIEDRICH ADOLPH SORGE [252]

IN HOBOKEN

London, 10 June 1891

Dear Sorge,

I am up to the eyes in the new edition of the *Origin of the Family, etc.*[a]; it has been necessary to go through all the relevant literature of the past 8 years and its quintessence must now be worked into the book, which is no joke, especially in view of the many interruptions. However the worst is behind me and I shall at last be able to get back to Volume III.[b] I have had to cut down on the whole of my correspondence, otherwise I should make no progress at all.

In Berlin — *strictly between ourselves,* for Schlüter must not know that it is *I* who have given you the information; he cannot always keep his mouth shut and if you tell him, he's sure to know that it comes from me — in Berlin, then, the chaps have finally come round to the view that Liebknecht is a windbag and nothing more. Earlier on the position was such that they *had* to give him the post of editor of the *Vorwärts* and at the same time make him an honorary member of the Executive. I had long been aware that this was bound to bring matters to a head; it was inevitable. They now find that he is editing the paper out of existence, for in the first place he does nothing himself and, in the second, he is standing in the way of others who *could* do something. So it's scandalous that he should allow his son-in-law Geiser to write botched leading articles for it, articles of such dreary arrogance and tedious ineffectiveness as to be beyond the capabilities of anyone save their author — and this is the Geiser who, morally speaking, was chucked out of the party at St Gallen.[253] For the moment there's no telling how the affair will end. They have offered Liebknecht another position in which he would act both as a popular

---

[a] the fourth German edition of *The Origin of the Family, Private Property and the State.* - [b] of *Capital*

speaker and in his earlier capacity of journalistic franc-tireur, but this he construes as a dismissal. Now they don't know how to set about pensioning him off in a decent manner, and to do so in such a way that he will accept — for that is what it really boils down to. The oddest part of all is that while the Anti-Socialist Law [11] was in force, precluding the outbreak of this conflict, Liebknecht hardly changed at all, or at most continued along a course upon which he had long since embarked, and that the chaps now find that, upon his transfer to Berlin from his Borsdorf retreat, he no longer bears the slightest resemblance to the Liebknecht of old — in other words Liebknecht as *they* had imagined him. The real point is that the *others* have progressed and now suddenly notice the difference; they imagine that it is *they* who have remained as they were, which is by no means the case.

Now for something else. Stanisław[a] writes to tell me that Anna[b] has approached Paris for money and has actually got some, or will be doing so; these attempts at extortion are really a bit thick, he says, and suggests we write to America lest there should be further useless expenditure over there on the young madame's behalf. Accordingly he has already written to you and asks me to do the same. He describes her, Anna's, way of going about things as downright blackmail.

Today we have at last had a semblance of summer; the vegetation is a whole month behind and in that respect the spring is not yet properly over, though otherwise we've seen no sign of it.

Thank you for the pirated American edition. Schlüter has told me some curious things about it.[254] Please thank him for his very detailed letter which I cannot unfortunately reply to just now.

Over here the movement is making fine progress. The UNION OF GAS-WORKERS and GENERAL LABOURERS [164] is gradually coming to the fore, thanks above all to Tussy. The movement is advancing English-fashion, systematically, slowly but surely, and it is an odd, if highly significant phenomenon that both here and in America the people who make themselves out to be orthodox Marxists and have changed the concept of our movement into a rigid dogma to be learned by rote — that these people should figure both here and over there as a *mere sect*. But what is even more significant is the fact that whereas in Amer-

---

[a] Stanisław Mendelson - [b] Stanisław Padlewski

ica these people are foreigners, i. e. Germans, over here they're Englishmen born and bred, i. e. Hyndman & Co. Tussy has just arrived
so I'll close.

Regard from her, Louise and your old friend to you, your wife[a]
and Schlüter,

F. E.

Tussy has just told me that at Whitsuntide — when she was on the
point of leaving for the GASWORKERS' congress in Dublin [247] — she too
received a letter from Anna similar to the one sent to the Paris people.
NO NOTICE TAKEN, of course.

First published in *Briefe und Auszüge aus
Briefen von Joh. Phil. Becker, Jos. Dietzgen,
Friedrich Engels, Karl Marx u. A. an
F. A. Sorge und Andere*, Stuttgart, 1906

Printed according to the original

Published in English in full for the
first time

109

ENGELS TO KARL KAUTSKY [255]

IN STUTTGART

London, 13 June 1891

Dear Kautsky,

Article on Peru [224] received with thanks. Perhaps you would allow
me to keep it here until I have completed the new edition [b] of the *Origin*. In another article on Negro customs in East Africa [c] I came across
a note to the effect that out there a woman's clitoris is cut off before
marriage; Sam Moore wrote and told me that this peculiar custom is
observed along the River Niger for a distance of more than a hundred
miles, though not in *his* locality where he has satisfied himself as to the
presence of the said organ.

---

[a] Katharina Sorge - [b] the fourth German edition - [c] A. Fleischmann, 'Rechtszustände
in Ost-Afrika', *Das Ausland*, Nos. 42, 43; 20 and 27 October 1890.

The introduction[a] to the new edition of the *Origin* is ready and I shall send it off to you next week in case you might wish to use it beforehand for the *Neue Zeit*. If so, please let me have the proofs — in fact, three lots —, the third will go to Ravé for the French translation which is finished so far as the old edition goes. Incidentally, Ravé doesn't know enough German, Strasbourger though he may be. He has made atrocious howlers, thereby involving Laura Lafargue in a colossal amount of work. I'm only surprised that she took it on at all.[b]

So you can inform Dietz that he won't have to wait much longer. But he might let me know the *number* of the new edition. The chaps have gone ahead so fast with the 5,000 copies printed in Zurich that I no longer have the slightest idea where I am. Is this the 2nd, 3rd, 4th or which edition?

The fee for Marx's article[c] received with thanks and already distributed. With regard to the payment for the new edition of the *Poverty of Philosophy* (and similarly for the *first edition as well* — for which we asked nothing at the time), perhaps you would be so good as to make provisional arrangements with Dietz. If, having done so, you then tell me what percentage of the *total fee* for the *new* edition ought to be allocated to *yourselves*, i. e. to you and Ede, and what percentage to *Marx's heirs*, I shall be able to form a better opinion. But the pair of you mustn't lose by it.

A stop ought to be put to Grillenberger's machinations, or at any rate he should be made to pay the fees. If he publishes Marx's speech on free trade[d] in your joint translation, you and Ede, not to mention Clara Zetkin, must protest and I should then do the same on behalf of the heirs — as a matter of principle.

As regards the *Origin*, I have been much delayed through having had to consult all the relevant literature. There is no bigger mutual assurance society than the specialists in prehistory. They're a bunch of scoundrels who indulge in camaraderie and cliquish boycotting on an international scale made possible by their relatively small numbers. Now, however, a new element has entered upon the scene in the

---

[a] The reference is to the preface to the fourth German edition of *The Origin of the Family, Private Property and the State* published in *Die Neue Zeit*, 9. Jg. 1890/91, 2. Bd., Nr. 41 under the title 'Zur Urgeschichte der Familie (Bachofen, McLennan, Morgan)' before the publication of the book. See also this volume, pp. 201, 204, 215-16, 232-33. - [b] See this volume, pp. 141, 144. - [c] *Critique of the Gotha Programme* - [d] K. Marx, 'Speech on the Question of Free Trade' (see present edition, Vol. 6, pp. 450-65).

shape of comparative jurisprudence and, while it has its bad aspects, it may well break up the old ring.

Yesterday Ede showed me Bebel's letter to you. You gave Simon his deserts.[256] Things never turn out particularly well if one aims at 'moderation'; a punch, however, hits home. Odd the way this chap behaves as though 100% of medical men were on his side instead of perhaps 1%.

Your 'Emancipation of the 4th Volume[a]' is nothing by comparison with the 'liberation from feudal *seats*[b]' they inflicted on me in the Berlin edition of the *Entwicklung des Sozialismus*.[c] Imagine what the evolution of socialism would look like had it happened[d] in Berlin!

Just let the chaps get on with their programme.[257] Bebel will make sure all right that none of the old Liebknechtian vulgar democratic and vulgar socialist catchwords find their way into it. It's quite a good thing that the people in Berlin should first discuss the subject amongst themselves; what they suggest can only be an improvement on the old programme and will still be open to discussion. The disenchantment of our friends who, after a 13 years' interval, are now obliged to meet Liebknecht face to face again and work with him, is really too comical. While the Anti-Socialist Law[11] was in force, he remained ensconced in Borsdorf, concerning himself with nothing save his correspondence. Now, 13 years later, the chaps find him completely changed. On the contrary, *he* has remained as he was; it is *they* who have progressed and are now aware that a great chasm exists. Now nothing happens without there being a rumpus, now they find that Liebknecht is editing the paper[e] out of existence. He did no better by the *Volksstaat*, etc., but then he was helped by the others to keep the paper afloat; now they have other things to do and now they have a Liebknechtian paper *tout pur*,[f] i.e. Liebknecht and *family*!

Lafargue's interpretation of the Bible is very pretty — callow but original, marking the final break with the now outmoded, German-rationalist philological method. As a beginning it's all one could ask for.[g]

The OMNIBUS STRIKE has been won![258] At any rate on the main issue. London without omnibuses was and is an odd sort of place. Ede

---

[a] *Band* (volume); misprint for *Stand* (estate). - [b] *Sessel* (seat); misprint for *Fessel* (bonds or shackles). - [c] *Socialism: Utopian and Scientific* - [d] In the original: *vorjefallen* (Berlin dialect). - [e] *Vorwärts* - [f] pure and simple - [g] P. Lafargue, 'Der Mythus von Adam und Eva. Ein Beitrag zur vergleichenden Mythologie', *Die Neue Zeit*, 9. Jg. 1890/91, 2. Bd., Nr. 34, 35.

ought to send you a description of it for the feuilleton; I shall tell him so tomorrow. He is enduring his grass widowhood with manly resignation, assisted by us.

Kindest regards.

Your

F. E.

First published in *Aus der Frühzeit des Marxismus. Engels Briefwechsel mit Kautsky,* Prag, 1935

Printed according to the original

Published in English in full for the first time

110

ENGELS TO LAURA LAFARGUE

AT LE PERREUX

London, 13 June 1891

My dear Laura,

I am sure I do not know how to thank you for the trouble you have taken with Ravé's blundering work. [199] I was rather surprised at your heroism in tackling it altogether; I sent you his specimen of Bebel, [a] and my notes, showing exactly the same class of mistakes and slovenly renderings — though not in such perfection — as in your anthology. May *'la génération infâme'* pursue him like the Erinnyes pursued Orestes!

Anyhow, I have just finished the introduction to the new edition which I shall send to Kautsky for the *Neue Zeit* if he likes to have it. [b] But before sending it off there is one point on which I should like to be sure. I state Bachofen's new discoveries to be these: 1) *hétairisme* as he calls it, 2) *Mutterrecht,* [c] as its necessary corollary, 3) women consequently held in high esteem in ancient times, and 4) that the transition to monogamy, where the woman belonged exclusively to *one* man, involved the violation of the ancient traditional right of the

---

[a] A. Bebel, *Die Frau in der Vergangenheit, Gegenwart und Zukunft* and *La Femme dans le passé, le présent & l'avenir.* Traduction française par Henri Ravé. - [b] See this volume, pp. 199, 204. - [c] mother right

other men to the same woman, a violation which had to be atoned for, or the toleration of which had to be purchased, by surrendering the woman for a limited period of time.[a]

Now as to this *point No. 4* I am not quite certain. You have no idea what thieves these prehistoric bookmakers are, and therefore all I recollect that *somewhere* I have found Bachofen quoted as the discoverer of this fact, and I believe even a reference to *Mutterrecht*,[b] preface p. XIX. But I cannot find it again. Now as you have my copy of Bachofen with you, would you mind (unless you remember it without looking) referring and letting me know whether I am, *generally speaking*, justified in attributing this discovery to Bachofen? It is so long since I have looked at the book, and as in defence of Morgan's claims I have to be rather severe on a lot of his exploiters, I should not like them to catch me in the wrong box. As soon as I have your answer, the ms. can go off and then Ravé can have a proof-sheet to go on with.

I had to read the whole literature on the subject (which *entre nous*[c] I had *not* done when I wrote the book — with a cheek worthy of my younger days) and to my great astonishment I find that I had *guessed* the contents of all these unread books pretty correctly — a good deal better luck than I had deserved. My contempt against the whole set — Bachofen and Morgan excepted — has considerably increased. There is no science where cliqueism and camaraderie are more dominant, and as the set is small, it can be carried on internationally and with success. Giraud Teulon[d] is as bad and as great an appropriator of other people's ideas as any Englishman amongst them. The only amusing fellow is Létourneau.[e] What a charming specimen of the Parisian philistine! And with what splendid self-complacency he proves to his own most intense satisfaction, that not only all the prehistoric tribes and present savages, in spite of all their '*excès*' *génétiques*'[f] as he calls it, are Parisian philistines at least, but so are, too, even the animals of the brute creation! The whole animated world one immense '*Marais*'[g] and boulevard du Temple, peopled by either contributors or readers of what the *Siècle* used to be under Louis Philippe, and the greatest authority on *les origines du mariage et de la famille* — Paul de Kock!

[a] The text of Point 4) is in German in the original. - [b] J.J. Bachofen, *Das Mutterrecht. Eine Untersuchung über die Gynaikokratie der alten Welt nach ihrer religiösen und rechtlichen Natur*. - [c] between ourselves - [d] See this volume, p. 193. - [e] Ch. Létourneau, *L'évolution du mariage et de la famille*. In: *Bibliothèque anthropologique*, Vol.VI. - [f] sexual excesses - [g] aristocratic district in Paris

De[a] Létourneau (evidently of the breed of *le petit étourneau d'Amé-rique — icterus pecoris — qui change de femelle au jour le jour,*[b] p. 33) to Ravé *il n'y a guère un pas.*[c] Ravé has a publisher, Carré, rue St André des Arts, could not that man be got to publish the new edition of the *Misère de la philosophie?* To hear Ravé, he seems very enterprising in our line.

I send you *The Workman's Times* regularly. It is the only working-class paper *belonging to working people.* It was started by the Northern Factory hands etc. and originally published at Huddersfield; now its headquarters are in London. It is a *non-political* paper, that is to say *it goes in for the formation of an independent working men's party* and Labour representation in all elective bodies. It is over-crowded with detail information, but giving *facts.* There is a regular crop of 'Labour' papers: *The Trade Unionist,* by Tom Mann — soft like Mann himself, who, for a Mann,[d] has one n too much in English and one too little in German; nice sincere fellow as he otherwise is, as far as a man without backbone can be so. Then *The Worker's Cry,* by Frank Smith, late Social Wing, Salvation Army.[259] — Then *The Labour World,* founded and abandoned by Michael Davitt and brought to speedy grief and extinction by Massingham, once of *The Star.* I shall send you specimens of these if they live.

Longuet's behaviour seems indeed worse than incomprehensible. At all events it is a good job for poor Mémé[e] that she is with you again. For the rest you leave us in the dark. *Si Longuet s'est refait une jeunesse auprès de Marie, Marie a-t-elle réussi à se refaire une virginité en même temps?*[f] And how are the boys[g] getting on? What's to become of them while he is gallivanting at Caen? How about the Conseil de Famille? etc., etc.

Louise keeps rummaging up all the papers, pamphlets, newspaper cuttings, etc., etc., brought over here from Maitland Park.[h] The letters *are* in tolerable order. Lassalle's will be published in Germany[260]; Bernstein is now using them for an introduction to Lassalle's works[178] to be published by the party. The Lassalleans will not like it, but since Liebknecht has taken Lassalle's party so much in the *Vor-*

---

[a] From - [b] little American starlings—*icterus pecoris*—who change females every day. - [c] there's only one step - [d] A pun in the original: Engels compares the English 'man' with the German 'Mann'. - [e] Jenny Longuet, daughter of Jenny and Charles Longuet - [f] If Longuet has recaptured his youth next to Marie, has Marie managed to recapture her virginity at the same time? - [g] Jean, Edgar and Marcel Longuet - [h] Marx's last residence

wärts, I am determined to have it out, and to use their own Lassalle-veneration as the peg whereupon to hang a criticism of the man.

Sam Moore suffers off and on from African fever here—has gone into the country. Very little news from Jollymeier. *Salut à* Paul. Grüsse von Louise.

Dein alter[a]
F. E.

First published, in the language of the original (English), in: F. Engels, P. et L. Lafargue, *Correspondance*, t. III, Paris, 1959

Reproduced from the original

111

ENGELS TO KARL KAUTSKY

IN STUTTGART

London, 16 June 1891

Dear Baron,

Herewith the ms.— I leave it entirely to you whether you print the *whole* of it or start on p. 2 below the line where the essay proper begins. For title one could put: *On the Early History of the Family: Bachofen, McLennan, Morgan.* By F. E., or something of the sort, followed by the note: introduction to the x-th edition of the *Origin,* etc.[b]

As the ms. ended up by being highly illegible, thanks to numerous interruptions, I do *beg* you to send me a proof—and, as already mentioned, an extra copy for Ravé who is all agog to get it.

The revision of the book itself is going ahead as quickly as my other correspondence permits. I'm itching to get on with it.

I almost wish that the Berliners would turn down Ede's introduction to the Lassalle[c] so that he can deal with the matter more thoroughly and with greater freedom in the *Neue Zeit.* How little is known in Germany of the *real* Lassalle is apparent from the case of Ede himself. Lassalle's letters to Marx, however innocuous they may

---

[a] Regards from Louise, Your old friend - [b] See this volume, pp. 199, 201, 215-16, 232-33. - [c] See previous letter.

seem to many people, as also the need to contemplate the man in the round, have thrown quite a new light on him so far as he, Ede, is concerned. But what the Berliners want more than anything else is *peace* in the party and that is hardly compatible with freedom to criticise. ,This is doubly disagreeable for them as they are at loggerheads with the Soldier [a] and as yet can see no way out of it. But in that case they ought to dispense with new editions of Lassalle. *Enfin,* [b] everything will doubtless get back on an even keel again.

Your

F. E.

First published in *Aus der Frühzeit des Marxismus. Engels Briefwechsel mit Kautsky,* Prag, 1935

Printed according to the original

Published in English for the first time

112

ENGELS TO PASQUALE MARTIGNETTI

IN BERGAMO

London, 19 June 1891

Dear Friend,

Today I am sending you

1. registered, your manuscript of the translation of *Wage Labour and Capital,* [c]
2. corrected proofs of the new edition [d] separately by book post,
3. Labriola's letter enclosed herewith.

I'm busy revising the new edition of the *Origin of the Family, etc.* [e] which will have numerous additions.

A new, complete edition of *Wage Labour and Capital* will follow as

---

[a] Wilhelm Liebknecht - [b] Still - [c] K. Marx, *Capitale e salario colla biografia dell'-autore e con una introduzione di F. Engels.* Prima traduzione italiana di P. Martignetti. - [d] K. Marx, *Lohnarbeit und Kapital.* Separat - Abdruck aus der *Neuen Rheinischen Zeitung* vom Jahre 1849. Mit einer Einleitung von Friedrich Engels. - [e] the fourth German edition of *The Origin of the Family, Private Property and the State.*

soon as I have got one. The principal additions are marked in pencil on the proofs.

I trust you are getting on all right in Bergamo; *l'e una bella città, la conossi — l'ha appresi di parlà 'l Meneghin, lu?* [a]

Saludi

F. Engels

First published in: Marx and Engels, *Works*, Second Russian Edition, Vol. 38, Moscow, 1965

Printed according to the original

Published in English for the first time

113

ENGELS TO VICTOR ADLER [261]

IN VIENNA

[Draft]

[London, 26 June 1891]

Dear Adler,

I would request you to pass on to the conveners of the Austrian Social-Democratic Party's Second Congress my sincere thanks for their kind invitation to this your party congress and to convey to them my regrets at being unable to attend in person as also my best wishes for a successful outcome to the proceedings.

Since Hainfeld, when the Austrian Workers' Party came into its own again, you have made immense progress. That is the best guarantee that your Second Party Congress will be the point of departure for even more significant triumphs.

How invincible is our party's inner strength is evident not only from the rapid succession of external victories, not only from the fact that last year in Germany, just as this year in Austria, it overcame the state of emergency. [262] This, its strength, is even more evident in the party's ability in every country to surmount obstacles and accomplish things in the face of which the other parties, who are recruited from

---

[a] It's a beautiful town, I know it—have you learnt how to talk like the Milanese?

the propertied classes, are helplessly halted in their tracks. While the propertied classes in France are engaged in an implacable struggle with the propertied classes in Germany, French and German Social-Democrats work hand in hand in full accord. And while in Austria the propertied classes in the various Crown Lands are forfeiting, in the mindless squabble over nationalities, the last vestige of their competence to rule, your Second Party Congress will project a picture of an Austria in which the squabble over nationalities is a thing of the past, of the Austria — of the working people. [263]

First published, with alterations, in *Arbeiter-Zeitung*, Nr. 27, Wien, 3. Juli 1891

Printed according to the original checked with the newspaper

Published in English for the first time

114

ENGELS TO PAUL LAFARGUE

AT LE PERREUX

Ryde, 28 June 1891

My dear Lafargue,

I have been staying here with Pumps for the past two days and shall remain until Thursday 2 July when I return to London. [264] Meanwhile Louise has sent me your letter of the 25th. [265] Fortunately I have a blank cheque which I can send you herewith made out for £20. Good luck! The preparations you have made for your defence strike me as excellent and I trust you will secure a seat in the Chamber without being sentenced.

Now for something else. Enclosed you will find a letter from *Field* (*Star*, 23 June) together with Burrows' reply, [266] evidently written by Hyndman. Is it true that, as Field maintains, *you authorised* him to do the idiotic thing he has done? We cannot believe it. But in any case you will see what a letter from you to this Field has given rise to, a letter that in itself may well be perfectly innocent. This Field, a good lad, but bursting to play a part of some sort — even at the cost of doing a disservice to the cause he wishes to serve — purports to be acting for *your* Party and, consequently, for ours. As an 'authorised' agent he makes appeals to the TRADES UNIONS, etc., and, *if he is known* at all, it is as a former collaborator of *Champion* who is now more despised than ever, thanks to his exploits in Australia!

The ground had therefore been too well prepared not to be exploited by Mr Hyndman. Witness his reply. Every idiotic utterance of Field's, every weak point in his letter is adroitly seized upon and all Field has done is to boost the Possibilists. [3]

Nobody here can take up the gauntlet. In the first place we don't know what transpired between you and Field. And then *The Star*, if they did accept a reply from us (which is doubtful, indeed more than doubtful), would close the correspondence after they had given Burrows another say. And Field has placed us in such an idiotic situation that we have no choice but to hope that the correspondence in *The Star* will be forgotten as quickly as possible.

In any case, if you want us to go on working *successfully* over here on behalf of the congress, you must *forbid* Field immediately and *categorically* to publish anything whatsoever that purports *to be authorised by the foreign secretary of the Workers' Party*. [a] And don't give anyone here a pretext to publish anything whatsoever authorised by you without having first consulted us. Otherwise we should do better to beat a retreat and leave everything to chance. To be placed under Champion's protection — that would be the last straw!

All was going well over here. We were working away quietly, if unremittingly, and a to-do in the press (we *have no newspaper*, remember) is the last thing we want if we are to succeed. However we have a right to expect that our own friends won't put a spoke in our wheel. We got all we wanted at Brussels, not without some difficulty, but we got it and we put it to good use. And that ought to be enough for you without the French Marxist party's affecting to play the part of convenor of the congress and arrogating to themselves a role to which they are not entitled. Anyhow, let us know what you wrote to Field so that we can try, if only by word of mouth, to mitigate the unfortunate effect of Field's stupidity.

Tussy still has Laura's letter about Longuet. I shall get it back on my return. Our thanks to Laura for this important information. At all events, the matter is about to be taken in hand although, having read the clauses in the Code, we doubt whether the Conseil de Fa-

---

[a] Paul Lafargue

mille can do very much other than appoint a guardian. Tussy must have written to Laura.

We have old Harney here. He has spent a month in Ventnor where he got rid of his chronic bronchitis but had a recurrence of rheumatic gout. We brought him here yesterday in a cab. He is full of aches and woes, poor devil, but perks up whenever the aches subside. He will be returning to Richmond in a day or so.

Pumps has a small but pretty house with a garden FRONT AND BACK, heaps of fruit of every kind, vegetables, even potatoes; greenhouse with vines laden with grapes, etc. It is splendid for the children, but will Percy manage to do any business? His brothers don't appear to be in any hurry to back him up with the necessary materials. Anyway we shall see.

Pumps, Percy and Harney send their best wishes to you and Laura as do I.

Yours ever,

F. E.

First published, in English, in *Labour Monthly*, No. 9, London, 1955

Printed according to the original

Translated from the French

115

ENGELS TO KARL KAUTSKY [267]

IN STUTTGART

[Ryde, 29 June 1891]

Dear Kautsky,

I have come down here to take refuge with Pumps for a few days [264] having been inundated with an intolerable amount of work. No sooner had I become happily engrossed in group marriage [268] than I was landed with the party programme, which *had* to be attended to. [269] I meant at first to try rewriting the preamble in rather more succinct form but want of time prevented my doing so, besides which I thought it more important to point out the shortcomings, some avoidable, others not, of the political part, as this would provide me with an opportunity to lash out at the conciliatory opportunism of the *Vorwärts* and the clean-devout-joyous-free [a] 'ingrowing' of the old canker 'into socialist society'. I have since heard of your proposal that there should be a new preamble; so much the better.

The party is going to print Lassalle's letters to Marx and myself, annotated by me [260] (thus precluding all censorship by the party). I can attend to this in the autumn, alongside Volume III. [b] (This *between ourselves.*)

I have taken refuge here in order to finish off part of my correspondence; on Thursday [c] I go home, when work on group marriage will be resumed. I was getting along so nicely — confound these interruptions!

Poverty of Philosophy — the position is that Dietz is to buy himself out for 450 marks, whereupon negotiations will be restricted to the four of us, so all is well and we shall be able to sort things out all right. But there can be no question of you two refusing to take *any* remuneration for the 2nd edition.

Dietz's plan for a volume of Marx's minor works won't do. Long ago Liebknecht cherished a pet project of this sort; it was to be put into effect by his latest protégé, Paul Ernst, who was also to publish other things of Marx's and, IN FACT, to be sent to me for a few months so that I could help him in this. The idea was for the thing to be published by the Berlin bookseller under the party's imprint — i. e. an edition of Marx alongside an edition of Lassalle. I turned this down categorically, which means that I can do no less where Dietz is concerned. I have *permitted* the party to publish a few minor things of Marx's in pamphlet form and as individual items, without notes or preface. Nor can I go any further than that. I cannot allow them to steal a march on me by bringing out in this piecemeal fashion the complete edition to whose ultimate publication *I* am committed.

Nor, for that matter, can I now contemplate a new edition of the *Condition, etc.,* [d] not, at any rate, until Volume III is completed. I am perfectly prepared to negotiate this with Dietz in due course, but the chaps have simply got to realise that I can take on absolutely nothing more until Volume III has gone to press. While it is in printing, arrangements can be made for something else. But until then I shall resist *all incitements* and pet projects, whether they emanate from

---

[a] A catchword used by German gymnasts. - [b] of *Capital* - [c] 2 July - [d] F. Engels, *The Condition of the Working-Class in England.*

Dietz or anyone else. After all, the chaps ought to have sense enough to exempt me till then from this sort of thing since it could only involve me in useless, time-consuming correspondence. As soon as I have finished revising the *Origin* I shall set to work on Volume III and then, come rain or shine, I'll carry on regardless.

Vollmar's speech [270] with its quite unnecessary concessions to the present Establishment and its still more unnecessary, and, what's more, unauthorised assurances that Social-Democrats would play their part if the Fatherland were attacked — i. e. would *help defend* the annexation of Alsace-Lorraine — has caused unmitigated glee amongst our opponents over here and in France. If it is allowed to pass, our chaps will have to pay very dearly for it in Brussels. [135] The Possibilists [3] and the Hyndmen are quarrying it for notes, after their usual fashion, nor can we over here do anything about it in the absence of an authentic statement denying Vollmar the right to speak in the name of the party. [271] Now, as Hyndman's man of straw, Bax has recently written on the subject in *Justice*; I haven't seen it yet. [272]

The meeting of women in labour in Hyde Park [273] has caused considerable merriment here and in London — the English version even more than the German because of the play on words in DEMANDING A REDUCTION OF THE HOURS OF LABOUR which, more specifically, can mean travail: A WOMAN IN LABOUR.

Ravé's address is Faubourg Rochereuil, Poitiers, France.

Pumps now lives down here; Percy has taken on an agency for his brothers. Their little house, The Firs, is in Brading Road, exactly one English mile outside the town. It's small but pretty and has a garden [with] [a] vegetables and fruit. Old Harney spent four weeks at Ventnor where he had a recurrence of gout and rheumatism. We fetched him over here on Saturday; he will probably travel back with me on Thursday and return to his headquarters in Richmond. He is terribly lame and out of sorts.

Schorlemmer will probably soon be with us. As you know, he's a very uncommunicative correspondent. While over here, Sam Moore has suffered from African malarial fever but is now better again. In August or September he will be returning to the Niger. In his heart of hearts, I believe, he yearns after the beautiful climate — despite the bouts of fever which recur with menstrual regularity.

---

[a] Manuscript damaged.

How could you possibly imagine I cared a rap about whether or not I'm given pride of place in the *Neue Zeit?* Simply suit yourself. Many regards from everyone here.

Your

F. E.

First published in *Aus der Frühzeit des Marxismus. Engels Briefwechsel mit Kautsky*, Prag, 1935

Printed according to the original

Published in English in full for the first time

116

ENGELS TO CONRAD SCHMIDT [267]

IN ZURICH

Ryde, Isle of Wight, 1 July 1891

Dear Schmidt,

I have taken refuge here for a few days. [264] Pumps is now living in this place where her husband has taken on an agency and, since my work had become altogether too much for me, I have come to stay with her for a few days if only to get a breath of fresh air and to deal with the most pressing correspondence. Tomorrow I go back to London again.

I have before me your two letters of 5 March and 18 June. You would be well-advised not to finish your work on the credit system and the money market until Volume III [a] comes out; in it you will find much that is new on these topics and still more that yet remains to be explored — new solutions, that is, and new tasks. As soon as my summer holiday is over, I shall set to work unremittingly on Volume III.— Your second project — the transitional stages on the way to a communist society — is worth thinking about, but my advice to you is *nonum prematur in annum* [b]; it's the most difficult subject on earth because conditions are constantly changing. For instance, every new

---

[a] of *Capital* - [b] Let it be kept quiet till the ninth year (Horace, *Ars Poetica*, 388).

trust causes them to change while the vantage points never remain the same from one decade to the next.

Your latest academic adventures in Zurich are exceedingly funny. [274] These gentlemen are everywhere alike. Well, I hope you will eventually succeed, to the mortification of the whole of that clique, and thus at long last be left in peace.

I found Barth's book[a] a great disappointment, having expected something a bit less superficial and makeshift. A man who assesses every philosopher, not in accordance with what is enduring and progressive in his work, but in accordance with what is of necessity transitory and reactionary, in accordance with the *system*, would have done better to hold his peace. For according to him the history of philosophy is nothing but a 'heap of rubble', the detritus of exploded systems. Old Hegel stands head and shoulders above this, his supposed critic! And then he believes himself to be criticising Hegel if here and there he succeeds in detecting one of the false starts which Hegel, like any other systematic philosopher, is bound to make in hammering out a system for himself! What a colossal discovery — that Hegel occasionally rolls into one what are contrary and contradictory opposites! I could put him on the track of some far better wheezes if only I could be bothered. The man's what we in the Rhineland call a *Korinthenscheisser*[b]; he reduces everything to insignificance and until he gets out of that habit he will, to use Hegel's words, 'come to nothing, from nothing, through nothing'.[c]

His critique of Marx is truly comical! First he concocts a materialistic theory of history such as, in his opinion, Marx *ought* to have had, only to discover that Marx's writings say something quite different. From this, however, he does not deduce that he, Barth, has put a wrong construction upon Marx — far from it; but that, on the contrary, Marx contradicts himself and is incapable of applying his own theory! 'Oh, if only these people could *read*!' as Marx used to exclaim when confronted by criticism of this kind.

I have not got the book here; if I had time I could point out to you hundreds more absurdities of the same nature. It is a pity, for one can see that the man might be capable of something if he were not in such a hurry to pass judgment. Let us hope he will soon write something

---

[a] P. Barth, *Die Geschichtsphilosophie Hegel's und der Hegelianer bis auf Marx und Hartmann.* -[b] i. e. someone who trivialises everything -[c] G. W. F. Hegel, *Wissenschaft der Logik*, Th. I, Abt. 2. In: *Werke*, Bd. IV, Berlin, 1841, S. 15, 75, 146.

upon which more attacks will be launched; a really sound drubbing would do him good.

As for me, I am very well — better than this time last year and shall, I think, be quite fit again after a bit of a holiday. If only one could work with fewer interruptions! 2 or 3 months ago I set to work on the new edition of the *Origin of the Family, etc.* [a] and should have finished it in a fortnight had it not been for the arrival of the new draft programme which they wanted me to criticise, [269] on top of which all sorts of little ineptitudes were perpetrated on the Continent, thus making it more difficult for us here in England — where the material is good but needs careful handling — to pave the way for the Brussels Congress, [135] etc. All this tends to throw me off course again and to distract me, and yet the thing must not only be almost entirely revised and brought up to date, but must also be *finished* if I am to get down to Volume III. WELL, since it's got to be managed somehow, managed it will be.

You'd almost think yourself in Prussia here. On Sunday [b] we encountered 4 or 5 sailors from the *Stosch*, splendid fellows, very well able to stand comparison with the English MAN-OF-WAR'S MEN; this morning, constant rumbling of guns and explosions of shells from the gunnery practice at the Portsmouth forts.

Many kind regards from Pumps, Percy and

Your old friend
F. Engels

First published in *Sozialistische Monatshefte*,   Printed according to the original
Nr. 22, Berlin, 1920

Published in English in full for the first time

---

[a] the fourth German edition of *The Origin of the Family, Private Property and the State* -
[b] 28 June

117

ENGELS TO LAURA LAFARGUE

AT LE PERREUX

[London,] 7 July 1891

My dear Laura,

That's bad for poor Paul, at least it looks bad at present.[275] Anyhow, he is not in prison yet. There is *cassation*, though that is one chance out of ten only in his favour. There *must* be some row in the *Chambre* about this infamous verdict, and I hope Millerand and Co. will not fail to make that row. I think it admirable policy of Paul to at once assume the offensive, revisit the battlefield of the North, and make himself as formidable to the government as he can. That is what the French always see better and clearer than our Germans, that, in order to make up for a reverse, you must attack at another point, but always attack, never show the white feather, never give way.

At all events his seat in the *Chambre* seems now pretty safe, and that would bring him out of prison if the election took place while he was in. *Le Nord nous appartient maintenant.*[a] What fools these governments are! To think they can put such a movement as ours down by repression. But with all his insolence M. Constans shows vacillation; the 'bus strike[276] showed him in quite a different light; there is no telling what he may not do, if he finds the effect of the verdict to be contrary to his expectations.

Ravé est à ravir.[b] I pity anyone who has to correct that man. What a work of Sisyphus it must have been for you![199] Anyhow it may give you an opening for translations with his publisher, and then your labour may bear fruit.

By the bye, the correct French expression for '*Schutzergebung*'—the technical, juridical word, is *commendation*.

I am finishing the revision of the *Ursprung* for the 4th edition. There will be considerable and important additions; especially a new introduction[c] (proof sent to Ravé, the text probably in the next *Neue Zeit*)

---

[a] North belongs to us now. - [b] Ravé is splendid.- [c] The reference is to the preface to the fourth German edition of *The Origin of the Family, Private Property and the State*, published in *Die Neue Zeit*, 9. Jg. 1890/91, 2. Bd., Nr. 41 under the title 'Zur Urgeschichte der Familie (Bachofen, McLennan, Morgan)'. See also this volume, pp. 199, 201, 204, 232-33.

and then in the chapter on the family. I think you will like them, my inspiring genius to a great extent has been Louise who is full of clear, transparent and original views on the subject. She wishes to be most kindly remembered to you and Paul.

Ever yours,

F. Engels

First published, in the language of the original (English), in: F. Engels, P. et L. Lafargue, *Correspondance*, t. III, Paris, 1959

Reproduced from the original

118

ENGELS TO JOHANN GUSTAV VOGT

IN LEIPZIG

[Draft]

London, 8 July 1891
122 Regent's Park Road, N. W.

Dear Sir,

If I have not replied until today to your esteemed letters of 20 June and 5 July,[277] this is due solely to the fact that I am still vainly awaiting a line from Liebknecht whom you gave as a reference and to whom, through Richard Fischer, his colleague on the Party Executive, I also sent a special request for information; this is the more necessary in that Bebel has only just made your acquaintance, whereas Liebknecht has known you for some time past.

Compliance with your request does not depend on me alone. It is Marx's heirs, for whom I merely act as agent, and also the publisher of *Capital*,[a] who must have the casting vote. As regards the latter I can, I believe, tell you straight away that he would in no circumstances give his consent to such a scheme. Nor would you be likely to fare better at the hands of Marx's heirs. Neither of his two surviving daughters[b] would agree to their father's writings being translated

---

[a] Otto Meissner - [b] Laura and Eleanor

from his own German into that of another author. Indeed, upon inquiry I have already been told as much.

I myself could not, with a good conscience, endorse your proposal. You have been kind enough to send us your writings — a new system of natural history. Since it is only in my spare time that I can turn my attention to the natural sciences, it will be some little while before I can venture to give an independent opinion on your mode of thought. As soon as time permits, I shall peruse your work and am most grateful to you for sending it to me. Even though it may not convince me, I shall certainly be able to learn something from it. But of that thorough command of political economy which must be the first prerequisite for your proposed task, there is no suggestion whatever in your writings.

Hence, aside from all other doubts and difficulties, I could give my consent solely on condition that the work be revised by me. In this way, however, it would become more or less *my* work and that would not suit you or, for that matter, myself since there are already far too many demands on my time.

So I can see absolutely no possibility of your attaining your goal with the consent of all concerned, nor can I conceal from you my opinion that Marx is best able to speak to Germans in his own German. Even the working men come to understand it in due course. They are far more intelligent and, indeed, more cultivated, than is generally supposed.

Yours faithfully

First published in: Marx and Engels, *Works*, First Russian Edition, Vol. XXVIII, Moscow, 1940

Printed according to the original

Published in English for the first time

119

ENGELS TO LAURA LAFARGUE

AT LE PERREUX

London, 12 July 1891

My dear Laura,

Paul sends me from Lille the enclosed.[278] As I do not know where he may be now, I return and reply to you.

First I have absolutely no time to do *un vrai travail*[a] for Duc-Quercy, in order that he may make out of it *un article à sensation*. I am finishing the *Origin*,[b] and then I shall go and recover a bit of nervous tension, as I do feel rather unstrung. And after that—the 3rd volume[c] and nothing else. That is settled long since and cannot and shall not be unsettled.

If I was to write on such a ticklish question and for such a ticklish public as the French, I should certainly do it myself under my name; but never allow a journalist to turn my letter into an interview and put into my mouth, French fashion, not what I did say but what in his opinion I ought to have said.

But finally I am not capable of writing on the 3 questions proposed in a style to please the French bourgeois and readers of the *Figaro*. I should have to remind them of the fact that by their submission, for 20 years, to the adventurer Louis Bonaparte they laid the foundation for all the wars that have come over us since 1850, including the Franco-German war; that that war originated, *en dernier lieu*,[d] in their claim to interfere in German internal affairs, a claim which they even now think they have a right to; that if they lost Alsace etc. *c'était la fortune de la guerre*[e] and that I do most distinctly object to the whole fate of Europe and of the working class being made subordinate to the question as to who is to have that miserable bit of country. All this might be very useful to tell them, but would they even listen to it without accusing me of having stolen a *pendule*?

---

[a] a great amount of work - [b] the fourth German edition of *The Origin of the Family, Private Property and the State* - [c] of *Capital* - [d] eventually - [e] it was the fortune of war

However that may be, I have no time and cannot submit to Duc-Quercy's manipulations. These are the two decisive points.

What Paul has written to me about Renard and his intended declaration, that *he* said the words attributed to Paul, he will have let you know even before me. I hope these things will help to smash up the verdict.[279]

Edward [a] is at St Margaret's Bay, he suffers from the kidneys again; so we shall have only Tussy and Sam Moore here. Wednesday [b] Louise intends going to Vienna, I expect Schorlemmer and then we will see what we may do. I have no fixed plans yet for the summer, but various nebulous projects are colliding in my brain.

Another thing. I should not like just now to speak about matters connected with the Vollmar affair [270] while the thing is being thrashed out in Germany. Anything I said in France might be used, misused and abused against them in Germany, and render their position more difficult. And it is well known to them all that I have refused to do any work for anybody until after the conclusion of Volume III.[c]

I believe I sent you the second batch of Field-Burrows letters in *The Star*.[280] Anyhow the matter has blown over—thanks to the accident of the Belgian Circular of 18th June.[281] This complete submission of the Belgians to the Halle Resolutions so upset all Hyndman's calculations that he is now in a towering rage against them, threatens them with his vengeance, but still holds back. In the meantime he ruins his last hopes in the East End by attacking the Gas Workers [164] (most of the leaders of whom are in the Social Democratic Federation [29]) and Tussy whom he calls Miss Marx. That's the degree of lowness he has come to.

Kind regards from Louise.

Ever yours,

F. E.

Tussy and I have just been talking over Nimmy's inscription. After various proposals of various epithets, to all of which objections may

---

[a] Aveling - [b] 15 July - [c] of *Capital*

be made, I incline to Tussy's proposal to put nothing but the name.
Then the inscription would run

In memory of
Jenny Marx
and of
Karl Marx
and of
Harry Longuet
also of
Helen Demuth
Born January 1st 1823, Died November 4th 1890

What do you think?

First published, in the language of the
original (English), in F. Engels, P. et
L. Lafargue, *Correspondance*, t. III, Paris,
1959

Reproduced from the original

120

ENGELS TO LAURA LAFARGUE

AT LE PERREUX

London, 20 July 1891

My dear Laura,

The Culine business is very bad indeed—worthy of the fellow's
name [282]—but what's to be done? With such a weapon in Constans'
hands, we can only hold our tongues.

Louise went on Wednesday[a] and Jollymeier came on Saturday,
but he is getting more and more Tristymeier, you have to work very
hard to get a smile out of him now. Anyhow I'll try my best.

Paul asks me to send you a cheque, so enclosed £20; please let me
know the receipt. I send it off quick because Jollymeier is still out at

---

[a] 15 July

his walk, so if I close this letter all of a sudden, you will know the reason why.

We are preparing a tour at sea, but have not made up our plans yet, and I have not yet finished my ms.[a]—but am at the last addition as far as I can see. Hope to have done by Wednesday[b] at latest.

Paul thinks Tussy is troubling herself more than necessary about Brussels[135]—I don't think so. Everything *may* go well, and probably *will* go well if everybody comes up to the scratch, but I have too much experience of such congresses, not to know how easily everything can go wrong. The Belgians have convoked for the *18th* August[281] *Tuesday*, instead of *Sunday 16th*—if our people come on the 18th and the (Possibilists) Broussists and Hyndmanites on the 16th, they can play ducks and drakes with everything. Tussy has written yesterday to Volders but these fellows never even reply! As to what the English will do, that's mere toss-up; from Germany almost certainly Vollmar will come and intrigue; what the small countries are you know: not to be trusted across the road. And one mistake on our part, one neglected opportunity, may cause us unnecessary but unavoidable work for years to come.

And then there is that irrepressible Bonnier who point-blank informed me that Guesde and he were going to go in for a restoration of the old International with a Central Council. I told him point-blank that that was putting everything in the hands of the Belgians (the only possible Central Council) knowing what sort of people they were; it was ruining every chance of the movement here in England for a couple of years by a foolish attempt to precipitate matters not ripe for action; and in fact the best means of setting French, English and Germans at loggerheads one with the other. He seemed abashed, but who can guess what he and Guesde may do in their enthusiasm?

Viele Grüsse von Jollymeier und

Deinem alten[c]

F. E.

First published, in the language of the original (English), in: F. Engels, P. et L. Lafargue, *Correspondance*, t. III, Paris, 1959

Reproduced from the original

---

[a] the fourth German edition of *The Origin of the Family, Private Property and the State* -
[b] 22 July - [c] Best greetings from Jollymeier and your old friend

121

ENGELS TO VICTOR ADLER

IN VIENNA

London, 22 July 1891

Dear Adler,

In order to give the Austrians more than an academic token of my sympathy, I have told Dietz to credit you—to use an Austrian expression [a]—with half the fees for the new edition [b] of the *Origin of the Family, etc.* for your party funds. Let us hope no drastic diarrhetic will be required to bring this about. When you will get it and how much you will get at a time (it may be paid by instalments), I cannot say. For every 1,000 copies printed he pays 50 marks, of which you will get 25.

When you enter this on your printed receipts, I should like you to put 'from F. E. in London, such and such a sum', without any further particulars.

Just one more thing: Louise has agreed, should you be able to procure her a mandate, which should surely not be difficult, to accompany you to the general mounting of the guard in Brussels.[155] But this was on the tacit understanding that she would bring you and Bebel or you, at any rate, back to London with her for a few days. And I hope she will succeed in doing so. I shall have returned here by then and shall eagerly await your advent. For in that case, who knows what you mightn't be able to persuade me to do next year? So not too much head-scratching—and bring your wife [c] with you!

Your old friend
F. Engels

First published in *Victor Adlers Aufsätze, Reden und Briefe*. Erstes Heft: *Victor Adler und Friedrich Engels*, Wien, 1922

Printed according to the book

Published in English for the first time

---

[a] Engels uses the word '*abführen*' which can also mean 'purge' - [b] the fourth German edition - [c] Emma Adler

122

ENGELS TO EMMA ADLER

IN VIENNA

London, 22 July 1891

Dear Mrs Adler,

This year, alas, nothing is likely to come of the trip to the Continent which I should dearly like to make, if only to come and see you at Lunz and convince you that I can indeed eat Austrian food, and with very good appetite, as Louise can testify; she never dresses a salad for me save after the Viennese fashion. But if I don't come and see you, there is, after all, another alternative. Perhaps you will accompany Victor to Brussels,[135] in which case we could make one another's acquaintance just as well here in London. Brussels is but a stone's throw from here, so what do you think? If, however, you should not go to Brussels, could you not authorise your husband to spend a few days over here to recuperate from the wear and tear of the world congress? That sort of thing is a tremendous strain, and spending a few days in London after it would greatly benefit his health.

The African Chief Justice, Sam Moore, has just arrived, and I must stop—do please come. Louise is sure to coax you into it—but if *you* cannot, then send your deputy.

Kisses to your dear children about whom Louise has told me so much.

Very sincerely yours,

F. Engels

First published in *Victor Adlers Aufsätze, Reden und Briefe*. Erstes Heft: *Victor Adler und Friedrich Engels*, Wien, 1922

Printed according to the book

Published in English for the first time

123

ENGELS TO FRIEDRICH ADOLPH SORGE [160]

IN MOUNT DESERT

Ryde, Isle of Wight, 9 August 1891

Dear Sorge,

Your two letters of 14 and 20 July have been forwarded to me here. I and Schorlemmer have been spending the past two weeks here with Pumps [264] whose husband is the agent here for his brothers. Shall be going home in about a week.

Am very grateful for the information *re* the *Journal of the Knights of Labor*—I have such a mass of newspapers to go through that, without such advice, I should often find it very difficult to get my bearings. Also *re* Gompers and Sanial [283]—most important, this, since I might run into them in London.

Anna [a] will have to look to her own future; this nonsense is really too much.

The Possibilist-Hyndmanian racket will probably take a hard knock at the Brussels Congress. [135] The split in the ranks of the Paris Possibilists [3] has completely cut the ground from under Brousse's feet. In the provinces they count for nothing while in Paris the majority support Allemane *against Brousse*. [53] This has resulted in the Possibilists of *both* complexions losing control of their last great vantage point, the *bourse du travail*. [57] Or so the *Socialiste* of 24 July says. [284] The Brussels chaps who are, in their heart of hearts, themselves Possibilists and have stood by the latter as long as they could, have made a complete *volte-face* [281]; they aim at becoming the General Council of a new International and are paying court to the all-transcendent 'Marxists'; hence the comical lamentations of the 'friends' they have left in the lurch in Paris and London. I fear, I fear that Mr Hyndman will cease to be our official 'enemy' and will try and make out that he

---

[a] Stanisław Padlewski

is our 'friend'. That would be a bad thing; we haven't got the time to keep a constant eye on a schemer like him.

Tussy, Aveling, Thorne and other members of the GASWORKERS,[164] Sanders (John Burns' secretary) and sundry others of our English supporters are going to Brussels. How things stand as regards the *old* TRADES UNIONS, I do not know.

The DOCKERS are going to pot. Though the success of their STRIKE was due solely and entirely to the £30,000, contributed in a fit of misguided enthusiasm by Australia, they imagine it was their own doing.[198] Hence they are making one mistake after another, the most recent being to close their lists and refuse to accept any more members, i. e. breed their own SCABS. Then they rejected a merger with the GASWORKERS. Many are DOCKERS in summer and GASWORKERS in winter. Having regard to these alternating occupations, the GASWORKERS proposed that a member's TICKET for *one* UNION should be valid for both—nothing doing! So far the GASWORKERS have nevertheless continued to honour the DOCKERS' TICKET—but how long they will do so is hard to say. Again, the DOCKERS are protesting vociferously against the immigration of FOREIGN PAUPERS (Russian Jews). Of their leaders, Tom Mann is a good chap but unbelievably weak, while his nomination as a member of the ROYAL COMMISSION ON LABOUR has all but turned his head; Ben Tillett is an ambitious intriguer, no funds are available, membership is rapidly dwindling, discipline gone by the board.

A week ago someone wrote to me from St Petersburg saying: 'WE ARE ON THE EVE OF A FAMINE.' [a] This was substantiated yesterday by the banning of the export of grain from Russia. In the first place, this will ensure us a year's peace; with famine in the land, the Tsar may well rattle his sabre, but he won't unsheathe it. But **if**, as seems probable, Gladstone comes to power here next year, an attempt will be made to persuade England and France to consent to the closing of the Dardanelles to *all* fleets, even in time of war, i. e. prevent the Sultan from obtaining assistance against Russia. So that's the next item on the oriental agenda.

In the second place, however, the Russian ban on the export of grain means *extending the famine to rye-eating Germany*; only Russia can make good Germany's colossal deficit in rye. But this would mean the complete collapse of Germany's grain tariff policy, which in turn would mean a whole series of political convulsions. For instance, the landed

---

[a] See this volume, p. 230.

aristocracy cannot forego its protective tariffs without also undermining the industrial tariffs of the middle classes. The protectionist parties will lose credit and the whole situation be totally altered. And *our party will grow tremendously* — the failure of this harvest will put us five years ahead of schedule, quite apart from the fact that it will prevent a war which would claim a hundred times more lives.

These two aspects will, in my opinion, temporarily dominate European politics, and if Schlüter would care to draw attention to this in the *Volkszeitung*,[a] it would be very useful. As soon as the Congress [135] is over, I shall also bring it up in the European press. Only I cannot, of course, be responsible for what others in Germany will make of the information I have supplied.

I am glad that Mount Desert is, as always, doing you good. I, too, am feeling the benefit of the sea air — only here in Europe the weather is so uncertain that one can't really plan anything. Schorlemmer sends his regards. I won't finish this letter off yet as there may be something more to tell you tomorrow.

11 August. The ban on the export of grain from Russia is not yet official but is almost a certainty; we may expect an official proclamation.

In East Prussia there have been 2 parliamentary elections — we gained an *enormous* number of votes. So we have at last opened up the rural areas — *cela marche*[b]! [285] With the help of the price rise we may well see something happen there by 1900, unless we kick the bucket first.

Louise Kautsky is in Vienna, will be going to Brussels with a Viennese mandate, and will bring Adler back to London with her and also perhaps Bebel; I have written to him in Switzerland but have not yet had a reply.

Tussy's report to the Brussels Congress on behalf of the GASWORKERS and others is very good [286]; I shall send it you. Tussy is going to Brussels with a mandate from the Dublin Congress [247] of the GASWORKERS and GENERAL LABOURERS and will thus be representing 100,000 men.

---

[a] *New Yorker Volkszeitung* - [b] Things have got going.

Aveling also has 3 or 4 mandates. It would seem that the *old* TRADES UNIONS will be poorly represented — all to the good on this occasion! Regards from Schorlemmer and myself to your wife.[a]

Your old friend

F. E.

First published abridged in *Briefe und Auszüge aus Briefen von Joh. Phil. Becker, Jos. Dietzgen, Friedrich Engels, Karl Marx u. A. an F. A. Sorge und Andere*, Stuttgart, 1906 and in full in: Marx and Engels, *Works*, First Russian Edition, Vol. XXVIII, Moscow, 1940

Printed according to the original

Published in English in full for the first time

124

ENGELS TO LAURA LAFARGUE

AT LE PERREUX

Ryde, 17 August 1891
The Firs, Brading Road

My dear Laura,

We are still here, Schorlemmer and I, awaiting fine weather which is very slow to come; now and then we have had a fine day and could venture on an excursion but on the whole we had our enterprising spirits damped by the glorious uncertainty which is common to the law and the climate of England; not a few times, too, damped and even wetted by but too certain rain. Anyhow we may thank our stars that our plan[s] of circumnavigating this island (not Wight, which we have twice sailed round but Great Britain) were nipped in the bud, for we should have caught it and well too. So we are here admiring the British Fleet which is moored opposite us and awaiting the French which is to come up the day after tomorrow.

So poor Paul has entered upon his term of Ste Pélagie [287] — I hope he'll keep his spirits up! It's a long bout of enforced rest, but then France *c'est l'imprévu*[b] and nobody knows what will turn up within

---

[a] Katharina Sorge - [b] is unpredictable

a twelvemonth. I am afraid you will find Le Perreux about as solitary as he will Ste Pélagie, well we must have you over here in London off and on, which may be done I hope without very great difficulties, for surely you will not be bound by your family of pigeons, hens, etc., etc. So I hope you will arrange to come by and bye after you have made Paul as comfortable as circumstances will permit.

Our Russian friend [a] wrote to me about 3 weeks ago: 'We are on the eve of a famine', and indeed that prophecy has been but too soon fulfilled. While the French Chauvins and Russian pan-Slavists fraternise and hurrah at each other, [288] this fact nullifies all their demonstrations. With a famine at home, the Czar cannot fight. The utmost he will do is to use the present mood of the French bourgeois for his own ends, by blustering and threatening, but he will not strike a blow, and if the French bourgeois should go too far, he will leave them to shift for themselves. What the Russian government aims at, at present, is the closing of the Dardanelles *in time of war to all navies*. That he will get the French to subscribe to, and then, when Gladstone comes in here, as is hoped, at next general election, the grand old Russophile is to be coaxed into agreeing to it too. With the two great naval powers bound hand and foot by such an agreement, the Czar is master of Constantinople which he can surprise any day, and the Sultan is but the Czar's care-taker on the Bosporus. That is the plan, to which the bourgeois republic at Paris is to act the part of cat's-paw, and when it has done its duty as such, it may go to the devil for aught the Czar cares. That is the reason why the Czar submitted to listen to the *Marseillaise* and to humour the representatives of a Republic.

Anyhow, peace is assured — unless some people turn crazy — for this and the greater part of next year. That is the principal effect of the famine in Russia.

But there are others. There will be internal commotions in Russia, and they *may* lead to a change; it is even likely they will cause *some* change, bring about some movement in that pool of stagnation; but it may be, that this is not only *le commencement de la fin mais la fin elle-même*.[b]

In Germany the failure of the crop seems certain too, and there the present and still rising famine prices will bring about the breakdown

---

[a] N. F. Danielson, see this volume, p. 230. - [b] the beginning of the end, but the end itself

of the Bismarckian fiscal policy and the protective duties. There, too, the old system will be shaken to its very foundations and nobody can tell how far that may go. Anyhow it will again swell our ranks amazingly, and help us to conquer the country districts where we are gaining ground wonderfully. There have been two by-elections in East Prussia on the borders of Russia, in thorough country districts, where two years ago we had about 400-500 votes together, this year we had about 3,000 [285]! And if we get the rural districts of the six eastern provinces of Prussia (where large landed property and large farming predominate) *the German army is ours.*

According to *The Standard* of to-day,[289] neither Hyndman nor Brousse had turned up, and Allemane was to take charge of the Possibilists.[3] So as far as *that* class of opposition is concerned, it looks like a walk-over for our people. That question once disposed of, there will remain but little real work for the Congress; unless the various velleities of a restoration of the 'International' venture to come out.[a] I hope they will not, for that would cause new splits and throw us back, here in England at least, for years to come. The thing is an absurdity in every respect, especially so long as neither in France nor in England there is one strong and united party. If that were the case, and both united heart and soul with the Germans, then the end would be obtained without any formal union, the moral effect of the three great western nations acting together would suffice. But so long as that cannot be, all attempts at restoring an International would bring one of the petty nations, probably the Belgians, into an undeserved prominency and end in quarrels. The fact is, the movement is too great, too vast to be confined by such hampering bonds. Still, there is a hankering after this restoration and Bonnier was full of it last time I saw him. Certainly he looked rather perplexed when I told him my objections and had not a word to say — but will that stop him and his friends in Brussels?

On Thursday[b] I expect to be back in London; Adler will come from Brussels for a few days, perhaps also Bebel. As soon as I am informed about the Brussels proceedings I shall send you a letter for Paul, in the meantime kind regards to both of you from Schorlemmer, the Pumpses and

Yours ever,

F. Engels

---

[a] See this volume, p. 221. - [b] 20 August

Had letter from Tussy from Brussels, but written before Sunday's meeting.[135] Shall not know anything of what happened by the time this has to be posted. 18th August, 11 in the morning.

First published, in the language of the original (English), in: F. Engels, P. et L. Lafargue, *Correspondance*, t. III, Paris, 1959

Reproduced from the original

125

ENGELS TO NIKOLAI DANIELSON

IN ST PETERSBURG

London, 2 September 1891

My dear Sir,

Today I return to you six more letters which include everything to end of 1878 — remainder will follow.[290]

Your prophecy about the famine has but too soon been verified, and we here in England, too, will have to suffer severely. The crop seemed excellent on the whole, when about 10 days ago terrible weather set in — just as corn cutting began in the South of England — and played terrible havoc with both cut and uncut corn, 20 to 30 per cent of the crop are said to be severely damaged if not ruined. There is but one advantage connected with this calamity: it will render a war impossible for some 20 months to come, and that, in the present state of universal armament and mutual distrust, is a blessing.

Allow me to return, on another occasion, to your very interesting communication of 1 May.[291] Today I am on the eve of a journey and my principal object is to request you in future to address all your letters to

Mrs Kautsky, 122 Regent's Park Road, N.W. London.

The letters will be handed to me *unopened*, so there is no necessity for a second cover (*enveloppe*). The fact is I shall be so often absent from London[264] that I am afraid letters addressed in the usual way might miscarry; I should have to trust to the intelligence and punctuality of servants.

My health is on the whole excellent; but I require once a year a holiday of about eight weeks and a considerable change of air. A sea voyage is always the best remedy for me. If I keep as well as I expect to be in a month, I shall set at once about the 3rd volume,[a] it *must* be finished. But I better not make any promises as to time.

Very truly yours,
P. W. Rosher[b]

First published, in Russian, in *Minuvshiye gody*, No. 2, St Petersburg, 1908

Reproduced from the original

Published in English for the first time

126

ENGELS TO FRIEDRICH ADOLPH SORGE[160]

IN HOBOKEN

London, 2 September 1891

Dear Sorge,

I have shown your letter about Mrs Schlüter[c] to Louise Kautsky who may be relied on implicitly and is acquainted with the circumstances. She takes the view that Mrs Schlüter has simply fired a warning shot and that she'll come back to him all right, providing Schlüter refuses to be intimidated. Nor does she believe that a third party would be required to nudge her into a decision of this kind. She did the same thing several times in Zurich — or something like it. Admittedly Schlüter's repeated infidelities have given her cause to rebel, but she regularly forgives him and the only people to suffer are those who take her wrath and her fulminations seriously. Louise is the last person to side with Schlüter in this affair or even excuse him — she and all of us know exactly what to expect of him in this respect — his

---

[a] of *Capital* - [b] Engels' conspiratorial pseudonym - [c] Anna Schlüter

cock regularly runs away with him. But, though his wife invariably threatens to leave him, she nevertheless falls into his arms again when it comes to the point—and thus there's nothing left for a third party to do.

The Bernsteins return from Eastbourne today. Sanial and Mac Vey are here and will be calling on me tomorrow. I was in Ryde[264] for a month staying with Pumps and accompanied by Schorlemmer who, however, is now back in Manchester. Every time he has a cold he goes extremely deaf and is no good for anything; otherwise there's nothing wrong with him. I am keeping well but shall have to get out and about a bit more if I am to bring myself fully up to the mark again. Adler from Vienna and also Bebel were here for 3 days, very cheerful and satisfied with the Congress.[135]

I have sent you a pile of documents as well as the *Weekly Dispatch* containing the interview Mother Crawford had with Liebknecht in Paris.[292] That interview will cause a rumpus; at any rate Liebknecht talked a great deal of nonsense. From all I hear he has grown quite thin! He looks rotten and is apparently at loggerheads with everyone; in Brussels he kept himself quite apart from the Germans and Austrians. Again, the best of our chaps are amazed at the disagreement that exists between him and the vast majority of the party on virtually every point. His editing of the *Vorwärts* has been quite deplorable, he has done nothing himself, has got Geiser to write leading articles for it, and has propounded the most peculiar views, in short there's the making of a catastrophe here and it may come all the sooner as a result of that interview.

The old dispute with the Broussists,[3] etc., has fizzled out; the Broussists were not represented at all in Brussels, nor did Hyndman dare go, while the people he did send squabbled and made asses of themselves; he now seeks a prop in Nieuwenhuis who has gone off his head, but that won't get him anywhere. In matters of principle as of tactics the Marxists have been victorious all along the line; the intriguing will still go on behind the scenes and their attacks on me, the Avelings, etc., in *Justice* will, I trust, continue as before, but there is no longer any public opposition to us as a whole.

The *Volks-Tribüne*'s account of the Congress is the most detailed.[a]

I have already read 6 proof-sheets of the new edition of the *Origin of*

---

[a] 'Internationaler sozialistischer Arbeiter-Kongreß', *Berliner Volks-Tribüne*, supplements, Nos. 34, 35; 22 and 29 August 1891.

the Family, etc.[a] Besides the new introduction, there will be many additions in Chapter 2[b] ('Family') and also a few later on. The Brussels Congress[135] has again ratified the Hague resolutions[293] in that it too has thrown out the anarchists. That ought to be emphasised in the press over there. On the other hand it has left the door wide open to the English TRADES UNIONS and no doubt the better ones among them will walk in through it before long. These are the two most important resolutions. It's delicious that the English should now be the most reactionary of all, and that for their sake things have to be toned down! But we can afford to do so, for it is now merely a question of months, or at most a year or two, before they come round. True, the next TRADES UNIONS Congress will try to overturn the LEGAL EIGHT HOURS resolution passed at Liverpool[27] but even if this succeeds—with the help of the textile workers who swear by 10 hours—it will only add more fuel to the flames. Things are moving—there's nothing more for us to do.

Kind regards to your wife.[c]

Your
F. E.

First published abridged in *Briefe und Auszüge aus Briefen von Joh. Phil. Becker, Jos. Dietzgen, Friedrich Engels, Karl Marx u. A. an F. A. Sorge und Andere*, Stuttgart, 1906 and in full in: Marx and Engels, *Works*, First Russian Edition, Vol. XXVIII, Moscow, 1940

Printed according to the original

Published in English in full for the first time

---

[a] the fourth German edition. See also this volume, pp. 199, 201, 204, 215-16. - [b] Chapter 3 in the manuscript - [c] Katharina Sorge

127

ENGELS TO PAUL LAFARGUE [294]

AT LE PERREUX

London, 2 September 1891

My dear Lafargue,

So you are back once more 'neath Madame Pélagie's [a] hallowed and sacrosanct vaults—in *la citta dolente fra le perduta gente* [b] but it won't last long, I trust, and before your 'year' is up we may have Constans there in your place. At all events it's a great pity that you weren't able to go to Brussels before you got nabbed; the effect would have been magnificent. But no matter; I am very happy about the congress [135] none the less. In the first place the total COLLAPSE of the Brousso-Hyndmanian opposition; it was as though it had never existed, as though the Possibilist congress of 1889 [52] had simply been a phantasmagoria. Heaven forbid that these gentlemen should become our 'friends'—if they did, they would become a pest; as enemies they would be a source of amusement, as in the past.

Next, the exclusion of the anarchists. The new International has resumed at the point where the old one broke off. Here, 19 years later, we have out-and-out confirmation of the resolutions at The Hague. [293]

Lastly, the door has been thrown wide open for the English TRADES UNIONS—a move which shows how well the situation has been understood. And the utterances committing the TRADES UNIONS to *the class struggle* and *the abolition of wage labour* mean that this did not even require our making any concessions.

Hence we have every reason to be pleased. The Nieuwenhuis incident has shown that the working men of Europe have at last progressed beyond an era dominated by high-falutin verbiage and that they are aware of the responsibilities incumbent on them: it is a class constituted as a *militant* party, a party which reckons with *facts*. [295] And the facts are taking an increasingly revolutionary turn.

In Russia there is already famine; in Germany there will be famine in a few months' time; the other countries will suffer less, this is why:

---

[a] Ste Pélagie—a prison in Paris. - [b] the city of woe, 'midst the lost ones below (Dante, *The Divine Comedy*, 'Inferno', III).

it is estimated that the 1891 harvest will be in deficit to the tune of 4 million QUARTERS ($11^1/_2$ million hectolitres) of wheat and 30-35 million QUARTERS (between 87 and $101^1/_2$ million hectolitres) of *rye*; in the latter case this enormous deficit affects mainly the two rye consuming countries, Russia and Germany.

That will give us a guarantee of peace until the spring of 1892. Russia won't make a move before then. Thus, assuming the absence of some inconceivable blunder on the part of Berlin or Paris, there won't be a war.

On the other hand, will Tsarism come through this crisis? I doubt it. There are so many rebellious elements in the big cities, especially in Petersburg, that they are bound to seize the opportunity, now to hand, of deposing that drunkard Alexander III, or of placing him under the control of a national assembly—perhaps it will be he himself who takes the initiative in convening it. Russia (i.e. the government and the young bourgeoisie) had done an enormous amount of work towards the creation of big industry on a national scale (see Plekhanov in the *Neue Zeit*[a]) and that industry will be stopped in its tracks because its only market—the domestic one—will be denied it on account of the famine. The Tsar will see what comes of having made Russia a SELF-SUFFICIENT COUNTRY independent of abroad; he will have an industrial crisis on top of an agricultural crisis.

In Germany the government will reach a decision, too late as always, to abolish or suspend the duty on corn. That will break the protectionist majority in the Reichstag. The big landowners, the *squirearchy*, will no longer want to support the duties on *industrial* products; they will want to buy IN THE CHEAPEST MARKET. Thus we shall probably see a repetition of what happened at the time of the vote on the Anti-Socialist Law [11]: a protectionist majority, itself divided by divergent interests arising out of the new situation, which finds it impossible to reach agreement on the details of a protectionist system, all the possible proposals being only minority ones; there will be either a reversion to the free trade system, which is just as impossible or—dissolution, displacement of the former parties and of the former majority, a new free trade majority opposed to the present government. That will mean the real and definitive end of the Bismarckian period and of stagnation in home affairs (I am not speaking here of our own party but of parties which might 'possibly' govern); there will be strife

[a] G. Plechanow, 'Die sozialpolitischen Zustände Rußlands im Jahre 1890', *Die Neue Zeit*, 9. Jg. 1890/91, 2. Bd., Nr. 47-51.

between the landed nobility and the bourgeoisie, and between the protectionist bourgeoisie (one section of the industrialists) and the bourgeoisie favouring free trade (the other section of the industrialists and the merchants); the stability of the ministries and of the country's domestic policy will be shattered, in other words there will be movement, struggle, vitality, and it is our party that will reap the whole benefit. If things take this turn, our party will be able to come to power round about 1898 (Bebel puts it as early as 1895).

There. I haven't discussed other countries because they are not so directly affected by the agricultural crisis. But suppose this agricultural crisis were to unleash, here in England, the acute industrial crisis we have been awaiting for the past 25 years, what then?

In a quarter of an hour we shall be leaving for Highgate to plant an ivy cutting on Marx's grave. Motteler brought it back three years ago from Ulrich von Hutten's grave (Island of Ufenau, Lake of Zurich) and it has grown marvellously on my balcony.

I have had Bebel and Adler from Vienna with me here for the past few days; they are very pleased about the congress.

Enjoy yourself and make good use of the opportunity you have been offered of 'concentrating' on work, as the Berlin journalist said when thrown into jug in 1841.

With best wishes,

Yours,

F. E.

First published abridged in *Le Socialiste*, No. 51, Paris, 12 septembre 1891 and in full in: Marx and Engels, *Works*, Second Russian Edition, Vol. 38, Moscow, 1965

Printed according to the original checked with the newspaper

Translated from the French

Published in English in full for the first time

128

ENGELS TO FRIEDRICH ADOLPH SORGE [267]

IN HOBOKEN

Helensburgh, Scotland, 14 September 1891

Dear Sorge,

I'm up here on a lightning tour [264] with Pumps and Louise Kautsky; the past week has been spent either in the Highlands or on the water and it has done me a power of good. We shall be home a week from now.

There's nothing one can do about the Schlüters. He can't help chasing after this petticoat or that and she[a] can't help burying the hatchet and forgiving him the moment she feels she has taken things as far as she dares. But if this time she nevertheless remains in Germany — which I'm inclined to doubt —, it will be because people there have talked her into it.

Mr Ferdinand Gilles, a scoundrelly man of letters, who was made to come over to us from the Party of Progress,[296] though we in Germany didn't want him, has joined forces in London with Hyndman & Co. and actually has a party all of his own in the Communist Society.[89] The man has been denounced to us as a police spy by a reliable source whose identity, however, cannot be divulged, which also explains his otherwise inexplicable source of funds (he contributes £6 a year to a school founded over here by Louise Michel). At the Brussels Congress [135] the fellow tried to gain currency among the Germans for the lies about Aveling being disseminated on the sly by Hyndman, Mother Besant, her lover Herbert Burrows and others to the effect that when Aveling married Tussy he had abandoned a wife and three children in a state of utter destitution and that his father-in-law was intent on beating his brains out. (Well, Aveling and his wife parted by mutual consent 8 years ago, she took back her fortune which brings her in over £500 a year, there were never any children and her father had died long before.) Since this fell flat, he sought to find a receptacle for these lies among the correspondents of the bourgeois newspapers and *that, of course, proved successful*. The entire press

---

[a] Anna Schlüter

was full of it. In Brussels Aveling could do nothing for fear of giving the Belgian police an excuse to disrupt the Congress. But when he returned to London and placed the whole matter before us, we unanimously fell in with his view that Gilles must be given a thrashing. After an attempt to do so in the German Society had been frustrated, Aveling, accompanied by Louise Kautsky as witness (lest he should falsely maintain that he had been floored by two *men*), proceeded to his house last Tuesday, the 8th, and gave him two hearty punches in the face. No doubt that will have a somewhat more salutary effect. Whether anything further came of the business I don't know, as we left the same day and have been unable to receive any news.

Aveling at once advised Liebknecht of the facts of the case for publication in the *Vorwärts* [a] [297] and so the affair will no doubt also be discussed in America.

Of the American delegates, those I saw were Mac Vey and Abraham Cahan, the apostle of the Jews; both of them pleased me much.

The Congress has proved a brilliant success for us AFTER ALL — the Broussists [3] stayed right away while Hyndman's chaps withdrew their opposition. And, best of all, the anarchists have been shown the door, just as they were at the Hague Congress. [293] The new, incomparably larger and avowedly Marxist International is beginning again at the precise spot where its predecessor left off.

The TRADES UNION Congress in Newcastle has also been a great victory. [298] The *old* UNIONS with the textile workers at their head, together with the entire reactionary party that exists among the workers, had mustered all their forces in order to overturn the eight hours resolution of 1890. They failed, having secured no more than one insignificant, fleeting concession. That is crucial. There is still much confusion, but there's no stopping things now and the bourgeois papers fully recognise the defeat of the *bourgeois labour party*, recognise it with dismay and a wailing and gnashing of teeth. The Scottish liberals in particular, the most intelligent and most classical bourgeois in

---

[a] E. Aveling, 'In der *Rheinisch-Westfälischen Zeitung* vom 22. Aug. findet sich ein Artikel...' and 'Der Urheber der über mich in der Deutschen Presse...', *Vorwärts*, Nos. 211 and 212; 10 and 11 September 1891; see also this volume, pp. 248, 251, 252-53.

the Empire, are unanimous in their lamentations over this great misfortune and the incorrigible perversity of the working man.

Warm regards to you and your wife.[a]

Your

F. E.

First published abridged in *Briefe und Auszüge aus Briefen von Joh. Phil. Becker, Jos. Dietzgen, Friedrich Engels, Karl Marx u. A. an F. A. Sorge und Andere*, Stuttgart, 1906 and in full in: Marx and Engels, *Works*, First Russian Edition, Vol. XXVIII, Moscow, 1940

Printed according to the original

Published in English in full for the first time

129

ENGELS TO KARL KAUTSKY

IN STUTTGART

London, 28 September 1891

Dear Kautsky,

I was on the point of writing to you about the programme when your letter arrived.

Your draft programme is *far better* than the official one and I note with pleasure that Bebel will propose it be accepted. I shall back him up there. You have avoided the only fault of your first draft — length — and have outdone the official one in brevity. However I should like to make the following suggestions [299]:

Section 1, pp. 785/86 of the *Neue Zeit*, para. 2, line 3: Growth of the *product* of human labour rather than yield. Marx has pointed out how ambiguous is the word '*yield*' which can mean not only the product itself but also its value, or even the total price that happens to be *realised*.

Further: Private ownership of *the* means of production throughout. What is meant, of course, are the social means of production in their

---

[a] Katharina Sorge

entirety or again those of one distinct working individual, peasant or artisan — in all these cases they are quite distinct and hence require the article. Omission of the article leaves one in doubt about the meaning, or so it seems to me, at any rate.

Section 2, *Neue Zeit*, p. 788, para. 1 has been edited somewhat inadequately. 'Which suffers under today's conditions' is much too weak. It would have been better to say that the ruling classes are also being intellectually and morally crippled by the class contradiction, more so indeed than the class that is oppressed. You could edit it into shape, provided you agree. The concluding sentence to the effect that the proletariat is the only class *whose interests, etc., ... are pressing* is also weak. I should prefer 'whose liberation is impossible without the socialisation of the means of production', or something of the sort.

Para. 2. ...'Without political rights they cannot embark on their economic struggles'—or establish *their organisation as a militant class* (what they need for their economic struggles and their organisation as a militant class is a measure of political freedom and equal rights that will grow with their successes?)—the remainder as in text.

Unfortunately I have no time for more than these brief suggestions as I'm inundated with jobs of every description.

I haven't yet managed to read Ede's article.[299]

In your first article you, too, dabble a bit in 'Utopia'. When and in what country did the things happen which you describe between p. 726 ('this metamorphosis was coincident with another') and p. 730? It seems to me that for the sake of convenience you dished up a grand pot-pourri of the times and places of various schools of thought. But there's nothing wrong in that; the great majority of your readers won't notice and each can take from it whatever suits his own particular book.

Thank you for the newspapers. It's a good thing that the party is strong enough to allow Liebknecht's speeches to pass, yet suffer no harm; as regards the paper,[a] which is more important, there will of course be a change before long. I must confess that the old man amazes me by the extent to which he has lagged behind. However we are now a power and as such are perfectly well able to lug along with us an heirloom of this kind and accord him the satisfaction of believing he has settled everything the moment he invents a formula that sets his mind at rest over whatever matter has happened to crop up.

[a] *Vorwärts*

Mr J. Wolf has also sent me concoction.[a] I have consigned it to my bookcase unread and there it will have to remain until I reach the preface to Volume III.[b] The letter you posted in Neumünster has now reached me. It reads:

'Zurich, 20 September 1891. Dear Sir, In the latest number of Conrad's *Jahrbücher für Nationalökonomie und Statistik*, a Jew from Brno by the name of Wolf, who teaches at the Polytechnic here, has the cheek to accuse you of having misconstrued Marx's theory of value and hence of intending to suppress Volume III. Shall you give him a box on the ears? An Admirer.'

Hardly that, but I shall have to take a look at the rubbish nevertheless.

I wrote at once telling Schmidt that, while his solution was *not* the Marxian one, the book[c] contains such excellent stuff in other respects that I thought it the most important thing to have been done in the field of political economy since Marx's death.[300] Now, however, as soon as I have attended to current business, I shall apply myself relentlessly to Volume III and everything else will be cast aside.

C. Schmidt was in Berlin and, during the holidays, made a very good job of editing the *Vorwärts*; no doubt he will now take up the lectureship in Zurich secured for him by Stössel in defiance of the professors.

You are right to go to the Congress.[301] The chaps will have a great deal of fault to find with the *Neue Zeit*, but that can't be helped. You should listen to everything, be as sparing as possible with your answers and afterwards go your own way. So long as Bebel is in charge there's no doubt that everything will get back onto an even keel again.

We over here will put the Gillesiad[d] to thoroughly good use. Hyndman & Co., who have seen the whole of their ambitious international intrigue with the Possibilists[3] come to grief in so lamentable a fashion, are furious, of course, and are at the back of the whole affair. Obviously we could want nothing better than that they should identify themselves with Gilles, though unfortunately they are already turn-

---

[a] J. Wolf, 'Das Rätsel der Durchschnittsprofitrate bei Marx'. *Jahrbücher für Nationalökonomie und Statistik*, 2. Bd., 3. Folge. - [b] of *Capital* - [c] C. Schmidt, *Die Durchschnittsprofitrate auf Grundlage des Marx'schen Werthgesetzes.* - [d] See this volume, pp. 237-38.

ing away. Courage is not the strong point of some of these gentlemen, as you know, nor is a box or two on the ears something they relish.

Regards from Louise.

Your

F. E.

First published in *Aus der Frühzeit des Marxismus. Engels Briefwechsel mit Kautsky*, Prag, 1935

Printed according to the original

Published in English for the first time

130

ENGELS TO AUGUST BEBEL[267]

IN BERLIN

London, 29 September 1891

Dear August,

We all of us very much liked your Russian article in the *Vorwärts*[302]; it should prove very effective. A point on which you and I are agreed is that there is an imminent threat of war, and this specifically from Russia; also that, if it materialises, everything possible should be done, especially by us and in our own interests, to crush Russia. Where we differ is in contending, you that the Russians want war, and I that all they want is to threaten without any definite intention of attacking, while at the same time being fully aware that things might nevertheless eventually get to that stage.

I have for years studied the methods and habits of Russian diplomats past and present and know that war, inasmuch as it is invariably unsolicited by the aforesaid diplomats, invariably spells a diplomatic defeat. For in the first place, victories obtained by diplomatic intimidation are cheaper and safer and, in the second, every new war merely goes to prove how relatively weak the Russian army is when it comes to conquest. So enormously do the military in Russia overrate their preparedness for war that, even after discounting 30% of their claims, the diplomats still pitch the army's efficiency too high. Of all the factors they must take into account, their own army is the most incalculable. Only in cases where others have to fight their battles for them (1813-14) do Russian diplomats willingly go to war.

If Gladstone comes to the helm over here, the Russian diplomats will be in a position more favourable than they could hope to achieve for decades to come. France an active ally, England a benevolent neutral — that's plenty to be going on with. That the Russians will make war-like gestures, I am in no doubt. But if they go to war it will not be intentionally.

There is no doubt whatever that the loan is a potential war loan. But that is merely a sign that the gentlemen are preparing themselves for *any* eventuality. As I see it, all the other signs you adduce — the ban on the export of rye, landing exercises in the Black Sea, etc.,— only go to prove the same thing. I would hazard a guess that, when it comes to the point, Europe, and the Triple Alliance in particular,[303] will be more afraid of a war than unassailable Russia will have need of one; whereupon Russia will be one up in the East while the French chauvinists will be the dupes.

You suggest that Russia is *bound* to attack because of difficulties at home. I do not think so — not, at any rate, in the sense in which you presumably understand it. In Russia three classes suffer — the land-owning aristocracy, the peasantry, the emergent proletariat. The latter is still, and the first is already, too weak for revolution, while all the peasantry could achieve would be local insurrections which would be fruitless unless given the necessary cohesion and moral support by a successful insurrection in urban centres. The new bourgeoisie, on the other hand, is flourishing as nowhere else; it is gradually moving towards the point at which it will inevitably clash with bureaucracy, but this may not be reached for years. The Russian bourgeoisie originated from farmers connected with vodka production and from army contractors plundering the state and is what it is because of the state — protective tariffs, subsidies, robbing of the state, licence and state protection for the most oppressive exploitation of labour. So things would have to get pretty bad before these people, whose turpitude far exceeds that of our own bourgeoisie, would undermine the rule of the Tsar.

If consideration for *this* particular bourgeoisie is conducive to war, it is only because it has translated pan-Slavism into materialist terms or, rather, has discovered the latter's material basis — the expansion of the home market by means of annexation. Hence the Slavophil fanaticism, hence the unbridled Germanophobia — up till 20 years ago, after all, Russia's trade and industry was almost exclusively in German hands — and hence the anti-Semitism. This really vile and ignorant bourgeoisie, unable to see beyond the end of its own nose, does indeed want war and is clamouring for it in the press. But *nowadays* no Tsar need go to war for fear of revolution at home. This may have been the case in the 70s when the decaying aristocracy in the *zemstvos*[a] was becoming aware and resentful of the situation to which it had everywhere been reduced. Today that same aristocracy is very much on its uppers, is being bought out of its landed property by the bourgeoisie and is altogether in the latter's financial clutches, while the bourgeoisie is Tsarism's new bulwark, particularly in the big cities which alone might present a threat. And nowadays a palace revolution or successful assassination attempt could only bring the bourgeoisie to power, no matter who had instigated the coup. Yet this self-same bourgeoisie would be even more likely than the Tsar to precipitate a war.

But that's beside the point. We both of us recognise the danger of war and, despite the famine in Russia, which you decidedly underrate, the reins may slip from the hands of the rulers, an eventuality for which we too must be prepared. I shall see what can be done in France; while it may be necessary to draw our people's attention to certain points, this should be done by the *French themselves*. Our people have got to realise that a war against Germany in alliance with Russia would first and foremost be a war against the strongest and most efficient socialist party in Europe, and that we should have no option but to fight with all our might against any assailant who went to Russia's aid. For either we should succumb, and that would put paid to the socialist movement in Europe for the next 20 years, or we should ourselves come to the helm and then the words of the *Marseillaise*,

'*Quoi, ces cohortes étrangères feraient la loi dans nos foyers?*'[b]

would apply to the *French*.

In neither case would the present regime in Germany survive a war; its defence would require too strenuous an effort and means that were too revolutionary.

---

[a] provincial assemblies - [b] What, shall these foreign cohorts lay down the law in our own homes?

You are right; if war comes we must call for the general arming of the population. But in co-ordination with the organisation already in existence and/or prepared for war. That would mean the embodiment of *hitherto untrained men* in the *Ersatzreserve* [304] and *Landsturm* [305] and, above all, the *immediate introduction of a rough-and-ready training programme* in addition to the arming of the population and its embodiment into permanent cadres.

The address to the French would have to assume a somewhat different form. [306] The Russian diplomats are not so stupid as to provoke war before the whole of Europe. On the contrary, things will be so arranged as to make either France or one of the Triple Alliance countries appear to be the offending party. The Russians always have dozens of such *casus belli* up their sleeves; what the exact answer to this should be depends on the pretext adduced for war. Whatever the case, we shall have to declare that since 1871 we have always been ready to come to a peaceable understanding with France, that as soon as our party comes to power it will not be able to exercise that power unless Alsace-Lorraine is free to decide its own future but that, should war be forced upon us, notably a war in alliance with *Russia*, we should regard it as an attack upon our existence and should have to defend ourselves with all available means and make use of all available positions—i.e. including Metz and Strasbourg.

As for the actual conduct of the war, there are two aspects which are of prime importance: Russia is weak in attack but enormously strong in defence, a thrust into the heartland is impossible. France is strong in attack but, after one or two defeats, is rendered impotent and incapable of attacking. Since I have no great opinion of Austrians as generals or of Italians as soldiers, our army will have to lead and sustain the main thrust. Containment of the Russians, defeat of the French, such must be the opening gambits in a war. Once the French offensive has been scotched, but hardly any sooner, a start can be made on the conquest of Poland up to the Dvina and the Dnieper. This must be effected by *revolutionary* means and, if necessary, by conceding to Poland, as ultimately constituted, part of Prussian Poland and the whole of Galicia. If all goes well, a *volte-face* may be expected in France. This should be our cue for insisting that Metz and Lorraine at any rate be accorded the French as a peace-offering.

But things probably won't go as smoothly as all that. The French won't simply let themselves be defeated. Their army is *very good* and better armed than ours nor, considering the kind of performance our generals put up, does it look to me as though very much is to be expected from that quarter. The French have shown this summer that they have learnt how to mobilise. Likewise that they have enough officers for the *first field army*, which is stronger than ours. Not until more troops move into the line will our numerical superiority in officers make itself felt. Moreover, the direct route between Berlin and Paris is heavily defended on both sides by fortifications. In short, and taking the most favourable view, it will probably turn out to be a campaign of changing fortunes in which both sides will continually bring in new reinforcements until one side is exhausted—or England actively intervenes, being able in the circumstances then obtaining to *starve out* the side, whether France or Germany, which it decides to oppose, and to compel it to sue for peace simply by cutting off its supply of corn. What happens meanwhile on the Russian border will depend largely on how the Austrians conduct the war, and is therefore unpredictable.

This much is, I believe, certain—if we are beaten, chauvinism and retaliatory warfare will flourish unchecked in Europe for years to come. If we are victorious, our party will take the helm. The victory of Germany, therefore, will be the victory of the revolution and, if war comes, we must not only desire that victory but promote it with all available means.

Ede's article[307] was intended as a reply to *Vollmar*[270] and, as such, would have been altogether appropriate. Instead, our good Ede dilly-dallied for so long that it appeared as a reply to the *Kronstadt fraternisation*[288] for which, of course, it was totally unsuitable, since the emphasis should have been laid on wholly different aspects. What certainly ought to have been said was that if France, as opposed to Germany, is the *formal* representative of revolution, Germany, by reason of its workers' party, is the *material* leader of revolution and that this would necessarily emerge in a war in which we—and with us the revolution—would either be suppressed or else come to the helm.

Apropos, I hear that you intend to put forward K. Kautsky's declaration of principles as your programme at the party congress. I too regard it in its present version (*Neue Zeit*, No. 51) as a great improvement on our draft. My only recommendation was that he should make a few alterations in the passage on p. 788.[a] He has obviously given the thing a great deal of thought and to good purpose. I have not

---

[a] See previous letter.

yet been able to read Ede's article concerning individual de-mands.[299] About Leibfried-Cuno[308] anon, in my next.

Regards from Louise and

Your

F. E.

1 October

I had meant to send off the above today, when your letter of the 29th turned up. I trust you read in the *original* the article by me which appeared in the *Socialiste*, for the rendering in the *Vorwärts* is atrocious and in places sheer nonsense.[a] Where the devil does Lieb-knecht unearth such appalling translators? — It is clear that the time is at hand when we shall be in the majority in Germany, or at any rate the only party strong enough to take the helm — *provided peace continues*. And for that very reason I would be reluctant to see this pro-cess of development interrupted by a crisis which might, it is true, curtail it by 2 or 3 years but which might equally well prolong it by 10 or even 20.

As regards my remarks concerning the undue consideration shown by you for your opponents' opinions, you alone are to blame; in your letter[b] you say of Ede's note[309]: '*For our opponents attack the work simply for being couched in tendentiously anti-Lassallean terms.*' This regularly reiterated argument about your opponents cannot but end by invit-ing the interpretation that those opponents can play ducks and drakes with us. Come to that, Marx and I used to say as long ago as 1848: 'What blunder of ours can have earned us our opponents' *praise?*' i. e. just as you do.

Whatever happens, you must keep Geiser away from the *Vorwärts*. After all, at St Gallen the man was the object of a formal vote of no confidence[253] so surely *he* cannot be allowed to take part in the edit-ing! Blos, too, is an alarmist and, what's more, a bore. — As regards the sixth leading article Liebknecht is to write, there's no need to worry your heads about it[310]; I'll wager that in 3 weeks' time he'll

---

[a] F. Engels, 'Le congrès de Bruxelles. La situation de l'Europe', *Le Socialiste*, No. 51, 12 September 1891 and 'Über den Brüsseler Kongreß und die Lage in Europa. (Aus ei-nem Brief an Paul Lafargue)', *Vorwärts*, No. 216, 16 September 1891 (see this volume, pp. 234-36 and also present edition, Vol. 27.) - [b] of 12 September 1891

have lost all enthusiasm for leading articles and will say, as he did in Leipzig in 1866, that anyone who supposes this to be the right time for writing leading articles cannot have a proper understanding of the times.

The Vienna *Arbeiterinnenblatt*[a] will doubtless be a thorn in the flesh of your women's paper ladies. The latter are all still very much 'beschacked'[b] and would like to have something specifically women's movementish and not confined to one feminine aspect of the labour movement. However, the latter standpoint is put forward with tremendous vigour in the Vienna journal and, if the women at home are as promising as you say, all this separate women's rights business—bourgeois trifling, no more,—will soon be pushed into the background. If the present spokeswomen are elbowed out by members of their own sex, no matter; but the Vienna paper must be given the credit for being the first of all women's papers to adopt and advocate this standpoint.

In failing to accept Aveling's anti-Gilles statement you have again proved that inside every German there lurks a bureaucrat who pops out the moment he holds some petty official post. Aveling considered it incompatible with his honour for Gilles' claim that he had likewise given him, Aveling, a licking, to go unchallenged in the German press. Aveling got Louise to attest the facts and they both of them put their names to the document. In any other country the reaction would have been: 'This is a matter in which those concerned must themselves know what they ought to do; I, the editor, though I may disapprove of their conduct, am bound to recognise their right to plead their own cause as they think fit.' With you, however, the editorial department sets itself up as censor, lays claim to complete infallibility, and forbids them to conduct their own case. The editorial department has a right to believe that *it* has finished and done with Gilles and need not *for its part* allude to him again, but if Aveling and Louise come forward in their own names, it ought not to use *this* view as a pretext for muzzling a *friend*. Incidentally, I do not in the least share your reservations—indeed it was I who drafted Louise's statement.[c]

Gilles at once proceeded to publish the enclosed leaflet. You will be getting Aveling's reply in a day or two. The business with Bradlaugh

---

[a] *Arbeiterinnen-Zeitung* (see also this volume, p. 252). - [b] derived from the name of Gertrud Guillaume-Schack - [c] See this volume, pp. 237-38, 251, 252.

was a stupendous blunder of Aveling's, but he was the innocent party. At the time Aveling was, so far as money matters and political negotiations were concerned, a thoroughly naïve, inexperienced and incredibly foolish young poet. Bradlaugh was aware of this and exploited him most outrageously; they started a Natural Science School and laboratory, the business side of which was managed by Bradlaugh while Aveling had to bear not only the brunt of the work but, towards the end, also the financial responsibility. When Aveling became a socialist and married Tussy, Bradlaugh falsely accused him of having engaged in dubious money transactions—Aveling was monstrously hoodwinked but altogether innocent—just unbelievably stupid. And when Bradlaugh published his circular letter, Aveling was stupid enough to keep silent and even by degrees repay Bradlaugh, by whom, for good measure, he had been cheated, something in the region of £ 200. It is now an old story, Bradlaugh is dead and, since he took care not to formulate any definite charges, there is nothing for it but for Aveling to make the circumstances known whenever the opportunity arises. As will happen the moment Mr Hyndman, who was originally responsible for raking up this tittle-tattle again, accepts Aveling's challenge to confront him in public.—The story of the Chicago telegram is also pure moonshine and again emanates from Hyndman. Our aim is to catch out the *latter*, for Gilles is simply his mouthpiece.

Many regards from Louise and myself to your wife[a] and yourself.

Your

F. E.

First published abridged in: F. Engels, *Politisches Vermächtnis. Aus unveröffentlichten Briefen*, Berlin, 1920 and in full in: Marx and Engels, *Works*, First Russian Edition, Vol. XXVIII, Moscow, 1940

Printed according to the original

Published in English in full for the first time

---

[a] Julie Bebel

131

ENGELS TO FRIEDRICH ADOLPH SORGE [160]

IN HOBOKEN

London, 30 September 1891

Dear Sorge,

I spent a fortnight in Scotland and Ireland with Pumps and Louise Kautsky [264] after which I attended to the proofs of the new edition [a] of the *Origin of the Family*; now I am dealing with arrears of correspondence, and shall then finish off Volume III. [b]

Meanwhile I enclose a business communication for Mother Wischnewetzky which you will, I trust, be able to pass on to her. Except by way of business I don't, of course, want to have anything to do with her.

I am sorry to see from your letter of the 15th that you are plagued with the gout. That being so, it's certainly a good thing that you should be eating less nitrogenous food and taking more physical exercise.

The Brussels Congress [135] did in fact go off better than you suppose. The only one of the Germans to behave boorishly was Liebknecht, but he had been most grossly provoked by Nieuwenhuis in the rudest, clerico-jesuitical way. Louise, who represented the working women of Vienna, says that Nieuwenhuis' base attacks and insinuations were utterly outrageous.

The TRADES UNION Congress was also a success. [298] The 'old' unions did everything in their power to get the Liverpudlian [27] eight hours resolution overturned and their failure to do more than whittle away a small fragment of it is of itself a defeat for them and their middle-class allies. You ought to have seen the liberal papers, in particular the Scottish ones, and the way they wrung their hands over the aberrations of the English working man and his lapse into socialism.

The People is quite impossible. It's ages since I have seen such a silly hotchpotch of a paper. Who has translated my *Entwicklung* [c]? [311] Jonas?

---

[a] the fourth German edition - [b] of *Capital* - [c] F. Engels, *Socialism: Utopian and Scientific.*

I'll send the necessary to the *Socialiste* and report back to you later.

Lafargue has been put up as candidate in Lille and is thus entitled to spend the 5 weeks of the *période électorale* out of prison and to engage in propaganda. He is unlikely to get in but, come the general election, he is sure of being returned in the Département du Nord.[312]

Abetted by Hyndman, Gilles continues his attempts to besmear Aveling — not a bad thing on the whole, firstly because he's such a colossal blackguard and secondly because we shall succeed increasingly in getting Hyndman out into the open.[a] More news of all sorts by the next post.

Warm regards to your wife[b] and yourself.

Your

F. E.

First published abridged in *Briefe und Auszüge aus Briefen von Joh. Phil. Becker, Jos. Dietzgen, Friedrich Engels, Karl Marx u. A. an F. A. Sorge und Andere*, Stuttgart, 1906 and in full in: Marx and Engels, *Works*, First Russian Edition, Vol. XXVIII, Moscow, 1940

Printed according to the original

Published in English in full for the first time

132

ENGELS TO LAURA LAFARGUE

AT LE PERREUX

London, 2 October 1891

My dear Laura,

Today I sent to you and to Ravé the sheets 7 to 12 (end) of *Ursprung*[c] with the alterations marked in red. I hope this will be the end of your trouble[199] for which I do not know how to thank you. May the effect be such as to reward you to some extent for your work.

---

[a] See this volume, pp. 237-38, 248-49, 252. - [b] Katharina Sorge - [c] the fourth German edition of *The Origin of the Family, Private Property and the State*

I hope Paul is out by this time, the furlough will be very useful to him and to the cause, 'le Nord' is hot and ought to be forged while it is so.[312]

Boulanger was *so* dead that he evidently could no longer bear life. He died as he lived—*en homme entretenu*.[a] The loss of his beloved M-me de Bonnemain he might have borne, but the loss of her fortune (which the English papers say was *not* left to him)—*ah, c'était autre chose*[b]!

Nobody will be more glad of this comical event than Rochefort, *le brav' général* had gradually become a veritable nightmare for him.

Now, my dear Laura, what in the name of all that used to be sacred am I to write to that *Almanach*[c] where, if the advertisements speak true, there is to be more than a *Sammelsurium*[d] of men, principles and things? The progress of socialism in Germany, why that's a book! And other interesting subjects? the most interesting and most important are such that in the mouth of a *foreigner* they would appear an insult to French readers. Besides you leave me in ignorance of when the thing is wanted, and how much space it is expected to occupy.[313] However I am fully occupied with work, urgent work so far and could not have written a scratch. So there is no time lost.

Last Monday[e] Percy brought the children over and since then we have had the whole family here. Lily has had a fall and hurt her back a little, so she is going to have a support made as a matter of precaution, and that will last a few days yet. Percy is leaving today.

Louise's Hyaena-paper[314] will not appear before 15th instant, your, Tussy's and Louise's articles will create a sensation among the women's rights women in Germany and Austria, as the real question has never been put and answered so plainly as you three do it. And both Louise and Tussy tell me they have *heiligen Schrecken vor den deutschen (Berliner) Frauenrechtsweibern*.[f] But the reign of these is not to last much longer. Bebel writes quite enthusiastically about the ardour with which the working women in Germany now rush into the movement, and if that is the case, the antiquated semi-bourgeois women's rights *ânesses*[g] will soon be ordered to the rear.

Gilles continues issuing flysheets against Edward. More in a day or two. We are trying to bring the slanders home to Hyndman who is us-

---

[a] souteneur -[b] that's another matter -[c] *Almanach du Parti Ouvrier* -[d] conglomeration -[e] 28 September -[f] sacred awe of the German (Berlin) women's rights women -[g] asses

ing Gilles as his tool — and who we hope will not be able to wash off the dirt which the dirty Gilles has spattered involuntarily on the man who uses such a tool.[a]

Love from Pumps and Louise and the children.

Ever yours,

F. E.

[From Louise Kautsky, in German]

My dear Laura,

Sincere thanks for your letter. As the General[b] has told you, our 'epoch-making' paper will not be coming out until 15/X, probably due to Victor's Bohemian court proceedings. When will I get some more? since I assume that you, dear Laura, having begun with A, will also say B. Anything will be welcome to us. With warm greetings to yourself and the M. P. for Lille.[c]

Yours,

Louise

First published, in the language of the original (English), in: F. Engels, P. et L. Lafargue, *Correspondance*, t. III, Paris, 1959

Reproduced from the original

133

ENGELS TO AUGUST BEBEL

IN BERLIN

London, 6 October 1891

Dear August,

Herewith what you need in regard to the Cuno-Leibfried case.[308]

But now I think you would be well-advised to stop bombarding poor Ede with letters about Lassalle[178]; he is becoming tremendously irritable because of them and so confused over what *you people*, on the one hand, are demanding and what *he*, on the other, considers to be his duty, that this sort of thing can only make matters worse and he'll end up by producing nothing but contradictory material. You are *as much to blame as Ede* for the fact that the note[309] is *in it at all*, and to

---

[a] See this volume, pp. 237-38, 248-49, 251. - [b] Engels' jocular name. - [c] Paul Lafargue

condemn this excellent work in its entirety because of one wretched note is surely not right. I told him not to let this deflect him from his purpose, but to continue wearing the velvet glove over the iron fist and I also said that you would be grateful to him in the long run for having criticised Lassalle in this way. For it's clear to me that were you to re-read Lassalle's stuff *now*, you yourselves would be surprised at what it contains and at the faith in the false hero which, out of courtesy, you forced yourselves to profess when consorting with the Lassalleans at the time of the Anti-Socialist Law.[11] I'm positive that you, as also a whole lot of chaps who still cling to the Lassallean tradition, no longer have any knowledge whatever of what the man said and wrote (indeed, said and wrote for the most part against his better judgment). And hence the new edition of Lassalle will have a thoroughly beneficial effect on you people as well, provided only that you read the works of the prophet's critic.

Lafargue is not yet out of prison, but if the government *doesn't* release him during election time, he will probably be elected in Lille.[312] The prospects are rosy; Delory would have got in all right at the last election had not the by now routed Boulangists collared a whole mass of working men's votes.

In Paris there could easily be a government crisis. Rouvier is a shady individual, more so than is tolerable and, now that Boulanger has met his end, Constans is no longer needed and is detested by Carnot because he wants to step into the latter's shoes. Freycinet & Co. also want to get rid of Rouvier and Constans and so it may easily come to a split when the Chamber assembles on the 15th.

I'm glad to see that Dietz has paid you my fee.

Louise asks me to tell you that the photographs have arrived; very many thanks from us all; she has taken one of the two identical ones and I the profile.

Warm regards to your wife[a] and yourself from Louise and

Your
F. E.

First published in: Marx and Engels, *Works*, First Russian Edition, Vol. XXVIII, Moscow, 1940

Printed according to the original

Published in English for the first time

---

[a] Julie Bebel

134

ENGELS TO PAUL LAFARGUE [141]

AT LE PERREUX

London, 13 October 1891

My dear Lafargue,

Why didn't you ask me for the cheque as soon as you needed it? Why expose Laura to such humiliations when you know that one word from you — or from her — would be enough to put a stop to them?

That dear man Constans would seem to be intent on making you deputy for Lille whatever the cost — so much the better, let's hope he pulls it off. If all you have for opponent is an Opportunist, you should have every chance of success. It is of the utmost importance that we should have you in the Chamber — the other socialist deputies don't seem to be UP TO SNUFF, they're feeble, feeble, feeble!

Constans will undoubtedly do his best to upset your plans — but in that case he will be working for you, just as Bismarck in Germany worked for us. For in my country it's not the socialists who work for the King of Prussia [a]; rather it's the King of Prussia [b] who works for the socialists. And it may well be that the fury aroused in Constans' breast by the boos and catcalls at Marseilles [315] will prove a powerful level in getting you elected. 'Above all, don't be too zealous,'[316] Mr Constans!!

I have a long letter to write to Bebel [c] today on the subject of the Erfurt Congress [301]; there are several very important questions to discuss. That's why I must cut this letter short. Keep smiling, try always to poke fun at your opponents, PUT YOUR TRUST IN THE HISTORICAL LUCK OF THE PARTY, AND KEEP YOUR POWDER DRY.

F. E.

---

[a] i.e. for nothing - [b] William II - [c] See next letter.

Likewise from Pumps and the children who are still here. The little girl[a] needs a steel brace for her back (she is growing too fast) and the man who is making it keeps dragging his feet from one day to the next.

First published in: F. Engels, P. et L. Lafargue, *Correspondance*, t. III, Paris, 1959

Printed according to the original
Translated from the French
Published in English for the first time

135

ENGELS TO AUGUST BEBEL

IN BERLIN

London, 13 October 1891

Dear August,

All I have time for today is to send you a reply about the Russians and in fact this is the only item of importance; the other business is over and done with.[317]

As to the likelihood of war breaking out early next year, there are in Russia three important currents. First you have the diplomats. Of the latter I have said all along that they look for victories without the expense or risk of war, but for that very reason see to it that *everything is placed on a warlike footing* in order that Russia's enormously favourable defensive position may be exploited to the full. This happens every time. They can then put forward outrageous demands and stick to them up to the last minute and then, without a shot being fired, extract the maximum profit from the enemy — who has more to lose — by playing upon his fear of war. Alongside the diplomats, however, you have the soldiers who, despite their numerous mishaps on the field of battle, are exceedingly cock-a-hoop and full of bluster — more so than anywhere else. They want to let fly. And, thirdly, you

---

[a] Lilian Rosher

have the new bourgeoisie to whom, as to the American bourgeoisie of
the 40s, the expansion of the market appears as MANIFEST DESTINY, as
Russia's historic mission, namely the liberation of the Slavs and
Greeks and the domination of the eastern continent. All three must
be taken into account; under Alexander III the diplomats have hitherto been consistently victorious. Now there is famine to be reckoned
with and in the east and south-east this is very severe. East of the line
Odessa-Nizhni Novgorod and Vyatka there is acute famine everywhere; to the west of this line the harvest showed a gradual improvement and in the west itself the wheat harvest was passable in places
though the rye harvest was consistently poor. In Russia potatoes are
not a staple food. The extremely acute form assumed by the famine in
the Volga basin shows how wretched Russia's communications still
are. For that reason it seems plain to me that you would expose yourself unnecessarily should you seek to place credence in the assurances
of those presenting the German military estimates when they tell you
that war may certainly be expected next spring. It is just as much the
job of Russia's diplomats to prepare for war with an assiduity that is
all the greater for their reluctance to embark on it, as it is the duty of
the General Staff to talk you people in the Reichstag into believing
that war will definitely break out in April '92. You are perfectly right
to pay careful attention to these statements and I shall be very grateful for any authentic information in this connection; however the
chaps also have their ulterior motives.

This point is not as academic as it seems. For it will assume the utmost importance the moment the government estimates are presented to the Reichstag. If we are positive that there'll be a bust up early
next year, we can hardly be opposed to these estimates *in principle*.
And that would be a pretty disastrous state of affairs so far as we are
concerned. For the arse-crawling parties would all be overjoyed that
they should have been proved right and that we should now have to
spurn our policy of the past twenty years. And so impromptu
a change of course would also cause enormous friction within the
party. And internationally as well.

On the other hand there *may* nevertheless be a war in the spring.
What then should our attitude to the estimates be?

In my view there can only be one attitude: 1. There's no longer
time in which to change our weapons. If peace prevails until new cannon and a rifle of even smaller calibre are introduced, peace will in
any case presumably continue to prevail. So these objections don't

hold water. 2. The same applies, if to an even greater extent, to new cadres for the standing army—I mean to the demand for new *regiments*. In view of the gigantic armies of today, the few new formations which may now be demanded are of no account and, if they are to serve as *training* cadres enabling more men to be recruited and trained, they can only do so during an extended period of peace and thus would be useless so far as a war next spring is concerned.—On the other hand we can, however, 3. vote estimates where the intention is to bring today's army closer to the concept of a whole people under arms, to strengthen the *defensive* side alone, to train and arm bodies of men of *any* age between 17 and 60 who have not yet been conscripted and to incorporate them into permanent cadres without a proliferation of pettifogging regulations. While the threat of war persists we cannot demand that the existing organisation of the army be revolutionised, but if we seek to prepare the vast mass of untrained but able-bodied men as best as we can and organise them in cadres— for actual battle, not for show or pettifoggery—that will bring us closer to our concept of a people's militia which alone is acceptable to us.

Should the threat of war increase, we can then tell the government that we should be prepared, if enabled to do so by decent treatment, to support them against a foreign enemy, provided they prosecuted the war ruthlessly and with all available means, including revolutionary ones. Should Germany be attacked from the east and west, all means of defence would be justified. It is a question not only of the nation's existence but also, in our own case, of asserting the position and the future prospects for which we have fought. The more revolutionary the prosecution of the war, the more it will be waged in accordance with our ideas. And it might happen that, in contrast to the cowardice of the bourgeoisie and Junkers, who want to save their property, *we* should turn out to be the only truly vigorous war party. Of course it might also happen that we should have to take the helm and do a 1794 in order to chuck out the Russians and their allies.

I must close so as to get this letter registered (cannot be done after 5 o'clock). From past experience I felt pretty sure that the first field army would be surreptitiously receiving substantial reinforcements but we are glad to have authentic confirmation of this point. So far as the Austrians are concerned, the men are *absolutely first-rate*, the junior officers possess pluck but vary greatly in the matter of battle-training, while the senior ranks are utterly unpredictable. A man can rise to the top there on the strength of his services as pimp to Francis Joseph.

I shall get something done for the French on the question of the war,[313] but it will be damned difficult not to do more harm than good; the chaps are so touchy.

Constans is doing all he can to promote Lafargue's candidature[312] by resorting to some typical Prussian chicanery; that is no good in France.

But how will things work out with the present war policy and with Liebknecht at the Foreign Office? His foreign policy — Parnell, Garibaldi festival in Nice, etc.— is beneath contempt.[318] What with his adoration of the 'Republic', there's the prospect of a nice old rumpus before long.

If you are so certain that war will break out in the spring, it seems to me that you ought at least to discuss the matter behind the scenes when you hold your party congress.[301]

Regards from Louise and

Your

F. E.

First published in: Marx and Engels, *Works*, First Russian Edition, Vol. XXVIII, Moscow, 1940

Printed according to the original

Published in English for the first time

136

ENGELS TO LAURA LAFARGUE

AT LE PERREUX

London, 13 October 1891

My dear Laura,

Herewith the cheque £20 — to turn your landlady out of your domicile.

Now as to your *Almanach*.[a] I am writing you an article[313] but as it will have a practical turn toward the end of it, I can hardly send it off, or give it its final shape, until a short time before publication. Therefore I *must* know when your *Almanach* is to appear. Otherwise the thing may turn stale, or even be completely upset by events. It won't be more than 2 or 3 pages, 4 at outside, so there will be no necessity to send it early — as far as *technical* matters are in question. But you will see that it is impossible to write *un article d'actualité* unless it be printed and published at once. So please let me know and I shall gladly do my best to oblige *nos amis de là-bas*.[b]

Thanks for the papers. That *Action de Lyon*[c] seems a splendid specimen of the present state of fusion and confusion amongst the French socialists, out of the midst of which arises, erect, unavoidable, *zudringlich, unausstehlich*,[d] the everlasting Adrien Veber, basking in his own conceit, in which he is hardly second to his worthy master Benoît Malon.[319] How does this new harmony of all the disharmonies work? I see in the *Secrétariat du travail*[320] there are all sorts, Possibilists A[53] and B,[3] aside of our people and a lot of others, and so far they seem to have respected each other's carcasses without coming to blows. I cannot imagine how it is done and what may be the upshot of it.

How much was the fine inflicted on Paul?[275] I cannot find it in the *Socialiste* and have not any other paper ready at hand — and what chances have you to evade it?

---

[a] *Almanach du Parti Ouvrier* - [b] our friends over there - [c] *L'Action* - [d] impertinent, intolerable

Love from Louise, Pumps, the children and your old ever thirsty (going to have a bear with Pumps)

F. Engels

First published, in the language of the
original (English), in: F. Engels, P. et
L. Lafargue, *Correspondance*, t. III, Paris,
1959

Reproduced from the original

137

ENGELS TO KARL KAUTSKY[321]

IN STUTTGART

London, 14 October 1891

Dear Kautsky,

On reading your draft as published in the *Vorwärts*,[322] I find to my great surprise 'one reactionary mass' cropping up all of a sudden. I am writing to you about it immediately though I very much fear that this will come too late. By striking a shrill, discordant note, this propagandist phrase utterly destroys the harmony of the concise, rigorously formulated scientific propositions. For it is a propagandist phrase and an excessively biassed one at that and hence — in its apodictically absolute form where alone it sounds effective — utterly false.

False because it presents an in itself correct *historical tendency* as a *fait accompli*. The moment the socialist revolution comes, all the other parties will *appear* as a reactionary mass by comparison with ourselves. Maybe that is what thay *are* already, being no longer capable of progressive action of any kind, although this is not necessarily the case. But *at this moment* we cannot say as much, not with the assurance with which we put forward the other propositions in our programme. Even in Germany circumstances may arise in which the parties of the Left, deplorable though they are, will be *compelled* to clear up part of the vast quantity of anti-bourgeois, bureaucratic and feudal rubbish that still remains there. In which case they could hardly be described as one reactionary mass.

Until we are strong enough to seize power ourselves and put our principles into practice there cannot, strictly speaking, be any question of *one* reactionary mass *by comparison with ourselves*. Otherwise the entire nation would be divided into a reactionary majority and an impotent minority.

Take the chaps who dismantled the system of small states in Germany, who provided the bourgeoisie with elbow-room in which to carry out its industrial revolution, who introduced a unified transport system — both for things and for persons —, thereby inevitably according greater freedom of movement to ourselves — were their actions those of a 'reactionary mass'?

Take the French bourgeois Republicans who between 1871 and '78 put paid once and for all to the monarchy and the rule of the clergy, who secured freedom of the press, of association and of assembly to an extent hitherto unknown in France in non-revolutionary times, who introduced compulsory schooling and standardised education, raising it to a level that might well serve as an example to us in Germany — were their measures those of a reactionary mass?

Take the Englishmen of the two official parties who have vastly extended the suffrage and brought about a fivefold increase in the number of voters, who have evened out the size of constituencies and introduced compulsory and improved schooling, who at every session still vote not only for bourgeois reforms but also for one concession after another in favour of the working man — their progress may be slow and sluggish but nobody can condemn them out of hand as '*one* reactionary mass'.

In short we have no right to present a tendency in gradual process of realisation as an already accomplished fact, the less so in that in England, for example, such a tendency will *never* quite get to the point of becoming a fact. Come the revolution over here, the bourgeoisie would still be prepared to introduce all sorts of minor reforms, though by then it would be quite pointless to insist on minor reforms in a system that was in the process of being overthrown.

Under certain circumstances the use in propaganda of Lassalle's phrase is justified, though in our case it has in fact been misused to an enormous extent, e. g. in the *Vorwärts* ever since 1 October 1890. But it *should not be included in the programme* where it would be utterly false and misleading. It would look like Bethmann the banker's wife on the balcony someone proposed to build onto his house for him. 'If you build me a balcony,' he said, 'my wife will go and sit there and muck up me whole façade!'

I can't comment on any other alterations in the *Vorwärts* version as I've mislaid the paper and this letter must go off.

The party congress[301] began on an illustrious date. The 14th of October is the anniversary of the battles of Jena and Auerstedt when the old, pre-revolutionary Prussia collapsed. Let's hope that the 14th of October 1891 will usher in for Prussianised Germany the '*domestic Jena*' predicted by Marx![323]

Your
F. Engels

First published abridged in *Die Neue Zeit*, Bd. I, Nr. 19, 1916-17 and in full in *Aus der Frühzeit des Marxismus. Engels Briefwechsel mit Kautsky*, Prag, 1935

Printed according to the original

138

ENGELS TO LAURA LAFARGUE

AT LE PERREUX

London, 22 October 1891

My dear Laura,

Herewith my article.[313] Please look it over and say what you think of it. If you think that it won't do, or not without essential alterations, please say so. If you think it will do, let it be judged by others, *quant au fond. Le fond*[a] once agreed upon, please tell me where that particular lady *la langue française* wants alterations. I could not, in a matter of this sort, where I should be held answerable for every word published, allow the Frenchies to make changes without seeing them myself first. If only formal changes are required, will you send me the

---

[a] as far as the substance is concerned. The substance

manuscript back with your proposed changes and then we can settle.
Kind regards to our prisoner.[a]
In great haste — *Postschluss!*[b]

Love from Louise and yours

ever

F. E.

First published, in the language of the
original (English), in: F. Engels, P. et
L. Lafargue, *Correspondance*, t. III, Paris,
1959

Reproduced from the original

139

ENGELS TO FRIEDRICH ADOLPH SORGE [267]

IN HOBOKEN

London, 24 October 1891

Dear Sorge,

I have in front of me your letters of 15 September and 2 and 9 October.

As regards Barondess' decamping (presumably with the funds?), perhaps you could send me some further details just in case the little man turns up here.

For heaven's sake do me a kindness and stop supplying me regularly with *any* American monthlies. I am dying to be able to read a *book* again; despite the fact that I can only take a proper look at $^1/_3$ of the newspapers that arrive here, they swallow up all my time — but the movement is now so huge and one must, after all, remain *au courant*[c]! On the other hand, please send me...[d]

That the movement is again in the doldrums over there I can readily believe. With you people it's one long succession of great UPS AND DOWNS. But with each UP you ultimately gain ground so that in the end it represents an advance. Thus the tremendous onward surge achieved by the KNIGHTS OF LABOR [324] and by the wave of STRIKES between

---

[a] Paul Lafargue - [b] time for the post - [c] informed - [d] Engels did not finish this sentence.
See this volume, p. 277.

1886 and 1888 did on the whole, and despite all setbacks, spell advancement for us. For, after all, the masses are stirring in a way they have never done before. Next time even more ground will be gained. But none the less the standard of living of the NATIVE AMERICAN WORKINGMAN is notably higher even than that of his English counterpart and this alone is enough to put him out of the running for some time to come. Again, there is the competition from immigrants and other factors besides. *When* the time comes over there, things will move with tremendous speed and dynamism, but that may not be for some while yet. Miracles never happen. And, in addition, there's the unfortunate business of your supercilious Germans who, wishing to double the role of schoolmaster with that of commanding officer, discourage the natives from learning even the best they have to offer.

I shall send the money to the *Socialiste* as soon as I know who it's for; Lafargue is in jug, as you know; I have not yet had an answer.

The *Entwicklung des Sozialismus*,[a] translated by Aveling and edited by me, is to appear over here in English (in Sonnenschein's Social Series); this authorised translation will pretty well neutralise the pirated American edition [311] which has been done into quite execrable English. And the thing isn't even complete — what they found too difficult they simply left out.

Needless to say, Mother Wischnewetzky gladly consented to Sonnenschein's publishing the *Condition, etc.*[b] in her translation. The fee, however, is to go to Mrs Foster-Amery. *Cela m'est bien égal.*[c] For the rest, she seems really pleased to have been able to establish contact again and tells me what a rotten time they are having, etc., etc.

I should like to have Bakunin's biography [325]; from it one could get some idea of how present-day anarchist tradition depicts that Messiah.

Letter of the 12th of this month now also received. Thanks.

In Erfurt everything went off very well.[301] I shall send you the official record as soon as it comes out; Bebel says that the reports of the speeches are very garbled. The insolent Berliners of the opposition, instead of acting as prosecutors, immediately became the accused, behaved with abysmal cowardice and will now have to get along *outside* the party if they propose to do anything. There are quite undeniably

---

[a] F. Engels, *Socialism: Utopian and Scientific.* - [b] F. Engels, *The Condition of the Working-Class in England in 1844.* Translated by Florence Kelley-Wischnewetzky. London: Swan Sonnenschein and C°, 1892. - [c] It's all the same to me.

police elements in their midst, while some are also *covert anarchists* who are out to surreptitiously convert our chaps; along with these are the jackasses, swollen-headed students and failed candidates, would-be bigwigs of all descriptions. Barely 200 of them all told.— Mr Vollmar likewise had to eat humble pie; the latter is far more dangerous than the former, being more cunning and tenacious as well as vain to the point of folly, and intent at all costs on playing a role. Bebel put up an excellent performance, as did Singer, Auer and Fischer (used to be on the *Sozialdemokrat* here, a really sterling chap, aside from being the bluntest of blunt Bavarians). To Liebknecht fell the bitter task of having to recommend Kautsky's draft programme which, with Bebel's and my support,[a] was accepted as the *basis* of the new programme's theoretical section. We have had the satisfaction of seeing Marx's critique[b] win all along the line. Even the last traces of Lassalleanism have been eliminated. With the exception of a few poorly written bits (though it's only the way they're put that is feeble and commonplace), there is nothing to complain of in the programme or not, at any rate, after a *first* reading.

You will have seen that Lafargue is standing in Lille, and will hear the result of tomorrow's election[c] long before you get this letter. If he isn't elected, he will be sure of a seat in the Département du Nord at the coming general election.[326]

The threat of war looms larger despite the famine in Russia. The Russians want to make prompt and thorough use of the diplomatic possibilities presented by the new French alliance[288] and, although I am convinced that the Russian diplomats do not want war and that the famine would make it seem an absurdity, the military and pan-Slav currents of opinion (the latter being now supported by the *very powerful* industrial bourgeoisie with an eye to expanding markets) may nevertheless prevail, while in Vienna, Berlin or Paris there might also be blunders which would lead to a war. Bebel and I have been corresponding about this and are of the opinion that if the Russians start a war against us, German socialists should lash out *à outrance*[d] at the Russians and their allies, whoever they may be.[e] If Germany is crushed, so shall we be, while at best the struggle will be so intense that only revolutionary means will enable Germany to hold its own, and hence there is every likelihood that we may be forced to take the

---

[a] See this volume, pp. 239 and 246-47. - [b] K. Marx, *Critique of the Gotha Programme*. - [c] See this volume, p. 269. - [d] with all their strength - [e] See this volume, pp. 242-47 and 256-59.

helm and play at 1793. Bebel made a speech to that effect in Berlin which attracted a great deal of attention in the French press.[327] I shall try and make all this clear to the French in their own language,[313] which won't be easy. But though I should regard it as a great misfortune if there were to be a war and it were to bring us to power prematurely, we have got to be prepared for that eventuality and I am glad that in this I have Bebel on my side, for he is by far the most efficient of our chaps.

Next week I start on Volume III.[a]

Warm regards to your wife[b] and to you yourself.

Your
F. E.

First published abridged in *Briefe und Auszüge aus Briefen von Joh. Phil. Becker, Jos. Dietzgen, Friedrich Engels, Karl Marx u. A. an F. A. Sorge und Andere*, Stuttgart, 1906 and in full in: Marx and Engels, *Works*, First Russian Edition, Vol. XXVIII, Moscow, 1940

Printed according to the original

Published in English in full for the first time

140

ENGELS TO AUGUST BEBEL[267]

IN BERLIN

London, 24 October 1891

Dear Bebel,

Many thanks for the postcards and packages without which it would have been difficult for us to follow the course of events in Erfurt.[301] Things really went off quite capitally — you, Auer, Singer and Fischer covered yourselves with glory, and the wretchedness of the opposition was the only thing you had to complain of, it being no pleasure to do battle with such small fry. At all events the gentlemen will now have to show what they are capable of outside the party,

---

[a] of *Capital* - [b] Katharina Sorge

where they are innocuous, and the better elements amongst the youthful rowdies will now be accorded time for reflection. The fact that Mr von Vollmar has seen fit to reject the new course in the arms of Caprivi, if without 'personal spite',[328] may provide temporary alleviation, but you are very far from being quit of the chap, and the more tense the situation becomes, the closer a watch you will have to keep upon him. However, every big party has *one* intriguer-in-chief and if you were to get rid of this one, another would take his place.

We were pleased that there should have been so much merriment on your side, and it made us laugh a lot — the sorry opposition and the worthy Vollmar are almost enough to send one to sleep.

On the *first* reading the programme makes an excellent impression, with the exception of a few weak spots to which I had already drawn K. Kautsky's attention earlier on.[a] It must have been a bitter pill for Liebknecht to swallow when *he* had to give an account of the new programme from which the last traces, not only of Lassalleanism, but also of his much-beloved People's Party[154] slogans had been eliminated. Indeed the speech — which, if the account in the *Vorwärts* is to be believed, he himself drafted — provides painful evidence of this. And then he suffered a further blow in the shape of Kunert's motion[329] on his son-in-law.[b] I hope Liebknecht may find a gently inclined plane down which he may slowly glide into retirement — he is remarkably outmoded in the party.

Monday, 26 October.— In the meantime another letter arrived from you this morning.[330] That Fischer had made enemies I am ready to believe, for it's something I know from my own experience. In my younger days I was just as inclined to be uppish at the wrong time and in the wrong place as he is, and in the same way I seldom detect a failing in the younger generation which I myself did not possess to a greater or lesser degree. It gradually wears off, provided one occasionally gets a slap in the eye which one has to admit is deserved.

I don't know whether you will in future be able to avoid settling such matters in public. I think it's better that you *should*, despite minor disadvantages and much personal unpleasantness. But there's no doubt that, unless your central organ[c] changes, you would be well-advised to hand it over entirely to the Berlin party and to acquire

---

[a] See this volume, pp. 239-41. - [b] Bruno Geiser - [c] *Vorwärts*

a national weekly advertiser which, however, should and would have to be properly edited.

It was most sensible to expend the 400 marks on Lafargue's election. This will come in *very handy* for the second ballot. Since unions and party are distinct in your case, it is perfectly all right if French and other STRIKES receive support *direct from the trades unions* in Germany, leaving the party funds free for political purposes. This being so, however, you should see to it that the unions do something for the glassworkers.[331] Quite a lot has been done for them from over here.

Lafargue is in a good position. He obtained 5,005 votes, the Opportunist and government candidate Depasse 2,928, the second Opportunist Bere (Beer or Bear, as you choose) 1,246, and the Radical Roche 2,272. *The latter is stepping down in favour of Lafargue.* That means that Depasse, his real competitor in the second ballot, could only get in if all Roche's voters were to abstain and if he were to poll, say, another 1,000 votes amongst the reserve of abstainers in the monarchist camp, or if 3,000 or more votes from that reserve were to more than outweigh the 5,005 + 2,272. I don't know how many registered electors there are and therefore am unable to judge; at all events the position is better than we had dared to hope.

Gilles is doing well for himself. The fellow must be living in clover at police expense. He has *bought* nearly everyone in the Communist Society[89] by lending them money and they *durst* not chuck him out. Since the fellow claims that, *as a member of that society*, he is *ipse facto* a *member of the German party*, it may be asked whether you people are prepared to put up with this particular 'comrade'. The funds available to him for his loans and his circulars — that sort of thing costs a pretty penny over here — can only emanate from the Embassy.

I have not yet seen anything about the Magdeburg meeting[332] either in the *Vorwärts* or in the *Echo*.[a] That the *Vorwärts* should suppress the opposition meeting in Berlin[333] was only to be expected in view of its previous practice. But it's abysmally stupid.

I am sending you an article by the great Paul Brousse from which you will see how that chief of all quarrel-pickers, mischief-mongers and authoritarians, now that he's been thoroughly trounced and reduced to a cipher, is holding forth to *you people*, whom he has combatted for years as his arch-enemies on the Continent, about peace and federation.

---

[a] *Hamburger Echo*

Herewith a few cuttings about the Russian famine which is spreading even farther west than I thought. Such things are to be found daily in the British press. The position is indeed a serious one and still more troops, or so Mendelson assured me yesterday, are being sent to the west simply in order that they may be fed. It would be madness for the Russians to go to war, but militarist parties always are mad and the Russian bourgeoisie is blinkered, stupid, ignorant, chauvinist and grasping in the extreme. If war there *must* be, then the sooner the better, for in that case the Russians would be treated to a rude awakening.

Since I thought it necessary to let the French know exactly what our position would be in case of war — a damned difficult task, mind you — I have written an article in French and sent it to Laura.[313] Today she writes to say that both she and Paul are absolutely delighted with the article and that it was exactly what was wanted for the French, etc. If Guesde is also of that opinion — he is still at Lille where he is doing duty for Lafargue with the electors — the article will be published. It was originally intended for the French socialist almanac[a] but may (I think will) be too strong for that paper's motley crew, in which case it will probably appear in the *Socialiste* which I trust you see. What I tell the chaps is this: We are virtually certain of coming to the helm within 10 years; we can neither seize power nor retain it without making good the wrongs done to other nationalities by our predecessors by 1. openly paving the way for the restoration of Poland and 2. putting the people of northern Silesia and Alsace-Lorraine in a position to decide freely where their allegiance lies. Between a socialist France and a socialist Germany, I go on, there is no such thing as an Alsace-Lorraine question. Hence there could be no grounds whatever for going to war over Alsace-Lorraine. But if the French bourgeois should begin such a war notwithstanding, and if to that end they should place themselves in the service of the Russian Tsar who, indeed, is the enemy of the *middle classes* throughout western Europe, this would represent a repudiation of France's revolutionary mission. We German socialists, on the other hand, who would come to power in 10 years' time provided peace is preserved, would be duty bound to assert the position acquired by us in the vanguard of the labour movement, not only against the internal, but also against the external, foe. If Russia were to win, we should be

---

[a] *Almanach du Parti Ouvrier*

crushed. So, have at 'em, if Russia goes to war, have at the Russians and their allies, *whoever they may be*. We should then have to ensure that the war be prosecuted with all available revolutionary means and that the existence of any government refusing to use those means be made impossible; alternatively that we ourselves take the lead at the crucial moment. We have not yet forgotten the glorious example set by the French in 1793 and, if our hand is forced, we might in fact celebrate the centenary of 1793 by showing that the German working men of 1893 are not unworthy of their predecessors the Sansculottes, in which case, should French soldiers cross our frontier, they will be welcomed with the cry:

> *Quoi ces cohortes étrangères*
> *Feraient la loi dans nos foyers?*[a] (*Marseillaise*)

That is the gist of the thing. As soon as the text has been finally decided on (I naturally anticipate that one or two minor amendments will be suggested) and printing has begun, I shall translate the article into German and we shall see what can be done with it. I'm not sure whether the conditions governing your press are such as to permit its publication in Germany; maybe if you qualified it a bit it might do — it'll be managed somehow. *My* articles are not in any case binding on the *party*, which is a great piece of luck for both of us, although Liebknecht supposes I regard it as a personal misfortune though this would never have occurred to me.

The reports quote you as saying that I had prognosticated the collapse of bourgeois society in 1898. There must have been a little mistake somewhere. All I said was that by '98 we might possibly have come to the helm. Should this *not* happen, bourgeois society might continue to potter along as it is for a bit, until such time as an impulse from without causes the whole rotten structure to come crashing down. In still air a dilapidated old wreck of that sort can survive for a couple of decades even when it is to all intents and purposes defunct. So I should have been exceedingly careful about making predictions of this nature. On the other hand, the possibility of our coming to power is merely a calculation of probability in accordance with mathematical laws.

Nevertheless, I hope that peace will prevail. Our position is such that we have no need to take a gamble — and war would compel us

---

[a] What, shall these foreign cohorts lay down the law in our own homes?

to do so. And again, ten years from now we shall be far better prepared. *Voici pourquoi*.[a]

If we are to take over and operate the means of production, we need people who are technically trained and plenty of them. These we have not got, and have even been pretty glad hitherto to have been largely spared the company of the 'educated'. Now things have changed. Now we are strong enough to absorb and digest any quantity of educated riff-raff and I would predict that in the next 8 or 10 years we shall recruit enough young technicians, doctors, jurists and schoolmasters for the factories and large estates to be managed for the nation by party members. In which case our accession to power will take place quite naturally and will run a — relatively — smooth course. If, on the other hand, we come to the helm prematurely and as a result of war, the technicians will be our principal opponents and will deceive and betray us at every turn; we should have to inaugurate a reign of terror against them and would lose out all the same. This is what *always* happened to the French revolutionaries, if on a smaller scale; even in everyday administration they had to leave the subordinate, really operative, posts to their former reactionary incumbents — men who hampered and paralysed everything. I therefore hope and pray that this splendid, unerring progress of ours, evolving with the impassivity and inexorability of a natural process, will continue along its appointed course.

Warm regards to your wife[b] and yourself.

Your
F. E.

First published in: Marx and Engels, *Works*, First Russian Edition, Vol. XXVIII, Moscow, 1940

Printed according to the original

Published in English in full for the first time

---

[a] That is why. - [b] Julie Bebel

141

ENGELS TO KARL KAUTSKY

IN STUTTGART

London, 25 October 1891

Dear K. K.,

My congratulations on the acceptance of your draft programme at Erfurt and on the deletion of 'one reactionary mass'.[a] I have not yet had time to compare your draft in detail with the programme as finally accepted.

I have proposed to Dietz that the fee for the 2nd edition of *The Poverty of Philosophy* be divided equally between all 5 concerned — 240 M for the 3 heirs and 160 M for the 2 translators, assuming 400 M to be the total, or pro rata if not. I hope you will agree to this so that we can get the business settled once and for all. The heirs are not entitled to the *whole* fee for this edition.

I have also asked Dietz to hand you on my behalf a copy of the new edition[b] of the *Origin, etc.*, a bound copy, that is.

Everything went off really splendidly at Erfurt.[301] Auer's and Fischer's speeches in particular caused us a great deal of merriment. But those two thoroughly deserved a chance to vent their wrath on the 'opposition'. Pit a Bavarian against a Berliner and there'll be damned little left of the Berliner at the finish. But the behaviour of these gentry, like that of Vollmar, shows how greatly that little crew had overestimated their own power. Retreats such as these are quite unheard of. But it could not fail to make an impact abroad, and over *here* it has meant a resounding defeat for Hyndman who first took Gilles publicly under his wing and obviously believed his boasts about the collapse of the German party — he would now like to disassociate himself from the scoundrel if he could. Incidentally, Gilles has been elevated in *Figaro* to the status of great man!

You may, if you wish, put an announcement in the *Neue Zeit* to the effect that the following will be coming out in Swan Sonnenschein's & Co.'s SOCIAL SERIES: 1. my *Condition of the Working-Class*[c] in *la* Wisch-

---

[a] See this volume, pp. 261-62. - [b] the fourth German edition - [c] *The Condition of the Working-Class in England in 1844*

newetzky's translation, 2. my *Entwicklung des Sozialismus*[a] translated by Aveling. 3. Ede's introduction to Lassalle translated by Tussy.[334]

Louise has suggested to me that it might be in the interest of the *Neue Zeit* to send a copy regularly to the editor of *The Review of Reviews*, W. T. Stead, Mowbray House, Norfolk Street, Strand, London, W. C. The thing has a sale of over 100,000 copies and prints extracts from reviews from all over the world together with the contents (titles of articles) of all of them, no less than 23 of these are from Germany, including the *Deutsche Revue, Ueber Land und Meer, Gartenlaube, Nord und Süd, Preußische Jahrbücher*, etc., etc. From the *Economic Journal* our draft programme's demands. Since Stead is a thoroughly mad sort of chap, albeit a brilliant businessman, it may well be of benefit to us and, on occasion, prove enormously effective if you were to send him copies — for whenever there's a chance of creating a sensation, he ruthlessly seizes on it, irrespective of the source. The thing would also be enormously useful to you people, costs only 6d. a month and contains a tremendous amount. It would save your reading *any other* English revue.

Now I must go out for a spot o' fresh air; the Avelings and Edes[b] will be arriving for luncheon shortly.

Your

F. E.

Monday.[c] I am sending you a copy of *The Review of Reviews* in which Stead butters up Mother Besant with the intention of instructing her in Christianity.[d] He obviously wants to win fame as the man who led her back to Jesus. There's one way to do that. For Mother Besant invariably shares the religion of the man who *downs* her. — Ede and Tussy agree to my proposal about the distribution of the fee.

Lafargue obtained 5,005 votes in Lille, the two Opportunists 4,174 together and the Radical, Roche, 2,272; the latter stepped down in favour of Lafargue. Hence, if an Opportunist is to get in, 3,000 ab-

---

[a] *Socialism: Utopian and Scientific* - [b] Eduard and Regina Bernstein - [c] 26 October - [d] 'Character Sketch: Mrs Annie Besant: — Portraits of the Leading Officials of the Theosophical Society', *The Review of Reviews*, Vol. IV, No. 22, October 1891.

staining Monarchists will have to *support* him in the second ballot. A most satisfactory position, therefore.[326]

First published in *Aus der Frühzeit des Marxismus. Engels Briefwechsel mit Kautsky*, Prag, 1935

Printed according to the original

Published in English for the first time

142

ENGELS TO LAURA LAFARGUE

AT LE PERREUX

London, 27 October 1891

Mein liebes[a] Löhr,

Das ist ja ein ganz famoses Resultat,[b] Paul heading the Poll — pretty Poll — you see enthusiasm makes me half mad and drives me into Pantomime puns, but when I came to 'pretty Poll' and remembered your name was Kakadou, that brought me to a dead stop, I might be accused of blasphemy and what not! *Au, au, sagt der Jud' in Berlin, wenn der christliche Germane auch einmal versucht einen Witz zu machen.*[c]

Well, if I only knew *le nombre des électeurs inscrits*,[d] I should make a shrewd guess. The *Défense* de Lille bragged with 6,000 monarchist and clerical votes, that I doubt very much, and so think Paul almost safe. We drank success to him last Sunday in 1868 Port, and I am sure at least the 5 votes over the 5,000 are due to our efforts. Never mind, next Sunday week we'll try another and more successful sort and that is sure to smash up all his opponents. What a fine country France is to be locked up! You attack the government, the government makes you M. P. (Pélagie) but Pélagie makes you M. P. (Parliament).[335] In Germany it's the other way about. You get elected into Parliament and then you may well write behind you name M. P. because that means Member of *Plötzensee* — the new monster prison near Berlin.

---

[a] My dear - [b] The result is absolutely splendid. - [c] Oh, oh, says the Jew in Berlin, if the German Christian ventures as much as once to make a joke. - [d] the number of registered electors

But *trève de bêtises*[a]! I am very glad indeed you and Paul like my article.[313] But will the *Kuddelmuddel*[b] people of the *Almanac*[c] be of the same mind? *Never* mind (another Pantomime effort, I shall soon be M. P. (Pantomime)), it can then go in the *Socialiste*.

Old Sorge who does not want to have the *Socialiste* without paying for it asks me to send 10s. for his subscription. I send a postal order, they sell readily in Vienna, as Louise tells me, so no doubt they will be legal tender in Paris.

Post mark:

I.
525, 490, 10/-   Regent's Park Road
38   24 September 91

Things in Erfurt went very well.[301] The execution of the insolent young student and *commis-voyageur* lot was very necessary. They will soon disappear now, and the next lot of the same sort will be less cheeky.

But now it's post-time and dinner-time too. Give Paul a hearty cheer in our name when you come into Pélagie, and take a hearty embrace yourself from Louise and

Your old incorrigible

General

First published, in the language of the original (English), in: F. Engels, P. et L. Lafargue, *Correspondance*, t. III, Paris, 1959

Reproduced from the original

---

[a] enough of stupidities - [b] mixed up - [c] *Almanach du Parti Ouvrier*

143

ENGELS TO FRIEDRICH ADOLPH SORGE

IN HOBOKEN

[London,] 29 October 1891

I was interrupted when on the point of asking you in my letter of Saturday 24 October[a] if you would from time to time send me a *women's paper* or magazine — from the bourgeois female's movement, needless to say. For the good of the *working women's* movement in Germany, Austria and over here, Louise is obliged to pay some slight heed to this stuff, too, and hence would very much like to take an *occasional* look at what these little ladies are up to in America.— Lafargue's prospects are rosy: 5,005 votes. Depasse, Opportunist, 2,928; Bère (read Beer), also Opportunist, 1,246; Roche, Radical, 2,272. The latter stepped down in favour of Lafargue who has the support of the extreme Radicals in the Chamber.[336] — In Germany the party congress takes pride of place over everything.[301] The few intriguers who were chucked out will attract no one save a number of stuck-up little students — GOOD RIDDANCE!

Regards to your wife.[b]

Your
F. E.

First published in *Briefe und Auszüge aus Briefen von Joh. Phil. Becker, Jos. Dietzgen, Friedrich Engels, Karl Marx u. A. an F. A. Sorge und Andere*, Stuttgart, 1906

Printed according to the original

Published in English for the first time

---

[a] See this volume, p. 264. - [b] Katharina Sorge

144

ENGELS TO NIKOLAI DANIELSON [337]

IN ST PETERSBURG

[London,] 29-31 October 1891

Dear Sir,

When your letter of 21 September arrived I was travelling in Scotland and Ireland [264]; only today I find time and leisure to reply to it.

Your letter of 20 January was indeed lost, which I regret doubly, first because the interesting information it contained was kept from me for so long, and second because it put you to the trouble of working it out again for me. Many thanks!

The '*Züchtung von Millionären*',[a] as Bismarck puts it, seems indeed to go on in your country with giant steps. Such profits as your official statistics show, are unheard of nowadays in English, French or German textile manufactories. 10, 15, at the outside 20%, average profits, and 25-30% in very very exceptional years of prosperity, are considered *good*. I was only in the childhood of modern industry that establishments with the very latest and best machinery, producing their goods with considerably less labour than was at the time socially necessary, were able to secure such rates of profit. At present, such profits are made only on lucky speculative undertakings with new inventions, that is to say on one undertaking out of a hundred, the rest mostly being dead failures.

The only country where similar, or approximatively similar profits are nowadays possible in staple industries, is the United States, America. There the protective tariff after the civil war, and now the Mackinley tariff,[338] have had similar results, and the profits must be, and are, enormous. The fact that this state of things depends entirely on tariff legislation, which may be altered from one day to another, is sufficient to prevent any large investment of *foreign* capital (large, in proportion to the quantity of domestic capital invested) in these industries, and thus to keep out the principal source of competition and lowering of profits.

Your description of the changes produced by this extension of mod-

---

[a] rearing of millionaires

ern industry in the life of the mass of the people, of the ruin of their home industry for the *direct consumption of the producers*, and by and by also of the home industry carried on for the capitalist purchaser, reminds me vividly of the chapter of our author on the *Herstellung des innern Markts*,[a][339] and of what took place in most places of Central and Western Europe from 1820 to 1840. This change, of course, with you has different effects to some extent. The French and German peasant proprietor dies hard, he lingers for two or three generations in the hands of the usurer before he is perfectly ripe for being sold out of his land and house; at least in the districts where modern industry has not penetrated. In Germany the peasantry are kept above water by all sorts of domestic industries — pipes, toys, baskets, etc.— carried on for account of capitalists; their spare time being of no value to them after they have tilled their little fields, they consider every kopek they receive for extra work as so much gain; hence the ruinously low wages and the inconceivable cheapness of such industrial products in Germany.

With you, there is the resistance of the *община*[b] to be overcome (although I should say that that must be giving way considerably in the constant struggle with modern Capitalism), there is the resource of farming land from the large proprietors which you describe in your letter of May l'st[291] — a means of securing surplus value to the proprietor but also of continuing a lingering existence to the peasant *as a peasant*; and the *kulaki*,[c] too, as far as I can see, on the whole prefer keeping the peasant in their clutches as a *sujet à exploitation*,[d] to ruining him once for all and getting his land transferred to them. So that it strikes me, the Russian peasant, where he is not wanted as a workman for the factory or the town, will also die hard, will take a deal of killing before he does die.

The enormous profits secured by the youthful bourgeoisie in Russia, and the dependence of these profits on a good crop (harvest) so well exposed by you, explain many things otherwise obscure. Thus what should I make out of this morning's statement in the Odessa correspondence of a London paper: the Russian commercial classes seem to be possessed of the one idea, that war is the only real panacea for the ever increasing depression and distrust from which all Russian industries are now suffering — what should I make of it and how explain it but for this coplete dependence of a tariff-made industry on

[a] creation of domestic market - [b] commune (Russ.) - [c] rich peasants in Russia - [d] object of exploitation

the home market and on the harvest of the agricultural districts on which depends the purchasing power of its only customers! And if this market fails, what seems more natural to naive people than its extension by a successful war?

Very interesting are your notes on the apparent contradiction that, with you, a good harvest does *not* necessarily mean a lowering of the price of corn. When we study the real economical relations in various countries and at various stages of civilization, how singularly erroneous and deficient appear the rationalistic generalizations of the 18th century—good old Adam Smith who took the conditions of Edinburgh and the Lothians as the normal ones of the universe! Well, Pushkin already knew that

и почему

Не нужно золота ему,
Когда простой продуктъ имѣетъ.
Отецъ понять его не могъ
И земли отдавалъ въ залогъ.[a]

Yours very sincerely,

P. W. Rosher[b]

Next Monday I begin again with Volume III[c]—and hope not to discontinue until complete.

This letter has been delayed until today 31 October in consequence of interruption.

First published, in Russian, in *Minuvshiye gody*, No. 2, St Petersburg, 1908   Reproduced from the original

---

[a] and why/it needs no gold if a supply/of *simple product* supplements it./His father failed to understand/and took a mortgage on his land. (A. Pushkin, *Eugene Onegin*, Ch. I.) - [b] Engels' conspiratorial pseudonym - [c] of *Capital*

145

ENGELS TO PAUL LAFARGUE

AT LE PERREUX

London, 31 October 1891

My dear Lafargue,

Louise and I send you our hearty congratulations on the result of last Sunday's[a] vote. 'It's magnificent' and it is 'war'.[340] True there may have been some 4,400 abstentions and missing voters, but more than 3,100 of those who abstained would have been needed to rally round your opponent if Dépasse was to surpass you by passing you (a pun, alas, passing through like an attack of diarrhoea, let's hope it will pass!). And no such thing has ever been known. And you yourself have won an intoxicating victory. So a week tomorrow we shall drink to your definitive victory[341] — though we shan't forget you tomorrow either.

I see from the newspapers sent me by you and Laura that the press, both governmental and of radical tendency, has at last been compelled to take notice of your election. The nonsense talked by *Le Temps*[b] cannot but be of use to you. Once the ice has been broken, anything these gentlemen may say will work in your favour. Even the worthy Pelletan of *La Justice* has had to come down on your side.

Should you be elected, that would be a further embarrassment to the Chamber: whether to vote or whether not to vote for your release.

What on earth is this new split that is about to happen amongst the Chamber's radicals, between Millerand, Hovelacque and Moreau, on the one hand, and the bulk of the Clemencists on the other? You speak of the possibility of joining forces with the former.[342] But up to what point are they keeping in step with you? To the best of my knowledge the nominally 'socialist' radicals in the Chamber have hitherto been merely the detritus of Proudhonism and, as such, the avowed opponents of the socialisation of the means of production. And in my view it would be impossible for us to effect a merger, form a *group*, with people who don't subscribe to that, at any rate in principle. Alternatively I believe we might enter into a more or less tempo-

---

[a] 25 October - [b] Presumably Engels has in mind the leader 'Il y avait trois élections hier...', *Le Temps*, No. 11118, 27 October 1891.

rary alliance with them, but not a merger. However there has evidently been some new development I don't know about and I shall await further word from you before forming an opinion. How truly splendid it would be if the radicals in the Chamber began to come over to our side — symptomatic indeed!

I'm delighted that you and Laura should have found my article [313] both good and topical — but what will the others — Argyriades & Co. of the *Almanach* [a] — say? In all my experience I have never had the good fortune to comply with the wishes of those gentlemen, those friends of all the world, having found that, whenever I have done an article at their request, it has always been quite different from the article they requested. Alongside the solemn lucubrations of Mr Bénoit Malon and other choragi of Parisian socialism, that would be well-nigh impossible. Besides it's all one to me. I warned Laura in advance that the situation would compel me to write things that many people would find distasteful. Well, she asked for it and I obliged. I know very well that the *Socialiste* won't hesitate, but as for the *Almanac*, that's another matter. Anyway we shall publish the thing one way or another and it will probably cause a rumpus.

At Erfurt everything went off very well. [301] The jackasses of the opposition left the representatives of the whole party in no doubt that they were indeed jackasses and poltroons undeserving of sympathy. They are either fools or covert anarchists or policemen. Last night there were meetings in Berlin at which delegates had to submit their reports, thereby probably demolishing the gentlemen of the opposition. [343] Vollmar, on the other hand, has had to recant, not only at Erfurt, but also, and more specifically, at Munich [344] before his own constituents. They rejected a resolution proposed by him in which he sought, without unduly infringing the resolutions passed against him at Erfurt, to introduce various passages acknowledging the point of view he had espoused in his reactionary speeches. Vollmar himself was forced to propose a fresh resolution, viz. outright submission to the Erfurt resolutions, and this was passed unanimously. As Bebel points out in a letter to me, whoever leaves the party or is shown the door by the party is, in political terms, dead. [345] Mr Vollmar is well aware of this and has taken good care not to do something that would place him in such a position. But that won't prevent him from being the most dangerous intriguer in our party.

---

[a] *Almanach du Parti Ouvrier*

First page of Engels' letter to Paul Lafargue
of 31 October 1891

Anyway things are going ahead in Germany and before long the same thing will happen in France. We shall, perhaps, avoid a war and, since we are slow and methodical, that may give the French a chance to overtake us again by pulling off some mighty coup. It augurs well for the '*fin de siècle*' and could put 1793 in the shade.

What idiots your bourgeois and the Russians are! In a war, England with her fleet and her command of the sea would hold the balance — which is why those gentry are impelling her into the arms of the Germans by teasing her on the subject of Egypt [346]!

Love to Laura — the Viennese women's paper [a] hasn't appeared yet — for want of money, no doubt.

Yours ever,

F. E.

First published, in Russian, in *Voprosy istorii KPSS*, No. 7, Moscow, 1965

Printed according to the original

Translated from the French

Published in English for the first time

146

ENGELS TO CONRAD SCHMIDT [267]

IN ZURICH

London, 1 November 1891

Dear Schmidt,

First of all, my congratulations on your engagement and, I hope, very imminent marriage. Let me know what the fateful day is to be so that we may drink to the health of yourself and your young bride, as we shall meanwhile be doing at lunchtime today with a glass of port.

May I also congratulate you on the agreement with Guttentag; it's a worthwhile undertaking but you will have to devote a good deal of time to it. [347] Next week I shall be tackling Volume III [b] (which part-

---

[a] *Arbeiterinnen-Zeitung* - [b] of *Capital*

ly explains this expeditious reply since all my correspondence must be polished off first), and won't, I think, have to stop till whole thing's polished off. Thus you will also be able to include this essential final section.

You cannot, of course, do without Hegel and he's another chap whom it will take you time to digest. The short paper on logic in the *Encyklopädie* would be quite good to start off with, but the edition you should have is that in Volume 6 of the *Werke* — not Rosenkranz's separate edition (1845) — since the former contains far more explanatory notes from the lectures, even if that idiot Henning himself frequently fails to understand the latter.

In the introduction, in §26, etc., you have first the critique of Wolf's version of Leibniz (metaphysics in the *historical* sense), then that of the English and French empiricists in §37, etc., then that of Kant, §40 et seqq. and, finally, that of Jacobi's mysticism, §61.— In the first section (Being), you ought not to linger too long over being and nothing — the last paragraphs on quality followed by quantity and measure are much nicer, but the theory of essence constitutes the main section: the dissolution of abstract opposites into their insubstantiality when, as soon as one tries to grasp one aspect alone, it changes imperceptibly into the other, etc. At the same time you can always clarify things by means of concrete examples. E. g. you, as a fiancé, and your affianced yourselves present an outstanding example of the indivisibility of identity and difference. It is quite impossible to ascertain whether sexual love is the pleasure derived from identity in difference or that derived from difference in identity. Remove the difference (in this case of sex) or the identity (the humanity of both), and what remains? I remember how tormented I used to be at first by this indivisibility of identity and difference, though we cannot take one step without stumbling over it.

On no account, however, should you read Hegel as Mr Barth has read him, namely so as to discover the paralogisms and shabby expedients that served him as tools for constructing his system. That is a schoolroom exercise, nothing more. What is far more important is to discover the truth and the genius beneath the falsity of the form and the factitious context. For instance, the transitions from one category or opposite to another are almost always arbitrary — and are often achieved by means of a joke, as in §120, when positive and negative 'fall to the ground' so that Hegel may proceed to the category 'ground'. To rack one's brains over this is a waste of time.

Since, in Hegel, each category represents a stage in the history of philosophy (as, indeed, he usually indicates), you would be well-advised to read the *Vorlesungen über Geschichte der Philosophie*—one of his most brilliant works—by way of comparison. For recreation I would commend the *Ästhetik*. Once you have gained some familiarity with it you will be amazed.

The inversion of Hegel's dialectics is based on the assumption that it is the 'self-development of the idea' of which, therefore, the dialectic of facts is only the image, while the dialectic in our minds is but the reflection of the actual development taking place in the natural world and human history in obedience to dialectical forms.

You should try comparing the Marxian progression from commodity to capital with the Hegelian from being to essence; this would give you quite a good parallel—on the one hand, the concrete development which follows from the facts, on the other, the abstract construction, in which extremely brilliant ideas and, in certain cases, very just transformations such as that of quality into quantity and vice versa, are elaborated to produce what appears to be the self-development of one notion out of another, of which, indeed, it would be possible to concoct a dozen of the same kind.

The noble Wolf has sent me his opus[a] in the form of an off-print. But, although asked by an anonymous 'admirer'[b] whether I intend to 'box the fellow's ears', I haven't looked at it yet. An academic of that sort can wait.

The party congress went off very well.[301] The amount of attention devoted to the 'opposition' did no harm; though it may have amused the philistines it undoubtedly had a very salutary effect upon the party.

Bebel and Adler spent a few days over here after the Brussels Congress,[135] when we were all very jolly. Bernstein's excellent introduction to Lassalle is coming out in English.[334]

---

[a] J. Wolf, 'Das Rätsel der Durchschnittsprofitrate bei Marx', *Jahrbücher für National-ökonomie und Statistik*, 2. Bd., 3. Folge. - [b] See this volume, p. 241.

Well, I hope that a whole lot of students, both male and female, will attend your first course of lectures.

Kindest regards.

Yours,

F. Engels

Mrs Kautsky sends you and likewise your fiancée her most sincere congratulations.

First published in *Sozialistische Monatshefte*, Nr. 22-23, Berlin, 1920

Printed according to the original

Published in English in full for the first time

147

ENGELS TO LAURA LAFARGUE

AT LE PERREUX

London, 9 November 1891

My dear Laura,

Victoire! Though hidden in one of its most desolate corners, amongst the paragraphs that help to make up columns, *The Daily News did* inform us that Paul had beaten Depasse (who now would do well to change the *a* of his name, source of so many calembours, into *i*) by 1,400 or thereabouts.[a] So the two toasts, in Port and Claret, offered up yesterday by us, were not without effect. Well, that's so much gained. And what is worth more than the victory itself almost, is the way in which it was won and which turns a common by-election into a great political action, a cause of incalculable effects. Paul may well back his Constans against the *roi de Prusse*[b] as an involuntary promoter of Socialism; but the real likeness lies between Constans and Bismarck, as it laid between Bismarck and Louis Bonaparte — they all partake of that short-sighted cleverness and *Dummschlauheit*[c] of the ordinary merchant and speculator who aims at one

---

[a] See this volume, p. 269. - [b] William I - [c] low cunning

thing, and by miscalculating causes and effects, arrives at effecting the very opposite.

Anyhow Constans' stupidity has resulted not only in Paul's election, which gives a tremendous *élan* to Socialism all over France, but also in loosening the coalition for the maintenance of the ministry which was formed against Boulangism at the Rue Cadet.[223] I don't think the mass of the *Clémencist* Radicals will as yet fall away from the ministry, they are held too tightly. But the old feeling of security does no longer exist since the *Roche*-debate.[348] And some, the more consistent elements like Millerand, can hardly keep within the ministerial alliance. That, and the personal ambitions and intrigues *within* the ministry will be sufficient to bring on a change — and every change loosens the bonds between the Czar[a] and French Chauvinists, and thus is in favour of peace. By the bye, what an irony of history that the Russian government, after having spent millions on Boulanger, must now spend fresh millions on the very people who upset Boulanger!

It was a nice exciting time and I have to thank you very much for enabling me to follow all the *péripéties* of it in the Paris press. What a miserable helpless political ass that Ranc has become. *Il doit être en train de s'enrichir, celui-là!*[b]

I have sent a few lines of humorous congratulations to Paul direct, so that *M. le directeur de la prison* might have the perusal of them.[153] If he should confiscate them I will send you a copy. But I hope and trust there will be more respect shown to *M. le député*.

I am anxious to see what Constans and the Chambre will do now. If they try to keep Paul in Ste-Pélagie, it will be all the worse for them.

It strikes me Mother Crawford is not far wrong in saying the strength of the present ministry is its having brought about outward signs of the French and Russian *entente*; and that this makes the Radicals[147] fear a dissolution.[c] But if, as is probable, *internal* dissensions break up the ministry, taking advantage of another such doubtful victory as that on Saturday week,[d] then everything changes. First, the Russian *entente* becomes very vapoury as soon as the instability of governments is evidenced again, and secondly, if the Cabinet splits up,

---

[a] Alexander III - [b] He must be getting rich now, that man. - [c] Engels has in mind E. Crawford's 'The French Ministry' in *The Daily News*, 9 November 1891. - [d] 31 October

either fragment will claim the merit of that *entente*. And thirdly, after a split nobody can tell either what the reconstruction may turn out to be, or how long it may last.

I have looked at the *Justice* of Clemenceau lately again more often, and it strikes me that at the bottom of the antiboulangist Alliance must have been the idea that there was only one way of taking the wind out of the sails of any present or future Boulanger, and that is: to close with Russia at any price and *then hasten on the guerre de revanche*.[a] That is the only conclusion I can draw from the tone of the *Justice: soyons plus patriotes que Boulanger!*[b] And no doubt that plan would suit them all: settle the account with Germany, raise France again to a position of supremacy (which Russia might allow them to show of, provided France gave her the reality) and then, but not before, settle our internal republican party quarrels. Unless that is the fact, I cannot make out either the language or the action of the Radicals. They may be fools, but there is a limit to all folly, outside the madhouse at least.

Louise is going to write a few lines, so I close with love

Ever yours,
F. E.

My dear Laura,

I am very proud that my definition of the letters M. P.[335] turned out right at last though you have been right before and are right as long as the things last. The notice about M. P. (in your sense) election was underneath a paragraph 'The murder of a wealthy widow'; General found it out, as I did not know, that the election of a Socialist ranges itself under the impression of a bourgeois...[c]

First published, in the language of the original (English), in: F. Engels, P. et L. Lafargue, *Correspondance*, t. III, Paris, 1959

Reproduced from the original

---

[a] retaliatory war - [b] let us be greater patriots than Boulanger! - [c] The end is missing.

148

ENGELS TO AUGUST BEBEL

IN BERLIN

London, 9 November 1891

Dear August,

Thank you for your letter of 29 October and the many other things you have sent me, including the postcard of 30 October.[349]

So Lafargue has won a victory.[330] It's quite an event, firstly because of the immediate impact on France, which will be very great, secondly, because on his occasion literally *all* the socialist parliamentary groups, including the Possibilists[3] — if sometimes wryly —, pulled together, and thirdly because, with a low cunning and brutality worthy of a Bismarck, M. Constans succeeded in turning what was merely a second ballot into a gripping political drama.

The government had two main vantage grounds: 1. Victory over the common threat, Boulanger. 2. The apparently deliberate display of an intimate relationship with Russia. Add to which a 3rd, namely the display, successful at any rate so far as the plebs were concerned, of France's newly restored military might during the big September manoeuvres. These 3 points enabled the government to compel the extreme Left to support it; the combined 'Republicans' constituted a majority vis-à-vis the combined Monarchists, Boulangists and to some extent also socialists. Then, contrary to the practice of 1869, Constans did not set Lafargue free to enable him to stand as candidate. In this the Radicals could not go along with him. Hence the big debate on the 31st October, following Roche's interpellation,[348] hence the government's Pyrrhic victory — 240 for the government, 160 against, but — 170 *monarchist abstentions*. In reality, therefore, anti-government majority of 90. Defection of Radicals[147] therefore = fall of the Cabinet the moment the Monarchists desire it and vote with the Radicals. After the division, needless to say, the alarm of the Radicals was as great as that of the government, especially since the latter threatened to dissolve parliament while giving the Radicals to understand that they would find the electorate far more pro-government than the present Chamber, as seems more than likely. In short, Constans' behaviour has shown the 'one Republican' mass that, after the disappearance of the only opponent capable of uniting them, there are internal questions which hopelessly divide them; the rift exists, cannot be patched up and, now that Constans is flouting all the republican conventions by his continued detention of Lafargue in Ste-Pélagie, things will liven up still more. Not that I anticipate the early demise of the government as a result of the Radicals' defection—on the contrary, there are likely to be a number of occasions on which the latter, having scored a victory despite themselves, will have to eat humble pie and beg the government's pardon; but within the government itself there is open warfare between Freycinet and Ribot on the one hand and Constans and Rouvier on the other, warfare which another doubtful division might bring to a head, thus inducing a split and, with it, a change of ministers, renewed instability in the Cabinet, i. e. a cooling off of Russia's ardour since what the Tsar needs is *stable* government in France; and finally—fresh elections under different circumstances and with different results.

While Liebknecht goes into ecstasies in the *Vorwärts* about the non-existence of chauvinism in France, the Paris press—which I have been able to study exhaustively during the period of the elections—and notably Clemenceau's *Justice* which Liebknecht, I believe, also sees every day, has convinced me that the secret behind the 'Republicans" (Opportunists, Radicals, Possibilists [3]) anti-Boulanger pact was the government's determination to outbid Boulanger in patriotism, to engineer the Russian alliance, to present the army to the world as ready for battle, to rattle its sabre and, should a retaliatory war ensue, to conduct it with might and main—in other words, to head as straight as maybe for a retaliatory war, the dearest wish of every French bourgeois. Just as the republic of 1849 and 1871 was the form most calculated to unite the Monarchists, so now retaliatory war is the issue that will most surely bring *all* Republicans, i. e. all *middle-class* ones—for the workers count only as election fodder—into the same fold, indeed the only issue that could bring this about once the republic had been attained and consolidated. Retaliation was the secret of the Boulangists' success—let us preach retaliation! The reacquisition of Alsace-Lorraine! If you compare *La Justice* of pre-Boulangist and Boulangist days with that of today, you would find it hard to draw any other conclusion. But that is against Liebknecht's principles. In France, a strong chauvinist tendency cannot be *allowed* to exist, it would fly in the face of the eternal principles and hence it is denied. If things go on like this, you people may have to pay dear-

ly for the policy pursued by the *Vorwärts*, and come to rue the fact
that the man who directs your foreign policy is colour-blind. I don't
know what ideas Hirsch may have on the subject; at one time he, too,
used sometimes to harbour curious views in regard to France. But no
doubt he will be open to discussion.

10 November. So Lafargue has been set free. For the period of the
session — and even Meyer Opper von Blowitz doubts whether he will
have to go back to Ste-Pélagie once it's over. That represents another
defeat for Constans. At first he and his Opportunists wanted to keep
Lafargue in gaol — but the conviction that, if they did, the Radicals
and Monarchists would form an *anti*-government majority and set
him at liberty, compelled the gentlemen to give way. So the extreme
Left has twice been compelled to disassociate itself from the government.— The politics of the French Chamber, by the by, are completely incomprehensible to anyone who fails to bear constantly in mind
that the government and the Opportunists are exploiting their term
of office for their personal enrichment in the most outrageous manner
and that the vast majority of Radicals are not only implicated but
have an *interest* in these goings-on, and are only waiting for the time
when *they* are strong enough to seize power themselves and skim off
the cream which is now the prerogative of the Opportunists.

Now for an example of the vicious stupidity of the French government: a few days before the second ballot at Lille a levy was made in
Fourmies as a result of which 30 young men were drafted into the battalion of the 145th Regiment garrisoned at Maubeuge, the regiment
which, on *May Day in Fourmies*, had opened fire on these same
men [243] — and among those 30 was the *brother of Marie Blondeau*, the
girl killed on May Day by this self-same battalion. You'd think you
were in Prussia. The *Vorwärts* chooses to ignore all this!

There was much rejoicing here over your victories in Berlin [349] and
Vollmar's most resounding and, for him, unpleasant defeat in Munich. [344] It will, I imagine, be some time before you have any more
trouble with defections and/or expulsions, and in the meantime the
party will grow to such an extent that *this particular* method of opposition might very well disappear altogether. But whether it will be
pleasanter for you when the cabalist crew remains within the bounds
of legality is another question.

The Zurich business [350] has shown you yet again how much of a drag on you the foreign associations are. Could you not seize on the opportunity and sort things out once and for all with that gang? The *Vorwärts* dealt admirably with Hans Müller, but that doesn't prevent these foreign idiots from presuming to subject you to a vote of no confidence. In this country the same thing applies to the Society[89] and Gilles.[a] Unless you counter Gilles' statement by *publicly* declaring how the said Society stands vis-à-vis the party, no amount of protests in private letters will be of any avail. That you people are responsible for the stupidities of this gang is simply taken for granted over here — and with justice, in view of the Society's past history, so long as you people remain silent.

We were very pleased about Stolp-Lauenburg and your article on the subject in the *Vorwärts*, which fully accords with my views.[351] The bulk of rural day labourers east of the Elbe (as also in England) are in fact still too much in thrall for our propaganda to have any real effect until they have been through the dame school of Progress.[296] It is the task of the men of Progress to pave the way for us there, and this they will surely do. So if in Berlin their inertia is such that, as opposed to ourselves, the men of Progress must be accounted part of the reactionary mass, in the rural areas their position is decidedly different at any rate as things are now. Admittedly this won't go on for long.

Though the term of the Reichstag has been extended to 5 years,[352] it is likely to be interrupted. Provided the pressure is kept up, the majority will disintegrate and the government will *have* to resign because it will have no alternative. Particularly in case of war. This very winter you may witness some ludicrous goings-on.

I am glad to hear that so much sympathy is already felt for us in technologically educated circles.[353] But from what I experienced in 1848 and 1870/71 of the French Republicans, who were after all themselves bourgeois, I know only too well just how far one gets with such silent hangers-on and sympathisers — in time of danger — and how horribly one can put one's foot in it, not to wish for a couple of years' respite in which to take a closer look at these gentlemen's qualifications and character, particularly in relation to so important a business as the socialisation of large-scale industry and large-scale agriculture. Not only would this save friction; it might also, at a moment of crisis, avert an otherwise inevitable and decisive defeat. There will

---

[a] See this volume, p. 269.

in any case be stupendous blunders, and plenty of them — that is inevitable. As you yourself have said, there are, among the postulants, plenty whose ambitions exceed their talents and knowledge, nor have I forgotten what Singer once said to me, *à propos* of Nonne, about students being driven into the arms of Social-Democracy by their fear of examinations. However, the very fact *of their coming* is a portent of what lies ahead.

In Russia the famine is assuming fearsome proportions. At Simbirsk, rebellious starvelings are given 500 lashes, i. e. flogged to death. The winter wheat in the south either could not be sown because of drought or else has been killed by an early frost. So there'll be more distress next year. It would seem to me that the Russians are bent on appeasement (Giers' trip to Milan), having also put a bit of a damper on the overhasty overtures of the French, and it was *precisely because of this* that the Tsar felt he could afford to travel across young William's domains without paying him a visit which is, after all, a flagrant case of *lèse-majesté*.[354] Only wait till the French Ministry begins to totter, and then you'll see how peace-loving the Tsar becomes — needless to say without desisting from his encroachments in the East and in Central Asia.

Yesterday Salisbury told the jackasses and speculators in the City that not one little cloud troubles the peaceful horizon. That would be a bad sign, for in 1870, a fortnight before the outbreak of war, the same thing was said by Granville, the Foreign Secretary.

The French September manoeuvres with 4 army corps were a fearful sham. Sir Charles Dilke, Parnell's colleague in adultery — albeit on a different basis — described them in enthusiastic Francophil terms, yet his article shows that there was much that was exceedingly rotten and much that had remained unchanged since 1870. Notably the inefficiency of the officers. Once the chaps begin to mobilise on a large scale, even more inadequacies will come to light.

Regards from Louise.

Your
F. Engels

The Russian loan[302] weighs heavily on the Paris bankers. Has dropped 4% below the issue price, and crowds of people *in this country* are busily disposing of other funds and shares so as to be able to make a fresh payment to the Russians on the 20th of this month in Paris.[a]

First published in: Marx and Engels, *Works*, First Russian Edition, Vol. XXVIII, Moscow, 1940

Printed according to the original

Published in English for the first time

149

ENGELS TO OSCAR HEIDFELD [355]

IN LIVERPOOL

[Draft]

[London,] 12 November 1891

Dear Sir,

...I still hold the documents mentioned in your letter [356] but they are of no value whatever now, the policy having lapsed long since through Mr Dronke's failing to pay the premiums as he ought to have done. The very first premium due in November 1877 I did pay expecting to be repaid by him, but when I applied for the money he never replied, nor have I been able ever since to make out his address, though my Manchester solicitors took every trouble to find him out. Under these circumstances, and in view of the almost certainty that the gradual payment with interest on the same and on the original loan would eat up more than any possible return for the policy, there was nothing left to me but to let the policy drop.

From what you tell me I must conclude that the same result would have been arrived at had he not pledged the policy.[b]

First published in: Marx and Engels, *Works*, Second Russian Edition, Vol. 37, Moscow, 1965

Printed according to the original

Published in English for the first time

---

[a] The postscript was written by Engels in the margin. - [b] The beginning and end of the letter are missing.

150

ENGELS TO FRIEDRICH ADOLPH SORGE

IN HOBOKEN

London, 14 November 1891

Dear Sorge,

A line or two in great haste before the last post goes. You will have heard by cablegram about Lafargue's victory.[330] It was brought about by M. Constans, who is as stupidly cunning and doltish as Bismarck, if not more so. 1. In a scandalously biassed trial he blamed Lafargue for the government's fusillade at Fourmies [243] and got him sentenced to a year's imprisonment. 2. Having thus made Lafargue enormously popular in the Département du Nord, and after the latter had been put up for the first seat to become vacant at Lille, Constans kept him in prison, contrary to the *precedent established* 22 years earlier *by the Empire itself*, instead of releasing him for the period of the election; 3. when, in the first ballot, Lafargue polled 5.005 votes, i. e. only 780 fewer than were needed for an absolute majority, Constans still did not release him, despite being severely rapped over the knuckles by the Chamber. Since the Radical candidate,[147] Roche, who had polled 2,274 votes, then proceeded to step down in favour of Lafargue, Lafargue's victory was assured.

But the best thing about it is that that idiot Constans further succeeded in making Lafargue's election into an *événement*,[a] thereby seriously endangering his own position. For on 31 October, when a demand for Lafargue's release was made in the Chamber by Millerand, the proposal to go over to the order of the day was carried by 240 votes against the Radicals' 160. *But only because 170 Monarchists did not vote.* This was the *first time the Radicals had voted against the government since the Boulangiade,* thus demonstrating that the government can be toppled at any moment by the combined votes of the Radicals and Mon-

---

[a] event

archists. And when, *after Lafargue's election*, a motion for his release was again tabled on 9 November, it was only the prospect of those combined votes that forced the government to abandon its intention of opposing the motion.

But now that the Cabinet is torn by dissension and Freycinet would rather obtain his majority *through* the Radicals, whereas Constans would rather do so through the Monarchists and *against the Radicals*, now that Constans has incurred the odium of the workers by his actions since May Day and his friend Rouvier is the most notorious and corrupt man in the Ministry, while Carnot, for his part, finds Constans intolerable because the latter is trying to succeed him, Carnot, as President of the Republic, all these parliamentary fluctuations assume significance. For the recurrence of ministerial instability in France is another guarantee of peace, since the Tsar would be chary of going to war arm-in-arm with a French government that is liable to topple any day.

Again, these symptoms are significant so far as France's domestic situation is concerned. A large number of Radicals — Millerand, Hovelacque, Moreau, etc.— realise that they simply can't do without the workers and that the government's duplicity in introducing into the Chamber bills ostensibly favourable to labour while ensuring that these are thrown out by the Senate, is something that just won't do. But if Lafargue should now get in and the small 7 or 8 strong socialist group — all of them small fry and incapable of any initiative — thus obtain a leader, things might soon begin to change. Only on condition, however, that Paul himself doesn't allow his eighth or twelfth part of negro blood to run away with him.

In Germany everything is going swimmingly. In Munich [344] itself Vollmar suffered an even more decisive defeat than at Erfurt.[301] The opposition [13] is virtually non-existent, and will soon be completely under the wing of the police. Any newspaper reports to the contrary, particularly such as are cabled to you, are false — I have seen some prime examples of this.

What will happen about the *Vorwärts* I cannot say. It has improved, but Hirsch isn't going to join it. Not that I really regard this as a misfortune.

Regards to your wife.[a]

Your

F. E.

First published abridged in *Briefe und Auszüge aus Briefen von Joh. Phil. Becker, Jos. Dietzgen, Friedrich Engels, Karl Marx u. A. an F. A. Sorge und Andere*, Stuttgart, 1906 and in full in: Marx and Engels, *Works*, First Russian Edition, Vol. XXVIII, Moscow, 1940

Printed according to the original

Published in English for the first time

151

ENGELS TO FRIEDRICH ADOLPH SORGE [357]

IN HOBOKEN

London, 21 November 1891

Dear Sorge,

Have had your letter of 6 and postcard of 8 November.

When Adler and Bebel came over here from Brussels, the former promised me that he would send you the Vienna *Arbeiter-Zeitung* regularly, and the Viennese stand by their word. Now that the Austrian movement is growing in importance, I am having to keep copies of the paper myself.

Der arme Teufel caused much merriment over here. Adler took the first Adolfinade with him and I sent the second to Bebel.

It goes without saying that you should publish Marx's letters to yourself if you want to, without asking me or anyone else. As soon as your articles on the American labour movement are complete, you ought to bring them out — booklet form [358] — in Dietz's Internationale Bibliothek, say — so that they can be kept permanently together.

---

[a] Katharina Sorge

If you like, I could do what is necessary to set the ball rolling with Dietz. He will, of course, have to pay for the things again.

Bakunin's biography [325] received with thanks — haven't looked at it yet.

In one of my letters [a] I asked you *not* to send me any middle-class American reviews — I can get all the *good* ones over here (from Mudie's) if there's anything in them — and Tussy keeps her eyes open. On the other hand I was about to add a request when I was interrupted and thus sent off the letter *as it stood*; namely, that you send me from time to time individual numbers of some women's rights organ — any old one. Louise looks at such stuff from time to time in order to keep herself — and hence also me — more or less informed about that racket.

In Berlin and other cities more victories in the municipal elections — in Berlin the number of votes has *trebled*. [359]

The *Jungen* [301] have formed an association [333] and are bringing out a rag, *Der Sozialist* — impertinent and silly. Nothing but tittle-tattle and lies. True, they would be easier to combat if Liebknecht didn't make so many blunders and edit the *Vorwärts* so deplorably.

So Mrs Schlüter intends to come back after all! Just as we thought.

In this country, too, we have scored sundry little victories in the municipal elections; in West Ham (it's called WEST BECAUSE EAST OF THE EAST END), Will Thorne, secretary of the Gasworkers Union [164] and a really splendid chap, was elected, etc., etc.

Warm regards to your wife [b] and yourself from

Your

F. Engels

First published abridged in *Briefe und Auszüge aus Briefen von Joh. Phil. Becker, Jos. Dietzgen, Friedrich Engels, Karl Marx u. A. an F.A. Sorge und Andere*, Stuttgart, 1906 and in full in: Marx and Engels, *Works*, First Russian Edition, Vol. XXVIII, Moscow, 1940

Printed according to the original

---

[a] See this volume, p. 264. - [b] Katharina Sorge

152

ENGELS TO AUGUST BEBEL

IN BERLIN

London, 25 November 1891

Dear Bebel,

I had been trying to find time, in the intervals of work on Volume III[a] now proceeding at a good, brisk pace, to answer your letter of the 15th, when some news arrived which compels me to write forthwith. At a meeting at Bordeaux on the 22nd[360] Lafargue is alleged to have said that in 1870 he had *servi le pays à sa manière en communiquant à M. Ranc des plans qui, si l'on en avait tenu compte, pouvaient complètement changer la face des choses. Ces plans lui étaient communiqués par des frères de l'Internationale en Allemagne, parmi lesquels se trouvaient plusieurs officiers de l'armée allemande.*[b] Now Lafargue *cannot* have said this, but I can't for the life of me think what he *did* say. However, the thing is so patently silly and the accusation so monstrous that you people probably ought to reply to it before you hear *what* Lafargue actually said. In order to ascertain the facts, I at once wrote yesterday, and again today, to Laura and to Lafargue himself,[153] to whom I also said that you would probably have to take immediate countermeasures and that if you showed a total lack of consideration for him, he would have to lump it. Not that he really deserves any; but all the same I would beg you not to act in anger which, as so often in my own case, always leads one to do something stupid; rather you should do all you can to ensure the continuance of concerted, or at any rate parallel, action with the French workers. You will, of course, repudiate any suggestion that the above preposterous assertion could apply to yourselves —that goes without saying. You did not yourselves, directly or in-

---

[a] of *Capital* - [b] served his country in his own fashion by communicating to M. Ranc plans which, had they been taken into account, might have completely changed the face of things. These plans had been passed on to him by *his brothers of the International in Germany, amongst whom were several German army officers.*

directly, send the French government in Bordeaux either military information or plans from German officers, having, so far as I know, had no connections of any kind with officers at that time. So the more vigorously you repudiate this truly insane accusation the better, though I would suggest that it would nevertheless be advisable, and also less conducive to eventual complications, for you to repudiate *only the report* as such, without as yet holding Lafargue responsible for it. After all, this would not preclude a further statement as soon as the text is known; I shall let you have this the moment I get it.

What Lafargue can have said and what he had in mind, I simply cannot conceive. For neither did we, the General Council of the International in this country, have any connections of any kind with German officers, and thus were never in a position to send him 'plans' of that description from gentlemen of that ilk. And even if he had been able to establish connections elsewhere in France upon his revisiting that country—I believe in 1868, after his marriage (or in 1869—I couldn't exactly say at the moment)—he concealed the fact from us so carefully that nothing whatever transpired before his return to France in 1880, nor, for that matter, has it done so since.

At all events, he has committed a quite unpardonable blunder—whether he told lies or tales out of school is something he himself must decide—and placed you people in a position such as might very well rob you of all desire for international intercourse. While I foresee the nature of the deluge that is about to engulf you, I cannot yet see how it is to be stemmed. I can only suppose that it's the eighth or sixteenth part of negro blood which flows in Lafargue's veins and occasionally gains the upper hand that has led him into this quite inexplicable folly—it is, to put it mildly, a quite inconceivable piece of stupidity.

In view of the large number of German officers who settled abroad in 1848/49 and after, there is always the possibility that something of the kind came into his hands, but to make the *frères d'Allemagne*[a] responsible really does take the cake.

Should you so wish, I shall at all times be prepared to testify that on no occasion during the war was the General Council of the International in a position to pass on to France information of any kind deriving from you, other than what was to be found in your own newspapers; indeed I should be prepared to make any statement that

---

[a] brothers in Germany

might help to clear you of the slightest suspicion of conniving at such foolishness. For if anything of the kind *did* happen, you people were as innocent of it as the unborn babe.

Nevertheless, these confounded vexations gave way to joy last night upon our learning from *The Evening Standard* of the victory in the Halle elections.[361] This does after all go to show that, despite all the blunders made by individuals, we as a mass continue to advance.

Apropos, what I wrote on the postcard [153]—I thought somebody over there would be able to read it—was Russian: *Da zdrávstvuyet Berlin!* Long live Berlin!

But now, luckily, it's time for the post—registered, which is safer, so I shall deal with the contents of your letter in my next. The Russians would appear to be drawing in their horns; the bankers in Paris have had difficulty moving the loan and the Russian government has had to take back a third or more as unplaceable [302]—on this occasion the unpatriotic character of capital again appears in a favourable light.

Writing to your wife[a] is another pleasure I shall have to keep in store. She will have had a letter from Louise.

Your
F. E.

First published in: Marx and Engels, *Works*, First Russian Edition, Vol. XXVIII, Moscow, 1940

Printed according to the original

Published in English for the first time

---

[a] Julie Bebel

153

ENGELS TO LAURA LAFARGUE

AT LE PERREUX

London, 27 November 1891

My dear Laura,

You need not be afraid that it ever entered my mind to think Paul capable of a wilfully mean and dishonorable action. That is entirely out of the question. But the man may be the very soul of honour, and yet commit an *étourderie*,[a] the consequences of which may be incalculable. And my letters contain no charge against Paul except the expression of the possibility that he *may* have been led into such an *étourderie*, and, besides, the attempt, supposing that to be the case, to help him out of it as much as lay in my power. To do which, it was absolutely necessary to make clear to him the full *portée*[b] of the words put into his mouth.

Now you yourself admit that it is just possible he *may* have been led to commit such a blunder.

To recall the facts. On Monday evening[c] *The Evening Standard* contains the *Reuter*[360] which showed to me the necessity of immediate action, 1) to obtain authentic information, 2) to prevent further blunders, in case one had been committed. Hence my letter to you[153] which I hope you will, on re-reading, find less unjustifiable than when you had read it first. Well, the same night, or next morning at latest, I receive from you 1) the enclosed cutting from a paper not named — from which report *Reuter* had evidently abridged, 2) an *Intransigeant* 25. Novembre where under the heading: 'Le cit. Lafargue à Bordeaux', it is equally stated that on 22 November Paul, *before a meeting of cinq ou six cents personnes ... dans la salle des Chats*, said *qu'à différentes reprises il avait (en 1870) remis à M. Ranc, alors directeur de la Sûreté générale, divers plans et documents importants sur la situation des armées allemandes qui lui avaient été communiqués par des socialistes allemands et qui auraient pu changer la face des choses*[d] etc. etc.

---

[a] error - [b] meaning - [c] 23 November - [d] ...*five or six hundred people in the Chats hall*, said that he (in 1870) provided M. Ranc, the then chief of the Secret Police, with different plans and important documents pertaining to *dislocations of the German armies*

From that I was forced to conclude that *you knew* the contents of these two reports, and that the very fact of your sending them to me *without a word of comment*, implied a tacit acknowledgement that they were in substance correct. On that conclusion, and moreover remembering certain expressions in the Lille speech, equally sent by you, and which expressions I considered *at least* uncalled for, I could not act otherwise than write to Paul my letter of Wednesday 25th.[153]

Now of course I see that you had never read a report of Paul's speech, and that my letters to you and to Paul gave you the first intimation of what had been put into his mouth. But now you will also see that this is a matter which must be attended to; that the statement about the action of some German socialists during the war of 1870/71—whether substantially true or substantially false—ought never under any circumstances to have been made, *if it was made*, and ought to be clearly and unmistakably disavowed, *at once*, if it was not made; that so long as this report is not completely and absolutely disposed of, it will be absurd to expect our German friends to place any confidence in our French friends; and that the government and bourgeois in Germany will at once exploit this report against our German party in a way which is absolutely incalculable; if it leads to nothing more than a renewal of the old Socialist law,[11] *it will be lucky!*

So if Paul has been slandered, if he is prepared to declare publicly that he never said a word implying in any way the assertion that German socialists, *either in or out of Germany*, provided him with military statements, plans, news or anything of the kind for the use of the French government during the war 1870/71—then let him send me that declaration *at once* and in a registered letter. But it must be plain, without reservation or qualification of any kind, or it will be useless and *may* turn out worse than useless.

If that plain declaration cannot, for one reason or another, be made, then I see no other way out of the mess but that you and Paul come over here at once and discuss by word of mouth such matters as will evidently be fitted for that mode of settlement alone. Your presence will be almost as necessary as his, to moderate our hot heads and to give us the views of your cool head on the situation in France; and also to help us in finding 'the way out' by your feminine sagacity and *souplesse*,[a] in cases where we male clumsy stick-in-the-muds are left in

which he received *from the German socialists* and which could have changed the course of events.

[a] pliancy

the dark. You see I am anxious as anxious can be, to keep Paul out of the difficulty if he has got himself into one; but the very first thing is to prevent the commission of fresh mistakes in case *one* has already been committed. Tomorrow his election [330] will be settled, on Monday at latest I shall have the first reports from Germany on the effect of this thunderbolt from a clear sky, so if you come on Sunday, to be here in the evening, we might succeed in dispersing at least the worst of the clouds on Monday. A telegram 'Coming to-night' would be agreeable, as we receive no letters on Sunday. And under all and any circumstances I do hope Paul will not take any public steps in a matter deeply concerning other people without first consulting these people, the slightest blunder might be fatal to himself, and he will see, I hope too, that this is no joking matter and must be got out of the world as soon as possible.

Ever yours affectionately,
F. E.

First published, in the language of the original (English), in: F. Engels, P. et L. Lafargue, *Correspondance*, t. III, Paris, 1959

Reproduced from the original

154

ENGELS TO AUGUST BEBEL

IN BERLIN

London, 1 December 1891

Dear August,

At last, after three exuberant days, my birthday mood may perhaps have subsided sufficiently for me to write a moderately rational letter again. First, then, the Lafargue affair has been settled. I have today heard from Laura—Lafargue has gone to Lyons,[362] having only been in Paris for a couple of hours on Saturday to attend to his scrutiny — who says:

'Paul authorises me to say, 1. that he confirms his letter to you' (see below); 2. 'that the meeting at which he spoke in Bordeaux was *private*',— a closed meeting for members of the Workers' Party—'that no reporters had been admitted and no official record exists; 3. *the incriminating statements are the invention of a reporter b r o d a n t s u r l e texte d' un article publié par Ranc'* (embroidering on the text of an article by Ranc); 4. 'the words used by Paul were as follows: "If I insisted upon the war being continued, this was because the information at my disposal led me to believe that Germany was not in a position to hold out for very much longer."'

She adds:

'*There was no question of plans obtained by Germans or through their agency*; in general Paul *declares* that, *throughout the war, he received no communications of any kind from Germany.* And Paul also says that he *subscribes to your demands*, and not only subscribes to them but *challenges any refutation of his above statement.*'

(Le Perreux, 28 November; only reached me today.) [363]

In his letter to me (Lyons, 26 November), Lafargue says that the purport of his speech had been such and such, that in 1870 the International in all countries had considered it its duty to prevent the crushing of the French Republic by Bismarck's troops, and that while the other Internationals had fought under Garibaldi, the Germans had protested against the continuation of the war and the rape of Alsace-Lorraine.

My demands to which he subscribes were for the repudiation, without reservation or qualification, of the statements ascribed to him and of their purport. These you now have and may *use as you think fit.*

So that's *one* weight off my mind, I'm glad to say. Thanks to the colossal stupidity of our enemies, they have lost this opportunity for a scandal, and now it is gone for ever. Should anything be brought up now, you will be forearmed and your assailants will look foolish in the extreme. But while the uncertainty lasted we over here were in a muck sweat, I can tell you, for fear that some reptile [364] or other should get his fangs into the thing before we knew what answer to make and *how* to give him the lie. But what idiots they are! As Tussy said only last Sunday, if *we* had got hold of some information like that about our enemies, what wouldn't we have done with it!

I missed the incident at Potsdam involving William II; what was it [365]? The affair would certainly seem to be assuming a growing pace, and every such straw in the wind is of interest. According to the papers over here, your Emperor intends to relinquish all the honorary colonelships he holds in the Russian army because of the impolite way in which Alexander travelled across his domains. [354] I should say that the Russians are trying to inveigle him into untimely escapades so that *he* may appear to be a disturber of the peace whilst *they*, who are pretty well unassailable, can afford to play for the highest stakes and allow him to purchase peace at the price of further concessions. That they really intend war seems to me impossible. The failure of the French loan [302]—instead of £20 million a bare £12; famine of unprecedented dimensions and intensity; the winter crops virtually destroyed by lack of seed and unfavourable weather; the wholesale death or slaughter of cattle and horses in the most fertile regions for lack of fodder, so that agriculture will be paralysed for years to come—all these are things which, in a semi-barbarous country like Russia, will deprive the army of any prospect of successful action. But despite all this, the Russians are not deterred from behaving politically as though they were deliberately heading for war; this they can permit themselves because of their strategic position and their expertise in betraying their friends. Of course, their little plan may always go awry — hence mobilisation and troop concentrations on a massive scale which, if things go off peacefully, can also serve as an instrument of diplomatic pressure.

Wonderful. France and Russia are confronting the Triple Alliance,[303] based 'on the existing status quo', with a Dual Alliance [288] which has 'a far loftier principle, namely the maintenance of the treaties!' Or so the papers say. Thus France, wishing to *break* the Treaty of Frankfurt, declares itself desirous of supporting it with the help of Russia, while Russia, which customarily breaks all treaties, enters into alliance with this self-same France because of the latter's steadfast demeanour. How stupid men such as *these* must consider the public to whom they address themselves.

Your budget speech was brilliant [366]—to judge by the *Vorwärts*. Do let us have the stenographic report. The allusion to *our* soldiers could not have been more apt. Why keep one's mouth shut about things our enemies know as well as we do?

The fact that Carl Hirsch isn't coming is not, to my mind, a disaster.[a] I didn't like to say anything once matters had been settled, but over here I at once remarked that it wouldn't work out. Hirsch is not only pig-headed but also embittered without reason, believing as he does that he was unfairly excluded from the editorship of the *Sozialdemokrat*; in fact, I believe that his resentment was directed more against Marx and myself than against you people.[367] For, as you will remember, what he wanted was that *we* should *press* him to accept, which had never ever crossed our minds. At all events he thereupon ceased to play any active role and has since accumulated such a mass

---

[a] See this volume, p. 299.

of grievances and crotchets that, if for no other reason, it might, I think, be better were he to void his costiveness elsewhere, after which he will gradually return to a more normal frame of mind and thus again become capable of doing something worthwhile. But I feel sure that Liebknecht and he would not have endured six weeks of each other's company without falling out. Schoenlank, too, has certain bees in his bonnet; so far as I can judge he hasn't nearly enough guts to put up the necessary resistance and will soon chalk up so many sins of omission as to make his chief editor his chief *in real earnest*. Well, we shall have to wait and see how things go — they can't get very much worse.

You are always comparing the situation in Germany with that of 1787-88; it is far more like that of 1847 in France and the scandals which brought about the downfall of Louis Philippe: Teste, the venal minister, the duc de Praslin, who murdered his wife, an equerry to the king who was caught cheating at cards in the Tuileries, or Fould who paid bribes in high places to get into the Légion D'Honneur, etc., etc. What's odd is the way people in Germany carry on about a bank crisis; for the few tin-pot firms that have gone to the wall are quite outside international trade as such — money brokers to civil servants, officers, landed aristocracy, petty bourgeoisie — to everyone in fact except wholesalers. If Anhalt & Wagener, Diskonto-Kommandit, Deutsche Bank, etc., were to put up their shutters, then it might be permissible to speak of a bank crisis. But even so, things aren't so dusty and, if the cloak falls, the Duke will soon come tumbling after.[a]

What you tell me about the kind of 'comrades' who are now presenting themselves is most interesting and also significant so far as the situation is concerned.[368] They have noticed that we are, to use a reptilian expression, becoming a 'factor' in the state and, since the Jews have more intelligence than the other bourgeois, they are the first to notice this — especially under the impulsion of anti-Semitism — and the first to come over to us. We can only be glad of the fact but, precisely *because* these chaps are brighter and have, as it were, been thrown back on and schooled in careerism by centuries of oppression, one has to be rather more on the qui vive.

Please will you convey my best thanks to the parliamentary group for their kind telegram of the 28th.[369] As soon as I get the photo-

---

[a] Paraphrased from Schiller's *Die Verschwörung des Fiesco zu Genua*.

graphs I shall endeavour to pay back in kind all the testimonies of friendship I have received.

Ede tells me you had suggested that he should spend more time at the Society.[89] I am firmly convinced that every minute he spends there would not only be completely wasted but would also discredit the party. He would have to consort with Gilles there and that is completely out of the question. But what he ought to do is frequent the English, get to know the chaps personally and enlighten them about things in Germany by conversing with them; as it is, he sits at home and forms an opinion of local affairs from the accounts he reads in *one* or at most *two* newspapers, there being no coffee houses or reading-rooms in his district.

Finally, let me assure you — as expressly requested — that Louise has executed her commission with a dignity worthy of a president of the Reichstag — at the very least; she had no opportunity for making bad jokes since I invariably forestalled her with some of my own. In other respects we were, however, exceedingly merry during the time in question, not least on account of your ostensible admirer[370] who, on the last page, revealed himself to be a 'Junger'[301] desirous of placing you on the shelf. The fellow is really priceless, with his ultra-High German.

Warm regards to Mrs Julie[a] and yourself from Louise and

Your
F. E.

First published in: Marx and Engels, *Works*, First Russian Edition, Vol. XXVIII, Moscow, 1940

Printed according to the original

Published in English for the first time

---

[a] Julie Bebel

155

ENGELS TO LAURA LAFARGUE

AT LE PERREUX

London, 1 December 1891

My dear Laura,

Your letter of the 28th, postmark Le Perreux 30th, arrived today and took an awful weight off my mind.[a] I have at once sent a translation to Bebel and authorized him to use it whenever necessary.[b]

Fortunately the stupidity of our enemies in Germany has been so colossal that they have, so far at least, seemingly overlooked the whole affair. What I was most afraid of, was that they should raise a storm in Germany before we had been able to ascertain the facts and to be armed with the materials for a crushing reply. Hesitation on the part of the German leaders, or random assertions that might be contradicted, would have been equally dangerous. Now the first danger is over, and although it is quite on the cards that the German Embassy in Paris may have sent reports which in consequence of the usual bureaucratic delays get into the press a week too late, we have a strong position and can meet the charge if it should come.

Still for that purpose it would be important to have Ranc's article. If it was possible to *broder*[c] such stuff upon it, it must form a peculiar canvas, and not only the false report of Paul's speech,[360] but also Ranc's words may be quoted; and we ought to know what they are. Paul merely wrote, Ranc had written in his favour with regard to Bordeaux 1870. Could you procure us the number, and if not, at least say what paper it appeared in, that we may try to hunt it up here?

Now as to other matters.

1) Some time ago I sent you 10s. for account of Sorge for the *Socialiste*; please say whether you have received it, you know how particular old Sorge is.

2) Have you received the copy of 4th edition *Ursprung der Familie*[d] I sent rather more than 3 weeks ago? I sent a lot of copies to the Continent and not one has been acknowledged. As the English Post sim-

---

[a] See this volume, pp. 306-07. - [b] Ibid., p. 307. - [c] embroider - [d] *The Origin of the Family, Private Property and the State*

ply confiscates book-post matter for abroad if a half-penny is short on the postage, I begin to feel rather anxious.

3) Tussy is bothered to death by Greenwood, the secretary of the glass-workers who has sent a lot of money for the French glass-workers on strike and cannot get a single acknowledgment of receipt. He says in a letter to Tussy November 28th that he has sent to Paul same day £49 for that purpose—will you please do your best to get Paul to acknowledge all sums sent through him and also to get Pierre Morrier of Lyons who has had several sums, to do the same? The Castleford Glass Bottle Makers have behaved very well to their French comrades, and the least these latter can do is to acknowledge receipt, so as to enable the senders to *account* for the money to their constituents. Unless this simple act is complied with, it will be doubtful whether the English Trades Unions will not get tired of supporting Continental strikes, and certainly nobody could blame them.

Bebel's speech on the budget was very good.[366] As soon as I get a pretty full report I shall send it you.

Last night a letter from Sam Moore; had arrived at Lagos in the Niger delta, and would be back in the arms of his black wife in about a week or ten days.

Yours ever,

F. Engels

First published, in the language of the original (English), in: F. Engels, P. et L. Lafargue, *Correspondance*, t. III, Paris, 1959

Reproduced from the original

156

ENGELS TO NATALIE LIEBKNECHT [371]

IN BERLIN

London, 2 December 1891

Dear Mrs Liebknecht,

Please accept my sincere thanks for your kind good wishes on yet another birthday [372]; they have, for the present at any rate, been pretty well granted, as I'm in the happy state of being physically fit and mentally alert and I trust this will so continue. We spent an exceedingly cheerful day and good wishes poured in from all sides; even Mr and Mrs Motteler paid us a visit while we were sitting down to our morning glass of beer. In the evening, however, we went to Tussy's where the Bernsteins were also present, and by doing so we frustrated a serenade which had been planned for me by the choir of the Workers' Society.[89] As I did not hear about this until Saturday morning, I was unfortunately not able to warn the gentlemen sooner.[373] All in all I was not sorry that it turned out as it did; I have a deep-rooted aversion to such demonstrations which are impossible to get out of if one's occupation is that of agitator, popular speaker or member of parliament. However I have been lucky enough to avoid them up till now and intend to do so in future.

Otherwise there's nothing particularly new to report; Tussy enjoys the not wholly unjustified reputation of being in charge of the Union of Gasworkers and General Labourers[164] and the week before last she was away for eight days on a propaganda trip to Northern Ireland. But they are in fact quite splendid chaps, these gasworkers, and their union is far more progressive than any of the others. Moreover they're so conversant with agitation 'in conformity with the law' that eighteen months ago in Leeds they fought and won two regular battles, first with the police and then with the police and dragoons, and forced the city council, the owners of the gasworks, to capitulate.[374] As an old soldier I'll say this for Will Thorne, General Secretary of the union, who was in command during these battles — I could not find the slightest fault either in his strategic or in his tactical dispositions.

For the rest, we are leading a somewhat quieter life than at the time when the *Sozialdemokrat* was functioning. Apart from the Avelings and Bernsteins, we see only few people; the Mottelers seldom go out, the Mendelsons are busy with their Polish club on Sunday evenings and, since March of this year, Pumps and her family have been living in Ryde on the Isle of Wight where her husband runs an agency business. I go down to see them occasionally and in July spent a month there, accompanied by Schorlemmer[264] just at the time when the French fleet was in. So far as one can judge from their external appearance, their ironclads, which are of the latest design, are far superior to those of the British. Pumps leads a delightful existence in a little house some 20 minutes' walk from the town and right out in the country, which is obviously an enormous advantage so far as the children are concerned. She is very fond of the life down there and if, as we hope, her husband does well, they will all benefit from having exchanged the air of London for that of the sea. The Isle of Wight is very pretty, indeed beautiful in parts; you can sail right round it in a steamer in seven hours, a very nice trip during which the tyro runs the risk of being seasick for about $2^1/_2$ hours.

Will you please give Liebknecht the enclosed notes and convey to him, as well as to your son,[a] my sincere thanks for their good wishes.

I trust that Berlin will continue to please you and that your health will permit you to enjoy the amenities of the 'imperial capital' in all its aspects. Meanwhile perhaps you will remember kindly

Yours sincerely,

F. Engels

Louise also sends her best wishes to you, Liebknecht and family.

First published in: Marx and Engels, *Works*, First Russian Edition, Vol. XXVIII, Moscow, 1940

Printed according to the original

Published in English in full for the first time

157

ENGELS TO KARL KAUTSKY [177]

IN STUTTGART

London, 3 December 1891

Dear Kautsky,

Your letter of 30 October has long been awaiting an answer; the blame for this must be placed upon Volume III[b] which I am once again sweating away at. I have just got to the most difficult part, i. e. the last chapters (six to eight or thereabouts) on money capital, banks, credit, etc., and, once having started, I shall have to keep at it

---

[a] Theodor Liebknecht - [b] of *Capital*

without a break and work through the relevant literature again, in short make myself completely *au fait*, if only so that I may — as is probable — eventually leave most of it as it stands, yet at the same time feel quite sure that I have committed no blunders either in the positive or the negative sense.

Very many thanks for the reports on Erfurt [301]; they were of value to me in many respects, the discussions of the programme committee being of particular interest. You describe the Executive's draft as *his*, Liebknecht's. Bebel sent me all the material relative to the genesis of this draft [269] from which it is evident that at each stage a fair portion of Liebknecht's initial work had been dropped and replaced with Bebel's propositions until in the end little or nothing remained. What did remain, however, was a lack of coherence, of rigour in the co-ordination of individual propositions, both being attributable to the consideration paid to Liebknecht's work. That was what gave your draft [299] the advantage, as everyone was bound to acknowledge at first glance, and it was that, too, along with Bebel's public admission of the fact, which immediately convinced the others.

The recent investigations, which have rendered obsolete Marx's chapter on the historical trend of capitalist accumulation,[375] are in any case the work of Geiser who is of course regarded in Breslau [a] as a genuine scientific authority. However it is also possible that in his embarrassment Liebknecht said (for he was obviously unaware that these propositions had been taken from *Capital*) the first 'bit of nonsense', as he would put it, that came into his head.

At any rate the theoretical part of the programme is now perfectly presentable; the main thing is that it should contain nothing that is theoretically controversial and in the main this aim has been achieved. The practical demands contain all kinds of snags; many of them seem philistine — if applied to conditions today — but now that we occupy a position of power we can reply quite rightly that they will certainly not be implemented until we come to the helm and that they will then assume quite a different character. As, for instance, free legal advice. A six hours' working day up till the age of 18 obviously ought to have gone in — as also the banning of night work for women and of any sort of work at the very least one month before and 6 weeks after a confinement.

I'm sorry for Liebknecht. For he had to sing the praises of the new

---

[a] Wrocław

programme although it was perfectly plain to everyone that he had had no part in it whatever. But he took on the job of his own accord, so what can one do about it?

What you say about Tölcke's speech is new to me and most interesting.[376] Ede's work[178] goaded the Old Lassalleans into a state of great activity at a time when Marx's letter[a] had already roused them from the complacency induced by the obligatory deification of Lassalle. Even Jacob Audorf, the discoverer of the path of boldness along which we were led by Baron Izzy[377] (as Marx used to call the chap), has been letting forth indignant battle cries amidst the Sunday chit-chat of the *Hamburger Echo*.[b] But they no longer count for anything. Incidentally, Ede got much more upset than he needed to over Bebel's, etc., criticism. Bebel was most reasonable, merely demanding that, so far as the *form* was concerned, his procedure should be such as not, at the very outset, to frighten off those readers with a tradition of Lassalle worship or to give the Old Lassalleans any justified grounds for complaint. To this was added the unfortunate circumstance that Ede had inserted a note that was admittedly quite uncalled for (because he turned it into a piece of tittle-tattle by using 'probably') about syphilis[309] and the worthy censors in Berlin *did not spot this note* until it was too late. The fact that *they* had made a hash of the business caused them, of course, to fly momentarily into a mighty Achillean rage whereupon Ede, of course, had to atone, not only for *his own* lapse but even more for *theirs*, by receiving a number of indignant letters. Naturally I have backed him up as best as I could throughout the whole affair.

The opposition press *lives* on the antithesis of the *national* Lassalle and the *unpatriotic* Social-Democrats. So they'll take care not to lay their hands on a book in which the legend of the nationalist Lassalle is so thoroughly demolished.

Ede's work is really very good and gave me great pleasure; it will elicit the major response it deserves in Germany — in the course of time — and, on completion of this edition, ought to be printed separately and/or expanded by Ede and divested of its special purpose. By then things will have progressed far enough for this to be perfectly feasible. In this country, too, it will have a good effect, for over here your socialistically inclined bourgeois is also seeking to oppose Marx by making a legend out of Lassalle.

---

[a] K. Marx, *Critique of the Gotha Programme.* - [b] [J. Audorf,] 'Zum Parteikongresse', *Hamburger Echo*, No. 245, 1st Supplement, 18 October 1891.

I shall take another look at the letter Labriola wrote to Tussy. My impression is that it would be better *not* to print it. Labriola is very dissatisfied with the way things are going in Italy and I'm not sure that it may not have something to do with his disappointment over the fact that *his* joining the movement did not immediately revive and revolutionise it. So far as I recall, the letter was of the kind that might have elicited dozens of replies. Some strange things are certainly going on there.

You will regret Lafargue's translation from Pélagie[a] to the Chamber. It will deprive you of many a nice article.

Addio.

Your
F. E.

Plekhanov's articles are excellent.[b]

First published in *Aus der Frühzeit des Marxismus. Engels Briefwechsel mit Kautsky*, Prag, 1935

Printed according to the original

Published in English in full for the first time

158

ENGELS TO PAUL LAFARGUE [141]

AT LE PERREUX

London, 3 December 1891

My dear Lafargue,

After your formal repudiation of all those passages in the Bordeaux report[c] of which I had a right to complain, it only remains for me to take back all the wounding words I may have used about you and outright to ask your forgiveness.

As my only excuse I shall describe for your benefit the situation in

---

[a] See this volume, pp. 297-98. - [b] G. W. Plechanow, 'Zu Hegel's sechzigstem Todestag', *Die Neue Zeit*, 10. Jg. 1891/92, 1. Bd., Nr. 7 - 9. - [c] See this volume, pp. 306-07.

which I found myself. One evening^a *The Evening Standard* arrived with the Reuters report you know about [360]; the next evening a bundle of newspapers from Laura, amongst them the *Intransigeant* with the report in question; then a cutting from yet another paper with the same report. All three versions were in agreement on the main point. So what conclusion could I have come to other than that Laura had read those reports and that, if she had sent them to me without a word of comment, they were to all intents and purposes accurate. Hence Paul must have said something of the sort.

Again, it contained things — whether true or not — which could only have been said by you or by Ranc. If said by Ranc, you would certainly not have hesitated to advise me of a fact that could have the gravest repercussions on the situation of the German socialists — well then?

Just so. For our friends in Germany it would mean at best the reintroduction of the Anti-Socialist Law,[11] frenziedly acclaimed by all the Chauvins in our ruling classes, the suppression of our newspapers and meetings, of all our literature and, in the event of war, the arrest of all the LEADERS at the very time when we would have most need of them to take advantage of the impending revolutionary moment. It would also mean the implantation of an element of discord, of mistrust, between French and German working men at the very moment when unity was more necessary than ever.

Thanks to the stupidity of our enemies, these accounts have not yet been cited in the German press. But the Embassy will undoubtedly have made use of them in its reports. And although your disavowal, which was at once passed on to Berlin,^b has lifted a terrible weight from my mind, there is always the danger that the German government will keep this accusation up its sleeve so as to imprison our best men at the outbreak of war and annihilate them with an accusation that would be doubly appalling at a time when chauvinist passions were running riot. So your disavowal would go only half way towards protecting them and this is why.

You say that the reporter embroidered the article by Ranc. But that embroidery, such as it is, would not have been possible had not Ranc at least *sketched out* the design on the canvas. I haven't set eyes on that canvas. So please be so kind as to send me either the article itself or at least a copy of the relevant passages; or else let me know the

---

^a 23 November - ^b See this volume, pp. 301 - 02.

name of the paper and the date of the number in which it appeared so
that I can seek it out here. Then we shall at least know what the attacks will be which we shall have to parry.

Yours ever,

F. Engels

First published in: Marx and Engels,
Works, First Russian Edition, Vol.
XXVIII, Moscow, 1940

Printed according to the original

Translated from the French

159

ENGELS TO LAURA LAFARGUE

AT LE PERREUX

London, 19 December 1891

My dear Laura,

Today I have just the time to inform you that the box with the
usual pudding, cake, etc., has been safely forwarded by the usual in-
strumentality yesterday and hope will reach you safely and in time.

20th December. You see I had *not* 'just the time' yesterday, for the
dinner-bell called me off, it being 5.20 and only ten minutes to spare
before closing of mail — so I thought it better to wait till today.

Schorlemmer cannot come this Christmas, and Pumps and family,
whom I saw at Ryde for a few days last week, are in the same position. So then it struck me; would it not be a bit of a change and rest
for you and Paul to come over and take possession of the top front
bedroom for a week or so? Surely you must want some interruption of
that restless sort of life which Paul's election [330] and its consequences
have thrown you both into. And the bright skies of Paris must make
you long for a good old-fashioned London fog such as is now overhang-
ing me. So I do hope you will make up your minds, and if Paul should
have engagements up to Christmas, you might come first, and he follow next week to spend at least the passage from '91 to '92 with us.

In the meantime I must not forget 'the compliments of the season' and the old-established form in which I ought to present them to you, namely the enclosed bit of pink paper which I hope you will do me the kindness to accept.

Schorlemmer is still suffering from deafness but hopes to be cured, if he can keep free from colds this winter. So I have not the heart to press him, especially as his ear-doctor says he always comes back from London worse than he went.

I am glad Paul has deposed a motion on the separation of Church and State. In his first speech, it appears to me as if the violent interruptions from all sides had prevented him from developing clearly and unmistakably what he intended to say, and that the Dumays and Radicals [147] and even Floquet tried to use that as a peg to hang on their cheap criticisms. This motion will re-establish clearness.[378]

My dear Laura, the fog is getting so perfect that I must give up writing in order not to ruin my eyes — writing by gas-light being still strictly prohibited. So in the hope of soon learning that you are getting ready for the road, and with kind regards from Louise, I remain

ever yours,

F. Engels

First published, in the language of the original (English), in: F. Engels, P. et L. Lafargue, *Correspondance*, t. III, Paris, 1959 and in full in: Marx and Engels, *Works*, First Russian Edition, Vol. XXVIII, Moscow, 1940

Printed according to the original

Published in English in full for the first time

160

ENGELS TO EDUARD BERNSTEIN

IN LONDON

[London,] Wednesday, 23 December 1891

Dear Ede,

Idiot that I am, it never crossed my mind yesterday that you might need some money after your mishap on Sunday[a] and, even though I believe there is some justification for my assuming that you would not have felt shy about mentioning the matter despite such gross remissness on my part, I shall, now that I see the whole thing clearly, hasten to make amends by offering you the unrestricted use of my balance at the bank and my CASH ON HAND. I still have about £5 here at home and tomorrow morning I shall draw some more — FOG PERMITTING.

Warm regards to you all.

Your

F. E.

Käte[b] could spend Friday night with us if you think that would be preferable. Won't be any bother.

First published, in Russian, in *Marx-Engels Archives*, Book 1, Moscow, 1924

Printed according to the original

Published in English for the first time

---

[a] See this volume, p. 324. - [b] Käte Schattner

161

ENGELS TO KARL KAUTSKY [177]

IN STUTTGART

London, 27 December 1891

Dear Baron,

A line or two in haste. I have fallen very far behind with everything as a result of a five-day fog which (abetted by tippling) has again affected my eyes somewhat and, on top of that, the following extras:

1. Proof correction of the English CONDITION OF THE WORKING-CLASS,[a] of which so far 6 sheets remain unread.

2. Revision of Aveling's translation of Entwicklung des Sozialismus,[b] which has got to be done properly; since I live in the place of publication I shall ineluctably be held responsible for every slip.

3. The colossal amount of correspondence, swollen by the festive season.

Not to mention a working day greatly curtailed by having to spare my eyes.

You will understand that, since work on Volume III[c] must be resumed as soon as possible and thereafter continued without interruption until finished, I shall only be able to run through your ms.[379] very cursorily, but what can be done I shall gladly do.

The new things about exchange value and value in the third edition of Capital[d] derive from handwritten addenda of Marx's, of which unfortunately there are very few, while such as there are were elaborated in the very difficult circumstances of illness. Marx spent a long time searching for the mot juste and made a lot of corrections.

So far as Fireman[380] is concerned, it is certainly quite plausible that, if $\frac{v}{c} = {}^1/_2 = {}^1/_3 = {}^1/_4 = {}^1/_5$, etc., occurs in practice, then one fraction or another should correspond to the proportion whereby profit and surplus value coincide (crudely speaking, for it is also subject to all manner of reservations). However, the chap is nevertheless to be commend-

---

[a] F. Engels, The Condition of the Working-Class in England in 1844. - [b] F. Engels, Socialism: Utopian and Scientific. - [c] of Capital - [d] K. Marx, Das Kapital. Kritik der politischen Oekonomie. Erster Band. Buch I: Der Produktionsprocess des Kapitals. Dritte vermehrte Auflage, Hamburg, 1883.

ed for having lighted on this idea. If he is agreeable, please send me his paper. It will, indeed, have to remain closeted in my desk until such time as I write the preface to Volume III,[a] at which point, *provided it is really worth the trouble*, I shall be able to accord it a place alongside other attempted solutions. I can do no more and with that Schmidt, too, was content.[381] If he doesn't like it, let him publish his paper and see what happens.

That poor R. Meyer should be reduced to taking refuge with us is almost tragic. POOR DEVIL, in addition to bad luck and diabetes, he has found out just what his conservative friends, wherever they may be, are like.[382]

Having boxed Gilles' ears, Aveling is in even less of a position to reply to his flysheets. Gilles doesn't of course publish that kind of filth in the press over here, and no one could expect Aveling to sue him for LIBEL and spend several hundred pounds on bringing a law-suit only to see Gilles vanish into thin air on the eve of the proceedings. Labouchère, when accused of LIBEL, was asked by defending counsel: 'HAVE YOU EVER BROUGHT AN ACTION FOR LIBEL?' 'No,' came the reply, 'I NEVER WAS SUCH A FOOL.' Whereat judge and lawyers alike pronounced him one of the leading authorities ON THE LAW OF LIBEL.

The Berliners, or Liebknecht at any rate, have made fools of us over the compositors' strike.[383] Mr Döblin, who came over here on behalf of the compositors, bearing letters of introduction from Liebknecht to everyone you can think of *save Ede and myself*, has not only ignored the German party over here, but has treated it *de haut en bas*[b] and denigrated it, at any rate in a *negative* sense. At Burns' he said the party had done *nothing whatever* for them, whereas it had in fact donated 20,000 marks. And when Sanders who was there asked him whether the entire party press hadn't backed them up, he was forced to admit that it had. And then Liebknecht writes[153] asking me to do everything I can for the compositors, but omitting to tell me what he and the party have done and not so much as mentioning the fact that one of the chaps' representatives is over here. In the circumstances I could not, of course, do anything — after all, it was only through the *English* press that I learnt what was afoot and I wasn't a fool as to impose myself on a man who had carefully shunned the party and dealt with the TRADES COUNCIL[196] direct. This, as you can imagine, was grist to the Hyndman-Gilles mill — 'Now you can see,' they say,

---

[a] In the ms: of the third edition - [b] with contempt

'that there's nothing whatever behind the much vaunted German party. Even the workers don't want to have anything to do with it and say it's no good.' And only this week we see the fruits thereof in the *Justice* in which Gilles publicly sides with the Independents.[a][333] A piece of good luck, as it happens, for it means that Hyndman will compromise himself and put his foot in it just as he did of yore with Brousse & Co.

The German bosses will be fools if they don't now introduce linotype machines which are increasingly being used by all the big newspapers both here and in New York.

Burns was horrified to learn that the compositors are given 21 M a week strike pay whereas here it's never more than 10 or 15sh. at the outside.

When the compositors sent someone over here, our Berlin chaps should either have *insisted* that he act in concert with Ede, the German party's representative here, or else have refused to co-operate. The party is no longer under any compulsion to throw itself at the heads of these aristocrats of the working class.

Last Sunday[b] Ede was burgled and lost £10, as you may already have heard. His nerves are in a very bad state and he needs rest and fresh air.

Thanks for your good wishes. Our entire household, including Tidlums, wish you and your wife[c] and your son[d] the best of health and happiness in the coming year. Tidlums has grown into a large, majestic tomcat, the sultan of all the female cats in Regent's Park Road and the terror of all competitors and rivals.

Your

F. Engels

First published in *Aus der Frühzeit des Marxismus. Engels Briefwechsel mit Kautsky*, Prag, 1935

Printed according to the original

Published in English in full for the first time

---

[a] F. Gilles, 'The Independent Socialists in Germany', *Justice*, No. 415, 26 December 1891. - [b] 20 December - [c] Luise Kautsky, née Ronsperger - [d] Felix Kautsky

162

ENGELS TO ANNA AND HERMANN SCHLÜTER [384]

IN HOBOKEN

London, 30 December 1891

A Happy New Year!

Louise
General

First published in: Marx and Engels, *Works*, Second Russian Edition, Vol. 50, Moscow, 1981

Printed according to the original

Published in English for the first time

1892

163

ENGELS TO THE LIEBKNECHT FAMILY [385]

IN BERLIN

[London, 1 January 1892]

A Happy New Year.
F. Engels, L. Kautsky, Gine Bernstein,
Eug. Oswald, Tussy, Edward,[a] *Ede.*

First published in: Marx and Engels, *Works*, Second Russian Edition, Vol. 38, Moscow, 1965

Printed according to the original

Published in English for the first time

164

ENGELS TO FRIEDRICH ADOLPH SORGE [386]

IN HOBOKEN

London, 6 January 1892

Dear Sorge,

I hope you received our New Year's greetings card. Today I shall reply to your letters of 20 and 23 November and 9 December.

I have happily survived my 71st birthday and am, all in all, healthier and stronger than 5 or 6 years since. If I go on till 1900 — though I don't know whether this would be a blessing or the reverse — I shall, I hope, still witness all manner of things. In America

---

[a] Aveling

you've got a movement which progresses by UPS AND DOWNS, frequently disappoints, and is therefore readily conducive to a mood of pessimism. If I incline to the opposite extreme, it is through having here, before my very eyes, a European movement which is on the whole making gigantic strides and has at its core the German movement, steadily forging ahead with the inexorability of a natural force. I have written something on the subject[a] for the French almanac and shall send it you as soon as I get another copy.

War with Russia has fortunately been delayed by another 3 or 4 years, provided nothing idiotic is done anywhere. Since a peaceful course of development in Germany promises victory for us under the *most favourable* circumstances — somewhat later perhaps, but all the more surely for that — there is no reason for us to stake our all on a gamble, as we would have to do should there be such a war.

I do not believe there is as yet room for a *third* party in America. In that vast area the disparity of interests, even in the *same* section of one class, is so great that completely different sections and interests are represented according to locality in each of the two big parties and that, to a very great extent, virtually every separate stratum of the propertied class has its representatives in each of the two parties, although *nowadays* big industrialists constitute the bulk of the Republicans as do the big Southern landowners that of the Democrats. The apparent fortuitousness of this amalgam is a first-rate breeding-ground for corruption and the exploitation of the state which thrive so wonderfully over there. Only when the land — the public lands — is entirely in the hands of speculators, i. e. when settlement has become increasingly difficult and/or subject to fraud, only then, or so it seems to me, will the time have come for a third party, provided, that is, things develop *peacefully*. Speculation is based on the *land* and the mania as also opportunity for speculation in America are the chief means whereby the native-born workers are kept in thrall to the bourgeoisie. Only when there is a race of native-born workers with *nothing more* to expect from speculation, shall we have firm ground beneath our feet in America. But then, who can expect things to develop *peacefully* in America? There you have sudden economic advances like the political ones in France — where they admittedly also have the same momentary set-backs.

[a] F. Engels, 'Le Socialisme en Allemagne', *Almanach du Parti ouvrier pour 1892*, Lille, 1892.

It seems improbable that the small farmers and the lower middle classes, consisting as these do of all-too rapidly changing elements, will ever succeed in forming a strong party; furthermore the farmer is often a migrant who cultivates 2, 3 or 4 farms in succession in various states and territories [387]; in both cases immigration and bankruptcy promote a steady turn-over of individuals, while economic dependence on creditors is yet another impediment to independence. On the other hand, however, they provide a first-rate element for politicians who make capital out of their discontent and then proceed to sell them to one of the big parties.

The 'doggedness' of the YANKEES who are actually resurrecting GREENBACK HUMBUG again [388] is a consequence of their theoretical backwardness and their Anglo-Saxon contempt for all theory. By way of retribution they are inflicted with a superstitious belief in any kind of philosophical and economic nonsense, and indulge in religious sectarianism and economically idiotic experiments, the benefit of which, however, is reaped by sundry bourgeois cliques.

Louise asks that you should send her *nothing but* the *Woman's Journal (Boston)* and this *only up till 31 March* unless otherwise advised by us. She needs it for the Vienna *Arbeiterinnen-Zeitung* (of which she, Laura and Tussy are the mainstays) and says it wouldn't occur to her to impose the foolish chit-chat of the American SWELL MOB LADIES on her working women. Thanks to your kindness in sending her the things, she is once more *au courant* and able to see that the said ladies are still as snotty and narrow-minded as ever they were and only wants to give this one paper a month or two's trial. In the meantime she thanks you most sincerely for your good offices.

At his first appearance in the Chamber Lafargue allowed himself to be somewhat flummoxed by the interjections and general uproar.[378] But he'll soon make up for it. The French always improve when engaged in hand-to-hand fighting.

The position as regards Gompers *is this*. He wrote, sending me detailed PAPERS concerning his association.[389] I was away a great deal at the time—during the summer [264]—besides being tremendously busy, nor had I any clear idea of what was afoot and supposed that *Iliacos extra peccatur muros et intra.*[a] Then I heard that Gompers was going to Brussels and might come here, so I thought things could be settled by word of mouth. Later, when he *didn't* turn up, I put off do-

---

[a] Sins were committed within as without the walls of Troy (Horace, *Epistles*, I, 2, 16).

ing anything. But I shall look out the papers and then reply to him; I thanked him for the list.

The other day I wrote to K. Kautsky [153] asking him to inquire from Dietz about the publication of your articles in book form [358] and am still awaiting a reply. More haste less speed, as they say in Germany, especially in Stuckert[a] on the Neckar's banks.

Blatchford has left *The Workman's Times*, which is a great relief. For that matter the paper evinces the defects that will always be inseparable from any such *private* undertaking in this country so long as it isn't backed by a party strong enough to control it.

I have now got to 1. read the proofs of the new edition of the CONDITION OF THE WORKING-CLASS IN ENGLAND 1844, 2. go over Aveling's translation of the *Entwicklung des Sozialismus*,[b] 3. attend to a few other oddments [390] and then 4. get down to Volume III[c] again, having now the most difficult chapters ahead of me. However, I think I shall manage if I vigorously exclude everything extraneous. What will then remain to be done will not, I believe, present any but formal difficulties.

Warm regards to your wife[d] and yourself from L. Kautsky and

Your

F. Engels

First published abridged in *Briefe und Auszüge aus Briefen von Joh. Phil. Becker, Jos. Dietzgen, Friedrich Engels, Karl Marx u. A. an F. A. Sorge und Andere*, Stuttgart, 1906 and in full in: Marx and Engels, *Works*, First Russian Edition, Vol. XXIX, Moscow, 1946

Printed according to the original

---

[a] Stuttgart - [b] F. Engels, *Socialism: Utopian and Scientific*. - [c] of *Capital* - [d] Katharina Sorge

165

ENGELS TO LAURA LAFARGUE

AT LE PERREUX

London, 6 January 1892

My dear Laura,

The pears have arrived in very good condition, the few that were urgently in want of being devoured, have been at once attended to, and the rest is being gradually, thankfully and pleasurably consumed. That the old Fry's Cocoa box should return to us with such agreeable contents, and as they say of expired directors in joint-stock companies, 'offer itself for re-election' next Christmas, was a pleasant surprise indeed.

Paul wants to know about the constitution of the Board of Health.[391] I will try to find it out, but am afraid I shall have to ask Tussy or Edward to hunt it up at the British Museum. If I only knew the year when the Board of Health was instituted, I might get the original Act of Parliament—if Sam was here, we should have it in a jiffy.

Your intermittent husband seems to be indeed seized with the fever of the wandering Jew—perhaps he wants to supersede him by the wandering Nigger[392]? Anyhow the proposition about separation of Church and State in the sense of the Commune[378] was the best thing he could do, it stops their mouths at once. Especially now when the French Clergy begin to face the eventuality and try to make it out that they ought to be, in that case, disestablished as the Church of Ireland was,[393] that is to say not only keep all their property, but have the salaries capitalised and bought off in a lump sum—*les milliards de l'Eglise! après ceux de M. Bismarck!*[a][394] The priests are too much in a hurry for to pronounce this is to make it impossible. If the thing was kept quiet, and sprung upon the people all at once in the shape of a government proposition, the surprise might pass, and the Radicals[147] would only be too glad to swallow it—but to have it discussed in public beforehand, is to ensure its failure. The French Republic, with its revolutionary principles of civil law, cannot *buy off*

---

[a] the thousands of millions of the Church! After those of Mr Bismarck!

the Church in the way the English semi-feudal monarchy did. Here the system developed by Lassalle in Vol. 1st of his *System der erworbenen Rechte* [166] is alone applicable, as it was exclusively applied by the Great Revolution. See Bernstein's Introduction to Lassalle's *Works*,[178] if you have not got it I'll try to get it. It is Lassalle's *only* juridical *Leistung*,[a] and not a great one, but quite correct *juridically*. *We* ought to start it in France, and *then* set Longuet to work the Radicals in that sense.

I have to interrupt again. Old Harney is laid up with bronchitis in Richmond — same complaint which last spring brought him to the grave's edge. I must go and see him, but hope to be back in time to finish that letter. I am crushed with work, there are 1) proof-sheets and new preface of new English edition of *Lage der arbeitenden Klassen in England*,[b] 2) revision of Edward's translation of *Entwicklung des Socialismus* — with another new preface, 3) German translation of my article[c] in the *Almanach before* anybody else seizes upon it, 4) a lot of letters to answer. And then *possibly* I may return to Vol. III[d] where just the very difficultest chapters of all await me.

4.30 p. m. Just returned from Richmond where I found old Harney much better — hope it will last.

I suppose you have got Louise's *Arbeiterinnen-Zeitung* with the Vienna *Arbeiter-Zeitung* direct from Vienna. Your article reads uncommonly well, Tussy's article will be in next number,[314] and as the paper is by its nature insatiable, I can only say that all further contributions will be thankfully received, in the meantime I send you Louise's thanks which like all thanks are double-edged, viz. 1) thanks for favours received, 2) 'a sense of favours to come', as the bourgeois said.

Poor Adler is sadly overworked, and moreover, the momentary rest he gets, he only gets as the nurse of his wife[e] who is seriously ill — they are at Salò, Lago di Garda, for the present. And as Victor is responsible for the filling of the paper, you do an indirect kindness to him and the Austrian party by helping to fill the women's paper with *good* matter; the *bourgeoises émancipées* would only be too glad of an opportunity of deposing their crotchets and nostrums in the working women's organ.

---

[a] achievement - [b] *The Condition of the Working-Class in England* - [c] F. Engels, 'Der Sozialismus in Deutschland'. - [d] of *Capital* - [e] Emma Adler

Pumps has been out of sorts a bit, so that she could not come during the holidays, but we shall have her and the children here in the course of this month.

What in the world made Vaillant fight that fool Gégout — *égout*[a]?

Love from Louise and myself to both of you. And do keep in mind the obligation you are under to come over here with Paul before long. It will do some of our working men good to see a live French *député socialiste*.

A vous de coeur[b]

F. E.

First published, in the language of the original (English), in: F. Engels, P. et L. Lafargue, *Correspondance*, t. III, Paris, 1959

Reproduced from the original

166

ENGELS TO LAURA LAFARGUE

AT LE PERREUX

London, 20 January 1892

My dear Laura,

Last night I had a letter from Paul from Bordeaux in which he writes me to send you a cheque to pay the *propriétaire*.[c] Now I should only be too glad to help you over this *mauvais quart d'heure*,[d] but the fact is, January and February are my worst months in the year, Christmas pumps one out almost completely, and I have next to nothing to come in before 1-5th March. In fact I do not yet see my way how to get over this awkward time myself, as besides the usual Christmas expenses, I had some considerable extra advances to make. Old Harney I had to lend money when he was ill, and Tussy and Edward have mortgaged with me the proceeds of four agreements with Sonnenschein, on which I advanced them a pretty round sum which comes in from Sonnenschein only gradually and at rather uncertain

---

[a] bastard - [b] Yours sincerely - [c] landlady - [d] bad spell

times—certainly not now when I want it most. In fact I am hard up myself. But if you can manage to find some one who, on my giving him my cheque for the amount, *dated say March 5th*, so that it cannot be presented before that date, will advance you the needful, then you can have my cheque with pleasure. I should think Deville might do that, as my cheque is absolutely safe. In that case please let me know what the amount is, for Paul merely speaks of '*un chèque*'.

My article[a] in the *Almanach* is appearing in Italian in the *Critica Sociale* and yesterday I was at last able to send to Bebel the German text of it — with a rather lengthy postscriptum on the Russian famine, which insures peace for a time and deprives my article of its most actual *actualité*.

The fight with Hyndman & Co. goes on here — at present the Kommunistischer Arbeiterverein[89] is the chief theatre, and there is a chance of Gilles being beaten and kicked out, and then Hyndman will have made with his German speculation (backing Gilles) even a worse *four*[b] than in his French speculation on Brousse.[395]

Hyndman you know is candidate for Parliament in Chelsea. When his meetings in Sloane Square were stopped by the police he was fined 1s. and paid it, and gave up Sloane Square. Now he makes the Federation[29] fight for a far worse place in Chelsea called *the World's End* (the name is enough to show it's no place for public meetings). Well they have had some 15-18 men summoned and sentenced, and now they tried to get the *other bodies* out to fight their battle, under the name of 'the right of public meeting in danger'. For Hyndman said, if he could keep this going on till the dissolution, *his seat was safe*. But it won't come off. The Gas Workers said they would send speakers to be arrested and tried, *if Hyndman on that occasion took the chair*[396]; and at a meeting last week where Burns, Edward and Tussy were, Hyndman was terribly taunted with his cowardice, and finally the whole attempt to rescue Hyndman by the intervention of the other Societies and Trades Unions was practically dropped. Croesel, one of our best Germans here, told Hyndman to his face he was a liar, in public delegate meeting, and he pocketed it.

Now I must go and see Ede Bernstein who has had the influenza, so good-bye. Louise says as Paul is always away you might use your spare time to write something for the *Arbeiterinnen-Zeitung* — you see she is awfully ambitious to make the Viennese paper beat the Stuttgart

---

[a] F. Engels, 'Le Socialisme en Allemagne. - [b] blunder

one[a] which however won't be difficult — that was first edited by Frau Ihrer, and damned badly, and now poor Clara Zetkin has it, and the first two Nos are certainly very poor and very slow. So if you have something to tell about *ces charmantes françaises*[b] and their movements, all the better.

I hope your animal family is going on all right — we have the influenza all round us, but so far our two servants here have only got a touch of it, Louise suffers from what my poor wife[c] used to call 'pains all over' (general muscular rheumatism) and I am not yet caught.

Ever yours,
F. Engels

First published in: Marx and Engels, *Works*, Second Russian Edition, Vol. 38, Moscow, 1965

Reproduced from the original

Published in English for the first time

167

ENGELS TO KARL KAUTSKY

IN STUTTGART

London, 26 January 1892

Dear Baron,

Proofs of the article[d] promptly returned yesterday. I cannot attend to those of the *Anti-Proudhon*[e] as I have got to tackle Volume III[f] without delay and look over the English translation of the *Entwicklung*[g], which I cannot refuse to do since it is I, after all, who will be held responsible for anything of that kind that appears in *London*; so I can take on *absolutely nothing else whatever*.

If the Berliners should object to anything in my article, I would ask you to substitute *dots*. There can be no question of toning things down

---

[a] *Die Gleichheit* - [b] these charming French ladies - [c] Lizzy Burns - [d] F. Engels, 'Der Sozialismus in Deutschland'. - [e] K. Marx, *The Poverty of Philosophy. Answer to the 'Philosophy of Poverty' by M. Proudhon*. - [f] of *Capital* - [g] F. Engels, *Socialism: Utopian and Scientific*.

because the French original is generally accessible and I might be accused of *falsifying* the text.

I should be grateful if you would send me the proofs of the *Poverty* — for I've got to take another look at the preface[a] in any case.

I have written and told Dietz,[153] by whom I've been saddled with a draft for an address to Bebel on the 25th anniversary of his entry into Parliament,[153] that in future *all* my fees are to be sent to Adler. As it is, the Berliners get the lion's share, since I can't deprive them of those accruing from what is published by the *Vorwärts* publishers. So it's only fair.

Well, the happy result of Julius'[b] underground activities was to get Gilles evicted from the Society[89] by 48 votes to 21, at 3 o'clock on Sunday morning.[c] He (Julius) conducted the campaign most ably and called in here on Sunday evening; he was full of beans and gave us a delightfully humorous account of his negotiations with the Society members whom he conjured up to the life. It was the same old story. At first the dullards thought they were only 7 strong, a figure which, on further investigation, turned out to be more like 50 — good men, if sluggardly—but once they'd been got together and galvanised into action, Gilles was done for. It's a matter of some significance because, in the eyes of the English, it has knocked the ground from under his feet; Hyndman is the only one who now has him hanging at his coat-tails, nor will he be able to shake him off.

Hyndman has also suffered some severe defeats. See the account in last week's *Workman's Times* of the delegates' negotiations at the So-CIAL DEMOCRATIC FEDERATION[29] HALL, Strand, concerning the FREE SPEECH MEETING at the World's End, Chelsea. On that occasion he was hard pressed by Shaw, Burns and Tussy. Burns said that, if it came to the point, he hoped it would not be necessary to go and look for speakers in the LAVATORIES (as for Hyndman in Trafalgar Square[397]), etc. Hyndman, he went on, could have saved the day if, instead of the untenable World's End (300 men constitute an OBSTRUCTION OF TRAFFIC, whereupon the police have *got* to intervene), he had stuck to Sloane Square which he had relinquished on being fined one SHILLING. The GASWORKERS said they would attend if there was any prospect of a fight, and would provide speakers if Hyndman would preside.[396] In short, his cowardice was at long last brought home to him. On Sunday he

---

[a] F. Engels, 'Marx and Rodbertus. Preface to the First German Edition of *The Poverty of Philosophy* by Karl Marx'. - [b] Julius Motteler - [c] 24 January

fared even worse at the delegates' meeting about the same subject. A SOCIAL DEMOCRATIC FEDERATION man said that the SOCIAL DEMOCRATIC FEDERATION was too weak to carry the thing off on its own and since it apparently was on its own, ought to drop it; someone else said that it wouldn't do for Hyndman to be arrested since the SOCIAL DEMOCRATIC FEDERATION was solely dependent on subsidies from MIDDLE—CLASS PEOPLE, ESPECIALLY Hyndman and Hunter Watts. The jackass has got so involved in his own intrigues that things may go badly for him. The real nub of the matter, as he himself had privately said, was this: if the squabbling over the World's End RIGHT OF MEETING could be kept going until the dissolution of Parliament, *it would ensure his being returned in Chelsea* (for which he is standing).

Many regards and my congratulations on the birth of your second son.[a] But surely it is now time you slowed down the tempo a bit? We are glad to hear that mother[b] and child are doing well. Over here influenza is still on the rampage; Percy had it, and pneumonia immediately afterwards; I anxiously await news of Pumps. Louise also had a touch of it, likewise Aveling.

Well, once again warm regards from Louise and

Your
General

First published in *Aus der Frühzeit des Marxismus. Engels Briefwechsel mit Kautsky*, Prag, 1935

Printed according to the original

Published in English for the first time

168

ENGELS TO KARL KAUTSKY

IN STUTTGART

London, 28 January 1892

Dear Baron,

Your omission of Bebel and Liebknecht ALL RIGHT.[398] It makes no difference at all to the thing.

---

[a] Karl - [b] Luise Kautsky (née Ronsperger)

Six Centuries, etc.[399] would probably be worth translating, more so at any rate than the same author's *Economic Interpretation of History*, most of which he undoubtedly cribbed from *Capital*; it is somewhat pedantically written although it does contain individual insights. In *Six Centuries* there is much that is unknown in Germany—genuine material but a number of false interpretations, as is inevitable with a bourgeois. But I should have thought you'd have found writing works of your own pleasanter and more necessary than translating.

Kindest regards from

Your

General

First published in *Aus der Frühzeit des Marxismus. Engels Briefwechsel mit Kautsky,* Prag, 1935

Printed according to the original

Published in English for the first time

169

ENGELS TO FLORENCE KELLEY-WISCHNEWETZKY

IN NEW YORK

London, 28 January [18]92

Dear Mrs Wischnewetzky,

1) The following is an abstract of my agreement with Swan Sonnenschein and Co.

a) we (that is I in yours and Mrs Aveling's name) transfer to them the *English* copyright of the *Condition*[a] etc.;

b) that they produce it in one volume in their Social Science Series;

c) that they pay us (i. e. you through me) $12^{1}/_{2}\%$ on full price (2s. 6d. per copy), 13 copies to be reckoned for 12;

d) the same for stereotype plates and copies sold for colonies;

---

[a] F. Engels, *The Condition of the Working-Class in England in 1844.*

e) the same on proceeds of copies sold by auction, or at reduced prices;

f) that we do not suffer from bad debts contracted by them;

g) that accounts be made up as on 30th June each year and settled within 3 months;

h) that we get 12 free copies.

----

2) The book is now printed, out of the appendix.[a] I have made a new preface for the British reader.[b] I have suppressed the preface of the American edition. On reading the proofs I have changed a few expressions, chiefly technical terms and evident misprints or slips of the press. As soon as I get our copies I shall send you six of them.

I had another tussle with Sonnenschein, but again had the best of him. On reading proof of title page, I found that he had struck out your name on the front and put it on the back in small print! Of course I at once protested, and asked Dr Aveling to see him about this, as I could not submit to have the translator, and the party *whose simple agent I was in this matter*, thus insulted. Of course the man gave in, but it seems impossible to do business with him without having to fight such little tricks. And all this on account of that unpronounceable Russian name which he fears might injure the sale of the book, as its bearer surely cannot be expected to know English!

3) I shall account and remit proceeds to you as soon as received every year.

4) Of course this arrangement with Swan Sonnenschein and Co. puts an end to the agency, for this book, of Reeves. I have, through the kindness of Dr Aveling who lives close to Reeves' shop, after a deal of trouble managed to get an account out of him, it amounts to about £5, and also part of the money; there are £4 to be paid yet, but the fellow has caught the influenza just in time to excuse delay, so that I do not expect to get it before next week — *if then,* for it is easier to get the truth out of a statesman than a farthing of cash

----

[a] F. Engels, *Appendix* [to *The Condition of the Working Class in England in 1844* (1887)]. -
[b] F. Engels, 'Preface to the 1892 English Edition of *The Condition of the Working-Class in England in 1844*'.

out of Reeves. This settlement therefore must be delayed til my next.

5) Sonnenschein asked me, would it be right for him to *send copies to America*? I replied certainly not, for the American edition was still on sale, and then I doubted whether you *could* give him a valid permission to do so even if you liked. But I said I would submit the matter to you, and of course in the meantime he does not send any copies.

So, this is I believe the whole budget of news I have to send you to-day, and as I am obliged to write about half a dozen long letters to-day, I must conclude.

Yours faithfully,
F. Engels

First published in: D. R. Blumberg, *Florence Kelly*, New York, 1966   Reproduced from the original

170

ENGELS TO HERMANN ENGELS

IN BARMEN

London, 28 January 1892

Dear Hermann,

I think it's high time I let you have some news of myself again, the more so because gently impelled thereto by business. For in your last statement you credited me with 79.40 marks, being a reimbursement by F. Engels & Co. This is presumably the cost of the power of attorney, certified by notary and consul at Rudolf's request. Otherwise everything seems to tally.

Then I should also like you to tell me how much the Schaaffhausens you are holding for me are actually worth today, i. e. the price and nominal value of my shares. The holding was reduced at one time and so I no longer know exactly how many I've got; there is a possibility I might prefer to get rid of the lot.

For the rest, I can't complain. My health is pretty good; my eye trouble has more or less cleared up and can be disregarded apart from the fact of my not writing by lamplight which admittedly is awkward in wintertime. I still enjoy eating and drinking, can still walk pretty briskly and am generally considered to be one of the youngest old men in London. On the other hand I have to restrict my smoking very considerably because, like good wine and, alas, Pilsener beer also, it tends to upset the cardiac nerves which, in turn, makes me sleep badly. But this only lasts from the New Year to the spring, during which time I take sulphonal once a week, and that sees me through the bad months as well—the sulphonal all comes from Bayers in Elberfeld—and, as soon as the weather is good and I can get out into the open air, things begin to look up again, and then comes the summer with holidays beside or on the sea, when I shall once again be on top of my form. Last summer I spent 4 weeks in the Isle of Wight followed by a fortnight in Scotland and Ireland,[264] mostly afloat; this is what always suits me best, now that riding is out of the question. If I could go riding here in winter and spend the summer at sea, then I should certainly be on top of my form again. But since this can't be done, I shall have to content myself with climbing London's Chimborazo, namely Hampstead Heath, which is about the same height above sea level as your house in Barmen, that is 150 metres. Fortunately this suffices at a pinch to keep one's spirits up.

So far I have fortunately missed having influenza which, however, is a veritable scourge over here; people in my street are going down like flies, though they most of them eventually recover; but it seems to be a wretched affliction, and makes everyone so terribly depressed that it quite takes one's appetite away.

But now it is your turn to tell me how things are with you, what you and Emma are doing and all the children and grandchildren, Rudolf, Hedwig and their not inconsiderable appurtenances, the Blanks, the Engelskirchen lot—indeed, all the innumerable hordes of whom one simply can't keep track over here. Since Rudolf Blank left this country I no longer get any news, particularly since marriages and christenings seem to have become fewer and further between; these used to provide as it were milestones which enabled one to keep tabs on what you were all of you up to.

With love to Emma and all your family, the Rudolfs, Hedwig & Co. & Co.

Your old
Friedrich

First published in *Deutsche Revue*, Jg. 46, Bd. III, Stuttgart-Leipzig, 1921

Printed according to the original

Published in English for the first time

171

ENGELS TO HERMANN ENGELS

IN BARMEN

London, 29 January 1892

Dear Hermann,

It is often said of women that what they really have to say never goes into the letter but into the postscript. But we old buffers are in even worse case—for hardly was yesterday's letter[a] in the post when I remembered the most important thing of all. Namely that, in strange contrast to the surplus of cash on the London money market, I am suffering from a slight shortage of that article and, since I can only expect small dividends up till 1 March, I should be grateful if, some time soon, you could send me some £30 of the balance you hold on my behalf. Then I shall make out quite well; between March and June money will again be coming in at a brisk pace.

Love from

Your
Friedrich

First published in *Deutsche Revue*, Jg. 46, Bd. III, Stuttgart-Leipzig, 1921 ·

Printed according to the original

Published in English for the first time

---

[a] See previous letter.

172

ENGELS TO KARL KAUTSKY

IN STUTTGART

London, 1 February 1892

Dear Baron,

Herewith Labriola's letter to Tussy; I don't believe that you could pull off publishing it without creating bad blood amongst divers persons in Italy, and in the end it would be the German party that would have to suffer for it, in as much as the *latter* would be held responsible for taking sides with or against those people who felt affronted by the article. For in Italy things are in such a mess that all kinds of people are sure to feel affronted, whether rightly or wrongly, as indeed I have written and told Labriola.[153] And those people would then be driven into the arms of the Possibilists,[3] Hyndmanists, Fabians[87] and God knows what other dogs-in-the-manger.

I have written and told Labriola that I thought it better not to publish but would leave the matter entirely in your hands and that you two should sort it out between you. At all events, *Tussy wants to have the letter back.*

It recently occurred to me that an account of *Luther* based on his actions and writings is urgently called for. In the first place a rectification not only of the Protestant legend, but also of the blinkered Catholic attack upon it by Janssen (who is now doing so well in Germany) would certainly not come amiss just now, and there is a distinct need for a demonstration, from *our* standpoint, of the extent to which the Reformation was a *bourgeois* movement. Also of particular importance would be a parallel between Luther *before* and Luther *after* Karlstad, the Anabaptists and the Peasant War,[400] on the one hand and, on the other, the bourgeoisie *before* 1848 and *after* that year. Likewise a detailed demonstration of how this transformation came about in Luther's case. There's still something to be accomplished in this field, and without any need for undue study; also it's something for which you are particularly fitted as a result of your

Thomas Morus.[a] And again you have in Stuckert[b] a library on Protestantism that is second to none. Surely that would be better than translating Rogers[399] whom any child could translate.

Greetings from one family to the other.

Your

F. E.

First published in *Aus Frühzeit des Marxismus. Engels Briefwechsel mit Kautsky*, Prag, 1935

Printed according to the original

Published in English for the first time

173

ENGELS TO AUGUST BEBEL

IN BERLIN

London, 2 February 1892

Dear August,

Am glad you liked the article.[c] I fully approve of the omission of the two names on the second occasion.[398] So far as France was concerned the repetition was necessary; in Germany it might do some harm and is in any case wholly superfluous.

Why, you ask, are the Russians still acting in a warlike manner and concentrating troops in the West? Nothing could be simpler. In my very first letter,[d] in which I maintained that the famine would put paid to Russia's desire for war, I told you that their sabre-rattling, far from ceasing, would tend to grow louder. It's what they always do. But only for the benefit of the public at home and abroad; foreign diplomats are not expected to *believe* but merely to *acquiesce* in it. The public is intended to see Russia's retreat as the retreat of the others before Russia.— But this time another factor is involved. The south-east

---

[a] K. Kautsky, *Thomas More und seine Utopie.* - [b] Stuttgart - [c] F. Engels, 'Der Sozialismus in Deutschland'. - [d] See this volume, pp. 242-46.

and the east are in a state of famine and cannot provision an army. The area where the harvest has failed is roughly bounded by the line which runs through Odessa, Moscow, Vyatka and Perm up to the Urals, then along this range to the northern extremity of the Caspian, from there to the eastern extremity of the Sea of Azov and back again to Odessa. Proof that only east [a] of the Odessa-Moscow line can large numbers of troops be provisioned; anywhere further north will itself need to be constantly supplied with corn. Besides, the Russians are now disseminating information about the movements of troops to the west that is downright *false*.

A comment in Sunday's [b] *Vorwärts* in no way tallies with what you say about your correspondence with Frenchmen regarding Alsace-Lorraine [401] and would seem to have been made without reference to you. However you would do well to keep a weather eye on *Figaro* which is a thoroughly blackguardly paper.

Your conversation with Köller [402] tickled us greatly. That's a typical Prussian for you. Herkner [c] had already dinned into the chaps how short-sighted it was to suck up to the Frenchified and rabidly French notables while antagonising the workers who don't even understand French and who by nature and language are still consummate Germans, thereby driving them into the arms of the Francophils. It would have been a splendid opportunity to practise demagogy from above and with enormous success. The mere imposition of German factory legislation and laws on association, etc., and a tolerant attitude towards the workers would have won them over within 10 years when, along with the Protestants and the wine and tobacco growers, they would have more than counterbalanced the Frenchified middle and lower middle classes and aristocracy. But how could that have been countenanced by the self-same people who were responsible for the Anti-Socialist Law [11] in Germany and who fought the workers at every turn? The German middle classes, you see, always arrive too late, and not even the Prussian government, which enjoys so much more elbow-room than they, would dare hazard *that* sort of Bonapartist policy. And as you say, your Prussian bureaucrat, soldier or Junker cannot, by his very nature, voluntarily surrender any position of power, however useless or, indeed, damaging to himself it may be—for would not the policy of petty oppression which is his be-all and end-all suffer in consequence?

---

[a] Should be: west. - [b] Should be: Saturday's. - [c] H. Herkner, *Die oberelsässische Baumwollindustrie und ihre Arbeiter...*

As you know, Gilles has at last been well and truly kicked out. But it was silly of the *Vorwärts* to have suppressed the name in *this* of all cases.[403] One ought not, after all, to take the shine off one's own achievements by playing them down in a report. And after all the Society[89] and those who induced it to act did at least deserve that an accurate account of what they had done for the party should appear in the official party organ. However, I realise that you can't do anything for the present, but it almost seems to me as though someone was intent on stirring up trouble.

My advising Julius[a] to be less verbose would be about as effective as your advising Liebknecht not to write indiscreet letters. I shall certainly not meddle in Julius' affairs unless absolutely *forced* to do so. Nor have I any alternative, considering the way the couple has deliberately cut itself off from us. His aunt[b] demands that visit be returned for visit, formal philistine etiquette, but among us communist bohemians that sort of thing is, first, simply not done and, second, simply impossible. Such philistine intercourse — known here as the SOCIAL TREADMILL — is admissible only for people with too much time on their hands; no one who wishes to work either can or does indulge in that sort of thing. I never conformed, even amongst the bourgeois in Manchester, and it is more than ever out of the question for me to do so now. Anyone wanting something of someone else goes and sees him, and that's that. But the fact that such is the case is what lies at the bottom of all the trouble in Hugo Road.[c]

I had suspected that Geiser was back at the *Vorwärts* from the unsurpassed dreariness, tedium and vacuity, for which he alone can be responsible, of certain articles. In other respects the *Vorwärts* has on occasion been noticeably better during the session of the Dresden Landtag.

Ah yes — the *Condition of the Working-Class*[d]! This is the umpteenth time the worthy Dietz has got someone to dun me, only to receive the same answer he has already had from me in writing, namely, that I'll be glad to oblige the moment Volume III of *Capital* is finished, but can take on absolutely nothing else before then. There are a lot of snags to your proposal that I should authorise him to negotiate with Wigand; hitherto I have always found that in such cases unnecessary and often irreparable mistakes tend to be made. Above all, I have got

---

[a] Julius Motteler - [b] Emilie Motteler - [c] Street in London where the Mottelers lived. - [d] F. Engels, *The Condition of the Working-Class in England*.

to know what my legal position is vis-à-vis Wigand. I enclose a résumé of the facts; if, as once before, you could obtain some legal advice as to this, we might resume negotiations. Your previous advice made it perfectly clear to me that, thanks to the lousy Saxon legislation whereby the publisher is protected at the author's expense, I was still very much in Wigand's hands; but what it failed to make clear, since the case did not then arise as now it might, was what my position would be, should Wigand refuse to bring out a new edition on the old terms. If it transpires that I should be as much in his clutches as ever, we shall *then* certainly have to see what can be done.[404]

The printers are reaping what they themselves have sown.[383] If it means they are driven to join the party, so much the better.

Yesterday, when I read Prince George of Saxony's Order of the Day,[405] I almost jumped onto the table for joy. How it will enrage the high and mighty! A thing like that, getting into the impious Social-Democratic press! Can it really be that those fellows are already in such close touch with 'my glorious army'? A telegram a column long has already appeared in today's *Daily News* about it — it will cause the dickens of a sensation all over the world. And they imagine that that kind of treatment will induce the troops to 'shoot down everything in sight', above all their own parents, brothers, etc.! *Sont-ils bêtes, ces Prussiens!* [a]

I am prepared to maintain, *envers et contre tous*[b] and despite anything that may be said to the contrary, that Louise is a very good housewife and, moreover, an excellent cook. I'm not quite sure that this housewifeliness isn't due in part to the fact of our not being married and, should this prove to be the case, it would be lucky for me because of the circumstance that the difference in our ages precludes marital no less than extra-marital relations, so that nothing remains but that self-same housewifeliness.

Warm regards to your wife and yourself from Louise and

Your

F. E.

Postscript. Louise is indignant because you reply to the letters she writes with six-page letters to me. I told her to write and tell you so herself, to which she replied that she was far too indignant to do any such thing.

---

[a] How stupid these Prussians are! - [b] against all comers

Herewith Gilles' latest masterpiece. The Society over here is distributing it by the hundred in the hope that it will prove his own undoing.

First published in: Marx and Engels, *Works*, First Russian Edition, Vol. XXIX, Moscow, 1946

Printed according to the original

Published in English for the first time

174

ENGELS TO LAURA LAFARGUE

AT LE PERREUX

London, 3 February 1892

My dear Laura,

Can you get me from the *Intransigeant* the London address of *Rochefort?* Wróblewski all of a sudden sends me a letter for that distinguished foreigner and supposes I know his address, but I will be hanged if I know anybody who can procure it me here — everybody advises me to write to Paris as the shortest and safest way to get it — so I suppose I must follow their advice and submit the case to you, especially as I have a slight suspicion that the poor devil of Wróblewski applies to Rochefort for cash, and would not have it said for the world that I was the cause of delaying even for one hour the — undoubtedly negative — answer he is sure (if any) to get from *le grand boulevardier*.

Here we have suffered from influenza right and left — I have been spared so far, but Louise and my servant have had a touch. Percy has had a pretty severe attack followed by pneumonia and is not yet on his legs again, Bernstein has been down, and E. Aveling is not quite himself. Our street and neighbourhood has suffered severely, cases right and left.

The latest scandal: all over London goes the rumour that the Duke of Clarence on his death had called his mother[a] and told her that 'May'[b] was in the family way by him. If true it is the only action

---

[a] Princess Alexandra - [b] Princess Victoria - Mary von Teck

for which I respect the boy. They say he was after her for a good time past, but the old queen[a] did not approve of the match at first. And if they did take the law into their own hands, it's more than I should have expected from 'Cuffs and Collars' and show that after all he was good for something.

Paul's migrations are very interesting,[392] but won't he soon get tired of it? It's very useful and very good work, but if he carries it on till May 1st, he will lose a deal of weight and come back, may be, to his parliamentary duties with the 'lean and hungry look', which, as a Cassius,[406] might become him in the eyes of the *épicier*.[b] At all events he has silenced the Brousses[3] and other *Neidhämmel*[c] who came down upon him for a slip of the tongue or two in his first speech.[378] The statistics about *Notre Dame de la fabrique* etc. are the best reply.

My article[d] from the *Almanach* has come out in Italian in the *Critica Sociale* di Milano and will appear in German in the *Neue Zeit* next No. with additions. Bebel has sent me some Alsatian papers with reports of his speech in Mülhausen,[407] one in French, I want to send it to you if I can find it (*Louise says she forwarded it to you*),[e] to show you what horrid French these 'patriots' of the *Industriel Alsacien* do perpetrate.

An awful row will be caused by the publication of the order of Prince George of Saxony to the 12th German (Saxon) Army Corps in yesterday's *Vorwärts*.[405] That shows how far our connexions in the army reach, and William[f] will be awfully vexed. It is sure to cause a deal of sensation in France, and if you can forward me Paris papers with comments on it, to be forwarded to Bebel and to be used in the Reichstag, it will be very very useful.

In great haste—kind regards from Louise and

ever yours,

F. E.

First published, in the language of the original (English), in: F. Engels, P. et L. Lafargue, *Correspondance*, t. III, Paris, 1959

Reproduced from the original

---

[a] Victoria - [b] grocer - [c] grudger - [d] F. Engels, 'Le Socialisme en Allemagne'. - [e] The words in brackets were inserted by Engels later. - [f] William II

175

ENGELS TO CONRAD SCHMIDT[267]

IN ZURICH

London, 4 February 1892

Dear Schmidt,

On the strength of your letter of 12 December we drank a toast on the 19th of the same month to you and your young wife and on the following day, Sunday, after we had had a meal with the Avelings, this was solemnly affirmed by us all in a fine 1868 port. I trust you are now comfortably settled in Zurich and have found that living with another is preferable to living alone.

Very many thanks for your anti-Wolf article.[408] However it also compelled me to read Wolf's opus[a] which I had quietly laid aside in my bookcase against a rainy day. Since the chap takes the view that the sole purpose of the German language is to conceal the emptiness of his mind, the perusal of this rubbish has been something of a job, though one soon discovers the void that lies behind it. You have stated the main points quite correctly and lucidly and were perfectly right to ignore the unessentials, all of which were put in, of course, simply for the purpose of getting the reader so snarled up that he overlooks the chief flaw. That the man has an aptitude for economic folly amounting to genius I already knew, having read an article of his in the *Neue Freie Presse* in which he seeks to put the Viennese bourgeois into an even worse state of confusion that they are in already. But this time he has exceeded even my expectations.

Let us reduce his argument to mathematical terms: C_1, C_2, two aggregate capitals whose respective variable components $= v_1$, v_2, and whose respective *quantities* of surplus value $= s_1$ and s_2. Given an equal rate of profit for both (profit and surplus value being provisionally taken to be equal), it may therefore be said that

$$C_1 : C_2 = s_1 : s_2, \quad \text{therefore} \quad \frac{C_1}{s_1} = \frac{C_2}{s_2}.$$

On this assumption we must now establish the necessary rate of

---

[a] J. Wolf, *Das Rätsel der Durchschnittsprofitrate bei Marx.*

surplus value, i.e. we multiply one side of the equation by $\dfrac{v_1}{v_1} = 1$ and the other by $\dfrac{v_2}{v_2} = 1$; thus

$$\frac{C_1 v_1}{s_1 v_1} = \frac{C_2 v_2}{s_2 v_2} = \frac{C_1}{v_1} \times \frac{v_1}{s_1} = \frac{C_2}{v_2} \times \frac{v_2}{s_2}.$$

If we bring the respective factors over to the other side of the equation, thereby inverting the fraction, we have

$$\frac{C_1}{v_1} \times \frac{s_2}{v_2} = \frac{C_2}{v_2} \times \frac{s_1}{v_1} \quad \text{or} \quad \frac{C_1}{v_1} : \frac{C_2}{v_2} = \frac{s_1}{v_1} : \frac{s_2}{v_2},$$

or, in order to produce Wolf's equal rate of profit, the rates of surplus value must be in proportion to the respective aggregate capitals divided by their respective variable components. If they are not, Wolf's equal rate of profit falls to the ground. But that they 1. *can* be and 2. *always must* be — this was the economic fact that it was up to Mr Wolf to prove. Instead he gives us a deduction in which the point to be proved *appears as an assumption*. For the equation of the rate of surplus value as set forth is simply another form of the equation of the equal rate of profit.

Example: $C_1 = 100, \quad v_1 = 40, \quad s_1 = 10$
$ C_2 = 100, \quad v_2 = 10, \quad s_2{}^a = 10$

$$\frac{C_1}{v_1} : \frac{C_2}{v_2} = \frac{s_1}{v_1} : \frac{s_2}{v_2}$$

$$\frac{100}{40} : \frac{100}{10} = \frac{10}{40} : \frac{10}{10} \quad \text{which is correct.}$$

Now it really seems to me that you go a bit too far when you claim absolute uniformity of rates of surplus value for large-scale production as a whole. The economic levers which impose uniformity upon the rate of profit are, I think, much stronger and more rapid in their

---

a s_1 in the ms.

effect than those whose pressure equalises the rates of surplus value. However the *tendency* is there and the differences are negligible in practice. All economic laws are, in the end, merely the expression of mutually incompatible tendencies which gradually assert themselves.

Mr. J. Wolf is in for a pleasant surprise when the turn of the preface to Volume III[a] comes round.

I'm extraordinarily glad that you have made such an encouraging start as a lecturer and trust it will so continue. It will give particular pleasure to Mr Wolf—serve him right.

It's certainly a very good thing that some of those student gentlemen of yours who have looked askance at the transactions of the party should now be resuming their studies. The more they learn, the more tolerant they will be towards people who hold really responsible positions and try to fill them conscientiously, and in time they will also probably realise that, if an important goal is to be attained and the immense army necessary to its attainment kept together, they must concentrate on the main issue and not allow themselves to be led astray by irrelevant squabbles. They may also discover that the 'education', by which they set so much store vis-à-vis the working man, still leaves a great deal to be desired and that the working man already possesses instinctively, 'immediately' *à la* Hegel, what they could only din into themselves at the cost of much toil. But the shameful business of 'Jungen' at Erfurt was truly deplorable [301] and their newspaper,[b] from what I have seen of it, is no more than a feeble imitation of the anarchist autonomy over here.

If you become 'bogged down' in Hegel, do not be discouraged; six months later you will discover firm stepping-stones in that self-same bog and be able to get across it without trouble. In Hegel the coherent sequence of stages in the development of a notion is part of the *system*, of what is transient, and I consider that this is where he is at his weakest—if also at his wittiest for at every difficult point he has recourse to a witticism: positive and negative fall to the *ground* and hence lead on to the category *'ground'*[c] (*Encyklopädie*[d]). Obviously this would require a different rendering for each language. Try trans-

---

[a] of *Capital* - [b] *Der Sozialist* - [c] A pun in the original: *zu Grunde gehen*—to perish; *Grund*—ground. - [d] G. W. F. Hegel, *Encyclopädie der philosophischen Wissenschaften im Grundrisse*, Theil 1: *Die Logik*, § 120.

lating the sequence in the *Lehre vom Wesen* into another language and you'll find the transitions for the most part impossible.

Many regards from

Yours,

F. Engels

First published in *Sozialistische Monatshefte*, Nr. 24, Berlin, 1920

Printed according to the original

Published in English in full for the first time

176

ENGELS TO HERMANN ENGELS

IN BARMEN

London, 4 February 1892

Dear Hermann,

On 1-2 February I received prompt payment of £ 30 ON DEMAND from Pferdmenges & Co., for which very many thanks; the money certainly came in most handy, for after the Christmas expenditure January and February are always a lean time for me and I have to economise. I take it the firm doesn't require an official receipt?

Many thanks too for your information about the Schaaffhausens.[a] I don't intend to get rid of them for the time being, but there is always the possibility that other companies over here might make me an allotment of shares at par which would give me a higher return and I wanted to know how to set about things should that happen.

I was very glad to hear all the news from home and to know that on the whole everyone is getting on so well. I am delighted to learn that Hedwig[b] intends to write to me again some time. When you next see her please tell her that I have chalked that up on my slate and shall hold her to her word.

And now I must say how very grateful I am for the pictures. You all certainly look pretty sprightly still, especially Emma,[c] nor have

---

[a] See this volume, p. 339. - [b] Hedwig Boelling - [c] Emma Engels

you yourself become more saturnine than you were years ago. Heaven knows, you and I always look so terribly serious in our photographs. I am getting my own back by enclosing two of myself which admittedly were taken a year ago (February 1891) but I don't think I have changed much since then — if the others want any they are very welcome to them, provided they reciprocate.

I don't know whether your procedure regarding the declaration of income-for-taxation-purposes[a] (a 13-syllable word!) varies very much from ours, but over here it is what we have been used to for the past 40 years or more and, between ourselves, I have yet to come across a case in which a firm makes a true declaration of income; as a rule it is understated by 30%, 40%, 50% and more. All this is allowed to pass, for immediately the authorities start making trouble with a *firm* on account of underdeclaration and demand that it produce its books — which they are entitled to do — there is a general outcry from the mercantile world at such inquisitorial goings-on and the entire press is up in arms. The only thing the authorities can do *in practice* is increase the assessment at their own discretion. If the firm concerned then refuses to accept it, it must produce its books. As often as not that is allowed to pass, but should the authorities adopt this stratagem with the wrong firm, namely a firm whose earnings for the current year have, for once, actually been at a rate no higher than that declared in previous years — then the uproar breaks out again. Traders, therefore, have a measure of protection, but we poor rentiers are made to bleed, for 1. tax on our dividends, mortgage interest, etc., is actually deducted before we receive the money and 2. woe betide us if we have any other sources of income and do not voluntarily notify the taxation authorities of them, if, indeed, we don't literally ram this notification down their throats. The £18 or £24 which must be expressly notified each year in respect of my income over there cause me more trouble than all the rest put together — so far as tax is concerned. So I should be most grateful if you would send me my statement as early as possible. We get the forms on 1 May and have to return them completed on the 20th and, in the event of my being messed

---

[a] *Einkommensteuerdeklarationsverfahren* in the original.

about, I shall have to produce that particular statement as evidence, so it has got to tally.

With love to you all in Upper and Lower Barmen.

Your old

Friedrich

First published in *Deutsche Revue*, Jg. 46, Bd. III, Stuttgart-Leipzig, 1921

Printed according to the original

Published in English for the first time

177

ENGELS TO FILIPPO TURATI

IN MILAN

London, 6 February 1892
122 Regent's Park Road, N. W.

Dear Sir,

Se io lo conosco,[a] the illustrious Bovio?[409] *Ma dopo molti anni, dopo la vecchia Internazionale*,[b] when I encountered his articles at every turn in Italian socialist literature. At the time, I used to read them, and the more I read the less clear they became — *ho capi nagott*.[c] To use his own words, *non ricordo tempo più confusionario*.[d] To make things worse, in the end I did not know which of the two of us, he or I, was the *confusionario*.[e] However, on the whole, he is a good fellow, a pedant, it is true, but a generous and amiable one (which is never the case with our German pedants) and, as you say, a Victor Hugo type, a grandiose character, a man of broad views, who reconciles you with his personality, even if you fight the party which he supports. I quite understand that he should be idolised by your youth. If I were young,

---

[a] Do I know him - [b] I do, I have known him for many years, ever since the old International - [c] indeed, I couldn't make tail or head of them - [d] I cannot remember a time more muddleheaded. - [e] muddleheaded

I would be mad about him, I would worship him, but unfortunately I am 71, not 17.

This is my answer. Naturally it is slightly touched with irony — without which I would be unable to communicate with him — but, I hope, it is a civil answer. Would you be so kind as to translate it into Italian?

Sempre suo[a]

F. Engels

First published in: Marx and Engels, *Works*, First Russian Edition, Vol. XXIX, Moscow, 1946

Printed according to the original

Translated from the French

Published in English for the first time

178

ENGELS TO STANISŁAW MENDELSON

IN LONDON

11 February 1892
122 Regent's Park Road, N. W.

Dear Citizen Mendelson,

Herewith the preface.[b] It isn't very much but unfortunately it's all I can let you have at the moment. By the time the new edition of the *Manifesto* is published, I hope to know enough of your language to have no difficulty in keeping up with the Polish working men's movement and shall then be able to speak more knowledgeably about it.

I am sending you by the same post two American papers[c] relating to S. Padlewski's suicide.

---

[a] Ever yours - [b] F. Engels, 'Preface to the Polish Edition (1892) of the *Manifesto of the Communist Party*'. - [c] *New Yorker Volkszeitung* and *The Sun*

Kindly convey my compliments, as also those of Mrs Kautsky, to your wife.[a]

Yours sincerely,

F. E.

First published in: Marx and Engels, *Works*, First Russian Edition, Vol. XXIX, Moscow, 1946

Printed according to the original

Translated from the French

Published in English for the first time

179

ENGELS TO FILIPPO TURATI [410]

IN MILAN

London, 13 February 1892

Splendid! Many thanks.[409]

Cheerio.

F. E.

First published in *Annali*, an I, Milano, 1958

Printed according to the original

Translated from the Italian

Published in English for the first time

---

[a] Maria Mendelson

180

ENGELS TO EDWARD AVELING

IN LONDON

[Draft]

[London, first half of February 1892]

My dear Edward,

It was a perfectly understood thing that I was to revise your trans-lation[a] in the ms. and that, having done so, I should give it the character of an authorized translation by writing a new preface to it.[b]

After the action taken by Messrs Swan Sonnenschein & Co. with-out consultation with either of us, and in direct contravention to the above understanding, I am bound to reconsider my position.

Your translation being made with the knowledge that I would re-vise it, is necessarily but a rough draft; moreover, you, as translator, would feel bound to stick to the letter of the original, when I, as the author, might deviate more or less from it and thus make the book read not as a translation but as an original work. To revise not the ms. but paged proofs in this spirit, would imply, more or less, the up-setting of the paging.

Now, as far as I can see at present, there are but two courses open to me:

Either I revise the proofs in full liberty, exactly as I would have re-vised your ms., regardless of the expense this may occasion. In that case our original understanding holds good, the translation is author-ized by me, and I write a preface. In that case we must have four more copies of proofs at least, and revise afterwards.

Or, I am to respect the proof-sheets, as far as the paging is con-cerned, and merely to make verbal changes within the limits of each page. In that case I will do my best to make the translation as good as I can, but I must decline being in any way connected with it before the public, and reserve to me the right of publicly declining any re-sponsibility for it if such would be imputed to me.

As a matter of course, the expense caused in either case would have

---

[a] of *Socialism: Utopian and Scientific*. See also this volume, p. 359. - [b] F. Engels, 'Intro-duction to the English Edition (1892) of *Socialism: Utopian and Scientific*'.

to be borne by Messrs Swan Sonnenschein & Co. who alone have brought it about.[a]

And on all these points I must ask for their decision in writing before I stir in the matter.

First published in: Marx and Engels, *Works*, First Russian Edition, Vol. XXIX, Moscow, 1946

Reproduced from the original

Published in English for the first time

181

ENGELS TO HERMANN ENGELS

IN BARMEN

[London,] 17 February 1892

Dear Hermann,

It will be perfectly all right if you send me the statement *before* 30 April, in which case perhaps you would be good enough to notify me *by postcard* when the relevant dividends have been paid in and how much they amount to. That is the best way of dealing with it.

Since yesterday we have been having glorious German winter weather, cold and snowy. I was in Richmond today, visiting an old friend [b] who is ill, and then in town. The weather has really toned up my nerves and the Pschorrbräu I drank afterwards tasted marvellous. Love to Emma [c] and all the others.

Your
Friedrich

First published in *Deutsche Revue*, Jg. 46, Bd. III, Stuttgart-Leipzig, 1921

Printed according to the original

Published in English for the first time

---

[a] See this volume, p. 359. - [b] George Julian Harney - [c] Emma Engels

182

ENGELS TO VICTOR ADLER

IN VIENNA

London, 19 February 1892

Dear Victor,

I was on the point of replying the other day to the letter you wrote me from Salo, when I was badly balked. Owing to the publisher's [a] malice, stupidity, or both, Aveling's translation of my *Entwicklung des Sozialismus*,[b] which I was supposed to revise while still in manuscript form, had already been set up and came to me in complete, made-up, paginated proof. In view of the law in this country which delivers up the author to the publisher bound hand and foot, I ran the risk of the thing coming before the public as it stood and thus of incurring discredit, for the ms. was only a rough draft. So everything else had to be left undone until the thing had been revised and the publisher persuaded by devious means to reconcile himself to the expenses for which he himself was to blame. Well, the worst is now over, and the first person to be sent a reply will be you.

We were overjoyed to learn that your wife [c] is better and that her recovery may be confidently anticipated. You have enough work, trials and tribulations as it is, and the Austrian movement is in far too great need of every ounce of your strength for us not to have given a sigh of relief on hearing that the worst of your worries was over, in this respect at any rate. But you will, I hope, permit us to rejoice, not only as party members but also as your personal friends, at the prospect that, having made a complete recovery, your wife will shortly be restored to you and that so fine a woman as your Emma is not to suffer the terrible fate which for a moment seemed to hang over her.

But if in the circumstances you succumbed to a mood which you yourself describe as dejected, it is only too understandable. Meanwhile circumstances have, it seems, helped you Austrians out of the deadlock which you had feared, and with good reason. The proposed haphazard reconstruction of Greater Vienna provided you with an opportunity upon which you, with your habitual flair, instantly seized and duly exploited in accordance with the model originally

---

[a] Swan Sonnenschein - [b] *Socialism: Utopian and Scientific* - [c] Emma Adler

placed before the Paris Municipal Council by Vaillant and our chaps.[411] (The Possibilists [3] did no more than hasten its passage through the Municipal Council by *selling themselves* to the bourgeois Radicals [147] in return for services rendered in other spheres thus, in their low cunning, doing *us* a service and, what's more, paving the way for their *own* destruction.) So in what direction I am supposed to give you the 'fillip' requested, if not actually demanded, of me in a letter to Louise, I fail to see. The French have a peculiar knack of giving the right political form to demands of this kind, and that is what happened in this case. In this country, too, some of the French demands have been adopted by the London GOUNTY COUNCIL, while others figure in the electoral manifestos of every Labour candidate.[412] See *The Workman's Times* of the past three weeks. Since the elections to the COUNTY COUNCIL are to take place on 5 March, these manifestos are playing an important role just now, and *The Workman's Times*, which I hope you get regularly, will thus provide you with propaganda material of all kinds. And the business ought to be exploited to the utmost, first in the interests of agitation generally and of potential individual victories, and secondly and more particularly in order to eliminate the otherwise inevitable hostility between the workers of Vienna and the starveling coolie and sweated labour imported from abroad. This is a point you brought out particularly well.

You will eventually get your daily paper, but it must in the main be *your own creation*. Considering the nature of your press laws, the step from weekly to daily would seem to me a very big one for which long, robust legs are required, and one which would also make you more vulnerable than ever to a government intent on ruining you by means of fines and legal costs. This is fresh proof of your government's cunning — always greater *in small matters*. The Prussians are too stupid for that sort of thing, relying as they do on brute force, while your politicians are stupid only when it comes to doing anything big. Personally, I rather doubt whether, in view of the fines you would incur, you would be able to keep a daily going for as much as six months and, were it to collapse, the defeat would be hard to get over.

But in order to do my bit for the Austrians, and since all my fees from stuff issued by the Vorwärts Publishers find their way willy-nilly into *German* party funds, I have decided that *all* fees from the stuff published by Dietz should go to you people and *have instructed him accordingly*.[153]

I feel sorry for Rudolf Meyer; to judge by your account and the news since received about his staying in Moravia instead of Palermo, he must be in a very poor way with his diabetes. For all his astonishing and often comical megalomania, he is the only Conservative to have risked anything for his social demagogic schemes and socialist sympathies and to have gone into exile because of them. And while in exile he has discovered that, though the Austrian and French aristocrats might be far more gentlemanly in social intercourse than the rotten Prussian Junkers, they are no less tenacious in the pursuit of their rents, ambitions, etc. Things have come to such a pass that he, the only remaining genuine Conservative, is now vainly searching for men with whom he might found a genuine Conservative party.

For the rest, affairs are taking a critical turn. In the German Reichstag a considerable crisis is brewing. Little Willie,[a] it seems, wishes for once to put his *regis voluntas*[413] to the test and is actually driving the deplorable members of the National Liberal Party[414] into the arms of the opposition; already there are signs of conflict. In addition, there is a ministerial crisis in France which is of great importance to us because Constans is rabidly anti-working class and his fall will bring about a number of changes in domestic affairs; also because the recurrence of instability in French government circles is very unwelcome to the Russian alliance which is in any case on its last legs.

The enclosed appeared in the *Critica Sociale*.[b]

Louise sends you the enclosed. She has spent the whole day disengaging oxygen — on paper; she is studying chemistry under circumstances aggravated by the English textbooks and the absence of experiments...[c]

First published, in part, in *Arbeiter-Zeitung*, Nr. 327, Wien, 28. November 1920 and in full in *Victor Adlers Aufsätze, Reden und Briefe*. Erstes Heft: *Victor Adler und Friedrich Engels*, Wien, 1922

Printed according to the book

Published in English for the first time

---

[a] William II - [b] F. Engels, 'Reply to the Honourable Giovanni Bovio'. - [c] The end of the letter is missing.

183

ENGELS TO AUGUST BEBEL [415]

IN BERLIN

London, 19 February 1892

Dear August,

First of all, my heartfelt congratulations on your birthday and MANY HAPPY RETURNS OF THE DAY, as they say over here; likewise on your 25th anniversary in Parliament and/or your silver wedding with parliamentarianism, which falls due very shortly.[416] Well, you could hardly have chosen a better time to show the chaps what an asset you are to them, and it gave us over here a great deal of pleasure.

Things are really coming to a head in Germany, indeed must have gone pretty far if the National Liberals [414] repeatedly evince strong oppositional tendencies and Richter can dream of a German 'great Liberal Party'.[417] A capitalist society which has not yet subordinated the state to itself formally which has left real government in the hands of an hereditary, monarchical-bureaucratic-Junker caste and must rest content if, by and large, its own interests nevertheless ultimately prevail — such a society, as situated in Germany, fluctuates between two tendencies — firstly the alliance of all official and propertied social classes against the proletariat; this tendency ultimately leads to the formation of the 'one reactionary mass' [322] and, if things go *smoothly*, will ultimately retain the upper hand. Secondly there is a tendency which is for ever reviving the old conflict, cravenly left unresolved, between the monarchy with its absolutist throw-backs, the landed aristocracy and the bureaucracy, which deems itself above all party, and, in opposition to all these, the industrial bourgeoisie whose material interests are impinged upon daily and hourly by the above outmoded elements. Which of these two tendencies will momentarily prevail will be determined by personal, local, etc., contingencies. Just now in Germany, the second would seem to be gaining the ascendancy, in which case the industrial magnates *à la* Stumm and the shareholders of industrial concerns will, of course, mainly side with outmoded reaction. However, this pale reflection of the old conflict of 1848, now resuscitated for the umpteenth time, can become serious only if the government and the landed aristocracy, presuming on their past successes, do something quite crazy. Not that I regard this as out of the question, since the curious personal aspirations up on high are lent support by the growing conviction of the Junkers that industry will *not* long be *capable of sustaining* the tariffs on raw materials and foodstuffs. But the lengths to which this conflict will be taken depends, as I have said, on personal contingencies.

One of its characteristic features is the time-honoured practice of belabouring the load in place of (or rather along with) the donkey. They belabour Social-Democracy but at the same time bring down a shower of blows on the bourgeoisie, politically at first, by attacking the liberal principles it has ostentatiously flaunted for the past 60 years and its *direct* if negligeable share in the administration; and later, if all goes well, also economically, by sacrificing its interests to those of landed property.

So a strong swing to the Right would now appear to be in progress, having for pretext the necessity of keeping back *our* advance. In what way can it affect *us*?

1. Anti-Socialist Law[11]? We overcame that and to do so now, when we are morally 100% and materially at least 50% stronger than on 1 October 1890,[a] would be child's play. Nor would it be very likely to secure a majority.

2. Reactionary amendments to the laws against the press, association and assembly? Would be unacceptable to the Centre[418] and impossible without it. To form a majority with 93 Conservatives of both factions[419] and 42 National Liberals would require 66 men of the Centre. If they went over, that would be the end of the Centre — a not unsatisfactory result. That and the colossal fury such retrograde measures would evoke in the people would more than compensate for the coercion we should have to endure.

3. Restriction of the suffrage and of the secret ballot? Completely out of the question so far as the Centre is concerned; the Clericals aren't so stupid as to cut their own throats. And without the Centre they would again be short of some 60 or 70 votes.

4. Coups d'état? No good because of the princes. Any infringement of the Constitution would threaten the Empire with dissolution, and release individual princes from all obligations thereto. And even if they could all be won over in such a case (which would *never* happen), the assent of their immediate heirs — most of them minors! — would

---

[a] The Anti-Socialist Law was valid until 1 October 1890.

be necessary to ensure the stability of the Empire. Out of the question, therefore.

5. Thus the only remaining possibility would seem to lie in increasingly rigorous administrative, police and legal measures, as foreshadowed in the outrageous sentence passed on Peus.[420] But we shall survive them and will soon learn to organise ourselves accordingly. They might even go one better and declare an ordinary state of emergency, but this would constitute a hazard only in the first few weeks; later on it would automatically fall into desuetude, quite apart from the fact that it could only be proclaimed for this or that part of the Empire; moreover the bourgeois would also tire of it, and thus perhaps be driven still further into opposition.

So unless our Prussian masters hit on other inventions of quite a new and brilliant kind — as it were intellectual and moral machine guns and Maxims — they may be able to harass us, but will always do us more good than harm. A bit of undisguised Junker rule would do no harm! But I'm rather afraid our chaps may not have enough backbone; ambitions and to spare but insufficient staying-power, for the spirit is willing but the flesh is weak. The sad thing about Germany is that both sides, Junkers no less than bourgeoisie, are so deplorably supine.

Last night I read with real delight the anti-Stumm speech you made on Friday 12 February [421]; it was a splendid piece of improvisation and one can see how successful it was. I also look forward immensely to reading the military speech which came today.[422]

We were very pleased by your announcement that you would be here round about the 10th or 11th of April — everything is ready for you and, should Schorlemmer turn up, we can accommodate him as well; that has been seen to. You are pretty sure to be given lobster mayonnaise again after the letter Louise got from you today; I had already hatched a little plan of my own to that end, though this will presumably no longer be needed. But *I* shall assume responsibility for the oysters and likewise for the choice of drinks. Luckily Louise revels in these two delicacies just as much as you and I do and, on such a basis, agreement can always be reached. That she is a witch she is herself aware and is not a little proud of the fact for, or so she says, in Vienna all witches are attractive. And, between you and me, I don't believe that, were she not a witch, you and I would get on so well with her.

Now as regards Otto Wigand, I can only repeat that, until the completion of Volume III of *Capital*, I cannot take on *anything that might involve me in work*. As it is, I am held back quite enough by the letters that daily come pouring in from all over the world and by other current business, so I do beg you to let me get this load off my shoulders at long last, thereby regaining some liberty of action. And I have just got to a section which, if I am to finish it, demands that I have a few months completely free of interruptions. If Dietz cares to discuss the matter personally with Wigand,[a] *without in any way committing me*, then let him, if he thinks anything is to be gained thereby. He can say he has reason to believe that I think he, Dietz, has better sales facilities for a new edition than Wigand, and that I am inclined to entrust publication to him, Dietz, provided he can come to an agreement with Wigand. Only I cannot 1. declare myself committed in advance by anything Dietz may say to Wigand, nor can 1, 2. send him to Wigand as my representative. Semi-officially but not officially! He should sound him out and, if the terms suit *him* (and are such as to leave me, i. e. for party purposes, a fee commensurate with the circumstances), should go ahead, in which case I should certainly not leave him in the lurch. But I don't want to find myself between two stools — i. e. an *unwilling* Wigand and a *hamstrung* Dietz!

It's a real joy to know that things are livening up again. Who can tell whether, with passions running so high, your Reichstag and the French Chamber won't both be dissolved? And what could be better for us? What I fail to understand, however, is that now, when really decisive battles are being fought in the Reichstag, Liebknecht should remain squatting in his Dresden froggery.[b] I myself would be willing to sacrifice ten Saxon mandates for the right to say a word in the Reichstag just now.

Anyway, who can tell whether we aren't both being accused in more timorous party circles of having spoken out of turn and conjured up the threat of reactionary measures? That my article in the *Neue Zeit*[c] found its mark is evident from the obstinate silence of the bourgeois and ministerial press which otherwise is so ready to attack anything like that. It has since appeared in Italian, Polish and Romanian and in Italy has involved me in a polemic with that benign old jackass Bovio.[d]

Unfortunately I shall not be able to reply to Mrs Julie's[e] kind letter

---

[a] See this volume, pp. 345-46. - [b] in the Saxon Landtag - [c] F. Engels, 'Socialism in Germany'. - [d] See this volume, p. 354. - [e] Bebel

today, having spent the whole of this morning in conference with Aveling, sorting out his translation of *Entwicklung des Sozialismus*[a] and, if this letter is to reach you on Monday, it will have to be sent off today, Saturday. However, I shall make good the omission at the first opportunity and in the meantime can only repeat how much we regret we shan't be seeing her here also. Well, it's something we can still look forward to.

Warm regards,

Your
F. E.

First published, in part, in: F. Engels, *Politisches Vermächtnis. Aus unveröffentlichten Briefen*, Berlin, 1920 and in full in: Marx and Engels, *Works*, First Russian Edition, Vol. XXIX, Moscow, 1946

Printed according to the original

Published in English in full for the first time

184

ENGELS TO LAURA LAFARGUE

AT LE PERREUX

London, 5 March 1892

My dear Laura,

Today I can do no more than fulfil my promise to Paul and send you the enclosed cheque for the rent — £15 — made out in your name, so that Paul's absence need not cause any delay. I have received your letter and shall reply in a few days — I am overwhelmed with work — Sonnenschein has by some blunder sent the rough draft of Edward's translation of my *Entwicklung des Sozialismus*[a] *to press* and now all the work of revising that rough draft falls upon me, and of course has to be done quick. — Then Percy was here all week, left yesterday, then other interferences with work — today Tussy has

---

[a] F. Engels, *Socialism: Utopian and Scientific*.

gone on *Union*[164] work to Plymouth and Edward will be all day with us, so I must get this letter closed and off before he comes.

I am glad of the news about the 'Daily'[a] and this time it may turn out a success, if our friends take the proper precautions not to be turned out again the very moment the paper begins to pay.[423] But things are better now, there is a power behind them now and that makes a difference — only they ought to take care to secure their position in the paper for all that.

I should be glad if Paul would let me know something of the position of the various socialist and '*Auch-Sozialisten*'[b] groups in the Chamber — the Blanquists, Possibilists,[3] Millerand lot,[336] and the ex-Boulangists. I see in yesterday's *Intransigeant* that Paul and Ferroul attended a meeting composed chiefly of the *Blanquist Boulangists*, and, if he works together with them, it's 100 to 1 that Hyndman will attack them in *Justice*, and anyhow the subject is sure to be discussed here and interpellations to come to me — so I ought to be prepared!

In my next you will also very probably receive a dunning letter from Louise for more contributions to the *Arbeiterinnen-Zeitung*.

Love to all your numerous family

Ever yours,
F. E.

First published, in the language of the original (English), in: F. Engels, P. et L. Lafargue, *Correspondance*, t. III, Paris, 1959

Reproduced from the original

185

ENGELS TO KARL KAUTSKY

IN STUTTGART

London, 5 March 1892

Dear Baron,

Your ms.[379] goes off by *registered* mail today. I have only been able to read the first 16 pages. If I were you I should omit the better part

---

[a] *Le Socialiste* - [b] 'partly socialist'

of this introduction. The reasons why a programme should have a commentary, etc., etc., in short, all those reflections of yours about *why* the pamphlet was written, only serve to weaken the impact and deter the reader from persevering. You must plunge straight into it — you could have no better justification. I cannot give an opinion of the way the rest, the major part, is arranged. So overwhelmed am I by work of all kinds that I don't know whether I'm coming or going. Nothing but trifles, but quite scandalously time-consuming. I long to have time for Volume III[a] and every day am invariably robbed of it. Well, we shall get round to it some time or other.

Ten copies of *Neue Zeit* containing my article[b] received with thanks.

Simply amend the name Hodgskin and the figure 1824 in the next edition, and include a note saying that in the original these read such and such, *obviously a slip of the pen or printer's error*.[424]

Menger is a jackass and will so remain. His critique of bourgeois law[c] is throughout nothing but a vindication of the 'police state' as opposed to the 'constitutional state'. True, the law, especially bourgeois law, is stricter and more rigorous than police despotism which may sometimes appear humane precisely because it is despotic. If I had the time, I should soon put paid to this empty talk which is possible only in backward countries such as Germany and Austria.

I am glad you are agreeable to the Luther idea.[d] There's no rush.

Cunow's letter returned with thanks. I look forward to seeing the ideas he has worked out about class.[425] He has made some very nice discoveries about the Peruvian gens. He had sent me the stuff and I thanked him for it.

You will also be getting the Peruvian community system[224] — I have just looked at it.

I don't think you are in any danger for the time being. So changeable and multifarious are the cravings in Berlin that none could really be satisfied; now all at once it's the liberal bourgeois who's the *bête noire*. Liberalism is at the root of all socialism, so if one is to act *radically* one has got to smash liberalism, whereupon socialism will automatically wither away. For the present we may observe this exceptionally cunning manoeuvre with quiet amusement. Once the liberal philistines have been driven wild — and they are, it seems, really being whipped into a fury willy-nilly — then there'll be no more false

---

[a] of *Capital* - [b] 'Der Sozialismus in Deutschland' - [c] A. Menger, *Das bürgerliche Recht und die besitzlosen Volksklassen*. - [d] See this volume, pp. 342-43.

alarms so far as we are concerned. Apart from the fact that in Germany there are also rulers to whom this wind from Berlin provides the not unwelcome opportunity of currying favour at little expense and thus extracting capital for particularism and reserved rights.[426] When the street rioting began in Berlin[427] I was somewhat concerned lest it result in the ardently desired fusillade, but when the rowdies cheered young William,[a] thereby placating him, I knew that all was well — but just let the *Kölner Zeitung* be locked up[428] along with Peus,[429] and we may well see some fun.

So in my view, in so far as there is any danger, it is primarily confined to Prussia, and the greater it becomes there, the better off you people in the small states will be.

Now I have got to write to Sorge[b] — the American mail goes today — so FAREWELL. Aveling, who has just come in, sends his best wishes. Regards from one household to the other.

Your
F. E.

First published in *Aus der Frühzeit des Marxismus. Engels Briefwechsel mit Kautsky*, Prag, 1935

Printed according to the original

Published in English for the first time

186

ENGELS TO FRIEDRICH ADOLPH SORGE[357]

IN HOBOKEN

London, 5 March 1892

Dear Sorge,

Have received your letters of 15, 22 and 29 January and postcards of 2, 4 and 13 February. Also the newspapers re Anna.[c] The latter has evidently succumbed to that fashionable complaint, megalomania. It's strange; these sort of people, the Hartmanns *et al*, are fit for *one*

---

[a] William II - [b] See next letter. - [c] Stanisław Padlewski

deed — GOOD, BAD OR INDIFFERENT — and, once that's done, are good for nowt else,[a] as Schorlemmer would say.

Though I haven't alas had time to read your last article in the *Neue Zeit*,[b] I must get round to doing so since it's only with your help that I can follow developments in America without going astray.

I am terribly overburdened with all kinds of tasks and tiresome odds and ends. You ought to see the mass of German, French, Italian, Spanish, Polish, Russian, Danish, American, English and, now and again, Romanian newspapers I get and must at any rate glance at if I am to keep *au courant* with the movement. Not to mention genuine tasks which swallow up the rest of my time. And the correspondence! I've got backlog enough to last me a week. And then I'm supposed to complete Volume III.[c] It's appalling. But it will be managed somehow. Only you people must be patient if I sometimes allow my correspondence to lapse.

In France things are going very well. Lafargue is using his expense allowance and his free railway pass to travel all over the place, from Lille to Toulouse, agitating and this with brilliant success. All the other socialist factions have been pushed into the background by ours and even in Paris the Possibilists[3] are continuing to beat a retreat, thanks to their internal squabbles and to vigorous action on the part of our own people. They again have in mind a daily journal as party organ, and this would now stand a better chance.[423] It's capital that Constans should have been sacked from the Ministry of the Interior; the chap was determined to provoke fusillades, by violence, and we can do without them. Since our May Day demonstration coincides with the municipal elections throughout France,[429] shooting is a luxury no minister could permit himself unless, like Constans, he was banking on a nine days' wonder.

Here the bickering continues as before, but nevertheless the cause is making headway in true Anglo-Saxon fashion, slowly but surely. Everything always subsides into small individual battles which cannot be assessed until actually resolved. At the moment these concern the May Day celebrations. On the one side our people, on the other, in opposition to us, the TRADES COUNCIL[196] (the stuffier TRADES UNIONS) and the SOCIAL DEMOCRATIC FEDERATION[29]; the two enemies of yesteryear have been forced to club together against us, which is in itself a vic-

---

[a] In the original: *nix mehr ze wolle* (South-German dialect) - [b] F. A. Sorge, 'Das Programm der Geldreformer in den Vereinigten Staaten'. - [c] of *Capital*

tory. *We* are in possession of Hyde Park and POSSESSION IS NINE POINTS OF THE LAW. How things will turn out remains to be seen. On our side we shall probably have the GASWORKERS,[164] a number of the smaller unions and the RADICAL CLUBS [430] (almost wholly working class) — what happens next must remain to be seen.

And now for Germany. Things are going so swimmingly there that we couldn't wish for anything better, although we shall no doubt experience some pretty hard knocks in the near future. From the outset Little Willie[a] has been a prime example of a 'last of the line' with a singular aptitude for ruining the dynasty and monarchy. But now his madness has taken on an acute form and his megalomania is such that he can neither sleep nor hold his tongue. As luck would have it, the *regis voluntas* which, at the drop of a hat, would become *suprema lex*,[413] is directed against us one day and the Liberals the next, and now he has actually discovered that it's the Liberals, whose progeny we are, that are the source of all evil — he's been taught as much by his clerical friends. And now he's prosecuting the *Kölnische Zeitung* for lèse-majesté [428] and will not rest content until he has hounded your tame German philistine into the opposition. What more could we ask? A month ago, when Stumm's speech was heard in the Reichstag,[421] it was still possible to envisage the re-introduction of the Anti-Socialist Law but that is no longer the case, for William is more incensed by the opposition of the bourgeoisie to his bill for the clericalisation of primary schools [431] than by all the Social-Democrats put together, and would sooner leave us alone than make any concessions to the other fellows. In both chambers it is, in fact, from the bourgeois parties that he encounters most opposition, not from our 35 members in the Reichstag; in the Prussian chamber we have no seats at all. Nevertheless, we, too, may run into some heavy weather — yet what could be better than for the Crown to place itself in an impossible position vis-à-vis the middle classes and the workers at one and the same time? The ministers are all second-rate or third-rate men, Caprivi is a staunch lout but unequal to his task, nor does Miquel grow any the wiser for his perpetual cheese-paring. In short, at this rate a crisis may be in the offing. In Prussia and in the Prusso-German Empire people cannot as in Bavaria afford to go on for years putting up with a demented monarch[b] and I shouldn't be surprised if, some time soon, they didn't erect a special madhouse for Little Willie. And then there'd be a Regency, which is exactly what we've been needing.

[a] William II - [b] Ludwig II

As regards Russia and *la haute politique*,[a] I have nothing to add to my article[b] in the *Neue Zeit*.

Warm regards from Aveling, who happens to be here just now — Tussy is off agitating in Plymouth. Louise will enclose a short note. Warm regards to your wife,[c] and look after yourselves.

Your
F. E.

First published abridged in *Briefe und Auszüge aus Briefen von Joh. Phil. Becker, Jos. Dietzgen, Friedrich Engels, Karl Marx u. A. an F. A. Sorge und Andere*, Stuttgart, 1906 and in full in: Marx and Engels, *Works*, First Russian Edition, Vol. XXIX, Moscow, 1946

Printed according to the original

187

ENGELS TO AUGUST BEBEL[432]

IN BERLIN

London, 8 March 1892

Dear August,

We were all very glad to hear that your parliamentary anniversary was such a jolly occasion.[416] So far as the address is concerned, I did, as requested, certainly send off a draft[153] which — since I had to take account of the wishes, specific but unknown to me, of a parliamentary group most of whose 35 members were likewise personally unknown to me — seemed to me distinctly flat nor, till that moment, had I heard anything about either it or its fate. The French wrote one for you, published in today's *Socialiste*, in which they could let themselves go a bit more.[433]

So Liebknecht has been chucked out of the Dresden froggery.[434] Considering how petty those philistines are, little else was to be ex-

---

[a] high politics - [b] 'Der Sozialismus in Deutschland' - [c] Katharina Sorge

pected. Pretexts are never wanting and, while the affair may have accorded their vindictiveness some small personal satisfaction, the jackasses have derived no advantage whatever therefrom. The *Vorwärts*, by the by, has shown a marked improvement of late.

I am glad that the rumpuses in Berlin are over and that our people have held themselves so strictly aloof.[427] There might very well have been a bit of shooting and that would have sufficed to make things awkward for us in all kinds of ways. Had there been shooting in Berlin, the National Liberals[414] would have been quite capable of enthusiastically supporting the Elementary School Bill[431] while the hitherto indeterminate anger of certain people would finally have been directed against ourselves. The one reactionary mass,[322] which is looming larger every day, is not much use to us as yet; so long as *we* cannot actively make history ourselves, our interests demand that historical developments should not stand still, and to that end it is necessary that the bourgeois parties remain at loggerheads. And here the present regime is invaluable in that it provides that very situation for us. But if the shooting starts *too soon*, i. e. before the old parties have become more closely locked in combat, it might drive them to seek a reconciliation with each other and to form a united front against us. It will happen some time, as surely as eggs is eggs and, if it happens when we are, say, twice as strong as at present, it will no longer matter very much. Though even were it to happen now, the exercise of personal power would undoubtedly see to it that the opponents fell out with each other again. But it's better to be on the safe side. Things are going so famously now that we can only hope they'll be allowed to proceed without interruption.

However, unemployment might well get worse next year. For protectionism has had exactly the same effect as free trade — the flooding of individual national markets and this almost everywhere, though it's not so bad over here as where you are. But in this country where we have come through two or three insidious little crises since 1867, we would at last seem to be heading for another acute one. The enormous cotton crops of the past 2 or 3 years (up to 9 million or more bales a year) have depressed prices to the same extent as in the worst days of the 1846 crisis, and are thus exerting tremendous pressure on production which means that the manufacturers here are having to overproduce because of overproduction by the American planters! At the same time they are steadily losing money because the falling price of raw materials invariably means that their product, spun from expensive cotton, has already fallen in value by the time it reaches the market. *Indeed, that is the reason for the cries of distress emanating from the German and Alsatian cotton spinners*, though no one has said anything about this in the Reichstag. Nor are other branches of industry faring much better over here. For the past 15 months there has been a marked decline in railway revenues and in the export of industrial goods so that in this country, too, the outlook for next winter is pretty bleak. No improvement can really be looked for in continental countries that have protective tariffs and, even though trade agreements might bring momentary relief, this will be offset before the year is out. And if next winter the same rumpus, but on a larger scale, recurs in Paris, Berlin, Vienna, Rome and Madrid and finds an echo in London and New York, a still more serious situation might arise. On the other hand, it's a blessing that Paris and London, at any rate, have municipal councils that are *all too aware* of their dependence on the Labour vote, and are the less inclined to put up any serious resistance to demands, realisable even today, such as employment on public works, shorter working hours, wages in accordance with trades union demands, etc., etc., in that these represent the best means of safeguarding the masses against worse socialist — *genuinely* socialist — heresies. It remains to be seen whether the municipal councillors of Berlin and Vienna, who owe their election to a suffrage that is based on class and property, are forced *nolentes volentes*,[a] to flounder along in their wake.

Yesterday's *Standard* carried a telegram from *St Petersburg* according to which, after William's[b] speech in the Brandenburg Landtag, one of the gentlemen pointed out that the 'glory' to which he had alluded was opposed by, inter alia, Russia. Whereat William replied: 'I SHALL PULVERIZE RUSSIA', or words to that effect. Shuvalov, it seems, got to hear of this and, having assured himself of the authenticity of the report, passed it on to *his* Emperor. Whereupon Alexander promptly sought occasion to reprimand Schweinitz, instructing him to tell his Emperor that 'should he again feel the urge to pulverise Russia, I shall have the pleasure of sending half a million soldiers across his borders'.

On Saturday[c] Russia won a victory here in London which, however, will no longer be of any use to it. In the County Council elections (in London what is known elsewhere as a municipal council is called County Council) the Liberals scored a resounding victory and

---

[a] willy-nilly - [b] William II - [c] 5 March

there is no longer any doubt — if indeed there ever was — that, after the next parliamentary elections, Gladstone will come to power. But Gladstone is fanatically pro-Russian, anti-Turk and anti-Austrian, and his accession would provide Alexander with a further incentive for war since it would mean England's benevolent neutrality, not to mention English pressure on Italy to keep her neutral as well. The famine and the internal conflicts which we may hope it will evoke in Russia will redress the balance — provided, that is, nothing silly is done on either side of the Russian border, a possibility which can never entirely be excluded.

For the rest, and so far as this country is concerned, the Liberal victory is not a bad thing. The Conservatives aren't up to much unless they have at their head a chap like Disraeli capable of leading the whole party by the nose and getting it to do the opposite of what it actually intended. The present leaders are nothing but fools and coxcombs who allow the local party leaders, i. e. the stupidest men on earth, to dictate what their programme should be. Moreover 6 years in office have exhausted and staled them. So there has got to be a change and that is what the whole of this farce ultimately boils down to.

Ede tells me he has had a letter from Mehring saying that neither the *Neue Zeit* nor the *Vorwärts* nor any other party newspaper has taken the slightest notice of his *anti-Richter* [a]; he considers this inexcusable, feels inclined to give up politics altogether, etc. I can see that, to an author accustomed to literary pretentiousness — this is not to imply any blame, for in the bourgeois press, even at its most literary, that sort of thing is not only the rule but a *sine qua non* — I can see, then, that to a man like this, who has grown up in the non-Social-Democratic press, these Social-Democratic customs could be highly objectionable. But then we should all of us have to raise our voices in complaint, for the same thing is done to you and me and all the rest. None the less, and however unpleasant it may sometimes be for the individual, I consider this haughty indifference on the part of our press to be one of its greatest merits. Mehring's stuff will be bought and read even if the *Vorwärts* doesn't puff and it is better not to boost anything than to boost the masses of party trash which, worse luck, are also launched upon the world. And if any one thing were

---

[a] F. Mehring, *Herr Eugen Richters Bilder aus der Gegenwart. Eine Entgegnung von Franz Mehring*.

to be singled out, 'equal rights for all' would be demanded for everything else, in accordance with time-honoured democratic custom.
That being so, I would rather put up with the equal right of being
passed over in silence.

But there is one thing your chaps might do — come to an equitable
arrangement with Mehring's publisher as regards regular and frequent advertising. That, however, is another example of the total
lack of business sense which is congenital to our newspapermen.

I recently got hold of a copy of the 3rd edition of Mehring's *Deutsche Socialdemokratie* and took a look at the historical part. I should
say that, in *Kapital und Presse*, he skates rather lightly over this incident.[435] But it's all one to *us* and *we've* got nothing to reproach him
with; whether he's got anything to reproach himself with is his own affair and no concern of ours. In his place *I* should have admitted my
change of heart quite openly, since there's nothing whatever for him
to be ashamed of and it would have saved him a great deal of time,
vexation and strife. It would, by the by, be absurd for him seriously to
consider withdrawing from politics since he would thereby only be
doing the ruling powers and the bourgeoisie a service; his leaders in the
Neue Zeit are indeed really first-rate and we eagerly await the appearance of each one. Such verve should not be allowed to wither away or
be wasted on rotten belletrists.

We all liked Siegel very much. He is yet another of those German
working men whom one would be proud to be seen with in any company. The fact that he left in order to escape quite exceptionally rigorous and systematic persecution is in no way reprehensible. It's just
because they are only now entering the movement that the miners are
being persecuted with especial rigour, nor can the victims in any way
rely on the support of their fellow workers — and for the same reason
solidarity has not yet gained general recognition. Cunninghame-
Graham and Keir Hardie have procured work for him in Scotland
and his family is following him there. The company he is working for
are advancing him the money and deducting it from his wages. Now,
it's not going to be easy for him to repay this. I have given him five
pounds for the journey to Scotland and to help him settle in, but cannot well do more. Would it not be appropriate for you people to grant
him a subsidy of, say, 100 or 150 marks? I have read the letters Schröder wrote him and there seems small likelihood of his getting anything from that quarter.[436] Think the matter over.

From the enclosed chit from the Witch's kitchen you will see that your lobster mayonnaise will, 'by virtue of the true elapse' of time (to use Arnold Ruge's words) put in an appearance only to disappear a moment later. Let us hope this dialectical process will then be crowned by a smoothly functioning negation of the negation.

Cordial regards.

Your
F. E.

The 10th of April is Palm Sunday. You should leave no later than the 8th, in which case you would be here by the evening of Saturday the 9th at the latest. That would be the best and most convenient arrangement. You won't be needed for the Queen's Speech. So we shall expect you here on the 9th.

First published in: Marx and Engels, *Works*, First Russian Edition, Vol. XXIX, Moscow, 1946

Printed according to the original

Published in English in full for the first time

188

ENGELS TO JULIE BEBEL [231]

IN BERLIN

London, 8 March 1892

Dear Mrs Bebel,

Unfortunately I have only today got round to answering your kind letter of 18 February, though at the same time I am sad to note that you have definitely decided to give your daughter[a] at St Gallen rather than us the pleasure of your company. Well, we can't blame you for preferring to visit Mrs Simon and console ourselves with the hope and the firm expectation that we shall be all the more certain of seeing you here in the spring (or summer?) of 1893. For in summer our fireplaces are screened off, plum puddings strictly forbidden, fogs only occur very rarely and so you'll see England looking her best,

---

[a] Frieda Simon

even though a malicious Frenchman once said that the English summer amounts to nothing more than three very hot days and a thunderstorm, after which it is all over. Next year I trust you will give us an opportunity to prove that this is a wilful exaggeration. You will also find that you can get on perfectly well over here, even though you speak no English.

But whether I come to Germany, as you surmise, will depend on all kinds of things over which, in view of these critical and changeable times, I have no control. Gone are the good old days of the new course's [437] calf love for anyone who aroused Bismarck's wrath, and there is no knowing what may not happen between now and the summer. So for the time being I shall leave everything in the lap of the gods and wait and see where fate may lead me this summer, whether to Germany, to Norway, to the Canary Islands, where they would also like to see me, or somewhere else. My one regret, should there be no real prospect of my making a pleasant summer visit to Germany, would be to miss yet another chance of making your personal acquaintance. I do so long to set eyes once again on a real, honest to goodness German proletarian woman, which is how people have always described you to me. My wife [a] was also of genuine Irish proletarian blood and her passionate feeling for her class, a feeling that was inborn, was of immeasurably greater value to me and has been a greater standby at all critical junctures than anything of which the priggishness and sophistry of the 'heddicated' and 'sensitive'[b] daughters of the bourgeois might have been capable. But my wife has now been dead for twelve years and more, while August is fortunate enough to have you still at his side; that is the difference.

Louise has just written another quite outrageous letter to August. You have absolutely no conception of how cocky the little woman has become now that she is once again standing on her own feet. You ought to be here sometime when we take our morning glass of Pilsener beer, and listen to our laughter and the kind of nonsense we talk. I'm happy that I can still join in such youthful tomfoolery; after all, one ages in so many ways that it is a real joy to find one has not yet lost the ability to laugh. And I really cannot thank Louise enough for all she is doing to ensure that my old Rhinelander's *joie de vivre* doesn't

---

[a] Lizzy Burns - [b] In the original: *jebildeten* and *jefühlsvollen* (Berlin dialect).

wither and die. And now once again my warm regards and the sincere hope that you will continue in good health.

Yours sincerely,

F. Engels

First published in: Marx and Engels, *Works*, First Russian Edition, Vol. XXIX, Moscow, 1946

Printed according to the original

Published in English in full for the first time

189

ENGELS TO LAURA LAFARGUE

AT LE PERREUX

London, 14 March 1892

My dear Laura,

I have a whole heap of your letters before me, such a heap that I hardly dare look at it without being ashamed of myself — but you have no idea how I have been worked, interrupted, *tracassé, embêté*[a] etc. etc. by all sorts of people. My best working time — January to April — has been frittered away and I have not had a moment to even look at the 3rd volume[b] which I was determined to advance a good bit — and over the critical point — by Easter. All vanity of vanities. Now, my time up to a week after Easter is already engaged (by 10 April I shall have Bebel here for a fortnight or so, before that time I must go to Ryde to see Pumps who has had a sore time of it, Percy had 1) influenza, 2) pneumonia and 3) and last is now laid up with pleurisy) and it will cost a damned effort of energy and a determination to reply to no letters whatever and do no work for no matter whom if I want to use May and June for the 3rd volume.

But damn all this, you don't want to hear my grumbling. I am glad there are prospects of a daily paper for Paris,[423] that will make up for many a mishap in other parts of the world. Though mishaps to our party are getting few and far between, unless we provoke them ourselves. We have such capital allies. Young William[c] brags about his

---

[a] harassed, annoyed - [b] of *Capital* - [c] William II

ally God who so arranged all things from the creat[ion of the][a] world, that they must turn out to the grea[test] glory of the Prussian monarchy in general and young William in particular. But the poor boy does not see that all the time he is a better ally *to us* than God ever was or will be to him; and even if he was to see it, he could not help it, it's the nature of the beast!

My article[b] of the *Almanach*[c] and *Neue Zeit* has now been translated into Italian (*Critica Sociale*—got me into a row with that *confusionario l'illustre*[d] Bovio[e]), Roumanian (*Revista Socială*[438]) Polish (*Przedświt*) and English (New York *People*).

We have just come back (3.30 p.m.) from Highgate, the cemetery is in a disgusting state of soft clay, we had half a hundredweight sticking to each foot. On the gr[ave] Tussy (I suppose) had planted a small cypress, and one of the old crocus bulbs has come out in flower. The sprig of ivy which Motteler had brought from Ulrich von Hutten's grave on Ufnau Island in the Lake of Zürich, and which we planted after poor Nimmy's burial, having trained it on our balcony, had already been robbed of its best part last summer, but what is left, now grows well and is rooted deeply in the soil, so that no further desecration is possible.

Here we are also busy about the 1st of May. It is a beautiful play of intrigues woven and cut to pieces and woven afresh, Penelopean fashion. The 8 Hours Committee[200] (Edward, Tussy and their friends) tried to be first in the field but the Trades Council,[196] that reactionary rel[ict of the] Old Trades Unions, was o[ut befor]e them. Now the Trades Council and the S. D. F.[29] are for the [nonce] friends, as against all the rest; at present they do not compete one with the other, and have common interests in putting down all 'outsiders'. So when the 8 Hours Committee proposed to act with the Trades Council, in the same way as last year, they got a complete rebuff. But then the 8 Hours Committee *secured the Park*[f] *for themselves*, before the Trades Council had thought of it, and then again offered co-operation with the Trades Council which was again haughtily declined. Then *both* bodies addressed the Metropolitan Radical Federation (of Radical clubs[430]) to co-operate with them; and the M. R. F. decided to *mediate*, but under all circumstances *to act with the 8 Hours Committee* to whom the whole movement from the origin was due. So that the

---

[a] Manuscript damaged.-[b] 'Socialism in Germany'-[c] *Almanach du Parti Ouvrier*-[d] notorious muddlehead-[e] See this volume, p. 354.-[f] Hyde Park (see also this volume, pp. 370-71.)

Trades Council and the Social-Democratic Federation, as usual over-estimating their strength, have put themselves in an awkward position: either they must knuckle under, or have a separate demonstration, and bear the responsibility of the split. At all events *our* demonstration is now an assured success, whatever the others may do.

Hyndman gets more foolish every day. His blind hatred of the Germans makes him support the Berlin '*Unabhängige*'[a][333] and keep as his German chief of staff that outrageous scamp Gilles who is evidently in the pay of the German Embassy and has been, with a lot of malcontents, turned out of the German Communist Club here (our old '*Verein*'[b][89]). So that he has now lost even the little foreign support he had; in Germany they used to have some little regard to his position as leader of at least a *section* of English socialists, but he has forfeited that; in France his friends Brousse and Co. are so down, that even Hyndman himself had to protest against their 'hygienic' programme for their next congress.[439] One does long for a good strong breath of revolutionary air to sweep away all these pettifogging *Jammerkerle*[c] — but it is coming, slowly, slowly as everything does come among these '*verdammten*[d] Schleswig-Holsteiners' (as Marx called the English) but when it comes it is *safe*.

I intended to enclose a line to Pau[l. I ha]d a letter from him from Marseilles — but it's getting dinner-time, and I am afraid of being stopped in the midst of it. I am afraid their new alliance with Granger and Co. will not turn out to their satisfaction. First of all, these men have shown that they are absolutely un[reliable] when they passed over to Boulanger, and we can only expect being betrayed by them on the first occasion. Secondly, Paul says we must reap where Boulanger has sown. Exactly so, but *reap the masses* and *discard the leaders*, as the plan was with the Possibilists[3]; but these leaders have no masses behind them, and are themselves highly undesirable bedfellows. Thirdly, they have crept into the Chambre *under false pretences* and are sure to be kicked out next election, so that it seems to me our friends are leaning upon an already broken reed. And as to *foreign policy*, fourthly, these men are *pledged Chauvinists* — otherwise they could not have got elected — and if Paul and friends form a party with them, they may be outvoted, kicked out, or driven to a split on the first occasion. I hope I may be wrong, but I am afraid I am not. The passage to Boulanger of these fellows was an unpardonable trea-

---

[a] Independents - [b] Society - [c] miserable people - [d] damned

son, and I'd rather have Vaillant than the whole lot of them — indeed I thought it a blessing that they had made themselves impossible.

Louise will write to you as soon as possible. She has been rather out of sorts for the last 8 days and is only just coming round again. To-morrow I must go to see old Harney at Richmond where he is ill with the windpipe and his rheumatic gout. And then you want me to say something to the Parisians about the 18 March.[440] I'll be hanged if I know what! *Mais nous verrons!* [a] Ever yours affectionately,

F. E.

[Ki]nd regards from Louise.

First published in *Labour Monthly*, No. 10, London, 1955   Reproduced from the original

190

ENGELS TO NIKOLAI DANIELSON[441]

IN ST PETERSBURG

London, 15 March 1892

Dear Sir,

I am almost ashamed to reply to your kind and interesting letters of the 12 and 21 November last. But I have been so overwhelmed with work, and I find that writing by gaslight is still so hurtful to my eyes (which otherwise keep quite serviceable) that this extra work and the shortness of daylight during our winter must be my excuse.

You are passing indeed through a momentous period for your country, the full importance of which can hardly be overestimated. From your letters it seems to me that you look upon the present неу-рожай [b] not as an accident, but as the necessary result, as one of the unavoidable concomitants of the economic development entered upon by Russia since 1861.[442] And that is my opinion too, as far as one can judge from a distance. With the year 1861 Russia entered

---

[a] But we shall see! - [b] crop failure (Russ.)

upon the development, on a scale worthy of a great nation, of Modern Industry. The conviction ripened that now-a-days no country can take a befitting rank among civilised nations without possessing steam-driven industrial machinery and providing, to a great extent at least, for its own wants of manufactured goods. And upon that conviction Russia has acted, and acted with great energy. That she surrounded herself with a rampart of protective duties, was but too natural, English competition forced that policy upon almost every great country, even Germany, where *une grande industrie* had successfully developed under *almost absolute free trade*, joined the chorus and turned protectionist, merely to accelerate the process of what Bismarck called *die Züchtung von Millionären*.[a] And if Germany entered upon this course even without any necessity, who can blame Russia for doing what to her *was* a necessity, as soon as the new industrial course was once determined upon?

To some extent your present situation appears to me to find a parallel in that of France under Louis XIV. There, too, manufactures were placed in a condition of vitality by Colbert's protective system; and within 20 or 30 years, it was found out that a national manufacturing industry, under the circumstances then existing, can be created only at the expense of the peasantry. The *Naturalwirtschaft*[b] of the peasants was broken up and supplanted by the *Geldwirtschaft*,[c] the home market was created and, at the same time, nearly destroyed again, at least for the time, by this process and the unprecedented violence with which economic necessity enforced itself, and by the increased taxation in money and in men, necessitated, then, by the introduction of standing armies by conscription, as it is now-a-days necessitated by the introduction of the Prussian military system of universal army service. And when at last a crop or two failed, then arose that universal state of discomfort all over the country which we find depicted in Boisguillebert and Marshal Vauban.[d]

But there is one immense difference: The difference between old '*Manufaktur*' and modern '*grande industrie*' which (in the action upon the peasant, the agricultural producer on a small scale and with his own means of production) is as the difference between the old smooth-bore flint-musket of 1680 and the modern repeating rifle, ca-

---

[a] raising of millionaires - [b] subsistence economy - [c] money economy - [d] [P.] Boisguillebert, *Le détail de la France* and S. Vauban, *Projet d'une dîme royale*. In: *Économistes financiers du XVIII-e siècle*.

libre 7.50 millimetres, of 1892. And moreover, whereas in 1680 agriculture on a small scale was still the normal mode of production, and
large estate-farming could only be a *rising* exception, but always an
exception, large farming with machinery is now the rule and becomes
more and more the only possible mode of agricultural production. So
that the peasant today appears to be doomed.

You remember what our author said in the letter on Joukow-
sky[a] — that if the line entered upon in 1861 was persevered in, the
peasants' *obščina*[b] must go to ruin. That seems to me to be in course of
fulfilment just now. The moment seems getting near, at least in some
districts, where the whole of the old social institutions of Russian
peasant life not only lose their value to the individual peasant but become a fetter, exactly as they have done in former times in Western
Europe. I am afraid we shall have to treat the община[b] as a dream of
the past, and reckon, in future, with a capitalist Russia. No doubt
a great chance is thus being lost, but against economic facts there is
no help. The only curious thing is that the very men in Russia who
never tire of defending the invaluable superiority of Russian primitive
institutions as compared with those of the rotten Occident, are doing
their very best to destroy those primitive institutions and to replace
them by those of the rotten Occident!

But if the Russian peasant is doomed to be transformed into a proletarian, industrial or agricultural, the помѣщикъ[c] does appear to be
doomed too. From what I gather, this class is even more in debt than
the peasants, and has to sell out gradually. And between the two seem
to step in a new class of landowners, village кулаки or town-
bourgeois — the fathers of, perhaps, a future Russian landed aristocracy??

The failure of last year's crop has brought all this out into glaring
daylight. And I am quite of your opinion that the causes are entirely
social. As to deforestation, that is as essentially, as is the ruin of the
peasants, a vital condition of bourgeois society. No European 'civilised' country but has felt it, and America,[*] and no doubt Russia, too,
feels it at this moment. Thus deforestation, in my eyes, is essentially

---

[*] In America I have seen it myself 4 years ago.[443] There great efforts are made to
counteract its effects and redress the mistake.

[a] K. Marx, 'Letter to *Otechestvenniye Zapiski*'. - [b] commune (Russ.) - [c] landowner (Russ.)

a social factor as well as a social result. But it is also a very common pretext for interested parties, to devolve the blame for economic mishaps upon a cause which apparently nobody can be made responsible for.

The failure of the crop, in my opinion, has only made *patent*, what was there already *latent*. But it has terribly accelerated the velocity of the process going on. The peasant, at seed-time this spring, will be infinitely weaker than he was at seed-time last autumn. And he will be called upon to recover strength under far more unfavourable circumstances. A pauper, over head and ears in debt, no cattle, what can he do — even in the places where he has got through the winter without having to leave his land? It therefore seems to me that it will take years before this calamity is completely overcome, and that when that point is reached, Russia will be a very different country from what she was even on 1 January 1891. And we will have to console ourselves with the idea that all this in the end must serve the cause of human progress.

I sent you last autumn a little book: *Ursprung der Familie*,[a] 4th edition, it was registered and my address outside on the wrapper, as it did not come back I hope you have received it.

I thank you very much for the many papers and reviews sent — the one of Mendelejeff's [b] was especially interesting. But I regret I cannot just now give to them all the attention they deserve, owing to hard work. How fast I was with extra work, you will conceive when I tell you that from New Year to now — generally my quietest time — I have not been able to give one minute to 3rd volume.[c]

Your congratulations were duly forwarded to Paris.[444]

With kind regards ever yours

P. W. Rosher [d]

No news from our mutual [e]?

First published, in Russian, in *Minuvshiye gody*, No. 2, St Petersburg, 1908

Reproduced from the original

---

[a] *The Origin of the Family*... - [b] Д. И. Менделѣевъ, *Толковый тарифъ или изслѣдованіе о развитіи промышленности Россіи въ связи съ ея общимъ таможеннымъ тарифомъ 1891 года.*- [c] of *Capital* - [d] Engels' conspiratorial pseudonym - [e] Hermann Lopatin

191

ENGELS TO AUGUST BEBEL

IN BERLIN

London, 16 March 1892

Dear August,

Today I have a request, namely that you send me the stenographic report of the session at which our chaps spoke about Alsace-Lorraine and Singer apparently made a statement on the same subject on behalf of the parliamentary group.[445] I'm sure to be questioned about it and should therefore like to be in possession of the *precise* facts.

Over here the usual struggle[a] has begun again in regard to May Day, but so far the outlook is favourable. What I am about to tell you *must not appear in the 'Vorwärts'*, for Gilles will interpret and manipulate it in his own way for Hyndman's benefit — i.e. in order to sing the praises of the Independents [333] and malign the parliamentary group and, since the struggle has still to be decided, anything that might be published could be used *against* us.

Well, the original 'Legal 8 Hours Committee',[200] presided over by Aveling, and the Trades Council [196] under Shipton (presently allied with Hyndman and the Social Democratic Federation [29]) tackled the matter almost simultaneously. The 8 Hours Committee invited the Trades Council to act in concert with them, as happened last year, but was rejected with contumely. At the same time it approached the Metropolitan Radical Federation (comprising more than 50 radically 'labour' and partly socialist clubs),[430] whereupon the latter was approached by the Trades Council. In the meantime Aveling had played the same trick on the Trades Council as they had played on him 2 years before [446] and secured first right to the Park.[b] Having assured itself of the Park, the 8 Hours Committee actually made a further approach to the Trades Council but was again rejected with contumely. Immediately afterwards, however, the Metropolitan Radical Federation, which on several occasions had also been treated by the Trades Council in a high-handed way (last year the Trades Council admitted only Trades Union people, not club speakers, to the plat-

---

[a] See this volume, pp. 370-71 and 380-81. - [b] Hyde Park

forms they had been allotted) resolved that, whatever happened, it should join forces with the 8 Hours Committee, but that there should be one more attempt at reconciliation with the Trades Council. The 8 Hours Committee met on Sunday[a] when it was agreed with the Metropolitan Radical Federation that the latter should make this attempt, after which a decision would be taken on further action. That is how matters stand. Up till now the 8 Hours Committee has been in a vastly superior position. It has the Park, the Gasworkers, a whole number of small East End unions and the Radical Clubs — in short, a number at least twice as large as that which supports the Trades Council and Hyndman's Federation. For the moment the latter is keeping as quiet as a mouse and letting the Trades Council do its work for it. Provided there are no blunders or indiscretions, the Trades Council will either have to back down or, as was the case 2 years ago, play second fiddle at the demonstration, and an ill-tempered fiddle at that.

I have now read Mehring's 'Lessing-Legende' in the *Neue Zeit* and derived much pleasure from it. It is a really excellent work. There is much that I should have accounted for differently or toned down a bit, but all in all he has hit the nail on the head. It is truly a pleasure to see that the materialist view of history, which for the past 20 years has — as a rule — had to pay the price of being used as vainglorious rhetoric in the writings of our younger party members, is at last beginning to be put to the use for which it was originally intended, i. e. as a guide for the student of history. Kautsky and Ede have produced some very nice stuff in this line but Mehring has made a much closer study of his special subject, namely Prussia's small segment of German history, and generally takes a less blinkered view; above all he expresses himself more positively and precisely. I hope the work will be published on its own as soon as it has finished appearing in the *Neue Zeit*. Never, to my knowledge, has the citadel of the Prussian legend been besieged so well and so forthrightly: for Lessing read old Fritz.[b] And it is vitally necessary to demolish the Prussian legend before Prussia is able to vanish into Germany. As regards the *preconditions* for Prussia east of the Elbe in German as well as in European and world history, I should sometimes have expressed myself differently but these are things which in fact Mehring merely touched upon.

But now I must go and eat so that the Witch can get on with her

---

[a] 13 March - [b] Frederick II

Witch's Latin. As to the EAST END business,[447] you mustn't let it worry you too much; I don't think that anything dangerous is being planned.

Warm regards to Mrs Julie[a] and yourself.

Your
F. E.

First published, in Russian, in *Bolshevik*, No. 22, Moscow, 1940

Printed according to the original

Published in English for the first time

192

ENGELS TO FILIPPO TURATI

IN MILAN

[London,] 18 March 1892

Dear Citizen Turati,

Thank you for the two copies of the *illustrious one's*[448] reply which you were kind enough to send me. Needless to say, I have no intention of letting him have an answer, for if he didn't mean to discuss and didn't discuss the German Socialists, what were his reasons for quoting my article[b] and appending his comments to his quotations? It's more incoherent than ever, but to be charitable, one must suppose that he had totally forgotten what he had written in the *Tribuna*.[449]

Kind regards,
F. E.

First published, in the language of the original (French), in: Karl Marx, Friedrich Engels, *Scritti italiani*, Milano-Roma, 1955

Printed according to the original

Translated from the French

Published in English for the first time

---

[a] Julie Bebel - [b] 'L'imminente trionfo del socialismo in Germania'

193

ENGELS TO KARL KAUTSKY [177]

IN STUTTGART

London, 30 March 1892

Dear Baron,

Yesterday evening I sent back to you the preface duly corrected and I also added a couple of lines to the 2nd edition.[450] I think that should do. The old preface will still serve the purpose of preventing the resurrection of the Rodbertus nonsense which, like any article of fashion, has a tendency to keep recurring. It certainly acted remarkably quickly, though it is no credit to me if the great men pitted against us are the sort of chaps who can be done to death in two prefaces. Besides, the economic arguments set out therein will still do the Germans some good; the awkwardness of many of our people when engaged in economic polemics is curious though hardly edifying.

Congratulations on the birth after a difficult confinement of your pamphlet on the programme.[379] The child will get on in the world all right. A new popular digest is always most useful; people's speeches frequently make one realise how necessary such refresher courses are; and a fat tome is the last thing they are either willing or able to read.

Rather than complain about the carelessness of German writers, you should adopt the principle of marking with coloured ink such articles as you intend to accept and returning them to the authors for correction; then they would soon mend their ways. Obviously if the editors are so obliging as to place their own style at the author's disposal, he will become more and more slovenly.

I can understand your complaining about your correspondence, for you speak to a fellow sufferer. But then you are also an editor, which I am not, and are entitled to confine yourself exclusively to business matters — after all, anything more you do is for your own personal pleasure — and that is precisely what is denied me.

Apropos, I did *not* read Marx's article on Proudhon from the Berlin *Social-Demokrat*[451] in proof; I had no time.

As regards Adler,[452] you learned rather more from Dietz than

I did. I therefore passed on your comments to Louise and asked her to prepare a memorandum on the affair for your own use — this I enclose. From her discretion towards me I gather, as no doubt you will, too, that this is a case which calls for the utmost discretion on the part of us all and where any incautious revelation could have the most dire consequences. Unfortunately, in a case like this, there are so many people who sympathise that out of sheer sympathy they are incapable of keeping their mouths shut. It's already quite bad enough that the affair should have been bandied about so freely in Berlin.

The Condition of the Working-Class[a] has at last come out over here. Unfortunately I have no copies to send you but have arranged for the *Neue Zeit* to be recommended to S. Sonnenschein & Co. *Socialism: Utopian and Scientific* is also finished, as far as it goes, but since the little book has turned out to be much too meagre for its price of 2s. 6d. (though the jackass of a publisher knew this from the beginning!), I am to swell it out with a long preface.[b] Well, we shall see. That, however, will be the last of my own jobs, after which I shall then get on with Volume III.[c] I have had word from Petersburg (this is *between ourselves*) that the *Origin of the Family* will probably be appearing in Russian shortly. The article on 'socialism in Germany' has now come out in Italian, Romanian (*Critica Socială*), English (*The People*, New York) and Polish (*Przedświt*, here), the last two having been taken from the *Neue Zeit*.

Kindest regards from one household to the other.

Your

General

First published in *Aus der Frühzeit des Marxismus. Engels Briefwechsel mit Kautsky*, Prag, 1935

Printed according to the original

Published in English in full for the first time

---

[a] *The Condition of the Working-Class in England in 1844* (1892) - [b] 'Introduction to the English Edition (1892) of *Socialism: Utopian and Scientific*' - [c] of *Capital*

194

ENGELS TO PASQUALE MARTIGNETTI

IN BENEVENTO

London, 30 March 1892

Dear Friend,

I can no longer lay my hands on the issue of *Lotta*[a] you mentioned in your postcard of the 26th, but in any case it would in my view be a mistake and an offence against the best interests of the party were a socialist to give the first subaltern who came along the opportunity of killing him.[453] By employing what for them would be the perfectly safe method of duelling with a socialist, it would be an easy matter for young officers to gain not only a great reputation for dash, but also rapid promotion, and, what's more, make away with our best people. We ought not to let ourselves in for that kind of thing.

Circumstances might arise in which even our own people might find that a duel was unavoidable; a French or Italian deputy might be forced to engage in a political duel should the refusal of a challenge be more injurious to the party than its acceptance, especially if it was our own deputy who was responsible for the affront. But to agree to a duel or even provoke one except in cases of dire necessity is, to my mind, absurd.

I am sending you the English translation of my *Die Lage der arbeitenden Klasse in England* which has just come out. I trust it will be of use to you in your English studies.

Yours ever,

F. Engels

First published, in Italian, in *Mefistofele*, Benevento, 29 aprile 1892

Printed according to the original

Published in English for the first time

---

[a] *Lotta di classe*

195

ENGELS TO HERMANN SCHLÜTER [267]

IN NEW YORK

London, 30 March 1892

Dear Schlüter,

First of all I must thank you for the letter you sent me last year,[454] which provided me with so much valuable information. Unfortunately I cannot repay you in the same coin. By and large enough can be learned about the general political situation in Europe from a carefully selected reading of the newspapers and in order to allow time for my work it behoves me to keep myself out of the internal affairs of individual socialist parties as much as possible, otherwise I should never get anything done. I cannot therefore give you any information about the sequence of events inside the parties in the various countries in so far as these take the form of squabbles amongst the leaders, as is usually the case, for even the little that I do know about it has as often as not been told me only on condition that I keep my mouth shut.

Had I known that the *Figaro* article [455] would have interested you people over there, I should have let you have it, for I was sent one by Lafargue. It has long since gone astray, departed into limbo, so I shall write to Paris but hardly imagine I shall be able to unearth another copy or get any real information out of Lafargue who has doubtless long since forgotten about it. Since his election he has been travelling indefatigably all over France on his free ticket, agitating and propagating (I don't mean the race) evidently with great success. May Day — since it coincides with the municipal elections [429] to be held throughout France except Paris — will on this occassion be a highly critical day for the French; they are spurred on by the ambition to emulate the Germans.

It seems to me that in America your great stumbling-block consists in the exceptional position of the native-born working man. Before 1848 one cannot speak of an established, native-born working class except by way of an exception; the few who constituted its beginnings in the cities of the east could always hope to become farmers or bour-

geois. Such a class has now come into being and has also largely organised itself along TRADES UNION lines. But it still adopts an aristocratic
attitude and whenever possible leaves the ordinary, ill-paid occupations to immigrants of whom only a small proportion enter the aristocratic TRADES. These immigrants, however, are split up into nationalities which understand neither each other nor, for the most part, the
language of the country. And over there your bourgeoisie is far more
adept than the Austrian government at playing off one nationality
against another — Jews, Italians, Bohemians, etc., against Germans
and Irishmen, and each against the other so that in New York the
workers' living standards vary, or so I understand, to an extent unheard of elsewhere. And on top of that you have the complete indifference of a society, which has grown up without any of the easy-going
background of feudalism and upon a purely capitalist basis, towards
human beings who have fallen victim to the competitive struggle;
THERE WILL BE PLENTY MORE, AND MORE THAN WE WANT, OF THESE DAMNED DUTCH-
MEN,[a] IRISHMEN, ITALIANS, JEWS AND HUNGARIANS — and in addition, standing in the background, you have JOHN CHINAMAN who far outdoes them
all in his ability to live on next to nothing.

In such a country repeated endeavours followed by no less certain
set-backs are inevitable. Except that the endeavours grow more and
more strenuous and the repulses less and less crippling, so that on the
whole the cause nevertheless advances. But one thing I regard as certain, namely that the purely bourgeois basis without any pre-
bourgeois humbug behind it, and the correspondingly colossal vigour
of a development which manifests itself despite the insane lengths to
which the present system of protective tariffs has been taken,[338]
will one day bring about a change that will astonish the whole
world. Once the Americans get going it will be with a vigour
and ferocity that will make us in Europe look like babes in arms
by comparison.

With kindest regards.

Your
F. Engels

---

[a] This is how Germans were called in the USA.

[From Louise Kautsky]

Dear Schlüter,

A woman does not usually lift a finger and hence only becomes affable when she wants something. What I should now like to have is some authentic information on the bourgeois women's movement in America, i. e. their relative privileges and voting rights in the various states as regards not only school or municipal elections but also political suffrage, etc. I, or rather the General on my behalf, gets through Sorge the 2 most prominent women's rights papers, *Woman's Journal* and *Woman's Tribune*. But I need more, I need a brief, concise but historically complete account of the struggle to attain women's civil rights, not the dreadful, dreary catchphrases of the female pioneers of women's civil rights. The book which you...[a]

First published in *Briefe und Auszüge aus Briefen von Joh. Phil. Becker, Jos. Dietzgen, Friedrich Engels, Karl Marx u. A. an F. A. Sorge und Andere*, Stuttgart, 1906

Printed according to the original

Published in English in full for the first time

196

ENGELS TO LAURA LAFARGUE

AT LE PERREUX

London, 4 April 1892

My dear Laura,

Today but two words to ask you to look after the *Éclair*.— On Friday[b] morning all of a sudden Émile Massard came down upon me with a demand for an interview for that iridescent paper. As he promised to submit the ms. to my correction, and as I thought to be thereby able to put a flea in the ear of the Parisian *gogo*,[c] I consented. Yesterday I looked over the ms. and *almost entirely recast it*. Would you be good enough to send me about 4-6 copies of the paper as soon as it appears? If correct I shall want them for various regions, if incorrect, I shall at once protest against the breach of faith.[456]

---

[a] The end of the letter is missing. - [b] 1 April - [c] juggins

Anyhow this new experience with the eternal interviewing nuisance will help me to refuse in future, as I always have to do the real work (from 11 to 3 yesterday, instead of being out this warm weather) and even then it's not what I want and does not bring out my ideas. Damn the lot of them.

I was in Ryde for a week,[457] has done me good. Pumps and the children are well, Percy has had influenza, pneumonia, pleurisy, inflamed throat, etc., one after the other and is only just recovering.

I am busy with an infernal preface[a] for the never-to-be-satisfied Swan Sonnenschein and Co. and that, as it will be long, will take me all week. As soon as finished you get a long letter.

Salut to the travelling parlamentarian[b] who is not only a peripatetic grass widower but also a grasshopper, and love from Louise and yours

everlasting old
General

Next week we expect Bebel here unless stopped by ill health — he seems a deal out of sorts by overwork and overexcitement.

First published, in the language of the original (English), in: F. Engels, P. et L. Lafargue, *Correspondance*, t. III, Paris, 1959

Reproduced from the original

---

[a] F. Engels, 'Introduction to the English Edition (1892) of *Socialism: Utopian and Scientific*'. - [b] Paul Lafargue

197

ENGELS TO HENRI BRISSAC

IN PARIS

[Draft]

[London, after 7 April 1892]

Dear Citizen,

I have just received your letter of the 7th inst. (postmarked yesterday). I am still awaiting the pamphlet[a] you were good enough to send me. I shall read it with interest. But I greatly regret that it will be impossible for me to render you the service you ask of me.[458] In the first place, if I were to write *on your behalf* a criticism of your work for publication, courtesy might, perhaps, preclude my speaking freely. Moreover, whatever I might do for you I should also be obliged to do for every other *bona fide* socialist, be he French, German, English, Italian, Spanish, Danish, etc., etc., and what would that lead to? I shouldn't have a single moment to call my own. And more important than any other consideration is the fact that I have before me a very difficult task which has been weighing on my conscience for years, namely the editing of Volume III of Marx's *Capital*. Several months ago I made a resolution not to take on any additional work whatsoever until I had discharged this urgent duty.

Yours sincerely

First published in: Marx and Engels, *Works*, First Russian Edition, Vol. XXIX, Moscow, 1946

Printed according to the original

Translated from the French

Published in English for the first time

---

[a] H. Brissac, *La Société collectiviste*.

198

ENGELS TO AUGUST BEBEL

IN ST GALLEN

London, 16 April 1892

Dear August,

I must say it was a damnable disappointment when your telegram arrived. Well, illness is something that can't be helped, and I only hope you had so far recovered as to manage the journey all right and that you are now enjoying the benefits of the mountain air. On the other hand you're now duty-bound to bring Mrs Julie[a] with you in May — something towards which I have done my bit in the enclosed note which I beg you to endorse in the strongest terms.

As regards the Parisians, two men turned up here before your letter had arrived. I arranged for them to come again the next day, Wednesday,[b] for I felt sure your letter would have arrived by then. When it came, I went to see Julius[c] and Louise went to see one of the men — somewhere at the back of beyond — but found no one and left a written message. At last, on Thursday evening, one of them turned up (the other having already departed on Wednesday morning), told me that, because of certain circumstances, the matter had been postponed, and said they hoped to manage without the assistance of you people to whom they would have recourse only in case of extreme need. We'll discuss it further when you come over. It isn't urgent.[459]

Why, on leaving St Gallen, you should first want to return to the imperial sand box,[d] we cannot understand. Once there, you'll resume your drudgery, day after day will go by and your health will begin to suffer again, whereupon the doctor will come and you'll be unceremoniously bundled off to Karlsbad[e] after all. I'm a passionate advocate of Karlsbad — for other people that is, not for myself — because I saw how it put Marx to rights again[460]; had he been able to take advantage of it eight years earlier, he might still be alive today. It is wonderfully effective for all disorders of the stomach and liver and I would strongly advise you to take these capital waters (capital because it yields physiological surplus value for you and economic sur-

---

[a] Julie Bebel - [b] 13 April - [c] Motteler - [d] Berlin - [e] Karlový Vary

plus value for the landlords of Karlsbad) for 4 or 6 weeks in June, when Dr Fleckles, Marx's and Tussy's friend — she will tell you about him — will provide what other entertainment you need; he is one of the wittiest men in Europe.

I should have written to you before, but in order to avoid odious slander, I have had to write a most odious foreword.[a] It's a typical English affair. Aveling translates my *Entwicklung des Sozialismus* for a SOCIAL SERIES of which each volume costs 2.50 marks. I say it's a swindle to sell the little thing at that price. No, says Aveling; the chap — the publisher — is quite aware of what he's doing — one booklet is too fat, the other too slim, and it ultimately averages out (particularly for anyone who happens to find nothing of interest except in the slim volumes). Moreover, the publisher, having seen the German original, knows all about it. Well and good. The thing's completed and, by dint of tremendous leading of type, they have managed to make some 117 pages of it. Now the publisher — he's called Sonnenschein[b] but at times seems unable to see, however bright the sunshine may be — discovers that it's insufficient after all and asks me to write a good, long foreword. Well, it's not as straightforward as all that. For the first time I have got, as it were, to put myself on show before the heddicated[c] British public, and it requires some thought. Anyway, what emerged was a long dissertation about this, that and t'other, through which ran a consistent leitmotif — scathing mockery of the British bourgeoisie. I look forward to seeing what the British philistine will have to say about it. I shall let the *Neue Zeit* have it in German[461] and hope it will amuse you all.

Well, to avoid missing the post, Louise and I would ask you to give our regards to Frieda[d] and Simon — perhaps they too will come to London some time? — while remaining

Yours, etc., or not etc., as the case may be,

F. E.

First published in: Marx and Engels, *Works*, First Russian Edition, Vol. XXIX, Moscow, 1946

Printed according to the original

Published in English for the first time

---

[a] An untranslatable pun, *Nachrede*—slander and *Vorrede*—foreword. - [b] Sunshine - [c] In the original: *jebildeten* (Berlin dialect). - [d] Bebel's daughter, married to Ferdinand B. Simon.

199

ENGELS TO LAURA LAFARGUE

AT LE PERREUX

[London,] 19 April 1892

My dear Laura,

At last—*ouf, je respire*[a]! When Sonnenschein saw that Edward's translation of *Socialisme Utopique etc.* after all possible leading of type did look awfully meagre for a 2/6 book (what I told him from the beginning) he insisted on my writing a lengthy preface. And as I *had* promised to write a preface, and had various matters on my mind which I felt a liking to explain to the British philistine, I set to work, and at last, it is done. It's I dare say about half as long as the whole book, and had to be done carefully, for the British philistine hates being made fun of by foreigners, yet I could not help it.

By the bye, have you heard anything of Ravé and his translation?[462] the thing ought to be out by this time.

Now to your last letter. I think that these two things ought to be kept separated: 1) our relations to the Blanquists' old school, and 2) those to the Boulanger-Blanquists.

First. I cannot help thinking that our differences with Vaillant began last April,[b] and that our people are not quite blameless. At that time Vaillant and we pulled together, the Allemanists[53] being third party, and wanting a full recognition by us. Then, our people, without consulting the Blanquists, started the plan of processions to the *Mairies* and Palais Bourbon[c] with deputations to interview the *élus*.[d] To that the Blanquists naturally objected as they would not meet their t r a î t r e s.[e] But our people insisted, and thus, as far as I can see, *drove* the Blanquists into the alliance with the Allemanists. It strikes me our people in that case did a bit of rather sharp practice which after all availed them nothing, for the whole plan fell through.

What happened since, I know very little of, but no doubt, this final

---

[a] I can breathe.-[b] See this volume, pp. 183, 189 and 190.-[c] the premises of the Chamber of Deputies-[d] deputies-[e] traitors

cause of mistrust between the Blanquists and our people once established, it would be easy for the tag-rag and bobtail of the Blanquists,
the Allemanists helping, to widen the breach and to fortify the alliance between Blanquists and Allemanists, which again set us down in
a hopeless minority in Paris. Now that would be no great misfortune
provided we conquered in the provinces, and for that purpose Paul
and Guesde have worked splendidly and we may expect, I hope,
great successes on 1st May,[429] and let Blanquists and Allemanists
cuire dans leur jus.[a]

But then comes this alliance with the ex-Boulangists of the Chamber. As I said before,[b] when the masses have been led into such a glaring mistake as that was with Boulanger, the break-up of the delusion
makes them all the fitter for listening to sense, and coming round to
us. *That* inheritance of Boulangism we were entitled to. But it appears
to me, that it is a very different thing to accept, at the same time, the
leaders of that movement, and not as private individuals, but at their
own valuation and with the rank they held in the Boulangist crew.
I cannot help holding in considerable contempt the men that allowed
themselves to fall into that trap — on no matter what pretext. There
is nothing that has damaged the reputation of the French, abroad, so
much as this infatuation for a new saviour of society, and such a one!
And had it been the bourgeois alone — but the great mass of the
working class too went down on their knees before this windbag!
What reliance can anyone in his senses place on the men that cast in
their lot with this *jouisseur*[c] who intrigued with extreme Republicans,
Clericals, Monarchists all at once and must have been quite as much
of a 'constitutional liar' as S. Sonnenschein said to Bax he, Sonnenschein, was! These men must be either deficient in character or in in-
tellect or both, and certainly not worth having. What possible good
can they be to us?

 1) We cannot rely on them for a day.

 2) If we form a party with them in the Chamber, they *outnumber us*
and can pass the most absurd resolutions over our heads which we
must either be bound by, or else secede again from them — which
leaves us in a worse position than before. If I am to knuckle under
a majority, after all I'd rather do so to one commanded by Vaillant,
than to one led by Granger and Co.

---

[a] stew in their own juice -[b] See this volume, pp. 381-82. -[c] bon viveur

3) As all these men got into Parliament on false pretences, they are almost sure to be kicked out next election — so was it worth while for us to identify ourselves with them?

And if Argyriades raves against the Germans, how about Rochefort and his paper[a] which evidently receives Russian money (at least some of the *rédacteurs*) and Russian articles?

The breach with the Blanquists' old school may have been unavoidable, and may be swallowed; but I do fail to see the slightest real advantage that can accrue to us from an alliance with the ex-Boulangist Radicals in the Chamber. Have we not, for the mere show of a group of some 25 men in Parliament, sacrificed very serious future chances?

However the thing is done and cannot be helped. I only hope our friends will not place too much confidence in their new allies. And I believe our party in France is now strong enough to bear without serious damage the consequences of a mistake or two.

That our new allies do not bring us any real strength in Paris, is shown by the fact that Paul and Guesde both go to the North on May 1st, which seems tantamount to our leaving the 1st of May in Paris entirely to the Blanquists and Possibilists.[3] As I said before, there would be no great harm in that, if we can beat them in the provinces; but if our new allies are not strong in Paris, where in the name of dickens *are* they strong?

Your article on the religious interference in factories seems to have been too much for the Austrian press law practice. Your last one on night-work[b] has appeared — Louise requests you not to blame her for one or two blunders they have put in in Vienna.

We expected Bebel here for Easter, but he fell ill (catarrh of the stomach and intestine) and was stopped by the doctor. He expects to come about middle of May. This is the third attack within a year and he has received a serious warning from the doctor — a specialist. He wants him to go to Karlsbad,[c] which I think would set him up again.

John Bull showed himself yesterday again in all his brutality at Hampstead Heath station, about 5 o'clock, rain threatening, a crowd rushed down the steps, and crushed eight people to death, mostly

[a] *L'Intransigeant* - [b] L. Lafargue, 'Nachtarbeit für die Frauen in Frankreich', *Arbeiterinnen-Zeitung*, No. 8, 15 April 1892. - [c] Karlový Vary

women and children, injuring a dozen more. Imagine a French crowd being guilty of that!

Ever yours,

F. Engels

Love from Louise.

How about a delegate or two to May 1st here? *The Possibilists will have two men here* (see *Chronicle* we sent you with Adolph Smith's letter to Shipton[463]). Edward wrote to you about it, if you cannot send a man, try to delegate Bonnier from the *Conseil National* of the Party and to send a letter. Don't allow the Possibilists to walk over the course as the representatives of France. But let it be done *officially*.[464]

First published, in Russian, in *Istorichesky arkhiv*, No. 2, Moscow, 1956   Reproduced from the original

200

ENGELS TO KARL KAUTSKY

IN STUTTGART

London, 20 April 1892

Dear Baron,

Needless to say you will be getting the introduction to the English version of *Sozialismus*[a] *etc.*— in German of course; it's got to come out and where else could I get anything as long as this published except in the *Neue Zeit*? It went off yesterday and so, until the proofs arrive, I shall be *hors de combat*. It's so infernally long because I've made it the vehicle for all sorts of old grudges against the English bourgeoisie and look forward to seeing what the British philistine has to say about it.

We over here are at last clear about what is to happen on May Day — or rather the reverse of clear. The TRADES COUNCIL[196] and the SOCIAL DEMOCRATIC FEDERATION[29] have done their utmost to ensure

---

[a] F. Engels, 'Introduction to the English Edition (1892) of *Socialism: Utopian and Scientific*'.

that on this occasion matters should be placed completely in their hands and, above all, that the Eight Hours League [200] be totally excluded. For just now the SOCIAL DEMOCRATIC FEDERATION is working hand in glove with the most reactionary elements — Shipton, etc. — in the TRADES COUNCIL, to which body it is wholly subordinating itself so far as the May Day demonstration is concerned; the TRADES COUNCIL is to conduct the campaign against the independent elements in the EAST END, while the SOCIAL DEMOCRATIC FEDERATION hopes to reap the fruits thereof. Those elements they sought to get rid of have, of course, found a rallying point in the Avelings, the latter's mainstay being 1. the GASWORKERS UNION, [164] 2. the METROPOLITAN RADICAL FEDERATION, [430] 3. a number of the smaller unions who would rather make their mark in the EIGHT HOURS LEAGUE that be forced to play second fiddle to the OLD, petty-bourgeois-minded UNIONS in the TRADES COUNCIL. There was a great deal of manoeuvring on both sides and, at a meeting of delegates from London's labour organisations — in which, of course, the majority was rigged —, the TRADES COUNCIL succeeded in assuming control of the demonstration. Nevertheless, although it had previously decided *not* to enter into any negotiations with the Eight Hours League, it had to climb down and admit into the Executive Committee first 1 and then 2 delegates from the Eight Hours League, besides placing two platforms in the Park [a] at the latter's disposal. In addition the METROPOLITAN RADICAL FEDERATION likewise has a couple, which are also ours, whereas the SOCIAL DEMOCRATIC FEDERATION only has two.

Now the eight-hour day advocated by the majority on the TRADES COUNCIL merely implies payment of the ordinary wage for 8 hours, any work over and above this being payable as overtime at one and a half times or twice the ordinary rate; *thus the eight hour day advocated by these people is quite different from our own*, which means that in the course of this year, after May Day, the conflict will flare up in real earnest and be fought out anew. Such is the issue that will at long last receive an airing over here. So don't allow yourself to be hoodwinked by anything anyone from the *Vorwärts*, etc., may say about May Day here; from our point of view the whole thing's a swindle; it's an eight hour day IN A PICKWICKIAN SENSE, as is bound to come out in the long run, whereupon the equivocal situation from which both the SOCIAL

---

[a] Hyde Park

DEMOCRATIC FEDERATION and the FABIANS [87] are profiting will cease to exist.

You should make use of *The Workman's Times only* for its factual material. The editor[a] is a provincial who is relapsing into belletrism, is anxious to keep in with everyone and both talks and accepts a great deal of bosh. But the *reports* are all done by working men, STUPID though the 'ERRAND BOY' and his mother, the 'MARXIAN' (an out-and-out duffer), and the 'PROLETARIAN', etc., may be.*

Mother Wischnewetzky has had to suffer all manner of rough treatment at her husband's hands, has got divorced, calls herself Mrs Kelley again and lives in Chicago with her 3 children of whom she is the legal custodian.

I wonder very much what results our Frenchmen will obtain in the municipal elections on 1 May.[429] It will be the first time they have been really put to the test.

Regards from one household to the other.

Your
F. E.

First published in *Aus der Frühzeit des Marxismus. Engels Briefwechsel mit Kautsky*, Prag, 1935

Printed according to the original

Published in English for the first time

201

ENGELS TO PASQUALE MARTIGNETTI

IN BENEVENTO

London, 21 April 1892

Dear Friend,

I am sorry that I cannot send you a German copy of the *Condition of the Working Class*.[b] The book has not been in the book-

---

* *The Workman's Times* has amalgamated with the former *Trade Unionist* and Nash, of whom you know, has become one of its editors. Thus the influence of Toynbee Hall,[465] of which you also know, has gained a footing there.

---

[a] Joseph Burgess - [b] F. Engels, *The Condition of the Working-Class in England in 1844*.

shops for the past 16 years and even old, second-hand copies are offered only very rarely in dealers' catalogues and are extremely dear (30-40 marks!). I intend to bring out a new edition as soon as I have completed Volume III of Marx's *Capital*.

I am pleased to see from your translation of the English preface in the *Critica Sociale*[466] that your English has progressed by leaps and bounds. However, I wouldn't advise you to translate the book from the English text; the translation is very clumsy and full of Americanisms, not all of which I have been able to eliminate.

Once you have got to the stage of being able to translate English rapidly and without a dictionary, let's hope that Labriola, Turati or some other friend will succeed in finding literary work for you so that you may at last get away from the poverty and isolation of Benevento. If only you could leave it and go to Rome or Milan, you would undoubtedly find something fairly quickly.

My preface was not at all easy to translate, containing as it did a number of expressions for which no definition, at any rate in the sense used by me, is to be found in the dictionary.

I cannot thank you enough for the assiduity with which you translate my works, thereby rendering a great service, not only to myself, but also to international relations between Italian and German socialists. You will shortly be getting something else from me, namely the English edition of *Die Entwicklung des Sozialismus*[a] with a long new introduction which is to appear in German in the *Neue Zeit*.[461]

From the outset Fantuzzi seemed a sham to me. You would, I think, be well-advised to ask him to return the mss and corrected proofs,[467] for who knows whether he has any intention of printing anything else.

Very sincerely yours,

F. Engels

First published, in the language of the original (German), in *La corrispondenza di Marx e Engels con italiani. 1848-1895*, Milano, 1964

Printed according to the original

Published in English for the first time

---

[a] F. Engels, *Socialism: Utopian and Scientific*.

202

ENGELS TO JOHANN HEINRICH WILHELM DIETZ[468]

IN STUTTGART

London, 23 April 1892

Dear Mr Dietz,

Herewith a brief note in case you should wish to place the same before O. Wigand.[a]

Once the preliminaries have been settled, printing could begin, providing you agree that the book should appear, not only unaltered, but also without any addition save for a new preface and at most an occasional note. In that case you could send me the proofs in galley form and I should insert the annotations (footnotes) that were required.

Since the English edition has just come out, I have been able to satisfy myself that nothing more than this is required. A series of notes or an appendix such as would bring the book up to date would double its size, demand a year's study (which I cannot afford) and thus delay publication indefinitely. Moreover, *Capital*, Volume I, does the job perfectly adequately. Today the book is an historical document describing a certain stage of development and that is enough, the more so since in Germany we have reached much the same sort of stage today. Anything that needs to be said about this will be said in the preface.

Have you got a copy from which it can be printed?

The English edition (i. e. the one newly published over here, a reprint of the American edition) has now come out.

Awaiting your esteemed reply, I remain, yours most cordially

F. Engels

First published in: Marx and Engels, *Works*, First Russian Edition, Vol. XXIX, Moscow, 1946

Printed according to the original

Published in English for the first time

---

[a] See next letter.

203

ENGELS TO JOHANN HEINRICH WILHELM DIETZ

IN STUTTGART

London, 23 April 1892
122 Regent's Park Road, N. W.

Dear Mr Dietz,

I beg to acknowledge your esteemed favour of the 20th inst. I also agree that you should, with Mr Otto Wigand's consent, arrange for the publication of the *Condition of the Working-Class in England* in your Internationale Bibliothek [469] on terms which remain to be settled in detail between ourselves.

I therefore look forward to seeing your proposals on the same and remain

Yours very sincerely,

F. Engels

First published in: Marx and Engels, *Works*, First Russian Edition, Vol. XXIX, Moscow, 1946

Printed according to the original

Published in English for the first time

204

ENGELS TO JOHANN HEINRICH WILHELM DIETZ [470]

IN STUTTGART

London, 27 April [a] 1892

Dear Mr Dietz,

I agree to the terms proposed in your esteemed favour of yesterday's date and shall later be sending you instructions regarding the amount of the fee.

If I understand you aright, we are also agreed that, while the book is to be published as it stands, I am to write 1. a new preface and 2. a brief footnote here and there as required to make the book *intelligible*, not bring it up to date.

This does not require express confirmation, provided my assumption is correct.

I have kept a reserve copy for printing purposes and am sending you this by registered book post.

With cordial regards,

Yours faithfully,
F. Engels

First published in: Marx and Engels, *Works*, First Russian Edition, Vol. XXIX, Moscow, 1946

Printed according to the original

Published in English for the first time

205

ENGELS TO NIKOLAI PETERSEN

[IN COPENHAGEN]

[London, 3 May 1892]

Dear Mr Petersen,

I understand that it is possible even in prison for you to receive letters, and so I could not refrain from expressing to you my genuine

---

[a] 26 April in the ms.

sympathy on your conviction and imprisonment. Things are now much the same in Denmark as in other countries: where others are acquitted, a socialist is found guilty, and where others are given a month in prison, a socialist gets a year or several years, and hard labour into the bargain. This is proof that they fear us more and more, but it makes it no less unfortunate for those who are the victims of reaction.

Many thanks also for sending me *Arbejderen*. As I only rarely see *Social-Demokraten*, your paper has been my sole source of information as far as the situation in Denmark is concerned, and that has made it even more welcome to me.

The May Day festival went off well. I wish that you had been able to see the 600,000 people who were in Hyde Park the day before yesterday.[471] Every year the May Day parade becomes more impressive, showing that the time is fast approaching when we shall be strong enough to let things come to a decisive battle.

And now farewell. I hope that you are no worse off than German comrades usually are on similar occasions, so that it is at least bearable. It can scarcely be as bad as in England and America, or as good as in Paris in Sainte Pélagie. In any case we all hope that you will leave prison with your health unimpaired and that you will be fit enough to be with us on the next May Day.

With best wishes from Mrs Kautsky and me myself,

Yours, as ever,

F. Engels

First published, in Danish, in *Arbejderen*, No. 28, Copenhagen, 1892

Printed according to the newspaper

Translated from the Danish

Published in English for the first time

206

ENGELS TO JOHANN HEINRICH WILHELM DIETZ

IN STUTTGART

London, 5 May 1892

Dear Mr Dietz,

In response to your favour of 28 April an unbound copy of the *Condition of the Working-Class in England* went off to you on the 2nd inst. *by registered mail*, done up in a strong wrapper; I trust you have received it.

From what you say, it is not clear *how much* of a free hand Wigand has given you as regards publication in the Internationale Bibliothek [469] — whether for one edition of a stipulated size or for as many, over as long a period, as you and I may agree. To judge by your afore-mentioned letter, the latter would appear to be the case. I would be much obliged if you could let me have further details; in matters of business it is important for me to know what my position is.

Cordial regards,

Yours,

F. Engels

First published in: Marx and Engels, *Works*, First Russian Edition, Vol. XXIX, Moscow, 1946

Printed according to the original

Published in English for the first time

207

ENGELS TO LAURA LAFARGUE

AT LE PERREUX

London, 5 May 1892

My dear Laura,

A few lines in a hurry. What was intended as a defeat for us here, has ended in a veritable triumph.[471] We had only two platforms on Sunday,[a] but they were the only ones that drew, both public and press. You will have seen our involuntary caricatures in the *Daily Graphic* I sent you.[472] Platform No. 14, the international platform, was the great success of the day. By a conspicuous piece of good luck, Roussel of the *Bourse du travail*[b] [57] was, it seems, sent out of the way of Prudent Dervillers and Argyriades by them and Adolphe Smith and came on our platform, so that we had *two* Frenchmen,[c] two Russians,[d] a German, Bernstein, an Austrian, Louise, a Pole, Mendelson and a Jew,[e] besides *la Española* Mrs C. Graham and the Britishers.[f]

The demonstration itself was immense, even compared with the two previous ones, and showed that things *are* moving here, though they move in that peculiar roundabout way in which the English delight.

In the evening we had the Mendelsons, Bernsteins, Tussy and Edward of course, and Bonnier brought Roussel, we were very jolly, had a Maibowle, and fat Roussel was effusively delighted, while Argyriades and Co. owned next morning to him, they had been bored to death in the company where they had, or rather had been, moved (*sans calembour*[g]!)

I am very anxiously awaiting the *Socialiste* to learn something about our electoral successes on May 1st in France,[429] the papers you sent me do not contain anything to go by, and surely if we had not secured majorities, we must have got in at least some minorities.

Anyhow I am glad the thing passed off quietly everywhere. The

---

[a] 1 May - [b] Labour Stock-Exchange - [c] Paul Lafargue and Ferdinand Roussel - [d] Felix Volkhovsky and Sergei Stepnyak-Kravchinsky - [e] Shajer - [f] Edward Aveling, Eleanor Marx-Aveling, William Morris, Thomas Mann, Peter Curran and others - [g] this is not a pun

idea that the 1st of May is to be a day of rows and riots is a mere trap set by the bourgeois and we have no interest whatever to fall into that trap. We want to show our strength, that's all, as to when we are to use that strength, that's our business, not that of our opponents, if we can help it.

Thanks for the papers—Dinner Bell! I have Pumps, Percy and family here, so cannot write much, must take them out to see some of the sights they have missed so long in the Isle of Wight. They send their kindest regards to you and Paul. Ditto from Louise.

Ever yours,

F. Engels

First published, in the language of the original (English), in: F. Engels, P. and L. Lafargue, *Correspondance*, t. III, Paris 1959

Reproduced from the original

208

ENGELS TO AUGUST BEBEL

IN BERLIN

London, 7 May 1892

Dear August,

So we can expect to see you here on Saturday,[a] a week today.[473] Let's hope you instil so much confidence into Paulus[b] while afloat that he will regard the crossing via Ostend as a trial trip for the crossing to Chicago.[474] For if he plucks up enough courage, he could go straight on to Chicago by water *all the way*—from Liverpool to Montreal on the St Lawrence and thence through the Great Lakes, after which he would for ever be immune; for on the big, inland lakes even the most seasoned old salts are sea-sick and, when the four of us survived a storm on Lake Erie without being affected in that way,[443] we were regarded as prodigies by the entire company.

But if you imagine I now intend to reply to your three letters in detail and in writing, you are mistaken. Louise has just come back from

---

town bringing with her a tremendous thirst, so that we have ventured on a second mid-morning glass of beer and are in exceedingly merry mood. For it is very warm outdoors and hence we must, to use a Prussian expression, bring about a change.

You will be meeting Mendelson and his wife[a] who were here last Sunday and will also be able to go and converse with them at their house.

The fact that we had good weather for May Day and you did not, serves you right. You should have been over here and then you'd have been able to see what it looks like when 600,000 people foregather in one place [471]; it was really tremendous; and an impression like that leaves one in no state to sustain even such criticism as is called for by the deplorable scheming and squabbling before the event, and yet sustain it one must.

When you come over here, your doctor's orders will safeguard you against any sort of public speechifying, always assuming that you yourself abide by the said orders. You know how it is — anyone who lets himself be talked round on just *one* occasion, is lost for good and all.

Laura Lafargue writes to say that, while our chaps have so far been victorious in the French municipal elections [429] at a number of places, the real results, because of the second ballot, won't be known until next week. So far I haven't seen much about it in the press.

Well, mind you bring with you a pair of good horny hands; we have already written to the BOARD OF WORKS, instructing them to put at our disposal sufficient ancient trees in the parks of London to enable you to uproot at least one a day for your breakfast.[475]

Cordial regards from Louise.

Your
F. E.

First published in: Marx and Engels, *Works*, First Russian Edition, Vol. XXIX, Moscow, 1946

Printed according to the original

Published in English for the first time

---

[a] Maria Mendelson

209

ENGELS TO JOHANN HEINRICH WILHELM DIETZ

IN STUTTGART

London, 12 May 1892

Dear Mr Dietz,

I am in complete agreement with your proposal of the 9th inst.[476] I for my part concede you the right, in so far as it is within my competence, to print 10,000 copies, in return for which you are to pay me the following fees:

for 2,500 copies M. 500 in the autumn of 1892, after printing;
" 2,500 " " 500 in the New Year of 1893;
" 5,000 " " 1,000 after printing this second half, but *not* *later than 6 months* after printing has *begun.*

In view of your agreement with Wigand which is, after all, still very vague, I think you have chosen the right procedure. Whether you now stipulate *one* edition or decide to do several is your own affair. I of course am much more concerned with placing the work before the public again than with the kudos of having numerous editions.

With cordial regards,

Yours,

F. Engels

First published in: Marx and Engels, *Works*, First Russian Edition, Vol. XXIX, Moscow, 1946

Printed according to the original

Published in English for the first time

210

ENGELS TO STANISŁAW MENDELSON

IN LONDON

[London,] 14 May 1892
122 Regent's Park Road, N.W.

Dear Citizen Mendelson,

Sorge has written from New York to say that, of the ten pounds (five of them from you) we sent him for Anna,[a] he still has 19 dollars 64 cents left; he has returned me this sum, namely £ 4. 8s., by postal order. I am therefore sending you herewith a cheque for £ 2. 4s. for your half.

Our friends Bebel and Singer arrive tomorrow and Bebel in particular has expressed a desire to see you — you and Mrs Mendelson. Perhaps you might care to do us the pleasure of having supper with us here on Sunday evening. If, by chance, you are engaged for Sunday, would you be so good as to fix a day and time when we could come and see you at your house.

With many good wishes from both Mrs Kautsky and me to Mrs Mendelson and yourself.

F. Engels

First published in: Marx and Engels, *Works*, Second Russian Edition, Vol. 38, Moscow, 1965

Printed according to the original

Translated from the French

Published in English for the first time

---

[a] Stanisław Padlewski

211

ENGELS TO KARL KAUTSKY

IN STUTTGART

London, 17 May 1892

Dear Kautsky,

You will have got the postcard about Werner-Weiler.[477] Meyer told me directly after the Edinburgh Congress [478] that he had spotted Weiler there.

To apply that epithet to me was really very silly.[479] You would be doing a kindness to me and certainly to others as well, if you pointed out to him, at any rate for his future guidance, that he must accustom himself to our less grandiose terminology, failing which you will have to correct his stuff accordingly.

Hirsch is in Frankfurt all right and Meyer is in his debt since at Meyer's request he used to shout out at appropriate moments the admonition: 'Mr Meyer, you ought not to drink so much.' It was the funniest bosom friendship between a Jew — and what an archetypal Jew! — and an anti-Semite I have ever known. It still makes me laugh, just writing about it.

Now as to the business of Louise, I should, if I were you, let the matter rest.[480] That she bears your name is the result of your own voluntary action. That you are no longer together is likewise the result of your own initiative. That there is a possibility of mistaken identity is again entirely your own doing. She is now using the only name she is entitled to bear under Austrian law and I can see absolutely no reason why she should evade that necessity.

Let me be perfectly frank with you. All of us here, not least myself, have grown very fond of Louise, as was already the case when you were over here together. When the business of the divorce began, she behaved from beginning to end with a magnanimity we could not admire too greatly and, since arriving in this country, she has become so dear to me that I regard her just as I do Pumps, Tussy or Laura, just as though she were my own child. When you were here, she showed you that she bore you no grudge whatsoever. But enough is enough.

Nobody can expect her to bear whatever unpleasant consequences may arise from *your* actions. Were you to put to her what you told me in your letter and were she to come and ask my advice, my answer would be an uncompromising 'No!'

Mistaken identity has also occurred on the other side, but she merely laughed about it. And supposing she did oblige you, what would be the result? Lo*u*ise Kautsky and L*ui*se Kautsky would be joined on the stage by yet a third Louise Strasser-Kautsky whereupon the comedy of errors would degenerate into pure farce. It would be of no help to *you*, while *she* would have to go into long explanations with all and sundry about the how, the who, the when and the wherefore.

So as I have said, let sleeping dogs lie. Your having parted is really quite a good thing and Louise is perfectly content with this state of affairs. But no one will ever be able to undo what you have done and it is you, after all, who must bear the consequences. And *this* particular consequence is really not so trying as to warrant any sort of fuss being made about it.

Tussy is of the same opinion and August, to whom I have shown both your letter and the foregoing,[473] is fully in agreement with it.

So don't worry, the whole thing will automatically right itself.

Your old friend,

F. Engels

First published in *Aus der Frühzeit des Marxismus. Engels Briefwechsel mit Kautsky*, Prag, 1935

Printed according to the original

Published in English for the first time

212

ENGELS TO LUDWIG SCHORLEMMER

IN DARMSTADT

London, 17 May 1892

Dear Mr Schorlemmer,

Not long ago I received the same curious letter from Carl [a] as you did, whereupon I approached his physician, Dr Gumpert, an old friend of Marx's and mine. He said that over a period there had been considerable changes in Carl's physical condition — as we had all noticed, added to which he had had a bout of influenza in the spring followed by all kinds of unpleasant after-effects. What struck him most of all was the very considerable time his system was taking to recoup the strength it had lost. It was not yet possible, he said, to diagnose any specific illness, but something appeared to be wrong and he would write again as soon as he had something more definite to tell me. Meanwhile there was no necessity for me to come to Manchester, as I had offered to do, nor did he himself wish it.

I haven't seen Carl since last summer; he was unable to come for Christmas on account of tinnitus which bothers him a great deal during lectures and examinations and is, he says, always aggravated by a trip to London. At Easter he went down with influenza and once again everything fell through. Dr Gumpert now says that, as soon as his condition permits, he will send him away from the smoke of Manchester. We may perhaps go somewhere together where the air is better, although I can't say anything about that yet.

I believe it would be best if you didn't let Carl know that we correspond about his health, for he seems to be very touchy. It would, I think, be best if you were again to write to him every now and then, giving him news from home and asking for news of himself. I shall be hearing from Gumpert from time to time, as promised, and shall then pass the information on to you with or without prompting.

August is over here and is staying with us. Paul the Stout [b] is also here, staying with the Bernsteins.[473] August is not available at this

---

[a] Carl Schorlemmer - [b] Paul Singer

moment, otherwise he would certainly have sent you his greetings; Mrs Kautsky warmly reciprocates your good wishes and I, too, should like to send you mine and would ask you to pass on my kindest regards to the rest of your family.

Yours,
F. Engels

My niece Mrs Rosher, known as Pumps, is also here and sends her best wishes to you all.

First published in: Marx and Engels, *Works*, First Russian Edition, Vol. XXIX, Moscow, 1946

Printed according to the original

Published in English for the first time

213

ENGELS TO VICTOR ADLER

IN VIENNA

London, 19 May 1892

Dear Victor,

I have reached an understanding with Dietz and he with Wigand in regard to a new edition of the *Condition of the Working-Class in England*, the initial benefit of which will be a fee of 1,000 marks. Dietz promises to pay $^1/_2$ in the autumn and $^1/_2$ in the New Year of 1893 but August, who is over here, believes we can get at least part of it out of him even sooner. Also an additional fee of some sort for *Neue Zeit* articles. Now I should like to pass this on to you Austrians but would take the liberty of making a few stipulations regarding its use; these I have discussed with August who agrees to them.

For even though I may be unfamiliar with the details, I know well enough for practical purposes that your activities on behalf of the Austrian party are being continually hampered by the inability of that self-same party to secure for you the material position that would permit you to devote all your time and energy to the cause. I also know that the misfortunes you have met with of late have involved you in expenditure and that the party is unable to offer you the means with which to meet it. So I regard it as one of the prime conditions for the continued growth of the Austrian movement that you should be given an opportunity firstly to weather the present period of exceptional expenditure and, secondly, to secure for yourself, if possible, the necessary increase in pay which cannot yet be provided over there. The former is the more essential, but the latter is bound up with it. I should now like to put a suggestion to you, namely that the above fees should be placed at your disposal for either the former or the latter purpose or both — how they are to be used will then depend entirely on circumstances which you alone will be competent to judge. I need hardly add that there would then be no grounds for acknowledging in public, say, receipt of these sums.

I trust you will do me the pleasure of accepting my proposal. I know from my own experience, even though that was long ago, how greatly one's ability to work, will to work and time for work is restricted by the economic struggle for existence and we three[a] here are all of the opinion that you can do the Austrian party no greater service than to fall in with this little scheme.

Your May Day celebrations made a very good impression over here, the more so since Paris did not in fact participate this year as a result of the squabbles going on there. However Lafargue writes to say that in 22 places (the biggest being Roubaix and Marseilles where we got *everyone* home) we gained a majority on the city council — four hundred seats in the first ballot and a further 200 in the second.[429] The effect this has had can be gathered from the Orleanist *Soleil* which I am sending you.

Many regards, then, from

Your
F. Engels

First published in *Victor Adlers Aufsätze, Reden und Briefe*. Erstes Heft: *Victor Adler und Friedrich Engels*, Wien, 1922

Printed according to the book

Published in English for the first time

---

[a] Frederick Engels, August Bebel and Paul Singer

To the Congress of the Austrian Social-Democratic Party.
Invitation sent to Engels. 1892

214

ENGELS TO PAUL LAFARGUE[141]

AT LE PERREUX

London, 19 May 1892

My dear Lafargue,

What a rottenly organised statistical service you have over there! In Germany we should have had the results 3-4 days after the 2nd ballot, whereas such information as is to be found in the *Socialiste* of the 15th is barely accurate and largely incomplete.[481] But that will come in time. You'll discover that nothing fires the imagination of the masses more than a splendid, well set out array of figures announcing electoral victories. In particular this is of prime importance when it comes to making workmen realise the extent to which universal suffrage lends strength to their arm. Don't forget to complete your statistics for 1 May 1892 — for comparison with the figures for the '93 parliamentary elections when they come out. If things improve, and of that I am convinced, you will see how effective it can be when friends and enemies alike are able to ascertain what advances have been made, how much ground has been won, in a year.

After all, the winning of 22 councils and 600 seats is not to be sneezed at![429] And the *Soleil* which you sent me and which, now that Bebel has finished with it here, is on its way to Adler in Vienna,[a] confirms as much in distinctly peevish terms. Bravo!

Now what have the others gained, the Broussists,[3] Allemanists,[53] Blanquists? The first must have had some success or lack of it at Chatellerault etc. etc., the second in the Ardennes, the Blanquists in Le Cher. Or did you include them in your list?

I congratulate you most of all on the fact that in France, too, Lassalle's 'single, compact, reactionary mass',[322] the all-party coalition opposed to the Socialists, is beginning to take shape. In Germany we have had this for years and in the big industrial centres the anti-Socialist mass is already mustering its forces for the 1st ballot so as to bar our way. The whole of Germany's official history, if we disregard the influence of young William's[b] entourage, a most heterogeneous

---

[a] See this volume, p. 420.- [b] William II

camarilla which leads him a pretty dance, is shaped, on the one hand, by Socialist influence which is causing the bourgeois parties to combine into one large party of straightforward resistance and, on the other, by the interplay of divergent interests amongst those parties, which draws them apart from one another. The Reichstag's legislation is simply the product, the result, of the conflict between these two opposing currents, the second of which, the disintegrative current, is gradually dwindling to a trickle.

Well, the same old game is beginning in France. There is no better sign of progress, for it shows that they fear you, not as a riotous force liable to act on the spur of the moment, but as a regular, organised, *political* force.

I have had misgivings similar to those you express about the inexperience of the new councillors. After the wholesale replacement of an administration there is a period of between 6 and 10 months when the seats of power are occupied by the council's permanent employees who are quite prepared to let their new masters burn their fingers in experiments of a more or less dangerous nature. This is particularly the case where the new incumbents are Socialists. They should be advised to bide their time until they feel they can stand on their own feet in their new surroundings. Otherwise the old reactionary officials will wreck everything, and the blame will fall on our people.

As for the daily newspaper,[423] a fresh start must be made. I hope you will succeed better NEXT TIME. In any case, you will be able to set up your editorial headquarters. Are you going to have a 'political editor' — Guesde?

Have you really formed a group in the Chamber or is the matter still up in the air?

A thousand greetings from Louise and Bebel [473] to Laura and you. Give her a hug in my behalf and tell her that as soon as the telephone has been properly installed, I will use it to have a cask of Pilsner sent to her.

Yours,
F. E.

Singer too is here, he is staying with the Bernsteins.

LOUISE SAYS SHE WISHES LAURA WOULD TELEPHONE HER AN ARTICLE FOR VIENNA.

I have just received a letter from Gumpert on Schorlemmer. You will know that the latter has been physically and mentally sick for

4 years now. In the last two years he has been unable to come here either for Christmas or for Easter. Last year, when we were to go on a sea voyage round the British Isles, he was put out of action within the first 24 hours. Recently he wrote his brother [a] and me to tell us not to write him since he was unable to answer. In reply to my enquiry Gumpert informed me that he found Schorlemmer extremely feeble after what was a rather light case of influenza. Today he has written to tell me that this feebleness, physical and intellectual, is growing worse daily, that it is, in fact, senility pure and simple, that he had made him draw up his will, that he fears that within a very short time Schorlemmer's mental powers will be gone, and that the end is approaching. Poor devil! A talent of the first order fading away. You would not have recognised him had you seen him during these last few years—all his vivacity and good spirits are gone, he no longer takes an interest in anything. I am writing to his brother—he will be desperate. Imagine Schorlemmer dying of senility while his mother lives on in good health!

First published in: F. Engels, P. et L. Lafargue, *Correspondance*, t. III, Paris, 1959

Printed according to the original

Translated from the French

215

ENGELS TO LUDWIG SCHORLEMMER

IN DARMSTADT

London, 19 May 1892
122 Regent's Park Road, N. W.

Dear Mr Schorlemmer,

I have just had a letter from Dr Gumpert who says that Carl's [b] condition has unfortunately changed for the worse. He tells me that Carl has become weaker and also less mentally alert, while the symptoms of paralysis in the left arm have grown steadily more marked over the past week. He very much doubts whether he will improve

---

[a] Ludwig Schorlemmer - [b] Carl Schorlemmer

sufficiently to be able to get away from Manchester to some place where he could build up his strength and breathe fresh air. Moreover his mental condition indicated so great a deterioration of his faculties that he (Gumpert) felt it essential to obtain from him the particulars required for a will; this was to have been drawn up by a solicitor yesterday and signed by Carl today. Apparently Carl is exceedingly apathetic and listless and expresses no desire whatever to receive any of his friends and Dr Gumpert has explicitly told me that, if I write to a member of his family in Germany, I am simply to say 'that no purpose would be served by any of the family's coming over'.

I hasten to inform you of this by the first post. I shall also write to Gumpert asking for further reports and, each time I get one, shall at once tell you what it says. Unfortunately the outlook is now very depressing and, since Gumpert is a highly skilled and, especially in diagnosis, highly experienced doctor, I fear we must be prepared for the worst. What will your poor old mother say, now that yet another of her sons is mortally ill? [482]

With warm regards,

Yours,

F. Engels

First published in: Marx and Engels, *Works*, First Russian Edition, Vol. XXIX, Moscow, 1946

Printed according to the original

Published in English for the first time

216

ENGELS TO PAUL AND LAURA LAFARGUE

AT LE PERREUX

London, 27 May 1892

My dear Lafargue,

I congratulate you on your success. With your daily now under way [423] (unless you get thrown out again, which would be *your* fault entirely this time), and with the provinces TO BACK YOU, you will conquer Paris under the noses of the Possibilo-Blanquists.

Bebel and Singer are here.[473] This morning I had a talk with Bebel on the subject of a German correspondent. If *you haven't yet written to Berlin about this matter*, we would ask you not to do so for the moment, but in the meantime to let us know what kind of information you require—reports on the situation in general and on that of the Party in particular?

As for me, I can only say that if you could get Bebel to act as your correspondent you would have reports of the utmost value. At the time of the Anti-Socialist Law [11] Bebel wrote a weekly report for Adler's *Arbeiter-Zeitung* in Vienna. Those reports were such that, before forming a definite opinion on an important fact or an important matter affecting Germany at that time, I would always try to read what Bebel had to say in his articles. It was clear, concise, TO THE POINT and always accurate.

Bebel would write in German and Laura would, I trust, translate. You would have *facts*, whereas all you would get out of Liebknecht would be hot air. And Liebknecht would pride himself on writing to you in French. You would correct his style and he would tell you that you had mangled his facts and ideas.

I shall write to Ravé as soon as I have received and read Roy's translation. It's a ticklish matter and I shouldn't like Laura's work to be wasted. What I have read of it is decidedly better than Roy's translation.[483] And then there's the question of a publisher! Has he got one? As for Ravé's promises, which he hasn't kept, he excuses himself on the grounds that he has been held up by the additions to the fourth edition. Anyway it's a pretty unpleasant business, which I can't really fathom at this moment. However we shall see.

*Now my dear Löhr a few words with you. In that new daily paper you are an absolutely necessary factor. If the thing is to be superior to the usual run of Parisian dailies, there must be somebody who follows closely from day to day, and reports on, from time to time, the English and German movement. And you are the only person in *toute la belle France*[a] who can do this. I have no doubt that you are perfectly ready to undertake this work, which fortunately can be done

---

[a] the whole fair country of France

very comfortably at Le Perreux, as it will not matter a bit whether *these* news, generally, are published a day sooner or a day later. But what I want to drive into you, poking your ribs with both my forefingers, is that you must be a regular member of the *rédaction*[a] and paid accordingly. Paul is too much of an hidalgo to think of, or to press, such matters, but '*it mun be done*' as they say in Lancashire, and I think it is my duty to call your and Paul's attention to it. The subject is too important to be neglected, and it will not be properly treated unless you are *rédactrice du Socialiste quotidien*[b] and charged with that special branch.

Bebel and Louise send their kindest regards.

Ever yours,*

F. E.

First published in: F. Engels, P. et L. Lafargue, *Correspondance*, t. III, Paris, 1959

Published according to the original

Translated from the French

217

ENGELS TO AUGUST SIEGEL

IN MUIRKIRK

London, 28 May 1892
122 Regent's Park Road, N. W.

Dear Comrade,

Mrs Aveling got back safe and sound on Saturday when we were glad to hear that the business had been settled so quickly and satisfactorily. Naturally it was not your fault that the colliery MANAGER should have duped you, but let that serve as a warning never to reach a final settlement with the colliery management without having first consulted the Scottish miners and us down here. In this country the Ger-

---

[a] editorial staff - [b] editress of the daily *Socialiste*

mans are now reputed, not without some justification, to depress wages and provide blackleg labour more than any other nation and that is why Messrs Burt, Fenwick, etc., were determined not to find you work over here. Were the Germans in Muirkirk now to do anything at all that might serve to support this old anti-German prejudice, it would represent a most serious threat to international relations between Germans and Englishmen generally, and this applies not merely to the miners, but to the workers in all branches of industry. So if you wish to continue operating in the spirit of the labour cause, you must do your best to learn enough English to enable you to talk things over with the Scots without risk of misunderstandings and to keep in daily, and if possible hourly, touch with the Scottish workers. You will find the Scottish workers very honest, very stalwart and, provided only that you can talk things over properly with them, very reliable, so it behoves you to get on really friendly terms with them. The colliery managements, on the other hand, are much more artful and mendacious than in Germany and thrice as experienced when it comes to exploitation. But until you feel really confident about your English it would definitely be advisable for you to write *in German* to Mrs Aveling, 65 Chancery Lane, London, W. C. whenever you are in doubt about anything. She will be glad to place her experience of labour relations over here at your disposal.

It was fortunate that we had two Reichstag deputies and members of the Party Executive over here at that particular moment,[473] as they were able to intervence at once and advance the necessary funds. Otherwise the affair might have ended unpleasantly and brought great discredit on German workers throughout this country.

Mrs Aveling will also have told you that people in Germany are saying Schröder induced you to leave by citing all kinds of inaccurate reports and that as a result you threw away an excellent position, although the danger was not nearly so great as people would have you believe. I must say that I had suspected as much all along and should be very happy were a man like you not to be entirely lost to the German miners' movement. After all, you would be pretty sure of a Reichstag mandate and if, in course of time, you were to return and then, after a month or two in jug, do your best to keep the German miners on the right lines, it could only be to our advantage.

You will be getting some newspapers shortly.

Warm regards from Mrs Kautsky and myself to your wife, about whom Mrs Aveling has told us a great many nice things, and to you yourself.

Yours,
F. Engels

I don't mean, of course, that you should return to Germany this very instant; on the contrary it will be extremely useful if you acquire an intimate knowledge of labour relations over here and then, drawing on your own experience, point out to the Germans how much better off they would be, even in a capitalist economy, if only they stood up for themselves.

First published in: Marx and Engels, *Works*, First Russian Edition, Vol. XXIX, Moscow, 1946

Printed according to the original

Published in English for the first time

218

ENGELS TO SIR HENRY ENFIELD ROSCOE

IN LONDON

[Draft]

[London,] 28 May [1892]

Dear Sir Henry,

Many thanks for your note of yesterday.[484] Gumpert has in fact given me a full report of the consultation with Dreschfeld, whom already 3 or 4 weeks ago he had proposed to Schorlemmer to call in, but Schorlemmer would not hear of it. As both medical men agree perfectly in their diagnosis, I am afraid there is but little hope left to us.

I have my friend Bebel of the German Reichstag here staying with me until middle of next week,[473] and intend driving over to Manchester about Thursday[485] unless called before by Gumpert.

If I do not reciprocate the style of address employed in your note,[486] it is simply because that note is in the handwriting of a third party, and therefore an unintentional mistake not quite excluded.

Yours truly

First published in: Marx and Engels, *Works*, First Russian Edition, Vol. XXIX, Moscow, 1946

Reproduced from the original

Published in English for the first time

219

ENGELS TO LUDWIG SCHORLEMMER

IN DARMSTADT

London, 28 May 1892

Dear Mr Schorlemmer,

I am not, alas, in a position to give you any better news today. Not only has Carl's[a] debility, both physical and mental, not diminished; it has actually increased, for which reason Gumpert has called in another physician, Dr Julius Dreschfeld of Mannheim, who is professor of medicine at Owens College[487] and is a great personal friend of Carl's. Unfortunately the opinion of this distinguished medical man is exactly the same as Gumpert's, namely that Carl's strength is gradually failing and that there is probably very little hope of his recovery. Since last Saturday Gumpert has kept him wholly confined to bed and has engaged a hospital nurse for him with whose work he declares himself completely satisfied. I myself propose, unless called before by Gumpert, to travel down to Manchester next Wednesday or Thursday[485] when, having seen for myself how things are, I should have more to tell you. But if Gumpert sends for me before then, I shall, of course, go down at once.

Bebel is still here and will be returning home with Singer in the middle of next week.[473] While here he has rallied very well, as was indeed essential for he was in fact very much run down. However, the doctor has forbidden him to speak in public for the next few months.

---

[a] Carl Schorlemmer

And Bebel's strength has got to be spared—he's such a splendid chap and we shall never get another like him.

In about three weeks' time our chaps in Paris will have a big daily that will be able to bear comparison with the best newspapers; it is to be under the control of Guesde and Lafargue.[423]

Mrs Kautsky joins me in sending kind regards to your mother and to the rest of the family.

Yours,

F. Engels

Carl has made his will in which he leaves everything to his mother. Should you receive inquiries from England regarding Carl's manuscripts, I would most strongly advise you to make no promises of any kind before finding out what is involved from Dr Gumpert, myself or someone else whom you know well.

First published in: Marx and Engels, *Works*, First Russian Edition, Vol. XXIX, Moscow, 1946

Printed according to the original

Published in English for the first time

220

ENGELS TO LUDWIG SCHORLEMMER

IN DARMSTADT

London, 5 June 1892

Dear Mr Schorlemmer,

I arrived back from Manchester yesterday evening[485] and am sorry to say that I cannot give you any better news of Carl.[a] He is in bed and very apathetic, wants peace and quiet, but otherwise suffers no pain at all; he is not quite clear in the head and his memory often fails him, besides which he frequently misunderstands what is being said to him. I visited him six times, never for longer than five or ten minutes which is about as much as he can stand.

---

[a] Carl Schorlemmer

I can now tell you something I have withheld from you hitherto, namely that in the past week or so he has been found beyond doubt to have developed a carcinogenic tumour of the right lung extending pretty much over the whole of the upper third of the organ. In consequence of the pressure of this tumour on the nerve ends and the larger blood vessels, the activity of the brain is impaired and the right arm paralysed and swollen. The existence of this tumour explains the earlier symptoms—the intense debility following his influenza and the failure to overcome that debility. But unhappily the discovery of the cause deprives us of all hope that he may recover and now all we can wish is that the painless condition he is now in persists until the end. Gumpert says this could come at any moment, though again Carl might, in the absence of any complications, continue in his present state but growing steadily weaker for several more weeks and possibly even longer.

I have made sure that he is well looked after. The hospital nurse obtained for him by Gumpert appears to know her business properly and to be taking great care of him, quite unlike the London nurses, my experience of whom has not been exactly happy. Also the owners of the house where he has been living for the past fourteen years are doing everything that lies within their power. The landlord showed me his fairly voluminous mss and promised me faithfully that he would hand them over to Carl's executors [a] and to no one else. I spoke to one of these two executors, a chemist and an old friend of ours,[b] and told him what I thought should be done first—at the very outset—to safeguard the manuscripts and the interests of the heirs thereto; he was in full accord with me, so that in that respect my mind is at rest. Since there are people about who would not be averse to pluming themselves with Carl's feathers and have, indeed, already made some attempt in that direction, I thought I ought to do all I could to frustrate them. More about this anon.

Should you or any other member of your family wish to set your minds at rest by coming over here and seeing with your own eyes how Carl is faring, Dr Gumpert would gladly do anything to make matters easier for you in Manchester, as I would here.

We have discovered that a niece of yours from Bordeaux is here in London, but have been unable to get her address out of Carl; would

---

[a] Philipp Klepsch and Ludwig Siebold - [b] Ludwig Siebold

you be so good as to let us have it? We might be able to be of some use to the young lady.

I would also ask you to be so kind as to write at once (in German) to Dr Gumpert, whose address I give below, to say whether a telegram addressed to Ludwig Schorlemmer, Darmstadt, would reach you or whether a more detailed address is necessary and, if so, what it is.

With kind regards to your mother and to your whole family, I remain,

Yours very sincerely,
F. Engels

Dr Gumpert,
203 High Street, Oxford Road,
Manchester, England

Bebel and Singer went back to Germany on Wednesday.[a]
Mrs Kautsky likewise sends her most cordial regards.

First published in: Marx and Engels, *Works*, First Russian Edition, Vol. XXIX, Moscow, 1946

Printed according to the original

Published in English for the first time

221

ENGELS TO LAURA LAFARGUE

AT LE PERREUX

London, 9 June 1892

My dear Löhr,

Your silence and Paul's is ominous—no news of any agreement signed on June 1st—are your intelligent capitalists after all recalcitrant? In the meantime Bax who is editor of *Justice* for 2 months, heard of your paper [423] at Mottelers, where he met Bebel, Singer and our

---

[a] 1 June

lot, and in spite of our precautions, cautions and remonstrances, has blabbed it out in last No.[488]

Well, I am likely to wait until I get news from you, fortunately the weather is so hot, that waiting is not so very difficult, and rather less so than any more active proceeding—in the meantime I am in the agreeable position to hand you a little cash viz. £2.18.4, one third of £8.15.- proceeds of 180 Marks sent by Dietz as share of honorarium, for Marx's heirs, of the German edition of the *Misère de la Philosophie*. The translators[a] have all at once come to the consciousness that, for the first edition of that work, Mohr's heirs were not paid anything, so I was called upon to say what they were to have for both editions now on the coming out of the 2nd edition. After some correspondence we agreed that of the 300 Marks paid for the second, the two translators were to have $2/5 = 120$ M. and the heirs 180 Marks $= 3/5$, which I believe is fair enough.[b] So herewith your cheque.

Tussy is in Plymouth for Gas Workers Annual Conference,[489] and Edward goes from there to Aberdeen, on an invitation to preach.[490]

I was in Manchester last week.[485] Poor Schorlemmer is dying. You know how changed he has been since that fall on boards the Flushing steamer which prevented his coming to Paris with Nimmy and Pumps. For the last two Christmases he could not come here. Even Easter he stopped at home and at last sent a letter: don't write, as I cannot reply! Then I wrote to Gumpert and learnt that he was getting weaker and that percussion brought out a dullness over the upper third of the right lung which, all other possibilities being excluded by the other symptoms, indicated the formation of a tumour. This diagnosis has turned out only too correct. Partial paralysis, oedema and low temperature of the right arm have set in in consequence of the pressure of the tumour on the *vena cava* and the *plexus brachialis*, while the left arm is relatively and the lower extremities perfectly free from these symptoms. His brain, too, is not quite clear, and sometimes very confused. At the same time he suffers no pain, hardly any uneasiness, and is gradually getting weaker. Gumpert thinks he may last some weeks yet, but may go off quite suddenly if any complication arises. It was impossible to converse with him more than 5-8 minutes, he wants rest, peace and quietness, and does not

---

[a] Eduard Bernstein and Karl Kautsky - [b] See this volume, pp. 199 and 273.

take any interest in anything. I hope he will be spared any sufferings. His mother is still alive, she is 81 years old.

Well, my dear girl, do give us news, even if they are not exactly what you would like them to be, we want to know what is going on.

Vaillant called here on Monday morning, but evaded all further invitations or occasions for meeting me, I whall try to find out what brought him here.

We had Bebel and Singer here for a fortnight, and were very jolly.[473] You will have received the *Pall Mall* interview we sent you.[491]

We also send you the *Elend der Philosophie*,[a] 2nd edition.

Love from Louise, who would be thankful for an article,

and yours affectionately
F. Engels

Ditto to *M. le député*.[b]

First published, in the language of the original (English), in: F. Engels, P. et L. Lafargue, *Correspondance*, t. III, Paris, 1959

Reproduced from the original

222

ENGELS TO KARL KAUTSKY

IN STUTTGART

London, 11 June 1892

Dear Baron,

I would have written to you about Schorlemmer before now had I not wished to go and see for myself first. This I did only last week[485], after August and Paul had left for home on Wednesday,[c] I went down to Manchester that same day. I had already heard from Gumpert, who is treating him, that he was confined to bed, was quite apathetic and was probably suffering from a carcinogenic tumour of

---

[a] *Poverty of Philosophy* - [b] Paul Lafargue - [c] 1 June

the right[a] lung. And so I found him, unresponsive, totally incurious, but entirely free from pain; at the same time his faculties were clouded and he often supposed himself to be somewhere else. More than 5 to 10 minutes' conversation (when for the most part he mechanically repeated what the other person said) was too much for him and rest was what he needed most. The tumour of the lung continuing to develop, there was a marked dullness on percussion, while pressure on the large blood vessels and on the plexus also produced, on the one hand, impaired activity of the brain and, on the other, paralysis and oedema of the right arm. While there is no oedema of the legs, they are exceedingly weak, the muscles being relaxed and wasted. He might last out for a few weeks in this condition, but again might be carried off any day by some complication or other. There is, of course, no hope. I have told his family as much as they need to know, and have made provisions for the safeguarding of his fairly extensive mss; this may give rise to some interesting arguments. Gumpert got him to make his will before it was too late.

So that's another of our best chaps on the way out. He had not been his old self for four years or more, and had increasingly lost interest in anything not immediately connected with his work, the mere pursuit of which cost him considerable labour. Moreover, he was often testy because of increasing deafness and a susceptibility to the draughts and chills by which that deafness was instantly aggravated. Last year I made one more attempt to induce him to take a sea trip to Scotland and Ireland, but before twenty-four hours were out he was laid low by relatively minor adversities and we had to abandon the project. The tumour of the lung, now plainly distinguishable, explains much of this, and likewise his debility after the bout of influenza last March, which marked the beginning of his final illness.

My translation of the introduction to the English version of SOCIALISM: UTOPIAN AND SCIENTIFIC is now finished; as soon as the book comes out (and why it isn't already out I cannot think), I shall send you the introduction for the Neue Zeit.[462] In the meantime I am sending you the Italian translation of the same book in the second edition published in Milan.

This country is swarming with congresses. On Thursday[b] Tussy and Aveling returned from the Gasworkers' Congress in Plymouth[489] where they couldn't have set a better example to the TRADE

---

[a] 'left' in the ms. -[b] 9 June

UNIONISTS of the old stamp. A *Liberal* candidate, having given £10 towards a gasworkers' strike, or rather towards that of one of their factory workers' sections, asked to be admitted to the congress as an unofficial guest, a request ordinarily granted as a matter of course. The gasworkers, however, said *quod non*,[a] they wanted no truck with middle-class candidates, and the man had no *locus standi*[b] at their congress.

We've also got the miners over here.[492] The day before yesterday the Germans, including a *český towaryš*,[c] came to call on me. It was particularly unfortunate that Tussy shouldn't have been here to interpret and advise; I need tell you no more than that the chaps had fallen into the clutches of Julius,[d] who failed to understand anything that went on either in English or in French and, though unacquainted with conditions and people over here, had to pretend he understood everything and was acquainted with everyone, thus isolating the chaps almost completely. On top of that, they had with them an Anglicised German who cannot speak either language and is hand in glove with the old TRADES UNIONS. Fortunately the Avelings were present on the last and most important day. The ignominy of the English is plain for all to see: The Continentals are demanding 8 hours for *everyone* employed in the mines, the English ask it only for those working underground! That has now been established and the vainglory of the English about their superior TRADES UNION ORGANISATION has been punctured by themselves.

Kindest regards from

Your

General

First published in *Aus der Frühzeit des Marxismus. Engels Briefwechsel mit Kautsky*, Prag, 1935

Printed according to the original

Published in English for the first time

---

[a] no - [b] place - [c] Czech comrade - [d] Julius Motteler

223

ENGELS TO LUDWIG SCHORLEMMER

IN DARMSTADT

London, 16 June 1892

Dear Mr Schorlemmer,

I have received your letter of the 7th this month and have also heard from Gumpert who tells me he has had a line or two from you. Of Carl[a] he further says:

'As before, he suffers no pain at all, takes enough nourishment and sleeps well on the whole. During the past few days his faculties have been very clouded and he often forgets what has just happened.'

Otherwise there was no change. Not having heard from Gumpert since, I cannot be sure whether or not there has been any material change, but thought I would allay your anxiety by passing on the above note.

With cordial regards, in which I am joined by Mrs Kautsky, to you and all your family.

Yours,
F. Engels

First published in: Marx and Engels, *Works*, First Russian Edition, Vol. XXIX, Moscow, 1946

Printed according to the original

Published in English for the first time

---

[a] Carl Schorlemmer

224

ENGELS TO NIKOLAI DANIELSON [493]
IN ST PETERSBURG

London, 18 June 1892

My dear Sir,

I have to thank you for your very interesting letters of 24 March, 30 April and 18 May,[494] and to ask your pardon for not replying to them sooner. But I have been extremely busy, so much so that I have not been able to devote one moment to III volume [a]—next week however I hope to return to it.

I believe that in reality we both agree perfectly as to the facts, and the bearing of these facts, which constitute the present economic condition of your country. Only you seem to have taken sundry *ironical* expressions of my last letter [b] as if they were seriously meant—especially what I said about sundry things serving in the end the cause of human progress. There is in reality no fact within history which does not serve human progress in one way or another, but it is after all an awfully round-about way. And so it may be with the present economic transformation of your country.

The fact I especially wanted to lay stress upon, is that the неурожай,[c] to use the official expression, of last year, is not an isolated and accidental occurrence, but a necessary consequence of the whole development since the close of the Crimean War, that it is a result of the passage from communal agriculture and domestic patriarchal industry to modern industry; and that it seems to me that this transformation must in the long run endanger the existence of the agricultural община [d] and introduce the capitalist system in agriculture too.

I conclude from your letters that, as to these facts themselves, you are agreed with me; as to the question whether we like them or not, that is another thing, and whether we do like them or not, the facts will continue to exist all the same. The more we leave our likings and dislikings out of the question, the better we shall be able to judge of the facts themselves and of their consequences.

There can be no doubt, but that the present sudden growth of modern '*grosse Industrie*' [e] in Russia has been caused by artificial

---

[a] of *Capital* - [b] See this volume, pp. 382-85. - [c] crop failure (Russ.) - [d] commune (Russ.) - [e] big industry

means, prohibitive duties, state subventions etc. The same has taken place in France, where the prohibitive system has existed ever since Colbert, in Spain, in Italy and, since 1878, even in Germany; although that country had almost completed its industrial transformation when, in 1878, the protective duties were introduced in order to enable the capitalists to compel their inland customers to pay them such high prices as would enable them to sell, abroad, for less than cost price. And America has done exactly the same, in order to shorten the period during which American manufacturers would not be in a position to compete on equal terms with England. That America, France, Germany and even Austria will be enabled to arrive at conditions where they can successfully fight English competition in the open market of the world at least in a number of important articles, of that I have no doubt. Already now France, America and Germany have broken the industrial monopoly of England to a certain extent, which is felt here very much. Will Russia be able to attain the same position? Of that I have my doubts, as Russia, like Italy, suffers from the absence of coal in industrially favourable localities, and moreover, as you develop so well in yours of 12 (24) March, has quite different historical conditions to contend with. But then we have the other question to answer: Could Russia, in the year 1890, have existed and held its own in the world, as a purely agricultural country, living upon the export of her corn and buying foreign industrial products with it? And there I believe we can safely reply: *no.* A nation of 100 millions that plays an important part in the history of the world, could not, under the present economic and industrial conditions, continue in the state in which Russia was up to the Crimean War. The introduction of steam engines and working machinery, the attempt to manufacture textile and metal products by modern means of production, at least for home consumption, *must* have been made sooner or later, but at all events at *some* period between 1856 and 1880. Had it not been made, your domestic patriarchal industry would have been destroyed all the same by English machine competition, and the end would have been—India, a country economically subject to the great central workshop, England. And even India has reacted by protective duties against English cotton goods; and all the rest of the British colonies, no sooner had they obtained self-government, than they protected their home manufactures against the overwhelming competition of the mother country. English interested writers cannot make it out, that their own free-trade example should be repudiated everywhere, and protective duties set up in return. Of course, they *dare* not see, that this, now almost universal, protective system is a— more or less intelligent and in some cases absolutely stupid—means of self-defence against this very English Free Trade, which brought the English manufacturing monopoly to its greatest height. (Stupid for instance in the case of Germany which had become a great industrial country under Free Trade and where protection is extended to agricultural produce and raw materials, thus raising cost of industrial production!) I do not consider this universal recurrence to protection as a mere accident, but as a reaction against the unbearable industrial monopoly of England; the *form* of this reaction, as I said, may be inadequate and even worse, but the historical necessity of such a reaction seems to me clear and evident.

All governments, be they ever so absolute, are *en dernier lieu*[a] but the executors of the economic necessities of the national situation. They may do this in various ways, good, bad and indifferent; they may accelerate or retard the economic development and its political and juridical consequences, but in the long run they must follow it. Whether the means by which the industrial revolution has been carried out in Russia, have been the best for the purpose, is a question by itself which it would lead too far to discuss. For my purpose it is sufficient if I can prove that this industrial revolution, in itself, was unavoidable.

What you say about the necessary accompaniments of such tremendous economic changes, is quite correct, but it applies more or less to all countries that have gone or are going through the same process. Exhaustion of the soil—*vide* America; deforestation—*vide* England, France, and at the present moment Germany and America; change of climate, drying-up of rivers is probably greater in Russia than anywhere else on account of the level nature of the country that supplies these enormous rivers with water, and the absence of an Alpine snow-reservoir such as feeds the Rhine, Danube, Rhône and Po. The destruction of the old conditions of agriculture, the gradual transition to capitalistic farming on large farms, are processes which are completed in England and East Germany and now proceeding everywhere else. And it seems to me evident that *la grande industrie en Russie tuera la commune agricole*,[b] unless other great changes occur

---

[a] in the end - [b] Russian big industry will do away with the agricultural commune

which may preserve the община.[a] The question is, will there be time for such a change in public opinion in Russia, as will make it possible, to graft modern industry and modern agriculture upon the община and at the same time to modify the latter in such a way that it may become a fit and proper instrument for the organization of this modern production and for the transformation of such production from a capitalistic to a socialised form? You will admit that to even think of carrying out such a change, a tremendous progress has first to be made by the public opinion of your country. Will there be time to effect this, before capitalistic production, aided by the effects of the present crisis, undermines the община too deeply? I have no doubt whatever that in a good many districts the община has recovered from the blow it received in 1861 (as described by V. V.[495]). But will it be able to resist the incessant blows dealt to it by the industrial transformation, by rampant capitalism, by the destruction of domestic industry, by the absence of communal rights of pasture and woods, by the transformation of the peasants' *Naturalwirtschaft*[b] into *Geldwirtschaft*,[c] by the growing wealth and power of кулаки[d] and мироеды[e]?

I have to thank you too for the books you were kind enough to send me, especially Kablukov and Karyshev.[f] At the present moment I am so overworked that I have not been able, for 6 months, to read through one single book in any language; I keep your books for my time of rest in August. What you say about Kablukov seems to me perfectly correct,[496] as far as I can follow it without reading the book itself. The agricultural labourer who has no land of his own, no hired land, finds employment for only a portion of the year, and if he is paid *for this work only*, must starve the whole unemployed time, unless he has other kinds of work to do during that time, but modern capitalist production takes every chance of such work from him. This difficulty is got over, as far as possible, in the following way in Western and Central Europe: 1) the farming capitalist or landowner keeps a portion of the labourers, all the year round, on his farm and feeds them as much as possible with its products, so as to spend but little actual money. This is done to a great extent in North East Germany, in a lesser degree here in England, where however the climate admits of

---

[a] commune (Russ.) - [b] subsistence economy - [c] money economy - [d] kulaks (Russ.) - [e] bloodsuckers (Russ.) - [f] Н. [А.] Каблуковъ, *Вопросъ о рабочихъ въ сельскомъ хозяйствѣ*; Н. [А.] Карышевъ, *Крестьянскія внѣнадѣльныя аренды*.

a good deal of agricultural work being carried on in winter. More-over, *in capitalist farming*, there is a good deal of work to be done on a farm even in winter.— 2) Whatever is still required to keep the agri-cultural labourers alive, and only just alive, during winter, is often enough procured by the work of the women and children in a fresh kind of domestic industry (see *Capital*, I vol., ch. 13, 8, d [a]). This is the case in the South and West of England, and for the small peasan-try, in Ireland and Germany.— Of course, while the transformation is proceeding, the disastrous effects of the separation of agriculture from domestic patriarchal manufacture are most striking, and that is the case with you just now.

This letter is already getting too long for me to enter into the de-tails of yours of 18th May, but it seems to me that there too your facts prove the ruin of the peasantry and with that, also, at least for a time, the exhaustion of the soil. I quite agree with you that both these things are now proceeding with increasing rapidity. If the present sys-tem continues the end must be the ruin of both помещики [b] and му-жики, [c] and the rise of a new class of bourgeois landed proprietors. But there is another side to the question which I am afraid *Вестникъ Финансовъ* [d] does not engross upon. That is the state of the public fi-nances. The last loan in Paris (1891) was to bring 20 millions £ st. They were oversubscribed several times, but the report goes here that in reality only 12 millions were paid up, and 8 millions never reached the Petersburg exchequer. [302] If that happened in France after Cron-stadt, [288] what is to happen when the next loan has to be negotiated? And can that new loan be long delayed after the tremendous sacri-fices that were forced on the treasury by the неурожай [e]? *Vyshnegradsky serait-il Calonne, et y aurait-il un Necker après lui?* [f]

Very sincerely yours,
P. W. Rosher [g]

First published, in Russian, in *Minuvshiye gody*, No. 2, St Petersburg, 1908

Reproduced from the original

Published in English in full for the first time

---

[a] See present edition, Vol. 35. - [b] landowners (Russ.) - [c] peasants - [d] *Financial Courier* - [e] crop failure (Russ.) - [f] Will Vyshnegradsky prove to be Calonne, and will there be a Necker after him? - [g] Engels' conspiratorial pseudonym

225

ENGELS TO FRIEDRICH ADOLPH SORGE

IN HOBOKEN

London, 18 June 1892

Dear Sorge,

I don't know whether I have already acknowledged receipt of your letter with money order postmarked 28 April and your card of 3 May; what with so much correspondence and other unforeseen events, I am somewhat at sea. The money arrived all right and I have repaid Mendelson the half that was due to him.[497]

During the second half of May we had Bebel here, likewise Singer who stayed with the Bernsteins.[474] We had a very jolly time and discussed everything there was to discuss relevant to the German movement. I am in complete accord with Bebel; we see eye to eye about almost everything and, if not, are quickly agreed, as indeed has been the case for years with this clear-sighted man who not only sees things as they really are but has also acquired a remarkable grasp of theory. Nor has he ever been any trouble to me. Singer possesses considerable practical vision and dexterity in his own sphere but if he departs from it, he's apt to blunder; however, in this respect he is perfectly willing to be guided by Bebel whose superiority he freely acknowledges. Both men have not only realised, but have learnt from practical experience, that Liebknecht is only fit for the scrapheap and has become a positive impediment to the party. He has been marking time for years, whereas the party has made tremendous strides — also in the field of theory, as all its literature (even the smaller newspapers, somewhat to my surprise) goes to show. This had been known to me for a long time, but what could I do? Upon the abolition of the Anti-Socialist Law,[11] Liebknecht *was*, quite ineluctably, editor of the *Vorwärts* which he now edits atrociously, and the worst of it is that they can't get rid of him without wreaking more havoc than he is doing already. I have advised them to pension him off as decently as they can but, aside from any other difficulties, he will dig his heels in. Well, we shall just have to let things take their course; luckily the party is now robust enough to withstand a good deal of stress, and in the end things will resolve themselves one way or the other.

The above is, of course, written *in the strictest confidence and solely for your own consumption.* You will realise to what lengths things have gone when I tell you that Liebknecht considers all the members of the Party Executive to be enemies who are intriguing against him — save, perhaps, for Singer who, however, sees just as plainly as anyone else what the position is. I feel sorry for Liebknecht, but I have seen this coming for years and he has only his own pig-headedness to blame. Any of our people would gladly make him a bridge of gold and we can only hope that he will eventually realise this.

The German and Austrian miners' delegates to the international congress here[492] have been to see me a couple of times — two Westphalians, a Rhinelander from the Saar, a Saxon and a Czech. For the most part good, sound men just as Siegel, who is now working in Scotland, was a good, sound chap. The miners make a splendid addition to our ranks — all sturdy chaps and most of them ex-soldiers and enfranchised. The only snag lies in the many Wasserpolacken[498] and other Poles (Dortmund district 22,000, Essen district 16-18,000), Ultramontanes to a man and stupid as they come, but it's only a transitory ill; in the long run they too will become involved and will then constitute a disaffected element in Upper Silesia, Posen[a] and West Prussia.

I look forward to hearing more about the gerrymandering in your presidential elections.[499] Never before have I had such an opportunity to observe the *modus operandi*[b] and this time I shall be on the qui vive. Having once thoroughly investigated the thing, one would know what was happening on subsequent occasions.

I have not yet written to Dietz about your business, firstly because your articles[500] are not yet ready, secondly because I have been having to correspond with him about his new edition, now shortly due, of the *Condition of the Working-Class in England*[c] and didn't want to get the two things mixed up, thirdly because Bebel told me that he, Dietz, had not done very well out of republishing stuff from the *Neue Zeit,* and fourthly because I may very possibly be going to Stuttgart with Bebel in August, when I should see Dietz in person.[d] However, I feel sure that someone will be glad to publish your work, particular-

---

[a] Polish name: Poznań - [b] method of operation - [c] F. Engels, *Die Lage der arbeitenden Klasse in England*, Stuttgart, 1892. - [d] See this volume, pp. 489-92.

ly if you include some new material and thus make it a third or half as long again. Should I fail to arrange things with Dietz (though I'm sure I won't), the *Vorwärts* book publishers in Berlin would take it. In my view, the additional bits should primarily aim at supplementing the factual material, while in the *book* you would be able to express yourself more freely about the follies of the German Socialist Labor Party [133] than you might have deemed advisable in the *Neue Zeit*.

I am glad that your wife [a] is getting better. Here too the winter has taken a heavy toll, notably as a result of influenza. Our friend Schorlemmer never recovered from his attack and now has cancer of the lung so that he's unlikely ever to get up again. A fortnight ago when I visited him, [485] the poor chap's physical and mental powers were failing him and he was confined to bed, but luckily he feels no pain and we can only hope that this will last up till the end which, alas, cannot be far off.

Warm regards to you and your wife from Louise and

Your
F. Engels

I have several times heard from Florence Kelley-Wischnewetzky.

First published abridged in *Briefe und Auszüge aus Briefen von Joh. Phil. Becker, Jos. Dietzgen, Friedrich Engels, Karl Marx u. A. an F. A. Sorge und Andere*, Stuttgart, 1906 and in full in: Marx and Engels, *Works*, First Russian Edition, Vol. XXIX, Moscow, 1946

Printed according to the original

Published in English for the first time

---

[a] Katharina Sorge

226

ENGELS TO AUGUST BEBEL [501]

IN BERLIN

London, 20 June 1892

Dear August,

Herewith the *Judenflinten* [502] under sealed cover, for if sent by book post they might well be confiscated.

Schorlemmer is still so-so. I found him weak, apathetic, his faculties slightly clouded, but not otherwise in pain. Gumpert writes to say that the lung tumour is growing slowly but surely, with (due to pressure on the big arteries which should carry back the blood from the upper part of the body to the heart) a concomitant disturbance of cerebral activity; also apathy and loss of memory. He is still taking sufficient nourishment, however, so that, barring accidents, things might go on as they are for some little while.

The fact that Warken is still holding his own in the *Saar* ought not to surprise you in view of the fact that Schröder is able to hold his own in the *Ruhr*. I wrote a line or two to Siegel telling him what Bunte had said to you about his flight.[a] Siegel sent that letter to Schröder along with a wholly guileless letter of his own saying that Bunte had been caught embezzling money, and Schröder gave me both of them — Siegel's and my own — to read. Whether it's true about Bunte I don't know. At all events you can see that Schröder is still firmly in the saddle. In the case of so young a movement as that of the miners, one ought always to consider carefully whether it wouldn't be better to give untried johnnies like Schröder and Warken enough rope to hang themselves, or at any rate enough to provide us with definite, tangible evidence against them. And there's really nothing new in that, for wherever the movement arises anew the first leaders to push their way to the fore are more often than not place-seekers and blackguards.

Bax is now editor of *Justice* and will remain so until the end of July; and it is now a decent paper; yesterday it gave a decent mention to Aveling's speeches in Aberdeen,[490] while internecine strife (i. e. indirectly Hyndman himself) was condemned.[503] Indeed, yesterday Bax

---

[a] See this volume, p. 429.

came hurrying round here in order to get his pat on the back, as the Witch, with her keen nose for such things, had prophesied the moment she set eyes on the paper. What Hyndman actually has in view is not yet very clear to me. Most likely he realises that he's been compromised by his previous policy and that a change of front is called for. His paper is running at a loss, his Social Democratic Federation [29] isn't getting anything like its share in the general growth of the movement over here — a share which would entitle it to take over the leadership; nor is it succeeding in its rivalry with the Fabians [87] — on the contrary, it has been left in the lurch, and will continue to be so left, by its foreign allies Brousse and Gilles. In short, he might well deem it advisable to turn elsewhere and seek a rapprochement with us. That would be very far from pleasant for, as I have told anybody who was prepared to listen, I would far sooner have Hyndman for an enemy (when he is virtually powerless) than for a friend (when one has to keep a constant and very time-consuming watch on him). Another thing that may have impelled him to adopt this course is the total loss of any electoral prospects in Chelsea from which he proposed to oust Sir Charles Dilke but where Quelch, the test candidate put forward by Hyndman in the County Council elections,[412] polled only 153 votes, since which time he has abandoned all hope. At all events Hyndman will find it difficult in August to resume the old attitude so publicly disavowed by Bax in the self-same paper, nor could or should he do so if he wishes to compete successfully with the Fabians. Well, we shall see.

Over here we are already in the thick of the electoral fray [504] and the Tories and Liberal Unionists [505] are proferring an abundance of money so as to provide Labour candidates with cash and thereby enable them to steal votes from the Liberals. Champion, one of the Tories' chief agents in this respect, offered Aveling the means to contest Labouchère's seat in Northampton but needless to say Aveling refused. These financial blandishments have put the Labour leaders into a state of tremendous excitation and such of the good fellows as think they can get something out of it are tussling with their consciences in an attempt to convince the latter that there is after all some honest way of accepting Tory money without blushing, though admittedly the blushing is mainly due to the fear of eventually doing themselves more harm than good. Knowing the extent to which all political life over here is riddled with parliamentary corruption, one can only wonder that the chaps should feel even this modicum of shame.

True, the Horlacherliesl[a] is closely related to the Witch; nevertheless, I still prefer the latter. Greatly though Anzengruber may on occasion idealise his Austrian peasant, and uncommonly restricted though the background may be against which his excellent dramas take place, nevertheless one is painfully aware of the separation of that splendid race from the rest of Germany and of the necessity for reunification which, however, only we are capable of bringing about.

Well, I wish I could drop Mrs Julie,[b] honorary bookkeeper,[506] a couple of lines to thank her for her last letters which have, alas, not yet had an answer, but I am up to my eyes in work. I have two more long and somewhat ticklish letters to write after which I intend at long last to get down to Volume III.[c] Hence I have got to put on one side all the correspondence that merely gives me pleasure and devote myself solely to business matters. So be my advocate with your wife and don't let her be too angry with me. I shall make up for it, if possible before I come to Berlin, but otherwise when I get there; I look forward so much to meeting her and know in advance that we shall get on very well. So warm regards to her and yourself from both of us.

Your old

General

First published in: Marx and Engels, *Works*, First Russian Edition, Vol. XXIX, Moscow, 1946

Printed according to the original

Published in English in full for the first time

---

[a] A personage from Ludvig Anzengruber's comedy *G'wissenswurm*. - [b] Julie Bebel - [c] of *Capital*

227

ENGELS TO KARL KAUTSKY

IN STUTTGART

London, 25 June 1892

Dear Baron,

As regards the business of the name,[480] you misunderstand me if you imagine that I looked upon Louise's acceptance of your proposal as a sacrifice she would be making on your behalf. What I wished to imply was that in my view a request of that kind ought not in the circumstances to have emanated from *you*. So far as you are concerned, Louise has unquestionably done more than anybody could have asked of her, on top of which she received you over here in a way that evidently came as a surprise to you yourself, and re-established you both on a footing that made social intercourse possible without embarrassment or constraint, both between the two of you and between us and yourselves. So why go and drag up the old business again for the sake of something so trivial? A divorced woman's social position is quite bad enough in any case, for if she is to rehabilitate herself, she must, in accordance with present-day ideas, show proof to all and sundry that *she* is not the 'guilty party'. And don't you see that a divorced woman must feel deeply hurt if the man from whom she is divorced demands that she bear in public, not her lawful name, but another which, furthermore, he presents to her cut and dried?

I know nothing about the practice of divorced women to which you refer. All I know is that Johanna, née Mockel, later wife of Matthieux (whom she divorced), and subsequently of Kinkel, used no other name than J. Matthieux from the time of her divorce up till her marriage to Kinkel and that all her published songs, etc., appeared under that name.

As to *la* Schack, she simply made use of the aristocratic privilege conferred on her by the Prussian Civil code. Part II, Title I, § 740 reads:

'If she (the divorced woman) has not been held to be the guilty party, she may revert to *the higher rank* she bore before her marriage.'

And § 741:

'In general the woman may choose, *especially in the case of § 740*, whether she wishes to reassume her former maiden name or her deceased husband's name.'

Even should *la* Schack have become or remained a Swiss, she could assert this right in Prussia and invoke it outside Prussia.

La Wischnewetzky *never* dropped the name of Kelley; if she has now dropped the Wischnewetzky, she was able to do so because in America they base themselves on English common law, according to which A MAN'S NAME IS WHAT HE IS KNOWN BY, as Sam Moore would say, and may be changed at will.

So none of this applies to Louise who, as it happens, is committed to the Austrian police state which will not permit her to bear any name other than your own.

But why on earth should Louise now be expected to oblige you by bearing in public a name other than her lawful one? Does that mean that every female Kautsky who appears in public must necessarily be your wife? And since the world is in any case unfamiliar with your present wife's Christian name,[a] ought not your mother[b] also to individualise herself by using a different name to indicate that she is not your wife? The world is divided into two parts—those who know your wife and those who don't. The former *know* that the London Louise Kautsky, the Louise Kautsky of the *Arbeiter-* and the *Arbeiterinnen-Zeitung*, is *not* your wife, while the latter will be in no way enlightened as to this by the proposed change of name, since they cannot know what your wife was 'née'.

I have informed Louise that you have told me the matter is dead and buried so far as you are concerned. I fear that so far as she is concerned that is not the case. I fear that by dragging up this business you have awakened so many memories that it will not be so easy to bury them again. By demanding what you did you have wounded Louise deeply, so deeply, I fear, that you will be unable to make amends. She has constantly nursed that wound and now intends to write to you herself.

Sonnenschein doesn't want to do anything about the English *Entwicklung*[c] until *after* the election.[504] But then comes the silly season over here, so nothing can really materialise until the end of September. I shall therefore again write to Sonnenschein asking for *definite* information and shall then send you the ms.[461] which you can have

---

[a] Luise - [b] Minna Kautsky - [c] F. Engels, *Socialism: Utopian and Scientific*.

set provisionally but *not publish* before the date of which I shall also then inform you.

I have heard nothing further about poor Schorlemmer; whatever has happened, there has been no significant change.

Very many thanks for your information *re* Sorge-Dietz.[500] It was important to me because Sorge has not yet reported on the progress of the negotiations being conducted through you and I had to know about this before I myself could do anything. Dietz is much too preoccupied with selling in bulk. If he wishes to be the publisher of the *scientific* socialists, he must set up a section where there is also room for books which sell more slowly, otherwise we must find someone else. Genuinely scientific literature cannot reach sales in the tens of thousands and the *publisher* must arrange things accordingly.

Much confusion still prevails in the elections here. Nevertheless the Liberals are being taught their *first* lesson by Labour.

Your
General

First published in *Aus der Frühzeit des Marxismus. Engels Briefwechsel mit Kautsky*, Prag, 1935

Printed according to the original

Published in English in full for the first time

228

ENGELS TO KARL KAUTSKY

IN STUTTGART

[London,] 27 June 1892

Our good Schorlemmer died peacefully this morning. I'm going down tomorrow.[507]

There will be an obituary in the *Vorwärts*.[a]

Your

F. E.

First published in *Aus der Frühzeit des Marxismus. Engels Briefwechsel mit Kautsky*, Prag, 1935

Printed according to the original

Published in English for the first time

229

ENGELS TO LUDWIG SCHORLEMMER

IN DARMSTADT

Manchester, 30 June 1892
203 High Street, Oxford Road

Dear Mr Schorlemmer,

The first news of Carl's death on the 27th of this month will already have reached you from Gumpert. I got here yesterday [507] and learnt that a post-mortem had been carried out at the request of the doctors and that the earlier diagnosis — cancer of the right lung — had been fully confirmed by the findings. In accordance with the wishes of the faculty who, along with the students, would like to attend but would be prevented from so doing by an important examination on Thursday, the funeral will not take place until Friday [b] at 11.30 a. m. Gumpert has already seen to the wreath you ordered by telegram and its

---

[a] F. Engels, 'Carl Schorlemmer', *Vorwärts*, No. 153, 3 July 1892. - [b] 1 July

ribbon will bear the words: 'To their dear Carl—his mother, brothers and sisters.'

I myself shall be laying a wreath on behalf of the Executive of the German Social-Democratic Party.

This afternoon I put his papers into some sort of order, in so far as they have to do with business matters, so that I shall be able to discuss the more important points with the executors.[a] I have also put his manuscripts in order so far as I could; there is a fair number of them, but I dare say a good many are already in print.

I did not see Carl again. By the time I got there this morning the coffin had already been screwed down.

There is one matter upon which you may all set your minds completely at rest—nowhere could he have received better care than the care that was given to him and no one could possibly have had a more painless illness or a more peaceful end. It only remains for us to keep his memory alive in our hearts and in the world at large. To-morrow I shall send an obituary to the *Vorwärts*.[b] The excellent obituary in the *Manchester Guardian* which Gumpert sent you was by Dr Schuster, a former student of his and more recently a colleague as lecturer in physics.

So good-bye for today. You will be with us in spirit on Friday and I shall certainly be thinking of his mother, brothers and sisters. It is a grievous and bitter loss to us all, but was a foregone conclusion months ago. With that we must console ourselves.

With warm regards to your mother and all his brothers and sisters.

Yours,

F. Engels

I shall write again after the funeral.[c]

First published in: Marx and Engels, *Works*, First Russian Edition, Vol. XXIX, Moscow, 1946

Printed according to the original

Published in English for the first time

---

[a] Philipp Klepsch and Ludwig Siebold-[b] F. Engels, 'Carl Schorlemmer', *Vorwärts*, No. 153, 3 July 1892.-[c] See next letter.

230

ENGELS TO LUDWIG SCHORLEMMER

IN DARMSTADT

[Manchester,] 1 July 1892
203 High Street, Oxford Road

Dear Mr Schorlemmer,

I am writing to you directly after Carl's[a] funeral which took place this morning. It was an imposing procession, first the carriages with personal friends, including the executors,[b] Dr Gumpert and Carl's landlord, then the faculty of Owens College,[487] virtually all of whom were represented, also Roscoe, then a large number of his students past and present. The executors had asked Mr Steinthal, a Unitarian (akin to our Free Congregations[508]) minister to conduct the burial service and say a few words at the graveside, which in fact he did most impressively — he was a good friend of Carl's. If the address doesn't appear in tomorrow's papers, Gumpert will send you a copy of it. Numerous very beautiful wreaths had been sent; apart from those from the family and the Party Executive in Berlin there was one huge and most beautiful wreath bearing the inscription: 'From the Germans in Manchester to their Illustrious Compatriot'; also one from his former students, one from the students of his last course, from his colleagues, etc.

I was asked on arrival whether I had any objections to the proposed arrangements for a funeral of this kind, maintaining as it did at least a semblance of Church practice. They felt that this was how they could best conform to the wishes of the family. I cannot say that I was particularly delighted with the plan, but circumstances being what they are here in Manchester, I had no alternative but to reply that it was up to the executors to decide and that if the ceremony was to be performed in a conventional setting, then Steinthal was undoubtedly by far the best man for it and he did, in fact, acquit himself quite admirably. Had I protested I might perhaps have been respon-

---

[a] Carl Schorlemmer - [b] Philipp Klepsch and Ludwig Siebold

sible for a wholly unecclesiastical funeral. But in the first place I did not know whether this would have been acceptable to *all* the members of your family. Secondly, the entire responsibility would in that case have devolved upon myself; *I* alone would have had to speak and the emphasis would not have been on Schorlemmer the chemist but on Schorlemmer the *Social-Democrat* and in the circumstances it was certainly preferable to play down the Social-Democrat in order that the chemist might be given his full due. The entire English bourgeois press would have said that I had exploited Carl's death for the purpose of a pointless and useless socialist demonstration in front of an audience that felt cool if not actually hostile towards *me* and towards socialism, yet was compelled to keep silent out of respect for the open grave. And since I dislike all demonstrations, however unavoidable, it would have been utterly repugnant to me to allow the funeral of a dear friend to degenerate into an intrusive demonstration. It would of course have been different had Carl himself made stipulations in his will. However the scarlet bows bearing the inscription 'From the Executive of the German Social-Democratic Party' were eloquent enough; they stood out in garish contrast to the white flowers and bows of the other wreaths and were in any case grossly at variance with British custom.

I have today shown Mr Philipp Klepsch, one of the executors (both are German), all the papers. We settled one or two further matters and discussed the more important points, which means that I can return to London tomorrow.

The will must now be registered at the Court of Probate and estate duty will have to be paid. Not until then can anything further be done.

I have arranged with Mr Klepsch that family letters should be returned to you. If you have any wishes regarding other mementoes, perhaps you would write to him,

Ph. Klepsch,

c/o Stadelbauer & Co., Manchester.

In case you might want them, I also suggested that he should keep for you the various writings Marx and I inscribed and presented to him.

As regards the manuscripts and publishers' contracts, more anon.
Warm regards to your mother and the whole family.

Yours,

F. Engels

First published in: Marx and Engels, *Works*, First Russian Edition, Vol. XXIX, Moscow, 1946

Printed according to the original

Published in English for the first time

231

ENGELS TO STANISŁAW MENDELSON

IN LONDON

[London,] 4 July 1892
122 Regent's Park Road, N. W.

Dear Citizen,

I have this minute received a letter from Bebel with a communication for you, which I am sending on at once.[509] I trust you will receive the money through the Deutsche Bank (which has, I believe, a branch here in London) and that you will be able to decipher Bebel's writing. If not, perhaps you might care to return me the letter so that I can transcribe it into characters of a more international nature.

My compliments, as also those of Mrs Kautsky, to Mrs Mendelson.[a]

Yours ever,

F. Engels

Bebel was not immediately able to lay his hands on your address, which is why he sent the bank's statement of sale to me.

First published in: Marx and Engels, *Works*, Second Russian Edition, Vol. 38, Moscow, 1965

Printed according to the original

Translated from the French

Published in English for the first time

---

[a] Maria Mendelson

232

ENGELS TO AUGUST BEBEL [501]

IN BERLIN

London, 5 July 1892

Dear August,

You forbid me to write to you,[510] i. e. I am to give up the only correspondence I always find enjoyable and, instead, hammer away at the letters which bore me. But I'm not going to do it simply to oblige you.

And even if I were so docile, the *Vorwärts'* colossal howlers[511] about the elections over here[504] would make me fly off the handle. To say nothing about it would be really too deplorable. For the *Vorwärts* has now actually succeeded in transforming South Paddington into a *rural district* of London — South Paddington which is situated right in the middle of the town, slightly to the north of Hyde Park and west of Regent's Park, and in which the only rural districts are a couple of green SQUARES — about as rural as the Dönhoffplatz[a]!

The England of the *Vorwärts* exists only in the imagination of the writer. The view that the TORIES of today are more favourable to the workers than are the Liberals is the reverse of the truth. On the contrary, all the Manchesterian prejudices[512] of the Liberals of 1850 are today articles of faith only to the TORIES, while the Liberals know very well that if they are to survive as a party they must capture the Labour vote. Because they are jackasses, the TORIES can, from time to time, be induced by an outstanding man such as Disraeli to carry out a bold coup of which the Liberals would not be capable; but in the absence of an outstanding man it's the jackasses among them who rule the roost, as at present. The TORIES are no longer simply the tail of the big landowners, as they were up till 1850, for between 1855 and 1870 the sons of the Cobdens, Brights, etc., of the upper middle classes and the Anti-Corn LAW men,[513] have one and all gone over to the TORY camp, and the strength of the Liberals now lies in the dis-

---

[a] a square in the centre of Berlin

senting middle and lower middle classes. And, since Gladstone's
HOME RULE BILL of 1886,[514] the last remnants of the Whigs and the
old Liberals (middle-class and university men) have gone over to
the Tory camp (as dissident or UNIONIST LIBERALS[505]).

Hence the need the Liberals face of making apparent or real concessions — primarily the former — to the workers. And nevertheless
they are too stupid to know *where* to begin, many of them being, after
all, still too hidebound by their antecedents.

So far the elections have proceeded as if in response to our orders.
The Liberals are obtaining a slender majority and in many places are
actually losing votes by comparison with the last election; thus there
has so far been no sign of the great Liberal wave that was to sweep
across England. Today is a very important day and the results will
probably be decisive; should the Liberals score a brilliant victory today, the vacillating philistine — by no means a rare animal — will
be driven over onto their side and that will give them the upper
hand. What we need is a moderate Liberal majority (including
the Irish) so that Gladstone is dependent on the Irish over here —
otherwise, if able to exist without them, he is sure to do the dirty
on them.

But it's capital that Keir Hardie, the Labour candidate in West
Ham in the East End of London,— one of the few who did not take
any money from the Liberals and did not therefore place himself
under an obligation to them — should so far be the only one to have
turned a Conservative majority of over 300 in the last election into an
anti-Conservative majority of 1,200. Excellent, too, that elsewhere —
in Aberdeen, etc.— the Labour candidates who stood *against* Liberals
and Conservatives should have obtained anything up to a thousand
votes. The Independent Labour Party is casting its shadow before
it.[515]

There are three kinds of Labour candidate here:

1. Those who were paid by the TORIES to filch Liberal votes.
Nearly all of these will fail and know it.

2. Those who take Liberal money and are bound to serve the Liberals. These are mostly put up in places where there is no prospect of
their getting in, and amongst their number there are also men who,
like the miners' candidates, are Liberals by nature.

3. The genuine Labour candidates, who are acting off their own
bat and do not ask themselves whether they are standing against Liberals or TORIES. Of these, the Liberals accept the ones they *have*

to (Keir Hardie and Burns) and try to undermine the others. In Scotland there are *many* such candidates, though it's difficult to say what their chances are. Goodbye and warm regards to your wife.[a]

Your old friend,

F. E.

First published in: Marx and Engels, *Works*, First Russian Edition, Vol. XXIX, Moscow, 1946

Printed according to the original

Published in English for the first time

233

ENGELS TO KARL KAUTSKY

IN STUTTGART

London, 5 July 1892

Dear Baron,

I got back from Manchester on Saturday,[b][507] Schorlemmer having been buried on Friday. Should you want an obituary for the *Neue Zeit*, the man to look out for would be a chemist who would be able to give a comprehensible account of his discoveries and his importance to science. This would certainly be excellent, but in addition the man would have to be familiar with the history of organic chemisry in the fifties and sixties.

I agree that I owe you an explanation as to how Louise found out about your intended proposal.[480] After getting your letter of 13 May, and although from the first I had taken the view that there was no reason why Louise should fall in with your idea, I nevertheless thought fit to sound her out. I asked her, as though, mind you, it was *my* idea, whether it mightn't be a good thing, so as to avoid confusion, to add her maiden name to her married one, as is often done in Western Germany and Switzerland, even by married persons of both sexes. She looked at me inquiringly before replying: 'You needn't

---

[a] Julie Bebel - [b] 2 July

bother; I know who's behind this — it's Karl and he's been egged on by his mother.' Nor could I persuade her otherwise. On the contrary, a little while later she told this to Gine[a] as an established fact, whereupon Gine told her quite innocently and naturally, as almost anyone would have done under the circumstances, that you had likewise written to Ede[b] about it, whereupon the two of them discussed the matter.

When Louise later remonstrated with me about this, I had really no alternative but to read out to her the relevant passage in your letter of 13 May which did at least put an end to any further conjectures and speculations and to that extent could only have a soothing effect. Besides, that particular passage looked to me as though it had been expressly written in such a way that it could, if necessary, be shown to Louise.

Such was the course of events. Not that I am in any way dissatisfied with it. For once you had suggested I consult Tussy and had at the same time written to Ede on the subject, one thing was plain, namely that if four people who, as it were, consorted daily with Louise were in the know, not many months would elapse before one of them let the cat out of the bag in her presence and that would have made matters ten times worse, for then she would have said: 'So that's how you people settle my affairs behind my back — affairs which concern only myself, etc.'

To be sure, Louise read me the letter she wrote you, or rather the draft thereof after it had gone off. It has shown me yet again that a third party should never intervene in the private affairs of married or erstwhile married couples since he can never know enough about the antecedents. For instance, it was only from this I learnt that, when your divorce was first mooted, you two had already discussed and decided upon the name to be used by Louise. If this is true, and I have no reason to suppose anything else, then I am sorry not to have known about it before. For in that case I should have immediately, and without reference to anyone else, have urged you at all costs to let sleeping dogs lie.

So as you see, Louise alone was responsible for her letter, as your familiarity with her independence of mind would be enough to tell you without specific assurances on my part. As for giving you my opin-

---

[a] Regina Bernstein - [b] Eduard Bernstein

ion of that letter, I do not regard myself as either called upon or competent to do so, this being a private matter between two divorced people. All I can say is that what has happened affects neither my relations with Louise nor those with you.

I am today sending you the introduction in German [461] by REGISTERED book post. Sonnenschein doesn't want the book to come out before September, so please don't put the thing in the *Neue Zeit before 1 September*; after that date it will be all one to me — the fool has kept me waiting long enough. Unfortunately the German is a pale reflection; the English is far livelier and you will like it better.

Many thanks for the information *re* Sorge.[500] I shall attend to this as soon as I have a moment to spare.

So far the elections over here have gone off capitally.[504] The Liberals are winning, but if things go on as they are today, they'll get only a *slender* majority, i.e. they will remain dependent on the Irish, which is a good thing, otherwise Gladstone would do the dirty on them again and the Irish question be perpetuated. While yesterday's polls showed a swing in favour of the Liberals, there was no trace of the powerful, all-engulfing Liberal wave that the Gladstonians were counting on. Indeed, the incipient LABOUR PARTY [515] is already proving a thorn in the flesh of the Liberals. The *only* candidate to have achieved a striking swing in the latter's favour is Keir Hardie in South West Ham, one of the few Labour candidates not to have taken *any* money from the Liberals or to have submitted to Liberal discipline. On the other hand Labour candidates in other places, in so far as they were competing with Liberals, deprived the latter of a great many votes and likewise gave them a portent of things to come. This will, I hope, be the last election contested by the two official parties *only*; next time the workers will play a very different sort of role.

Your
General

First published in *Aus der Frühzeit des Marxismus. Engels Briefwechsel mit Kautsky*, Prag, 1935

Printed according to the original

Published in English for the first time

234

ENGELS TO AUGUST BEBEL

IN BERLIN

London, 6 July 1892

Dear August,

Here be I again,[a] as you can see. With my obituary of Schorlemmer,[b] I enclosed a note to the *Vorwärts* asking them to send me 12 copies of that edition — i. e. only the page the thing was in, not all the supplements and such. I need these copies for people in Manchester and for leading chemists over here who ought to know where, outside of chemistry, Schorlemmer's allegiance lay. Needless to say, I have not had *a single copy*. Would you tell the chaps — the note may have been completely overlooked — that important party interests are at stake, and that they should send me what I asked before it is too late and the public over here has turned its attention elsewhere.

The elections here [504] have proved a disappointment for the Liberals. So far they have gained 9 votes, i. e. the government's majority has been reduced from 68 to 50 (68 − 9 = 59 TORIES; 0 + 9 Liberals = 9; 59 − 9 = 50 at the poll). Yesterday's elections didn't bring them a single gain, but with 25 more votes, the 50 − 25 would be cancelled out by the + 25, and it would be simply splendid if neither the Right nor the Left were to end up with a proper majority. However, the Liberals are likely to obtain a small majority and even that wouldn't be too bad.

Your Bismarck rumpus gets nicer every day [516] — the fellow must be quite mad. According to today's telegram he's absolutely intent on getting Caprivi's scalp. Well, we may see some fun. If only our papers weren't always pointing out that it's really a case for the courts! Must we really play the bureaucrat, policeman and public prosecutor like our opponents? Couldn't we, just for once, allow that old, broken-winded jackass Bismarck to make a fool of himself to his heart's content? And wouldn't three days in jug turn him into a martyr? It is almost beyond belief how ultra-Prussian the chaps are!

The *Vorwärts* has gone quite insane. Today it says that England,

---

[a] In the original: *mir sein* (Saxon dialect). - [b] F. Engels, 'Carl Schorlemmer', *Vorwärts*, No. 153, 3 July 1892.

Wales, Scotland, Ireland, the colonies and India are all of them called Great Britain [517]! But that name comprises only England, Wales and Scotland — *not even Ireland*, let alone anything else (the official title is THE UNITED KINGDOM OF GREAT BRITAIN *AND IRELAND*). Are the fellows absolutely intent on making a universal laughing-stock of themselves and of us?

Downstairs the Witch is contemplating a baby belonging to our former housemaid, and so deeply has she been engrossed for the past two hours in this act of worship that I can't winkle her out to send you her greetings. So unless she turns up at the last minute before the post goes, I shall have to send you and Mrs Julie [a] my warmest regards all on my own.

Your old friend,
F. E.

[From Louise Kautsky]

The General is only testifying to his own inadequacy for if, as he maintains, the baby-worship went on for two hours, he must have spent a full two hours writing the letter; an interpretation more flattering to me would be that, even though it was you he was writing to, the time seemed so long to him. However that may be, the child has gone, as you see, so that I can myself send my love to Mrs Julie who, of you three, is certainly best able to understand the attraction exerted by children. Same to you.

The Witch

[From Engels]

How fanciful of the Witch to say (as she does) that I have spent two hours writing this letter. I was doing a very difficult legal task for Schorlemmer's executors [b] on the subject of his literary estate, while she was giving the baby her fingers to suck. So it must have sucked away all her wits!

[From Louise Kautsky]

I've never heard the likes of it — the baby's sucking from my finger the wisdom which enabled the General to write his legal piece — blessed is he who believes.

[From Engels]

She has to have the last word.

---

[a] Julie Bebel - [b] Philipp Klepsch and Ludwig Siebold

[From Louise Kautsky]

Written word.

[From Engels]

Nichevo.[a]

First published in: Marx and Engels *Works*, First Russian Edition, Vol. XXIX, Moscow, 1946

Printed according to the original

Published in English for the first time

235

ENGELS TO JOHN BURNS

AT BATTERSEA[b]

[Telegram][518]

London, 6 July 1892
122, Regent's Park Road, N. W.

Wish you success and victory
Engels
Kautsky
Burns 108 Lavender Hill Battersea

First published in: Marx and Engels, *Works*, Second Russian Edition, Vol. 50, Moscow, 1981

Printed according to the telegraph form

Published in English for the first time

---

[a] Engels gives the Russian word 'ничего' ('not bad') in Latin letters.- [b] district of London

236

ENGELS TO AUGUST BEBEL

IN BERLIN

London, 7 July 1892

Dear August,

This is what comes of your forbidding me to write to you![510] Yet another letter. The obituary numbers of the *Vorwärts* turned up this morning,[a] so all is well in that quarter.

The elections are going swimmingly.[504]

1. The Liberal victories are such minor ones and so much offset by counter-victories and other unmistakable symptoms (diminished majorities, often to the extent of being virtually non-existent, etc.) that the next parliament is likely to show at most a *narrow* majority for Gladstone, and maybe none at all (i. e. practically none at all) either for him or for the TORIES. That would mean early dissolution and another election, but also *preparations* for the latter in the shape of legislation which would ensure extra votes for the Liberals, and those could only be new Labour votes. In fact even were the TORIES to remain at the helm — which hardly seems likely — they would have to try and strengthen their position by acquiring additional votes and these again they could only get from the workers. So there's a prospect of 1. a cessation of the harassment which has hitherto made it difficult for individual workers to assert their right to the universal suffrage they have been conceded[519] and 2. social measures favourable to the workers.

The Liberals have won 16 of their opponents' seats: the last government majority was 68. If you take away the 16 seats lost and also the above 16 won from their opponents, you get 32. That still leaves a TORY majority of 36. So if another 18 seats are won, the parties will be all square. I believe that a few more will be won; the so-called country boroughs are those in which opposition to the feudal pressure exerted by the big country landowners is strongest and where the lower middle classes do not therefore, as here in London and in other large towns, vote Conservative out of opposition to the now enfran-

---

[a] F. Engels, 'Carl Schorlemmer', *Vorwärts*. No. 153, 3 July 1892. See also this volume, p. 464.

chised workers and out of philistine habit. Gladstone might quite likely obtain a majority of 20, including, of course, the Irish, and he won't be able to govern with that. The Irish are bound to demand HOME RULE and a majority of 20 won't enable him to put that through in the teeth of the Upper House. And that will mean a rumpus.

2. The only startling victories are those of the *new Labour Party*. Keir Hardie has turned what was, in the last elections, a TORY majority of 300 into a majority of 1,200 for himself. John Burns — whose Liberal predecessor had a majority of 186 — has got one of 1,560. And in Middlesbrough (the iron-working district of Yorkshire) Wilson, Secretary of the UNION of Seamen and Coal Trimmers — a careerist but pledged neck and crop to the new unionism,[520] obtained 4,691 votes, thus beating the Liberals (4,062) *and* the TORY (3,333). The measly Liberal majorities look pitiful by comparison.

3. In three places where a Labour candidature, etc., was both apposite and had been properly prepared for in advance, the Labour candidates were in fact beaten, but they *also caused the downfall of the Liberals*.

In Salford, Hall, Labour, obtained 553 votes but the Liberal was beaten by *only 37*.

In Glasgow (Camlachie) Cunninghame-Graham was beaten (906 votes), but so was the Liberal who needed 371 votes to obtain a majority.

In Glasgow (Tradeston) the Labour candidate Burleigh (in other respects a ne'er-do-weel) got 783 votes while the Liberal got 169 fewer than the TORY.

What's more, in a number of other places (Aberdeen, Glasgow — College —, Bradford), though the Liberals did in fact win, they nevertheless forfeited anything from 990 to 2,749 votes to Labour candidates standing against *both* parties, which means that next time Labour will constitute a direct threat.

In short, the Labour Party has proclaimed itself clearly and unmistakably and that means that next time both the old parties will have to make it offers of alliance. The TORIES may be ruled out so long as they are led by the present jackasses. But the Liberals are bound to make an approach. And likewise the Irish. When Parnell was sent to Coventry over the absurd affair of the divorce,[521] he suddenly turned pro-Labour, and so will the Irish gents in Parliament when they realise it is only Labour that can procure them HOME RULE. Then the compromising will begin, and then, too, the FABIANS [87] — in these elections conspicuous by their absence — will again put in an appearance, but over here that sort of thing just can't be avoided. However, we're making progress, as you can see, and that's the main thing.

By a splendid quirk of history, *both* of the two old parties have now got to appeal to Labour and make concessions to Labour if they want to retain or take the helm, and at the same time each of them senses that by so doing they are giving a leg up to their own successors. And yet they can't help it! What is our little jest compared with the colossal jest now emerging from the turn history is taking?

Many regards from Louise and myself to Mrs Julie[a] and yourself.

Your
F. E.

If you write to Shaw you might recommend Conrad Schmidt's article in the *Neue Zeit*[b] as a refutation of their 'AUSTRIAN THEORY OF VALUE'.[522]

First published in: Marx and Engels, *Works*, First Russian Edition, Vol. XXIX. Moscow, 1946

Printed according to the original

Published in English for the first time

237

ENGELS TO LAURA LAFARGUE

AT LE PERREUX

London, 7 July 1892

My dear Laura,

I went at once to Manchester[507] on the telegram of Schorlemmer's death, on Friday last week 1st July we buried him and on Saturday I returned. The last weeks of his life he remained in the same half-conscious and very oblivious, but absolutely painless state in which I had found him when there in the beginning of June,[485] and on Monday morning 27th June[c] he expired quietly and without any

---

[a] Julie Bebel - [b] C. Schmidt, 'Die psychologische Richtung in der neueren National-Oekonomie', *Die Neue Zeit*, 10 Jg. 1891/92, 2. Bd., Nr. 40, 41. - [c] In the original '29 June', which is a slip of the pen.

struggle. A *post mortem* entirely confirmed the diagnosis of Gumpert: a carcinomatous tumour in the right lung, of the size of a small orange, sufficient, by its pressure on the vena cava and the plexus brachialis to account for the deficient action of the brain and the partial paralysis and oedema of the right arm. The large vein of that arm contained a considerable thrombus, there were distinct though small carcinomatous places in the brain, and the heart was beginning to show fatty degeneration. Under these circumstances we may congratulate ourselves that he was spared longer and perhaps acute sufferings.

Gumpert had got him in May already to make a will, he left everything to his mother. The manuscripts he left may cause some trouble. The most interesting one is on the history of chemistry, 1) Ancients, 2) Alchemy, 3) Jatrochemistry,[523] up to the 17th century; a fragment of the 3rd part not completed, but still full of new views and discoveries. Then a lot of work on organic chemistry. But as he has *two* works in the press at the same time: 1) his own organic chemistry, 2) his and Roscoe's big book[a];—it will be pretty hard to distinguish which belongs to which. One of his executors is a chemist (Siebold) but hardly knows enough about the theory of the science to distinguish. And Roscoe's red-hot after the ms., as he knows too well that *he* cannot finish the book. I have told the executors in my opinion they might let Roscoe have what belongs to the Roscoe-Schorlemmer book on binding himself to let the heirs participate in the profits of the pending volume (German and English) in the same way as Schorlemmer himself would have done. As Roscoe was elected yesterday for Manchester, he will no doubt pounce upon the executors at once, so I wrote them yesterday giving a full account of what I considered ought to be done in the matter.

A short notice I wrote in the *Vorwärts*[b] I send you today.

Here we are in the midst of the elections.[504] They go remarkably well for us—under the circumstances. First, the immense Liberal Wave which was to carry Gladstone triumphantly to power, is all bosh. He will probably get a small majority, and it is not even certain whether there will be a majority for anybody. This will make *both* official parties dependent, for the next election, which may come *very* soon, upon the working men. Secondly the *new* working-class move-

---

[a] C. Schorlemmer, *The Rise and Development of Organic Chemistry*; H. E. Roscoe and C. Schorlemmer, *Ausführliches Lehrbuch der Chemie*, Bd. I-V; H. E. Roscoe and C. Schorlemmer, *A Treatise on Chemistry.* - [b] F. Engels, 'Carl Schorlemmer', *Vorwärts*, No. 153, 3 July 1892.

ment enters Parliament triumphantly. On Monday[a] Keir Hardie was elected with 1,200 majority in the East-End (West Ham) — last member a Tory[b] with 300 majority! Yesterday John Burns at Battersea with 1,600 majority — last member a bourgeois Liberal[c] with only 186 majority. And then at Middlesborough in Yorkshire J. H. Wilson, secretary of the Sailors and Firemen's Union (a *Streber*[d] but deeply engaged and mortgaged to *new* Unionism[520]) beat *both* a Liberal *and* a Tory! These are the only éclatant victories in the whole election and all gained by working men: in two cases the Liberals *dared* not oppose one of their own, and in the third when they did, they were *battus à plate couture*.[e] And third: wherever a working man's candidature had been well selected and prepared, it either considerably diminished the Liberal majority, so as to warn them to be more careful and not to risk losing the seat next time, or it *made* the Liberals lose the seat. Thus in 2 divisions of Glasgow, Cunninghame-Graham was beaten, *but so was his Liberal competitor*. Thus in Salford, Hall, an S. D.F.[29] man, but said to be good, had only 554 votes, but these deprived the Liberal of his seat. And thus, 3 Liberal seats lost merely because they would thrust bourgeois members upon working-class constituencies.

The election has done already what I maintained was all we had a right to expect from it: give fair and unmistakable warning to the Liberals that the *Independent Working Men's Party*[515] was approaching, that it cast its shadow before it, and that this was to be the last general election carried on between two parties only, the Ins and the Outs. And therefore I am quite satisfied, especially so, as we shall get a parliament with which no stable government is possible.

From your silence I conclude that Bonnier is right when he writes to Tussy [:] *le journal pend toujours à un fil*.[423] Let us hope the *fil*[g] will not snap but on the contrary grow into a rope and even a hawser.

Love from Louise. Prosperity and eloquence to M. *le député*.[h]

Ever yours
F. Engels

First published, in the language of the original (English), in: F. Engels, P. et L. Lafargue, *Correspondance*, t. III, Paris, 1959

Reproduced from the original

---

[a] 4 July - [b] Georges Banes - [c] O. W. Morgan - [d] careerist - [e] beaten hollow - [f] The paper is in a perilous state. - [g] thread - [h] Paul Lafargue

238

ENGELS TO PANAYOTTIS ARGYRIADES

IN PARIS

[Draft]

[London, beginning of July 1892]

Dear Citizen,

I have received the *Almanach de la Question Sociale* for 1891 and '92, for which I send you my thanks.

You hope to be able to number me amongst your contributors for 1893. However I see that, without my knowledge, you have already named me as a contributor for 1892.[524] If there is to be a contribution from me to the 1893 *Almanach*, it will, I fear, be an involuntary contribution as before. A month ago, when our friends in Austria asked me for an article for their yearbook,[a] I had to tell them

1. that I was unable to undertake any further work, whether large or small, until I had seen to the publication of Vol. III of Marx's *Capital*, which is now ten years overdue;

2. that a contribution to this or that Socialist yearbook would, in the interests of impartiality, necessitate my contributing to most of the remainder and that accordingly my time would no longer be my own.

True, I made an exception last year in the case of the French *Almanach du Parti Ouvrier*.[525] But on that occasion it would have been dangerous to hold back. That was the time when at Kronstadt[288] the official French republic kow-towed to the Tsar,[b] the hereditary leader of European reaction. War was imminent and in my view was prevented only by the famine in Russia. At that critical juncture it was up to me to do all in my power to remove any possibility of a mis-

---

[a] *Österreichischer Arbeiter-Kalender* - [b] Alexander III

understanding between French and German working men.[a] I took advantage of the occasion and spoke up; that is all.

First published in: Marx and Engels, *Works*, First Russian Edition, Vol. XXIX, Moscow, 1946

Printed according to the original

Translated from the French

Published in English for the first time

239

ENGELS TO HERMANN ENGELS

IN BARMEN

London, 12 July 1892

Dear Hermann,

Thank you very much for your letter of 23 June. The Schaafhausen dividend has been debited to you—many thanks.[b] I hope you enjoy your Italian trip; I shall probably go there myself some time.

TodayI am just writing to ask which of you is going to be in Engelskirchen on or about the 10th or 12th August, and whether you could do with me there for a couple of days round about that time. I shall probably be paying another visit to the Continent then and, although unlikely to take in Barmen, should like for once to get another breath of Engelskirchen air. I'd be glad if you wouldn't mention this unless you have to or else certain people might expect me to go to Barmen as well, and that might not fit in with my other plans.

For the rest, all is well with me but I too am beginning to feel the need for relaxation. That's the trouble with London; in July it becomes sultry and unbearable and one longs to get right away from it.

---

[a] In the original there follows a phrase 'I spoke to the French proletariat', which is crossed out. - [b] See this volume, pp. 339 and 352.

But I still have heaps of urgent jobs to do.

Love to Emma[a] and your children and grandchildren.

Your

Friedrich

First published in *Deutsche Revue*, Jg. 46, Bd. III, Stuttgart-Leipzig, 1921

Printed according to the original

Published in English for the first time

240

ENGELS TO EDUARD BERNSTEIN

IN ZURICH

London, 14 July 1892

Dear Ede,

Your and Gine's postcard of 24 June 1892 (I reproduce the postmark for want of any other date) and letter of 2 July have reached me safely. I feel sure that the prospects for your harvest have in the meantime improved to such an extent that you are now worth, not 50 raps but 1 franc, and, since the value of money—whether paid or not—does after all represent ± [b] physical labour, I am equally sure that your health can only benefit from your haymaking. But why you sweat physically in the heat of the afternoon and mentally in the cool of the morning is not very clear unless it's a slimming cure you are after and of that, after all, you have no need. However, you are now in Zurich, so that all these comments will arrive after the event and your haymaking will presumably have given way to *nutrimentum spiritus*[c] (to stick to old Fritz's[d] Latin) in the museum or the Tonhalle or whatever the places are called there. But you should take *spriritus* in the form *vini aut cerevisiae*[e] rather than in that of more abstract spiritous material, otherwise it won't be a real summer holiday. As for what's happening in the English elections,[504] the *Vorwärts* is in any case far better informed than the two of us put together.[f]

---

[a] Emma Engels - [b] more or less - [c] spiritual nourishment - [d] Frederick II - [e] of wine or beer - [f] See this volume, pp. 459-60 and 464.

Bax's editorship of *Justice* would seem to be over. After the one number,[503] in which he radically changed the paper's tone,[a] there was a hitch; the tone reverted—at any rate in the negative sense of ignoring the movement in France, Germany, etc.—to what it had been, even though the earlier onslaughts were not resumed. But the last number is again Hyndman ALL OVER; Keir Hardie is attacked, Burns ignored and all the leading articles are supplied by Hyndman. Over here it is said that Bax's attack on Stanley of Africa[526] (who suddenly turned up in North Lambeth[b] to oppose the Gladstonians as UNIONIST candidate) has brought about a breach between him and Hyndman and that Hyndman has led the SOCIAL DEMOCRATIC FEDERATION[29] in a fervent pro-Stanley campaign in the latter's constituency. I am passing this on to you as related to me. No doubt you will be seeing Bax in Zurich in about a fortnight's time but whether, having resigned from the editorship of *Justice*, he will pay me a call before then, I cannot say.

Typical characteristics of the elections are: 1. A complete lack of enthusiasm for HOME RULE in England.

2. The granting of suffrage to working men has driven vast numbers of petty bourgeois into the Conservative camp, at any rate in the larger cities. Your petty bourgeois is beginning to be afraid of the workers, or at any rate does not want to be mistaken for one of them; CONSERVATIVE IS RESPECTABLE and hence he votes against Gladstone.

3. The strength of the Liberal Party lies in the middle and lower middle classes of the smaller towns and COUNTIES where the pressure exerted by the semi-feudal landowners and the High Church[527] clergy is still a force to be reckoned with. In the larger cities even the DISSENTERS, traditional mainstay of the Liberal Party, are beginning to vacillate—cf. for instance Birmingham.

4. Now that the two bourgeois parties are on an almost exactly equal footing (today of 3,300,000 votes cast, the opposition's majority over the government amounts *in all* to no more than about 76,000), it is Labour which is beginning to call the tune. And only in the election of Labour candidates—Keir Hardie, Burns, Wilson and others—was there any show of enthusiasm. Even before the elections[c] I had said that these would be the last to be fought out between the two official parties, but that they would give the Liberals a foretaste of

---

[a] See this volume, pp. 448-49 - [b] district of London - [c] See this volume, p. 463.

things to come. As has happened in full measure. Even at the next elections the Labour Party will put up quite a different show. The current elections *must* have filled it with confidence in its own strength.

5. The new Parliament is a provisional one. Gladstone will not get a majority without the support of the Irish and Labour members, which means an early dissolution. So much the better.

Apropos. Tussy intends to send the *Neue Zeit* an article on the elections [a] in which, however, only such internal matters will be discussed as could be known to someone *over here,* and then not to *all and sundry.* So don't let it deter you from writing in the *Neue Zeit* about the general results as you see them. Her information, on the other hand, consists of specific facts relating to the skulduggery of the various parties, something quite different to what you will be writing.

Warm regards from Louise and myself to both of you.

Your
F. E.

First published in: Marx and Engels, *Works*, First Russian Edition, Vol. XXIX, Moscow, 1946

Printed according to the original

Published in English for the first time

241

ENGELS TO PAUL LAFARGUE [141]

AT LE PERREUX

London, 22 July 1892

My dear Lafargue,

Let's hope that this time the Battle of *Eylau* will not, like its predecessor, be a DRAWN BATTLE [528] and that whatever Mr *Weinschenk* decants for you will be wine of a respectable sort. [b] I begin to understand

---

[a] E. Aveling and E. Marx-Aveling, 'Die Wahlen in Großbritannien', *Die Neue Zeit,* 10. Jg. 1891/92, 2. Bd., Nr. 45. - [b] A pun in the original: *verser* means 'to decant' and 'to invest capital', Weinschenk is a surname and also means 'vintner'.

French anti-Semitism when I see how these Jews of Polish origin with German names are insinuating themselves everywhere, claiming everything as their own, pushing themselves forward even to the extent of shaping public opinion in the City of Light,[a] a city of which your Parisian simpleton is so proud that he believes it to be the supreme power in the universe.

At all events, it's not a symptom to be overlooked if these gentlemen are now of the opinion that a socialist newspaper is a sound investment. We're quoted on the Stock Exchange! That really is a sign of progress.

I believe Millerand is right in advising you to deposit 25 or, better still, 50 thousand fr. in your name at a good bank. That is the only guarantee, but take care that the bank places it to your credit *without any conditions*. They should send you a formal letter, stating that the sum of ... has been placed to your credit and that you are at liberty to dispose of it whenever you wish. Moreover, in the contract with you and Guesde, Weinschenk should authorise you to withdraw this sum *in the event of his breaking the contract*. For otherwise the private contract between him and the two of you would not be binding on the company to be floated — unless the latter had expressly accepted it. But these are legal niceties and Millerand will doubtless advise you properly.

As regards the cholera, it is virtually certain to arrive here. Meanwhile it is completing the work of peace begun in 1891 by the famine in Russia.[b] What is beyond my comprehension is the stupidity of your French bourgeois who evidently believes that Russia is a power capable of doing anything whatever for France. If he had only a modicum of common sense he would see that at this moment the alliance with France is absolutely indispensible to Russia and that whatever France wanted, Russia would have to concede. But in all western countries the attitude of our official politicians to Russia is stupid beyond belief. France, in the shape of her army, has all the safeguards she needs. I have been reading an article by an English officer, not one of your generals of the old school, who owe their promotion to their ignorance, but a colonel who knows his business and who speaks of the French army with an envy that is genuinely felt — he is envious because he knows that the advantages it enjoys are impracticable in England by reason of the fundamental difference between the two mil-

[a] Paris - [b] See this volume, pp. 242, 343-44 and 374-75.

itary institutions. But he says that the French army is truly democratic — in the regiments, namely its vital organisation —, that officers
and men respect one another and work together towards the same
end, that all ranks know their trade, that even the territorials [529]
have made better soldiers than might have been expected, that *real*
discipline is excellent and based on the good will of all, that military
training is confined to things which are really necessary in war, but
that within those limits such training is perfectly adequate, and that
all superfluous parades are rigidly eschewed. In short, if you except
the better training received by the French, *it is a description of the Prussian army as reorganised after 1807* under Scharnhorst and that's the
greatest compliment one could pay the French army. I'm beginning
to believe that battalion for battalion it's just as good as the German
army, if not better. The Germans' superiority lies in the large number
of officers on the reserve, the superiority of the French in the good relationship between the men and their officers. In our case the men are
shamefully ill treated.

You are right. Next week I am off to Ryde.[530] Louise departs next
Sunday for Vienna and I shall probably depart on Wednesday.[a] So if
you write after Tuesday, the address is: The Firs, Brading Road,
Ryde.

I trust Laura is well; we haven't heard a word from her.[531] Since
distance precludes my giving her a kiss, give her a kiss on my behalf.

My regards, Mr Wandering Jew,[392]

F. E.

First published in: F. Engels, P. et
L. Lafargue, *Correspondance*, t. III, Paris,
1959

Printed according to the original

Translated from the French

---

[a] 27 July

242

ENGELS TO AUGUST BEBEL

IN BERLIN

London, 23 July 1892

Dear August,

With your usual perspicacity you rightly guessed that I would be sending you this letter via the Witch. So to begin with let me thank you for the Imperial and Royal Railway Timetable and assure you that I shall set my 'new course' by the above right royal document. I have already fathomed a few of the mysterious signs and wonders to be found therein and within the next fortnight hope to get to the bottom of them all, thereby ensuring that I don't find myself stuck anywhere.

Well, my plans are as follows: Next Wednesday [a] I go to Pumps in Ryde [530] whither all letters will be forwarded. Shall stay there until about 10-15 August, depending on circumstances, for I am awaiting a letter from Barmen,[b] the contents of which will determine the day of departure. I shan't go to Barmen, as I have so many nephews and nieces there that duty visits alone would take more than a fortnight. But I want to spend a few days in Engelskirchen where my brothers go in turn for the summer holidays. Thence, on or about the 18th or 19th, to Zurich where I must pay a visit I have been promising for years to my cousin Mrs Beust and family. I shall let you know as soon as I arrive and shall then go on to St Gallen on the 24th or 25th. If you fetch me, so much the better. We would then set out for Stuckert[c] on the Neckar's banks, pick up Uncle Georg and carry on to Munich and — via the Alps if possible — to Vienna, etc. She will be able to tell you the rest by word of mouth (I don't mean Mrs Beust who is the grammatical subject but the Witch who is in any case a most ungrammatical one).

According to Tussy, the elections [504] here in the East End of London have aroused wild enthusiasm. The workers have at last realised that they are capable of something if only they have the will. The Liberal spell has been broken and, what's more, correspondents from

___
[a] 27 July - [b] See this volume, p. 473. - [c] Stuttgart

far and wide have been proclaiming in the *Workman's Times* that an
INDEPENDENT LABOUR PARTY is all that is needed. Facts and facts alone
are what impress hard-headed John Bull and these cannot fail to
do so.

The Vollmariad provides further proof that the man has completely lost touch with the Party.[532] A break with him is bound to
come, probably this year or next; he seems intent on ramming state socialist inanities down the Party's throat. But since he is an artful intriguer and since I have had wide experience of campaigning against
people of this sort — Marx and I often made tactical blunders when
confronted by this kind and had to pay dearly for it — I shall now
take the liberty of offering you a few tips.

What these people are mainly after is to put us *formally* in the
wrong and that we must prevent. Otherwise they'll keep harping on
this side-issue in order to obscure the main issue of whose weakness
they are aware. So be careful what you say both in public and in private. You will have noticed how cleverly the fellow made use of your
remark about Liebknecht[533] so as to foment trouble between
him (Liebknecht) and yourself — after all he is perfectly well
aware of your attitude to one another! — and thus place you in a
quandary.

Secondly, since it is important to them to obscure the main issue,
you must avoid giving them any cause to do so; any side-issue *they*
may raise should be dealt with as briefly and conclusively as possible
so that it is disposed of once and for all. As for *yourself*, however, you
must if at all possible ignore all side-issues or red herrings that may
arise, whatever the temptations. Otherwise the debate will range ever
wider and the original bone of contention will gradually disappear
from view. In which case there will no longer be any chance of a
decisive victory. So far as the intriguers are concerned, that might
be success enough, but for us, at any rate, it would be a moral
defeat.

Thirdly, it follows from 1. and 2. that, when confronted by such
people, *purely defensive tactics* are best until such time as they land
themselves in a real predicament — then you open up with short,
devastating artillery bombardment before going in with the bayonet
for the coup de grâce. Here, as nowhere else, it is a matter of husban-
ding one's ammunition and reserves until the last moment.

Every time we departed from these rules when fighting the Bakuninists, Proudhonists, German academics and other such riff-raff, we

had to suffer for it and that is why I now submit them to you again for your consideration.

Well, warm regards to yourself and Mrs Julie[a] from

Your

General

Siegel's last letter is enclosed at his request.

First published in *Bolshevik*, No. 14, Moscow, 1935

Printed according to the original

Published in English for the first time

243

ENGELS TO REGINA BERNSTEIN

IN ZURICH

London, 25 July 1892

Dear Gine,

We were delighted to get your and Ede's letter and showed it to Tussy yesterday. From the picture the château[b] has the appearance of a really splendid little castle; a garden restaurant for some 500 people and, next to a couple of giant poplars, a few mysterious trees that look like unassuming palms; on the slope below the vines whence comes the sour wine.[c] Still, one gets used to that too and in any case it's better than London ALE, while the air up there must be a lot better than in Highgate. I'm glad it's doing Ede good and that you can hope to˙ bring him back with his nerves functioning in such a way that he is no longer conscious of them.

Here too the summer holidays have started. Louise left for Cologne yesterday afternoon and by now — 5 p.m. — will doubtless be very close to Berlin. The day after tomorrow I set off for a fortnight's stay with Pumps,[530] after which I shall pay another visit to the dear fatherland about the time you will be preparing to leave; indeed it is not

---

[a] Julie Bebel - [b] In the original: *Schlössli* (Swiss dialect). - [c] In the original: *sure Wi chömmt* (Swiss dialect).

impossible that I may venture as far as Zurich shortly after you have gone—that, however, is entirely between ourselves. But why did you buy those confounded return tickets? They are the main obstacle that prevents us from sauntering along the lake together. I'm glad to hear that your mama is still such a doughty mountaineer. If I really do get to Berlin—alas, the dream is far too beautiful for one to believe it might come true—I shall in any case see her there.

Tell Ede that Louise was so overwhelmed on hearing that he had said *Massel* and *Broche*[a] three times on her behalf that I had to administer a potent draught of cognac before she set off on her journey to help her recover from the shock.

What follows next is for Ede. Namely, in the first place, Tussy's and Edward's article[b] was ready by Sunday (a week ago yesterday) and was sent off to Stuckert.[c]

Secondly, our successes in the elections[504] have now been generally acknowledged over here. The present situation is that, in view of the marked preponderance of the *Radical* wing in his party, Gladstone must largely rejuvenate his cabinet if it is to survive;

further, that his Home Rule Bill will at once be thrown out by the Upper House;

but that to be able to dissolve with any certainty of success, he must at the same time introduce one man one vote by drawing up a sensible electoral register which will ensure the workers do in fact get what was promised them on paper in general terms in 1867 and 1884 but was subsequently retracted in matters of detail,[519] i.e. a $1\text{-}1\frac{1}{2}$ million increase in the Labour electorate—and perhaps a second ballot;

and that not until *this* has gone through will he dissolve.

So it is a splendid situation so far as we are concerned.

Many regards to Ede and you yourself,

Yours

General

First published, in Russian, in *Marx-Engels Archives*, Book I, Moscow, 1924

Printed according to the original

Published in English for the first time

---

[a] good fortune and blessings - [b] E. Aveling and E. Marx - Aveling, 'Die Wahlen in Großbritannien', *Die Neue Zeit*, 10. Jg. 1891/92, 2. Bd., Nr. 45. - [c] Stuttgart

244

ENGELS TO PASQUALE MARTIGNETTI

IN BENEVENTO

London, 25 July 1892

Dear Friend,

I have not replied to your letter of 13 May sooner because I wished to include with my reply a material token of my sympathy. At the time, however, I myself was short of funds and it is only now that I find myself in a position to send you the enclosed money-order for three pounds sterling. I know only too well that your troubles all derive from the struggle for existence and I'm only sorry that I cannot do more to make that struggle easier for you.

Meanwhile I'm glad to learn from your letter of 1 July that your health is improving and that there is no longer any fear of the neurasthenia that was threatening to take hold. I hope the improvement will continue, so that you will soon be able to look round for remunerative employment again.

I shall ask Aveling tomorrow about the *Students' Marx*; he is unlikely to raise any objections.[534]

You will have heard that in the elections[504] here we scored positive triumphs *over* both the old parties and that even where we lost we gave the Liberals a taste of our power. The movement is gaining more and more ground, thanks in particular to the resolution regarding eight hours demonstrations adopted by the Paris Congress.[51] The First of May has '*fait merveille*',[a] immeasurably more so than did the *Chassepots* at Mentana,[535] which have long since been consigned to the scrapheap.

With sincere regards,

Yours,

F. Engels

First published, in the language of the original (German), in *La corrispondenza di Marx e Engels con italiani. 1848-1895*, Milano, 1964

Printed according to the original

Published in English for the first time

---

[a] worked marvels

245

ENGELS TO LUDWIG SCHORLEMMER

IN DARMSTADT

London, 25 July 1892

My dear Schorlemmer,

Do please let us drop the ceremonious 'Mr' in future. I'm glad you were satisfied with the obituary in the *Vorwärts*.[a] I had to write it in great haste and without any external aids on the afternoon before the funeral. Had I been able to wait until I got back to London I could have gone into greater detail. But in cases like these one must work exactly like a journalist, i. e. quickly, making do with the material to hand.

Justice, the English Socialist paper, also published an excerpt from the obituary.[536] This paper is the organ of Mr Hyndman who is in personal control of the Social Democratic Federation,[29] a society that is Marxist in principle and anti-Marxist in practice. Hyndman is a petty-minded intriguer who looks down on the German party with indescribable envy because his little society is incapable of achieving what our own people can pull off without a second thought and who therefore allies himself with anyone who opposes the German party — over here with the noble *Gilles*, for example, with the French Possibilists of Broussian persuasion,[3] etc. Two months ago, however, he stepped down as editor in favour of Bax who is a talented and in other respects decent fellow with a complete mastery of German, and who often visits me and the Avelings. Hyndman hoped that he would thereby get him into his clutches, but apparently Bax has decided that there is nothing doing in that quarter so far as he is concerned — at all events it was he who published the notice in the last number he edited; he knew Carl[b] very well and often used to meet him at my house and elsewhere. — Shall try and send you the number.

But now I had better speak to you about one or two business mat-

---

[a] F. Engels, 'Carl Schorlemmer', *Vorwärts*, No. 153, 3 July 1892. - [b] Carl Schorlemmer

ters connected with the estate, as will probably be some time before you hear from Manchester.

In accordance with the law over here, every will must be deposited with the Court of Probate where anyone may inspect it on payment of one shilling = 1 M. But before it gets as far as that, it must be approved by the Court of Probate and estate duty must be deducted and paid, the amount in your case being 1% or 3% — I cannot say exactly which — of the gross assets. The executors must swear to the value of the estate they have declared, and all in all this is the kind of case that requires the attention of a solicitor from start to finish if one is not to be atrociously rooked. So you will doubtless have to be patient a little longer and will also have to reckon on expenses that are very high by German standards. That, however, is inevitable.

The books, etc, he left will fetch little when sold. The chief items in the estate consist in cash on deposit at the bank and the copyrights.

The former will amount to about £1,800 from which must be deducted the cost of the funeral, current petty debts, estate duty, court and solicitor's expenses, etc., which may amount in all to between £200 and £250; I am unable to assess it from here, but it's nevertheless my opinion that you can reckon on a net sum of at least £1,500 = 30,000 marks.

So far as works on chemistry are concerned, the value of the book rights is only of very limited duration. Science is making such rapid strides that things become outdated in a year or two unless they are constantly revised. And then again the death of an important chemist always provides younger men of varying quality with an opportunity to take upon themselves the preparation of new editions, which also means that they receive most of the profit. The same thing will happen here. The executors are consulting me in the course of their negotiations, likewise Gumpert, so we may be sure that nothing precipitate will be done. Moreover I have backed them up in their view that nothing final should be decided in this respect without the consent of the family. That is not only their duty but also an excellent way of bringing pressure to bear on the opposing side. The latter, publishers no less than collaborators such as Roscoe, is in a hurry to bring matters to a conclusion, while the executors, on the other hand, have plenty of time and can therefore wait for these people to approach them and contribute towards a quick settlement by making this or that further concession. So here too it would be in your own interest not to press for a quick settlement.

I hear from Gumpert that you have written and told him your mother is unwell and has taken to her bed. I hope for the best but she is very old and Carl's death will have hit her very very hard. But I hope that despite everything you will be able to send me better news before long.

Yours very sincerely,

F. Engels

First published in: Marx and Engels, *Works*, First Russian Edition, Vol. XXIX, Moscow, 1946

Printed according to the original

Published in English for the first time

246

ENGELS TO LAURA LAFARGUE

AL LE PERREUX

London, 26 July 1892

My dear Laura,

I receive this minute, 9.45 evening — Sonnenschein's account which results in £5.9.2., 3/5-ths of which go to Mohr's heirs, that is £ 1.1.10 each, of which cheque enclosed.

I hear from Tussy that you are very much out of sorts just now, hope you will mend soon!

To-morrow I am off to Ryde for a fortnight,[530] address:

F. E.

The Firs, Brading Road, Ryde

Louise left on Sunday[a] for Austria.

Ever yours,

F. Engels

First published in: Marx and Engels, *Works*, Second Russian Edition, Vol. 38, Moscow, 1965

Reproduced from the original

Published in English for the first time

247

ENGELS TO LUDWIG SCHORLEMMER

IN DARMSTADT

Ryde, Isle of Wight, 28 July 1892
The Firs, Brading Road

My dear Schorlemmer,

I had hardly expected that my forebodings about your mother would be realised so soon. But the blow she suffered from Carl's[b] death must nevertheless have been too much for the old lady, ailing and debilitated as she was; on the other hand she was certainly still too mentally alert for the news to have been concealed from her. So one family misfortune has been followed by another and we can only hope that this will be the last. I can sympathise only too well with you in your loss, for eighteen years ago I too lost my mother,[c] who was then 77, and I know what a peculiar bond is formed among the members of a large family by the maternal home and how irreplaceable this is, however united the children may be. The maternal home keeps the whole of that same younger generation together as one

---

[a] 24 July - [b] Carl Schorlemmer - [c] Elisabeth Franziska Engels

large family. Once the mother dies, each of these younger families feels much more independent and involuntarily tends to draw apart from the others. That is in the natural course of things but it is a drastic change none the less and when, in my case as in yours, the mother outlives the father by many years, this makes the added loss of the mother doubly distressing.

Please convey my sincere condolences to your brothers and their families.

To you yourself I send my wishes for your daughter's speedy and complete recovery.

I arrived here yesterday to spend ten days or so with my niece.[530] She also knew your mother and would like to add a line or two.

Yours very sincerely,

F. Engels

[From Mary Ellen Rosher]

I cannot let this letter from my uncle go off without sending to you and all your family my condolences on the death of your dear mother. With warm regards to you all from

Yours,

Ellen Rosher

First published in: Marx and Engels, *Works*, First Russian Edition, Vol. XXIX, Moscow, 1946

Printed according to the original

Published in English for the first time

248

ENGELS TO HERMANN ENGELS

IN BARMEN

Ryde, Isle of Wight, 28 July 1892
The Firs, Brading Road

Dear Hermann,

Very many thanks for your letters. I'm sorry that my plans should have clashed to some extent with yours, but because of other arrangements I was more or less tied to a fixed date and could not very well upset these so long as there was no positive word from you. Everything is now in order and, unless I advise you to the contrary, I shall arrive on the 12th (probably by the first train from Cologne) and shall in any case telegraph from there.

I have been here since yesterday and intend to stay until the 9th, or at any rate the 8th, of August.[530] The weather is magnificent, cloudless sky, temperature 16-17 Réaumur, a fresh easterly wind, flowers and beautiful trees outside my window, wonderful air, barely a kilometre from the sea though nearly 200 ft above it, and with hills and coppices all around.

So here's to our meeting. Meanwhile my love to Emma[a] and the children.

Your old
Friedrich

First published in *Deutsche Revue*, Jg. 46, Bd. III, Stuttgart-Leipzig, 1921

Printed according to the original

Published in English for the first time

---

[a] Hermann Engels' wife

249

ENGELS TO AUGUST BEBEL

IN BERLIN

Ryde, England, 8 August 1892
The Firs, Brading Road

Dear August,

Your card received this morning. My dear fellow, the whole thing
has fallen through and I am the odd man out! My old trouble, which
obliges me to wear a complicated bandage and about which I have
told you various details, has reared its head again after five years of
inactivity and all at once completely crippled me. I had already suspected something of the kind during your visit,[474] but it was so insignificant that I paid no attention to it, thinking that, as it had often
done on previous occasions, it would finally clear up of its own accord
here in the sea air. On Saturday[a] I walked about $1\,^3/_4$ kilometres,
rested for half an hour or so and then came back — a mere $3\,^1/_2$ km in
all — and by the evening realised that the crisis was upon me and that
instead of going to Germany I should have to spend a month here,
resting and abstaining from alcohol, if I was to get myself up to
the mark again. At this moment I should merely have to walk a thousand paces to be banished to a sofa for 8 or 10 days. Thus do the best
laid plans come to nothing!

As to the cause, all I can say is that since last August I have been
addressing myself to the bottle more liberally than for many years
and that the accumulated effect eventually brought about this result.
Anyhow, I can find no other explanation for the thing, especially
since it is a condition of the cure that one must abstain from alcohol
during such time as symptoms of localised inflammation are noticeable. How delighted your son-in-law[b] will be! — though the conclusion he'll doubtless draw will not be shared by me.

At any rate I am totally incapable of making the projected trip in
this condition. At most I might get as far as my brothers in Engelskirchen, but certainly not Zurich and so, despite this rotten bit of luck,
I cannot but congratulate myself that the attack did not happen on

_____
[a] 6 August - [b] Ferdinand Simon

my travels, leaving me completely *hors de combat* in a foreign land. Now I can at least doctor myself here at Pumps' and in a month's time I shall, I imagine, be fairly mobile again. The thing is of no consequence, save for the tedium; I have weathered it three or four times already and am familiar with the treatment, the more so through having devised it myself as a result of my own experience, since the good doctors were, with one exception, and he is dead, all of them utterly mystified by the case.

I at once wrote to Louise yesterday, telling her that she should make no changes whatever in her plans and on no account hasten her return even by so much as a day.[153] However it is highly probable that you, like her, will now prefer to make other arrangements, in which case you will have to resume your correspondence about it.

Tell your wife and daughter[a] that I am doubly sorry that, as a result of what has happened, I shall be deprived of the pleasure of making their personal acquaintance as also that of your son-in-law. But to postpone is not to put off for ever, and the bitter experience of the present year will make me a wiser man in the next when, I trust, I shall still be alive and once again nimble on my pins. And then we shall make the same trip, if not an even better one.

My address up till the end of August will be as on the letterhead. Rosher's name is not necessary, but letters will be delayed unless addressed to The Firs, Brading Road.

So my warm regards to you all, and do please drink to my recovery. Since I am now abstaining in his stead, Dr Simon might even permit himself a sip for once!

Your old friend
F. Engels

First published in: Marx and Engels, *Works*, First Russian Edition, Vol. XXIX, Moscow, 1946

Printed according to the original

Published in English for the first time

---

[a] Julie Bebel and Frieda Simon

250

ENGELS TO HERMANN ENGELS

IN ENGELSKIRCHEN

Ryde, 8 August 1892
The Firs, Brading Road

Dear Hermann,

After all the preparations and letter writing, my trip has finally fallen through. The old trouble with my groin, which originally began when I came down with my horse while out fox hunting and which became bothersome ten years ago but lay dormant during the latter five, has suddenly sprung to life again. The bandages are no longer of any use and after walking about 2 English miles = 3 kilometres last Saturday[a] I was pretty well incapable of going any further. I know what to do. For the next month I must take a complete rest and abstain from beer and wine, after which all will be well, but travelling is out of the question. I wrote yesterday to Rudolf[b] in Barmen,[153] but am sending this note to Engelskrichen today in case you are still there.

I'm terribly sorry that things should have turned out in this way. But it can't be helped and I must resign myself. So I shall be staying here (address overleaf) until the end of August.[530]

Time for the post. Much love to you all. In haste.

Your
Friedrich

First published in *Deutsche Revue*, Jg. 46, Bd. III, Stuttgart-Leipzig, 1921

Printed according to the original

Published in English for the first time

---

[a] 6 August - [b] Engels

251

ENGELS TO KARL KAUTSKY[501]

IN STUTTGART

Ryde, 12 August 1892
The Firs, Brading Road

Dear Baron,

Herewith the proofs, returned with thanks.[537]

August will already have told you that my trip to Germany has fallen through. The after-effects of the old trouble, which laid me up 9 years ago when you came to visit me on my birthday, have once more asserted themselves and at just the wrong time so that I have got to lie here on the sofa instead of tippling with you. Luckily I can breathe good sea air here — the house is right out in the country, high up, with a view of the sea — and this, together with rest and abstinence from alcohol will no doubt set me on my legs again within 3 or 4 weeks. But it's a pity it should have happened just now. Well, to postpone isn't to put off indefinitely.

Thank you for your book[a] — unfortunately I have so far been prevented from reading it by the upsets of the past few days.

A pity that the bits in Tussy's article about the SOCIAL DEMOCRATIC FEDERATION[29] and the FABIANS,[87] and also about Taylor's candidature,[b] didn't go in.[538] I saw these in ms. after the event and they are *virtually indispensable* if you are to have a complete picture of the elections. The total collapse of the SOCIAL DEMOCRATIC FEDERATION the moment it was really put to the test was significant in view of the boasting which that 'one and only' Social-Democratic organisation and One True Church has for years indulged in. I don't know whether you saw Bax in Zurich, but he's a very indifferent authority on the SOCIAL DEMOCRATIC FEDERATION. He edited *Justice* for 6 weeks and got rid of all its many vulgarisms but was wholly incapable (for otherwise he would surely have done so) of giving the paper a character that was anything but sectarian. For the SOCIAL DEMOCRATIC FEDERATION is in fact a sect pure and simple. It has ossified Marxism into a hard and fast dogma and, by repudiating *any* labour movement that isn't

---

[a] K. Kautsky, *Das Erfurter Programm in seinem grundsätzlichen Theil erläutert.* - [b] See this volume, pp. 497 and 515.

orthodox Marxist (and, what's more, Marxist in a very wrong-head-ed way) — i. e. pursuing a policy exactly the reverse of that recom-mended by the *Manifesto*,[a] has put itself in such a position that it can never become anything other than a sect. There were many reasons why Bax should have got into touch with these people again, but if they go on as they are it won't be long before he discovers that they are trying to exploit him politically and financially and that he is un-able to assume any responsibility for them. But that's something he will have to learn from personal experience; for the time being he has so far compromised himself as to be obliged in some measure to be their advocate. Come to that, Bax is *completely out of touch with the workers as such*.

The FABIANS have become a real stumbling-block, tailing along behind the big Liberal Party on the pretext, so they say, of imposing their candidates upon it. They may pull this off for a time in the case of the COUNTY COUNCIL,[412] where they can dabble in Possibilist pro-grammes of municipal reform,[539] but even there the pious sham will pass muster only until such time as it is rumbled by the middle classes. In the case of parliamentary elections none of this applies, for here the Liberals will give the FABIANS, like all other self-styled Labour candi-dates, only such constituencies as are *hopeless*. If one wants to impose Labour candidates upon the Liberals, it must be done after the man-ner of Burns and Keir Hardie, by holding a pistol to their heads, and not after the manner of the FABIANS, by sucking up to them under false pretences. Fortunately the call for an INDEPENDENT LABOUR PARTY is now already so loud and so general that even the bland inducements of Fabian cajolery and Fabian cash will eventually be overcome.

Burgess, the *Workman's Times* man, now proposes to found an INDE-PENDENT LABOUR PARTY himself— yet another competitor for the other two [b]! Burgess is a vain, ambitious johnny, hitherto most unreliable. Whether and to what extent he will make out remains to be seen. At all events his present action is a straw in the wind.

A very good bit of news: So proud were the factory workers of the North of their old TEN HOURS BILL that it was largely they who opposed the eight hour day (cf. Newcastle TRADES UNION Congress [298]). This is now changing; the masses are gradually being converted to 8 hours while the leaders with their 10 hours are beginning to find themselves

---

[a] *The Manifesto of the Communist Party* - [b] the Social Democratic Federation and the Fabian Society

out on a limb. This will no doubt be more or less in evidence at this year's TRADES UNION congress.[540]

The Avelings have gone to Norway. Just before they left, Tussy got a letter from Greulich in which the latter requested her on behalf of the Zurich International Congress Committee [541] to oblige them with an English draft of the invitation to the English TRADES UNION Congress, and to translate all their other stuff into English. So Mr Seidel's machinations, aimed at getting the confounded Marxists cold-shouldered on that occasion (which could only have led to the installation of Mr Adolphe Smith Headingley), would seem to have been happily nipped in the bud.

Pumps and Percy send their kindest regards.

Your
F. E.

First published in *Aus der Frühzeit des Marxismus. Engels Briefwechsel mit Kautsky*, Prag, 1935

Printed according to the original

Published in English in full for the first time

252

ENGELS TO AUGUST BEBEL

IN BERLIN

Ryde, 14 August 1892
The Firs, Brading Road

Dear August,

I share your hope that by the beginning of September I shall have so far recovered as to be able to travel at least as far as Berlin. *Should* this be the case, I shall without fail pay a flying visit to Berlin — my sole destination in fact, for by then the Engelskirchen folk will have dispersed to the four winds.

The only question is whether it is going to be possible. And of that I cannot as yet give you any idea. I know from experience that in such cases 3 or 4 weeks' rest is absolutely essential if I am to recover my mobility, and any premature exertion or excessive exercise, however slight, will set me back by a week or a fortnight. But unfortunately one cannot tell until it's too late whether the exertion is premature or the exercise excessive.

On top of that I am, after all, 5 or 6 years older than I was at the time of the last bout, and have undeniably allowed more alcohol to pass through the inner man this year than I normally do in three. So I shall have to resign myself to a somewhat longer cure, even if the inflammatory symptoms have not resulted in any organic changes in the shape of adhesions or lesions or scarring.

At all events it will not be until very late in the day that I shall be able to tell from observations what the position is. You must keep me properly informed of the addresses at which my letters and, if needs be, telegrams, can reach you, especially in the case of Vienna, and how long you propose to stay there, so that Louise doesn't leave for London at the same time as I for Berlin.

Last Monday^a and Tuesday I was in London where I saw the Avelings and put my house in order. Thus the cure was interrupted until Wednesday. Now I am lying absolutely still and, of course, feel correspondingly better. I hope in a week's time to be able with impunity to allow myself at least a *modicum* of exercise. I shall let you have a bulletin as soon as there is anything to report.

Needless to say, I shall now have to observe 'sobriety and moderation' in regard to alcohol. I had indeed been surprised at my continued ability to tolerate the stuff so well, and had grown overconfident as a result. Well, we must hope that the consequences do not persist too long. I must revert to my former principle of abstaining for a fortnight or a month every so often. Not that I regard abstaining from drink as any more of a hardship than refraining from smoking, provided there is good reason for it.

I have not had an answer from Louise to the letter I wrote to her a week ago today.[153] The Sunday postal arrangements over here are abominable.

One good piece of news: Mr Seidel's intrigues, aimed at preventing the accursed Marxists from having any say in the preparations for the Zurich Congress,[541] would seem definitely to have misfired.

Greulich wrote to Tussy on behalf of the Zurich Committee re-

---

^a 8 August

questing her to draft a letter of invitation to the English TRADES
UNION Congress [540] and also to do their English translations. The letter
arrived when the Avelings were on the point of leaving for Norway
and Tussy, of course, immediately drafted the invitation, and generally placed herself at the committee's disposal; she sent me Greulich's
letter when she was actually on board the steamer.

And now for another: a period of slack trade and the manufacturers' threats to knock 10 per cent off wages has suddenly cured the
Lancashire cotton operatives of their enthusiasm for 10 hours and
opened their eyes to the advantages of the 8 hour day. Even the leaders are already said to have switched horses. Thus the 8 hour day
has triumphed in England. The resistance of those factory hands who
enjoyed the protection of the 10 hour day was the principal weapon
in the bourgeois arsenal. They'll lose it, come the September
congress. [540]

K. Kautsky did not make use of the enclosed passages from the
Avelings' article in the Neue Zeit. [538] When he wrote, he said this had
had to be done for *technical* reasons; may be, but again it may have
had something to do with Ede's comical respect for the FABIANS [87] and
Bax's (he's in Zurich) interest in the SOCIAL DEMOCRATIC FEDERATION. [29]
At all events, you'll find the passages interesting and they form an essential part of the overall picture.

You might get the *Vorwärts* to print the following questions:

1. Is it true that the 'Independents' in London, i. e. those who
were thrown out of the Communist Workers' Educational Society, [89]
have founded a club and rented Grafton Hall, a large building in
Fitzroy Square, for the purpose?

2. That to help raise the considerable sum required for this,
Mr Baginski, who earns at most £3 a week, made a contribution of
£500 sterling = 10,000 marks?

3. That Mr Hochgürtel, likewise a working man, contributed
another £500 and that, to the question as to where he had got the
money, he returned the strange reply that he had divorced his wife,
and thus obtained *h e r* money?

4. That the brewer who supplies beer to the club advanced another £1,200?

5. If all this be true, where did this money come from and who provided the brewer with the collateral without which no one would be so stupid as to advance so large a sum?

Warm regards to your wife[a] and children,

Your
F. E.

The Roshers send their kindest regards.

First published in: Marx and Engels, *Works*, First Russian Edition, Vol. XXIX, Moscow, 1946

Printed according to the original

Published in English for the first time

253

ENGELS TO REGINA BERNSTEIN

IN ZURICH

The Firs, Brading Road,
Ryde, England (that suffices)
15 August 1892

Dear Gine,

I and all the rest of us here are very sorry that your summer holiday should have been so sadly disrupted, but we all of us hope that all danger is now past, for otherwise I should certainly have heard from you. Unfortunately, my projected trip has also been completely ruined; just when I was about to get ready, I detected the unmistakable symptoms of an old disorder which I thought I had got the better of five years ago and which precluded all exercise for at least a fortnight if not a month. So I have got to remain stuck here in Ryde,[530] but first I had to spend a couple of days in London to put all my affairs in order there, and this, together with the many letters arising out of the 'catastrophe ordained by God', has so flummoxed me that I have not been able to write to you until today.

I can well believe that Ernst[b] is very down as a result of typhoid.

---

[a] Julie Bebel - [b] Ernst Schattner

Do give him time to recover completely before letting him go back to the exertions of school. But you have so many doctors on both sides of the family that I really ought to keep my mouth shut.

Since I have been here, we have been having marvellous weather and I am able to spend nearly all day, usually until 6 or 7 o'clock, sitting out in the garden in an armchair; there have been only 2 wet days in almost three weeks. Let us hope it lasts, since fresh air, along with rest, is my best medicine.

I am glad to hear that Ede is to make, or is already making, one more excursion into the Alps. He undoubtedly needs it, although it was with great pleasure that I saw from the *Neue Zeit* that he was his old self again.[542] His critique of Proudhon is *very nice indeed*, and his sense of humour is also returning. But it's better to be safe than sorry, i. e. to get properly well while he's got the chance, and thoroughly shake off his vexation over the Lassalle business [a] which was, after all, at the root of the whole thing. And you, too, ought to have a spell in which to recover from the difficult days and nights which have wrought such havoc with the peace and quiet of your holiday.

In other respects all is well here — that is, Pumps is as well as 'circumstances' allow, the event being expected in October. The children are far healthier than they used to be in London. This is a very large family: 2 dogs, 3 cats, a canary, a rabbit, two guinea pigs, a cock and 14 hens.

Many regards from the Roshers and especially from myself to you and Ede and Ernst.

Your old friend,

The General

First published, in Russian, in *Marx-Engels Archives*, Book I, Moscow, 1924

Printed according to the original

Published in English for the first time

---

[a] See this volume, pp. 253-54, 316.

254

ENGELS TO VICTOR ADLER [543]

IN LUNZ

Ryde, England, 19 August 1892
The Firs, Brading Road

Dear Victor,

That's what comes of exuberance. Instead of gallivanting round with you and yours in Lunz or Vienna, I have got to stay here in Ryde, miserably cossetting what Heine called 'my not altogether healthy body'; though walking and drinking are forbidden, boredom evidently is not. I had so very much looked forward to seeing Vienna at last, to being with you and all the others and, in particular, to becoming personally acquainted with your wife [a] and children, and now this confounded business crops up. Besides, I had also intended to obtain the opinion of a Viennese or — possibly *also* — a Berlin doctor on this somewhat obscure case and to ask you, after acquainting you with the facts, which specialist you would recommend. For over here there are as many medical faculties as there are hospitals, and the only men whom family doctors recommend are those from the hospital where they themselves did their training; this is not altogether a bad thing because they are the men they know best, but it narrows down the field of possible consultants very considerably and reduces the medical world of London to the dimensions of a small German university town. Accordingly, this sudden relapse is, in addition, positively detrimental to me.

Well, if there's one consolation — it is that to postpone is not to defer indefinitely, and what has misfired one year may perhaps come off the next. At all events this has taught me a lesson which I shall not soon forget. To be completely done out of my summer trip — and what a trip! — is bad enough and I shall have cause enough to rue it this winter, for I know all too well that the slight change of air from London to Ryde [530] does not have anything like the same effect on my old carcase as a trip to the Continent and to the Alps in particular. My health will not be as good this year as it was after the trips I made, first to America, [441] then to Norway [544] and, last year, to

---

[a] Emma Adler

Scotland and Ireland. [264] But I hope we'll get over it, in which case we shall definitely fix things up next year. For I have got to go to Vienna and, if possible, also to the Austrian Alps; the Swiss Alps harbour too many Swiss and have already been turned into too much of a showplace, so I really would prefer Anzengruber's peasants. And, by then, or so I hope, I should find you and your wife in perfect health, while I myself would again be in case to go climbing about in the mountains. Until next year, then!

While here I've been dabbling in early Christianity and am reading Renan[a] and the Bible. [545] Though shockingly superficial, Renan is a man of the world and as such his outlook is wider than that of the German scholastic theologians. Otherwise his book is a novel and what he said of Philostratus is equally applicable to himself, namely that it could be used as an historical source in the same way as, say, the novels of Alexandre Dumas *père* could be used as a source on the period of the Fronde. [546] In matters of detail I have caught him making the most shocking howlers. Moreover, he plagiarises the Germans with unparalleled effrontery.

Louise will have passed on to you the information I sent her the day before yesterday about the cotton operatives in Lancashire and their sudden conversion to the eight hour day. [b] [153] The same sort of thing is happening daily. Yesterday meetings of delegates representing entire districts again voted unanimously in favour of the 48 hour week, while in other districts the motion was carried in *all* cases with a majority, usually of two thirds. This has finally broken the back of the opposition *in the working class*.

The Russians are unfortunate. First they have a famine which will recur again this year, if in more chronic form, and then the cholera. And now, when their friend Gladstone has come to the helm here, he has to appoint Rosebery, who refuses to have any truck with Gladstone's Russophilia, as his Foreign Secretary.

August wants me to go to Berlin if at all possible. Well, I should like to, but can it be done? For the past ten days I have hardly set foot outside the garden gate and don't yet know whether I am really on the mend. For the fact is that, if I bestir myself just a little too soon or a little too much, I may find myself back where I started. And I have got to make up my mind in ten days or a fortnight at the latest — well, we shall see.

---

[a] E. Renan, *Histoire des origines du christianisme.* - [b] See this volume, pp. 497, 503-04.

So give my regards to all our friends and above all to your wife and children, and tell them how sorry I am not to have been able to come over this year. But next year I hope to make up for it. And warm regards to yourself from your crippled old

F. E.

I shall be staying here at least until the 31st of this month. [530]

First published in *Victor Adlers Aufsätze, Reden und Briefe*. Erstes Heft: *Victor Adler und Friedrich Engels*, Wien, 1922

Printed according to the book

Published in English in full for the first time

255

ENGELS TO AUGUST BEBEL

IN ST GALLEN

Ryde, 20 August 1892

Dear August,

Your letter of the 17th arrived this morning. I am replying at once because, tomorrow being Sunday and this being England, there would otherwise be no certainty of my note reaching you while you are still in St. Gallen. For I wanted to ask you to observe caution vis-à-vis K. Kautsky in regard to Ede. The latter is definitely on the mend, as his article in the *Neue Zeit* goes to show, [542] and we must do nothing that might interfere with this. Where his friendship with Ede is concerned, K. Kautsky isn't exactly the soul of discretion and should his letters suggest to Ede that we were secretly conspiring to counteract his enthusiasm for Fabianism, [87] it might bring about a serious relapse. Neurasthenics are mistrustful, and in my view his vexation over the Lassalle business [a] was not only the first symptom of his illness but also quite definitely the cause of its onset. So we must see that there isn't a recurrence. I also suspect that his unduly high opi-

---

[a] See this volume, pp. 253-54, 316.

nion of the FABIANS is partly attributable to his illness and that this will subside provided we don't keep harping on the subject.

Yesterday at long last a letter arrived from the Witch in which she grumbles about my not coming. But how could I help it? And what would she have said if I had been stricken down in Engelskirchen or Zurich, as I surely would have been had I set out? And far worse stricken than here, where I could deal with the thing in good time. She also tells me that, whatever happens, she will accompany you to Berlin.

I am *very* glad that I need not embark on the journey, if it comes off, before 7 September. That gives me a whole month's rest, by which time I hope I'll be fit to travel again. Since yesterday I have at last noted signs of improvement — very slight, but something at any rate. So we shall have to see.

Apropos — have we still got lawyers in Cologne who are members of the party? I still don't quite trust my Prussians and if I had the address of one such I should be armed against all eventualities.

I was very distressed by what you wrote and told me about Victor. [547] Let's hope you'll be able to find some solution. His wife's health also depends on this — worry about the future is said to have been largely responsible for her illness. I had no idea that things were so bad. But the Austrians are like the French and Irish, none of whom are capable of collecting contributions *regularly*. What is asserting itself here is the Celtic blood of their forebears, the Norici, [548] who were first Romanised and then Germanised. If you want to get an idea of how the General Council of the International fared with the French and their contributions, you should read Paul's two Epistles — especially the second — to the Corinthians, [a] throughout which he complains that *les cotisations ne rentrent pas.* [b]

Couldn't you vote the Austrian party a regular subsidy on condition that it goes to Victor? He would, after all, soon be kicked out of Germany since, unlike K. Kautsky, he'd be obliged to work, not on a learned journal [c] but on a propagandist paper.

The Lancashire cotton operatives are almost literally falling over each other to vote for the 8-hour day (48-hour week). Today the delegates are meeting in Manchester. Yesterday in Preston, there were 3,600 for and 600 against. But this is a question that Lancashire will

---

[a] 2 Corinthians, Ch. 7-9 - [b] the contributions are not coming in - [c] *Die Neue Zeit*

decide for the rest of England because last year it was still the seat of concerted opposition.

It was Mrs Croesel (she's even better than her husband) who told Tussy the stories about the London Independents' Club. [a] But no harm will be done if we save the thing up until we are all back in London again. As regards the source of the money, there might still be some interest left over from the Guelph funds, [236] and the stupidity of the police is beyond all bounds. At all events, Gilles had and may *still* have a great deal of money at his disposal. The other chaps are his men of straw.

Today comes the pleasing news that William [b] refuses to have any truck with the proposal for a two-year period of military service. [549] But since this carrot *has* already been dangled before the noses of the philistines, even the National Liberals [414] will find it hard to relinquish it. And this means better chances for a dissolution of the Reichstag.

What pitiful creatures these German bourgeois are! With the government's financial requirements increasing year by year, they could no be better placed to purchase a concession of political power in return for each grant of supply, as the English have been doing in a small way from time immemorial. But they don't *want* to; they leave all the power in the hands of the government and are content to haggle over a few paltry pence.

Cordial regards to Mrs Julie [c] and to Mrs Frieda and husband. [d]

Your old friend,

F. E.

The Roshers send their kindest regards.

I shall be staying here at any rate until the 31st. [530]

First published in: Marx and Engels, *Works*, First Russian Edition, Vol. XXIX, Moscow, 1946

Printed according to the original

Published in English for the first time

---

[a] See this volume, pp. 497-98. - [b] William II - [c] Julie Bebel - [d] Frieda and Ferdinand Simon

256

ENGELS TO LAURA LAFARGUE

AT LE PERREUX

Ryde, 22 August 1892
The Firs, Brading Road

My dear Laura,

I had hoped to hear from you how the preparations for the great event are progressing, as the day of October 1 is drawing near [550]; and especially would it interest me to learn that the fr. 25,000 — the guarantee-fund that business is meant — have been paid in to the Crédit Lyonnais. [551] But perhaps I shall now hear in a few days, the sacramental date of the 20 *Août*[a] with its 250,000 *en espèces et tout l'outillage*,[b] having passed. [552]

I have had an attack of my old complaint which from 1883 to 1887 laid me up lame from time to time, and had left me pretty well undisturbed for five years. Unfortunately at the wrong time it returned. I was to have left about 10 days ago, gone to Zürich to see the Beusts, thence with Bebel who is at St Gallen, to Stuttgart, Munich, Vienna, where we were to take up Louise and go to Berlin, and thence return to London. All this *ist ins Wasser gefallen*.[c] Bebel will have to do the Vienna trip alone, but wants me to come at least to Berlin if possible. Now as I am gradually mending, it is not quite impossible that I should be in a condition to undertake that bit of a journey. But so far I cannot tell, I want at the very least another fortnight's rest. Fortunately the fine weather allows me to spend all my lame time in the garden, and the splendid air here does me a deal of good.

Tussy, just before she was off for Norway, had a letter from Greulich, in the name of the Zürich Congress Committee, [541] asking her to send them a draft invitation, for the International Congress, to the Glasgow Trades Union Congress, [540] and to do all their English translation work. I suppose you know that some months ago Seidel intrigued to have this job given to one who was not connected with the damned Marxists. Louise in Berlin on her road to Vienna told Bebel, and Bebel at once wrote to Zürich, and this is the result.

---

[a] August - [b] in cash and all the equipment - [c] failed to come off

I have to shut up. It's dinner-time, and the cloth must be laid where I write. Immediately after dinner the mail-boxes are cleared (3 p. m.). So *gehab dich wohl!*[a] When shall we see you again here in England? I hope this autumn even if you cannot bring the *député-directeur politique*[b] with you.

Pumps, Percy and the little ones send their love.

Ever yours,

F. Engels

Hope you had my last with Louise Kautsky's Vienna address. [153]

First published, in the language of the original (English), in: F. Engels, P. et L. Lafargue, *Correspondance*, t. III, Paris, 1959

Reproduced from the original

257

ENGELS TO PASQUALE MARTIGNETTI [553]

IN BENEVENTO

Ryde, 22 August 1892

...I imagine there must be some error in regard to the Duchess,[c] *nata*[d] Leffler. I have never heard Mrs E. Marx-Aveling mention that lady. At this moment Mrs Aveling is in Norway; on her return I shall ask her and then send you further news.

Yours,

F. Engels

(London address still holds good.)

First published, in the language of the original (German), in *La corrispondenza di Marx e Engels con italiani. 1848-1895.* Milano, 1964

Printed according to the original

Published in English for the first time

---

[a] keep well and healthy -[b] Paul Lafargue -[c] di Caianiello -[d] née

258

ENGELS TO FRIEDRICH ADOLPH SORGE [357]

IN HOBOKEN

Ryde, Isle of Wight, 23 August 1892

Dear Sorge,

If I have not yet begun negotiations with Dietz regarding your book, [500] it is because I was prevented by the following circumstances:

I had arranged with L. Kautsky, who is in Vienna, and with Bebel, who is staying with his son-in-law [a] in St Gallen, that at the end of this month Bebel and I should go to Stuttgart together and thence to Berlin via Vienna, where we were to collect Louise Kautsky and take her with us. While in Stuttgart I had intended to settle the matter *verbally* with Dietz.

Now during my stay here in Ryde with Pumps, [530] the old trouble in my groin, which had ceased to bother me for five years past, has suddenly made itself felt again — and to such good purpose that for the past twelve days or so I have been crippled and unable to move. This put paid to my journey and now, although I am visibly better, I don't know whether I shall be in good enough shape to undertake a shorter tour. In any case I should not take in Stuttgart and hence shall shortly begin negotiations with Dietz by letter — as soon, that is, as I know that he hasn't gone off on a lightning tour with Bebel. The matter as such is already settled; all we are concerned with are the details, so you can go ahead with your addenda and the more comprehensive you make them the better. Notably, should you propose to do a more detailed account of the post-1870 period, you might well include the vicissitudes of the *professedly* socialist (German) party [133] and the blunders it has made. For you should remember that you are writing for a public that knows nothing whatever about transatlantic matters and has got to be told what's what. And even if this elicits a snarl from the worthy leaders in New York and Cincinnati, it needn't worry you, for after all you have long been used to that sort of thing.

Here is a piece of news which you must keep secret, above all from

---

[a] Ferdinand Simon

the gentlemen of the press, until I write and tell you more. Guesde and Lafargue have signed a contract with some capitalists whereby they are to bring out a daily in the grand manner and be its *directeurs politiques*. 500 000 fr. are to be expended on it and it is to appear on 1 October. [423] But being always somewhat sceptical in such matters and not having heard from Paris lately, I feel that something may yet intervene and that's why *nothing whatever must get into the papers*.

As you will have seen from the municipal elections in May [428] and the departmental elections in July, [554] the French are increasingly following in the footsteps of the Germans and learning to make use of universal suffrage instead of inveighing against it. And the cause is proving a great draw. At the Marseilles Congress [555] the 'Marxists' will acquire a standing such as they have never had before.

Add to which the splendid progress made here in England. The elections were a great success. [504] You will have noticed how different the tone of the *Workman's Times* has been since the beginning of July, and how Mr Burgess (Autolycus) is already attempting to found a separate 'INDEPENDENT LABOUR RARTY' under *his own* leadership, alongside the one which the SOCIALIST DEMOCRATIC FEDERATION [29] claims to lead. You will have gleaned the essentials from Louise Kautsky's [556] and Tussy's [538] articles in the Vienna *Arbeiter-Zeitung* and the *Neue Zeit* and will find a certain amount more in the preface to the new edition of the *Condition of the Working Class in England*[a] which I shall be sending you as soon as I get back to London. The TRADES UNION Congress to be held in Glasgow in a fortnight's time [540] will mark a great step forward: 1. because of the impact of the elections which has been all the greater in that the PARLIAMENTARY COMMITTEE [557] elected last year in Newcastle, [298] and consisting oddly enough entirely of former OLD UNIONISTS, has treated with disdain all the political resolutions of the self-same Congress, and has implemented none of them; and 2. because of the conversion of the textile workers who, last year, went to make up the bulk of the opposition to the 8-hour day but have now, because of the poor state of trade, suddenly and en masse declared themselves *in favour of 8 hours*. Last week the whole of Lancashire voted in *all* districts for 8 hours instead of 10, usually by a very big

---

[a] F. Engels, 'Preface to the Second German Edition (1892) of *The Condition of the Working-Class in England*'.

majority. In short, here too the cause is going ahead quite famously and next year, not only Austria and France, but also England, will be marching behind Germany, which in turn cannot fail to have the desired effect on your Anglo-Americans, particularly if your militia does a bit more shooting, by finally purging the chaps of some of their republican and GREAT COUNTRY arrogance.

In Germany everything is going splendidly; if you follow the party news in the *Vorwärts* you will see that we are making tremendous headway amongst the rural population — *even in the east* where it is most necessary.

And now you want me to tell you whether I shall be coming over next year. It's not out of the question, though it certainly won't be in the heat of July and August — one August in New York was quite enough for me. [441] Bebel is thinking of visiting America after the Zurich Congress, [541] i. e. in September or October. If he does, I might accompany him. But these are castles in the air. For, as you can see, even the plan I made for this year fell through a fortnight after it had been definitely decided upon, so how can I be expected to make plans a whole year in advance?

I realised long ago that some time you'd find it necessary to break with that madman Hepner. The man's got a mass of bees in his bonnet and either learns nothing or else gets it all wrong.

Cordial regards to your wife. [a]

Your
F. E.

My regards to Schlüter also.

First published abridged in *Briefe und Auszüge aus Briefen von Joh. Phil. Becker, Jos. Dietzgen, Friedrich Engels, Karl Marx u. A. an F. A. Sorge und Andere*, Stuttgart, 1906 and in full in: Marx and Engels, *Works*, First Russian Edition, Vol. XXIX, Moscow, 1946

Printed according to the original

Published in English in full for the first time

---

[a] Katharina Sorge

259

ENGELS TO AUGUST BEBEL

IN LUNZ

Ryde, 25 August 1892

Dear August,

Your letter dated 23, St Gallen, arrived this morning. I know perfectly well that the Prussians cannot do me any serious harm, but better safe than sorry and one never knows what chicanery those gents may not get up to. Some bright busybody of a policeman might at any time take it into his head to make things awkward for me under some bogus pretext or other and, perhaps, improve the shining hour by getting hold of certain letters from Miquel to Marx.[a] And, as you know, the Prussians make it a rule not to humiliate in public any official who commits a blunder, but at most quietly to haul him over the coals after having publicly whitewashed what he has done.

By the by, my projected journey is once more very much in the air. During the last day or two I have once or twice ambled along to the nearest post office some three hundred paces from the house and this trial of strength has again resulted in a total if temporary inability to walk more than a few steps, extraordinary sensitivity to pressure from the bandage in the inguinal region, etc.— which means that I'm laid up again. Today there is some improvement as a result of my having rested, but whether, in the 13 days between now and the 7th, things will have improved enough for me to be able to undertake the trip is, I think, very questionable. Well, we shall see.

No further news from Louise. On the other hand, I was delighted to hear from Dietz that, at your request, he had paid the second instalment of the fee for the *Condition*,[b] namely 500 M., to Victor.[c] At the beginning of September there is going to be something else of mine in the *Neue Zeit*,[d] the fee for which will be paid to Victor, and I have like-

---

[a] See Marx's letter to E. S. Beesly of 12 June 1871 (present edition, Vol. 44). -[b] second German edition (1892) of *The Condition of the Working-Class in England* - [c] Adler -[d] F. Engels, 'Introduction to the English Edition (1892) of *Socialism: Utopian and Scientific*'.

wise instructed Dietz to pay him *all* balances accruing to me with his firm. I have *got* to finish the third volume of *Capital* this winter and then, having rid myself of that burden, I shall be able to earn some more money again.

You are perfectly right about it's being sheer madness for the government to make the military estimates an occasion for dissolving the Reichstag, should the two year period of military service be turned down.[a] Nevertheless we cannot exclude the possibility that something of the kind may happen—considering the nature of the 'determining' factors in the German Empire today.

That Russia cannot go to war in Europe is evident from her activities in Central Asia—the other horn of her dilemma.[558] And there she is being very foolish. It will not intimidate the British but arouse their wrath and make it impossible for Mr Gladstone to give free rein to his Russophilia. While Gladstone might be prepared to sacrifice Constantinople, he could in no circumstances tolerate a threat to India; that would never do.

To me, the Isle of Wight seems intolerably boring when I think of you setting out alone on the journey on which I should have accompanied you. And then Louise goes and imagines I'm only shamming sick! Instead of sending this letter to Lunz, I should a thousand times rather have come in person. Today is the 15th day I have been confined to this little house and garden as to a prison, having in the last four days only made three excursions of three hundred paces down the road—with the result that I am again under the most stringent house and garden arrest. Today there is a flower show on the pier and tomorrow a regatta, and all the Pumpses will be going, while I shall have to stick at home—what a thrill! The only thing I am really glad about is that this trouble didn't come upon me while I was on my travels—that really would have been a pretty kettle of fish.

Well, give my regards to Victor and to his wife[b] and children; likewise to the Witch who will, I presume, have written to me in the meantime, and tell them all how very sorry I am not to be able to

---

come out and join you. But next year, if I am still alive, I shall assuredly come.

Your
F. E.

First published in: Marx and Engels, *Works*, First Russian Edition, Vol. XXIX, Moscow, 1946

Printed according to the original

Published in English for the first time

260

ENGELS TO VICTOR ADLER

IN LUNZ

Ryde, 30 August 1892

Dear Victor,

I was unable to reply yesterday to all the points in your letter, partly because there was no room on the page, partly because I had no time — our mid-day meal is at 2 and the post goes at 3. But now that sweet, impatient Oberdöbling[a] has sent me a postcard pestering me for a letter, I can write to you today about the rest.

What you say about tactics is only too true.[559] But there are all too many who, for convenience sake and to save themselves the trouble of racking their brains, would like to carry on indefinitely employing tactics that are appropriate only to the moment. We don't fashion our tactics out of nothing, but out of changing circumstances. In our present situation we must all too often allow our opponents to dictate them to us.

You are also right about the Independents.[560] I still recall the years — at the time I was still corresponding officially with Liebknecht — when I had to engage in a ceaseless struggle against the all-pervading, typically German petty bourgeois mentality. By and large we are safely over that in Imperial Germany, but as for the petty bourgeois in the parliamentary group, what a crew! — and more and

---

[a] Louise Kautsky (Oberdöbling forms part of Vienna).

more keep on arriving. In circumstances such as these a workers' party has no choice other than between the working man who is promptly made to suffer for it, in which case he readily deteriorates into a party pensioner, and the petty bourgeois who, though self-supporting, brings discredit on the party. And by comparison with them your Independent is a pearl beyond price.

What you say about the rapid industrial advance of Austria and Hungary has pleased me immensely. That is the only solid basis for the advancement of our movement. And it is also the only good aspect of protectionism — at any rate in the case of most of the continental countries and of America. Large-scale industry, big capitalists and large masses of the proletarians are being artificially nurtured, the centralisation of capital is being speeded up and the middle classes destroyed. In Germany protective tariffs were, in fact, unnecessary, having been introduced at the precise moment when Germany was establishing herself in the world market and it is *that* process which they have disrupted, though to make up for it they have filled a number of gaps in German industry which would otherwise have long remained unfilled and, were Germany to be compelled to sacrifice her protective tariffs to her position in the world market, she would be far better able to compete than hitherto. Both in Germany and in America protective tariffs are now simply a hindrance because they hinder those countries from taking their proper place in the world market. In America, therefore, they are bound to be abandoned before long and Germany is bound to follow suit.

By promoting your industry, however, you will be doing England a service; the more quickly her domination of the world market is utterly destroyed, the sooner will the workers over here come to power. Continental and American competition (and likewise Indian) has finally precipitated a crisis in Lancashire, the first of its consequences being the prompt conversion of the workers to the eight-hour day. [a]

Cooperation with the Czechs is necessary also from the political viewpoint. These people live in the middle of Germany, we are linked to them as they are to us, and it is in the interests of us all not to let them turn into a young Czech-cum-Russian-cum-pan-Slav preserve. True, there are means of coping even with that in the long run, but it is better to be safe than sorry. And since these people can get anything out of us they may need or want *quoad*[b] national autonomy *on*

---

[a] See this volume, pp. 503-04 and 508-09. - [b] in regard to

Czech territory, there is in fact no danger. (As you see, in none of this do I take any account of their temporary political separation from Germany.)

I return to London next week; although I'm better today, it is nevertheless unlikely that anything will come of my trip to Berlin.

Many regards to everyone on the editorial staff.[a]

Your
F. E.

First published in *Victor Adlers Aufsätze, Reden und Briefe*, Erstes Heft: *Victor Adler und Friedrich Engels*, Wien, 1922

Printed according to the book

Published in English for the first time

261

ENGELS TO KARL KAUTSKY[439]

IN STUTTGART

Ryde, 4 September 1892

Dear Baron,

Ede wants to know when I shall be back in London, but instead of giving me his address he merely states that he has left Kilchberg and is en route to Zurich; moreover, all the times he gives are so vague as to make it quite impossible to correspond with him at this range. As I imagine that you are better informed than I am, perhaps you would tell him that I return to London the day after tomorrow, the 6th.[530]

My lameness still rules out any possibility of my travelling further than that. In London I shall probably have to spend another two weeks lying on the sofa, but otherwise the thing is of no significance.

Sorge's article on Homestead naturally takes precedence. Come to that, I am in no great hurry provided the German text appears at the same time as the English one or a *little* later.[561] Needless to say I have heard nothing about the latter for the past two months.

Had you been here during the last election,[504] you would have

---

[a] of the *Arbeiter-Zeitung*

spoken differently about the FABIANS.[87] As regards our tactics we have one firm rule for all modern countries and for all times and that is to prevail upon the workers to form their own independent party in opposition to all bourgeois parties. At the last election the English workers, impelled by the course of events, took, if still only instinctively, their first decisive step in this direction; that step proved surprisingly successful and contributed more towards the development of the workers' minds than any other event of the past 20 years. And what did the FABIANS do — not this or that individual but the FABIAN SOCIETY as a whole? It preached and practised *the affiliation of the workers to the Liberals*, the result being what one might expect. The Liberals assigned them four seats, none of which could possibly have been won and the Fabian candidates met with a resounding defeat. That paradoxical man of letters, Shaw — extremely talented and witty as a writer but utterly useless as an economist and politician, though an honourable man nevertheless and no careerist — wrote to Bebel saying that if they didn't pursue this policy of imposing their candidates upon the Liberals, they would reap nothing but DEFEAT AND DISGRACE (as though defeat was not often more honourable than victory) — and now, having pursued this policy, they have reaped both.

That is the crux of the whole matter. Now that, for the first time, the workers are taking an independent stand, the FABIAN SOCIETY is urging them to remain an appendage of the Liberals. And this must be made abundantly clear to the continental Socialists; to hush it up would be to connive at it. And that is why I am sorry that the Avelings' postscript should have failed to appear.[538] It was not written *post festum*,[a] not as an afterthought, but was overlooked in the hurry to get the article off. The article is incomplete without the description of the attitude of the two Socialist organisations[b] in regard to the elections — and the readers of the *Neue Zeit* have a right to hear about this.

I believe that I myself told you in my last letter that both in the SOCIAL DEMOCRATIC FEDERATION[29] and in the FABIAN SOCIETY the provincial members are better than the central body. But that won't do any good so long as the attitude of the central body determines that of the Society. As to the rest of those sterling fellows, I know none of them apart from Banner. Since joining the FABIAN SOCIETY Banner has not, oddly enough, put in an appearance at my house. I imagine he was

---

[a] after the event - [b] The Fabian Society and the Social Democratic Federation

impelled by disgust at the Social Democratic Federation and the need for some kind of organisation—perhaps also by a few illusions. But this particular swallow doesn't make a summer.

You feel that there is something half-baked about the Fabian Society. On the contrary, the chaps are only *too well* done, a clique of middle class 'socialists' of varying calibre from the careerist to the sentimental socialist and the philanthropist, who are united only in their fear of impending Labour rule and are moving heaven and earth to avert this threat by consolidating their *own* leadership—the leadership of the 'heddicated'.[a] If they then admit a working man or two to their central executive, thereby enabling the latter to perform an Albert *ouvrier*[b] of 1848 act in the shape of a constantly outvoted minority, that ought to deceive nobody.

The means employed by the Fabian Society are indistinguishable from those employed in corrupt parliamentary politics: money, intrigue, careerism, i.e. after the English fashion where it is taken for granted that every political party (save only, it seems, in the case of Labour!) should pay its agents in one way or another or reward them with posts. These chaps are up to their eyes in the intrigues of the Liberal party and hold office in it, one such being Sydney Webb who is altogether a typical British politician. There is nothing one can tell the workers to beware of that these chaps are not already practising.

This is not to suggest, of course, that you should treat these people as enemies. But in my view they should no more be shielded from criticism than anyone else. And that is what the omission from the Avelings' article of the passage relating to them certainly looked like. But if you would like the Avelings to supply you with an article on the history and attitude of the various socialist organisations in England, you have only to say so and I shall suggest it to them.

I was very taken with your article on Vollmar[c]; it will do him more harm than any amount of wrangling in the *Vorwärts*.[532] Moreover, the endless threats of expulsion ought no longer to remain uncensured. Today they are wholly uncalled for reminders of the dictatorial period of the Anti-Socialist Law.[11] One must now give the rotten elements time to become so rotten that they defect virtually of their own accord. The discipline of a party numbered in millions is quite differ-

---

[a] The Berlin dialect in the original. - [b] Albert the working man - [c] K. Kautsky, 'Vollmar und der Staatssozialismus', *Die Neue Zeit*, 10. Jg. 1891/92, 2. Bd., Nr. 49.

ent from that of a sect numbered in hundreds. What you might have
gone into a bit further is the way in which 'state socialism as such' *necessarily* turns in practice into fiscality, and this in the only land
where it is practicable, namely Prussia (which you expound very
nicely).

Ede's critique of Proudhon [542] was also very nice. I was especially
glad to see that he is his old self again.

Your
F. E.

First published in *Aus der Frühzeit des Marxismus. Engels Briefwechsel mit Kautsky*, Prag, 1935

Printed according to the original

Published in English for the first time

262

ENGELS TO KARL KAUTSKY

IN STUTTGART

[Ryde, 5 September 1892]

Dear Baron,

I forgot to reply to you about Bonnier the day before yesterday.[562]
If you look at the reports on England and Germany over the signature 'B' or Bernard in the *Socialiste*, it will enable you to judge to
what extent you can make use of him. Bonnier is a sterling fellow, but
his German studies have somewhat spoiled the Frenchman in him,
something I have observed more than once in his fellow countrymen.
He lives in a world of books and will find it difficult accurately to
weigh the facts of the living movement one against the other. Moreover he resides at Oxford, far removed from all the activity, besides
which he has an unshakeable faith in Guesde. Guesde's illusions and
optimism are in many respects of great value within the movement itself, in much the same way as are Liebknecht's; neither is prone to despair. But these qualities are hardly suited to the reporting of current
activities. However Bonnier, with his native intelligence, is bound

gradually to gain in refinement — not that I have seen much of him of late. If the others on the daily [423] are finding more than enough to do, you really haven't much alternative — provided that Bonnier, too, is not fully occupied in that quarter.

Regards from Pumps and Percy.

Your
F. E.

I return to London tomorrow. [530]

First published in *Aus der Frühzeit des Marxismus. Engels Briefwechsel mit Kautsky*, Prag, 1935

Printed according to the original

Published in English for the first time

263

ENGELS TO LUDWIG KUGELMANN

IN AHLBECK

Ryde, 5 September 1892

Dear Kugelmann,

There will be no trip to Germany for me this year. I have gone lame and must take it easy for the next fortnight at least before I can so much as begin to move about again. Meanwhile I shall be returning to London tomorrow. [530] However I still intend to make another tour of inspection of my native land next year, but whether I shall also manage to take in Hanover is impossible to say so far in advance, the more so as I have seen this summer how quickly all such plans can come to nothing, for this year I have been cheated out of a long and delightful trip and who can tell whether we shall still be alive next year. But you may rest assured that I shall leave the 'Pomeranian grandees' [563] to others. The last of them I saw was an alleged Baron Grumbkow, a seedy looking individual who in the role of professional beggar tried to touch me for a loan some six months ago but was thrown out. *Cela me suffit.*[a] With many regards.

Your
F. Engels

Please let Singer have the enclosed.

First published in: Marx and Engels, *Works*, First Russian Edition, Vol. XXIX, Moscow, 1946

Printed according to the original

Published in English for the first time

264

ENGELS TO LAURA LAFARGUE

AT LE PERREUX

London, 11 September 1892

My dear Laura,

I am here again since last Tuesday,[b] still house-bound, but mending. Louise I expect back on Wednesday, Bebel fetched her from Vienna to Berlin and there she is now.

Thanks for the news about the paper.[423] Then Luce being out of it, I take it that the old agreement has lost its binding power over the other signatories too, unless expressly renewed by them. With Luce, too, his friend Vignaud has, I suppose, also gone out (the man is unknown to me). Anyhow it looks as if a new combination was being tried — let us hope it will be successful and the last of its race.

Here we have had a very important event which will occupy *all* the Socialist parties of the Continent. As you will see from enclosed report, the Trades Union Congress [540] deliberately rejected the invitation to the Zurich Congress [541] and resolved to call together '*immediately*' an Eight Hours Congress of its own — and an international

---

[a] That was enough for me. - [b] 6 September

one too! This requires action on our part, and if possible, *concerted action of the whole Continent.*

The English workmen are so deeply infected with the Parliamentary spirit of compromise that they cannot do a step in advance without at the same time taking $^3/_4$ or $^7/_8$ of a step backwards. Thus the sudden awakening of the Eight Hours' enthusiasm (3 years ago considered an impossibility, you know, by the very people who now clamour loudest after it) has almost succeeded in giving a reactionary character to that cry. It is to be the universal panacea, the one thing to be thought of. In their exultation at having secured so soon such a large and unexpected majority, the mass of the 8 hours' men now sacrifice everything that goes further, to the newly-converted 'Old' Unionists. This massacre of the Socialist Innocents is submitted to all the easier as the 'New' elements [520] are divided, without general organisation, personally unknown to each other, and have not as yet had the time to develop men enjoying the confidence of all; as you know, this can only be obtained here in Britain by what Ruge called *die Kraft der wiederholten Erscheinung,*[a] the effect of hawking your own person constantly for years before the public, *teste* Shipton, Cremer, Howell, etc.

Anyhow the fact is there. The T. U. C. by a deliberate vote of 189 to 97, nearly 2 to 1, has placed itself outside the universal working men's movement and resolved to march apart. With every possible insult our invitation has been flung back in our faces. Not even an order to the Parliamentary Committee [557] to reply politely. Not even a formal motion based on the invitation; a counter-motion is brought in, and then the invitation has to slip in as an amendment, otherwise it would not have been noticed at all. You will see from the full report I shall send you what a trouble Will Thorne had *to get it even brought before the Congress!* In fact the insult is complete.

Now what's to be done? This has to be considered seriously, and first of all by the French as their Marseille Congress [555] is before the Berlin one (16 October [564]). If we reply to the insult in the way it deserves, the Possibilists [3] and Blanquists, *who are sure to go to the Trades Union Congress,* will make capital out of it. On the other hand, if the Possibilists and Blanquists go, and are *alone* of all Continental Socialists, then all the better for us. Therefore I consider it of the highest importance that our French friends *at once agree upon a common line of*

---

[a] the impact of repeated appearance

action with Bebel and the German Executive. If Germany and France act together, Spain, Austria, Italy, Switzerland, probably Belgium, will follow, and Domela[a] may go if he likes.

At present—I have not yet had Edward's personal report on the affair (he was there)—my opinion is this:

1) France and Germany ought at Marseille and Berlin to proclaim their intention to ignore this pseudo-Congress altogether.

2) They ought to do this in a resolution of firm, but quiet and not hostile language, which, if possible, should be identical for both and a model for the other nationalities; leaving the door open to future T. U. Congresses, and to single Trades Unions even at present, to return to the fold. This they are sure to do, I am sure many will regret their vote before many days are over.

3) If *mild* counsels should prevail, and it should be resolved to be present at this British Congress, for the sake of peace, then *one* delegate from each country ought to go and no more. And he must, *as a matter of form*, be elected and *mandaté* by the *Trades Union Congress*, or *Executive thereof* and be a *bona fide* workman or *he will not be admitted*. And this one delegate should depose a distinct protest.

I shall write to Bebel tomorrow on this matter.[b] In the meantime please let me know *where* your people are and what can be done to come to an understanding with the Germans.

I enclose you a specimen of the French correspondence the *Vorwärts* is now printing and Liebknecht will excuse it, no doubt, saying that if our people will not send reports he must take them where he can get them.

If I hear anything more from Edward before this letter goes, I shall put it in.

Ever yours,
F. E.

In a day or two I send you 2 books of mine.[c]
The Scotch paper goes by the same post as this.

First published in *Labour Monthly*, No. 10, London, 1955

Reproduced from the original

---

[a] Ferdinand Domela Nieuwenhuis - [b] See next letter. - [c] *Socialism: Utopian and Scientific*, London, New York, 1892, and *Die Lage der arbeitenden Klasse in England*, Stuttgart, 1892.

265

ENGELS TO AUGUST BEBEL

London, 11 September 1892

Dear August,

So you intend to keep the Witch with you for one more day. No doubt in order to instruct her how best to manage the General in regard to his drinking and other sins; meanwhile you carry on urging me to keep an eye on her — but you mustn't imagine that I don't see through you. You want to stir up trouble between us, though what your perfidious motives may be, heaven knows, but you wait, my lad, it isn't as simple as all that. By way of revenge I shall bombard you with more work than you want and shall start straight away.

The TRADES Congress in Glasgow [540] has declared war on us Continentals. Malice on the part of the leaders of the old unions and, on the part of the new,[520] stupidity combined with a want of confidence either in themselves or each other — hence, too, of organisation *as a party* at the Congress where for decades the old unions have constituted a tightly knit group. When the chaps realise what they have done, most of them will regret it.

Well, the Zurich Committee had sent to the Parliamentary Committee [557] a letter addressed *to the Congress* containing an invitation to Zurich in 1893 [541]; this had been composed by Tussy.[a] The Parliamentary Committee attempted to suppress the letter. Will Thorne vainly pressed for news of it and demanded that it be read out, but met with repeated refusals on the grounds that the Congress must leave it to the Parliamentary Committee to decide which documents it should produce!! In the end Matkin (Liverpool) moved that the TRADES UNION Congress should convene an *international congress* for 1 May 1893 to adopt resolutions and pave the way for an international legal eight hour day.— Parnell, who had been in Paris,[b] was against it. They should, he said, send delegates to the Zurich Congress and settle the matter there. A big debate ensued in the course of

---

[a] See this volume, pp. 495 and 496-97. - [b] at the 1889 International Socialist Congress

which the 'old' unionists kept asking what point there was in going to Zurich, whether it was desirable to identify oneself with the continental socialists' WILD schemes, etc.— There was a further demand that the Zurich letter be read out and at last it was resolved that this should be done. And so, to save appearances, the Zurich letter was finally read out, whereupon a vote was taken and Matkin's resolution regarding the congress (which, however, is to be held IMMEDIATELY instead of on 1 May 1893) was adopted by 189 to 97. Thus, with hardly a second thought, the Zurich invitation was not so much rejected as consigned to the waste paper basket. In return, however, the 'ill-organised' continental proletariat was most graciously permitted to attend a congress in England, there to be lectured, indoctrinated and organised by the true leaders of the 8 hours movement— by those who only the day before had been engaging them in mortal combat. You will see from the detailed report in a Scottish paper, which I shall send you as soon as I get it, that the old unionists have insulted us for all they were worth while the young ones have acted like schoolboys.

Meanwhile I enclose the only report I have to hand.

However one must not take it too hard. The new unions are so delighted with the old unions' conversion to the legal 8 hours that they have allowed themselves to be caught napping over this issue. Most of them are undoubtedly regretting it already, as will they all as soon as they realise what they have done. In my view it is up to the Continentals to bring this home to them, and provided the former act together, the affair will end badly for the 'old' unions.

1. France and Germany must act together. All the rest will then follow suit. Accordingly I am today proposing to the French through. Laura that they should get in touch with you people in order that the aforesaid resolution should be followed by resolution couched, *if possible in identical terms*,[a] at your congresses in Marseilles[555] and Berlin.[564] So far as I can judge at this moment (I haven't yet seen Aveling who was present at Glasgow, nor have I consulted anyone else), your best plan would be to point out in firm but calm and not unfriendly language that you *utterly reject* the newly-fledged eight hours congress, while, at the same time, renewing your invitation to the individual TRADES UNIONS to send delegates to the Zurich Congress.

---

[a] See this volume, p. 521.

(The Zurich Committee would also have to do the same, that is to say in a circular — Tussy will be writing to them about it but a push from you people would also be a help.)

2. If, however, one wants to go further and heap coals of fire on the heads of infants who don't know what they are about, then it would be up to the French and Germans to send *one man each* to explain the position and register a protest against the Glasgow resolution. They will have to be delegated by the Central *Trades Union* Committee and be, or have been, *bona fide working men, otherwise they won't be admitted.*

If Marseilles and Berlin are at one, Austria, Spain and Italy will follow. Switzerland is a certainty, for she was the immediate recipient of the affront; Belgium will probably follow and likewise the Scandinavians. In which case Mr Nieuwenhuis, the Possibilists [3] and the Blanquists are welcome to go and visit the Trades Unions, whereupon they really will find themselves outside the great European movement.

That, provisionally, is my opinion just now. As soon as I hear anything further I shall write again. Meanwhile you people might think the matter over. At all events the arrogance of the 'old' unions and the spinelessness of the new afford you a splendid opportunity to explain your point of view to the English and to show them that the class-conscious continental proletariat has no intention of placing itself under the leadership of people who regard the wage system as an eternal and immutable universal institution.

It is a real blessing that the blinkered, biassed, *exclusively* trades union movement should now have exposed its reactionary nature in so merciless a light.

One more vignette: as a result of a formal resolution at the last conference of the Social Democratic Federation,[565] Mr Hyndman was requested (unanimously so it is said) to keep himself more in the background and to discontinue his activities at the head of the Social Democratic Federation.

The main concern of us all is that Marseilles and Berlin should act resolutely and in concert. All else is of secondary importance. If both of them pass identical resolutions, these will be adopted throughout Europe and that's the kind of thing that finds its way into all the papers over here. Your trades union congresses ought also to protest.

The Scottish paper with report is going off to you by *this* post. Warm regards to Mrs Julie,[a] the Witch, you yourself and all my friends.

Yours

F. E.

First published in: Marx and Engels, *Works*, First Russian Edition, Vol. XXIX, Moscow, 1946

Printed according to the original

Published in English for the first time

266

ENGELS TO CONRAD SCHMIDT [177]

IN ZURICH

London, 12 September 1892

Dear Schmidt,

A few days ago I came back from Ryde where I had been paying an involuntary six-week visit to Pumps.[530] A tiresome but otherwise insignificant complaint ruined both my holiday and a continental tour in the course of which you might otherwise have very possibly seen me in Zurich.

I look forward to seeing your other papers on the rate of profit. Fireman didn't send me his article[b] — can one get hold of that particular number? If so, I shall order it, provided you can tell me exactly which number it was, and also the title of the article. To print the section on the rate of profit separately and in advance is quite out of the question, for you should know that in Marx everything is so interrelated that nothing can be torn out of context. In any case — always provided my health holds out and *I am left in peace* — I shall be done with Volume III[c] this winter (but please don't breathe a word about this; I know how often something has intervened),

---

[a] Julie Bebel - [b] P. Fireman, 'Kritik der Marx'schen Werttheorie', *Jahrbücher für Nationalökonomie und Statistik*, 3. Folge, Bd. 3, Jena, 1892. - [c] of *Capital*

whereupon the poor professorial soul will be set at rest upon that count, only to be plunged instantly into an even worse state of agitation.

As regards Marx's view of history, you will find an article of mine about it in the next number of the *Neue Zeit* — it has already appeared over here in English.[462]

The Germans are utterly useless on the subject of money and credit. Many years ago Marx himself mercilessly ridiculed Knies.[566] The most useful things in English are Tooke's *An Inquiry into the Currency Principle*, 1844 and Fullarton's *On the Regulation of Currencies*, 2nd ed., 1845, both of which are only to be had second-hand. Everything there is to be said about money *qua* money may be found in the first volume of *Capital*. In the third there will, of course, be a great deal about credit and credit money; it is that particular section that is giving me most trouble.

Roger's *Economic Interpretation of History* is in many respects a very instructive book, if exceedingly superficial theoretically speaking. There is, of course, no question of an interpretation à la Marx.

Your essay in the *Neue Zeit*[a] gave me great pleasure. It's as if cut out for this country, since the FABIAN SOCIETY[87] positively pullulates with Jevons-Mengerians[522] who look down with infinite contempt on a Marx they have long since outdistanced. If there were a review over here that would take it, I would, with your permission, get Aveling to translate it under my supervision. But *just now* nothing is likely to come of this, there being no such review.

As regards the worthy Independents,[333] their fate is of their own making. For years the party has endured their yapping with truly angelic patience and even at Erfurt[301] it gave them ample opportunity to substantiate their mendacious tittle-tattle, but a million people cannot go on forever putting up with the obstructionism of fifty young whippersnappers who reserve the right to cast aspersions without having to substantiate them. Now that they've been chucked out, now that they have the chance of showing what they are capable of, all we get is endless lies and vituperation. And what, may I ask, has been achieved by those who showed some promise — the Kampff-

---

[a] C. Schmidt, 'Die psychologische Richtung in der neueren National-Oekonomie', *Die Neue Zeit*, 10. Jg. 1891/92, 2. Bd., Nr. 40, 41.

meyers, Ernsts, Müllers et al.— now that they are no longer under the thumb of the party leadership? Their paper[a] is utterly without substance and apart from that they produce nothing. If these gentlemen believe they are capable of something, why don't they do it? Nor is the case in any way altered by the fact that, in polemicising against them, as in so much else, the *Vorwärts* is sometimes clumsy and all too often overshoots the mark. Did not these gentlemen, even *before* the split, treat the parliamentary group and the party leadership to language no less intemperate than that used by the *Vorwärts* against themselves? In addition they are by and large *completely harmless*. In Germany they are as moribund as anyone else who detaches himself from the big movement. Now that the movement has grown strong actually inside Germany and is directed from within that country, the societies abroad are the only favourable breeding-ground for the kind of wrangles I have had to endure for 45 years in the society over here.[89] Up till 1860 the best chaps were, as a rule, abroad; now the position is reversed. The societies abroad consist of very impermanent elements who very seldom attain the average level of those at home, stand outside the movement in Germany to which they are merely extraneous appendages, and, since they rarely have any genuine occupation, are bored and hence far more susceptible to petty squabbling.

I am aware that you have many childhood and university friends amongst the Jungen, but it's something you must come to terms with. Indeed it's perfectly possible to remain good friends despite political differences. But we've all had to go through the same thing, in my case, in my own pious ultra-reactionary family. And then there is always the possibility of exerting a beneficial influence on your old friends by guiding their footsteps towards study rather than rodomontade. If the gentlemen would only go on with their studies, the more serviceable amongst them would soon come to their senses. But I'm afraid that the chronic megalomania so rampant among these people will prevent them from so doing. And as for provocation and embitterment, these are things that are unavoidable in the circumstances. 'I came not to send peace but a sword.'[b]

[a] *Der Sozialist* - [b] Matthew 10:34

In the next few days I shall let you have the *Condition of the Working-Class*.[a]

With kind regards

Your

F. Engels

First published in *Sozialistische Monatshefte*, Nr. 24, Berlin, 1920

Printed according to the original

Published in English in full for the first time

267

ENGELS TO KARL KAUTSKY

IN STUTTGART

London, 16 September 1892

Dear Baron,

Ede has asked me to send you a copy of a passage from the *Deutsch-Französische Jahrbücher*.[567] He gives only the opening words, but doesn't say *how much* is wanted, so you will find herewith a copy of the thing up to the end of the letter and you'll have to see how much of it is usable.

Kovalevsky, who is over here, says he would probably be prepared to let you have an article for the *Neue Zeit* on Lavrov's great Russian work *Zadači istoriji mysli*, *The Functions of the History of Thought*; but he would have to write it in French. If you would like to have the article, please let me know.[568]

There was high old confusion at the Trades Union Congress[540] in Glasgow.[b] The 'old' unions did everything in their power to achieve victory and, being organised and known to one another and of old repute, they were largely successful vis-à-vis the 'new' ones,[520] which didn't yet know the ropes, fell foul of the rules of procedure, were known neither to one another nor to many of the more honest elements amongst the 'old' unions, and hence possessed few personalities

---

[a] F. Engels, *Die Lage der arbeitenden Klasse in England*, Stuttgart, 1892. - [b] See this volume, pp. 519-20 and 522-24.

who, aside from their particular standing in the party, were personally respected by all concerned.* So it came about that the majority of those elected to the PARLIAMENTARY COMMITTEE [557] consisted of 'old' unionists, while Fenwick was re-elected secretary. The fact that the old unionists had given up as hopeless their opposition to the 8 hour day and continued to oppose the *legal* 8 hour day only *pro forma*, for the sake of appearances, quite delighted the majority of new unionists who, in their glee over the victory of the LEGAL 8 HOURS, were prepared to surrender everything else. So it came about that they not only demanded steps be taken to combat the immigration of 'PAUPERS', but turned down with contumely, and in a manner directly insulting to us, the invitation to the Zurich Congress [541] (amongst other things, because that Congress had not been convoked by the English TRADES UNION Congress!!); and at the same time resolved that an international eight hours congress be convoked immediately. What happened during this debate you will see from the Scottish paper Tussy has sent you.

It is now evident that our Continentals must take up the cudgels against this. It's a good opportunity for them to show the snooty TRADES UNIONS what their standpoint is. A start will doubtless be made by the French at Marseilles. [555]

Unfortunately I shall not be able to send you the *Workman's Times* for some little while, at any rate. For a time Burgess sent copies to Bebel and sundry other Continentals, but has suddenly ceased to do so — since the jackass doesn't want to have any truck with Continentals who 'do not even possess a TRADES ORGANISATION'. Now I shall have to send Bebel the copy which in the past has been available for you, since the Executive has *got* to have one and I can't very well alter before November the number of copies on order; I have trouble enough as it is in getting the right number of copies ordered. In November I shall be renewing my subscription, on which occasion I shall be able to make other arrangements.

At the last conference of the SOCIAL DEMOCRATIC FEDERATION [565] Hyndman was requested — unanimously, it is said — to resign from the leadership of the SOCIAL DEMOCRATIC FEDERATION and to confine his activities to writing. We shall see whether it lasts. But it's hard on him.

---

* Neither Hardie nor Tom Mann enjoy popularity in *broader* circles. Burns, who might have handled many things differently, wasn't there.

It's a pity that Ede should also have missed the TRADES UNION Congress, but it couldn't be helped. So far as he himself is concerned, it's all to the good that his holiday should have been prolonged.

Though still housebound, I am slowly improving.

Your

F. E.

First published in *Aus der Frühzeit des Marxismus. Engels Briefwechsel mit Kautsky*, Prag, 1935

Printed according to the original

Published in English for the first time

268

ENGELS TO REGINA AND EDUARD BERNSTEIN [357]

IN ZURICH

London, 17 September 1892

Dear Gine,

From Louise, who came back here on Wednesday,[a] I have learned that you are still in Zurich and that Käte[b] is already in this country, and yesterday the letter from you and Ede at last enabled me to connect up the broken telegraph wires again. We are most sorry that you should still be so unwell but that is something that will eventually pass, and in the meantime Ede can continue to recuperate in the open air for a while longer, which will be most beneficial for him and do the party no harm, now that he has in any case missed the TRADES UNION Congress.[540] The latter was the scene of considerable confusion. The most interesting session from our point of view was the one on Thursday[c] on the question of the Congress.[d] If we had known your address, we'd have sent Ede a Scottish paper containing an account of it, but as it is, the few copies we had have been sent elsewhere.

---

[a] 14 September - [b] Käte Schattner - [c] 8 September - [d] See this volume, pp. 519-20, 522-24 and 528-29.

When, despite continuous prodding from Thorne, the letter of invitation from Zurich 'to the Trade Union Congress' in Glasgow had obstinately been withheld for 4 whole days, Matkin tabled a motion, clearly concocted in conjunction with the 'old' unionists with a view to preventing attendance at Zurich, in which he called for the convocation of an international 8 hours congress of their own. Parnell, on the other hand, proposed an amendment to the effect that it would be better to go to Zurich. According to Ed. Aveling, Parnell and Quelch spoke very well. At that, all the old unionists went mad. The continental workers, they said, were weak and badly organised, but if the English took them under their wing all might go well; in any case the Zurich Congress had not been convoked by the English Trades Unions. Besides, who would want to associate himself with all the wild theories and the kind of socialism that throve on the Continent, etc.? (This latter anxiety, in particular, being voiced in rasping tones by a Lancashire weaver,[a] one of the new converts to the 8 hour day.)

In short, in their delight that there should now be almost no opposition to the 8 hours day, and by way of a sop to the weak in spirit — the Lancashire cotton operatives — they unceremoniously consigned the Continentals' invitation to the waste paper basket, and by 189 votes to 97, no less!

Now this, although most of them were probably unaware of what they were doing, was in fact a disgusting insult and a slap in the face for the entire continental Labour movement. We instantly broadcast the news here, there and everywhere and no doubt the first riposte will come from the French in a few days' time at Marseilles.[555] It's a heaven-sent opportunity — without making too much of the matter — for putting a damper on the self-conceit of the *old* trades unionists who are proving ever more reactionary.

Herewith a *Pall Mall* containing an article of Aveling's about the Hamburg socialists and the cholera.[b]

In the *Daily Chronicle* there was a long review, which no doubt you will have seen, of Socialism Utopian, etc.[c] What a canny lot they are!

The French daily has not yet emerged from the embryonic

---

[a] David Holmes - [b] E. Aveling, 'The Cholera and the Hamburg Socialists', *The Pall Mall Gazette*, No. 8577, 16 September 1892. - [c] the English edition (1892) of F. Engels' *Socialism: Utopian and Scientific*

stage; negotiations are still proceeding but this is better than if the chaps were again to rush headlong into some short-lived venture.[423]

Louise came back in a very cheerful mood, having found her mother and Ignaz very hale and hearty. She sends her warm regards.

Now for a note to Ede, so farewell for today.

With warm regards,

Yours,
F. Engels

Dear Ede,

The relevant passage went off to K. Kautsky[a] yesterday — indeed the *entire* letter from the point at which you began to quote; I told K. Kautsky that *he* would know how much to use, whether the whole thing or only a part, and which part.

At the last conference of the SOCIAL DEMOCRATIC FEDERATION [565] (BANK HOLIDAY,[569] the first Monday in August), Taylor, the unsuccessful candidate for Hackney,[b] proposed that Hyndman be thrown out. This met with great acclaim, particularly among the provincial delegates; however, Taylor was persuaded to tone down his motion in order that as large a majority as possible might be obtained. And thus it was resolved (unanimously, according to Taylor) that Hyndman be requested to resign from the leadership of the SOCIAL DEMOCRATIC FEDERATION and devote himself to written propaganda. How long this will continue remains to be seen. At all events it is a bitter blow for the megalomaniac. Cahan of New York, who called on him without knowing about this, found him in a very despondent, chastened frame of mind and remarkably conciliatory towards all those he had hitherto torn to shreds.

The *Workman's Times*, i. e. Burgess, now also wishes to become party leader. You will have seen that the £400, which he placed at the disposal of Burns, Keir Hardie, Taylor and Ben Ellis during the elections, emanated from Champion (or rather, through him, from Hudson's Soap).

---

[a] See this volume, p. 528. - [b] district of London

In short, there have been a good many changes here during your absence and you will find the chaps engaged in a variety of interesting pursuits.

Many regards,

Your

F. E.

.I haven't yet seen Käte.

First published, in Russian, in *Marx-Engels Archives*, Book I, Moscow, 1924   Printed according to the original

269

ENGELS TO PAUL LAFARGUE [141]

AT LE PERREUX

London, 17 September 1892

My dear Lafargue,

Your opinion that we should take advantage of the opportunity of teaching the old English TRADES UNIONS a lesson is also shared by Bebel. If Liebknecht goes to Marseilles,[555] you will have a good chance of coming to an understanding with him. At the same time you might ask him why the *Vorwärts* is packed with news about the doings and sayings of the Broussists,[3] Allemanists[53] and Blanquists, yet is virtually silent on the subject of our own people. However they are saying in Berlin that the cholera is rampant in Marseilles and that might put a stop to his trip.

Since the English TRADES UNIONS recognise only *bona fide* WORKING MEN and then only those who are organised in trade unions, it is of the utmost importance that not only the Workers' Party Congress, but also, and in particular, the French trade unions,[570] who will be holding their congress a few days before ours, should take a firm stand on the presumption of the English in seeking to ignore the *existing* movement on the Continent so as to start another one under their own leadership and based on their own views. French trade unionists will as-

suredly protest against what was said in Glasgow [540] about themselves and other continental working men.

(Woods M. P.)

'that the organisations on the Continent OF EUROPE WERE VERY INEFFECTIVE, BUT
HE FELT SURE THAT IF THE POWERFUL ORGANISATION IN ENGLAND WOULD *ONLY EXTEND
THE HAND OF FELLOWSHIP AND SYMPATHY* AND BROTHERHOOD' (what, nothing
more?!) 'TO THEIR FRIENDS ON THE CONTINENT, THEY COULD MINIMISE THE DIFFICUL-
TIES' ETC.!

Foster OF Durham, MINER:

'HE WAS STRUCK WITH THE REMARKS OF MR. WOODS, THAT THEIR EFFORTS IN
THIS COUNTRY WERE TO A CERTAIN EXTENT NEUTRALISED BY THEIR FELLOW-WORKMEN
IN OTHER COUNTRIES WHO WERE NOT ORGANISED SO WELL AS THOSE IN THIS COUNTRY;
THEIR SOCIAL POSITION WAS NOT EQUAL TO OURS' (!!!) ...'IF THEY COULD GET THEIR FEL-
LOW-WORKMEN ON THE CONTINENT *TO SHOW THE SAME CONSENSUS OF OPINION AS THOSE
IN THIS COUNTRY* WHEN THEY MADE UP THEIR MIND TO A PARTICULAR ACTION

(he is referring to the 8 Hours and you know how strongly the
English opposed it when the Continent was already unanimous — those
selfsame Englishmen who, one after another, are now giving tongue!)

'THEY WOULD THEN KNOW THAT THE POWER OF LABOUR COULD ACHIEVE THE OBJECT'
ETC.

Holmes, Burnley (cotton weaver, newly converted to the 8 Hours
and anxious to prove that this change of front hasn't turned him into
a socialist cannibal):

'WERE THERE SOME ADVANCED, OR AS THEY CALLED THEM, SOCIALIST MOVEMENTS
ON THE CONTINENT, THAT THEY WANTED TO DRAG THEM INTO (at Zurich).[541] HE ASKED
THOSE GENTLEMEN IF THEY WANTED TO GO TO THAT CONGRESS IN THE NAME OF THIS
BODY TO ADVOCATE MANY OF THE WILD SCHEMES WHICH THEY KNEW WERE GOING ON ON
THE CONTINENT?'

Conner, London:

'THOUGH THERE WERE TWO INTERNATIONAL CONGRESSES ALREADY ARRANGED
FOR (ZURICH AND CHICAGO [571]) NEITHER OF THEM *WERE ARRANGED BY, OR UNDER THE
AUTHORITY OF, THE TRADES CONGRESS* (!!)'

There. That ought to be enough in the way of insults to quicken
the pulse of your French trade unionists.

I repeat: *So far as the moral effect it would create here in England is
concerned*, a *Trades Union Congress* resolution rejecting the divisive tendency inherent in the Glasgow resolution would be far more important than one emanating from the *Socialist Congress*. So do the best
you can. Tussy has sent a newspaper report to Delecluze.

Give the French comrades my kind regards and keep up the good work, as at Lille.[38] Tussy says that the Working Men's Congress there was the most BUSINESS LIKE one she has ever attended.

Yours ever,

F. Engels

First published in: F. Engels, P. et L. Lafargue, *Correspondance*, t. III, Paris, 1959

Printed according to the original

Translated from the French

270

ENGELS TO NIKOLAI DANIELSON [267]

IN ST PETERSBURG

London, 22 September 1892

My dear Sir,

So far, then, we agree upon this one point, that Russia, in 1892, could not exist as a purely agricultural country, that her agricultural production must be complemented by industrial production.

Now I maintain, that industrial production nowadays, means *grande industrie*, steam, electricity, selfacting-mules, power-looms, finally machines that produce machinery. From the day Russia introduced railways, the introduction of these modern means of production was a foregone conclusion. You *must* be able to repair your own locomotives, waggons, railways, and that can only be done cheaply if you are able to *construct* those things at home, that you intend to repair. From the moment, warfare became a branch of *grande industrie* (ironclad ships, rifled artillery, quickfiring and repeating cannon, repeating rifles, steelcovered bullets, smokeless powder etc.) *la grande industrie* without which all these things cannot be made became a political necessity. All these things cannot be had without a highly developed metal manufacture. And that manufacture cannot be had without a corresponding development in all other branches of manufacture, especially textile.

I quite agree with you in fixing the beginning of the new industrial era of your country about 1861. It was the hopeless struggle of a nation, with primitive forms of production, against nations with modern production, which characterized the Crimean war. The Russian people understood this perfectly; hence their transition to modern forms, a transition rendered irrevocable by the emancipation act of 1861.[441]

This necessity of the transition from the primitive methods of production that prevailed in 1854, to the modern methods that are now beginning to prevail — this necessity once conceded, it becomes a secondary question whether the hot-house-process of fostering the industrial revolution by protective and prohibitive duties was advantageous or even necessary, or otherwise.

This industrial hot-house-atmosphere renders the process acute, which otherwise might have retained a more chronic form. It crams into twenty years a development, which otherwise might have taken sixty or more years. But it does not affect the nature of the process itself, which, as you say, dates from 1861.

One thing is certain: if Russia really required, and was determined to have, a *grande industrie* of her own, she could not have it at all, except under *some* degree of protection and this you admit. From this point of view too, then, the question of protection is one of *degree* only, not of principle; the principle was unavoidable.

Another thing is certain: if Russia required after the Crimean war a *grande industrie* of her own, she could have it in one form only: the *capitalistic form*. And along with that form, she was obliged to take over all the consequences which accompany capitalistic *grande industrie* in all other countries.

Now I cannot see that the results of the industrial revolution which is taking place in Russia under our eyes, are in any way different from what they are, or have been, in England, Germany, America. In America the conditions of agriculture and landed property are different, and this *does* make some difference.

You complain of the slow increase of hands employed in textile industry, when compared with the increase of quantity of product.— The same is taking place everywhere else. Otherwise, whence our redundant 'industrial reserve'? (*Capital*, c. 23, sect. 3 and 4 [a]).

You prove the gradual replacing of men's work by that of women and children — *Capital*, c. 13 (sect. 3, a).[b]

---

[a] *Capital*, Part VII, Ch. XXV, Sections 3, 4 (present edition, Vol. 35). - [b] *Ibid.*, Part IV, Ch. XXV, Section 3 (present edition, Vol. 35).

You complain that the machine-made goods supersede the products of domestic industry and thus destroy a supplementary production, without which the peasant cannot live. But we have here an absolutely necessary consequence of capitalistic *grande industrie*: the creation of the home-market (*Capital*, c. 24, sect. 5 [a]) and which has taken place in Germany during my lifetime and under my eyes. Even what you say, that the introduction of cotton-goods destroys not only the domestic spinning and weaving of the peasants, but also their *flax culture* has been seen in Germany between 1820 and now. And as far as this side of the question: the destruction of home-industry and the branches of agriculture subservient to it — as far as this is concerned, the real question for you seems to me this: that the Russians had to decide whether *their own grande industrie* was to destroy their domestic manufacture, or whether *the import of English goods* was to accomplish this. *With* protection, the *Russians* effected it, *without* protection, the *English*. That seems to me perfectly evident.

Your calculation that the sum of the textile products of *grande industrie* and of domestic industry does not increase, but remains the same and even diminishes, is not only quite correct, but would not be correct if it came to another result. So long as Russian manufacture is confined to the home market, its product can only cover home consumption. And that can only slowly increase, and, as it seems to me, ought even to decrease under present Russian conditions.

For it is one of the necessary corollaries of *grande industrie*, that it *destroys* its own home market by the very process by which it *creates* it. It creates it by destroying the basis of the domestic industry of the peasantry. But without domestic industry the peasantry cannot live. They are ruined, *as peasants*; their purchasing power is reduced to a minimum; and until they, as *proletarians*, have settled down into new conditions of existence, they will furnish a very poor market for the newly-arisen factories.

Capitalist production being a transitory economical phase, is full of internal contradictions which develop and become evident in proportion as it develops. This tendency to destroy its own market at the same time it creates it, is one of them. Another is the безвыходное положение [b] to which it leads, and which is developed sooner in a country *without* a foreign market, like Russia, than in countries which more or less are capable of competing on the open world-market. This sit-

---

[a] *Ibid.*, Part VIII, Ch. XXX (present edition, Vol. 35). - [b] desperate position (Russ.)

uation without an apparent issue finds its issue, for the latter countries, in commercial revulsions, in the forcible opening of new markets. But even then the cul-de-sac stares one in the face. Look at England. The last new market which could bring on a temporary revival
of prosperity by its being thrown open to English commerce, is
China. Therefore English capital insists upon constructing Chinese
railways. But Chinese railways mean the destruction of the whole
basis of Chinese small agriculture and domestic industry, and, as
there will not even be the counterpoise of a Chinese *grande industrie*,
hundreds of millions of people will be placed in the impossibility of
living. The consequence will be a wholesale emigration such as the
world has not yet seen, a flooding of America, Asia and Europe by the
hated Chinaman, a competition for work with the American, Aus-
tralian and European workman on the basis of the Chinese standard
of life, the lowest of all — and if the system of production has not been
changed in Europe before that time, it wil have to be changed then.

Capitalistic production works its own ruin, and you may be sure it
will do so in Russia too. It may, and if it lasts long enough, it will surely produce a fundamental agrarian revolution — I mean a revolution in the condition of landed property, which will ruin both the по-
мещикъ [a] and the мужикъ, [b] and replace them by a new class of large
landed proprietors drawn from the кулаки [c] of the villages and the
bourgeois speculators of the towns. At all events, I am sure the conservative people who have introduced capitalism into Russia, will be
one day terribly astonished at the consequences of their own doings.

Yours very truly,

P. W. Rosher [d]

First published, in Russian, in the *Minuv-shiye gody*, No. 2, St Petersburg, 1908

Reproduced from the original

Published in English in full for the first time

---

[a] landlord (Russ.) - [b] peasant - [c] kulaks - [d] Engels' conspiratorial pseudonym

271

ENGELS TO VICTOR ADLER

IN VIENNA

London, 25 September 1892

Dear Victor,

Your business with Stepnyak[572] has been settled, as indeed it had been before your telegram and two letters got here. For Stepnyak* sent me your letter of the 15th with the comment that he had now obtained Sonnenschein's formal consent and would be coming tomorrow (i. e. last Thursday, the 22nd) to exchange this document for the £15 sterling credited to me. Although not previously advised by you, I am far too good a business man not to honour the signature of so reputable a firm as V. Adler, even if not as yet actually in receipt of a formal advice. For you had held a pistol, not only to Stepnyak's head, but also in some measure to my own; otherwise had there been any other way out, I should for *your* sake have tried to avoid making any payment just now. And this merely on the grounds that you have now paid Stepnyak *all* that *he* is entitled to; but, as it is, his interest in seeing your translation published will no longer be of a pecuniary but merely of a literary nature and, if I know my Russians, that is not, I should say, the right way to get the stuff for the second volume out of him. However, there was nothing further I could do. I might have asked him to give me a written undertaking to the effect that he would deliver the goods within a given period, but it would have been worse than useless since you already have enough from him in writing in any case, and another scrap of paper would not have induced him to work any faster.

So I must content myself with his promise, made in Louise's presence, to let you have the goods in question within 2 weeks at the outside (*va-t-en voir s'ils viennent,*[a] *Jean*) and with having paid him, against the enclosed note and Sonnenschein's perfectly adequate declaration, the £15 sterling you had promised him and told him to claim from me. You wrote:

---

* after Louise, at your behest, had requested him to attend to the matter

---

[a] go and see if they are coming

'YOU CAN ALSO HAND THE FORMAL PAPER TO MR ENGELS, AND YOU *WILL RECEIVE IM-MEDIATELY FROM HIM* THE SUM OF 15 POUNDS.'

So you see, the categorical wording left me no other alternative.*

I also took occasion to explain to Stepnyak that, by dawdling as he has done, he had cheated himself and that, had he behaved rationally, S. Sonnenschein & Co. might well have been content with £5 STERLING *if not less*, which would have meant more for him, Stepnyak, to pocket. (Aveling maintains that S. Sonnenschein & Co. would in fact have given their permission *gratis*, the translation being in any case a good advertisement for the book.) None of this had occurred to him and he will no doubt take note of it. But it's you who have come off worst.

Summa summarum: should such a case arise in future, you would do well to inform me beforehand, in which case I could either give you my humble opinion or else I could at once enter into negotiations over here on your behalf, whether direct or through Louise or the Avelings. In the literary business 'local knowledge' is absolutely essential if you don't want to get stung.

We are glad to hear how much better your wife[a] is and hope the improvement will continue. Our thoughts are always with you.

We have seen nothing of Andreas Scheu for years, heard nothing of him for months and had no converse about him here for ages and ages. We know absolutely nothing about him. There's no need for you to worry about Uncle Julius and Aunt[b]— now that they systematically cut themselves off from us we scarcely ever see them, let alone tell them anything.

The story about Hyndman ought not to have been printed.[573] It was uncorroborated, confidential information and may, *formally speaking*, contain inaccuracies. *In essence* it is correct; Hyndman has been deposed, though in as considerate a fashion as possible. The mere *threat* of such a motion supported by a majority of the delegates may have sufficed. The worst of it is that we can't reply to the démenti without placing him in a more favourable position. Indeed

---

* You are wrong in saying that you had demanded the surrender of *his* stuff 'prior to payment'. I wish the wording had been such as to allow me to make that demand. But you made payment, and 'IMMEDIATELY' at that, solely dependent on Sonnenschein's FORMAL PAPER.

---

[a] Emma Adler - [b] Julius Motteler and his wife Emilie

there's something of his in *Justice* expressing the expectation that the *Vorwärts* won't publish his letter.[574] Now he has made an ass of himself.

You will be getting two copies of *Soziales aus Rußland*.[a] Of *The Bakuninists at Work* I have so far been able to find only *one* copy (bound up with other stuff), namely my handwritten one. I have perforce had to desist from lending things for propaganda purposes, and would advise you to do the same. Never again shall I allow the tools of my trade to leave the house.

My health 'continues slowly to improve'. Louise says you had asked how long this business had been going on — it manifested itself some ten years ago as a result of over-indulgence. The trouble originated some 25 years since when I came down with my horse while riding to hounds. For your further information only a few years after the thing had declared itself, I was forced by disagreeable sensations in the inguinal canal to wear a bandage with hernial pads and there would also seem to be a slight *varice*[b] in that region, on the left hand side. During the past few days I believe I have taken a distinct turn for the better although there is still some sensitivity to pressure, particularly after any time spent standing or walking; at all events I shall have to be patient and go on resting for a while longer. Louise said you were going to do me the kindness of inquiring about a specialist over here; I should be most grateful, the more so since every...[c]

First published in *Victor Adlers Aufsätze, Reden und Briefe*. Erstes Heft: *Victor Adler und Friedrich Engels*, Wien, 1922

Printed according to the book

Published in English for the first time

---

[a] F. Engels, *Refugee Literature. V. On Social Relations in Russia*. - [b] varicose veins - [c] The end of the letter is missing.

272

ENGELS TO KARL KAUTSKY

IN STUTTGART

London, 26 September 1892

Dear Baron,

Herewith what I consider to be indispensable amendments[a] to the two passages.[575]

I. As regards the adoption on the last day of a resolution to attend the Zurich Congress[541] after all, I have neither read anything to that effect, nor have I heard anything from Aveling who was present. Something of the kind is said to have appeared in the *Daily Telegraph* but this cannot be ascertained today. Aveling, who was intending to come here, has *not* so far, 4.40, turned up, so I am unable to ask him. The report in the *Daily News* says nothing of the kind. Nor does that in the *Workman's Times*. Bebel may have seen something of the sort in the *Frankfurter*.[b] Consequently, I think it might be safest to qualify the passage as you have done.

II. It is true that a meeting of people describing themselves as the INDEPENDENT LABOUR PARTY took place in Glasgow under the chairmanship of Keir Hardie. It is, however, the INDEPENDENT LABOUR PARTY which Burgess (Autolycus) of the *Workman's Times* is attempting to constitute off his own bat, and in no sense a genuine, recognised party like, say, our own in Germany or Austria; rather it is a sect like the SOCIAL DEMOCRATIC FEDERATION[29] with which it is in competition. Bebel was probably misled by Keir Hardie's name into taking the thing more seriously than it deserved. But Keir Hardie is a Scot and his diplomacy is too canny by half; moreover he has an urge to make the most of his new position as M. P. (thereby occasionally making a fool of himself) but will probably turn out well once he's had a chance to sow his wild oats. To my mind he is better than he *seems* to be just now.

---

[a] See this volume, pp. 545-46. - [b] *Frankfurter Zeitung und Handelsblatt*

I shall write to Bebel[a] about this, in fact shall do so now. More anon. Ede should be back tomorrow or on Wednesday. Your commissions shall be carried out.

Your
F. E.

First published in *Aus der Frühzeit des Marxismus. Engels Briefwechsel mit Kautsky,* Prag, 1935

Printed according to the original

Published in English for the first time

273

ENGELS TO AUGUST BEBEL

IN BERLIN

London, 26 September 1892

Dear August,

Louise will already have told you something about Kugelmann. At first, during the 60s, he was on very friendly terms with Marx and did a great deal towards breaking the newspapers' conspiracy of silence over *Capital, Volume I.* It was also he who persuaded Marx to go to Karlsbad,[b] which did him a lot of good,[460] but after they had been there for a while there was a final parting of the ways. Since Marx's death he has written to me several times, but I have tried to keep my distance, not being convinced of his reliability. At all events he has more than one foot in more than one camp.

As regards the copies of *Herr Vogt,* I have written and told him [153] that he must first let me know how many he has got. There are all sorts of people wanting it. I believe that not even Tussy or Laura have got a copy. You, too, will be given preference if at all possible.

Arndt is a student who used to be in Geneva, and then went to Spain where he frequented our people in Madrid before coming to this country. While here he was taken under Julius'[c] wing and he

---

[a] See this volume, pp. 543-47. - [b] Karlový Vary - [c] Julius Motteler

would occasionaly come and see us. Then he suddenly went to Paris. He never said a word to us about his intention to write for the *Vorwärts* — presumably this was arranged by Julius. I gave him a card for Laura but have never heard whether he presented himself; I shall ask her. Laura would have referred him to Vaillant and, since the latter was in Paris and Lafargue was nearly always away, this would account for the consideration currently being shown to the Blanquists and their allies, the Allemanists.[53] Can you get hold of Arndt's address for me? After the Congress,[555] and particularly when the daily[423] comes out, Lafargue will be spending more time in Paris and the man will have to be referred to him and Guesde direct.

I rather think I remember seeing Meyer[a] in St Louis, but there are so many people of that name. I trust that Kugelmann, who is forever bragging about his connections, will be able to find something out.

Pieper was at one time tutor to the Rothschilds in this country and is now a grammar school teacher in Hanover. Marx once — in 1867, I think — ran into him in the street, by which time he had become a bloated philistine.

I completely agree that you should go on with the *annual* party conference. If only for constitutional reasons you, as an Executive, should adhere to it, otherwise what a fine pretext it would provide for malcontents. And it's also important that once a year the party itself should be able to express itself as a body; this is generally applicable but doubly so just now — vis-à-vis both the 'Independents'[333] and Vollmar.

It is a great pity that you people should have been in such a hurry to put what I told you about Hyndman[b] into the paper.[573] Let me therefore expressly point out once and for all that in future anything I pass on to you in private letters is intended solely for your information and, where necessary — subject to the usual reservations — for the correction and prevention of inaccuracies or misconceptions in the *Vorwärts*; not for *immediate publication*, however, except when this is *expressly stated*. Otherwise I should have to keep my mouth shut about everything I could not actually substantiate, or else, in most cases, run the risk of having to betray my sources, thus causing these to dry up for the future.

Basically the information as such is quite *definitely correct*, as every number of *Justice* goes to show; gone are the attacks on individuals in

---

[a] Hermann Meyer - [b] See this volume, pp. 524, 529, 532 and 540-41.

this country or on the Continent, nor is anything left of the Hynd-manian spirit. But it's very possible that my information may have contained *formal* errors and that the mere *threat* of a resolution was enough to make Hyndman resign, etc. The only cause for regret is first, that this business will mean this and other sources on the doings of the SOCIAL DEMOCRATIC FEDERATION [29] will be closed to us, secondly, that Hyndman's position has been improved thereby and, thirdly, that any further attempt to put a stop to this can only improve it still more.

In *Justice* there's a piece by Hyndman expressing the expectation that you people would *not* print his letter, and to that extent he has made an ass of himself.[574] I shall try and get hold of a copy for you.

I have written and told Kugelmann that, so far as *I* was competent to say, you were authorised to read the letters from Marx to him.[153] Also that he would be getting *The Knight of the Noble Consciousness*.[a]

I have today received proofs of your article from K. Kautsky with queries about two passages.[575]

I. There was nothing in the *Daily News* about the adoption in Glasgow of a resolution that delegates should after all be sent to Zu-rich, nor had Aveling heard anything of the kind, otherwise he's have said so. He was intending to come here today but hasn't turned up. Louise say that on her way here she had seen something of that nature in the *Daily Telegraph*. In the circumstances I advised K. Kautsky to insert the words: *if the relevant newspaper report is true*. That covers you completely.

II. 'The Independent Labour Party now coming into being — whose supporters assembled for the first time after the end of the Glasgow Congress to constitute them-selves —', etc., etc.

I advised K. Kautsky at all costs to delete the words between dashes: '— whose ... constitute themselves —'. The Independent La-bour Party now coming into being over here is still very far from con-stituting itself, nor is it desirable that it should yet attempt to do so. It is not yet mature enough. The INDEPENDENT LABOUR PARTY, whose ad-herents more or less constituted themselves a party in Glasgow under Keir Hardie's chairmanship, is the sect founded by Autolycus (Joseph Burgess) of the *Workman's Times*, a sect which so far boasts 2,000 members and competes with the SOCIAL DEMOCRATIC FEDERATION in re-

---

[a] K. Marx, *The Knight of the Noble Consciousness*.

cruiting socialistically minded workers. At present it is no more *the* Independent Labour Party than is the SOCIAL DEMOCRATIC FEDERATION, nor is it either better or worse than the latter. What will come of it remains to be seen, but on no account should *we* proclaim it as a matter of course to be *the* one and only genuine Independent Labour Party, otherwise we might burn our fingers badly.

Since his election Keir Hardie has been pushing himself to the fore and putting on airs in a way that is both ludicrous and discreditable. Success has gone to his head and he will have to sow his wild oats for a while. He is evidently intent on pushing Burns into the background; the latter is behaving with great fortitude and restraint (he asked leave to call on me in order to consult me about the attitude he should adopt). I think it will all even itself out in the end — Keir Hardie is better than he makes himself out to be, but you should by no means conclude as a matter of course that someting is commendable because *he* happens to be taking part in it.

Otherwise I find your article quite unexceptionable — composed, dignified and emphatic.

At Marseilles the TRADES UNIONS Congress (*Congrès des syndicats*) [570] passed a resolution which I had put to Lafargue,[a] namely *that they should not take part in the international congress convoked by the TRADES UNIONS but should invite the latter to attend the Zurich Congress.*[541] This isn't the exact wording which I have yet to receive. Liebknecht will probably send it you as he had just turned up when Lafargue was in the act of writing. The Congress of the Workers' Party [555] will adopt a similar resolution. I drew Lafargue's attention to the fact that the TRADES UNIONS do not recognise the validity of Labour Party congresses and resolutions while according respect of a very different order to those of the trades unions. If you in Germany could get the trades unions to adopt resolutions along the same lines, this could not fail to make an impact over here; it's something that should certainly not be neglected.

You might send about 12 copies of your article to *us* for distribution to the papers over here. For their people very seldom understand foreign languages, and whether they would so much as look at it is a complete toss-up. To get anything into the press over here one must employ different methods. If, for instance, Aveling were to take *the finished article* to the *Pall Mall*,[b] he would probably get it in [576];

---

[a] See this volume, pp. 533-35. - [b] *The Pall Mall Gazette*

that same evening we should send copies to the other papers so that they would *all* be served at the same time and there might still be a possibility of its getting a mention in one paper or another. But once *one* paper has discussed any such subject, none of the others will subsequently take it up — such is the rule over here. That is why we, who are here on the spot, must be able to determine the moment of distribution. On the other hand you could certainly send copies, specially designated *as coming from you*, to the French press; it might possibly have some pull over there, particularly since in France we haven't got a single daily in which we are able to publish anything. You could send it to *L'Éclair* (the paper most likely to take it), *Le Figaro, Le Temps, Le Matin, La Justice, L'Intransigeant, Le Parti Ouvrier* (Possibilist) and *Le Parti Socialiste* (49, rue de Rivoli, Blanquist — weekly).

Please let me know whether or not the *Workman's Times* is still being sent you by the editorial department. Here it is being said that all complimentary copies for countries abroad have been cancelled. If this is true, I shall send it to you instead of to Fischer who can read it at your house or after you have done with it.

Well, I should have liked to write a word or two to your wife,[a] but it is already past 9 p. m. and, contrary to doctor's orders, I have already spent over-long writing by lamplight. I have also had to write to Victor[b] and to Karl Kautsky which has taken me all day,[c] so please ask her to excuse me. But she will be getting a letter all to herself from me. Till then, please give her my warm regards.

Your
General

I have just heard from Louise that you have not been getting an official copy of the *Workman's Times* for some while past. So that is one thing settled.

First published in: Marx and Engels, *Works*, First Russian Edition, Vol. XXIX, Moscow, 1946

Printed according to the original

Published in English for the first time

---

[a] Julie Bebel - [b] Victor Adler - [c] See this volume, pp. 539-41 and 542-43.

274

ENGELS TO VICTOR ADLER

IN VIENNA

London, 27 September 1892

Dear Victor,

Barely had my (registered) letter gone off yesterday [a] than a messenger arrived from the Crédit Lyonnais [551] and handed me the £15 in question in settlement of my loan. Receipt of this is hereby gratefully acknowledged.

The Marseilles Trades Unions (*syndicats*) Congress,[570] which *preceded* the one held by the Workers' Party,[555] resolved *not* to send delegates to the Eight Hours [b] Congress in Glasgow [540] convoked by the TRADES UNIONS, but instead to invite the TRADES UNIONS to Zurich. Lafargue writes to say that the party congress will pass a similar resolution. Were your trades unions to make a pronouncement along the same lines, it would create an impression over here. In the eyes of the bumptious gentlemen of the *old* TRADES UNIONS, resolutions adopted by *political* working men's congresses don't count!

Regards from Louise to your wife [c] and children and yourself, and likewise from

Your

F. E.

First published in *Victor Adlers Aufsätze, Reden und Briefe*, Erstes Heft: *Victor Adler und Friedrich Engels*, Wien, 1922

Printed according to the book

Published in English for the first time

---

[a] See this volume, pp. 539-41. - [b] See this volume, pp. 519-20, 522-24, 528-29, 530-31 and 533-35. - [c] Emma Adler

275

ENGELS TO FRANZ MEHRING

IN BERLIN [577]

London, 28 September 1892

Dear Mr Mehring,

Kautsky has sent me part of one of your letters with an inquiry addressed to me.[578] If you feel somewhat hesitant about writing to me because of my failure many years ago to answer two of your letters, I have no right to complain. At the time we were, of course, in different camps and the Anti-Socialist Law [11] was in force, imposing upon us the rule that 'he who is not for us is against us'. Moreover, if I remember rightly you yourself said in one of the letters that you could hardly venture to expect a reply.[579] However that was a long time ago and since then we have found ourselves in the same camp. You have also done excellent work for the *Neue Zeit*, a subject on which I have been far from parsimonious in my tributes when writing to e. g. Bebel.[a] Accordingly I shall be glad to take this opportunity of replying to you direct.

The claim that the discovery of the materialist view of history should be ascribed to the Prussian Romantics of the historical school is certainly new to me. I myself have Marwitz's *Nachlass* and I read the book a few years ago but found nothing in it other than some splendid stuff about cavalry and an unshakeable belief in the magic powers of five cuts of the whip when administered to the plebs by the nobility. Otherwise I have been a complete stranger to such literature since 1841-42 — I only applied myself to it very superficially — and am certainly in no way indebted to it so far as the present discussion is concerned. Marx became acquainted during his Bonn and Berlin days [580] with Adam Müller and Mr von Haller's *Restauration*, etc., and was always somewhat scornful of that vapid, cliché-ridden caricature of the French Romantics, Joseph de Maistre and Cardinal Bonald. But even had he come upon passages such as the one you cite from Lavergne-Peguilhen,[581] they could at that time have made absolutely no impression on him, always assuming he understood what the chaps were trying to say in the first place. Marx was then a He-

---

[a] See this volume, pp. 375-76 and 387.

gelian to whom that passage would have been downright heresy; he knew absolutely nothing about political economy and thus could not have made anything at all of a term such as 'economic system'. Hence the passage in question, even *if* he had known of it, would have gone in at one ear and out of the other without leaving any noticeable trace in his memory. But I very much doubt whether any such allusions were to be found in the historico-Romantic works read by Marx between 1837 and 1842.

It is indeed a highly remarkable passage and I should like to see the quotation verified. I am not familiar with the book, though the author is, of course, known to me as an adherent of the 'historical school'. The passage diverges from the modern view on two counts, 1. in that it derives production and distribution of production from the economic system instead of vice-versa, i. e. the economic system from production, and, 2. in the role it assigns to the 'proper administration' of the economic system, this being open to any number of interpretations, so long as one is unable oneself to see from the book what the author means.

But the strangest thing of all is that the correct concept of history *in abstracto* should be found among the very people who have most abused history *in concreto* — both theoretically and practically. In the case of feudalism the chaps may have seen that *here* the political system evolved out of the economic system because here it is, so to speak, plain as a pikestaff. I say *may* because apart from the above-mentioned unverified passage — you told me yourself that someone *gave* it to you — all I have ever been able to discover about it is that the theoreticians of feudalism are, needless to say, less abstract than the bourgeois liberals. So if, from this concept of the connection between the political system and the spread of civilisation on the one hand and the economic system within feudal society on the other, one of them proceeds to the generalisation that this applies to *all* economic and political systems, how then explain the total myopia of this self-same Romantic, the moment he is faced with *other* economic systems, with the bourgeois economic system and the political systems corresponding to its various stages of development — medieval craft fraternities, absolute monarchy, constitutional monarchy, republic? That is certainly difficult to fathom. And the same chap who regards the economic system as the basis of social and political organisation as a whole, also adheres to the school to whom the absolute monarchy of the 17th and 18th centuries already signifies the fall of man and a betrayal of true political doctrine!

Admittedly he also says that the political system emanates from the economic system and its *proper administration* as inevitably as does a child from the coupling of man and woman. Having regard to the widely known teaching of the author's school, I can only explain this as follows: The true economic system is the feudal one. But since human malice conspires against that system, it must be properly administered in such a way that its existence is protected against these attacks and perpetuated, and that the political system, etc., continues to correspond to it, i.e. is kept, so far as possible, as it was in the 13th and 14th centuries. Then the best of all possible worlds and the finest of historical theories would each be realised, while the Lavergne-Peguilhenian generalisation to the effect that feudal society engenders a feudal polity would be reduced to its true essentials.[582]

For the time being I can only assume that Lavergne-Peguilhen didn't know what he was saying. According to the proverb, certain animals occasionally discover pearls and among the Prussian Romantics such creatures are strongly represented. Incidentally, it might nevertheless be advisable to compare them with their French prototypes — to see whether this has not also been borrowed.

I can only say how grateful I am to you for drawing my attention to this point which I cannot unfortunately pursue further at this moment.

Yours very sincerely,

F. Engels

First published in: Marx and Engels, *Works*, First Russian Edition, Vol. XXIX, Moscow, 1946

Printed according to the original

276

ENGELS TO KARL KAUTSKY

IN STUTTGART

London, 29 September 1892

Dear Baron,

Ede and Gine are the most surprising people I have ever met. This morning a postcard dated Berne 27.9.92 with a view of the Schänzli arrived from them and at 1.30 this afternoon they burst in on me in person; both looked very well, especially Gine, despite the fact that she is still receiving treatment for her throat and, most important of all, Ede gives the impression of having got over his neurasthenia. Considering that they have of late been so extraordinarily efficient in the matter of supplying addresses, I shall steal a march on them by informing you that for the time being they are living at 23 Compton Terrace, Highbury, N., quite close to Highbury and Islington Station, North London Railway.

Mehring's letter, which I return herewith, made it necessary for me to reply to him direct if I did not wish to give offence, which would, of course, never occur to me. I did so on the enclosed sheet, which kindly forward to him.[a]

I told Kovalevsky on Friday that he should send you the article.[b]

We see the *Centralblatt*[c] here at home and also at the Avelings. Evidently the Brauns of the male sex cannot help keeping one foot in the armchair socialist camp. Respectability!

Since you have written to me about the article on the history of socialist organisations in England, I would commend Tussy to you, she being the only person capable of doing the thing with E. Aveling. The relevant literature is all very inadequate albeit voluminous, nor does it contain anything about what has actually happened and concerning which the public was supposed to be kept in ignorance. No one who was not a participant *can* express an opinion about it, i. e. be knowledgeable about individual events and record them objectively. Ede, for example, would have to go through all the numbers of *Justice*, *To-Day*, *Labour Elector*, *Commonweal*, etc. which appeared before his arrival in London, and even so he would have to ask Tussy to ex-

---

[a] See this volume, pp. 549-51. - [b] See this volume, p. 528. - [c] *Sozialpolitisches Central-blatt*

plain to him the significance of what had happened and in that case the whole thing would, after all, be at second hand. However it will be a ticklish job explaining this to Ede who has only just got over his neurasthenia and, since the matter is not urgent, I shall let it rest for the time being. You have seen more of Ede than I have and if you believe that the business would not upset him unduly, it might perhaps be best if the suggestion were to come from you. At all events I leave it in your hands.

Bebel's article,[a] on which I made the necessary comments in yesterday's letter,[b] is very good.

I fully agree that my article[c] should not have appeared until now. I don't even know whether the book has come out yet. Mendelson tells me he ordered it but received the reply that it was not yet available. There was a curious Fabian review in the *Daily Chronicle*, mostly excerpts, running to $2\frac{1}{2}$ columns.

From what C. Schmidt tells me, he has not succeeded in solving the puzzle. Nevertheless I shall wait and see what he says in the article.[d] His article on the Menger-Jevonsiad[e] was very nice. Unfortunately there's nobody one can place it with over here.[f]

Mehring's contributions, both the leaders [583] and the Lessing, strike me as quite excellent and I derive much enjoyment from them.

Your
F. E.

First published in full in *Aus der Frühzeit des Marxismus. Engels Briefwechsel mit Kautsky*, Prag, 1935

Printed according to the book

Published in English for the first time

---

[a] A. Bebel, 'Ein internationaler Kongreß für den Achtstundentag', *Die Neue Zeit*, 11. Jg. 1892/93, 1. Bd., Nr. 2. - [b] See this volume, 542-43. - [c] 'Introduction to the English Edition (1892) of *Socialism: Utopian and Scientific*'. - [d] C. Schmidt, 'Die Durchschnittsprofitrate und das Marx'sche Werthgesetz', *Die Neue Zeit*, 11. Jg. 1892/93, 1. Bd., Nr. 3, 4. - [e] C. Schmidt, 'Die psychologische Richtung in der neueren National-Oekonomie', *Die Neue Zeit*, 10. Jg. 1891/92, 2. Bd., Nr. 40, 41. - [f] See this volume, p. 526.

APPENDICES

1

WILLIAM THORNE AND ELEANOR MARX-AVELING TO SAMUEL GOMPERS [584]

IN NEW YORK

National-union of
Gasworkers and General Labourers
of Great Britain and Ireland.

Registered Office—144, Barking Road, E.

W. Watkinson, President
W. Byford, Treasurer
W. Thorne, ˙General Secretary
W. H. Ward, Assistant Secretary

[London,] 25 January 1891

Mr Samuel Gompers
for the American Federation of Labour [84]

Dear Comrade,

During the recent visit of Comrades Bebel, Liebknecht and Singer on the occasion of Frederick Engels' 70th birthday, they met representatives of the Gas Workers and General Labourers Union [164] (comprising about 100,000 men and women belonging to over seventy trades) and of several other Unions and Organisations, besides John Burns, Cunninghame Graham, M. P., and others. At this meeting the feeling was very strong that the time had come to bring about a close and organised relation between the labour parties of the different countries. The most immediate question is that of preventing the introduction from one country to another of unfair labour, i. e. of workers who not knowing the conditions of the labour-struggle in a particular country, are imported into that country by the Capitalists, in order to reduce wages, or lengthen the hours of labour, or both. The most practical way of carrying this out appears to be the appointing in each country of an International Secretary, who shall be in communication with all the other International Secretaries. Thus, the moment any difficulty between capitalists and labourers occurs in any country, the International Labour Secretaries of all the other countries should be at once communicated with, and will make it their business to try to prevent the exportation from their particular country of any labourers to take the place on unfair terms, of those locked-out or on strike in the country where the difficulty has occured. Whilst this is the most immediate and most obvious matter to be dealt with, it is hoped that an arrangement of the kind proposed, will in every way facilitate the interchange of ideas on all questions between the workers of every nation that is becoming every day and every hour the most pressing necessity of the working-class movement.

If your organisation [84] agrees with the views of the Gasworkers and General Labourers Union, will you at once communicate with us, and give us the name of the Secretary appointed by it to take part in this important movement?

Yours fraternally,

W. Thorne

(General Secretary)

Eleanor Marx-Aveling

(On the behalf of the Executive Committee)

First published in: Ivonne Kapp, *Eleanor Marx*, Volume II, *The Crowded Years*, London, 1976

Reproduced from the original

2

LOUISE KAUTSKY TO AUGUST ENDERS

IN ERFURT

London, 15 December [1891]
122 Regent's Park Road, N.W.

Dear Comrade,

When your letter arrived yesterday, Engels was on the point of leaving. However he read your letter and asked me to reply. In the first place your letter arrived much too late for the circular to be translated and put into the papers. In this instance the bourgeois papers were sooner and better advised of the Germans' intentions than were the comrades over here. To the best of my knowledge Mr Döblin, the German delegate, has not yet seen any of the more prominent comrades, besides which the London TRADES COUNCIL [196] has taken charge of the affair. According to today's papers there was a meeting yesterday at which not one German spoke English well enough to be able to translate. A letter from Mr Liebknecht was read out. At this stage we should only make ourselves look silly were we to tag along behind the rest in the name of the German Party and hence we might as well save ourselves the trouble. So far as I can see from the papers, the meeting went well for the compositors. The English trades unions will do everything they can. If in future you have anything of this kind, will you please send it to Bernstein first. Over here we say, as do the Avelings everywhere, that it is he who represents the German Party and in my view Döblin ought to have gone to Bernstein. Please don't regard this letter as an answer from Engels. He merely agreed that the things should not be published.

With Social-Democratic Greetings,

Louise Kautsky

Mrs Aveling, who is as familiar as anyone with English affairs, is in full agreement with what I have written.

Published for the first time   Printed according to the original

3

ELEANOR MARX-AVELING
TO PAUL LAFARGUE

AT LE PERREUX

[London,] 15 April 1892
65 Chancery Lane, W. C.

My dear Paul,

We sent you some days ago a copy of the *Chronicle*[a] containing a statement with regard to Adolphe Smith and the representation of the French Workers at the forthcoming demonstration in Hyde Park.[463] In the *Workman's Times* of this week—I send you a second copy tho' I believe you get one regularly—you will see some notes referring to this under the heading of (I think) 'London notes', and in any case over the signature of Autolycus—i. e. Burgess, Editor of the *Workman's Times*. Now the result of this paragraph has been much greater and much more unpleasant than you can probably imagine, and unless very disagreeable complications are to follow, you *must absolutely* write to the *Chronicle* and the *Workman's Times* on the subject. That is, of course, if the organisations for which M. Adolphe is the mouthpiece are, as we surmise, simply the Possibilist ones.

You know that 2 years ago, when in the face of violent opposition we managed to *force* a demonstration,[585] you came and spoke from the platforms of the Demonstration Committee. You know that last year your Party was again invited by us, and your letter, stating the reasons why you could not send a delegate was publicly read at the Demonstration. During all this time the London Trades Council[196] working then as now with Mr Hyndman and the English Possibilists, refused to have anything to do with the 'foreigners'. And do not forget the very important fact that the Legal Eight Hours Day demanded by Shipton and Co. is not *our* Legal Eight Hours Day. *They* only want the 8 hours day legalised *in order that over-time may be more highly paid*.

Now seeing all this our Committee[200] who have held steadfastly to the whole Paris programme,[586] and specially the strongest body not only on our Committee, but the strongest of the New Unions[164]— that of the 'Gas Workers and General Labourers'[520]—are deeply

---

[a] *Daily Chronicle*

hurt and surprised at the insult offered them in the *Chronicle*. Thorne came up here on Wednesday and said that he thought it doubly strange as his Union, long before the International Secretariats were thought about, had entered into correspondence with the French Parti Ouvrier,[146] and he wanted to know why they were now to be insulted. This is only one case out of many. I can't tell you the disastrous effect this will have if you don't reply.

Yesterday I had a long talk with the General on the subject (Edward is very ill with a bad throat)—and we both agreed, that you, as foreign Secretary of the 'Parti', *must* send a line to the *Chronicle*. The delay you can easily explain by the fact that you have been visiting your constituents and Fourmies. You should write—if that is the fact—that M. A. Smith speaks only for the Possibilists[3] who are the reactionary party and represent—you know what. That the Parti Ouvrier attended the 1st demonstration of the Legal Eight Hours Committee, that although it could send no delegate, it was at one with that Committee last year, and (this we *all* hope) that your Party will be represented on our platforms this year. The Possibilists are sending *2* delegates. Surely you could send one. Could not Delecluze come? It would cost *very* little to come from Calais? And you could also nominate Bonnier. Those 2 (I know you *can't* come) would counterbalance the others.

In any case, my dear Paul, you *must* write a line to the *Chronicle* (or better still let Laura write it!) and copy that and send it, with *further details if need be*, to the *Workman's Times*. But this must be done *at once*.

Yours,

Tussy

Why *don't* you get your *Verriers*[a] to join the International Bottle-makers' Society? Their not doing so is a great pity—and 'tis only 4d. (8 sous!) *per annum* per member!!

First published in: Marx and Engels, *Works*, Second Russian Edition, Vol. 38, Moscow, 1965

Reproduced from the original

Published in English for the first time

---

[a] glassworkers

4

ELEANOR MARX-AVELING
TO LAURA LAFARGUE

AT LE PERREUX

[London,] 22 April 1892

My dear Laura,

Enclosed a reply from the sweat Adolphe[a] to Paul's very excellent letter. I am writing to you from the General's, as I wished to ask his opinion before writing to you on the matter. He agrees with me that some answer should go, if you can induce Paul to send it. I know, of course, he is busy, but you may be sure that a reply *is* necessary here. It need not be long.

But *who* sends Lavy? Is it the *Broussists*,[3] or is it, as Smith[463] writes, the *joint Committee*? That makes all the difference. But a few facts as to the real strength of the Parti Ouvrier would have a good effect here, and anyhow I hope the elections of May lst[429] will show our real strength.

Get Paul to write, or rather, as I said before, do *you* write. (We all recognised your 'Roman hand' in the *Chronicle* article.)

Just time to catch the post. Love from the General and Louise and

Yours,

Tussy

First published in: Marx and Engels, *Works*, Second Russian Edition, Vol. 38, Moscow, 1965

Reproduced from the original

Published in English for the first time

---

[a] Adolphe Smith

5

GEORGE BERNARD SHAW
TO AUGUST BEBEL

IN BERLIN

29 May 1892

Our aims are as advanced as those of any other body of Social Democrats in England or in Germany, and our methods are as like the German party methods as is possible in view of the facts that we have no second ballot in England as you have in Germany, whilst on the other hand our House of Commons has command of the army, so that when we capture that we capture everything. The result is that whereas you can always run your S. D. candidate against both Liberal & Tory (as we should call them) with the certainty of winning at the 2nd ballot *if you have a majority as against the Tory, we in England would be defeated at the 1st ballot by the division of the labour vote between the Liberal and the S. D., both being beaten by the Tory. Therefore,* our only chance where the workers are not completely organized is to force the Liberals to accept our men as their party candidates. At the last *City Council* election the S. D. F.[29] ran independent candidates and they were all badly beaten, the Fabian Society[87] ran 6 of its members as 'Progressives' and they were all triumphantly successful. Meanwhile we are agitating for the introduction of the 2nd ballot here and urging the workers to organize themselves independently and break loose from the Liberals. If you and Paul Singer were to take the command of the Fabian Society, you would find yourselves compelled to take the same course and if you make a careful study of the work that has been done for some years past in spreading the S. D. idea in this country, I am sure that you will find that the Fabians who are a small and a *poor body* of men, have done as much as any other body in forwarding that work. You will readily understand that those enthusiastic socialists who have had no experience of practical political work accuse us of compromising our principles and intriguing with the Liberal party. I have already explained to you how we find ourselves as *Possibilists,* compelled for the present either to force our candidates on the Liberals or to suffer defeat *and disgrace* at every election.

Published for the first time   Reproduced   from   the   original

NOTES
AND
INDEXES

NOTES

[1] The letter is written on a postcard. The address is on the back: Herrn W. Lieb-knecht, Südplatz 11, Leipzig, Germany.— 3, 17

[2] Presumably Liebknecht had asked Engels (see Engels' letter to him of 30 June 1890; present edition, Vol. 48) to write a refutation to *Justice* in connection with an item headlined 'Make a Note of This!' published in its issue 336 on 21 June 1890. Citing Paul Brousse, a Possibilist leader, as his source, the author had attributed to Lieb-knecht the statement 'We are no revolutionists', which, he alleged, had been made on behalf of the German Social-Democratic Party. Social-Democracy in Germany, the *Justice* writer claimed, was pinning its hopes on propaganda rather than revolutionary action. The next issue of *Justice* (No. 337, 28 June) carried a letter to the Editor from Ferdinand Gilles headlined 'German Social-Democrats Still Revolutionists'. It declared that if Liebknecht had in fact made this statement, he was not speaking for the whole party, which at its every congress had confirmed its loyalty to revolutionary principles.

Liebknecht's reply to these items was published in *People's Press*, No. 22, 2 August 1890.— 3

[3] The *Possibilists* (or Broussists) were a trend in the French socialist movement. Their leaders — Paul Brousse, Benoît Malon and others — advocated the gradual transformation of the capitalist system into a socialist one by means of reform, through a 'policy of pursuing the possible'. In 1882 they caused a split in the French Workers' Party (see Note 146) and formed a new party named Fédéracion des Travailleurs socialistes. In the 1890s the Possibilists lost a great deal of their influence; in 1902 the majority of them joined the reformist French Socialist Party, founded by Jean Léon Jaurès.— 3, 24, 126, 140, 155, 162, 164, 167, 183, 186, 190, 193, 208, 211, 224, 229, 238, 241, 260, 291, 292, 342, 348, 360, 367, 370, 381, 401, 423, 484, 520, 524, 533, 561, 562

[4] This refers to preparations to make the journal *Neue Zeit* a weekly. It began appearing on a weekly basis in October 1890.— 5

⁵ In a letter of 3 July 1890 Karl Kautsky, discussing his plans for *Neue Zeit*, had asked Engels to write something for the journal: 'Of course I should very much like to promise something by you, indeed to begin with a contribution from you straight away.' Engels fulfilled his promise much later. His work *On the History of Early Christianity* was completed in July 1894 and published in *Die Neue Zeit*, 13. Jg., 1894/95, 1. Bd., Nr. 1, 2 (see present edition, Vol. 27, pp. 445-69). In the same letter Kautsky asked Engels to send him the address of Friedrich Adolph Sorge, whom he wanted to contribute to the journal.— 5

⁶ An extract from this letter was published in *Berliner Volks-Tribüne*, No. 39, 27 September 1890. Part of the letter first appeared in English in: Karl Marx and Frederick Engels. *Correspondence. 1846-1895*, Lawrence and Wishart, London, 1934, pp. 472-74.— 6

⁷ This refers to Conrad Schmidt's letter to Engels of 25 June 1890, in which Schmidt spoke of his literary plans. He mentioned in particular having promised to Kautsky a review of G. F. Knapp's book *Die Bauern-Befreiung und der Ursprung der Landarbeiter in den älteren Theilen Preußens*, published in Leipzig in 1887. However, the review never materialised. Schmidt also described his impressions of P. Barth's book *Die Geschichtsphilosophie Hegel's und der Hegelianer bis auf Marx und Hartmann*, Leipzig, 1890.— 6

⁸ *Blue Books* (so called after the traditional blue cover) is the general title of the collections of proceedings of the British Parliament and documents of the Foreign Office. They have been published since the 17th century and are the main official source on Great Britain's economic and diplomatic history. Marx used the Blue Books in particular for his work on *Capital*.— 6

⁹ Engels obviously means his letter to Eduard Bernstein of 2-3 November 1882 (see present edition, Vol. 46) in which he mentions a conversation Marx had with Paul Lafargue. In discussing the state of scientific socialist thought in France, Marx told Lafargue ironically: 'If anything is certain it is that I myself am not a Marxist.'— 7, 22

¹⁰ Between 14 June and 12 July 1890 *Berliner Volks-Tribüne*, in a discussion series headlined 'Jedem der volle Ertrag seiner Arbeit', published articles by Ferdinand Domela Nieuwenhuis, Paul Ernst, Paul Fischer, and also an article signed *Von einem Arbeiter*. On 12 July the paper summed up the discussion in an item headlined 'Schlußwort zur Debatte'.— 7

¹¹ The *Anti-Socialist Law*, initiated by the Bismarck government and passed by the Reichstag on 21 October 1878, was directed against the socialist and working-class movement. The Social-Democratic Party of Germany was virtually driven into the underground. All party and mass working-class organisations and their press were banned, socialist literature was subject to confiscation, Social-Democrats made the object of reprisals. However, with the active help of Marx and Engels, the Social-Democratic Party succeeded in overcoming both the opportunist (Eduard Bernstein et al.) and 'ultra-Left' (J. Most et al.) tendencies within its ranks and was able, by combining underground activities with an efficient utilisation of legal means, to use the period of the operation of the law for considerably strengthening and expanding its influence among the masses. Prolonged in 1881, 1884, 1886 and 1888, the Anti-Socialist Law was repealed on 1 October 1890. For Engels' assessment of it

see his article 'Bismarck and the German Working Men's Party' (present edition, Vol. 24, pp. 407-09).—8, 11, 14, 19, 47, 130, 134, 174, 180, 197, 200, 235, 254, 305, 318, 344, 363, 427, 516, 549

[12] The first *Congress of German Social-Democracy* to be held after the repeal of the Anti-Socialist Law met in Halle between 12 and 18 October 1890. It was attended by 413 delegates and 17 guests. The congress endorsed the new party Rules adapted to the task of turning the party, under the conditions of legality, into a mass working-class organisation. It abandoned the party's hitherto operative, Lassallean programme and, on Liebknecht's proposal, decided to have a new programme drafted for the next party congress, which was to be held in Erfurt, and published three months before the congress for discussion by local party organisations and in the press. The congress also discussed the party press (*Berliner Volksblatt* was made the central organ) and the party's stance on strikes and boycotts. The party adopted the name *Sozialdemokratische Partei Deutschlands* (Social-Democratic Party of Germany).— 11, 22, 24, 26, 46, 52, 55, 73, 95, 98

[13] In late March 1890 the Jungen, a group of Berlin Social-Democrats, including Max Schippel, published an appeal under the title 'Was soll am 1. Mai geschehen?', urging the workers to hold a strike on the 1st of May. The appeal reflected the specific attitude of the Jungen, crystallised in 1890, as a petty-bourgeois semi-anarchist opposition group within the German Social-Democracy. The hard core of the group was made up of students and young literati (hence the group's name) who claimed the role of the party's theoreticians and leaders. Paul Ernst, Paul Kampffmeyer, Hans Müller, Bruno Wille and others were the group's ideologues. The Jungen ignored the change in the conditions for the party's activity after the repeal of the Anti-Socialist Law. They denied the need for using legal forms of struggle, opposed participation in parliamentary elections and the use of the parliamentary platform by the Social-Democrats and demagogically accused the party and its Executive of opportunism, violation of party democracy and promotion of the interests of the petty bourgeoisie. In October 1891 the Erfurt Congress expelled some of the opposition leaders from the party.

A reply to the above-mentioned appeal of the Jungen was given on the party's behalf by the Social-Democratic parliamentary group in a statement entitled, 'An die Arbeiter und Arbeiterinnen Deutschlands!' (adopted in Halle on 13 April 1890).— 11, 20, 21, 25

[14] Engels refers to Bebel's 'Erklärung' in *Berliner Volksblatt*, No. 173, 29 July 1890, in which Bebel took issue with the article 'Der 1. Oktober' published in *Sächsische Arbeiter-Zeitung*, No. 88, 23 July 1890. In his statement Bebel pointed out: '...if you are sure that you have grounds for accusations, you must give the names and the facts you challenge so that those concerned may answer you. This is the mode of operation of honorable men. Any other mode of operation is sheer insolence.'— 11

[15] This refers to the item 'Tell Tale Straws' in *Justice*, No. 337, 28 June 1890.— 12

[16] A letter from Paul Lafargue of 4 August 1890.— 12

[17] The draft Rules of the Social-Democratic Party of Germany, framed by the Social-Democratic parliamentary group, was published for discussion in August 1890. The party congress in Halle (see Note 12) adopted them with a number of amendments.

These concerned, in particular, the provisions which had been criticised by Engels — on the procedure for fixing salaries for members of the Executive, on the representation of the party branches at congresses, and on the functions of the Social-Democratic group in the Reichstag.— 13

18 The fragment of this letter was published earlier in: Karl Marx and Frederick Engels, *Selected Works*, Progress Publishers, Moscow, 1968, pp. 690-91 and in: Karl Marx and Frederick Engels, *Selected Works*, International Publishers, N.Y., 1968, pp. 690-91.— 18

19 In a letter dated 16 August 1890 Otto von Boenigk, who was planning to give a lecture on socialism, asked for Engels' view on the expediency and possibility of socialist reform given the existing distinctions in the level of education, political awareness, etc., of the different social classes. Von Boenigk's other question concerned the family of Jenny Marx.— 18

20 This letter was first published in English in: Frederick Engels, Paul and Laura Lafargue, *Correspondence*, Vol. 2, 1887-1890, Foreign Languages Publishing House, Moscow, 1960. A passage from this letter was first published in French in: *Le Socialiste*, No. 115, 24 November 1900.— 21

21 The *École spéciale militaire*, founded in Fontainbleau in 1803 and transferred to Saint-Cyr near Versailles in 1808, trained infantry and cavalry officers. The whole course of studies took two years — a circumstance Engels was probably hinting at to show the graduates' inadequate knowledge.— 21

22 The Social-Democratic meetings mentioned by Engels were held respectively: the one in Dresden on 10 August 1890, that in Magdeburg on 13 August and that in Berlin — scheduled for 20 August — on 25 August. All three fully endorsed the policy of Bebel and the Reichstag Social-Democratic group, led by him.— 22

23 On 20 August 1890 *Le Figaro* launched a series of articles under the title 'Les Coulisses du boulangisme', signed x. The author was the ex-Boulangist journalist Mermeix.— 22

24 The second ballot in Paris on 27 January 1889 was contested by Georges Boulanger for the Rightists, Jacques for the Republican Party, and Boulés, a navvy, for the Workers' Party and the Blanquists. The Possibilists backed Jacques. The campaign was marked by high tension. Boulanger scored a major victory with a vote of about 250,000. Boulés polled 17,000 votes.— 22

25 This letter was first published in English in: Frederick Engels, Paul and Laura Lafargue, *Correspondence*, Vol. 2, 1887-1890, Foreign Languages Publishing House, Moscow, 1960.— 23, 42, 65, 82

26 In the autumn of 1890 the General Council of the Belgian Workers' Party, acting on a mandate from the Possibilist congress (see Note 53), sent out invitations for an international workers' congress to be held in Brussels in 1891. Since the executive committee of Swiss socialists set up on the instructions of the 1889 Paris International Socialist Workers' Congress (see Note 51) for the purpose of convoking another congress had failed to take any action until September 1890, the danger arose of two international congresses being held simultaneously in 1891.— 23, 26, 28, 46, 74

²⁷ The Congress of the British Trades Unions in Liverpool met from 1 to 6 September 1890. It was attended by 460 delegates representing more than 1.4 million organised workers. A considerable number of delegates represented new trades unions, in which a certain influence was wielded by the British socialists.

Despite resistance from the leaders of the old trades unions the congress adopted a resolution urging the legal introduction of the eight-hour working day and recognised as desirable the participation of trades unions in international workers' associations. It also decided to send delegates to the International Socialist Workers' Congress which was due to meet in Brussels (see Note 135).—23, 25, 46, 167, 185, 233, 250

²⁸ The *International Socialist Conference in Halle* was held on 16 and 17 October 1890, while the Congress of German Social-Democracy was meeting there (see Note 12). The conference was attended by German Social-Democrats and the representatives of nine socialist parties who took part in the congress as guests. In keeping with Engels' recommendation, the conference decided to hold a united socialist congress in Brussels in 1891 (see Note 135) which was to be attended, among others, by the Possibilists and their supporters. The Possibilists' participation was made contingent on their recognising the complete sovereignty of the congress—none of the decisions of the earlier congresses, the 1889 Possibilist congress included, was to be binding on it. For details see Engels' article 'The International Workers' Congress of 1891' (present edition, Vol. 27, pp. 72-75).—24, 29, 40, 46, 49, 52, 54, 57, 74, 98

²⁹ The *Social Democratic Federation*, set up in August 1884, consisted of English socialists of different orientations, mostly intellectuals. For a long time the leadership of the Federation was in the hands of reformists led by Hyndman, an opportunist sectarian. In opposition to them, the revolutionary Marxists within the Federation (Eleanor Marx-Aveling, Edward Aveling, Tom Mann and others) worked for close ties with the revolutionary labour movement. In the autumn of 1884—following a split and the establishment by the Left wing of an independent organisation, the Socialist League (see Note 49)—the opportunists' influence in the Federation increased. However, revolutionary elements, discontented with the opportunist leadership, continued to form within the Federation, under the impact of the masses.— 24, 43, 57, 123, 126, 131, 140, 155, 185, 190, 219, 333, 335, 370, 380, 386, 402, 449, 471, 475, 484, 493, 497, 508, 515, 542, 545, 563

³⁰ In his letter to Engels of 8 September 1890 Karl Kautsky said he intended, after the Halle party congress (see Note 12), to publish in *Neue Zeit* a series of articles criticising the party programme adopted at the Gotha congress in 1875. The prospective authors included Engels, Bebel, Auer, Bernstein and others.—25

³¹ In his letter of 8 September Kautsky told Engels that he was looking for a deputy editor to work simultaneously for *Neue Zeit* and *Schwäbische Tagwacht*, and asked Engels to help him in this matter. He mentioned Conrad Schmidt as a possible candidate.—25

³² In a letter of 16 September 1890 Paul Lafargue told Engels the French socialists considered it possible to hold an international socialist congress in Brussels in 1891

since the Possibilists had lost all influence among the Belgians and Dutch and there were no grounds to fear for the success of the congress.— 28

[33] Engels' letter to Bebel has not been found. In his reply, dated 23 October, Bebel wrote: 'Holding a sort of conference in Halle would be a good thing and easy to arrange because apart from the French and Nieuwenhuis there would be three or four Austrians there.'— 29

[34] Engels evidently means the position of non-interference adopted by the Workers' Party during the Boulangist crisis and the press reports concerning Boulanger's receiving financial aid from the royalists. He may also be referring to the Boulangists' defeat at the municipal elections held between 27 April and 4 May 1890.— 30

[35] This refers to the leading article, 'The Death of a Hero', in *Justice*, No. 349, 20 September 1890.— 30

[36] In a letter of 17 September Charles Caron asked Engels' permission to publish translations of works by Marx and Engels in *L'Oeuvre socialiste. Revue politique et littéraire.*— 31

[37] In a letter dated 19 September 1890 Paul Lafargue warned Engels against allowing Charles Caron to publish Marx's *The Poverty of Philosophy*. Caron, he wrote, was a private publisher and had long since drifted away from the labour movement.— 32

[38] The *Eighth Congress of the French Workers' Party* met in Lille on 11 and 12 October 1890. It was attended by about 70 delegates, representing more than 200 party groups and trades unions from 97 towns and localities. The congress revised the party Rules and finally determined the composition and functions of the National Council. The following persons were elected to the Council for the period 1890-91: Jules Guesde, Louis Simon Dereure, Leon Camescasse, Quesnel, Georges Edouard Crépin, Paul Lafargue and Joseph Ferroul. *Le Socialiste* was made the party's official organ. The congress called for a peaceful demonstration to be held on 1 May 1891. It rejected the proposal for a general strike put forward by the 1888 Bordeaux trade union congress and pronounced for an international strike of miners as the vanguard of the working class capable of representing the interests of all workers. On the Workers' Party see Note 146.— 32, 46, 52, 54, 459

[39] During the International Socialist Workers' Congress in Paris in July 1889 the French delegates, numbering 206, twice met separately from the congress. They established the National Council of the French Workers' Party, composed of Jules Guesde, Gabriel Deville, Louis Simon Dereure, Leon Camescasse, Georges Edouard Crépin, Paul Lafargue and Lenoel. The Council was to give practical leadership to the party and call its next congress.— 32

[40] This letter was first published in English in full in: S. Hook, *Towards the Understanding of Karl Marx. A Revolutionary Interpretation.* The John Day Company, New York, 1933.— 33

[41] In his letter of 3 September 1890 Joseph Bloch put two questions to Engels. The first concerned the interpretation of Roman historian Cornelius Nepos' statements on consanguine marriage in Ancient Greece. The second was formulated thus: 'Are

economic relations the *only* determining moment or do they merely form, in a certain sense, a solid basis for all other relations, which can then become factors in their own right?' — 33

⁴² In a letter to Engels of 19 September 1890 Jules Guesde pointed out an inaccuracy in Engels' letter of 2 September to the leaders of the French Workers' Party (see present edition, Vol. 27, pp. 233-34) concerning the resolution of the 1889 Paris International Socialist Workers' Congress on the procedure for the convocation of the next congress. Engels considered that authorisation to call it had been given to both the Swiss and the Belgian socialists. Formally it was the executive committee, to be set up by the Swiss socialists, that had to decide where to call the congress, in Switzerland or in Belgium. In essence, however, Engels was right since the executive could not function without agreeing its steps with the Belgians (see also Note 26).— 40

⁴³ This refers to the *International Socialist Conference* held in The Hague on 28 February 1889. Attended by representatives of the socialist movement in Germany, France, Belgium, Holland and Switzerland, it had been called, on Engels' initiative, by the Social-Democratic group in the German Reichstag with a view to formulating the terms for the convocation of the International Socialist Workers' Congress in Paris. The Possibilists stayed away from the conference and refused to recognise its decisions. The conference determined the powers, the date and the agenda of the congress.— 40

⁴⁴ This letter of Engels has not been found. On 29 September 1890 August Bebel wrote to him: 'Today we discussed matters relating to the international conference. We could not make up our minds to send out further invitations, if only to avoid creating the impression that we wanted to give our congress a special air of spectacularity through international representation. We are also definitely short of time.

'So besides the Austrians, the French and the Dutch we shall have one Belgian and one Swiss committee member. The latter decided last week to declare in favour of Belgium so as to preclude a breach. I trust with these representatives it will be possible to reach agreement on all questions in our sense. I believe things similar to those that happened last year in Paris are ruled out.' — 40

⁴⁵ This article, 'Ein ernstes Wort', was published in *Neue Preußische Zeitung* (evening issue) on 22 September 1890 and reprinted in the Viennese *Arbeiter-Zeitung*, No. 39, 26 September 1890, in the column *Ausland. Deutschland*, under the heading 'Berlin, den 23. September'.— 42

⁴⁶ The Danish Social-Democratic Party, formed in 1876, had a reformist and a revolutionary wing. The latter, led by Gerson Trier and Nikolai Petersen, was grouped round the newspaper *Arbejderen*. In 1889 the revolutionary minority was expelled from the party and formed an organisation of its own. However, due to the sectarian mistakes of its leaders, it failed to develop into a mass proletarian party.— 42

⁴⁷ The *Parliamentary Committee* was the Executive of the British Trades Union Congress (formed in 1868). From 1871, the Committee was elected annually by the Trades Union Congresses and acted as the unions' centre between congresses. It nominated union candidates for Parliament, organised support for pro-union bills and prepared the regular congresses. The Committee was dominated by reformists devoted to the old, conservative trade unionism and drawing their support from the

working-class aristocracy. From 1875 to 1890 the secretaryship of the Committee was held by Broadhurst. In 1921 the Parliamentary Committee was replaced by the General Council of the TUC.— 43

[48] This refers to the *Central Committee* of representatives of radical and socialist clubs and 'new' trades unions which was set up in the spring of 1890 to organise a demonstration in London on 4 May. In the subsequent months the Committee continued its activity, its aim now being to organise the struggle for a legal eight-hour working day, the implementation of the resolutions of the 1889 International Socialist Workers' Congress and the establishment of a workers' party. In the summer of 1890 the Legal Eight Hours and International Labour League (see Note 200) was formed on its basis.— 43

[49] The *Socialist League* was an organisation set up in December 1884 by a group of English socialists who had withdrawn from the Social Democratic Federation on account of its leaders' opportunist policies. The founders of the League included Eleanor Marx-Aveling, Edward Aveling, Ernest Belfort Bax, William Morris and others. In its early years the League took an active part in the labour movement. However, anarchist elements soon gained the upper hand in the League, forcing many of its organisers, among them the Avelings, to resign. In the early nineties the League disintegrated.— 43

[50] Engels means the *London International Trades Union Congress* held in November 1888. Representatives of Belgian, British, Danish, Dutch, Italian and pro-Possibilist French trades unions attended. The organisers of the congress had made participation conditional on the official election of delegates by trades unions and thereby denied access to the German and Austrian Social-Democrats and French Marxists. However, the reformist leaders of the British Trades Unions failed to impose their line. Despite their resistance, the congress appealed to the working people to fight for labour protection legislation and a legal eight-hour working day. The congress decided to call an international workers' congress in Paris in 1889, entrusting the Possibilists with its organisation.— 43

[51] The *International Socialist Workers' Congress* in Paris — virtually the inaugural congress of the Second International — opened on 14 July 1889, the centenary of the capture of the Bastille. Some 400 delegates from 20 countries of Europe and America attended. The congress heard the reports of the representatives of socialist parties on the state of the labour movement in their respective countries and worked out the fundamentals of international labour legislation, demanding a legal eight-hour day, the outlawing of child labour, and measures to protect working women and juveniles. It stressed the need for the political organisation of the proletariat and a struggle to ensure satisfaction of the workers' democratic demands. It also spoke out for the disbandment of standing armies and the universal arming of the people. The congress's most important resolution was the decision to hold demonstrations and meetings in all countries on 1 May 1890 to back up demands for an eight-hour working day and labour legislation. The anarchists opposed the congress resolutions but were overwhelmingly outvoted.— 43, 46, 97, 127, 139, 140, 483

[52] This refers to the campaign launched by the Possibilists in France and their supporters within the Social Democratic Federation (see notes 3 and 29) to discredit the International Socialist Workers' Congress (see Note 51). Another congress, called on the Possibilists' initiative, was being held in Paris at the time. It was only attend-

ed by 13 foreign delegations, most of them representing fictitious organisations. The attempt to bring the two congresses together failed because the Possibilist congress made merger conditional on a revision of the credentials of the delegates attending the Marxist congress. The Possibilist congress declared for the restoration of the International. It decided to hold the next congress in Brussels in 1891 and instructed the Belgian Workers' Party to convoke it.— 43, 234

53 Engels means the signs of a forthcoming dissociation within the Possibilist Workers' Party (see Note 3). At their congress in Châtellerault, 9 to 15 October 1890, the Possibilists split into two groups—the Broussists and the Allemanists. The latter formed an organisation of their own, the *Socialist Revolutionary Workers' Party*. The Allemanists retained the Possibilists' ideological and tactical principles but, in contrast to them, attached great importance to propaganda within the trades unions, which they regarded as the workers' principal form of organisation. The Allemanists' ultimate weapon was the call for a general strike. Like the Possibilists, they denied the need for a united, centralised party and advocated autonomy and the struggle to win seats on the municipal councils.— 43, 46, 49, 52, 53, 74, 98, 117, 139, 155, 164, 167, 183, 189, 190, 224, 260, 399, 430, 533, 544

54 This probably refers to Edward Aveling's article 'The New Era in German Socialism' in *The Daily Chronicle and Clerkenwell News*, No. 8903, 25 September 1890, which contained excerpts from Engels' article 'What Now?', published in the last issue of the *Sozialdemokrat* (see present edition, Vol. 27, pp. 7-10).

Aveling's interview with Eduard Bernstein was published in *The Star*, No. 832, 29 September 1890, under the heading 'Germany Flooded with Papers from Kentish Town.— A Talk with the Editor'.— 44

55 A reference to an article by Julius Grunzig headlined 'Die Vorgänge im Lager der deutschen Socialdemokratie', in *New Yorker Volkszeitung*, No. 217, 10 September 1890. It stated views in the spirit of the Jungen.— 45

56 The *National Congress of Trade Unions*, meeting in Calais from 13 to 18 October 1890, supported the resolutions of the Lille Congress (see Note 38) calling for a demonstration on 1 May and a miners' strike.— 46, 52

57 The *labour exchanges* in France, manned by representatives of various trades unions, were mostly operated by the municipalities in large cities. The government gave them support and, not infrequently, financial aid, seeking to exploit them for diverting the workers from the class struggle. The labour exchanges created jobs for the unemployed, founded trades unions, trained union activists and organised strikes.— 47, 224, 411

58 The Possibilists refused to take part in the demonstration on 1 May 1890 on the grounds that Boulangist and other agents of the reaction were going to participate and that the demonstration might harm the cause of the working class.— 47

59 The passage that had puzzled Engels in Sorge's letter of 23 September was explained to him in Sorge's letter of 14 October. Sorge had meant that Eleanor Marx-Aveling, delegated to the Liverpool Trades Union Congress by the Gas Workers and General Labourers Union, had been deprived of the right to vote on the far-fetched pretext of not being a wage labourer herself. Sorge probably drew this information from *People's Press* of 13 September, which carried Eleanor Marx-

Aveling's letter 'To the Editor of the *People's Press*', demonstrating the injustice of the refusal to recognise her credentials.— 49

⁶⁰ Fearing a strike at their enterprises, the owners of the Gas Light and Coke Company in Becton intended to call out troops to intimidate the workers. An army unit stationed at Chatham was put on the alert on 3 October 1890, but there followed no orders to leave the barracks. The government's readiness to make troops available for action against strikers was sharply condemned at many workers' meetings in different areas of London.— 51

⁶¹ This letter was first published in: F. Engels, P. et L. Lafargue, *Correspondance*, t. II, Paris, 1956.— 52

⁶² Engels means the congresses in Lille, Calais and Halle (see notes 12, 38 and 56).— 53

⁶³ This refers to the merger of two trends in the German working-class movement— the Social-Democratic Workers' Party (the Eisenach group), led by August Bebel and Wilhelm Liebknecht, and the Lassallean General Association of German Workers, led by Wilhelm Hasselmann, Wilhelm Hasenclever and others— which took place at a congress in Gotha, 22-27 May 1875. The party thus formed adopted the name of Socialist Workers' Party of Germany. Thus the split within the German working class was overcome. However, the draft programme of the united party (formulated basically by Wilhelm Liebknecht, whose main concern was reconciliation) contained serious mistakes and fundamental concessions to the Lassalleans. Marx, in his *Critique of the Gotha Programme* (see present edition, Vol. 24, pp. 75-99) and in his letter to Wilhelm Bracke of 5 May 1875 (ibid., Vol. 45, pp. 69-73) and Engels, in his letter to Bebel of 18-28 March 1875 (ibid., Vol. 45, pp. 60-66), approved the establishment of a united socialist party in Germany, but warned the Eisenach leaders against precipitate action and ideological compromises with the Lassalleans. They criticised the erroneous propositions in the draft programme, but the congress adopted it, with only minor amendments.— 53, 97, 117, 119, 123, 126, 161, 164, 168, 176, 179, 180

⁶⁴ This refers to the refusal of the Possibilists (see Note 3) to participate in the socialist congress in Troyes (23-30 December 1888), which originally had been called as a congress of the Possibilist party. The refusal was due to the fact that the convocation of the congress had been entrusted to the Troyes socialist organisations, consisting mostly of supporters of the Workers' Party (Guesdists), so that both parties had been invited.— 54

⁶⁵ Eleanor Marx-Aveling had attended the congresses of the French Workers' Party in Lille (see Note 38) and of the German Social-Democrats in Halle (see Note 12).— 54

⁶⁶ This refers to the opposition group of the Jungen (see Note 13).— 54

⁶⁷ On 17 October 1890 the newspaper *Gil Blas* carried an interview allegedly granted to its correspondent by August Bebel. Engels sent a copy of the text and a letter (which has not been found) to Bebel. The latter replied that he had granted no such interview and the *Gil Blas* text was a hoax from beginning to end. Seeing that this was the case, Paul Lafargue disavowed the interview in a note headlined 'Le Gil Blas interviewer' (*Le Socialiste*, No. 6, 26 October 1890).— 54

[68] In a letter to Engels of 16 October 1890 Lafargue said that almost all the delegates to the Lille Congress (see Note 38) had been victimised by the bourgeoisie: they had lost their living and were forced to engage in petty trade and the like. He also stressed that many of them held elective positions on municipal councils and similar bodies, which was proof of the growing influence of the French Workers' Party.— 54

[69] This letter is written on a postcard. The address — Mr. W. Liebknecht, Kanstraße 160, Charlottenburg-Berlin, Germany — is on the back.— 56

[70] This refers to the *French section of 1871* formed by French refugees in London in September 1871. Its leaders maintained close ties with the Bakuninists in Switzerland and joined in their attacks on the organisational principles of the International. When the General Council suggested that the section should bring its Rules into conformity with those of the International, the section came out against the Council, questioning its powers. In the spring of 1872, part of the section's following, jointly with English bourgeois republicans (including Adolphe Smith Headingley) and Lassalleans expelled from the International for their splitting activities, formed the so-called Universal Federalist Council, which claimed the role of leader of the International.— 56

[71] The greater part of this letter was first published, in German, in the supplement to *Leipziger Volkszeitung*, No. 250, 26 September 1895. The first, abridged, English publication was in: S. Hook, *Towards the Understanding of Karl Marx. A Revolutionary Interpretation*. The John Day Company, New York, 1933.— 57

[72] In a letter of 20 October 1890 Conrad Schmidt advised Engels that he, Schmidt, had been offered the position of stock exchange editor of *Züricher Post*. Somewhat later he began working for the newspaper, but in a different capacity — as its foreign news editor. On 18 June 1891 he informed Engels that he had relinquished his post.— 57

[73] Engels has in mind his sojourn in Manchester, 1842 to 1844, as a business apprentice at the Ermen & Engels cotton mill.— 58

[74] In his letter of 20 October Conrad Schmidt gave a high appraisal of P. Barth's book *Die Geschichtsphilosophie Hegel's und der Hegelianer bis auf Marx und Hartmann. Ein Kritischer Versuch*, Leipzig, 1890. He pointed to the author's convincing attempts to prove, with historical data, the effect of extraeconomic factors on the economic basis, and suggested that, unless it could be shown that these factors, above all the political ones, were conditioned economically, 'it would be difficult to uphold Marx's conception of history in its *strictest sense*'. This conclusion of Schmidt's worried Engels, hence his detailed reply.— 59

[75] *Code Napoléon* — system of bourgeois law adopted under Napoleon I between 1804 and 1810. It comprises five codes: civil, civil-procedural, commercial, criminal and criminal-procedural.— 61

[76] This refers to the *1688 coup d'état* in Britain which deposed the Stuart dynasty and established a constitutional monarchy with William of Orange on the throne (from 1689). The new system was based on a compromise between the landed aristocracy and the big bourgeoisie. British bourgeois historiographers call this coup the Glorious Revolution.— 62

[77] The *deists* recognise God as the impersonal rational primal cause of the world, but

see him as refraining from any intervention in the life of Nature and society. In contrast to feudal and church ideology, deism tends to take a rationalistic attitude, criticising the medieval theological world-outlook. At the same time, it compromises with institutionalised religion, holding that it should be retained for the masses in a rationalistic form.— 62

[78] See *Capital*, Volume I, Chapter 10, 'The Working Day', and the whole of Part VIII, 'The So-Called Primitive Accumulation' (present edition, Vol. 35).— 63

[79] On 16 September 1890 the *Volksstimme* carried an article by Paul Ernst distorting Engels' statements and alleging that he was in solidarity with the Jungen (see Note 13). In this connection Engels published his 'Reply to Mr. Paul Ernst' (see present edition, Vol. 27, pp. 80-85), in which he quoted part of his letter to Ernst of 5 June 1890 (see Vol. 48).— 63

[80] Conrad Schmidt had published an extract from Engels' letter to him of 5 August 1890 in the *Berliner Volks-Tribüne*, No. 39, 27 September 1890 (see this volume, pp. 6-9).— 64

[81] This letter was first published in English in: K. Marx and F. Engels, *Letters to Americans. 1848-1895. A Selection*, International Publishers, New York, 1953.— 67

[82] This letter has only reached us in the form of extracts published in Gustav Mayer's book *Friedrich Engels. Eine Biographie*, Vol. 2, The Hague, 1934. Part of the letter is given in Mayer's rendering. Engels wrote the letter under the immediate impact of the death and funeral of Helene Demuth, in reply to Louise Kautsky's telegram of condolences. In his letter Engels expressed his hope that Louise would move to London in order to keep house for him and be his secretary. However, not wanting to force her hand, he suggested that Louise should come to London for a short stay and make her decision there.— 68

[83] Engels wrote this letter in his capacity as executor of Helene Demuth.— 69

[84] The *American Federation of Labor* — leading US trade-union centre, formed in December 1886. Composed mostly of skilled workers, it initially played a positive part as a rallying point for the American working class, particularly in the struggle for the eight hours day. Its programme bore an imprint of socialist ideas.— 74, 113, 557, 558

[85] Sorge's first contribution to *Neue Zeit* (No. 8, 1890) was the article 'Briefe aus Nordamerika'.— 74

[86] The *Nationalists* were members of a social movement in the USA which sought to relieve society of the worst evils of capitalism through the nationalisation of production and distribution and a peaceful transition from capitalism to socialism. The first Nationalist club was set up in Boston in 1888, under the impact of Edward Bellamy's Utopian novel *Looking Backward 2000-1887*. By 1891 there were more than 160 such clubs all over the country. The clubs, consisting mostly of members of the petty and middle bourgeoisie, were vehicles for the propagation of Nationalist views. In 1889, the newspaper *Nationalist* began to appear. The Nationalist movement exerted a certain influence on America's socialists. For instance, the newspaper *Sozialist*, organ of the Socialist Labor Party of North America (see Note 133), echoed its propaganda, and Daniel de Leon, one of the party's leaders, held Nationalist views. Engels compared the Nationalists to the Fabians (see Note 87).

That the *Nationalists* boycotted Engels' works, ignoring them or declaring them harmful, was told to Engels by Sorge in a letter of 14 October 1890.— 75, 113

[87] The *Fabian Society* was a British reformist organisation set up by a group of intellectuals in 1884 and led by Sidney and Beatrice Webb. The Society's name derives from Fabius Maximus, a Roman general of the 3rd century B. C. nicknamed Cunctator (Delayer) for his tactic of evading a set battle in the war against Hannibal.— 75, 113, 342, 404, 449, 468, 493, 497, 502, 515, 526, 563

[88] This presumably refers to an article in *Paterson Labor Standard* of 11 October 1890 mentioned by Sorge in his letter to Engels of 14 October.— 75

[89] Engels means the *German Workers' Educational Society* in London, which was founded by Karl Schapper, Joseph Moll, Heinrich Bauer and other members of the League of the Just in 1840. After the establishment of the Communist League, its local branches played the leading role in the Society. In 1847 and 1849-50, Marx and Engels took an active part in its work. On 17 September 1850, they and a number of their followers retired from the Society because most of its members had sided with the adventurist sectarian minority (the Willich-Schapper faction) which was challenging the Marx- and Engels-led majority in the Central Authority of the Communist League. Marx and Engels resumed their work in the Society in the late 1850s. When the First International Working Men's Association was founded, the Society — then led, among others, by Friedrich Lessner — became its member. The London Educational Society was closed by the British government in 1918.— 76, 237, 269, 294, 310, 313, 333, 335, 345, 381, 497, 527

[90] The meeting took place at Edward and Eleanor Avelings' house in London on 1 December 1890. It was attended by German Social-Democratic leaders Wilhelm Liebknecht, August Bebel and Paul Singer and British socialist and labour leaders Robert Cunninghame-Graham, John Burns, Bill Thorne, Ben Cooper, Maxwell and Morrison Davidson, as well as by Engels and the Avelings. Cunninghame-Graham published an account of the meeting, 'Eight Hours "Blokes" in Council', in *People's Press*, No. 40, saying that 'the object of our meeting was to combine the attack against surplus value, to endeavour to bring about friendly relations between the sweated of all nations, and to push on the general eight hours day by legislative action...'.— 77

[91] A draft of this letter, roughly similar in content, also exists. The different readings are indicated in footnotes.— 77

[92] By the Dutch Labour Party Engels means the *Social-Democratic Union of the Netherlands*, founded in 1882, which united all Dutch socialists. In the late 1880s the anarchists and reformists succeeded in building up their influence within the Union. Government reprisals and the sectarian policy of the Union's leaders, in particular Ferdinand Domela Nieuwenhuis, led to a split in the Union and the establishment, in 1894, of the Social-Democratic Labour Party, joined by the remainder of the Social-Democratic Union in 1900.— 77

[93] *The Congress of Hungarian Workers' Organisations* met in Budapest on 7 and 8 December 1890. It was attended by 121 delegates (87 for Budapest and 34 for the provinces). The congress discussed the state of the working-class movement in Hungary, the political condition and rights of the workers, their attitude to social reform, the condition of the agricultural labourers, the role of trade unions and other questions. It

formed a workers' party, which was to be called the Social-Democratic Party of Hungary, and adopted a declaration of principle (the party programme).

Engels did not attend the congress. In reply to the invitation, he sent a message of greetings to the newspapers *Arbeiter-Wochen-Chronik* and *Népszava* (see present edition, Vol. 27, pp. 89-90).— 79

⁹⁴ *Opportunists* — the name given in the early 1880s to the party of moderate republicans in France, which reflected the interests of the big bourgeoisie.— 83

⁹⁵ This letter was first published in English in: K. Marx, F. Engels, V. I. Lenin, *The Communist View on Morality*, Novosti, Moscow, 1974.— 84

⁹⁶ In his preface to the fourth German edition of Volume I of *Capital* in June 1890 (see present edition, Vol. 35) Engels described in detail Marx's 1872 polemic with the German economist Lujo Brentano, who had accused Marx of misquoting a passage from Gladstone's parliamentary speech of 16 April 1863 in reproducing it in the *Inaugural Address of the Working Men's International Association* and in Volume I of *Capital*. Brentano's reaction to Engels' presentation of the case was the pamphlet *Meine Polemik mit Karl Marx*, Berlin, 1890, the introduction to which was published in *Deutsches Wochenblatt*, No. 45, 6 November 1890. On 4 December this journal carried a note containing two passages from Gladstone's letters to Brentano of 22 and 28 November 1890 in which Gladstone asserted that Brentano was right.

Engels replied in a brief article, 'In the Case of Brentano Versus Marx' (*Die Neue Zeit*, 9. Jg., 1890/91, 1. Bd., Nr. 13) and, at greater length, in a pamphlet of the same title, published in April 1891, which contained a large number of documents, including the above-mentioned article (see present edition, Vol. 27).— 85, 90, 93, 95, 103, 132, 146, 148, 158, 163, 172

⁹⁷ Engels presumably means his stay with his family in connection with his mother's death in the autumn of 1873.— 86

⁹⁸ Part of this letter was first published in the journal *Die Gesellschaft*, No. 5, 1932.— 90, 103, 107, 118, 129

⁹⁹ In all likelihood, this refers to Karl Kautsky's letters of 7 and 25 November 1890. The letter of 7 November has not been found. That of 25 November concerned Kautsky's help in the work on Volume IV of *Capital*.— 90

¹⁰⁰ Engels means the manuscript *Theories of Surplus-Value*, the only rough draft, made by Marx in 1862-63, of the concluding — historical and critical — part of *Capital*. In the last few years of his life Engels, realising that he would have no time to prepare it for publication, enlisted the help of Eduard Bernstein and Karl Kautsky. *Theories of Surplus-Value*, virtually the fourth book of *Capital*, was first published by Kautsky in 1905-10.— 90

¹⁰¹ General Seliverstov, chief of the Tsarist secret police in Paris, was killed by the Polish socialist S. Padlewski on 18 November 1890.— 92, 102, 108

¹⁰² Paul Lafargue was in negotiation with the chairman of the Paris municipal council's education board on the organisation of a course in the history of labour. The idea of such a course was first mooted by Marie Édouard Vaillant.— 92

¹⁰³ Laura Lafargue began preparing the second French edition of Marx's *The Poverty of Philosophy. Answer to the 'Philosophy of Poverty' by M. Proudhon* (see present edition, Vol. 6, pp. 105-212) in 1884, but things got stalled. In 1887 Paul Lafargue re-

sumed the negotiations on this edition, however it did not materialise until 1896.—
92

[104] Lafargue gave his version of the Rothschilds' role in the bankruptcy of the Bering Bank in his letter to Engels of 19 November 1890. See F. Engels, P. et L. Lafargue, *Correspondance*, t. II, Paris, 1956, pp. 440-41.— 92

[105] Wilhelm Liebknecht intended to reprint—under the title 'Ein Briefwechsel von 1843'—Marx's correspondence with Arnold Ruge published in the *Deutsch-Französische Jahrbücher* in Paris in 1844 (see present edition, Vol. 3, pp. 133-45).— 94

[106] Wilhelm Liebknecht quotes from Vol. 4 of Heinrich von Sybel's *Die Begründung des deutschen Reiches durch Wilhelm I*, pp. 411-14, where Sybel suggests that Bismarck might be willing to compensate France territorially—a willingness expressed in his pamphlet *Die Emser Depesche oder: Wie Kriege gemacht werden.*— 94

[107] In a letter of 2 December 1890, Sorge asked Engels' permission to make use of his letters in articles for *Neue Zeit.*— 95

[108] After the death of Helene Demuth, Sorge invited Engels to move to his place in Hoboken.— 96, 113

[109] This letter, written in German, has not been found.— 96

[110] In a letter of 23 December 1890, Frankel asked Engels to describe the position in the French working-class movement brought about by the split in the Workers' Party between the revolutionary, Marxist wing, led by Jules Guesde, and the Possibilists (see Note 3).— 96

[111] Engels is mistaken here. Wilhelm Hasselmann was expelled from the Socialist Workers' Party with Johann Most at the Wyden Congress in 1880 for adopting an anarchist stance.— 97

[112] This presumably refers to Frankel's article devoted to Engels' 70th birthday.— 99

[113] This is Engels' reply to the greetings conveyed to him on the occasion of his 70th birthday by the congress of mutual aid funds held in Berlin on 8 to 11 December 1890.— 99

[114] This letter to the Social-Democratic Reichstag deputy Georg Schumacher has reached us in the form of a publication in *Rheinische Zeitung*, No. 47, 24 February 1906, headlined 'Ein Brief von Friedrich Engels'. It is introduced by the following editorial note:

'A copy of a letter from Frederick Engels has been made available to us by the addressee, Comrade Georg Schumacher in Solingen. It is our great fighter's reply to the gift presented to him on the occasion of his 70th birthday. The gift was a knife, a real work of art, made by Comrade Fritz Studer of Solingen.'

The Social-Democratic group in the German Reichstag sent Engels an album with the photos of 35 of its members.— 100

[115] On these events see Engels' article 'Elberfeld', present edition, Vol. 9, pp. 447-49.— 100

[116] Engels means his postcard of 20 December 1890 (see this volume, pp. 94-96), which was his reply to Sorge's letter of 9 December.— 101

[117] In his letter of 2 December 1890 Sorge complained that the Paris newspaper *Le Socialiste* was being sent to him irregularly and asked Engels to pass this on to the French socialist leaders.— 102

[118] This refers to Marx's *Critique of the Gotha Programme* (see present edition, Vol. 24, pp. 75-99), prepared by Engels for publication in the journal *Neue Zeit*. By publishing this programme document of scientific socialism, a model of uncompromising struggle against opportunism, Engels sought to deal a blow at the increasingly active reformist elements in German Social-Democracy. It was especially important to do this in view of the forthcoming Erfurt party congress (see Note 301), which was to adopt a new programme to replace the Gotha one. In having the *Critique* published Engels had to overcome some opposition from the leaders of German Social-Democracy. The publication was deplored by the Social-Democratic group in the Reichstag and the editorial board of *Vorwärts*. At the same time, as Engels had foreseen, Marx's work was welcomed both within the German party itself and by socialists in other countries, who regarded it as a programme document for the entire international socialist movement. The *Critique of the Gotha Programme*, along with Marx's letter to Wilhelm Bracke of 5 May 1875 (see present edition, Vol. 24, pp. 75-99) and Engels' preface, was printed in *Die Neue Zeit*, 9. Jg., 1890/91, 1. Bd., Nr. 18.— 103

[119] See present edition, Vol. 24, pp. 91-92.— 103

[120] This letter to August Bebel (presumably of 15 January 1891) has not been found. As can be seen from Bebel's reply (21 January 1891), Engels had informed him of the forthcoming publication of *Critique of the Gotha Programme* and asked whether he knew of any objections by Marx to the compromise Gotha programme. Bebel answered that he had heard nothing to this effect during his imprisonment (up to 1 April 1875) or thereafter, but had written to Wilhelm Liebknecht from prison saying that the programme would not stand up to criticism and suggesting amendments.— 107

[121] This refers to Wilhelm Liebknecht's report on the programme of German Social-Democracy at the Halle party congress, which met 12 to 18 October 1890 (see Note 12). In discussing the Gotha programme Liebknecht made use of some propositions from Marx's manuscript devoted to it, without mentioning his name.— 107, 134, 176

[122] Stanisław Mendelson was arrested on charges of complicity in Padlewski's case (see Note 101). After an enquiry of several weeks the French authorities, threatening expulsion, compelled Mendelson and his wife to leave France.— 107

[123] Engels means Mendelson's and his wife's presence at a meeting of one of the branches of the Social Democratic Federation (see Note 29), which was reported in *Justice*, No. 364, 3 January 1891 ('Mendelson in London').— 108

[124] On 14 January 1891 *Vorwärts* carried a report by the Berlin correspondent of *The Daily Chronicle* exposing Theodor Reuß as a former police agent. The correspondent referred to an article on Reuß's spying activities published by *Sozialdemokrat* as early as December 1887. There had been another article on the same subject, 'Wie John Neve der preußischen Polizei in die Hände geliefert wurde', in *Sozialdemokrat*, No. 20, 13 May 1887.— 109

¹²⁵ This presumably refers to Jules Guesde's article 'Une interpellation nécessaire', published in *Le Socialiste*, No. 17, 14 January 1891. It said that the Russian secret police had set up a central office in Paris, which was despatching agents to other European cities too.— 110

¹²⁶ A letter headlined 'A Warning' appeared over the signature of Stanisław Mendelson in *Justice* No. 367 on 24 January 1891. It urged English socialists to be on the look-out for possible provocations by agents of the Tsarist secret police in London.— 110

¹²⁷ 'We German Socialists are proud of the fact that we are descended not only from Saint-Simon, Fourier and Owen, but also from Kant, Fichte and Hegel. The German working-class movement is the heir of German classical philosophy. London, 4 January 1891. Frederick Engels.'

Engels presumably made this inscription at the request of Heinrich Scheu, who was working on his portrait in 1891. The first sentence is from the preface to the German edition of *Socialism: Utopian and Scientific* (see present edition, Vol. 24, pp. 457-59), the second concludes Engels' *Ludwig Feuerbach and the End of Classical German Philosophy* (see present edition, Vol. 26, pp. 353-98).

The portrait and inscription were first published in the Sunday supplement to *Arbeiter-Zeitung* of 18 August 1895, in connection with Engels' death.— 110-11

¹²⁸ This letter was found among the leaves of Schorlemmer's unfinished manuscript *Geschichte der Chemie*, on which he had worked in the last few years of his life. Written in German and comprising 650 pages, the manuscript is preserved in the library of Manchester University.— 111

¹²⁹ In his letter of 10 January 1891 Heinrich Scheu informed Engels that, as well as making a woodcarving of Marx, he intended to portray Engels. For this purpose he requested Engels to send him a photograph.— 112

¹³⁰ This letter was first published in English in *Science and Society*, New York, 1948, Vol. 2, No. 3.— 113

¹³¹ This refers to *Pionier. Illustrierter Volks-Kalender für 1891*, New York. The calendar, an annual one, was published by *New Yorker Volkszeitung*. Hermann Schlüter was its editor, F. A. Sorge one of the contributors. As can be seen from Schlüter's letters to Engels of 3 June and 19 November 1890, the calendar for 1891 was to include, with Engels' permission, Marx's biography written by Engels in 1878 (see present edition, Vol. 24, pp. 183-95), with addenda by Schlüter.— 113

¹³² In his letter of 19 November 1890 Hermann Schlüter informed Engels that he had the possibility to buy a set of *The New American Cyclopedia* and asked whether Engels too needed one and whether Marx's articles in the *Cyclopedia* were of a theoretical nature.— 113

¹³³ The *Socialist Labor Party of North America* was formed at the union congress in Philadelphia in 1876 through the merger of the American sections of the First International and other US socialist organisations. The majority of the party members were immigrants (mostly Germans) who had only loose ties with America's native-born workers. Within the party a struggle was going on between the reformist leadership, consisting mostly of Lassalleans, and the Marxist wing, led by

Friedrich Adolph Sorge, an associate of Marx and Engels. The party's proclaimed goal was socialism. However, owing to the sectarian policy of its leaders, who ignored America's mass workers' organisations, above all the trade unions, it failed to become a truly revolutionary mass Marxist party.— 113, 167, 186, 447, 507

[134] This refers to the conflict between the Socialist Labor Party of North America (see Note 133) and the American Federation of Labor (see Note 84), of which Engels had been informed by Sorge in his letters of 9 December 1890 and 16 January 1891 and by Samuel Gompers in a letter of 9 January of the same year. The Socialist Party demanded for itself official representation in the trade unions. Gompers declared on behalf of the Federation's leadership that the Socialist Party, as a political organisation, could not be part of the Federation and proposed that party members should participate in the work of the trade unions as individuals. The Socialist leaders' rejection of the Federation's proposal and their attempts to counterpose the party to what was then the largest US workers' organisation were seen by Engels as a manifestation of sectarianism which objectively strengthened the reformists' influence in the working-class movement.— 113

[135] The *International Socialist Workers' Congress* met in Brussels, 16-22 August 1891. The 337 delegates represented the socialist parties and organisations and numerous trades unions in many European countries and the USA. By a majority vote the congress debarred the anarchists from taking part in its deliberations. Representatives of British trades unions attended. The American delegates included trades unionists, as well as socialists.

The congress discussed labour legislation, strike action and boycott, militarism and the celebration of May Day.

The resolution on the first question called on workers the world over to join forces for the fight against capitalist rule and, where workers possessed political rights, to use these to free themselves from wage slavery. The resolution on strikes and boycott recommended the workers to make use of these methods of struggle and stressed that trades unions were absolutely essential to the workers.

The attitude of the working class to militarism was in the centre of the congress deliberations. Wilhelm Liebknecht's and Edouard Vaillant's reports on this issue and the draft resolution tabled by Liebknecht pointed out that militarism was an inevitable product of the capitalist system, that socialist society alone could put an end to it and bring about international peace and that the socialists were the true party of peace.

The leader of the Dutch Social-Democrats, Ferdinand Domela Nieuwenhuis, who took a semi-anarchist stand, tabled an alternative resolution, under which socialists in all countries should, in the event of war, call on their respective people to proclaim a general strike. The vast majority of the delegates voted for the resolution tabled by Liebknecht.

Referring to the resolutions of the Brussels Congress, Engels pointed out that 'in matters of principle as of tactics the Marxists have been victorious all along the line' (Engels to F. A. Sorge, 2 September 1891).— 114, 155, 161, 164, 171, 211, 214, 221-24, 226, 230, 232-34, 237, 250, 287

[136] In his letters of 3 June and 19 November 1890 Schlüter said he had sent Engels material on the debasement of the silver coinage in the USA.— 114

[137] *Bimetallism* or *dual currency*, is a monetary system using both gold and silver as the standard of value.— 114

[138] Engels means the fourth German edition of Volume I of *Capital* (see present edition, Vol. 35).— 114

[139] In his letter to Engels of 19 November 1890 Schlüter said he had recently read the German translation of Marx's speech, 'The Protectionists, the Free Traders and the Working Class', made in 1846 by Joseph Weydemeyer, a friend and associate of Marx and Engels. The speech was first published in the Belgian newspaper *Atelier démocratique* on 29 September 1847.

In reply to Engels' questions, Schlüter wrote, on 10 March 1891, that Weydemeyer's translation had appeared, alongside that of Marx's 'Speech on the Question of Free Trade' (see present edition, Vol. 6, pp. 450-65) in Hamm in 1848, as a pamphlet entitled *Zwei Reden über die Freihandels- und Schutzzollfrage von Karl Marx*. Schlüter also gave a detailed description of the pamphlet.— 114, 150

[140] The *German Workers' Society* in Brussels was founded by Marx and Engels at the end of August 1847, its aim being to provide a political education for German workers living in Belgium and to spread the ideas of scientific socialism among them. Led by Marx, Engels and their followers, the Society became a legal centre rallying German revolutionary proletarian forces in Belgium and maintaining direct contact with Flemish and Walloon workers' clubs. Its most active members belonged to the Brussels community of the Communist League. The Society played an important part in founding the Brussels Democratic Association. Its activities ceased soon after the February 1848 revolution in France, when its members were arrested and deported by the Belgian police.— 144

[141] This letter was first published in English in: Frederick Engels, Paul and Laura Lafargue, *Correspondence*. Vol. 3. 1891-1895, Foreign Languages Publishing House, Moscow, 1963.— 115, 121, 122, 140, 161, 190, 193, 255, 317, 423, 476, 533

[142] On 30 January 1891 Paul Lafargue wrote to tell Engels that a report in the Paris press said the executive of the German Social-Democratic Party had decided to call on the socialist parties in other countries to put off the celebration of May Day to Sunday, 3 May 1891. Lafargue objected to the postponement and asked Engels to state his opinion of the German socialists' attitude on the matter.— 115

[143] A report in Supplement I to *Vorwärts*, No. 24, 29 January 1891, said that on 28 January 1891 the Social-Democratic group in the Reichstag had decided to recommend that the May Day celebration in Germany should be held on the first Sunday in May. The motives for this were to be explained in a special address of the group (see Note 163).— 115

[144] Engels' letter to Richard Fischer mentioned here is not extant. Fischer's answer, written on 4 February 1891, is quoted by Engels in his letter to Paul Lafargue of 6 February (see this volume, pp. 120-22).— 116

[145] This refers to Charles Bonnier's letter to Engels of 18 January 1891 stating that the French socialists intended to celebrate May Day on 1 May.— 116

[146] Engels refers to the various trends within the socialist movement in France.

The *Marxist trend*, headed by Jules Guesde (hence its other name, Guesdists) and Paul Lafargue, was represented by the Workers' Party, founded in 1879. From the outset this trend was torn by a sharp ideological struggle, as a result of which the party, at its St.-Étienne Congress in 1882, split up into two groups— the Guesdists and the Possibilists (or Broussists). The Guesdists retained the name of Workers' Party. Its programme, adopted at the Havre Congress in 1880, was drawn up with the participation of Marx. The Guesdists' strongholds were France's industrial centres. More specifically, they relied on individual groups of workers at the large plants of Paris. The party saw one of its principal tasks in winning the backing of the working masses. In the 1880s and 90s it achieved a measure of success in propagating Marxist ideas among France's workers. An important role in this was played by *Le Socialiste*, the party's newspaper. Marxists were active in the trades unions and led the workers' strike struggle. The party mounted a large-scale campaign in support of Paul Lafargue, whose election to the Chamber of Deputies in 1891 was a major success for the French socialists. The party also did a great deal to promote international socialist ties and expose the aggressive nature of the foreign policy of the French bourgeois republic, in particular of the 1891-93 Franco-Prussian alliance.

But the party's leaders did not always pursue a consistently Marxist policy and made opportunistic mistakes, particularly on the peasant question in the 1890s. Marx and Engels criticised them on various issues, helping them to work out a correct line for the working-class movement.

For the *Possibilists* (or Broussists) — see Note 3.— 116

[147] The *radicals* were a parliamentary group in France in the 1880s and 90s which had split away from the bourgeois party of moderate republicans (the 'opportunists' or 'Gambettists'). They continued to uphold a number of bourgeois-democratic demands virtually dropped by the republicans: abolition of the Senate, separation of the Church from the State, introduction of a progressive income tax, and others. They also demanded a limitation of the working day, pensions for the disabled, and other socio-economic measures. In 1901 the radicals set up a party of their own. It spoke, above all, for the middle and petty bourgeoisie.— 116, 289, 291, 297, 320, 330, 360

[148] Presumably an allusion to the leading article, 'Zum 1. Mai 1891', published in *Arbeiter-Zeitung*, No. 2, 9 January 1891.— 117

[149] In his 'Briefe aus Frankreich' ('Letters from France'), published in *Vorwärts*, Nos 23 and 25 on 28 and 30 January 1891, Jules Guesde exposed the policy of the moderate bourgeois republicans (the 'opportunists') led by Jean Antoine Constans, Pierre Maurice Rouvier and others. He showed that it aimed at suppressing the working-class movement in the country and compromised the republic.— 117, 130

[150] Engels means the article 'L'Avortement' (from the series 'Hygiène capitaliste') published by Paul Lafargue under the pen-name *Dr. Z.* in *Le Socialiste*, No. 17, 14 January 1891. Lafargue exposes the hypocrisy of the bourgeois judiciary, using as an illustration the trial of Fouroux, the Mayor of Toulon, and V. Jonquières, his

mistress, whom Fouroux had compelled to have an abortion, then banned by law.— 117

[151] Marx's *Critique of the Gotha Programme* was reprinted, without Engels' preface, in supplements to the newspaper *Vorwärts*, Nos 27 and 28, 1 and 3 February 1891 from *Die Neue Zeit*, 9. Jg., 1890/91, 1. Bd., Nr. 18.— 118

[152] This refers to the attempt by Wilhelm Liebknecht and other leaders of German Social-Democracy to prevent the distribution of No. 18 of *Die Neue Zeit*, which contained Marx's *Critique of the Gotha Programme* (see this volume, pp. 126 and 181). For the *Anti-Socialist Law* see Note 11.— 118

[153] The Editors are not in possession of the original of this letter.— 118, 129, 171, 289, 301, 303, 304, 305, 323, 329, 335, 342, 360, 372, 491, 492, 496, 501, 506, 543, 544

[154] The *People's Party* in Germany was formed in 1865. It consisted of petty bourgeois and bourgeois-democratic elements and was predominantly active in the South German states of Württemberg, Baden and Bavaria. The party put forward general democratic demands and opposed Prussian hegemony in Germany. Expressing the particularist attitude of certain German states, it advocated a German federation and rejected unity in the form of a centralised democratic republic.— 119, 180, 268

[155] In the autumn of 1878 the German Reichstag discussed a bill on import duties. In July 1879, new customs tariffs imposing considerably higher duties on industrial and agricultural imports were introduced.— 121

[156] In his letter to Engels of 7 February 1891 Paul Lafargue spoke of the German socialists' inconsistency in the matter of the 1891 May Day celebration: at the 1889 Paris International Socialist Workers' Congress (see Note 51) they had unanimously voted for having the May Day celebrations generally on May 1st, even though the Anti-Socialist Law was still in force then; now, after its repeal, they intended to have the celebration on May 3rd.— 122

[157] Paul Lafargue had told Engels (in his letter of 7 February 1891) that *Le Socialiste*, the organ of the Workers' Party, was rapidly increasing its readership.— 123

[158] In his letter of 7 February 1891 Lafargue had asked for Engels' opinion of his article, 'La propriété féodale', published under the pen-name Fergus in *La Nouvelle Revue* of 1 February 1891.— 123

[159] During the November 1885 parliamentary elections Hyndman and Champion accepted money from the leadership of the Conservative Party to finance the campaign of the Social Democratic Federation.— 124, 127

[160] An excerpt from this letter was first published in English in *The Labour Monthly*, No. 6, 1934.— 125, 224, 231, 250

[161] On 6 February 1891, the Vienna *Arbeiter-Zeitung*, No. 6, reported from Berlin, in the column 'Deutschland', that a document of great theoretical and practical importance, Marx's critique of the programme adopted by the German party at its 1875 Gotha Congress, had been published by Engels in Germany. Speaking of the service rendered by Engels, the author of the report, Adolf Braun, pointed out: 'The time has come to formulate the theoretical foundations of our party with full

clarity and uncompromisingly, so the present publication is very timely indeed.'—
126, 129

¹⁶² On 13 February 1891 *Vorwärts* (No. 37) carried a leading article, 'Der Marx'sche Programm-Brief', written by Wilhelm Liebknecht, in which the Reichstag Social-Democratic group expressed disagreement with the assessment of the Gotha programme and Lassalle's role given in Marx's *Critique*.— 126, 130, 135, 137, 146, 148, 166, 176

¹⁶³ The proclamation 'Parteigenossen!', issued by the Reichstag Social-Democratic group, was published in *Vorwärts*, No. 31, on 6 February 1891. The group urged the German workers to observe May Day on May 3rd rather than May 1st and, to substantiate its stand, cited the relevant resolution of the Paris International Socialist Workers' Congress (see Note 51) which said that 'workers in different countries will have to organise the celebration in a form suitable to the local conditions'. Engels criticised the proclamation for the tendency, manifest in it, to fix the first Sunday of May as the official day for the workers' May Day celebrations for all time.— 127

¹⁶⁴ The *Union of Gas Workers and General Labourers*, Britain's first trades union of unskilled workers, was set up in late March-early April 1889, against the background of the rising strike movement of the 1880s and 90s. Eleanor Marx-Aveling and Edward Aveling played an important role in organising and leading the union. It put forward the demand for an eight-hour working day and within a short time became very influential among large sections of the working class. About 100,000 gas workers joined it during the first year. The union gave great help in organising the famous London dock strike in 1889 (see Note 198). The strike and the Gas Union's activities gave rise to the Dockers' Union, another large organisation of unskilled workers, which in its turn contributed significantly to the establishment of more mass trades unions, to the fight for the eight-hour day and to the organisation of May Day demonstrations of British workers in the 1890s.

The gas workers readily responded to socialist and internationalist ideas, preached to them above all by Eleanor Marx-Aveling, and exerted an important influence on the labour movement in Ireland, where they initiated mass trades unions embracing, among others, farm labourers. The National Union of Gas Workers and General Labourers of Great Britain and Ireland (the union's full name) maintained links with workers' organisations in other countries. Eleanor Marx-Aveling and William Thorne represented it as delegates at the International Socialist Workers' Congress in Brussels (see Note 135).— 128, 138, 167, 197, 219, 225, 300, 313, 367, 371, 403, 557, 560

¹⁶⁵ This refers to Kautsky's letters of 6 and 9 February 1891, in which he informed Engels of reactions in Social-Democratic circles to the publication of *Critique of the Gotha Programme* in *Neue Zeit* and of Bebel and Liebknecht's attempt to prevent the publication.— 129

¹⁶⁶ The article in question, headlined 'Zur Kritik des sozialdemokratischen Programms' (*Hamburger Echo*, No. 33, 8 February 1891), noted the importance of Marx's programmatic letter, published by Engels, for the working out of German Social-Democracy's new programme.— 129, 331

¹⁶⁷ Engels' mention of the *system of acquired rights* is an allusion to Lassalle's work of the

same title, *Das System der erworbenen Rechte. Eine Versöhnung des positiven Rechts und der Rechtsphilosophie.* In zwei Theilen. Leipzig, 1861. For an assessment of this work see present edition, Vol. 41, pp. 330-31.— 129

[168] This article by Paul Lafargue, intended for *Neue Zeit*, did not appear in it. In his letter to Engels of 6 February Kautsky characterised it as slipshod and containing serious mistakes, and asked what he should do with it. The article was published later in *La Revue socialiste*, t. XVI, No. 93, 1892, under the title 'La théorie de la valeur et de la plus-value de Marx et les économistes bourgeois'. For Engels' assessment of it see this volume, pp. 140-42.— 129, 141, 159, 174

[169] This refers to August Bebel's, Wilhelm Liebknecht's and Paul Singer's stay in London, from 27 November to early December 1890, as Engels' guests on the occasion of his seventieth birthday (see also Note 90).— 130

[170] This refers to a letter from Bebel to Kautsky, which the latter had enclosed with his letter to Engels of 18 February. As can be seen from Kautsky's comments, Bebel said in his letter that the publication of *Critique of the Gotha Programme* had evoked a negative reaction in the party.— 131

[171] *Die Neue Zeit* (9. Jg., 1890/91, 1. Bd., Nr. 21) reprinted the leading article from *Vorwärts*, No. 37, 13 February 1891 (see Note 162), adding a brief introduction and the following note: 'It is a fact that we of course did not feel obliged to submit Marx's letter for approval to the party leadership or the parliamentary group..., but it is also a fact that we made no secret of our intention to publish it. The responsibility for the publication is ours entirely.'— 132, 133, 146

[172] This letter was first published in English in: K. Marx, *Critique of the Gotha Programme*, Lawrence & Wishart, London, 1933.— 133

[173] For the reaction of the Vienna *Arbeiter-Zeitung* see Note 161.
    The *Sächsische Arbeiter-Zeitung* reprinted Marx's work in its Nos 30, 31, 33 and 35; 6, 7, 10 and 12 February 1891, with an editorial introductory note emphasising the special significance of this programmatic letter for German Social-Democracy.
    Züricher Post, No. 34, 10 February 1891, carried an editorial (written by Franz Mehring) headlined 'Hängen und Würgen', which stressed that the publication of Marx's work testified to the strength and fighting spirit of German Social-Democracy which, with the objectivity and self-criticism characteristic of it, sought to clarify for itself the goals of its struggle.— 133

[174] This refers to Countess Sophie Hatzfeldt's divorce suit, conducted by Lassalle from 1846 to 1854.— 134

[175] In a letter of 20 February 1891 Richard Fischer informed Engels of the party Executive's decision to bring out new editions of Marx's *The Civil War in France* and *Wage Labour and Capital* and Engels' *Socialism: Utopian and Scientific* and asked Engels to write prefaces to these works.— 136

[176] This is an excerpt from Engels' reply—which has not survived—to Antonio Labriola's letter of 21 February 1891 conveying the request by the anarchist German poet John Henry Mackay, a devotee of the German Young Hegelian philosopher Max Stirner and collector of his works, to be allowed to familiarise himself with Marx and Engels' unpublished manuscript on Stirner, i. e. with *The German Ideology.*

The bulk of it is made up of the section 'Saint Max', which is a critique of Stirner's work *Der Einzige und sein Eigenthum*, published in 1844.

The German Ideology was first published, in German, in *MEGA*, Erste Abteilung, Band 5, Moscow-Leningrad, 1933 (present edition, Vol. 5, pp. 19-539).— 136

177 An excerpt from this letter was first published in English in: K. Marx and F. Engels, *Letters on 'Capital'*, New Park, London, 1983.— 137, 314, 322, 389, 525

178 In 1891 the Executive of the Social-Democratic Party of Germany decided to publish the collected works of Ferdinand Lassalle. They appeared under the title *Reden und Schriften. Neue Gesammt-Ausgabe. Mit einer biographischen Einleitung herausgegeben von Ed. Bernstein*, London, vols I-III, Berlin, 1892-93. In his introduction, entitled 'Ferdinand Lassalle und seine Bedeutung in der Geschichte der Sozialdemokratie', Bernstein gave a by and large correct assessment of Lassalle's role in the German working-class movement and provided a critical analysis of his theoretical views and political line. In his later edition of Lassalle's works Bernstein changed his views.— 138, 203, 253, 316, 331

179 Engels means the slander campaign against him launched by Hyndman in connection with the publication of *Critique of the Gotha Programme*. In February 1891 Hyndman published several items in the newspaper *Justice* describing Engels as the leader of 'the Marxist clique' engaged in plotting and intrigues fraught with the danger of a split. Hyndman supported the stand taken by the Reichstag Social-Democratic group and the editorial board of *Vorwärts* in regard of the publication of Marx's work (see Note 162).

To prevent Edward Aveling's nomination in Northampton (see this volume, pp. 120, 123-24, 126-27) Hyndman publicised in *Justice* the slanderous accusations levelled at Aveling by the Executive Committee of the Socialist Labor Party of North America ('The Northampton Election', 'Dr Aveling?', 'Dr Aveling Again') (see Note 133). The Committee, which had financed a US lecture tour by Edward Aveling, Eleanor Marx-Aveling and Wilhelm Liebknecht in September-December 1886, had charged Aveling with excessive expenditure and the forging of bills.— 138, 140, 155

180 Wilhelm Rosenberg and his followers pursued a sectarian policy underestimating the party's work in America's mass labour organisations, above all in the trades unions. In September 1889 they were removed from the leadership of the Socialist Labor Party of North America.— 138

181 In February 1891 Victoria, the widow of the German Emperor Frederick III, paid an unofficial visit to Paris. Nominally private, the visit pursued a specific political purpose— to bring about a rapprochement between Germany and France predicated on the latter's recognition of the results of the Franco-Prussian war, i. e. its giving up Alsace-Lorraine. The very fact of Victoria's sudden appearance in Paris (the visit had not been agreed with the French government), her demonstrative pilgrimages to sites associated with German military victories, hurt the national feelings of the French and provoked anti-German demonstrations. The visit caused a serious Franco-German diplomatic conflict.— 140

182 Engels was informed of the Broussists' (see Note 3) adhesion to the committee set up by the Marxists to organise a joint demonstration in Paris on 1 May 1891 by

Paul Lafargue (letter of 5 March 1891) and Charles Bonnier (letter of 4 March).—
140

[183] See present edition, Vol. 29, pp. 292-302.— 141

[184] This is Engels' summary of his answer to French journalist Henri Ravé's letter of
3 March 1891, jotted down by Engels on this letter. In his message, written at Paul
Lafargue's advice, Ravé informed Engels that he had completed a translation into
French of August Bebel's work *Die Frau in der Vergangenheit, Gegenwart und Zukunft*,
and asked Engels' permission to translate into French *The Origin of the Family,
Private Property and the State*. To form an idea of Ravé as a translator, Engels request-
ed him to send some proofs of the French version of Bebel's work.
Engels' letter proper is not extant.— 142

[185] This text was written by Engels on a postcard. The part of it which bore the stamp
is missing, some of the words are damaged.— 142

[186] Along with his letter of 26 August 1891 the Italian socialist Pasquale Martignetti
sent Engels a copy of the journal *Critica Sociale*, No. 3, 20 February 1891, containing a notice on the forthcoming issue, by Fantuzzi Publishers, Milan, of a new
Italian translation of the *Manifesto of the Communist Party*.— 142

[187] In his letter of 23 February 1891 Filippo Turati asked Engels' permission to translate and publish in Italian a number of works by Marx and Engels. He also approved, on the whole, of the publication of Marx's *Critique of the Gotha Programme* in
Neue Zeit.— 143

[188] Engels was corresponding secretary for Italy on the General Council of the International in 1871-72 and the General Council's provisional representative for Italy
in 1873. He visited Lombardy between May and mid-September 1841, on a tour
of North Italy. He described his impressions in the essay 'Wanderings in Lombardy', published in the journal *Athenäum*, Nos 48 and 49, 4 and 11 December
1841 (see present edition, Vol. 2, pp. 170-80).— 143

[189] The following notes are Engels' summary of his reply to a letter from Ravé of
8 March 1891, jotted down by Engels on this letter. In his letter, Ravé acknowledged receipt of Engels' letter of 6 March 1891. He wrote that he was enclosing with
his letter two proof sheets of his translation of August Bebel's *Die Frau in der Vergangenheit, Gegenwart und Zukunft*, which Engels had requested, and asked about Engels'
terms regarding the proposed translation into French of *The Origin of the Family,
Private Property and the State*. In his answer Engels suggested that Ravé should make
a trial translation of several pages from Chapter IX of this work.
Engels' letter itself is not extant.— 144

[190] The passages indicated by Engels will be found on pp. 256, 272 and 273 of Vol. 26
of the present edition.— 144, 154

[191] An excerpt from this letter was first published in German in the journal *Die Gesellschaft*, No. 5, 1932; the first—partial—English publication was in: Karl
Marx and Frederick Engels, *Letters on 'Capital'*, New Park, London, 1983.— 145

[192] In his letter to Engels of 9 January 1891 Karl Kautsky related a curious episode:
the translator of Oscar Peschel's book, *Völkerkunde* (*The Races of Man, and their
Geographical Distribution*, New York, 1876), had rendered the phrase 'blüthenlose

Pflanzen' (cryptogams) as 'organisms, devoid of blood such as plants' (the translator confused the German word 'Blüthen' [blossoms] with 'Blut' [blood]).— 146

193 In his letter to Engels of 2 March 1891 Sorge condemned the mistaken stand taken by the Social-Democratic group in the German Reichstag and by the editorial board of *Vorwärts* in regard of the publication of *Critique of the Gotha Programme* (see notes 118 and 162) but added: 'Only do not get involved in any further debates with these lads, you have more important things to do.'— 146, 148

194 This presumably refers to the article, 'Marx' Kritik des Parteiprogramms', published in *New Yorker Volkszeitung*, No. 51, 28 February 1891. It condemned the attitude taken by *Vorwärts* on the publication of Marx's *Critique of the Gotha Programme* (see Note 162) and emphasised the vast importance of this work.— 146

195 In his letter of 10 March 1891 Hermann Schlüter, describing the position in the Socialist Labor Party of North America (see Note 133), noted the weakness of its links with the mass working-class organisations. This, he said, had a negative effect on the strike struggle, in particular that of the building workers.— 149

196 The *London Trades Council* (the Council of all London Trades Unions) was formed in May 1860 at a conference of various London trades unions. The Council was composed of the leaders of the biggest ones. In the earlier half of the 1860s it headed the workers' campaigns against British intervention in the USA and in support of Poland and Italy. Later it fought for the legalisation of the unions. In the early 1890s the Council, which embraced mostly old-established unions, opposed the movement for the formation of new ones and for the eight-hour working day, but popular pressure compelled it to take part in the May Day demonstrations.— 150, 155, 167, 185, 323, 370, 380, 386, 402, 559, 560

197 Part of this letter was first published in German in: Friedrich Engels, *Politisches Vermächtnis. Aus unveröffentlichten Briefen*, Berlin, 1920; an excerpt first appeared in English in: Karl Marx and Frederick Engels, *Letters on 'Capital'*, New Park, London, 1983.— 151

198 The *London dock strike*, 12 August to 14 September 1889, was a landmark in the British working-class movement of the late 19th century. It involved 30,000 dockers and over 30,000 workers of other trades; the majority of the strikers were unskilled labourers not belonging to any trades union. Thanks to their fortitude and good organisation, the strikers secured satisfaction of their demands for higher wages and better working conditions. The action promoted working-class solidarity (about £50,000 was raised for the strike fund) and organisation; a dockers' union and several large unskilled workers' unions were set up; in 1890 the overall number of trades unions more than doubled (see Note 164).— 152, 186, 225

199 Laura Lafargue undertook to edit the French translation of Engels' *The Origin of the Family, Private Property and the State*, made by the French socialist Henri Ravé. She invested a great deal of effort to improve Ravé's translation. Engels looked through the edited translation and admired her work. The French edition came out in 1893.— 154, 201, 215, 251

200 The *Legal Eight Hours and International Labour League* was founded in 1890, with Engels' participation, by a group of British socialists led by Edward and Eleanor Aveling. Based on the committee which had organised the first May Day demonstration in England (1890), the League saw its task in obtaining the eight-hour

working day and other legislative measures tending towards the ultimate emancipation of the working classes and in implementing the resolutions of the Paris Congress of the Second International (see Note 51). It organised the British workers' May Day demonstrations in 1891 and 1892, which were also held under the slogan of the eight-hour day. League representatives took part in organising (1893) the Independent Labour Party of Britain (see Note 515).— 155, 167, 380, 386, 403

201 Paul Lafargue acknowledged receipt of this information in his letter to Engels of 30 March 1891. Paul and Laura Lafargue gave Engels detailed information on the preparations for the May Day demonstration in France in their letters of 5 and 30 March and 9 and 18 April 1891.— 155

202 Engels was sending Mendelson a copy of the letter from J. Wierzejski of 28 March 1891, written from Nice on the instructions of the sick Walery Wróblewski. The writer informed Engels of the gravity of Wróblewski's material conditions and asked Engels to remind Mendelson to return the money he owed Wróblewski.— 156

203 Bebel had corresponded with Engels from May 1873. He first met Marx and Engels in December 1880, when he visited London with Eduard Bernstein and Paul Singer to discuss questions relating to the editing of *Sozialdemokrat* with them.— 158

204 An allusion to the fact that Engels had published Marx's *Critique of the Gotha Programme* without having advised Bebel in advance.— 158

205 In his letter to Engels of 30 March 1891 Bebel said that he was prepared to forget the conflict that had developed between the two over the publication of *Critique of the Gotha Programme* (see also Note 232).— 158

206 Engels' Introduction appeared in *Die Neue Zeit*, 9. Jg., 1890/91, 2. Bd., Nr. 28, under the heading 'Ueber den Bürgerkrieg in Frankreich', with this editorial note: 'Following is the Introduction to the third edition—due to be put out shortly by the publishing house of our central organ—of the *Address of the General Council of the International on "the Civil War in France"*. The Address was written by Karl Marx. Thanks to Engels' kindness we are in a position to print his Introduction in *Neue Zeit*.'— 159

207 In his letter of 11 March 1891 Pasquale Martignetti asked Engels' permission to bring out a new Italian edition, in Fantuzzi's publishing house in Milan, of Engels' *Socialism: Utopian and Scientific* and *The Origin of the Family, Private Property and the State* in the series The Socialist's Popular Library. In sending Engels a copy of the Italian edition of the *Manifesto of the Communist Party* published by Fantuzzi, Martignetti drew his attention to the preface, the author of which, the anarchist Gori, had interpreted the work of Marx and Engels in the spirit of his own views.— 159

208 The 1883 Italian edition of *Socialism: Utopian and Scientific* contains no sketch of Engels' life. Engels probably means the biography published in the 1885 Italian edition of *The Origin of the Family, Private Property and the State* (see also this volume, p. 161).— 159

209 This letter has reached us in the form of a rough draft written by Engels on Fantuzzi's letter of 18 March 1891. Fantuzzi was asking Engels' permission to reprint *Socialism: Utopian and Scientific* in Italian and requested him to send a sketch of his life, which was to open the planned edition. The work in question appeared in

Martignetti's translation in Milan in 1892. Engels' letter proper is not extant.— 160

210 In his letter of 30 March 1891 Paul Lafargue informed Engels of the Allemanists' (see Note 53) reluctance to admit the Broussists (see Note 3) to the Marxists' committee in charge of May Day preparations.— 161

211 The French political writer Hippolite Buffenoir had been invited to contribute to *Vorwärts*, organ of the German Social-Democratic Party, and did so from October to December 1877. In a letter to Johann Philipp Becker of 11 January 1878 Engels described Buffenoir as a shady character playing no role whatever among the Paris workers (see present edition, Vol. 45).— 162

212 This refers to the attempt, staged in Sofia on 27 March 1891, on the life of Stephan Stambulov, head of the Bulgarian government, in which Minister of Finance Belchev, who was accompanying him, was killed. Stambulov oriented his foreign policy on Austria-Hungary and opposed Russian interference in Bulgarian affairs. The assassination was widely commented upon in the democratic press, which traced it to Russian diplomatic intrigues and the increased danger of war.— 162

213 In his letter of 30 March 1891 Lafargue informed Engels that the Allemanists (see Note 53) had tried to oppose the Guesdists (Marxists) in a number of places in the provinces. Members of the Workers' Party in Rouen published a letter protesting against the Allemanists' line. The letter appeared in *Le Parti Ouvrier* of 10 and 11 March 1891, not in *Le Socialiste*, as Lafargue had mistakenly told Engels.— 163

214 In his letter to Engels of 5 April 1891 Kautsky wrote to say that Conrad Schmidt had declined an invitation to join the editorial board of *Neue Zeit*.— 163

215 Engels means the article by Karl Kautsky and Wilhelm Eichhoff, 'Wie Brentano Marx vernichtet', published in *Die Neue Zeit*, 9. Jg., 1890/91, 2. Bd., Nr. 32. It was a review of the fourth German edition of Volume I of *Capital* and of Engels' work *In the Case of Brentano Versus Marx* (see present edition, Vol. 27).— 163

216 In his letter to Engels of 5 April 1891 Kautsky said he was afraid Lafargue had not written for *Neue Zeit* for a long time because the journal had failed to publish his article on pre-Marxian theories of value (see Note 168).— 164

217 This letter has reached us in the form of a rough draft written by Engels on Henri Ravé's letter to him of 1 April 1891. Engels' letter proper is not extant. — 165

218 An excerpt from this letter was first published in English in *The Socialist Review*, London, March-August, 1908.— 165

219 In a letter of 2 April 1891, Paul Singer, chairman of the Executive of the Social-Democratic Party of Germany, advised Engels of August Bebel's forthcoming silver wedding (6 April 1891) and asked Engels to send his congratulations.
For Bebel's letter mentioned here (written on 30 March), see Note 232.— 166

220 The *International Miners' Congress*, held in Paris from 31 March to 4 April 1891, was attended by 99 delegates from 5 countries, representing about 900,000 (according to other sources, 600,000) workers. It resolved to set up an international association of miners and elected a commission to draw up its Rules. There was a heated debate over the proposal of the Belgian delegation that a general miners' strike should be called internationally to press the demand for an eight-hour working

day. There was strong opposition to this, particularly from the British delegation, which insisted that the vote on this issue should be based on the number of workers represented by each delegation. The congress voted for a general strike in principle, but contrary to the Belgians' proposal refused to call one immediately.— 168, 171

221 In his letter of 8 April 1891 Heinrich Scheu had asked Engels to send him a sample of Marx's signature, which he intended to reproduce under the portrait of Marx he was working on at the time.— 170

222 Leo Frankel had requested Engels (letter of 16 April 1891) to write an article for the May Day issue of *Bataille*, a Left radical newspaper published by the French historian Prosper Olivier Lissagaray.— 171

223 An allusion to the *Society of the Rights of Man and Citizen*, whose offices were in the Rue Cadet, Paris. It was founded by the radicals (see Note 147) and moderate republicans on 25 May 1888 to combat the common danger, Boulangism. Eventually the Possibilists (see Note 3) joined it, too.— 171, 289

224 The reference is to Heinrich Cunow's article 'Die altperuanischen Dorf- und Markgenossenschaften', published in the journal *Das Ausland*, Nos 42-44, 20 and 27 October and 3 November 1890, of which Kautsky had informed Engels in his letter of 5 April 1891. Engels made use of Cunow's article in preparing the fourth edition of *The Origin of the Family, Private Property and the State*.— 173, 198, 368

225 What follows is, presumably, an excerpt from Engels' letter to Henri Ravé of 7 April 1891, which is not extant in full (see this volume, p. 165).— 173

226 This refers to the *Instructions for the Delegates of the Provisional General Council. The Different Questions* (see present edition, Vol. 20, pp. 185-94) drawn up by Marx for the delegates to the Geneva Congress of the First International (3 to 8 September 1866). In connection with the discussion on the programme of German Social-Democracy, Kautsky offered to publish the *Instructions* in *Neue Zeit*, along with the programme of the French Workers' Party, the theoretical introduction to which had been written by Karl Marx (see present edition, Vol. 24, pp. 340 and 638). In his letter of 25 April Kautsky suggested that Engels might write the commentary and notes to the projected publication.— 174

227 Engels probably has in mind the leading article on the miners' strike (see Note 228), headlined 'Sie haben's erreicht!', and the article 'Der Streik der Bergarbeiter', published in *Vorwärts*, respectively No. 96, 26 April, and No. 97, 28 April 1891.— 174, 182

228 The miners' strike in question started spontaneously in the Ruhr on 16 April 1891, spreading eventually to almost the whole of the Rhine-Westphalia coal region. The strikers' main demands were for higher wages and an eight-hour working day. The strike ended in defeat for the workers at the beginning of May. In his letter of 25 April Kautsky criticised the stand taken by *Vorwärts*, which was demoralising the strikers by predicting their defeat.— 174, 182

229 In his letter of 25 April 1891 Kautsky told Engels that, writing to him, Paul Lafargue had remarked critically on *Neue Zeit* after it had become a weekly, pointing

out that it was carrying few serious and independent articles. Kautsky also said he intended to order Lafargue an article on Émile Zola.— 174

230 In his letter of 25 April Kautsky asked for Engels' opinion of the US militia system and expressed the view that the Social-Democrats must favour conscription and the universal arming of the people.— 175

231 Part of this letter was first published in English in: K. Marx, F. Engels, V. I. Lenin, *The Communist View on Morality*, Novosti, Moscow, 1974.— 175, 377

232 In his letter of 30 March 1891 Bebel, explaining his long silence, said that he had been reluctant to write immediately after the publication of Marx's letter to Bracke of 5 May 1875 concerning the party programme because he had been put out by the manner of publication, and later he had been kept busy by Reichstag matters. Bebel considered the publication ill-advised because, in his opinion, Marx's letter concerned not the programme but the party leadership. Its publication, he said, had provided a weapon to the enemies of socialism, and the sharp criticism of Lassalle was incomprehensible to young party members and offensive to former Lassalleans now belonging to the party.

In his letter of 25 April Bebel informed Engels about the state of the working-class movement in Germany, in particular, about the strike of the Rhine-Westphalian miners (see Note 228). He considered the strike ill-timed because under the obtaining economic crisis it was being exploited by the mine owners to prevent a decline in the price of coal.— 175

233 This assertion was contained in a report published in the column 'Politische Uebersicht', *Vorwärts*, No. 48, 26 February 1891.— 176

234 A leading article in *Vorwärts*, No. 37, 13 February 1891 (see Note 162) maintained that the addressees of Marx's letter on the Gotha Programme had replied to his recommendations with a 'categorical no'.— 179

235 Engels means the refrain of Jacob Audorf's *Lied der deutschen Arbeiter* (Arbeiter-Marseillaise), written in 1864: 'Nicht zählen wir den Feind, nicht die Gefahren all! Der kühnen Bahn nur folgen wir, die uns geführt Lassalle!' ('We do not count the foes, the dangers—not at all! We boldly forge ahead along the path shown by Lassalle!').— 180

236 This refers to the revelations concerning the *Guelphic Fund*, which had far-reaching repercussions in Germany and caused a scandal in government circles.

The Fund, set up by the former Hanover royal court and, at the time in question, managed by Bismarck, was used to bribe the press. In March 1891 it became known that State Secretary Bötticher had received 360,000 marks out of it to pay the debts of his father-in-law, Bismarck. In this connection *Vorwärts* published a number of articles exposing corruption within the ruling classes (Nos 70, 71 and 74; 24, 25 and 29 March 1891).— 182, 504

237 At *Sedan*, one of the major battles of the Franco-Prussian war was fought on 1 and 2 September 1870. It ended in the rout of the French forces. Under the peace treaty signed in Frankfurt am Main on 10 May 1871 France ceded Alsace and East Lorraine to Germany and undertook to pay an indemnity of 5,000 million francs. The Alsace-Lorraine question was a permanent cause of Franco-German friction and international tension in the 1880s and 90s.— 182

[238] Engels means the speeches made by the Social-Democratic deputies, above all August Bebel, Paul Singer and Wilhelm Liebknecht, in the Reichstag in February and April 1891 in the course of the debate on a bill to amend the trades regulations. The bill was part of the Prussian government's 'labour protection legislation'. The Social-Democratic group voted against the bill in its third reading. Bebel criticised the bill and analysed the Social-Democrats' counterproposals in an article headlined 'Die Gewerbeordnungs-Novelle', published in *Die Neue Zeit*, 9. Jg., 1890/91, 2. Bd., Nr. 37-39.— 182

[239] This form of May Day demonstration had been decided upon by the congress of the French Workers' Party in Lille, 11-12 October 1890 (see Note 38) and endorsed by the congress of French trade unions in Calais, 13-18 October 1890 (see Note 56).— 183, 189

[240] During the 1891 May Day demonstration and meeting in London, held on May 3, Engels was on Platform 6, as reporter for *Neue Zeit*. Evidence of this is his press ticket, reproduced in this volume on p. 187.— 185

[241] Engels quotes the dictum 'c'est magnifique, mais ce n'est pas la guerre' ('magnificent, but this is not war'), which is attributed to the French general (subsequently marshal) Pierre Bosquet. He is supposed to have used it to characterise the reckless, self-destructive bravery of the British cavalry in the famous charge of the light brigade at Balaklava in the Crimean War.— 189

[242] This refers to the German *Freisinnige* (Freethinkers') Party, formed in 1884 as a result of the merger of the Party of Progress (see Note 296) with the Left wing of the National Liberals (see Note 414). The *Freisinnige* spoke for the middle and petty bourgeoisie and opposed the ruling quarters on certain matters.— 189

[243] During the 1891 May Day demonstration in the town of Fourmies, Département du Nord, France, arrests were made among the marchers. As a result, another demonstration, demanding the release of the detainees gathered in front of the Town Hall. Troops opened fire on the demonstration without warning, injuring 30 and killing 10 people, including women and children.
   On the subsequent persecution of socialists see Note 275.— 191, 293, 297

[244] On 18 May 1891 Paul Lafargue informed Engels that he had sent a letter of protest to *Le Temps*, which on 14 May had reprinted (from the provincial newspaper *Observateur d'Avesnes*) distorted excerpts from speeches he and Hippolyte Culine had made in the course of the pre-May Day agitation in Fourmies. *Le Temps* did not publish the letter, it appeared in *Le Socialiste*, No. 36, 27 May 1891.— 191

[245] Engels presumably means the miners' general strike in Charleroi, Liège, Mons, Borinage and other industrial centers of Belgium started in early May 1891. The strikers' principal demands were universal suffrage, the eight-hour working day and higher wages. The strike, involving about 100,000 miners and a large number of steel workers, lasted for several weeks. In some areas strikers clashed with government troops. Although supported by miners abroad, the walkout failed. However, the struggle for universal suffrage continued. It was introduced in Belgium on 12 April 1893.— 191

[246] Speaking in the Chamber of Deputies on 8 May 1891, Georges Benjamin Clemen-

ceau demagogically demanded an amnesty for the May Day demonstrators (see Note 243).— 191

[247] *The Second Congress of the National Union of Gas Workers and General Labourers of Great Britain and Ireland* (see Note 164) met in Dublin on 17 May 1891. Eleanor Marx-Aveling and Edward Aveling played an important part in preparing and holding it. The Congress decided that the Union should take part in the forthcoming International Socialist Workers' Congress in Brussels (see Note 135), and elected Eleanor Marx-Aveling and William Thorne as delegates.— 191, 198, 226

[248] Robert Cunninghame-Graham was expelled from France for having taken part in the May Day demonstration and in meetings of protest against the Fourmies massacre (see Note 243).

Père Duchesne is an imaginary character who was very popular with French revolutionary journalists in the late 18th and throughout the 19th century. *Le Père Duchesne* was the name of several political and satirical newspapers, published at different times, distinguished by their popular style and, sometimes, rude treatment of political opponents.— 192

[249] On 11 May 1891 a Japanese police officer made an attempt on the life of the heir to the Russian throne, the future Tsar Nicholas II, during his visit to the town of Obsu, near Kioto.— 192

[250] The letter contained detailed information on the massacre of the May Day demonstration in Fourmies (see Note 243).— 193

[251] On Sunday, 24 May, the traditional procession to the Mur des Fédérés (the Confederates' Wall in the Père Lachaise cemetery) took place. The speakers were Dumay, Vaillant and Allemane.— 193

[252] An excerpt from this letter was first published in: Karl Marx and Frederick Engels, *Letters to Americans. 1848-1895. A Selection*, International Publishers, New York, 1953.— 193

[253] The St Gallen (Switzerland) Congress of the Socialist Workers' Party of Germany (2-6 October 1887) discussed the conduct of a group of Social-Democratic Reichstag deputies who had refused to sign the appeal for the convocation of the congress for fear of reprisals. The congress unanimously passed a resolution censuring those deputies who had had no valid grounds for behaving in this manner and expressed the hope that no responsible party posts would be given them in the future. Bruno Geiser was among those censured.— 196, 247

[254] In sending a copy of the US edition of Volume I of *Capital* published without Engels' knowledge in New York in 1890, Hermann Schlüter wrote to tell Engels on 11 May 1891 that the book had been sold out quickly since the publisher had advertised it as being about 'how to accumulate capital'.— 197

[255] A quotation from this letter, in English translation, is contained in R. H. Dominick's book, *Wilhelm Liebknecht and the Founding of the German Social-Democratic Party*, Chapel Hill, The University of North Carolina Press, 1982.— 198

[256] This concerns the polemic, in the columns of *Neue Zeit* in 1891, between Karl Kautsky and the German physician Ferdinand Simon (son-in-law of August Bebel) on the need to combat alcoholism. Simon advocated total abstinence for workers.— 200

257 Engels means the new programme of German Social-Democracy being drawn up by the party Executive in accordance with a decision of the Halle party congress (see Note 12). Kautsky, in his letter to Engels of 4 June 1891, doubted the Executive's ability to work out a satisfactory programme.— 200

258 A strike of omnibus and tram drivers and conductors, caused by bad working conditions, took place from 7 to 13 June 1891. It was almost general in character, involving as it did 3,000 workers. Their principal demands were a reduction of working hours and higher wages. The walkout ended in a victory for the strikers— the working day was reduced to 12 hours.— 200

259 The *Salvation Army*— a religious philanthropic organisation founded by the preacher William Booth in England in 1865. In later years it spread its activities abroad, adopting its present name in 1878, after its reorganisation along military lines. It carries on large-scale religious propaganda and maintains a network of charity institutions in many countries.— 203

260 An edition of Lassalle's letters to Marx and Engels, which Engels intended to prepare, annotated and provided with a preface, did not materialise in his lifetime. The letters were brought out by Franz Mehring in 1902 under the title, *Aus dem literarischen Nachlass von Karl Marx, Friedrich Engels und Ferdinand Lassalle. Vierter Band: Briefe von Ferdinand Lassalle an Karl Marx und Friedrich Engels. 1849 bis 1862*, Stuttgart, 1902.— 203, 210

261 This letter, extant in the form of a rough draft, was first published, with minor alterations, as a message of greetings to the Second Congress of the Social-Democratic Workers' Party of Austria (see present edition, Vol. 27, p. 215).

The congress met in Vienna from 28 to 30 June 1891, with 193 delegates attending. The issues discussed included the party's condition and activities, the movement for universal, equal and direct suffrage, the celebration of May Day, the party's participation in the 1891 Brussels International Socialist Workers' Congress, trades union matters and social reform in Austria. A leading article headlined 'Unser Parteitag zu Wien' in *Arbeiter-Zeitung* of 3 July 1891 pointed out that Austria's Social-Democracy could be pleased with its congress as it had brought out the party's internationalist character, clarity of vision and unity on questions of tactics.

The *Unity Congress in Hainfeld*, held from 30 December 1888 to 1 January 1889 and attended by 73 delegates representing the socialists of almost every province of the Empire, was a milestone in the development of the socialist movement in Austria. It founded the Social-Democratic Workers' Party of Austria and adopted as its programme a *Prinzipienerklärung* (Declaration of Principle), based largely on the *Communist Manifesto*.— 206

262 Engels means the repeal of the anti-socialist laws introduced by the reactionary governments of Germany and Austria-Hungary to fight the socialist and working-class movement.

For the Anti-Socialist Law in Germany see Note 11. In Austria a law of this kind, called *Anarchistengesetz*, was adopted in 1884. It sanctioned the police persecution and prohibition of socialist and trades union newspapers and organisations and the expulsion of their leaders. In June 1891 the rising strike movement and the workers' mass May Day action forced Count von Taaffe's government to repeal it.— 206

263 Note in Engels' hand on the draft: 'To Adler. Re 2nd Austr. Party Congress'.— 207

264 In the summer and autumn of 1891 Engels repeatedly interrupted his work and left London owing to overstrain. From 26 June to 24 August (with intervals) he rested with Carl Schorlemmer and George Julian Harney in Ryde (Isle of Wight) at the home of Mary Ellen Rosher (Pumps), the niece of his wife, and roughly between 8 and 23 September he toured Ireland and Scotland with Mary Ellen Rosher and Louise Kautsky.— 207, 209, 212, 224, 230, 232, 237, 250, 278, 313, 328, 340, 501

265 In his letter to Engels of 25 June 1891 Paul Lafargue suggested that the forthcoming trial in connection with the events in Fourmies (see Note 275) might arouse public opinion and facilitate his election to the Chamber of Deputies.— 207

266 On 23 June 1891 *The Star* carried an article by Arthur Field headlined 'International Labour Congress'. The author declared that the secretary of the French Workers' Party for international relations had empowered him to elucidate all the details of the preparations for the Brussels Congress to the British labour organisations.

On 25 June there appeared in *The Star*, under the same heading, Herbert Burrows' reply stating that a secretary of the French Workers' Party had no business to concern himself with the problems of a congress convened by the Possibilists (see Note 3).— 207

267 Part of this letter was first published in: Karl Marx and Frederick Engels, *Correspondence. 1846-1895*. Lawrence & Wishart, London, 1934.— 209, 212, 237, 242, 264, 267, 285, 349, 392, 535

268 At the time, Engels was working on Chapter II, 'The Family', of the fourth edition of *The Origin of the Family, Private Property and the State* (see present edition, Vol. 26, pp. 129-276).— 209

269 As can be seen from the letters of August Bebel and Richard Fischer of 18 June 1891, the following items relating to the drafting of a new programme of German Social-Democracy to be adopted by the party congress in Erfurt had been sent to Engels for consideration: the draft programme compiled by Wilhelm Liebknecht; a copy of it with amendments in Bebel's hand, Liebknecht's second draft, taking into account Bebel's amendments; and the draft proper as endorsed by the party Executive. At the Executive's decision, copies of the draft were sent to Engels and other working-class and socialist leaders and also to the Social-Democratic Reichstag deputies.

Engels gave a detailed analysis of the document in 'A Critique of the Draft Social-Democratic Programme of 1891' (see present edition, Vol. 27, pp. 217-34). For a long time the copy of the draft sent to Engels had been considered lost. It was first published in the journal *Beiträge zur Geschichte der Arbeiterbewegung* (Berlin), 1968, Sonderheft, pp. 173-74. In the present edition it will be found in Volume 27, Note 184. The extent to which Engels' criticisms on the version of the draft programme sent him were taken into account can be seen from the draft programme published by the party Executive in *Vorwärts* on 4 July 1891, soon after the receipt of Engels' comments (see present edition, Vol. 27, Note 184), and from Bebel's letter of 12 July 1891. Another draft programme, written by Karl Kautsky, was put forward by the editorial board of *Neue Zeit*. These documents show that account had been taken of Engels' criticism pertaining to the general theoretical propositions and to the section stating the economic demands. No changes of substance were made in the political demands section. The draft contained no mention of the conquest of political power by the proletariat, of the democratic republic, of remodelling Germany's political system or of the need to combat the survivals of feudalism and absolutism.— 209, 214, 315

270 Addressing a public Social-Democratic meeting at the Eldorado hall in Munich on 1 June 1891, Georg von Vollmar, leader of the Bavarian Social-Democrats, delivered a speech 'On the Immediate Tasks of German Social-Democracy' in the context of the 'new course' of the Caprivi government. He advocated an opportunistic tactics of co-operation with the ruling classes in home and foreign policy, in particular in the event of war with Russia. This tactics was supposed to result in a gradual reform of society. The speech, applauded by the bourgeois press, was criticized at party meetings, in most party periodicals and, later, at the Erfurt Congress, especially in the addresses of August Bebel and Paul Singer (see Note 301).— 211, 219, 246

271 On 1 July 1891 *Vorwärts* published an official statement of the party Executive of 30 June 1891 denying Georg von Vollmar the right to speak on behalf of the party.— 211

272 On 27 June 1891 *Justice* (No. 389) carried an article by Ernest Bax, 'The German Party — Its Misfortunes and Its Faults', which, referring to Vollmar's speech, accused all German Social-Democracy of chauvinism and revenge-mongering.— 211

273 Engels plays on a misprint in the report on a meeting of London workwomen in Hyde Park quoted by Clara Zetkin in her first article of the series, 'Die Frage des Arbeitsschutzes für Frauen', published in the *Arbeiterin* on 6 June 1891. The report read: 'The women in childbed (*Wöchnerinnen*) demanded a reduction of the hours of labour.' The word that ought to have been used is *Wäscherinnen* — washerwomen. The issue of *Arbeiterin* in question had been sent to Engels by Karl Kautsky.— 211

274 Conrad Schmidt had applied for a lectureship at the Zurich University. Julius Wolf, a professor of political economy, raised serious objections to his admission on the grounds that Schmidt was an editor of the Social-Democratic newspaper *Berliner Volks-Tribüne*.— 213

275 Following the massacre of the May Day demonstration in Fourmies (see Note 243) the French government, anxious to absolve itself from the responsibility, clamped down on the socialists, accusing them of fomenting demonstrations and murder. Paul Lafargue was put on trial charged with having, in his speech in Wignehies on 14 April 1891, called on the workers to fight their masters arms in hand. Hippolyte Culine, the secretary of the Fourmies socialist organisation, was arrested too. On 4 July 1891 a jury in Douai (Département du Nord) pronounced Lafargue guilty. He was sentenced to one year in prison and a fine of 100 francs. Culine was condemned to six years' imprisonment.

In July Lafargue and Guesde toured Northern France (Wignehies, Fourmies, Lille, Roubaix and other cities) and gave a series of talks on the subject 'Modern

Socialism. Answer to the Indictment'. Resolutions condemning the sentences and demanding that they be quashed were adopted at various meetings.— 215, 260

276　The strike of omnibus and tram drivers and conductors in Paris, 25 to 27 May 1891, involved about 7,000 people. The strikers demanded shorter hours, higher wages and the reinstatement of workers dismissed for taking part in the May Day demonstration. The strike failed owing to the indecision of the trade union leaders, intimidated by Minister of the Interior Constans' threat to withdraw the *Companie omnibus générale*'s transportation monopoly if the strike continued.— 215

277　In a letter of 20 June 1891 the German philosopher Johann Gustav Vogt asked Engels' permission to publish a rendering of *Capital* under the title *Karl Marx's 'Capital', According to the Exact Text of the Original, Popularly Presented by J. G. Vogt.*— 216

278　This refers to a letter from the French socialist journalist Albert Duc-Quercy, enclosed by Lafargue with his letter to Engels of 10 July 1891. Presumably, Albert Duc-Quercy had asked Engels, via Lafargue, to state his views on certain aspects of France's foreign policy; these pronouncements were to be published in the form of an interview in *Le Figaro.*— 218

279　In a letter to Engels of 10 July 1891 Paul Lafargue wrote: 'I have been sentenced for *direct incitement* to murder; for direct incitement to be the case, the persons to be killed must be specifically named; and the indictment charges me only with having said that one must get rid of the employers as of vermin with an insecticide.

'But there is another point. This phrase, the only one where the word kill is used, was in the first instance attributed to Hippolyte Culine by an official newspaper; the indictment puts it down to me; and on Monday, when I arrived at Fourmies station, I met Renard, who had spoken at that meeting on April 11th and he showed me a letter which he was sending to the Minister of Justice in which he stated that it was he who had spoken these words and that he accepted all the consequences.' For the trial of Lafargue see Note 275.— 219

280　Engels must have sent Laura Lafargue a copy of *The Star* of 27 June 1891 containing another letter of Arthur Field on the Brussels Congress, headlined 'The International Labour Congress', and a copy of the same paper of 2 July 1891, carrying, under the same headline, Burrows' answer (see Note 266).— 219

281　This refers to the circular of the Belgian Workers' Party of 17 June 1891, headlined 'Congrès international ouvrier socialiste de 1891' and signed by Jean Volders. The circular, published in *Vorwärts* on 26 June 1891 and in *Le Socialiste*, No. 41, 1 July 1891, contained an invitation to the International Socialist Congress due to meet in Brussels on 18 August 1891. It signified the virtual recognition by the Belgian socialists, who formerly supported the Possibilists, of the decisions adopted at the international conference in Halle (see Note 28).— 219, 221, 224

282　Hippolyte Culine, condemned with Paul Lafargue at the trial in Douai (see Note 275), had appealed for pardon to Minister of the Interior Constans, thus complicating for himself and Lafargue the campaign for the quashing of the unwarranted sentence.

In referring to Culine's name Engels hints at its similarity to the French verb 'culer', which means 'to retreat'.— 220

283　In his letters of 14 and 20 July 1891, Sorge, referring to the forthcoming International Socialist Congress in Brussels, said the Socialist Labor Party of North America (see Note 133) would probably be represented by Lucien Sanial, and the American Federation of Labor (see Note 84) by Samuel Gompers. In this connection Sorge expressed his fear that the two, being ideological opponents, might use the congress as an additional platform for their controversy.— 224

284 Engels obviously means the item headlined 'Enfin!' in *Le Socialiste*, No. 45, 29 July 1891, which said that 'from a stronghold of the Possibilists, which it has been so far, the Labour Exchange has become what it is called upon to be — the *common house* of all workers without distinction of doctrine or grouping'.— 224

285 On 27 July 1891 Reichstag elections were held in Tilsit (Gumbinn, First Constituency) and Memel-Heydekrug (Königsberg, First Constituency). In Tilsit, the Social-Democrats polled 925 votes as against 119 on 20 February 1890. In Memel, the Social-Democratic candidate, Lorenz, got 1,571 votes.— 226, 229

286 This refers to the *Report from Great Britain and Ireland to the Delegates of the Brussels International Congress, 1891*, published as a pamphlet in London in 1891. Compiled by Eleanor Marx-Aveling on behalf of the Gas Workers and General Labourers Union (see Note 164), the Legal Eight Hours and International Labour League (see Note 200), the Bloomsbury Socialist Society and the Battersea Labour League, it gave a detailed review of the working-class movement in Britain from the 1889 International Socialist Workers' Congress (see Note 51) and a characterisation of various socialist and labour organisations. The report emphasised the importance of the new trades unions, which were introducing the workers to socialism and thus contributing to the formation of a workers' socialist party in Britain.— 226

287 Paul Lafargue was kept at Ste Pélagie prison in Paris from late July to 10 November 1891 (see Note 275). He was released in connection with his election to the Chamber of Deputies (see Note 326).— 227

288 A French naval squadron visiting Kronstadt in July and early August 1891 was accorded an elaborately solemn welcome — a demonstration of a rapprochement between Tsarist Russia and France. At the same time, diplomatic negotiations were in progress which culminated in the signing, in August 1892, of a treaty under which France and Russia undertook to consult each other on international matters and co-operate in the event of a threat of an attack on either of them. This agreement was a landmark on the way to the final formalisation, in 1893, of the Franco-Russian alliance, set up in opposition to the Triple Alliance (see Note 303).— 228, 246, 266, 308, 444, 472

289 *The Standard* of 17 August 1891 carried a Reuters report, 'Socialist Congress in Brussels', on the Brussels International Socialist Workers' Congress (see Note 135).— 229

290 This refers to Marx' letters to Danielson which the latter had sent to Engels for copying (see present edition, Vol. 48).— 230

291 In his letter of 1 May 1891 Danielson sent Engels statistics on the development of capitalism in Russia.— 230, 279

292 Subsequently Engels learnt, from a letter from Laura Lafargue written on 3 September 1891, that the so-called Liebknecht interview published in the radical

Weekly Dispatch of 30 August 1891 was a concoction by the paper's Paris correspondent, Emily Crawford. Liebknecht disavowed the interview, declaring in *Vorwärts*, No. 206, 4 September 1891, that he had not met any correspondents or granted any interviews during his latest visit to Paris.— 232

293 This refers to the *Hague Congress of the International Working Men's Association*, held 2-7 September 1872. It marked the culmination of the struggle Marx, Engels and their comrades-in-arms had waged for many years against every kind of petty-bourgeois sectarianism in the working-class movement. The congress condemned the Anarchists' splitting activities and expelled their leaders from the International.— 233, 234, 238

294 This letter was first published abridged and with editorial changes in *Le Socialiste*, No. 51, 12 September 1891, in the form of an article headlined 'Le congrès de Bruxelles', which was reprinted in German translation in *Vorwärts*, No. 216, 16 September 1891,— in the column 'Politische Uebersicht'— under the headline 'Über den Brüsseler Kongreß und die Lage in Europa (Aus einem Brief an Paul Lafargue)' (see present edition, Vol. 27, pp. 233-34). In English an excerpt from this letter was first published in: Frederick Engels, Paul and Laura Lafargue, *Correspondence*, Vol. 3, 1891-1895, Foreign Languages Publishing House, Moscow, 1963.— 234

295 Addressing the Brussels Congress (see Note 135) in the course of a debate on the proletariat's attitude to militarism on 21 August 1891, Ferdinand Domela Nieuwenhuis, the leader of the Dutch socialists, tabled a resolution urging socialists in all countries to call a nation-wide general strike in the event of a declaration of war. The congress turned down the resolution.— 234

296 The Party of Progress, founded in June 1861, advocated German unity under Prussia's aegis, the convocation of an all-German parliament, and a strong liberal ministry responsible to a chamber of deputies. In 1866, the party's Right wing, capitulating to Bismarck, split away and formed the National Liberal Party (see Note 414). In contrast to it the Progressists continued to describe themselves as an opposition party even after Germany's unification (1871). This attitude, however, was a merely notional one. In 1884 the Progressists merged with the split-away Left-wing National Liberals, forming the Freisinnige Party (see Note 242).— 237, 294

297 On 10 September 1891 *Vorwärts* (No. 211) carried a long statement by Edward Aveling rejecting Ferdinand Gilles' slanders. On the following day, the paper published a note by Aveling on the thrashing he had given Gilles.— 238

298 This refers to the twenty-fourth annual Congress of British Trades Unions, held in Newcastle from 7 to 12 September 1891. It was attended by 552 delegates, representing about 1,300,000 (according to other sources, about 2,000,000) organised workers. The majority of the delegates came from new unions.

The delegates speaking for the old, conservative unions made an attempt to secure the cancellation of the resolution on the eight-hour working day adopted by the previous, Liverpool Congress (see Note 27), but were defeated by 232 votes against 163. The congress voted for the unions' participation in the forthcoming parliamentary elections.— 238, 250, 494, 508

299 The Editorial Board of *Neue Zeit*, in Nos 49-52 of the journal (1891), published four articles giving a detailed critique of the draft programme of the Social-Democratic

Party of Germany published by the party Executive on 4 July 1891 (see Note 269). The first three articles, dealing with the theoretical section of the programme, were by Kautsky, the fourth, analysing the practical demands, was by Bernstein. The various criticisms were summarised in the form of a new draft programme, given in the concluding part of the fourth article (see also Note 322).— 239, 240, 247, 315

[300] Presumably Engels means his letter to Conrad Schmidt of 17 October 1889 (see present edition, Vol. 48).— 241

[301] The Erfurt Congress of the Social-Democratic Party of Germany met from 14 to 21 October 1891. It was attended by 258 delegates.

The congress was preceded by a sharp ideological struggle between the party's revolutionary hard core and the Right- and Left-wing opportunists, who had stepped up their activities and created the atmosphere of a party crisis in German Social-Democracy.

There had been sharp debates at meetings and in the press on the party's programme and tactics, set off by the public pronouncements of Georg von Vollmar, leader of the Bavarian Social-Democrats, who sought to impose an opportunist reformist tactics and lead the party away from class proletarian positions (see Note 270).

Vollmar's campaign provided a pretext for fresh attacks on the party (summer and autumn 1891) by the Jungen, a petty-bourgeois semi-anarchist opposition group within German Social-Democracy formed in 1890. Their stronghold being the Social-Democratic organisation of Berlin, they were also known as the Berlin opposition. The group's specific character was determined by students and young literati claiming the role of the party's theoreticians and leaders. Foremost among them were Paul Ernst, Hans Müller, Paul Kampffmeyer, Bruno Wille, Karl Wilderberger and Wilhelm Werner. The Jungen ignored the fact that the repeal of the Anti-Socialist Law had changed the conditions the party was operating in. They denied the need to employ legal forms of struggle, opposed Social-Democracy's participation in parliamentary elections and use of the parliamentary platform and demagogically accused the party and its Executive of protecting the interests of the petty bourgeoisie, of opportunism and of violating party democracy. The leaders of the Berlin opposition levelled especially fierce attacks at the party's leaders — Bebel and Liebknecht. The sectarian anarchist activities of the Jungen held a grave danger to the party's unity. The paramount task facing the Erfurt Congress was to overcome the crisis in the party and consolidate its ranks.

The congress discussed the report of the party Executive, the activities of Social-Democratic deputies in the Reichstag, the party's tactics, the draft of its new programme, and various organisational questions.

The ideological struggle continued at the congress too, especially over party tactics. A report on this issue was presented by Bebel. He — in his report and speeches — as well as other speakers (above all Singer, Liebknecht and Fischer) gave a resolute rebuff both to the Left and to the Right opportunist elements. By a majority vote the congress endorsed Bebel's draft resolution on tactics. It pointed out that the main objective of the working-class movement was the conquest of political power by the proletariat and that this end would be attained not through a chance concatenation of circumstances but through persevering work with the masses and skillful employment of every form and method of proletarian class struggle. The resolution emphasised that the German Social-Democratic Party was a fighting party employing the traditional revolutionary tactics. Vollmar and his supporters, finding themselves in isolation, were forced to retreat. The congress expelled two leaders of the Jungen — Werner and Wilderberger — from the party for their splitting activities and slander; a number of other Jungen leaders announced their resignation from the party and walked out of the congress.

The main achievement of the congress was the adoption of a new programme for German Social-Democracy. A report on it was presented by Liebknecht.

The Erfurt Programme being essentially Marxist, was an important step forward compared with the Gotha Programme. The Lassallean reformist dogmas had been dropped. The new programme scientifically substantiated the inevitability of the collapse of capitalism and its replacement with socialism, and pointed out that, in order to be able to restructure society along socialist lines, the proletariat must win political power.

At the same time, the programme had serious shortcomings, the principal one being its failure to state that the dictatorship of the proletariat was the instrument of the socialist transformation of society. Also missing were propositions concerning the overthrow of the monarchy and the establishment of a democratic republic, the remoulding of Germany's political system and other important matters. In this respect, the criticisms made by Engels in *A Critique of the Draft Social-Democratic Programme of 1891* (see present edition, Vol. 27, pp. 217-34) also apply to the version of the programme adopted in Erfurt.

The resolutions of the Erfurt congress showed that Marxism had firmly taken root in Germany's working-class movement.— 241, 255, 259, 263, 265, 267, 273, 276, 277, 282, 287, 298, 310, 315, 351, 526

[302] In this letter — written in reply to Bebel's letter of 12 September 1891 — Engels analyses Bebel's article 'Die russische Anleihe' published in *Vorwärts*, No. 226, 27 September. The article dealt with Russia's 3 per cent loan in France, agreement on which had been reached in September 1891. Bebel characterised it as a military loan. The sum stipulated was 500 million francs (125 million gold roubles). Initially a great success, the loan was only realised to the amount of about 96 million roubles owing to the sharp decline of Russian securities at the European stock exchanges caused by the aggravation of Russia's economic situation in connection with the 1891 famine.— 242, 295, 303, 308, 444

[303] The *Triple Alliance*, embracing Germany, Austria-Hungary and Italy, was a military-political bloc directed against France and Russia. It finally took shape in 1882 when Italy joined the Austro-German military alliance, formed in 1879. The Triple Alliance treaty, concluded for five years, was renewed in 1887 and 1891 and automatically extended in 1902 and 1912. The establishment of the Triple Alliance marked the first step towards the division of Europe into two large military camps and ultimately led to the first imperialist world war (1914-18). Italy withdrew from the Alliance at the outbreak of the war and in 1915 joined the powers fighting against Germany and Austria-Hungary.— 243, 308

[304] The *Ersatzreserve* (replacement reserve) — set up under the law of 2 May 1874 (*Reichs-Militärgesetz*) — was the part of the Prussian army reserve consisting of men of call-up age who, for various reasons, were granted deferment of military service in peacetime. The *Ersatzreserve* was to supply personnel for the army during call-ups.— 245

305 The *Landsturm* was a militia started in Prussia in 1813-14. Under a law of 1867 it was to be formed of men liable for call-up, aged 17 to 42, who had not served in either army or navy. It was only to be called up given the danger of a foreign invasion.— 245

306 In his letter to Engels of 12 September 1891 Bebel put forward a number of considerations on the Social-Democrats' tactics in the event of Germany waging war against Russia and France: the Reichstag Social-Democratic group would have to demand the general arming of the people; the purpose of the war would have to be to facilitate the overthrow of Tsarism; simultaneously there should be an appeal to the French to renounce the alliance with Russia. The appeal should point out the negative consequences of a Russian victory for the whole of Europe and argue that France's failure to renounce the alliance would result in support for the war against France, since the very national existence of Germany would be at stake.— 245

307 The reference is to Eduard Bernstein's article of 29 August, 'Briefe aus England', published in *Die Neue Zeit*, 9. Jg., 1890/91, 2. Bd., Nr. 50. The article attacked the Triple Alliance (see Note 303) and Germany's stance in it. Bebel, in a letter to Engels of 12 September, criticised Bernstein, suggesting that he underestimated the danger the future war would hold to Germany's national existence.— 246

308 This refers to the inheritance lawsuit involving Alphonse Cuno and the notary Leibfried in Luxembourg.— 247, 253

309 An allusion to the fact that in his preface to Lassalle's works (see Note 178) Eduard Bernstein, speaking of Lassalle's chronic disease, appended a footnote reading, 'presumably syphilis'.— 247, 253, 316

310 In his letter of 29 September 1891 August Bebel advised Engels that a decision had been taken under which the six leading articles published in *Vorwärts* every week were to be written by August Bebel, Ignaz Auer, Gustav Keßler and Wilhelm Liebknecht (one each) and Bruno Schoenlank (two). This implied that there were to be no further contributions by Bruno Geiser and Wilhelm Blos.— 247

311 Engels means the English translation of his *Socialism: Utopian and Scientific*, commissioned without his knowledge by the Socialist Labor Party of North America (see Note 133) and published in *The People* in 1891. As can be seen from Sorge's letters to Engels of 9 and 12 October 1891, the translation was made by Daniel De Leon and H. Vogt (presumably from the German edition of 1883) and printed also as a pamphlet.— 250, 265

312 In a letter of 23 September 1891 Laura Lafargue told Engels that the French Workers' Party had put up Paul Lafargue as its candidate for the Chamber of Deputies in a by-election in Lille to replace the deceased deputy Werquin. This enabled Lafargue to get out of prison and conduct the election campaign in North France. He was elected to the Chamber on 8 November 1891 and did not have to go back to prison.— 251, 252, 254, 259

313 On 23 September 1891 Laura Lafargue, on behalf of the French Workers' Party, requested Engels to write an article for the *Almanach du Parti Ouvrier pour 1892*. As a theme, she said, Jules Guesde and Paul Lafargue had suggested 'Socialism in Germany'. Engels replied positively. The article he wrote, 'Le Socialisme en Allemagne', appeared in *Almanach* in early December 1891. Somewhat later Engels

translated it into German for *Neue Zeit*, adding a brief introduction and a concluding section. The article was published in *Die Neue Zeit*, 10. Jg. 1891/92, 1. Bd., Nr. 19 under the heading 'Der Sozialismus in Deutschland' (see present edition, Vol. 27, pp. 235-50).— 252, 259, 260, 263, 267, 270, 276, 282

314 This refers to the Viennese *Arbeiterinnen-Zeitung*. Engels' phrase 'Hyaena-paper' is based on Schiller's *Song of the Bell*, which compares women revolutionaries to hyaenas.

The first issue of the newspaper, which appeared on 1 January 1892, carried contributions by Laura Lafargue, 'Ein Gruß aus Frankreich', and Louise Kautsky, 'Aus England'. On 5 February an article by Eleanor Marx-Aveling, 'Wie sollen wir organisieren?', was published.— 252, 331

315 On 8 October 1891 Marseilles' democratic forces staged a mass demonstration against Constans, who had arrived with other ministers for the start of city services improvement works. Despite numerous arrests and attempts to disperse the crowds with military force the demonstration was resumed. Throughout their route the ministers were met with boos and calls of 'Down with Constans!' and 'Down with the Fourmies murderers!' Incensed by the hostile reception, Constans demanded that the Mayor should take the most drastic measures against the demonstrators.— 255

316 This is a paraphrase of Talleyrand's saying, 'Surtout, Messieurs. Point de zèle' (Above all, sirs, not too much zeal).— 255

317 In his letter of 9 October 1891, which Engels is answering, Bebel noted the increasing threat of war and suggested that, in all probability, the hostilities would be unleashed by Russia, with France to join in next.— 256

318 In his letter of 12 September 1891 Bebel informed Engels of forthcoming changes on the editorial board of *Vorwärts*. He wrote: 'Hirsch will become, with our support, Editor-in-Chief proper, while Liebknecht will retire to his reserved property and get the Foreign Ministry...'—259

319 The newspaper *L'Action* of 11 October 1891 carried an article by Adrien Veber, 'Le socialisme intégral', which was a review of the book of the same title by the Possibilist Benoît Malon. Veber praised it beyond measure, calling the author 'the most significant mind of modern socialism'.— 260

320 The *Secrétariat du travail* was set up in France in early October 1891 in conformity with the decision of the Brussels International Socialist Workers' Congress (see Note 135) decreeing the establishment of such bodies in every country. The secretariats were to study the workers' living and working conditions, gather and publicise data on these matters, mediate in industrial disputes, etc.

The French Secretariat of Labour, composed of representatives of conflicting groups and parties, failed to produce positive results and was disbanded in 1896.— 260

321 This letter was published in English for the first time in *The Labour Monthly*, London, 1939, Vol. 21, No. 2, II.— 261

322 In connection with the forthcoming Erfurt Congress of the German Social-Democratic Party its Executive reprinted — in Supplement I to *Vorwärts*, No. 233, 6 October 1891—its own draft of the party programme and that put forward by

the Editorial Board of *Neue Zeit* (see Note 299), and published, in the same supplement, a number of other drafts and proposals submitted by party organisations and individuals in the course of the debate on the programme.

The proposition concerning 'one reactionary mass', criticised here by Engels, figured in the programme of German Social-Democracy adopted at the union congress in Gotha in 1875 (see Note 63). It was not included into the programme adopted in Erfurt.— 261, 362, 373, 423

³²³ Engels presumably means the closing words of Marx's *Revelations Concerning the Communist Trial in Cologne* (see present edition, Vol. 11, p. 457).

The *battles of Jena* and *Auerstedt*, both fought on 14 October 1806 and often referred to collectively as the battle of Jena, ended in defeat for the Prussian forces. As a result, Prussia, a member of the Fourth Coalition, surrendered to Napoleonic France. The Jena defeat brought out the whole rottenness of the socio-political system of the Hohenzollern feudal monarchy.— 263

³²⁴ The *Noble Order of the Knights of Labor*, an organisation of US workers, was founded in Philadelphia in 1869 and was a secret society until 1878. The Order consisted mostly of unskilled workers and included many Afro-Americans and women. It organised co-operatives and mutual aid societies and took part in many campaigns of the working class, in particular, the strike movement of 1886-88. Despite a ban imposed by its leadership, the Order's rank and file participated in the 1886 national strike. The leaders of the Order pursued a policy of class collaboration and, to all practical purposes, rejected workers' participation in political struggle. Its influence on the working masses declining, the Order disintegrated in the late 1890s. Its significance lies in the fact that it sought to bring the US working class together in a single national organisation.— 264

³²⁵ This refers to the series of articles headlined 'Zur Biographie Bakunins' which appeared in the anarchist newspaper *Freiheit*, Nos 1-10 and 12-16; 3, 10, 17, 24 and 31 January, 7, 14, 21 and 28 February, 7, 21 and 28 March and 4, 11 and 18 April 1891. Sorge advised Engels of the publication of the series in his letter of 9 October 1891 and later, at Engels' request, sent him all the relevant issues of *Freiheit*. The Bakunin biography was published under the sign **. In Sorge's opinion, the author was a Russian anarchist.— 265, 300

³²⁶ In the second round of the elections to the Chamber of Deputies in Lille, on 8 November 1891, Paul Lafargue defeated the government-backed candidate, Lucien-Hector Depassi, by 6, 470 votes against 5,175. In view of Lafargue's election to the Chamber, the government was forced to release him from prison on 9 November.— 266, 275

³²⁷ Engels means the speech 'Die europäische Lage und der Sozialismus', which Bebel made at a meeting in Berlin's Constituency No. 4 on 5 October 1891. A report on the speech appeared in *Vorwärts*, No. 235, 8 October. Surveying the foreign policy of European states from the Franco-Prussian war onwards Bebel noted that his views on the matter, in particular on the policy of Russia, coincided with those of Marx and Engels. This remark was omitted in the newspaper report. In his letter to Engels of 9 October Bebel deplored the omission.— 267

³²⁸ Engels ironically quotes a phrase used by Georg von Vollmar at the Erfurt Congress (see Note 301). Discussing Bebel's draft resolution on the party's tactics the

delegate Carl Oertel proposed adding to it a special paragraph stating that the party did not share von Vollmar's view on the tasks and tactics of German Social-Democracy and considered them dangerous to its further development. Von Vollmar characterised Oertel's amendment as motivated by 'personal spite' and declared that he supported the resolution, but without the amendment.— 268

³²⁹ At the Erfurt Congress (see Note 301) the delegate Fritz Kunert proposed rescinding the resolution on Bruno Geiser (Liebknecht's son-in-law) adopted at the St Gallen party congress (see Note 253). After a debate, the motion was rejected.— 268

³³⁰ In his letter of 24 October 1891 Bebel informed Engels about the results of the Erfurt Congress. He also advised him of the party Executive's decision, adopted at his, Bebel's, proposal, to make available 400 marks for Lafargue's election campaign.— 268, 291, 297, 306, 319

³³¹ In January 1891, glassworkers in the Rhone department struck for uniform rates and shorter hours. By the autumn the strike had spread throughout France, involving nearly 6,000 workers.— 269

³³² A Social-Democratic meeting was held in Magdeburg on 21 October 1891. It heard a report on the Erfurt Congress and endorsed its decisions, including the one on the expulsion of the leaders of the Jungen (see Note 301).— 269

³³³ On 20 October 1891 Karl Wilderberger and Wilhelm Werner—leaders of the Jungen expelled from the party at the Erfurt Congress (see Note 301) — called a meeting in Berlin. Since the Berlin party leaders refusing to co-operate with this opposition group were at the congress, the two considered this an opportune moment for an attempt to win the support of the Berlin party organisation and have it condemn the decision of the congress. When news of their activities reached Erfurt (a telegram had been sent from Berlin and read out at the congress), the Berlin delegates sent a letter to Berlin protesting against the decisions of the congress being discussed before its conclusion. The letter, signed by Theodor Metzner, was published under the heading 'An die Parteigenossen Berlins!' in *Vorwärts*, No. 246, 21 October 1891.

On 8 November the Berlin opposition called another meeting at which it constituted itself the Union of Independent Socialists (1891-94). Its organ was *Der Sozialist*, which appeared from 1891 to 1899. In the summer of 1893 the newspaper was taken over by the anarchists.— 269, 300, 324, 381, 386, 526, 544

³³⁴ An announcement on the forthcoming publication of Engels' works here mentioned appeared in *Die Neue Zeit*, 10. Jg., 1891/92, 2. Bd., Nr. 9, S. 283.

An English edition of Bernstein's preface to the works of Lassalle (see Note 178) appeared in Eleanor Marx-Aveling's translation in 1893 under the title 'Ferdinand Lassalle as a Social Reformer'.— 274, 287

³³⁵ In connection with Paul Lafargue's nomination as a candidate for the French Chamber of Deputies Louise Kautsky called him M. P. In her letter to Engels of 16 October 1891 Laura Lafargue jokingly remarked in this context that in France M. P. meant 'membre de Pélagie' — an allusion to the fact that Paul Lafargue was serving a sentence at Ste Pélagie prison. Engels plays on this joke.— 275, 290

³³⁶ Engels means the 'Independent Socialists' in the Chamber of Deputies. Led by Étienne-Alexandre Millerand, the group consisted mostly of bourgeois radicals

(see note 147) who had joined the socialist movement following the events in Four-mies (see Note 243) and formed the opportunist wing of the socialist faction in parliament. The 'Independent Socialists' supported Lafargue's candidature and demanded his release from prison (see this volume, pp. 269 and 274-75).— 277, 367

337 This letter was first published in the language of the original (English) in: K. Marx, F. Engels, *Ausgewählte Briefe*, Dietz Verlag, Berlin, 1953.— 278

338 Mackinley was one of the leaders of the US Republican Party. The protectionist tariff initiated by him was introduced in 1890. An instrument of the monopolies, it sharply raised the import duties on manufactures, the results being a rise in the price of consumer goods and a deterioration of the condition of the working class. Engels discussed the Mackinley tariff in his article 'The American Presidential Election' (see present edition, Vol. 27, pp. 329-31).— 278, 393

339 This refers to Part VIII, Chapter XXX, 'Reaction of the Agricultural Revolution on Industry. Creation of the Home-Market for Industrial Capital', Vol. I of Marx's *Capital* (see present edition, Vol. 35).— 279

340 Engels paraphrases a saying attributed to the French general Bosquet (see Note 241).— 281

341 Engels means the runoff election, which was due on 8 November 1891.— 281

342 In his letter of 24 October 1891 Lafargue told Engels that, if elected to the Chamber of Deputies, he intended to form a single group of 60 to 80 M. P.s, consisting of socialists and those radicals who had supported him at the elections (see Note 336).— 281

343 Five large Social-Democratic meetings were held in Berlin on 30 October 1891, with delegates to the Erfurt Congress speaking. The speakers included, among others, August Bebel, Wilhelm Liebknecht, Paul Singer and Ignaz Auer. The main topic discussed was the congress decision on the opposition of the Jungen (see Note 301). The vast majority of the audience supported the Erfurt resolutions.— 282

344 Reporting on the Erfurt Congress at a Social-Democratic meeting in Munich on 26 October 1891, Vollmar regretted the expulsion by the congress of some of the leaders of the Jungen from the party (see Note 301). The meeting rejected Vollmar's draft resolution on party tactics. In its unanimously adopted resolution on the report, submitted by Carl Oertel, it declared itself in agreement with the congress decision on tactics and recommended all party members to take it as a guide.— 282, 293, 298

345 The reference is to Bebel's letter of 29 October 1891.— 282

346 Engels means the presence of British troops in Egypt, which was part of the Ottoman Empire. France and Russia were trying to make Turkey demand their withdrawal.— 285

347 In his letter of 25 October 1891 Conrad Schmidt informed Engels of his intention to write a book entitled *Karl Marx, seine Lehre und seine Stellung in der Wissenschaft*, which was to be put out by Guttentag in Berlin. 'In particular,' Schmidt wrote, 'I want to make an exact study of the method applied in *Capital*, to prove that it is the only correct one, and to examine the influence Hegel's dialectics exerted on it.' Obviously the work did not materialise.— 285

[348] On 31 October 1891 the Chamber of Deputies discussed an interpellation by Ernest Roche, who had demanded that the government state its motives for keeping Lafargue in prison and thus denying him the possibility to campaign in the election. The government's conduct was criticised by Étienne Alexandre Millerand and Georges Benjamin Clemenceau. The Radicals voted against the government's proposal to proceed to other business. The Monarchists abstained. As a result, the government's proposal was passed with only a small majority.— 289, 291

[349] In his letters of 29 and 30 October 1891 Bebel informed Engels that Social-Democratic meetings held in Berlin and other cities had approved the decisions of the Erfurt party congress directed against the opposition (see Note 301).— 291, 293

[350] On 31 October 1891 an open meeting of German Social-Democratic émigrés in Zurich adopted a resolution, tabled by Hans Müller, expressing disagreement with the expulsion of leaders of the Jungen by the Erfurt party congress (see Note 301) and urging the next congress to rescind this decision. In its report on the meeting, *Vorwärts*, No. 259, 5 November, pointed out that the Erfurt Congress had been attended by people more competent in party matters than Hans Müller.— 293

[351] On 28 October 1891 a Reichstag by-election was held in the Stolp-Lauenburg constituency in Pomerania. Bebel analysed its outcome in an article headlined 'Die Reichstagswahl in Stolp-Lauenburg', printed in *Vorwärts*, No. 256, 1 November. He interpreted the victory of the candidate of the Freisinnige Party (see Note 242) in a constituency which had consistently elected conservatives from 1867 onwards, as important evidence of the weakening of the reactionary forces in rural constituencies.— 294

[352] In February 1888 the term of the German Reichstag was extended from three to five years. Attempts by the Bismarck government to win such an extension in 1881 and 1885 had ended in failure. A longer term for the Reichstag meant a restriction of the voters' rights.— 294

[353] In his letter to Engels of 26 October 1891 Bebel wrote that revolutionary views were taking hold on people's minds, so that the intellectuals would, in his opinion, side with the Social-Democrats when the time was ripe. Scientists, teachers, officials and technicians, he said, bitterly resented the government pressure.— 294

[354] In the course of a diplomatic tour of Europe in the autumn of 1891, the Russian Foreign Minister N. K. Giers visited Milan, where he had talks with King Umberto I and Prime Minister Rudini on 12 and 13 October. In the opinion of the European press, he tried to persuade Italy to quit the Triple Alliance (see Note 303).

On his way back from Denmark in late October 1891 Tsar Alexander III visited the German port of Danzig and Berlin, but evaded a meeting with William II. The pointed omission of a visit to the German Emperor (though a meeting had already been announced in the press) was interpreted by European newspapers, in particular English ones, as evidence of tension between Russia and Germany.— 295, 307

[355] The whereabouts of Engels' letter to Oscar Heidfeld are unknown. Engels' copy reproduced here only contains excerpts from it.— 296

[356] In his letter of 11 November 1891 Oscar Heidfeld advised Engels of Ernst Dronke's

death and of the financial documents left among his papers (see also present edition, Vol. 45).— 296

[357] This letter was published in English for the first time in *The Labour Monthly*, London, 1934, No. 10, pp. 629-32.— 299, 507, 530

[358] Between 1890 and 1895 Sorge published a series of articles on the US working-class movement over the period 1830-94 in *Neue Zeit*. They were to be put out in book form. This edition never materialised.— 299, 329

[359] On 17 November 1891 elections to the City Assembly were held in Berlin. In the first round the Social-Democrats retained their three seats and won another three. In the runoff, on 15 December, they gained a seventh seat.— 300

[360] Engels means the slanted account of Paul Lafargue's speech in Bordeaux on 22 November 1891 published in *The Evening Standard* of 23 November under the heading 'The Lille Election' (see also this volume, pp. 306-07).— 301, 304, 311, 318

[361] On 24 November 1891 *The Evening Standard* mistakenly reported that the Reichstag by-election in the 11th Constituency (Halle, Oehrungen, Warisberg, Backnaug) had been won by the Social-Democrat Hartmann. Hartmann had in fact been elected, but he was not a Social-Democrat.— 303

[362] In Lyons, the ninth congress of the French Workers' Party was held from 26 to 28 November 1891. It adopted a municipal programme and determined the party's tactics for the municipal elections due on 1 May 1892. It also endorsed the composition of the Secretariat of Labour formed in October 1891 (see Note 320).— 306

[363] Laura Lafargue's letter to Engels of 28 November 1891 is not extant.— 307

[364] The reference is to the 'reptile press', the press dependent on the Bismarck government. The name derives from the 'Reptile Fund', the assets provided to the Elector of Hesse, ex-King George V of Hanover, in compensation for the incorporation of Hanover (an ally of Austria) into Prussia after the Austro-Prussian war. The fund was sequestered after it had become known that the Hesse Elector engaged in anti-Prussian activities in France. In his speech to the Prussian Landtag on 30 January 1869 Bismarck maintained that the fund would be used to combat the intrigues of the former Hanover King and his agents, whom he called 'reptiles'. Actually, a considerable part of the means was used by Bismarck to bribe certain periodicals and individual journalists. The words 'reptile' and 'reptile press' became synonyms of a government-bribed press.— 307

[365] In his letter of 7 December 1891 Bebel told Engels that on one occasion William II arrived without notice at a cavalry barracks in Potsdam, secretly removed the guards and had them arrested, with the exception of the bugler. He then ordered the alarm to be sounded and watched with satisfaction the confusion of the officers at not finding the guards at their posts. These practical jokes of the young emperor, shrugged off by the generals, were causing discontent among the officers and ranks.— 307

[366] Engels means Bebel's speech on the military budget delivered at the Reichstag on 28 November 1891. The speech was reported in Supplement I to *Vorwärts*, No. 280, 29 November. Taking issue with those deputies who advocated a more numerous army and larger military appropriations on the plea that internal riots

were to be feared in view of the grown influence of the Social-Democrats in the army, Bebel said: 'Things are developing to our advantage of themselves, and if you have to raise millions of men, up to the *Landsturm* (home reserve) of the second call, needless to say there will be hundreds of thousands of Social-Democrats among them.'—308, 312

367 See K. Marx and F. Engels, 'Circular Letter to August Bebel, Wilhelm Lieb-knecht, Wilhelm Bracke and Others' (present edition, Vol. 24, pp. 253-69).—308

368 In his letter of 15 November 1891 Bebel named some intellectuals and bourgeois who had declared themselves members of the Social-Democratic Party.—309

369 On 28 November 1891, on the occasion of Engels' birthday, the Reichstag Social-Democratic deputies sent Engels the following message: 'The Social-Democratic group of the German Reichstag wishes its staunch and indefatigable champion many happy returns of the day.'—309

370 An allusion to an anonymous anti-Socialist pamphlet, *August Bebel der Arbeiter-Bismarck. Von einem Socialisten*, Berlin, 1890.—310

371 Part of this letter was published in English for the first time in: K. Marx and F. Engels, *Ireland and the Irish Question*, put out simultaneously, in 1971, by Progress Publishers, Moscow, and International Publishers, New York.—312

372 In a message of birthday greetings on 26 November 1891 Natalie Liebknecht wished Engels many happy returns on her own behalf and that of Wilhelm Liebknecht and their son, Theodor.—312

373 See also F. Engels, 'To the Choir Club of the Communist German Workers' Educational Society. Tottenham Street' (see present edition, Vol. 27, pp. 254-55).—313

374 The owners of the Leeds gas works stipulated that workers should initially be employed for four months, during which period they were not allowed to take part in strikes. The workers were also required, within a shift of eight hours, to perform 25 per cent more work than they had previously, when the working day was longer. These terms, practically meaning the abolition of the gas workers' union in Leeds and the cancellation of the eight-hour day won by the workers, aroused the latter's anger and resistance. Early in July 1890 strikers fought pitched battles against strikebreakers and troops, and ultimately carried the day. The employers were forced to withdraw their terms.—313

375 This refers to Chapter XXV, 'The General Law of Capitalist Accumulation', of Volume I of *Capital* (see present edition, Vol. 35).—315

376 In his speech at the Erfurt Congress of the Social-Democratic Party of Germany (see Note 301) the Dortmund delegate Karl Wilhelm Tölcke attacked Eduard Bernstein for his critique of Ferdinand Lassalle (see Note 178). He also tried to present Lassalle's views on universal suffrage, the tactics of the working-class movement and other matters.—316

377 Here Engels paraphrases the refrain of Jacob Audorf's *Lied der deutschen Arbeiter (Arbeiter-Marseillaise)* (see Note 235).—316

378 On 17 December 1891 Paul Lafargue, on behalf of the French Workers' Party, submitted to the Chamber of Deputies a bill on the separation of the Church from

the State, which was, by and large, based on the decree of the Paris Commune of 2 April 1871. It envisaged the cancellation of the cults budget, the confiscation of Church property, with the means thus obtained to be used for popular education and social security, and a ban on the building of churches and the involvement of workers in religious societies. The bill was published in *Le Socialiste*, No. 66, 26 December 1891.

Lafargue's maiden speech in the Chamber of Deputies (8 December 1891) was a substantiation of his bill on a full amnesty for persons charged with political offences. The speech was repeatedly interrupted by noise and heckling from bourgeois deputies. It was published verbatim in *Le Socialiste*, No. 65, 19 December 1891.— 320, 328, 330, 348

[379] This refers to Kautsky's brochure, *Das Erfurter Programm in seinem grundsätzlichen Theil erläutert*, published in Stuttgart in 1892.— 322, 367, 389

[380] Peter Fireman had sent Kautsky the manuscript of his article 'Kritik der Marx'schen Werttheorie'. In his letter of 7 December 1891 Kautsky informed Engels of its contents. The article was published in *Jahrbücher der Nationalökonomie und Statistik*, Dritte Folge, 3. Bd., 1892. Engels analysed it in the Preface to Vol. III of *Capital* (see present edition, Vol. 37).— 322

[381] This refers to Conrad Schmidt's work *Die Durchschnittsprofitrate auf Grundlage des Marx'schen Werthgesetzes* (Stuttgart, 1889), which Engels analyses in his preface to Volume III ot *Capital* (see present edition, Vol. 37).— 323

[382] In his letter to Engels of 3 December 1891 Kautsky said in its next issue *Neue Zeit* would carry an article by Rudolf Meyer ('Anbaupolitik und Nahrungsmittel', *Die Neue Zeit*, 10. Jg., 1891/92, 1. Bd., Nr. 11, 12. He also wrote that Meyer was ill and being boycotted by the conservative press.— 323

[383] The *compositors' strike* in Germany began on 8 November 1891 and involved 10,000 printers. The strikers demanded a 12.5 per cent pay rise and a nine-hour working day. The strike continued until 14 January 1892 but, despite support from workers of other industries in Germany and abroad, ended in failure.— 323, 346

[384] This message of greetings was written by Louise Kautsky on a postcard. The address is in Engels' hand: Mr. und Mrs. Schlüter 382 Washington St. *Hoboken N. Y. U. S. America.*— 325

[385] This message of greetings was written by Engels on a postcard. The address— Familie Liebknecht, 160 Kantstr., Charlottenburg, Berlin, Germany—is also in his hand.— 326

[386] Part of this letter was published in English for the first time in *The Labour Monthly*, London, 1934, No. 10. The letter appeared in English in full for the first time in *Science and Society*, New York, 1938, Vol. 2, No. 3.—326

[387] *Territories* was the designation of newly developed areas in the USA, mostly in the West, which did not form part of any of the states and were governed by the President or the Senate. As a rule, they were admitted to the Union as states upon attaining a certain population number.— 328

[388] An allusion to the *Greenback Party*. Formed in the West of the USA in 1874, it consisted mostly of farmers. The party opposed the withdrawal of the paper money (popularly called greenbacks) emitted during the 1861-65 Civil War and, being

devalued, no longer convertible into gold. The Greenbackers laboured under the illusion that keeping a large amount of paper money in circulation would lead to a rise in the price of farming produce. The party obtained over a million votes at the 1878 elections. It virtually disintegrated following a defeat at the polls in 1884.— 328

389 On 9 January 1891 Samuel Gompers, President of the American Federation of Labor (see Note 84), wrote to Engels asking him what he thought of the conflict between the Federation and the Socialist Labor Party of North America (see Note 133). Engels' reply to Gompers is not extant.— 328

390 Presumably Engels means the editing and translation into German of his article 'Socialism in Germany' (see present edition, Vol. 27) and his work on 'Preface to the 1892 English Edition of *The Condition of the Working-Class in England in 1844*' (see present edition, Vol. 27, pp. 257-69).— 329

391 The *Boards of Health* were municipal bodies in Britain concerned with health, sanitation and social security. In his letter of 31 December 1891 Paul Lafargue asked Engels to tell him about the Board of Health in London because he intended to submit to the Chamber of Deputies a proposal for the establishment of similar bodies in France.— 330

392 Between December 1891 and early February 1892 Paul Lafargue made several canvassing tours in France, addressing rallies and workers' meetings in Lille, Lyons, Boulogne, Bordeaux, Nantes, Toulouse and other cities. As he told Engels in his letter of 26 December, these tours were, above all, part of the campaign for the municipal elections due on 1 May 1892.

Referring to the tours in a letter to Engels on 28 December, Laura Lafargue jokingly called her husband the wandering Jew. Engels, in his reply, alludes to Lafargue's black origin.— 330, 348, 478

393 The bill on the disestablishment of the Church in Ireland (1869) applied solely to the Church of England, which had an insignificant following in Ireland. The bill put an end to the privileges of the Anglican Church and placed it, legally and financially, on an equal footing with the Catholic and the Presbyterian Church. It abolished tithes and various ecclesiastical offices. The Church of England also had to relinquish a small part of its land holdings, whose revenue was now to be used for charity and assistance to Ireland's other Churches and also to raise the salaries of the remaining Anglican priests. The bill on the disestablishment of the Church in Ireland was passed by the Gladstone government, alongside other measures, to pacify the Irish national movement.— 330

394 This refers to the 5,000 million francs which France paid in indemnities to Germany under the peace treaty after the 1870-71 Franco-Prussian war.— 330

395 Henry Mayers Hyndman supported Paul Brousse when the French Possibilists split up in October 1890. See *Broussists* (Note 3) and *Allemanists* (Note 53).— 333

396 At a joint session of the freedom of speech committee and representatives of socialist and workers' organisations on 24 January 1890, the delegates of the Union of Gas Workers and General Labourers (see Note 164) declared that they were not going officially to participate in meetings at the World's End.— 333, 335

397 On 13 November 1887 the British socialists organised a demonstration in London.

About 10,000 workers marched to Trafalgar Square, where a rally was to be held. Arriving there, they found the square occupied by 4,000 police. In the ensuing clashes several hundred demonstrators were injured (three fatally), some of the organisers of the rally were arrested. These events went down in the history of the British labour movement as Bloody Sunday.— 335

398 In reprinting, in German, Engels' article 'Socialism in Germany' in *Die Neue Zeit*, 10. Jg., 1891/92, 1. Bd., Nr. 19 (see present edition, Vol. 27, pp. 235-50), the Editors omitted the names of Bebel and Liebknecht in the following passage: 'More than once entire groups of Lassalleans went over en masse, drums beating and banners flying, to Bebel's and Liebknecht's new party, called the Eisenach party.'— 336, 343

399 On 26 January 1892 Kautsky informed Engels that J. H. W. Dietz had requested him to translate James E. Thorold Rogers' *Six Centuries of Work and Wages. The History of English Labour* (London, 1886). In this connection Kautsky asked for Engels' opinion of the book.— 337, 343

400 Engels means the evolution of Martin Luther's views. In his early, radical period Luther formulated his teaching, in which the masses of the people saw a reflection of their revolutionary sentiments. In late 1521 the Reformation led by Luther began to distance itself from the plebeian and peasant elements, with Luther himself gravitating to the side of the German princes who supported the Reformation.

This split in the Reformation camp was reflected, among other things, in Luther's critique, in December 1521, of the radical Church reforms carried out by the theologian Andreas Rudolf Karlstadt in Wittenberg, the centre of the Reformation.

During the *Peasant War* in Germany (1524-26) Luther openly sided with the enemies of the insurgent peasants, his attitude reflecting that of the majority of German burghers, who had gone over to the side of the feudal lords for fear of revolutionary action by the masses.— 342

401 In the second half of January 1892 several French newspapers, including *Figaro*, asked Bebel to state the terms that would make possible a Franco-German agreement on Alsace and Lorraine, both annexed by Germany in 1871. In a letter to Engels of 27 January Bebel summarised his reply to *Figaro* as follows: 'The public, I said, knew what I and our party thought about the annexation; it also knew that we favoured a reconciliation with France, and certainly also that we considered one possible; but our party still lacked the strength to bring about a decision, and outside the party there might be individuals who likewise wanted a reconciliation, but none of these were people of influence; hence any real action promising success was out of the question.'

A note headlined 'Ueber den Rückkauf Elsaß-Lothringes' published in the 'Parteinachrichten' column of the supplement to *Vorwärts*, No. 25, 30 January 1892, said Bebel had declared that the Social-Democratic Party would accept a Franco-German agreement on Alsace and Lorraine on any terms.— 344

402 In his letter of 27 January 1892 Bebel told Engels about a conversation he had just had with Ernst Matthias von Köller, deputy state secretary for Alsace-Lorraine at the Prussian Ministry of the Interior, on the position in that province. Köller said Bebel had only him to thank for having been able to address a meeting in Mul-

house on 6 January (see Note 407). In the course of the conversation Bebel sharply criticised the German government's police reprisals.— 344

403 A report headlined 'Aus London', in *Vorwärts*, No. 25, 30 January 1892, said elements hostile to German Social-Democracy had been expelled from the German Workers' Educational Society (see this volume, pp. 333 and 335). It did not say, however, that the person expelled was Ferdinand Gilles.— 345

404 This refers to a legal statement, sent by Bebel to Engels on 7 February 1885, concerning the possibility of bringing out another printing of Engels' *The Condition of the Working-Class in England*, published by Otto Wigand in Leipzig in 1845. This possibility was first discussed by Engels in his letters to Liebknecht of 15-22 May 1872 and 12 February 1873 (see present edition, Vol. 44, pp. 373-77 and 477-78). Under statement, a second edition could only be issued by a publishing house in a country which had no copyright convention with Germany.

However, Wigand ceded his rights in regard of Engels' book to Dietz of his own accord (see this volume, pp. 406, 410, 414 and Notes 468, 470 and 476).— 346

405 This Order of the Day by Prince George of Saxony, commander-in-chief of the Saxon army, dated 8 June 1891, was published in *Vorwärts*, No. 26, 31 January 1892, under the title 'Zu den bevorstehenden Reichstags-Verhandlungen über den Militär-Etat'. It summed up the findings of a court martial investigation into complaints about the brutal treatment of soldiers.— 346, 348

406 An allusion to a passage in Shakespeare's *Julius Caesar*, Act I, Scene 2: 'Yond' Cassius has a lean and hungry look; He thinks too much: such men are dangerous!' — 348

407 On 6 January 1892 Bebel addressed a workers' meeting in the Alsatian town of Mulhouse. He spoke mostly about the economic condition of Alsace. His attempts to proceed to political questions were cut short by the police commissioner, who threatened to close the meeting. A report on the meeting was published in *Vorwärts* on 9 January 1892.— 348

408 Engels means Conrad Schmidt's article 'Noch einmal das Rätsel der Durchschnittsprofitrate' in *Jahrbücher für Nationalökonomie und Statistik*, 3. Folge, 2. Bd., Jena 1891. Schmidt had enclosed a copy of the article in his letter to Engels of 12 December 1891.

Engels gives a critical analysis of Julius Wolf's article in his preface to Vol. III of *Capital* (see present edition, Vol. 37, Part I).— 349

409 On 2 February 1892 Filippo Turati sent Engels an article by the Italian philosopher and political leader Giovanni Bovio published in *La Tribuna*. The article contained a critique of the first instalment of Engels' 'Socialism in Germany' (see present edition, Vol. 27, pp. 235-50) as printed by Turati in the socialist journal *Critica Sociale*, No. 2, 16 January 1892. Turati, editor of the journal, reproduced Engels' work in translation from its French version published in *Almanach du Parti Ouvrier*. Turati requested Engels to reply to Bovio's article. Engels wrote his counterblast in French (see 'Reply to the Honourable Giovanni Bovio', present edition, Vol. 27, pp. 270-72) and sent it with a covering letter to Turati. Turati's Italian translation of Engels' reply, endorsed by the latter in a letter to Turati of 13 February (see this volume, p. 356), was published in *Critica Sociale*, No. 4, 16 February 1892 under

the title 'Federico Engels — Giovanni Bovio' and was reprinted by several Italian newspapers.— 354, 356

[410] Engels wrote these words on a postcard which bears — in his hand — the address: Sigr. avvo, Filippo Turati, Portici, Galleria V. E., Milano, Italy.— 356

[411] In connection with the Greater Vienna reconstruction project *Arbeiter-Zeitung* campaigned in January and February 1892 for due consideration to be given to the interests of the city's working people, and exposed the demagogy and machinations of the building companies and the authorities. For instance, Victor Adler, in an article headlined 'Die Verkehrsanlagen von Groß-Wien und die Wiener Arbeiter', published in *Arbeiter-Zeitung*, No. 2, 8 January, proposed setting up a trade-union association to protect the interests of the building workers.

In November 1888 Marie-Édouard Vaillant submitted to the Paris municipality a building project to improve the sanitation facilities in working-class neighbourhoods.— 360

[412] During the campaign to elect the London County Council, working-class candidates demanded in their manifesto that the Council be turned into a municipal body which would really protect the workers' interests. In particular, they insisted on the municipalisation of the gas, water and power supply and of the city transport (the omnibus and tram service), then in private hands. They also urged measures to improve the health service and working and living conditions. The funds to finance these measures were to be obtained through heavier taxation of the land-owners.

The London County Council collected taxes and disposed of the local budget. All persons eligible to vote for Parliament and all women over 30 years of age were entitled to vote for it.— 360, 449, 494

[413] During a visit to the Munich City Hall, in the autumn of 1891 Emperor William II made the following entry in the Book of Honour: 'Regis voluntas — suprema lex' (The King's will is the supreme law).— 361, 371

[414] The *National Liberal Party* — originally Prussian and later (from 1871) all-German — existed from 1866 to 1918. It was based on the Right wing of the Party of Progress (see Note 296), which split off in the autumn of 1866. The National Liberals were a pillar of the Junker-bourgeois bloc. One of the party's major objectives was the union of the German states under the aegis of Prussia. Soon after this was achieved, the party finally took shape as the spokesman of the big bourgeoisie, above all the industrial magnates. Its programme called for equality and bourgeois-democratic liberties but, faced with the mounting working-class movement, the party gave up the struggle for these demands and contented itself with Bismarck's half-hearted reforms.— 361, 373, 504

[415] Part of this letter was published in English for the first time in *Marx and Engels on Reactionary Prussianism*, Foreign Languages Publishing House, Moscow, 1943.— 362

[416] The twenty-fifth anniversary of Bebel's parliamentary activity was observed in Berlin on 22 February 1892. The celebration was attended by almost the entire Reichstag Social-Democratic group, the staff of the Editorial Board and the printshop of *Vorwärts* and by representatives of the Berlin party branch.— 362, 372

[417] On 22 January 1891, in the course of a Reichstag debate on a commercial treaty

with Switzerland, Bennigsen, the leader of the National Liberals (see Note 414), expressed the hope that the treaty could help form close ties between the German liberal parties. On 23 January Eugen Richter, leader of the Freisinnige Party (see Note 242), supported Bennigsen's idea in his speech. The Social-Democratic deputy Max Schippel, speaking on the same day (the speech was published in *Vorwärts* on 24 January), ridiculed these hopes, pointing out that there was no basis for them in view of the contradictions dividing the various sections of the German bourgeoisie.— 362

[418] The *Centre* (1870-1933) was a bourgeois political party in Germany formed through the merger of the Catholic factions in the Prussian Landtag and the German Reichstag (these factions had their seats in the centre of the respective assembly halls) on the eve of Germany's unification. The Centre united, under the banner of Catholicism, different social strata: clergymen, landowners, bourgeois and part of the peasantry, predominantly of the small and medium-sized states in west and southwest Germany, whose particularist tendencies it supported. The Centre was in opposition to the government, but voted for its measures directed against the working-class and socialist movement. The late 1870s brought a certain rapprochement between the ruling quarters and the Centre. With the country's industrial progress big industrialists came to play a more important part in the party's leadership. Engels characterises the Centre in detail in *The Role of Force in History* (see present edition, Vol. 26, pp. 453-510) and in the article 'What Now?' (see present edition, Vol. 27).— 363

[419] The *Conservative Party* expressed the interests of the Prussian Junkerdom, the military, the upper echelons of the bureaucracy and the Lutheran clergy. It traced its origin from the extreme Right monarchist faction in the Prussian National Assembly of 1848 and was initially called the party of *Kreuz-Zeitung*. After the establishment of the North German Confederation and in the early years of the German Empire it attacked the Bismarck government from the Right, opposing bourgeois reform and the expansion of the competence of the Imperial authorities, since it considered Prussia's hegemony in the Empire insufficiently consolidated. However, as early as 1866 there was a split in the party, resulting in the secession of the Free Conservative Party, which spoke for the big landowners and a section of the industrial community and unreservedly backed Bismarck.

In 1876 the Conservatives united with other Right-wing groups to form the all-German Conservative Party (1876-1918), which inherited the Conservatives' home and foreign policy.— 363

[420] On 15 February 1892 the Social-Democrat Wilhelm Peus was sentenced to 26 'months' imprisonment and 5 years of suspension of civil rights for *lèse-majesté*. Speaking in Magdeburg on 26 October 1891, he had declared that the monarchy served no useful purpose and its abolition was no crime.— 364, 369

[421] On 12 February 1892 Karl Ferdinand von Stumm-Halberg, an important German industrialist and Conservative deputy, sharply attacked the Social-Democratic Party in the Reichstag, accusing it, among other things, of preparing the forcible overthrow of the monarchy, violation of the oath, and preaching free love. In his reply Bebel exposed Stumm's speech as a provocation designed to prepare the ground for a new anti-Socialist law, and clarified the policy of German Social-Democracy.— 364, 371

[422] On 15 February 1892 Bebel spoke in the Reichstag debate on the military budget. He concentrated on the appropriations for the military legal department and on the cruel treatment of soldiers in the German army. An extract from the speech was published in *Vorwärts* on 16 February.— 364

[423] This concerns the plan for turning *Le Socialiste*, the weekly newspaper of the French Workers' Party (see Note 146), into a daily. Engels had asked Laura and Paul Lafargue to keep him informed of the progress of the negotiations. The plan failed to materialise.— 367, 370, 379, 424, 426, 432, 434, 471, 518, 519, 532, 544

[424] This refers to the correction of inaccuracies in the first French edition of Marx's *The Poverty of Philosophy* (1847) and reproduced in the 1885 German edition. The corrections in question were mentioned by Engels in his 'Preface to the Second German Edition of Karl Marx's *The Poverty of Philosophy*' (see present edition, Vol. 27) in 1892. These inaccuracies were used by the Austrian bourgeois sociologist and lawyer Anton Menger, in his book *Das Recht auf den vollen Arbeitsertrag in geschichtlicher Darstellung* (1886), to cast aspersions on Marx's and Engels' scholarship and integrity. Menger's insinuations were exposed in 'Lawyers' Socialism', a polemic written jointly by Engels and Kautsky (see present edition, Vol. 26, pp. 597-616).— 368

[425] In his letter of 19 February 1892 Kautsky told Engels that Heinrich Cunow was going to write a work on the 'class organisation' of the Australoids. It appeared under the title *Die Verwandtschaftsorganisation der Australneger* (1894).— 368

[426] This refers to the special rights (independent administration of the postal service, telegraphy and railways, a degree of autonomy in military matters, and other rights) of the south German states, mainly Bavaria, Württemberg and Saxony, incorporated in their treaties of accession to the North German Confederation (November 1870) and in the Constitution of the German Empire (April 1871). Representatives of Bavaria, Württemberg and Saxony on the Council of the Confederation formed a special foreign policy committee vested with the right of veto.— 369

[427] Demonstrations and rallies of unemployed took place in central Berlin, particularly in front of the royal palace, on 25, 26 and 27 February 1892. Accompanied by serious lumpen-proletarian violence, they were broken up by the police. The German Social-Democratic Party emphatically condemned the outrages and urged the workers to stay away from these demonstrations.— 369, 373

[428] On 2 March 1892, it was announced in Berlin that proceedings had been instituted against *Kölnische Zeitung* on charges of *lèse-majesté*. An article published in the newspaper contained critical remarks in regard of William II's speech at the annual banquet of the Brandenburg Landtag on 24 February 1892, in which the emperor sharply attacked the 'criticasters' and opponents of the government policy. The prosecution of *Kölnische Zeitung*, followed by charges against and the confiscation of other newspapers, was seen by the German and European public as marking the imperial authorities' transition to a policy of open police reprisals.— 369, 371

[429] At the municipal elections held in France between 1 and 8 May 1892 the Workers' Party scored a considerable success, polling over 100,000 votes and getting 635 socialists elected. In 26 towns the socialists obtained more seats than any other party

and in Roubaix, Marseille, Narbonne and Toulon they headed the municipal councils.— 370, 392, 400, 404, 411, 413, 420, 423

⁴³⁰ The *radical clubs* were democratic associations in Britain in the second half of the nineteenth century. They consisted mostly of workers and were formally connected with the Liberal Party. The clubs exerted a certain influence on the British working class. In the late 1880s, in connection with the rise of the labour movement in the country, their number increased and socialist ideas won wide currency among their members. In 1885, the Metropolitan Radical Federation was set up, which united the Radical Clubs of London.— 371, 380, 386, 403

⁴³¹ At the end of January 1892 the Prussian government submitted a bill on the primary schools to the Landtag. All primary schools providing general education were to be turned into religious schools, all newly opened schools were to be religious ones, and the entire system of primary education was to be supervised by the clergy. The bill, reflecting the interests of the Centre (see Note 418), encountered strong criticism from the Liberals which, in March 1892, forced the Prussian Cabinet to resign. The new Cabinet withdrew the bill.— 371, 373

⁴³² Part of this letter was published in English for the first time in: K. Marx and F. Engels, *Selected Correspondence*, Progress Publishers, Moscow, 1965.— 372

⁴³³ The message of greetings of the French Workers' Party (see Note 146), and the Editorial Board of *Le Socialiste* on the occasion of Bebel's twenty-fifth anniversary in parliament was published in *Le Socialiste*, No. 76, 6 March 1892. It noted Bebel's outstanding contribution to the struggle for the triumph of socialist ideas and pointed out that his activities did honour not only to the German Social-Democratic Party, but the whole international socialist movement.— 372

⁴³⁴ On 2 March 1892 the Saxon Landtag deprived Liebknecht of his seat on the grounds that he permanently lived in Berlin and not in Saxony.— 372

⁴³⁵ In *Kapital und Presse. Ein Nachspiel zum Fall Lindau*, Berlin, 1891, Franz Mehring explained why he had gone over to anti-Social-Democratic positions after 1876. His change of heart was especially evident in the third, revised edition (1879) of his *Die Deutsche Socialdemokratie. Ihre Geschichte und ihre Lehre*.— 376

⁴³⁶ In his letter of 20 March 1892 August Siegel told Engels that the Executive of the German Miners' Association had provided 120 marks to his wife to cover travelling expenses. In addition, he had received £16 from the British miners.— 376

⁴³⁷ The *new course* in Germany's foreign and home policy, proclaimed by Emperor William II in March 1890 after the resignation of Bismarck, was associated with Chancellor Leo von Caprivi (1890-94). In regard to the working-class movement it brought a policy of reform, notably in labour legislation (the introduction of free Sundays and holidays in industry, a ban on work by children under thirteen, and other measures). However, this did not mean a total renunciation of reprisals against workers' organisations.

   In Germany's foreign policy the new course brought imperialist tendencies.— 378

⁴³⁸ This is an inaccuracy. The *Revista Socială* appeared from 1884 to 1887. Engels' article was published in the Romanian Social-Democratic journal *Critica Socială*, Nos 2 and 3, 1892, under the headline 'Socialismul in Germania'.— 380

⁴³⁹ Engels means the congress of the Possibilists (see Note 3) which was to meet in Paris in July 1892. It was to deal mostly with municipal organisation and social hygiene.— 381

⁴⁴⁰ For 18 March 1892 Engels wrote 'Greetings to the French Workers on the Occasion of the 21st Anniversary of the Paris Commune' (see present edition, Vol. 27, pp. 275-76), published in *Le Socialiste*, No. 79, 26 March 1892.— 382

⁴⁴¹ This letter was published in English for the first time in: K. Marx and F. Engels, *Selected Correspondence*, Foreign Languages Publishing House, Moscow, 1955.— 382

⁴⁴² Engels means the Peasant Reform of 19 February 1861 (*Statute on Peasants Emerging from Serfhood*), which abolished serfdom in Russia. As a result of the reform about 22.5 million peasants were liberated, part of whom, however, were obliged to do corvée service or pay quit-rent for the use of land (so-called temporarily liable peasants). It was not until 28 December 1881 that a law decreeing the obligatory redemption by the peasants (as of 1 January 1881) of the plots they used was promulgated. Corvée and quit-rent were formally abolished but in effect continued to exist in the form of the labour service system until the 1900s.— 382

⁴⁴³ Engels toured the United States and Canada with Eleanor Marx-Aveling, Edward Aveling and Carl Schorlemmer in August-September 1888. For Engels' impressions of the journey see present edition, Vol. 26, pp. 581-86.— 384, 412

⁴⁴⁴ In his letter of 12 (24) November 1891 Danielson requested Engels to congratulate Paul Lafargue on his election to the Chamber of Deputies.— 385

⁴⁴⁵ During the Reichstag debate on a bill concerning martial law in Alsace-Lorraine on 3 March 1892, the Conservative deputy Karl Alwin Hartmann alleged that there existed differences on the Alsace-Lorraine issue within the German Social-Democratic Party between Wilhelm Liebknecht and Georg von Vollmar. In his reply Paul Singer, speaking on behalf of the Social-Democratic deputies rejected this assertion and declared that, as far as the Social-Democratic Party was concerned, the Alsace-Lorraine issue did not exist at all. The charge that Liebknecht advocated the return of Alsace and Lorraine to France, he said, was a lie.— 386

⁴⁴⁶ The London Trades Council and Social-Democratic Federation (see notes 196 and 29) had attempted to bar the Marxist-led working-class organisations from participation in the 1890 May Day demonstration in London. For details see Engels' article 'May 4 in London' (present edition, Vol. 27, pp. 61-66).— 386

⁴⁴⁷ Bebel was to address a workers' meeting in the East End at Eleanor Marx-Aveling's request during his planned visit to London (see Note 473).— 388

⁴⁴⁸ On 4 March 1892 Turati sent Engels two copies of the journal *Critica Sociale* of 1 March, which contained Giovanni Bovio's answer to Engels' article 'Reply to the Honourable Giovanni Bovio' (see present edition, Vol. 27, pp. 270-72).— 388

⁴⁴⁹ The Roman newspaper *La Tribuna* of 2 February 1892 carried a critical article by Giovanni Bovio about Engels' work 'Socialism in Germany' (see Note 409). Engels quotes from the article in his 'Reply to the Honourable Giovanni Bovio' (see present edition, Vol. 27, pp. 270-72).— 388

⁴⁵⁰ This refers to Engels' work 'Marx and Rodbertus. Preface to the First German Edition of *The Poverty of Philosophy* by Karl Marx' (see present edition, Vol. 26),

which was included in the second German edition of Marx's book (1892), and to Engels' special 'Preface to the Second German Edition of Karl Marx's *The Poverty of Philosophy*' (see present edition, Vol. 27, p. 277 and this volume, Note 424).— 389

[451] Marx's article 'On Proudhon' (see present edition, Vol. 20) was published in the Berlin *Social-Demokrat*, organ of the Lassallean General Association of German Workers, on 1, 3 and 5 February 1865, Nos 16-18. It was reprinted in the first and second German editions—both prepared by Engels—of Marx's *The Poverty of Philosophy*, which appeared in 1885 and 1892.— 389

[452] On 27 March 1892 Kautsky wrote to tell Engels that Victor Adler was in financial straits, and his wife, Emma, was seriously ill.— 389

[453] In a postcard of 26 March 1892 Martignetti asked Engels to state his views on duelling in connection with a report in the *Lotto di classe* that a young Italian socialist, Arturo Zambianchi, had challenged an officer for an affront.— 391

[454] Engels probably means Schlüter's letter of 11 May 1891, which contained a great deal of information on the US working-class movement and Schlüter's own activities.— 392

[455] The Paris *Figaro* had published an article by Paul Lafargue containing a definition of socialism. In his letter of 14 March 1892 Schlüter asked Engels to send him a copy of the issue in question.— 392

[456] Engels granted the interview to Émile Massard on 1 April 1892 (see present edition, Vol. 27, pp. 533-38). On 3 April he almost completely rewrote Massard's manuscript. The interview appeared in *Éclair* on 6 April. Judging by the fact that it was reprinted, even if abridged, in *Le Socialiste* (No. 82, 16 April), the newspaper of the French Workers' Party, it may be assumed that Engels regarded the *Éclair* text as satisfactory.— 394

[457] Engels holidayed in Ryde (Isle of Wight) from 20 to 26 March 1892.— 395

[458] On 7 April 1892 Henri Brissac asked Engels to review his pamphlet *La Société collectiviste* (Paris, 1892), which was a collection of his articles published in *Revue Socialiste*.— 396

[459] This refers to a plan for the merger of two groups of Russian revolutionary émigrés—the *Emancipation of Labour Group* and the *Circle of People's Will Veterans*. The plan had the support of the German Social-Democratic Party, which was willing to provide the necessary funds. The talks between the two groups were to take place in London in the spring of 1892, with Frederick Engels, August Bebel and Georgi Plekhanov participating. The plan failed to materialise.— 397

[460] Marx went for treatment to the Karlsbad (now Karlovy Vary) spa in August-September 1874, August-September 1875 and August-September 1876.— 397, 543

[461] Engels wrote the 'Introduction to the English Edition (1892) of *Socialism: Utopian and Scientific*' (see present edition, Vol. 27, pp. 278-302) in April 1892. In June he translated it into German and in July sent it to *Neue Zeit*, which reprinted it, slightly abridged, under the heading 'Ueber historischen Materialismus', 1. Bd., Nr. 1, 2, 1892-1893.— 398, 405, 452, 463

462 This refers to the French edition of Engels' *The Origin of the Family, Private Property and the State* (see also Note 199).— 399

463 In his letter to George Shipton, published in *Daily Chronicle* of 11 April 1892 in the column 'The Eight Hour Demonstration', Adolph Smith wrote about his talks with the leaders of the Possibilists (see Note 3) in Paris on sending delegates to the May Day demonstrations being organised by the London Trades Council (see Note 196). The idea was to give the demonstration an international character and deal a blow to the prestige of the Marxist-led Legal Eight Hours and International Labour League (see Note 200).— 402, 562

464 Paul Lafargue took part in the May Day demonstration in London in 1892 as a representative of the French Workers' Party (see also this volume, pp. 410-11).— 402

465 *Toynbee Hall*, in London's East End, was named after Arnold Toynbee, the English social reformer and economist, who died in 1883. The hall was used as a meeting place by his followers, Christian philanthropists, who sought to win over students and intellectuals for the propagation of Christian socialism among workers.— 404

466 Extracts from Engels' 'Preface to the 1892 English Edition of *The Condition of the Working-Class in England in 1844*' (see present edition, Vol. 27, pp. 257-59) were published in Martignetti's Italian translation in *Critica Sociale*, No. 8, 16 April 1892, under the heading 'A proposito della lotta di classe'.— 405

467 This refers to the second Italian edition of Engels' *Socialism: Utopian and Scientific* in Martignetti's translation (the first edition appeared in 1883). The issue of a second edition had been proposed by Romualdo Fantuzzi and Martignetti in March 1891, to which Engels gave his consent (see this volume, pp. 159 and 160). In the summer of 1891 the type was set, and the proofs read by Pasquale Martignetti and Antonio Labriola. But then the publisher delayed the printing without any explanation, which made Engels contemplate abrogating his contract with Fantuzzi. Despite the delay, the brochure did appear in 1892.— 405

468 In his letter of 20 April 1892 J. H. W. Dietz informed Engels of his intention to bring out a second edition of *The Condition of the Working-Class in England* (see Note 404) and of Otto Wigand's willingness to cede the copyright to him. Dietz asked Engels to advise him of his consent by a special letter. Engels agreed to Dietz's proposal. The latter's letter bears Engels' inscription: '*Yes*, reprint with the most essential notes and a new preface. Begin at once. Corrections to be made in the proofs so that I can insert the notes.'— 406

469 The *Internationale Bibliothek* (International Library) was published by J. H. W. Dietz, in Stuttgart and later in Berlin, from 1887 to 1923. A total of 67 instalments appeared, including the most important works of Marx, Engels, Bebel, Bernstein, Kautsky, Mehring, Aveling, Plekhanov, Lissagaray and other socialists.

The 14th instalment, published in 1892, contained the second edition of Engels' *Condition of the Working-Class in England*.— 407, 410

470 In his letter of 26 April 1892 Dietz informed Engels that the matter with Otto Wigand had been settled (see this volume, pp. 406-07) and the printing of the second edition of *The Condition of the Working-Class in England* could be proceeded with

at once. The letter bears Engels' note: '*Accepted.* Unless the answer is *No*, I shall write 1. the preface, 2. brief notes.'— 408

[471] The powerful May Day demonstration of 1892, in which Engels took part, had been staged jointly by London's working-class and socialist organisations. The festival lasted for two and a half hours and was attended by workers' and socialist representatives from several European countries.— 409, 411, 413

[472] The *Daily Graphic* of 2 May 1892 carried a drawing representing platform 14 at the 1892 May Day demonstration in London's Hyde Park.— 411

[473] August Bebel and Paul Singer visited Engels in London approximately between 14 May and 1 June 1892.— 412, 417, 418, 424, 427, 429, 430, 436, 490

[474] Paul Singer intended to visit Chicago as a member of a Berlin deputation in the summer of 1893.— 412

[475] In his letter of 5 May 1892 Bebel told Engels that he was well again and could, if necessary, 'uproot a few oaks'.— 413

[476] Answering Engels' question of 5 May 1892 (see this volume, p. 410) Dietz, in his letter of 9 May, wrote that Wigand had conceded him the right to publish *The Condition of the Working-Class in England* without any limitation of the number of copies. Dietz also informed Engels that he was going to print 10,000 copies and stated the terms concerning the fees, which Engels accepts in the present letter. Written on Dietz's letter in Engels' hand is the following note:
'Accepted.
'1/4 of the fee by autumn '92, after printing
'1/4 "   " 1 Jan. 93
'1/2 "   after printing the second 5,000, but not later than 6 months after printing has begun.'— 414

[477] Rudolf Hermann Meyer, in his article 'Der große Generalstab und die nörgelnden Zeitungsschreiber' intended for *Neue Zeit* (see Note 479), mentioned a carpenter by the name of Werner as one of the German representatives at the 1879 Edinburgh Congress of the British Trades Unions (see Note 478). According to Meyer, Werner set forth Marx's ideas at the congress. In his letter to Engels of 13 May 1892 Kautsky suggested that in reality it may have been Adam Weiler and asked Engels whether this was so.
The Editors do not have Engels' postcard mentioned here at their disposal.— 416

[478] The *Edinburgh Congress* of British Trades Unions (14-20 September 1879) concerned itself mostly with workers' participation in parliamentary elections. Its resolutions demanded longer voting time, a redistribution of constituencies and the abolition of distinctions between rural and urban constituencies. The congress also pronounced itself in favour of putting up working-class candidates at parliamentary elections.— 416

[479] In his letter of 13 May 1892 Kautsky wrote that Rudolf Meyer had described Engels as the 'oldest and greatest of the living political economists' in his article (see Note 477). Despite Engels' objections, the phrase was kept. The article appeared in *Die Neue Zeit*, 10. Jg., 1891/92, 2. Bd., Nr. 35, 36.— 416

[480] In his letter of 13 May 1892 Karl Kautsky expressed the desire that Louise Kaut-

sky, his former wife, should use the double name Strasser-Kautsky (Strasser was her maiden name) in her public activities.— 416, 451, 461

[481] On 15 May 1892, *Le Socialiste* (No. 86), the newspaper of the French Workers' Party, published an official report of the Party's National Council on the showing of the party's candidates in the first round of the municipal elections held on 1 May 1892 (see Note 429).— 423

[482] The scientist Friedrich Schorlemmer, elder brother of Carl and Ludwig Schorlemmer, died young.— 426

[483] This refers to the French edition of Engels' *The Origin of the Family, Private Property and the State* (see Note 199). Joseph Roy's French translation of the book was not published in full. Part of it— Chapter IX, 'Barbarism and Civilisation', and Chapter V, 'The Emergence of the Athenian State'— appeared in the July and August issues of *L'Ère Nouvelle* in 1893. In the same year Chapter IX was published by *L'Ère Nouvelle* as a separate edition.— 427

[484] On 27 May 1892 Henry Enfield Roscoe informed Engels of the doctors' pessimistic assessment of Carl Schorlemmer's condition and expressed his regret at being unable to go to Manchester.— 430

[485] Engels visited Manchester on 2 to 4 June 1892 (see also this volume, pp. 435 and 436-37).— 430, 432, 435, 436, 447, 469

[486] In his note of 27 May 1892 H. E. Roscoe uses the phrase 'Dear Engels'.— 431

[487] *Owens College* was founded in 1851 with money bequeathed for the purpose by the Manchester merchant John Owens. It is part of Manchester's Victoria University, founded in 1880.— 431, 456

[488] On 4 June 1892, *Justice* (No. 438), reported that a socialist daily was due to be published in France under the editorship of Jules Guesde and Paul Lafargue.— 435

[489] The annual congress of the National Union of Gas Workers and General Labourers of Great Britain and Ireland (see Note 164) was held in Plymouth at the beginning of June 1892. It decided that the Union should put up independent working-class candidates at parliamentary and municipal elections and take part in the 1893 International Socialist Workers' Congress in Zurich. The congress also discussed the Union's structure and finances.— 435, 437

[490] According to *Justice* of 18 June 1892 ('Socialism in Aberdeen'), Edward Aveling addressed socialist meetings in Aberdeen on 10 and 12 June.— 435, 448

[491] On 28 May 1892 the *Pall Mall Gazette* (No. 8482) carried an interview with August Bebel and Paul Singer headlined 'The Prospects of Socialism'. In the interview, granted during their stay in London earlier in May (see Note 473), Bebel and Singer briefly characterised the working-class movement in Germany and emphasised the significance of the success scored by the French Workers' Party at the May 1892 municipal elections (see Note 429).— 436

[492] Engels means the third International Miners' Congress, held in London from 7 to 10 June 1892. Attended by representatives of over 900,000 British, German, Austrian, Belgian and French workers, the congress discussed, above all, the establishment of an international miners' association and the struggle for an eight-hour working day for all miners.— 438, 446

⁴⁹³ Part of this letter was first published, in the language of the original (English), in: K. Marx, F. Engels, *Ausgewählte Briefe*, Dietz Verlag, Berlin, 1953.— 440

⁴⁹⁴ In these letters Danielson continues his discussion of the paths of Russia's economic development (see this volume, pp. 278-80 and 382-85) and gives his opinion of two books he sent Engels on 30 April and 18 May 1892: N. Kablukov, *Vopros o rabochikh v selskom khoziaistve* (Concerning Agricultural Labourers), Moscow, 1884, and N. Karyshev, *Krestianskie vnenadelniye arendy* (Rent of Land by Peasants Holding Communal Plots), Derpt, 1892.— 440

⁴⁹⁵ Engels means the book *Krestianskaya obshchina*, Moscow, 1892, by the Russian Narodist economist V. V. (V. P. Vorontsov), a copy of which Danielson sent him in March 1892.— 443

⁴⁹⁶ In his letter to Engels of 30 April 1892 Danielson pointed out that N. Kablukov, in his book *Vopros o rabochikh v selskom khoziaistve* (Concerning Agricultural Labourers) failed to take into account that the agricultural labourers were, in effect, day labourers employed only at periods when the big landowners needed labour and that their work did not provide them the necessary means of subsistence.— 443

⁴⁹⁷ In March 1891 Engels, on his own behalf and Mendelson's, sent Sorge some money for Stanisław Padlewski. After Padlewski's suicide the remainder of this money was returned to Engels and Mendelson (see also this volume, p. 415).— 445

⁴⁹⁸ *Wasserpolacken* (Water-Polacks) was a name (used from the 17th century) for Poles native to Upper Silesia who floated timber down the Oder. Subsequently, all the Poles of Upper Silesia, who had lived under Prussian rule for centuries, were called by this nickname.— 446

⁴⁹⁹ Engels means the US presidential election which was due on 8 November 1892. At the polls, the Republican Benjamin Harrison lost the Presidency to the Democrat Grover Cleveland. Engels displayed a great interest in the contest and in November 1892 wrote the article 'The American Presidential Election' (see present edition, Vol. 27, pp. 329-31).— 446

⁵⁰⁰ This refers to the projected publication of a collection of Sorge's articles on the US labour movement which had appeared in *Neue Zeit* from October 1890 (see Note 358). On 20 June Kautsky informed Engels about his negotiations with J. H. W. Dietz on this matter. He said Dietz objected in principle to the separate edition of articles from *Neue Zeit* because of their bad sales. Dietz was, however, prepared to consider Sorge's proposal, provided that the articles were revised and expanded. The project did not materialise.— 446, 453, 463, 507

⁵⁰¹ Part of this letter was first published in: Karl Marx and Frederick Engels, *On Britain*, Foreign Languages Publishing House, Moscow, 1953.— 448, 459, 493

⁵⁰² This refers to the anti-Semitic pamphlet by Hermann Ahlwardt, *Neue Enthüllungen. Judenflinten*, Dresden, 1892, an 'exposé' of underhand dealings allegedly engaged in by the Isidor Löwe firm in supplying arms to the German army. The pamphlet was confiscated under a court ruling. Bebel had sent a copy of the pamphlet to Engels.— 448

⁵⁰³ Engels refers to Bax's editorial, 'Internecine Divisions in the Socialist Party', published in *Justice*, No. 440, 18 June 1892. It urged co-operation between Britain's different socialist groups.— 448, 475

[504] The summer 1892 parliamentary election in Britain was won by the Liberals. The campaign brought success to the workers' and socialist organisations, which had put up a considerable number of independent candidates. Three of them—James Keir Hardie, John Burns and John Havelock Wilson—were elected.— 449, 459, 463, 464, 467, 470, 474, 479, 482, 483, 508, 514

[505] The *Liberal Unionists* were a group of anti-Home Rule Liberals led by Joseph Chamberlain who in 1886 broke away from the Liberal Party because of differences over Ireland. They virtually merged with the Conservative Party, formalising their accession a few years later.— 449, 460

[506] Bebel had called his wife 'honorary bookkeeper' in his letter to Engels of 4 June 1892. Julia Bebel helped her husband in the performance of his duties as treasurer of the Executive of the German Social-Democratic Party.— 450

[507] Engels visited Manchester for Carl Schorlemmer's funeral between 29 June and 2 July 1892.— 454, 461, 469

[508] *Unitarianism* is a system of Christian thought and religious observance deriving its name from its doctrine of the single personality of God the Father, in contrast with Trinitarianism or the concept of one God in three persons. Modern Unitarianism is an outgrowth of Humanism and of the Reformation. Unitarianism made its way to England and America in the seventeenth century. Nineteenth-century Unitarianism laid special emphasis on the moral aspect of religion and opposed every preoccupation with the external, ritualistic aspect.
   The *Free Congregations* (Freie Gemeinden) were communities that had separated from the official Protestant Church in 1846-47 under the influence of the *Friends of Light*, a religious trend, formed in 1841, that questioned the pietism, with its extreme mysticism and hypocrisy, dominating the Protestant Church. On 30 March 1847 Free Congregations were granted the right to independent worship.— 456

[509] In his letter of 1 July 1892 Bebel asked Engels to forward to Stanisław Mendelson a letter containing the receipt for a sum of money the German Social-Democratic Party had provided by way of material aid to a Polish student who carried on revolutionary work among Poles in Germany.— 458

[510] Writing to Engels on 29 June 1892 Bebel, presumably in reply to Engels' letter of 20 June concerning the pressure of work (see this volume, p. 450), remarked that he did not expect an answer to his letter.— 459, 467

[511] Engels means the note headlined 'Die englischen Wahlen' in *Vorwärts*, No. 152, 2 July 1892. For the 1892 elections in Britain see Note 504.— 459

[512] This refers to the *Manchester School*—a trend in political economy reflecting the interests of the industrial bourgeoisie. It favoured Free Trade and non-interference by the State in the economy. The Free Traders' stronghold was Manchester, where the movement was led by Richard Cobden and John Bright, two textile manufacturers who founded the Anti-Corn Law League in 1838. In the 1840s and 1850s the Free Traders were an independent political group which later formed the Left wing of the Liberal Party.— 459

[513] The *Corn Laws* imposed high import duties on agricultural produce in the interests of the landowners, in order to maintain high prices for their products on the home

market. In 1838 the Manchester factory owners Richard Cobden and John Bright founded the Anti-Corn Law League, which demanded the lifting of the corn tariffs and urged unlimited freedom of trade for the purpose of weakening the economic and political power of the landed aristocracy and reducing workers' wages. The struggle between the industrial bourgeoisie and the landed aristocracy over the Corn Laws ended in 1846 with their repeal.— 459

514 Under the *Home Rule Bill*, submitted by the Gladstone government in April 1886 with a view to winning the support of the Irish M. P.s and putting an end to the Irish national liberation movement, Ireland was to be turned into a self-governing colony with its own parliament and government, the latter to be accountable to the British Cabinet, which was to retain control of foreign, military and customs matters. The Bill was opposed by the Right-wing Liberals, known as the Liberal Unionists (see Note 505), and caused a split in the Liberal Party. On 7 June 1886, Parliament rejected Home Rule by the votes of the Conservatives and Liberal Unionists.— 460

515 The *Independent Labour Party* was founded by the leaders of the New Trades Unions (see Note 520) in 1893 against the background of spreading strikes and a growing movement for an independent policy of the British working class vis-à-vis the bourgeois parties. Led by James Keir Hardie, the party included members of new and old trades unions and Fabian-influenced intellectuals and petty bourgeois. Its programme called for collective ownership of all means of production, distribution and exchange, an eight-hour working day, a ban on child labour, introduction of social insurance and unemployment benefits, and other measures. Engels greeted the establishment of the Independent Labour Party, hoping that it would avoid repeating the sectarian mistakes of the Social Democratic Federation (see Note 29) and become a genuinely mass working-class party. But the Independent Labour leaders took a bourgeois reformist stand from the very beginning, placing the emphasis on parliamentary forms of struggle and readily compromising with the Liberal Party. In 1900 the Independent Labour Party joined the Labour Party.— 460, 463, 471

516 In June 1892 Bismarck, in Vienna for his son's wedding, criticised the policy of his successor, Chancellor Leo von Caprivi (see Note 437). He did so in public speeches and in an interview for the Viennese *Neue Freie Presse*, published on 24 June.— 464

517 Engels means the note 'Die englischen Wahlen', published in *Vörwarts*, No. 154, 5 July 1892.— 465

518 This telegram was sent in connection with Burns' election to Parliament from Battersea on 6 July 1892.— 466

519 This refers to the second and third electoral reforms in Britain.
Under the *reform of 1867* the suffrage in urban areas was granted to all house-owners and house tenants, and also to apartment tenants who had resided at the place in question for no less than a year and paid no less than £10 rent. The property qualification for voters in the counties was reduced to £12 rent a year. As a result of the reform a section of the industrial workers obtained the vote. In 1872 balloting was introduced. The *1884* reform extended the provisions of the 1867 reform to the rural constituencies, thus making part of the rural population eligible to vote. However, even after these reforms the voters made up only 13 per cent of the

country's population. The urban and rural poor and all women still had no access to the ballot box.— 467, 482

520 This refers to the New Trades Unions, which were called into being by the rise of the British working-class movement in the late 1880s and early 1890s. One of the biggest among them was the Union of Gas Workers and General Labourers, founded in 1889 (see Note 164). In contrast to the 'old' unions which, as a rule, consisted of workers of only one trade, the new ones were based on the production principle (workers of different trades in one industry could belong to the same union). The new unions opened their doors to unskilled workers, who hitherto had remained outside the union movement. An important part in the formation of the new unions was played by British socialists, who had the direct assistance of Engels. He characterised the New Trades Unions in his article 'May 4 in London' and in his 'Preface to the 1892 English Edition of *The Condition of the Working-Class in England in 1844* (see present edition, Vol. 27, pp. 257-69).— 468, 471, 520, 522, 528

521 In December 1889 Charles Stewart Parnell was put on trial on charges of 'cohabitation' with Mrs O'Shea, with whom he had lived in factual wedlock from 1881. Supporters of the Liberal Party took advantage of this to achieve their political ends. Gladstone demanded Parnell's resignation as leader of the Home Rule Party. Some Home Rulers joined Gladstone. This led to a split in the Irish Parliamentary group, with 45 members demanding Parnell's resignation from the leadership. The split among the Home Rulers and Parnell's death (6 October 1891) temporarily weakened the Irish national movement.— 468

522 This refers to the *theory of marginal utility*, a school of thought in vulgar political economy which rejected the labour theory of value in favour of the view that the value of commodities is determined by their utility, which is assessed subjectively. The theory of maximum utility took shape in the 1870s. In the last third of the 19th century and at the beginning of the 20th, its leading proponents included Karl Menger and Eugen Böhm-Bawerk of the 'Austrian school', William Stanley Jevons and others.

See also Engels' Preface to Volume III of *Capital* (present edition, Vol. 37).— 469, 562

523 *Jatrochemistry* (iatrochemistry) was a school in natural science and medicine which saw the main cause of diseases in the obstruction of chemical processes in the organism and looked for chemical means of treatment. Its rise (16th century) and development are associated with the names of Paracelsus, J. B. van Helmont and F. de la Boë Sylvius.

The Jatrochemists studied many processes in the human organism and discovered and introduced into medical practice a large number of chemical compounds. Jatrochemistry played an important part in overcoming the dogmas of medieval medicine. It ceased to exist as an independent medical school in the second half of the 18th century.— 470

524 In its issue for 1892 *Almanach de la Question Sociale*, published by Panayottis Argyriades, listed Engels on the title page as one of its principal contributors. Printed in French in that issue, without Engels' knowledge and considerably abridged, was his 'Introduction to Karl Marx's *Wage Labour and Capital* (1891 Edition)' (see present edition, Vol. 27, pp. 194-201).— 472

525 Engels means the publication in the *Almanach du Parti Ouvrier pour 1892* of the most important section of his work 'Socialism in Germany', written in October 1891 (see present edition, Vol. 27, pp. 235-50).— 472

526 Two editorial notes in *Justice*, No. 443, 9 July 1892—'Stanley Goes Under' and 'Stanley Must Be Kept Under'— urged voters to oppose Henry Morton Stanley as a reactionary and colonialist.— 475

527 The *High Church*— a group in the Anglican Church (mostly members of the aristocracy) that emphasised the doctrine of apostolic succession and attached great importance to ritual and symbols.— 475

528 A pun on the geographic name Eylau and the name of a financier with whom the French socialists were negotiating over the establishment of a daily newspaper.

The *battle of Eylau*, in Eastern Prussia, 7-8 February 1807, between the French and Russian troops was one of the bloodiest in the war of the fourth coalition against France. Despite heavy losses Napoleon's army failed to achieve a decisive victory.— 476

529 The *territorial army* came into being during the Franco-Prussian war of 1870-71. From 1872 it was a component of France's armed forces formed for rear, garrison and guard service in wartime. Men were enlisted in the territorial army for six (until 1892 nine) years, after active service and seven years in the reserve. Upon expiry of this period, they were transferred for another nine years to the territorial army reserve.— 478

530 Engels came to Ryde for a holiday on 27 July 1892. Illness made him stay on until 6 September.— 478, 481, 487, 488, 489, 492, 498, 500, 502, 504, 507, 514, 518, 525

531 Engels' letter bears this addition in Laura Lafargue's hand: 'I replied to Engels this evening. The ear is getting better. L. L. I have received the money.'— 478

532 Engels means the polemic between *Vorwärts* and Georg von Vollmar provoked by his article 'Le socialisme de M. Bismarck et le socialisme de l'empereur Guillaume', published in the June 1892 issue of the French *Revue bleu. Revue politique et littéraire*. Vollmar maintained in this article that some propositions of the Erfurt programme approximated to the state socialism of Bismarck and William II. The article caused a broad polemic in the Social-Democratic press. *Vorwärts* rebuffed Vollmar in a series of editorials, headlined 'Staatssozialismus', in its Nos 155, 160, 168 and 169; 6, 12, 21 and 22 July 1892.— 480, 516

533 To disprove Vollmar's assertions that Bebel was interfering in the affairs of *Vorwärts*, Bebel stated in a private letter to Vollmar that he had not seen Liebknecht, the editor of *Vorwärts*, for a whole fortnight. However, Vollmar, in his article 'In eigener Sache' published in *Münchener Post*, No. 161, on 19 July 1892, distorted this in a way suggesting that Bebel was accusing Liebknecht of neglecting his duties. Bebel denied Vollmar's allegations in *Vorwärts*, No. 168, on 21 July 1892.— 480

534 This refers to Edward Aveling's book, *The Students' Marx. An Introduction to the Study of Karl Marx' 'Capital'* (London, 1892), a popular summary of Volume I of *Capital*. In his letter to Engels of 1 July 1892 Martignetti said he intended to translate the book into Italian, and asked for a copy. At Engels' request one was sent him in August.— 483

535 At Mentana, on 3 November 1867, French troops in co-operation with the Pope's

mercenary guards defeated Garibaldi's forces, which were on their second march on Rome to reunite the papal domain with Italy.

Engels ironically quotes General Pierre Louis Charles de Failly, the French commander, who, referring to the efficacy of his soldiers' Chassepots (guns of a new system), reported: 'Nos fusils Chassepots ont fait merveille' ('Our Chassepots have worked a miracle').— 483

[536] Excerpts from the obituary 'Carl Schorlemmer' by Engels were published under the heading 'A Socialist F.R.S.' in *Justice*, No. 445, on 23 July 1892.— 484

[537] This refers to the proofs of the German translation of Engels' 'Introduction to the English Edition (1892) of *Socialism: Utopian and Scientific*' (see present edition, Vol. 27, pp. 278-302), which was being published in *Neue Zeit* (see also Note 461). Kautsky had sent the proofs to Engels on 8 August 1892.— 493

[538] Engels means the article 'Die Wahlen in Großbritannien' by Edward Aveling and Eleanor Marx-Aveling, published in *Die Neue Zeit*, 10. Jg., 1891/92, 2. Bd., Nr. 45. In editing it, Karl Kautsky had omitted the passages in which the authors criticised the sectarianism and opportunism of the Social Democratic Federation and the Fabian Society (see this volume, pp. 497 and 515).

On 8 August 1892 Kautsky wrote to tell Engels that the article had remained unread for some time owing to his absence, with the result that publication had been delayed by a week and the article had had to be abridged for lack of space.— 493, 497, 508, 515

[539] Engels refers to one of the basic propositions of the Possibilists (see Note 3) — the gradual solution of the social problem through the take-over of the municipalities by workers' representatives. The Possibilists' municipal programme was worked out at their regional congress in Paris in 1885. It provided, among other things, for public works to end unemployment, and special municipal controlled shops. The national Possibilist congress held in Paris in July 1892 also discussed the municipalities' tasks in public health and the provisioning of workers.— 494

[540] The 1892 annual Trades Union Congress, held in Glasgow from 5 to 10 September, discussed labour representation in Parliament, co-operation, factory inspection and other questions and pronounced itself in favour of introducing the eight-hour working day. At the same time it turned down an invitation to the third International Socialist Workers' Congress in Zurich (1893) received from its preparatory committee, and decided to call another international congress — on the eight-hour day issue. This could interfere with the congress of the Second International being prepared by the Marxists and split the international working-class movement.

Engels emphatically opposed these actions of the British union leaders. He sent letters to Germany, Austria, Spain and France recommending the socialist parties to publicly condemn them (see present edition, Vol. 27, and this volume, pp. 522-24, 528-29, 530-31, 533-35).— 495, 497, 505, 508, 519, 522, 528, 530, 534, 548

[541] This refers to the third International Socialist Workers' Congress, held in Zurich, 6 to 12 August 1893.— 495, 496, 505, 509, 519, 522, 529, 534, 542, 546

[542] In 1892, after a long interval caused by Eduard Bernstein's nervous disease, *Neue Zeit* resumed the publication of a series of articles of his entitled *Die soziale Doktrin des Anarchismus*. The third instalment of the series, headlined 'Proudhon und der

Mutualismus', appeared between late July and the first half of August in *Die Neue Zeit*, 10. Jg., 1891/92, 2. Bd., Nr. 45-47.—499, 502, 517

543 Part of this letter was published in English for the first time in: Karl Marx, Frederick Engels, *On Literature and Art*, Progress Publishers, Moscow, 1976.—500

544 Engels made a trip to Norway with Carl Schorlemmer in July 1890.—500

545 Engels summarised the results of his many years' research into the origin and essence of Christianity in 1894 in his work *On the History of Early Christianity* (see present edition, Vol. 27). It was published in *Die Neue Zeit*, 13. Jg., 1894/95, 1. Bd., Nr. 1-2.—501

546 The *Fronde* (1648-53) was an anti-absolutist movement in France involving different social sections—from radical peasant and plebeian elements to aristocrats—which in many cases pursued opposite aims. The defeat of the Fronde resulted in the consolidation of the absolutist regime.—501

547 In his letter of 17 August 1892 Bebel told Engels that Victor Adler and his family were in grave financial straits.—503

548 The *Norici* were inhabitants of Noricum, an area south of the Danube corresponding to part of Austria (Styria, Carinthia, Salzburg) and Germany (Bavaria). The Norici were of Illyrian origin and later were dominated by various Celtic tribes. In 15 B. C. Noricum was conquered by the Romans and made a Roman province.—503

549 In a speech before the senior officers of the German army on 18 August 1892 William II condemned the government's plan for reducing the term of active military service in the infantry to two years. The emperor's speech caused a political crisis in Germany and gave rise to rumours about the imminent resignation of Chancellor Leo von Caprivi, who advocated a shorter term of service. Nevertheless, the proposed two-year term was retained in the draft of the new military law, which was passed on 15 July 1893 by the new Reichstag, elected in June 1893 (after the dissolution of the old Reichstag, which had rejected the draft in May 1893).—504

550 On 1 October 1892 the first issue of *Le Socialiste*, the daily newspaper of the French Workers' Party (see Note 423) was due to appear.—505

551 *Crédit Lyonnais*—one of France's biggest depositary banks (founded 1863).—505, 548

552 By 20 August 1892, the financiers with whose money the daily newspaper of the French Workers' Party was being founded were to make available part of their contributions—fr. 250,000—and deliver the equipment for the printing-house.—505

553 This letter is written on a postcard part of which, including the stamp, is torn off. The beginning of the letter is not extant.—506

554 Departmental elections were held in France on 31 July and 7 August 1892. The Workers' Party (see Note 146) polled more than 100,000 votes on election day and in the runoffs and won 27 seats on the district councils and the general councils of the departments.—508

555 The tenth congress of the French Workers' Party was held in Marseilles from 24 to 28 September 1892. It discussed the party's position and activities, in particular its

work in the countryside, the celebration of May Day, the party's participation in the International Socialist Workers' Congress in Zurich in 1893 (see Note 541) and in the forthcoming parliamentary elections, and other matters. The congress adopted an agrarian programme which contained a number of specific demands reflecting the interests of the farm labourers and small peasants. The congress decided against the party's participation in the international congress called by the British trades unions to discuss the eight-hour working day (see Note 540) and for inviting British trade unionists to the Zurich Congress.— 508, 520, 523, 529, 531, 533, 544, 548

556 Louise Kautsky's article on the parliamentary election in Britain was published untitled in *Arbeiter-Zeitung*, No. 32, 5 August 1892.— 508

557 The *Parliamentary Committee* was the executive body of the 1868-formed Trades Union Congress of Great Britain. From 1871 it was elected by the annual trades union congresses, and was regarded as the unions' guiding centre in the intervals between congresses. Its functions included the nomination of trades union candidates for Parliament, the backing of Bills submitted in the interests of the trades unions, and the preparation of the annual congresses. In 1921 the Parliamentary Committee was replaced by the General Council of the Trades Union Congress.— 508, 520, 522, 529

558 In the summer of 1891 and 1892 small Russian army detachments, commanded by Colonel Ionov, undertook two expeditions to the Pamir. Under the 1872-73 Anglo-Russian agreements, this region, highly important strategically, had been recognised as lying within Russia's sphere of influence. The two expeditions were to consolidate Russia's hold on the region. They caused diplomatic friction between Russia and Britain, which was apprehensive of Russia's advance towards India. Negotiations in the subsequent years and the delineation of borders resulted in the Russo-British agreement of 27 February (11 March) 1895, which recognised the greater part of Pamir to be the possession of Russia.— 511

559 In his letter of 25 August 1892, to which Engels is replying, Adler said that he intended to write a pamphlet on party tactics in which he would take issue with Ferdinand Domela Nieuwenhuis and Georg von Vollmar. In this connection he pointed out that the critics of Social-Democracy's tactics regarded them as immutable, while actually they should change depending on the circumstances.— 512

560 In his letter of 25 August 1892 Adler wrote, referring to the 'Independent' Socialists in Austria (for the 'Independents' in Germany see Note 333), that philistinism held the 'greatest danger' to them and therefore 'if there were no Left opposition, it would have to be invented'.— 512

561 In his letter to Engels of 31 August 1892 Kautsky wrote that in the next issue of *Neue Zeit* he intended to start printing F. A. Sorge's article 'Homestead und Coeur d'Alène', which dealt with the steel workers' strike in Homestead (USA). He was therefore postponing the printing of Engels' 'Introduction to the English Edition (1892) of *Socialism: Utopian and Scientific*' (see Note 461). Sorge's article appeared in *Die Neue Zeit*, 10. Jg., 1891/92, 2. Bd., Nr. 50, 51.

The workers of the Carnegie Steel Company in Homestead went on strike at the end of June 1892 in protest against the lockout announced by the administration to force the workers to disband their trade union and accept lower pay rates.

Armed strikebreakers and troops were brought in against the strikers, who had the backing of workers at neighbouring plants and of other trade unions. After a series of clashes involving many casualties on both sides, government troops took over the plants and legal proceedings were instituted against the strike leaders. The strike ended in late November. The workers were compelled to accept the company's terms after the administration had succeeded in starting production with the help of strikebreakers.

At the time of the Homestead strike, the silver and lead miners of the Coeur d'Alêne area staged a walkout in protest against wage cuts. In July 1892 clashes occurred between the strikers and armed strikebreakers, with the former carrying the day. Eventually the strike was crushed with the help of government troops. Its leaders were arrested and the miners' union prosecuted.— 514

562 In his letter of 31 August 1892 Kautsky asked what Engels thought of inviting Bonnier to write reviews of current events in France for *Neue Zeit.*— 517

563 *Pomeranian grandees* was the phrase Ludwig Kugelmann, then at the Baltic resort of Ahlbeck, in Pomerania, used in his letter to Engels of 21 August 1892 to refer to the Prussian Junkers.— 518

564 The Berlin Congress of the German Social-Democratic Party (14-21 November 1892) discussed the reports of the party's Executive and the Reichstag group, the preparations for and celebration of May Day in 1893, the forthcoming International Socialist Workers' Congress in Zurich (1893), the use of boycott, and the So-cial-Democrats' attitude to so-called state socialism. After a long debate the congress pronounced against state socialism. It turned down the invitation to send delegates to the international congress called by the Trades Union Congress in Glasgow (see Note 540) and resolved to take part in the Zurich Congress. It also urged the German working class to fight against militarism and the build-up of armaments, which it described in its resolution as the main threat to international peace.— 520, 523

565 This refers to the twelfth annual conference of the Social Democratic Federation (see Note 29), held in London on 1 August 1892. It heard the reports on the Federation's activities and finances and discussed addenda to its programme, the Federation's attitude to the Independent Labour Party, then being formed (see Note 515), its participation in the 1893 International Socialist Workers' Congress in Zurich (see Note 541) and other matters.— 524, 529, 532

566 Marx commented on Carl Knies' book, *Geld und Credit. Erste Abtheilung. Das Geld. Darlegung der Grundlehren von dem Gelde* (Berlin, 1873), in his letter to Engels of 25 July 1877 (see present edition, Vol. 45, pp. 250-53).— 526

567 Bernstein requested Engels to send Kautsky the following excerpt from Marx's letter to Arnold Ruge written in September 1843: 'In that case we do not confront the world in a doctrinaire way with a new principle: Here is the truth, kneel down before it! We develop new principles for the world out of the world's own principles. We do not say to the world: Cease your struggles, they are foolish; we will give you the true slogan of struggle. We merely show the world what it is really fighting for, and consciousness is something that it *has to* acquire, even if it does not want to' (see present edition, Vol. 3, p. 144). The letter had been published in the only issue of *Deutsch-Französische Jahrbücher* to have appeared, in the section 'Ein Briefwechsel

von 1843'. Kautsky made use of the excerpt in the editorial 'Zum zehnjährigen Bestand der "Neuen Zeit"', published in his journal, Vol. I, No. 1, 1892-1893.— 528

[568] On 19 September 1892 Kautsky accepted Engels' proposal. However, Kovalevsky's article did not appear in *Neue Zeit*.— 528

[569] *Bank holidays*, in the United Kingdom, are those days which by the Bank Holidays Act, 1871, and the Holidays Extension Act, 1875, are kept as close holidays in all banks in England, Wales, Northern Ireland and Scotland, respectively.— 532

[570] The fifth congress of the National Federation of Trade Unions, held in Marseilles, 19-23 September 1892, discussed, among other matters (the questions of the general strike, of May Day celebrations, of women's and child labour in industry), the decision of the Glasgow Congress of British Trades Unions (see Note 540). The congress resolved to stay away from the international congress on the eight-hour working day called by the British trades unions and instead invite their representatives to the 1893 International Socialist Workers' Congress in Zurich (see Note 541).— 533, 546, 548

[571] This refers to the Congress of the American Federation of Labor (see Note 84) then being prepared. Held in Chicago in December 1893, it decided to submit for discussion to the trade unions a programme containing a number of socialist principles, and also the question of the workers' independent political activity. On the basis of this discussion, a final decision was to be taken at a congress in Denver in December 1894. The programme called for the nationalisation of the railways, the means of communication and mines, for obligatory schooling, for a legal eight-hour working day for all categories of workers, for home and factory sanitary inspection, for the transfer of all the instruments and means of production and distribution to the collective ownership of the people, and for other measures.— 534

[572] The reference is to Adler's German translation of Volume I of S. M. Kravchinsky's (Stepnyak's) book, *The Russian Peasantry. Their Agrarian Condition, Social Life and Religion*, published by Swan Sonnenschein & Co. in London in 1888. In a letter of 22 September 1892 Adler asked Engels to obtain through Stepnyak Sonnenschein's formal permission to the publication of the German translation and pay the author and publisher the fees due to them. Stepnyak read Adler's translation and wrote a brief preface to the German edition. The book appeared under the title *Der russische Bauer* at the Dietz publishing house in Stuttgart in 1893.— 539

[573] An article headlined 'Aus England' in *Vorwärts*, No. 216, 15 September 1892, cited a report to the effect that the twelfth conference of the Social Democratic Federation (see Note 565) had resolved to remove Henry Mayers Hyndman from the Federation's leadership. See also this volume, pp. 524, 529, 532.— 540, 544

[574] This refers to Hyndman's protest against the report published in *Vorwärts* (see Note 573). The protest appeared in *Vorwärts*, No. 220, 20 September 1892. Hyndman's letter in *Justice* was published in its No. 454, on 24 September 1892.— 541, 545

[575] In his letter of 24 September 1892 Kautsky asked Engels to elucidate several passages in an article on the Glasgow Trades Union Congress (see Note 540), written by Bebel for *Neue Zeit*. The article was published under the headline 'Ein internationa-

ler Kongreß für den Achtstundentag' in *Die Neue Zeit*, 11. Jg., 1892/93, 1. Bd., Nr. 2. Engels' remarks had been taken into account.— 542, 545

576 Edward Aveling quoted a considerable part of Bebel's article in his article 'Discord in "The International"'. Continental Opinion on the British Trades Unionists', published in *Pall Mall Gazette*, No. 8598, 11 October 1892.— 546

577 Part of this letter was first published by Mehring, with Engels' permission (see Engels' letter to him of 11 April 1893; present edition, Vol. 50), in Mehring's essay 'Ueber den historischen Materialismus'. The essay was appended to the first separate edition of his book *Die Lessing-Legende* (Stuttgart, 1893).

For the first English publication of the letter see Note 441.— 549

578 Mehring, who was working on an essay about historical materialism (see Note 577), had directed a relevant question to Engels via Kautsky. The latter forwarded it to Engels on 24 September 1892.— 549

579 Engels means Mehring's letters to him of 3 June 1884 and 16 January 1885, in which Mehring asked for material for a biography of Marx. These letters opened the Mehring-Engels correspondence.— 549

580 This refers to Marx's years of study at Bonn (October 1835-October 1836) and Berlin (October 1836-March 1841) universities.— 549

581 Engels refers to the book by the German historian Moritz von Lavergne-Peguilhen, *Grundzüge der Gesellschaftswissenschaft. Erster Theil. Die Bewegungs- und Productionsgesetze*, Königsberg, 1838. It contains a passage, on p. 225, about the effect of the form of economy on the form of the state.

This passage, referred to by Engels, is quoted in Mehring's essay 'Ueber den historischen Materialismus', appended to the separate edition of his *Lessing-Legende*.— 549

582 In his letter to Mehring of 11 April 1893 (see present edition, Vol. 50) Engels asked him to alter this passage, when quoting it in the appendix to the *Lessing-Legende* (see Note 577), as follows: '... while the Lavergne-Peguilhenian generalisation would be reduced to its true content, namely that feudal society engenders a feudal world order'.— 551

583 From 1 June 1891 Franz Mehring had contributed weekly editorials to *Neue Zeit*, providing a Marxist analysis of current political events. These articles formed an important stage in Mehring's development as a Marxist historian and journalist.— 553

584 This letter was addressed to the leaders of the American Federation of Labor (see Note 84). Similar letters were sent to other countries. The proposal they contained for appointing in each country a secretary for international ties met with a broad response. In her letter to Samuel Gompers of 26 March 1891 Eleanor Marx-Aveling listed the names of the secretaries appointed in ten countries.— 557

585 This refers to the 1890 May Day demonstration in London, which Engels described in his article 'May 4 in London' (see present edition, Vol. 27).— 560

586 Eleanor Marx-Aveling means the demands for international labour legislation put forward by the 1889 Paris International Socialist Workers' Congress (see Note 51).— 560

NAME INDEX

A

Adler, Emma (née Braun) (1858-1935) — Victor Adler's wife.— 87-88, 223, 331, 359, 500, 502, 503, 511, 540, 548

Adler, Victor (1852-1918) — a leader of Austrian Social-Democrats, corresponded with Engels in 1889-95, editor of the Arbeiter-Zeitung, delegate to the international socialist workers' congresses of 1889, 1891 and 1893.— 5, 24, 55, 69, 71-73, 87-89, 103, 117, 118, 126, 129, 206-07, 220, 221, 226, 229, 232, 236, 253, 287, 299, 331, 335, 359-61, 389, 419-20, 423, 427, 500-02, 503, 510-14, 539-41, 547, 548

Ahlwardt, Hermann (1846-1914) — German journalist and politician, deputy to the Reichstag (1892-1903); author of the anti-Semitic pamphlet Neue Enthüllungen. Judenflinten. — 448

Albert (pseudonym of Martin, Alexandre) (1815-1895) — French worker, a leader of secret revolutionary societies during the July monarchy; member of the Provisional Government (1848).— 516

Albert Victor Christian Edward, Duke of Clarence and Avondale and Earl of Athlone (1864-1892) — Queen Victoria's grandson.— 347

Alexander III (1845-1894) — Emperor of Russia (1881-94).— 92, 228, 235, 244, 257, 270, 289, 292, 295, 298, 307, 374, 375, 472

Alexandra (1844-1925) — daughter of King Christian IX of Denmark; wife (from 1863) of Prince of Wales (King Edward VII of England from 1901); mother of Duke of Clarence.— 347

Allemane, Jean (1843-1935) — French socialist; printer; member of the Paris Commune, served a penal sentence after its suppression, was granted an amnesty in 1880; Possibilist in the 1880s, leader (1890) of the semi-anarchist syndicalist Parti ouvrier socialiste révolutionnaire, which separated from the Possibilists.— 47, 51, 74, 98, 193, 224, 229

(1886-92), candidate at the parliamentary elections of 1892.— 471

Banner, Robert— Scottish socialist, member of the Fabian Society, founder of the Edinburgh branch of the Social Democratic Federation (1882).— 515

Banting, William (1797-1878) — English entrepreneur, the author of *A Letter on Corpulence, Addressed to the Public*, which was first published in 1863 and then went through several editions; system of diet recommended in it is known as 'banting'.— 166

Baring Brothers and C°— an English banking-house.— 92-93

Barondess, Joseph (1867-1928) — American Jewish labour organiser and Zionist leader.— 264

Barth, Ernst Emil Paul (1858-1922) — German philosopher, sociologist and pedagogue, taught at Leipzig University from 1890.— 7, 8, 63, 213, 286

Bax, Ernest Belfort (1854-1926) — English socialist, historian, philosopher and journalist; was among the first to disseminate Marxism in England; Left-wing activist of the Social Democratic Federation, a founder of the Socialist League; was on friendly terms with Engels from 1883.— 211, 434, 448, 449, 475, 484, 493, 494, 497

Bebel, Ferdinand August (1840-1913) — a leading figure in the German and international working-class movement, turner; President of the Union of German Workers' Associations from 1867; member of the First International, deputy to the Reichstag from 1867, a founder (1869) and leader of the Social-Democratic Workers' Party, opposed the Lassalleans, took an internationalist stand during the Franco-Prussian War of 1870-71, came out in support of the Paris Commune, friend and associate of Marx and Engels.— 5,

11, 20, 22, 25, 29, 40, 42, 47, 54-56, 64, 73, 76, 77, 89, 107, 116, 118, 129-32, 134, 142, 145, 146, 157-58, 164, 166, 174, 175-84, 200, 201, 216, 220, 226, 229, 232, 236, 239, 242-49, 252-59, 265-72, 282, 287, 291-96, 299, 301-03, 306-12, 315, 316, 333, 335, 336, 343-47, 348, 362-66, 372-77, 386-88, 395, 397-98, 401, 412-13, 415, 420, 423, 427-28, 430-32, 434, 436, 445-50, 458-61, 464-65, 467-69, 479-81, 490-91, 495-98, 502-04, 505, 507, 509-12, 515, 519, 521-25, 529, 533, 542-47, 549, 553, 557, 563

Bebel, Frieda— see Simon, Frieda

Bebel, Johanna Caroline Julie (1843-1910) — August Bebel's wife.— 157, 184, 249, 254, 272, 303, 310, 346, 365, 377-79, 388, 397, 450, 461, 465, 469, 481, 491, 498, 504, 525, 547

Beesly, Edward Spencer (1831-1915) — British historian and politician, Radical, positivist philosopher, professor at London University, supported the International and the Paris Commune in 1870-71.— 510

Bère— French politician, moderate republican.— 269, 277

Bernstein, Eduard (1850-1932) — German Social-Democrat, journalist, editor of the *Sozialdemokrat* (1881-90), contributor to *Die Neue Zeit* (the 1890s), after Engels' death came out with the reformist revision of Marxism (second half of the 1890s).— 5, 7, 12, 26, 30, 41, 44, 47, 48, 55, 63, 98, 108, 115, 118, 138, 150, 155, 184, 189, 191, 199-201, 203-05, 232, 240, 246, 247, 253, 274, 287, 310, 313, 316, 321, 324, 326, 331, 333, 347, 375, 411, 418, 424, 435, 445, 462, 474-76, 481-82, 497, 499, 502, 514, 517, 528, 530-33, 543, 552, 553, 559

Bernstein, Regina (Gine) (née Zadek; Schattner by her first husband) — Eduard Bernstein's wife.— 184, 189, 232, 274,

Boenigk, Otto, Baron von — German public figure.— 18-20

Boisguillebert, Pierre le Pesant, sieur de (1646-1714) — French economist, predecessor of the Physiocrats, founder of classical bourgeois political economy in France.— 141, 383

Bonald, Louis Gabriel Ambroise, vicomte de (1754-1840) — French politician and writer, monarchist, an ideologist of aristocratic and clerical reaction during the Restoration.— 549

Bonaparte — see Napoleon I

Bonnemains, Marguerite de (née Rouget) (d. 1891) — Boulanger's sweetheart.— 252

Bonnier, Charles (b. 1863) — French socialist, journalist, active member of the Workers' Party; lived in England for a long time, contributed to the socialist press, took part in preparations for the international socialist workers' congresses of 1889 and 1891, delegate to the congresses of 1891 and 1893.— 23, 24, 29, 30, 40, 116, 221, 229, 402, 411, 471, 517, 518, 561

Boulanger, Georges Ernest Jean Marie (1837-1891) — French general, War Minister (1886-87), strove to establish military dictatorship in France.— 22, 30, 162, 183, 252, 254, 289-92, 381, 400

Bovio, Giovanni (1841-1903) — Italian idealist philosopher and politician, republican and anti-clerical, M. P. from 1876, professor at Naples University.— 354, 361, 365, 380, 388

Bracke, Wilhelm (1842-1880) — German Social-Democrat, journalist, publisher of socialist literature in Brunswick; a founder (1869) and leader of the Social-Democratic Workers' Party (Eisenachers), deputy to the Reichstag (1877-79).— 129

Bradlaugh, Charles (1833-1891) — English journalist and politician,

radical; editor of The National Reformer weekly.— 120, 126, 131, 248, 249

Braun, Adolf (1862-1929) — German Social-Democrat, journalist, took part in the working-class movement in Germany and Austria-Hungary, an editor of the Vorwärts and other German and Austrian Social-Democratic newspapers in the 1890s, author of several works on the trade union movement.— 126, 129

Braun, Heinrich (1854-1927) — German Social-Democrat, journalist, a founder of Die Neue Zeit, editor of the Archiv für soziale Gesetzgebung und Statistik and other publications.— 7, 552

Brentano, Lujo (Ludwig Joseph) (1844-1931) — German economist; one of the major representatives of armchair socialism.— 25-26, 85, 90, 93, 95, 103, 141, 146, 148, 158, 163, 172

Brett — English wine merchant.— 37

Bright, John (1811-1889) — English manufacturer and politician, a leader of the Free Traders and founder of the Anti-Corn Law League; M. P. (from 1843), leader of the Left wing of the Liberal Party from the early 1860s, held several ministerial posts.— 459

Brissac, Henri (1826-1906) — French socialist, journalist, member of the Paris Commune, was exiled to New Caledonia after its defeat, returned to France after amnesty in 1879, member of the French Workers' Party.— 396

Brousse, Paul Louis Marie (1844-1912) — French socialist; physician; took part in the Paris Commune, sided with the anarchists, member of the French Workers' Party from 1879, a leader of the Possibilists.— 46-47, 52, 53, 56, 74, 97-99, 108, 155-56, 224, 229, 269, 324, 333, 381, 449

Buffenoir, Hippolyte François Philibert (1847-1928) — French journalist and writer, contributed to the *Vorwärts* in the 1870s.— 162

Bunte, Friedrich — German Social-Democrat, a leader of the Ruhr miners' strike in 1889.— 448

Burgess, Joseph (pseudonym *Autolycus*) (b. 1853) — prominent figure in the English working-class movement, knitter; an editor of *The Workman's Times* newspaper in 1891-94, a founder of the Independent Labour Party (1893).— 404, 494, 508, 529, 532, 542, 545, 560

Burleigh — workers' candidate for Glasgow at the parliamentary elections in 1892.— 468

Burns, John Elliott (1858-1943) — prominent figure in the English working-class movement, a leader of the New Trade Unions in the 1880s, leader of the London dockers' strike (1889), adopted the liberal trade union stand in the 1890s, M. P. from 1892, held ministerial posts in Liberal cabinets. — 77, 190, 225, 323, 333, 335, 461, 466, 468, 471, 475, 494, 529, 532, 546, 557

Burns, Lydia (*Lizzy, Lizzie*) (1827-1878) — Irish working woman, Frederick Engels' second wife.— 334, 378

Burrows, Herbert (1845-1922) — English official, radical, a founder of the Social Democratic Federation, organised the trade union movement of the unskilled workers in the 1880s-1890s.— 175, 207, 208, 219, 237

Burt, Thomas (1837-1922) — English miner, prominent figure in the English trade union movement, secretary of the Northumberland Miners' Association, delegate to international miners' congresses, M. P. (1874-1918), secretary of the Board of Trade.— 429

Byford, William — treasurer of the National Gas Workers and General Labourers Union of Great Britain and Ireland.— 557

C

Cahan, Abraham (1860-1951) — American socialist, Russian émigré, edited the New York Jewish workers' newspaper, delegate to the International Socialist Workers' Congress of 1891, wrote several books on the life of Jewish immigrants in the USA.— 238, 532

Calonne, Charles Alexandre de (1734-1802) — French statesman, Controller-General of Finance (1783-87), retired after abortive attempts to reduce the deficit of the national budget.— 444

Caprivi, Leo, count of (1831-1899) — German statesman, military figure, general, Chancellor of the German Empire (1890-94).— 268, 371, 464

Caria, Gustave (pseudonym *Léopold*) (b. 1841) — French adventurer, took part in the Paris Commune, was involved in robberies, emigrated to England after the defeat of the Commune, member of the French section of 1871 in London, slandered the participants of the Commune, was expelled for this from the Société des Réfugiés in 1872.— 56

Carnot, Marie François Sadi (1837-1894) — French statesman, moderate republican, held ministerial posts several times, President of the Republic (1887-94).— 254, 298

Caron, Charles — French publisher.— 29, 31-32

Carré — owner of a publishing house in Paris.— 203

Champion, Henry Hyde (1859-1928) — English socialist, publisher and journalist; member of the Social Democratic Federation till 1887, later a leader of the Labour Electoral Association in London, edited and pub-

Engels, Caspar (1816-1889) — Frederick Engels' cousin, manufacturer in Barmen.— 86

Engels, Elisabeth Franziska Mauritia (née *van Haar*) (1797-1873) — Frederick Engels' mother.— 487-88

Engels, Emma (née *Croon*) (1834-1916) — Hermann Engels' wife, Frederick Engels' sister-in-law.— 340, 341, 352, 358, 474, 489

Engels, Friedrich (1796-1860) — Frederick Engels' father.— 488

Engels, Hedwig (in marriage: *Boelling*) (1830-1904) — Frederick Engels' sister.— 340-41, 352

Engels, Hermann (1822-1905) — Frederick Engels' brother, manufacturer in Barmen, a partner in the firm Ermen & Engels in Engelskirchen.— 37-38, 87, 339-41, 352-54, 358, 473-74, 489, 492

Engels, Johann Caspar (1753-1821) — Frederick Engels' grandfather, manufacturer in Barmen.— 86

Engels, Luise Friederike (née *Noot*) (1762-1822) — Frederick Engels' grandmother.— 86

Engels, Rudolf (1831-1903) — Frederick Engels' brother, manufacturer in Barmen, a partner in the firm Ermen & Engels in Engelskirchen.— 86, 339, 340, 492

Ernst — see *Schattner, Ernst*

Ernst, Paul (1866-1933) — German journalist, critic, writer and playwright; sided with the Social-Democrats in the late 1880s, a leader of the Jungen in the early 1890s, editor of the *Berliner Volks-Tribüne* (mid-December 1890 to mid-November 1891); withdrew from the Social-Democratic Party in 1891; later he took Rightist, anti-Marxist stand.— 63, 94, 109, 210, 527

F

Faillet, Marius Eugène (pseudonym *Dumont*) (1840-1912) — prominent figure in the French working-class movement, took part in the Paris Commune, delegate to the Hague Congress of the International (1872), subsequently member of the French Workers' Party.— 51

Fantuzzi, Romualdo — brother of Flaminio Fantuzzi (Italian publisher).— 159-61, 405

Fenwick, Charles (1850-1918) — miner, prominent figure in the English working-class movement, a leader of the Miners' National Union, M. P. (from 1885), secretary of the Parliamentary Committee of the Trades Union Congress (1890-94), championed liberal labour policy.— 429, 529

Fergus — see *Lafargue, Paul*

Ferroul, Joseph Antoine Jean Frédéric Ernest (pseudonym *Léon Stern*) (1853-1921) — French physician, socialist, member of the Chamber of Deputies from 1888, delegate to the international socialist workers' congresses of 1889 and 1891.— 367

Ferry, Jules François Camille (1832-1893) — French lawyer, journalist and politician, a leader of moderate republicans, member of the Government of National Defence, Mayor of Paris (1870-71), premier (1880-81 and 1883-85), pursued a policy of colonial expansion.— 214

Feuerbach, Ludwig Andreas von (1804-1872) — German materialist philosopher.— 36, 63

Field, Arthur (b. 1869) — English journalist, socialist, member of the Social

Socialist Workers' Congress of 1893.— 312

Greulich, Hermann (1842-1925) — German book-binder, member of the Swiss section of the International from 1867, founder and editor of the newspaper *Tagwacht* (1869-80), a founder of the Swiss Social-Democratic Party (1888), leader of its Right wing.— 45, 495-97, 505

Grillenberger, Karl (1848-1897) — German worker, later journalist, Social-Democrat; deputy to the Reichstag from 1881, belonged to the opportunist wing of the German Social-Democratic Party.— 199

Grunzig, Julius (b. 1855) — German Social-Democrat, emigrated to the USA during the operation of the Anti-Socialist Law, contributed to the *New Yorker Volkszeitung*.— 45

Guesde, Jules (real name *Mathieu, Jules Bazile*) (1845-1922) — prominent figure in the French and the international working-class and socialist movement, initially republican, sided with the anarchists in the first half of the 1870s, later a founder of the French Workers' Party (1879); for a number of years a leader of the revolutionary wing in the French socialist movement.— 23, 29, 30, 32, 40-41, 49, 51, 117, 130, 155, 193, 221, 270, 400, 401, 424, 432, 477, 508, 517, 544

Guillaume-Schack, Gertrud (née *Countess of Schack*) (1845-1903) — German socialist, prominent figure in the German women's movement.— 248, 451-52

Gumpert, Eduard (d. 1893) — German physician, resident in Manchester, a friend of Marx and Engels.— 154, 162, 418, 424-26, 430-39, 448, 454-56, 470, 485, 486

Guttentag — book publisher in Berlin.— 285

H

Hall, Leonard (b. 1866) — English socialist, worker, later journalist, member of the Social Democratic Federation, subsequently of the Independent Labour Party.— 468, 471

Haller, Karl Ludwig von (1768-1854) — Swiss lawyer and historian, absolutist.— 549

Hardie, James Keir (1856-1915) — miner, prominent figure in the English working-class movement, journalist, founder and leader of the Scottish Labour Party (from 1888) and of the Independent Labour Party (from 1893), first workers' independent candidate elected to Parliament (1892).— 376, 460, 461, 463, 468, 471, 475, 494, 529, 532, 542, 545-46

Harney, George Julian (1817-1897) — prominent figure in the English labour movement, a leader of the Chartist Left wing, edited *The Northern Star, Democratic Review, Red Republican* and *Friend of the People*, lived in the USA from 1862 to 1888 with intervals, member of the First International; associate of Marx and Engels.— 192, 194, 209, 211, 331-32, 358, 382

Hartmann, Lev Nikolayevich (1850-1913) — Russian revolutionary, Narodnik, took part in a terroristic act of the Narodnaya Volya organisation against Alexander II in 1879, after which emigrated to France, later to England and to the USA in 1881.— 369

Hasselmann, Wilhelm (b. 1844) — a leader of the Lassallean General Association of German Workers; editor of the *Neuer Social Demokrat* in 1871-75,

166, 167, 175, 186, 198, 207-08, 211, 219, 221, 224, 229, 232, 237, 238, 241, 249, 251, 252, 273, 323, 333, 356-57, 367, 381, 386, 448, 449, 475, 484, 524, 529, 532, 540, 544, 545, 560

I

Ibsen, Henrik (1828-1906) — Norwegian playwright.— 10, 27

Ihrer, Emma (1857-1911) — prominent figure in the German women's and trade union movement, founded the *Arbeiterin* journal (1891), delegate to the international socialist workers' congresses of 1889 and 1891.— 334

Itzig — see *Lassalle, Ferdinand*

J

Jacobi, Friedrich Heinrich (1743-1819) — German fideist philosopher.— 286

Jakins — houseowner in London.— 38-39

Janssen, Johannes (1829-1891) — German historian and theologian, author of works on German history.— 342

Jean — see *Longuet, Jean Laurent Frédéric*

Jevons, William Stanley (1835-1882) — English economist and philosopher.— 526, 553

Jodko-Narkiewicz, Tomasz Witold (*Rabin*) (1864-1924) — Polish journalist, a founder of the Polish Socialist Party and leader of its revolutionary wing, member of the Proletariat Party in the 1880s, contributor to the magazine *Przedświt* in the 1890s, its editor in 1893-1906.— 106, 110

Joffrin, Jules Louis Alexandre (1846-1890) — French mechanic, socialist; member of the Paris Commune; later émigré in England, on his return to France a Possibilist leader, member of the Paris City Council from 1882, member of the Chamber of Deputies from 1889.— 30, 47

Jollymeier — see *Schorlemmer, Carl*

Jonas, Alexander (c. 1839-1912) — German-born American journalist, socialist, editor-in-chief of the *New Yorker Volkszeitung* from 1878.— 20, 45, 250

K

Kablukov, Nikolai Alexeyevich (1849-1919) — Russian economist and statistician, Narodnik, professor at Moscow University, author of several works on economy and statistics.— 443

Kampffmeyer, Paul (1864-1945) — German journalist, Social-Democrat from the late 1880s, a leader of the Jungen group and the Union of Independent Socialists in the early 1890s; later revisionist.— 526

Kant, Immanuel (1724-1804) — German philosopher.— 62, 286

Karlstadt, Andreas Rudolf (real name *Bodenstein*) (1480-1541) — German theologian, Reformer.— 342

Karyshev, Nikolai Alexandrovich (1855-1905) — Russian economist, statistician and public figure, professor at Yuriev (Tartu) University (1891-93) and Moscow Agricultural Institute (1895-1904), wrote several works on economy and statistics which propagated views of Liberal Narodniks.— 443

Kasprowicz, E. Ł. — publisher of the first volume of *Capital* in Polish.— 75

Käte — see *Schattner, Käte*

Kautsky, Felix (1891-1953) — Karl Kautsky's son by his second wife.— 131, 324

Kautsky, Karl (1854-1938) — German Social-Democrat, journalist, editor of *Die Neue Zeit* (1883-1917), adhered to

ethnographer and lawyer, author of a number of works on history of the primitive society.— 22-23, 124, 528, 552

Kravchinsky, Sergei Mikhailovich (penname *Stepnyak*) (1851-1895) — Russian writer and journalist, prominent figure in the revolutionary Narodnik movement of the 1870s; emigrated after committing a terrorist act against the chief of gendarmes in St Petersburg in 1878; lived in England from 1884.— 144, 411, 539, 540

Kugelmann, Ludwig (1828-1902) — German physician; took part in the 1848-49 revolution in Germany, member of the First International, Marx's regular correspondent (1862-74). — 518-19, 543-45

Kunert, Fritz (1850-1931) — German Social-Democrat, journalist, edited several Social-Democratic newspapers in the 1880s-90s, an editor of the *Vorwärts* (1894-1917), repeatedly elected deputy to the Reichstag (from 1890), delegate to the Erfurt Party Congress of 1891.— 268

L

Labouchère, Henry de Pré (1831-1912) — French-born English politician, diplomat and journalist, Liberal M. P., one of the owners of *The Daily News* (from the late 1860s).— 323, 449

Labriola, Antonio (1843-1904) — Italian philosopher and journalist, one of the first to disseminate Marxism in Italy.— 136, 205, 317, 342, 405

Labruyère, Georges de — French journalist, contributor to *Le Cri du Peuple*; Boulangist in the late 1880s.— 92, 107

Lafargue, Laura (*Löhr*) (1845-1911) — Karl Marx's second daughter, Paul Lafargue's wife from 1868, participant in the French working-class move-

ment.— 21, 23, 25, 29, 30, 41-42, 44-45, 52-55, 66, 70, 76-77, 91-93, 117, 120, 125, 141, 154-56, 161-63, 172, 185-90, 192, 195, 199, 201-04, 208, 209, 215-16, 227-30, 251-53, 260-61, 263-64, 270, 275-76, 281, 282, 288-90, 301, 304-06, 311-12, 318-20, 328-34, 347-48, 366-67, 379-82, 394-95, 399-402, 411-12, 413, 416, 424, 426-28, 434-36, 469-71, 478, 486-87, 505-06, 519-21, 523, 543, 544, 561-62

Lafargue, Paul (1842-1911) — prominent figure in the international and French working-class movement, member of the General Council of the International, Corresponding Secretary for Spain (1866-69); a founder of the Workers' Party in France; disciple and associate of Marx and Engels; husband of Marx's daughter Laura.— 12, 21-25, 28-33, 42-43, 47, 49, 53-55, 65-66, 92, 93, 108, 115-17, 121-25, 129, 140-42, 144, 154, 156, 159, 161-63, 164, 165, 167, 174, 183, 189-95, 200, 204, 207-09, 215, 216, 218, 219-21, 227, 229, 234-36, 251, 252, 253-55, 259, 260, 264, 265, 266, 269, 270, 274-77, 281-85, 288-89, 291-93, 297, 298, 301-07, 311-12, 317-20, 328, 330-33, 348, 366-67, 370, 381, 392, 395, 400, 401, 412, 420-28, 432, 434, 436, 471, 476-78, 506, 508, 533-35, 544, 546, 548, 560-62

Lassalle, Ferdinand (1825-1864) — German journalist and lawyer, socialist; took part in the democratic movement of the Rhine Province (1848-49); founder of the General Association of German Workers (1863-64) and its president.— 130, 134-35, 138, 145, 180, 181, 203-05, 210, 247, 253, 274, 287, 316, 331, 423, 499, 502

Laura — see *Lafargue, Laura*

Lavergne-Peguilhen, Moritz von (1801-1870) — German historian and economist, belonged to the so-called Romantic School.— 549, 551

French trade union movement, representative of the Glass Workers' Trade Union in Lyons (1891).— 312

Morris, William (1834-1896) — English poet, writer and artist; participant in the working-class and socialist movement in the 1880s-90s, a leader of the Socialist League (1884-89); shared anarchist views (from the late 1880s).— 411

Motteler, Emilie — Julius Motteler's wife.— 41, 150, 313, 345, 434, 540

Motteler, Julius (1838-1907) — German Social-Democrat; member of the Reichstag (1874-79), émigré in Zurich and then in London during the operation of the Anti-Socialist Law; supervised the delivery of *Der Sozialdemokrat* and illegal Social-Democratic literature to Germany.— 13, 30, 41, 115, 150, 236, 313, 335, 345, 380, 397, 434, 438, 540, 543-44

Mudie, Charles Edward (1818-1890) — English publisher and founder of Mudie's lending library (1842).— 300

Müller, Adam Heinrich, von Nitterdorf (1779-1829) — German journalist and economist, representative of the so-called Romantic School.— 549

Müller, Hans (1867-1950) — German journalist and writer, studied in Zurich in the late 1880s and sided with the German Social-Democrats, a leader of the Jungen in the early 1890s, contributed to a number of Social-Democratic papers.— 294, 527

N

Napoleon I (Bonaparte) (1769-1821) — Emperor of the French (1804-14 and 1815).— 61

Napoleon III (Charles Louis Napoleon Bonaparte) (1808-1873) — Napoleon I's nephew, President of the Second Republic (1848-51), Emperor of the French (1852-70).— 218, 288

Nash — English Christian socialist, member of *The Workman's Times* editorial board from 1892.— 404

Necker, Jacques (1732-1804) — French banker and politician, several times Controller-General of Finance in the 1770s and 1780s, attempted to carry out reforms.— 444

Nicholas Alexandrovich (1868-1918) — heir to the Russian throne, then Emperor Nicholas II (1894-1917). — 192

Nieuwenhuis — Ferdinand Domela Nieuwenhuis's son.— 78

Nieuwenhuis, Ferdinand Domela (1846-1919) — prominent figure in the Dutch working-class movement; a founder of the Dutch Social-Democratic Party; became an anarchist in the 1890s.— 24, 49, 77-78, 232, 234, 250, 521, 524

Nim, Nimmy — see *Demuth, Helene*

Nonne, Heinrich — German student, resident in Paris; was exposed as a Prussian agent provocateur in 1884.— 295

O

Oppenheim, Max — Ludwig Kugelmann's brother-in-law.— 151-53

Oswald, Eugen (1826-1912) — German democratic journalist; took part in the 1848-49 revolution in Baden; emigrated to England after its defeat.— 76, 326

Ottenbruch — houseowner, neighbour of the Engels family in Bruch.— 86

Owens, John (1790-1846) — English merchant, founder of the Owens College in Manchester.— 431, 456

P

Packard — English physician.— 66

Padlewski, Stanisław (1856-1891) — Polish socialist, assassinated in Paris Nikolai Seliverstov, Russian general and chief of the gendarmes, in 1890; emigrated to London and then to the USA where committed suicide. — 91-92, 102, 107, 127, 129, 138, 147, 197, 198, 224, 355, 369, 415

Parnell, Charles Stewart (1846-1891) — Irish politician and statesman, Liberal; M. P. from 1875; leader of the Home Rule Party from 1877.— 128, 259, 295, 468

Parnell, William — English trade union figure, joiner, leader of the Cabinet-Makers' Union, delegate to the International Socialist Workers' Congress of 1891.— 522, 531

Paul — see *Lafargue, Paul*

Pauli, Ida — Philipp Victor Pauli's wife.— 76

Pauli, Philipp Victor (1836-d. after 1916) — German chemist, Carl Schorlemmer's friend.— 76

Pelletan, Charles Camille (1846-1915) — French politician, journalist, editor-in-chief of *La Justice* (from 1880), belonged to the Left wing of the Radical Party.— 281

Percy — see *Rosher, Percy White*

Peschel, Oskar (1826-1875) — German geographer and historian, professor at Leipzig University.— 146

Petersen, Nikolai (1854-c. 1916) — a prominent figure in the Danish working-class movement; a leader of the Left wing of the Social-Democratic Party of Denmark, delegate to the International Socialist Workers' Congress of 1889.— 408-09

Petty, Sir William (1623-1687) — English economist and statistician, founder of English classical political economy.— 141

Peus, Heinrich Wilhelm (1862-1937) — German writer, Social-Democrat (from 1890), later revisionist, was condemned for *lèse-majesté* (1892).— 364, 369

Philostratus (c. 170-245) — Greek rhetorician, sophist philosopher and writer.— 501

Pieper, Wilhelm (born c. 1826-1899) — German philologist and journalist, member of the Communist League; emigrated to London; was close to Marx and Engels in 1850-53.— 544

Plekhanov, Georgi Valentinovich (1856-1918) — prominent figure in the Russian and international working-class movement, philosopher and propagandist of Marxism in Russia, founder of the first Russian Marxist organisation — Emancipation of Labour group (1883), delegate to the International Socialist Workers' Congress of 1889 and to a number of other congresses of the Second International.— 235, 317

Praslin, Altarice Rosalba Fanny (née Sèbastiani) (1807-1847) — wife of Charles Praslin, Duke of Choiseul.— 309

Praslin, Charles Laure Hugues Théobald, duc de Choiseul (1805-1847) — French aristocrat; Peer of France; was accused of murdering his wife (1847); committed suicide.— 309

Proudhon, Pierre Joseph (1809-1865) — French writer, economist and sociologist, a founder of anarchism.— 389, 499, 517

Ptolemy — name of the Macedonian Kings who ruled Egypt for three hundred years (305-30 B. C.).— 33

Pumps — see *Rosher, Mary Ellen*

Pushkin, Alexander Sergeyevich (1799-1837) — Russian poet.— 280

radical journalist and philosopher, Young Hegelian; deputy to the Frankfurt National Assembly (Left wing) in 1848; a leader of German petty-bourgeois refugees in England in the 1850s; became a National-Liberal after 1866.— 94, 377, 520

S

Salisbury, Robert Arthur Talbot Gascoyne-Cecil, Marquis de (1830-1903) — British statesman, leader of the Conservatives; Secretary of State for India (1866-67 and 1874-78), Foreign Secretary (1878-80), Prime Minister (1885-86, 1886-92, 1895-1902).— 295

Sam — see *Moore, Samuel*

Sanders, William Stephen (b. 1871) — English socialist, a leader of the Legal Eight Hours and International Labour League, member of the Fabian Society; delegate to the International Socialist Workers' Congress of 1891.— 225, 323

Sanial, Lucien Delabarre (1835-d. after 1925) — American socialist, member of the Socialist Labor Party, editor and publisher of several socialist papers, delegate to the international socialist workers' congresses of 1891 and 1893.— 224, 232

Say, Jean Baptiste (1767-1832) — French economist, representative of vulgar political economy.— 141

Schack — see *Guillaume-Schack, Gertrud*

Scharnhorst, Gerhard Johann David von (1755-1813) — Prussian general and politician; after the defeat of the Prussian army by Napoleon I in 1806, head of the commission for a reform of the army; War Minister (1807-10) and Chief of Staff (1810-13); took an active part in the liberation war of the German people against Napoleonic rule.— 478

Schattner, Ernst (born c. 1879) — Regina Bernstein's son by first husband.— 498, 499

Schattner, Käte (born c. 1881) — Regina Bernstein's daughter by first husband.— 321, 530

Scheu, Andreas (1844-1927) — a leader of the Austrian and British socialist movement, editor of the newspaper *Gleichheit* (1870-74); member of the International; emigrated to England in 1874; a founder of the Social Democratic Federation.— 540

Scheu, Heinrich (1845-1926) — Austrian Social-Democrat, member of the International; delegate to the Hague Congress (1872), emigrated to England in 1873, artist, delegate to the International Socialist Workers' Congress of 1891, Andreas Scheu's brother.— 112, 125, 170

Schewitsch, Serge von — Russian-born American socialist; member of the *New Yorker Volkszeitung* editorial board in the 1870s-80s; editor of *The Leader* from 1886.— 20, 45

Schiller, Johann Christoph Friedrich von (1759-1805) — German poet.— 309

Schippel, Max (1859-1928) — German economist and journalist, Social-Democrat from 1886, was close to the Jungen opposition group; delegate to the International Socialist Workers' Congress of 1893.— 11, 129, 130, 174

Schlüter, Anna — Hermann Schlüter's wife.— 12, 67, 109, 113-15, 150, 151, 231, 237, 300, 325

Schlüter, Hermann (1851-1919) — German Social-Democrat, leader of the Social-Democratic publishing house in Zurich in the 1880s, a founder of the archives of German Social-Democracy; in 1889 emigrat-

ed to the USA where he joined socialist movement; author of several
works on the history of the working-
class movement in Great Britain and
America.— 12, 67, 74, 95, 109, 113-15,
146, 149-51, 168, 196-98, 226, 231,
237, 325, 392-94, 509

Schmidt— Conrad Schmidt's wife.— 285,
288, 349

Schmidt, Conrad (1863-1932) — German
economist and philosopher, Social-
Democrat, was close to Marxism in the
1880s-90s, later became a Neo-
Kantian and a revisionist.— 6-9, 25,
57-65, 109, 163, 172, 212-14, 241, 285-
88, 323, 349-52, 469, 525-28, 553

Schoemann, Georg Friedrich (1793-
1879) — German philologist and historian, author of several works on the
history of Ancient Greece.— 36

Schönlank, Bruno (1859-1901) — German
Social-Democrat, journalist; deputy to
the Reichstag (1893); contributed to
the *Vorwärts* in the 1890s.— 95, 309

Schorlemmer— Carl and Ludwig Schorlemmer's mother.— 425, 426, 432, 434,
436, 455, 458, 470, 486, 487

Schorlemmer, Carl (*Jollymeier*) (1834-
1892) — German organic chemist, professor in Manchester; member of the
German Social-Democratic Workers'
Party; friend of Marx and Engels.— 5,
6, 10, 12, 27, 30, 41, 44, 48-50, 96, 104,
111, 154, 159, 163, 168, 204, 211, 219,
220, 221, 224, 226, 227, 229, 232, 313,
319-20, 364, 370, 418, 425, 426, 430-
33, 435, 436, 439, 447, 448, 453-58,
461, 464-65, 469, 470, 484-87

Schorlemmer, Johanna— Ludwig Schorlemmer's daughter.— 488

Schorlemmer, Ludwig— Carl Schorlemmer's brother.— 81-82, 418-19, 425-
26, 431-34, 439, 454-58, 484-88

Schramm, Carl August (1830-
1905) — German Social-Democrat,

economist, criticised Marxism, withdrew from the party in the 1880s.—
132

Schröder, Ludwig (1849-1914) — German
Social-Democrat, one of the organisers
and leaders of the miners' movement in
the Ruhr area.— 376, 429, 448

Schumacher, Georg Gerber (1844-
1917) — German Social-Democrat,
tanner, later businessman; deputy to
the Reichstag from 1884, adhered to
the party's opportunist wing, delegate
to the International Socialist Workers'
Congress of 1891; expelled from the
Social-Democratic Party in 1898.—
100

Schuster— professor of physics in Manchester, Carl Schorlemmer's
student.— 455

Schweinitz, Hans Lothar (1822-
1901) — German general, diplomat
and military writer, Ambassador to
Vienna (1869-76) and St Petersburg
(1876-92); advocated rapprochement
between Germany and Russia.— 374

Schweitzer, Johann Baptist von (1833-
1875) — German lawyer; a Lassallean
leader; editor of *Der Social-Demokrat*
(1864-67), President of the General Association of German Workers (1867-
71), supported unification of Germany
under Prussia's supremacy; fought
against the Social-Democratic Workers' Party; expelled from the General
Association for his contacts with the
Prussian authorities (1872).— 11, 97

Seidel, Robert (1850-1933) — Swiss Social-Democrat, teacher, editor of the
Arbeiterstimme in the 1890s, delegate to
the International Socialist Workers'
Congress of 1893.— 495, 496, 505

Seliverstov, Nikolai Dmitrievich (1830-
1890) — Russian general, chief of gendarmes, murdered in Paris by the Polish socialist Stanisław Padlewski.— 92,
102

sections of the First International; Secretary of the Federal Council; delegate to the Hague Congress (1872); member of the General Council in New York and its General Secretary (1872-74), a founder of the Socialist Labor Party (1876); propagandist of Marxism; a friend and associate of Marx and Engels.— 5, 10-12, 20-21, 45-48, 51-52, 67, 73-75, 95-96, 101-02, 109, 113, 123, 125-28, 137-39, 146-50, 165-68, 196-98, 224-27, 231-33, 237-39, 250-51, 264-67, 277, 297-300, 311, 326-29, 369-72, 394, 415, 445-47, 453, 463, 507-09, 514

Sorge, Katharina— Friedrich Adolph Sorge's wife.— 12, 48, 49, 67, 75, 96, 101, 103, 109, 125, 128, 139, 149, 168, 198, 227, 233, 239, 251, 267, 277, 299, 300, 329, 372, 447, 509

Stambulov, Stefan (1854-1895) —Bulgarian statesman; deputy (from 1880) and Chairman of the National Assembly (1884-86), head of government (1887-94), advocate of the anti-Russian foreign policy.— 162

Stanley, Sir Henry Morton (real name John Rowlands) (1841-1904) — one of the explorers of Africa; leader of the English expedition to the Equatorial Africa (1887-89); M. P. (1895-1900).— 475

Stead, William Thomas (1849-1912) — English journalist and writer; Liberal; editor of the Pall Mall Gazette (1883-89); editor of the Review of Reviews in the 1890s.— 274

Steinthal— Unitarian clergyman in Manchester, Engels' acquaintance.— 456

Stepnyak— see Kravchinsky, Sergei Mikhailovich

Steuart, Sir James (afterwards Denham) (1712-1780) — British economist, one of the last Mercantilists.— 141

Stinzleih.— 99

Stirner, Max (real name Johann Caspar Schmidt) (1806-1856) — German philosopher, Young Hegelian, an ideologist of individualism and anarchism.— 136

Stößel— Swiss government official in Zurich.— 241

Strabo (63 B.C.-A.D. c. 20) — Greek geographer and historian.— 34

Strasser— Louise Kautsky's mother.— 88, 532

Stumm-Halberg, Karl Ferdinand, Baron von (1836-1901) — German manufacturer and conservative politician.— 362, 364, 371

Sybel, Heinrich von (1817-1895) — German historian and politician, National-Liberal from 1867.— 94

T

Tacitus, Publius Cornelius (c. 55-c. 120) — Roman historian and orator.— 22

Tauscher, Leonhard (1840-1914) — German Social-Democrat, compositor; during the operation of the Anti-Socialist Law took part in printing Der Sozialdemokrat in Zurich, then in London; later an editor of Social-Democratic periodicals in Stuttgart. — 30, 41, 104, 114

Taylor, H. R.— member of the London Trades Union Council and of the Social Democratic Federation, delegate to the International Socialist Workers' Congress of 1891, candidate at the parliamentary elections of 1892.— 493, 532

Taylor, Sedley (latter half of the 19th cent.-early 20th cent.) — British economist, armchair socialist; took part in the co-operative movement in England, advocated workers' sharing in the capitalists' profits; in the 1880s

INDEX OF LITERARY AND MYTHOLOGICAL NAMES

INDEX OF QUOTED
AND MENTIONED LITERATURE

WORKS BY KARL MARX AND FREDERICK ENGELS

Marx, Karl

Capital. A Critique of Political Economy (present edition, vols 35-37).— 36, 137, 172, 216, 337

Capital. A Critique of Political Economy. Volume I, Book I: The Process of Production of Capital (present edition, Vol. 35).— 63, 279, 314, 406, 444, 526, 536-37

— Das Kapital. Kritik der politischen Oekonomie. Erster Band. Buch I: Der Produktionsprocess des Kapitals. Hamburg, 1867.— 543

— Das Kapital. Kritik der politischen Oekonomie. Erster Band, Buch I: Der Produktionsprocess des Kapitals. Dritte vermehrte Auflage. Hamburg, 1883.— 322

— Capital: a critical analysis of capitalist production. Translated from the third German edition by Samuel Moore and Edward Aveling and edited by Frederick Engels. Vol. I [part 1-2]. London, 1887.— 30, 160

— Das Kapital. Kritik der politischen Oekonomie. Erster Band. Buch I: Der Produktionsprocess des Kapitals. Vierte, durchgesehene Auflage. Herausgegeben von Friedrich Engels. Hamburg, 1890.— 30, 48, 93, 109, 114, 126, 146, 158, 163

— Capital: a critical analysis of capitalist production. Translated from the third German edition by Samuel Moore and Edward Aveling. And edited by Frederick Engels. New York, [1890].— 125, 197

— Kapitał. Krytyka ekonomii politycznej. Tom pierwszy. Księga I. Wytwarzanie kapitału. Lipsk, 1884-1889 [1890].— 75

Capital. A Critique of Political Economy. Volume II, Book II: The Process of Circulation of Capital (present edition, Vol. 36)

— Das Kapital. Kritik der politischen Oekonomie. Zweiter Band. Buch II: Der Cirkulationsprocess des Kapitals. Herausgegeben von Friedrich Engels. Hamburg, 1885.— 141, 159

Capital. A Critique of Political Economy. Volume III. Book III: The Process of Capitalist Production as a Whole (present edition, Vol. 37)
— Das Kapital. Kritik der politischen Oekonomie. Herausgegeben von Friedrich Engels. Dritter Band, Theile 1-2. Buch III. Der Gesammtprocess der kapitalistischen Produktion. Hamburg, 1894.— 50, 63, 94, 144, 149, 153, 171, 173, 184, 196, 210, 211, 212, 214, 218, 219, 231, 241, 250, 267, 280, 285, 301, 314, 322-23, 329, 331, 334, 345, 351, 365, 368, 370, 379, 385, 390, 396, 405, 439, 450, 472, 511, 525

The Civil War in France (present edition, Vol. 22)
— Der Bürgerkrieg in Frankreich. Adresse des Generalraths der Internationalen Arbeiter-Association. Dritte deutsche Auflage vermehrt durch die beiden Adressen des Generalraths über den deutsch-französischen Krieg und durch eine Einleitung von Friedrich Engels. Berlin, 1891.— 137, 144, 145, 146, 148, 159, 171

A Contribution to the Critique of Political Economy. Part One (present edition, Vol. 29)
— Zur Kritik der politischen Oekonomie. Erstes Heft. Berlin, 1859.— 141, 159

Critique of the Gotha Programme (present edition, Vol. 24).— 90, 97, 103, 107, 109, 118, 119, 129, 133, 134, 161, 167, 173, 179, 266, 316
— Randglossen zum Programm der deutschen Arbeiterpartei. In: *Die Neue Zeit*, 9. Jg. 1890/91, 1. Bd., Nr. 18.— 103, 107, 109, 118, 119, 123, 126, 133-37, 143, 150, 176, 199
— Randglossen zum Programm der deutschen Arbeiterpartei. In: *Vorwärts. Berliner Volksblatt*, Nr. 27-28 (1. Beilage), 1., 3. Februar 1891.— 118, 123
— Randglossen zum Programm der deutschen Arbeiterpartei. In: *Sächsische Arbeiter-Zeitung*, Nr. 30, 31, 33, 35; 6., 7., 10., 12. Februar 1891.— 133

The Eighteenth Brumaire of Louis Bonaparte (present edition, Vol. 11).— 36, 63, 92
— Le Dix-huit Brumaire de Louis Bonaparte. In: *Le Socialiste*, No. 16-24, 26-29, 37-39, 41, 42, 44-47, 49, 51-56, 58, 59, 61; 7, 14, 21, 28 janvier, 4, 11, 18, 25 février, 4, 18, 25 mars, 1, 8 avril, 3, 10, 17 juin, 1, 8, 22, 29 juillet, 5, 12, 26 août, 12, 19, 26 septembre, 3, 10, 17, 31 octobre, 7, 21 novembre 1891.— 92

First Address of the General Council of the International Working Men's Association on the Franco-Prussian War (present edition, Vol. 22)
— The General Council of the International Workingmen's Association on the War. To the Members of the International Workingmen's Association in Europe and the United States. July 23rd, 1870, [London,] 1870.— 137, 145
— Erste Adresse des Generalraths über den deutsch-französischen Krieg. In: Marx, K. *Der Bürgerkrieg in Frankreich.* Dritte deutsche Auflage. Berlin, 1891.— 137, 145

Herr Vogt (present edition, Vol. 17)
— Herr Vogt. London, 1860.— 543

Instructions for the Delegates of the Provisional General Council. The Different Questions (present edition, Vol. 20)
— Instructions for the Delegates of the Provisional General Council. In: *The International Courier*, Nos. 6/7 and Nos. 8/10, February 20 and March 13, 1867.— 173
— Rapport du conseil central. Sur les différentes questions mises à l'étude par la conférence de septembre 1864. In: *Le Courrier international*, Nos. 8/10 and 11; 9 and 16 mars, 1867.— 173

The Knight of the Noble Consciousness (present edition, Vol. 12)
— Der Ritter vom edelmüthigen Bewußtsein. [New York, 1854].—545

[*Letter to 'Otechestvenniye Zapiski'*] (present edition, Vol. 24)
— [Letter to 'Otechestvenniye Zapiski'.] In: *Вѣстникъ Народной Воли*, No. 5, 1886.—384

Letters from the 'Deutsch-Französische Jahrbücher' (present edition, Vol. 3)
— Ein Briefwechsel von 1843. M[arx] an R [uge], im März 1843; Köln, im Mai 1843; Kreuznach, im September 1843. In: *Deutsch-Französische Jahrbücher*, hrsg. von Arnold Ruge und Karl Marx. Lfg. 1/2. Paris, 1844.—94

On Proudhon [Letter to J. B. Schweitzer] (present edition, Vol. 20)
— Über P.-J. Proudhon. In: *Der Social-Demokrat*, Nr. 16-18, 1., 3., 5. Februar 1865.—389
— Karl Marx über Proudhon (Veröffentlicht in Berliner *Sozialdemokrat*, 1865). In: Marx, K. *Das Elend der Philosophie. Antwort auf Proudhon's 'Philosophie des Elends'*. Deutsch von E. Bernstein und K. Kautsky. Mit Vorwort und Noten von Friedrich Engels. Zweite Auflage. Stuttgart, 1892.—389

The Poverty of Philosophy. Answer to the 'Philosophy of Poverty' by M. Proudhon (present edition, Vol. 6).—92
— Das Elend der Philosophie. Antwort auf Proudhon's 'Philosophie des Elends'. Deutsch von E. Bernstein und K. Kautsky. Mit Vorwort und Noten von Friedrich Engels. Stuttgart, 1885.—199, 368, 435
— Das Elend der Philosophie. Antwort auf Proudhon's 'Philosophie des Elends'. Deutsch von E. Bernstein und K. Kautsky. Mit Vorwort und Noten von Friedrich Engels. Zweite Auflage. Stuttgart, 1892.—210, 273
— Misère de la philosophie. Réponse à la philosophie de la misère de M. Proudhon. Avec une préface de Friedrich Engels. Paris, 1896.—92, 203

The Protectionists, the Free Traders and the Working Class (present edition, Vol. 6)
— Die Schutzzöllner, die Freihandelsmänner und die arbeitende Klasse. In: Marx, K. *Zwei Reden über die Freihandels- und Schutz-zollfrage aus dem Französischen übersetzt und mit einem Vorwort und erläuternden Anmerkungen versehen von J. Weydemeyer*. Hamm, 1848.—114, 150

Second Address of the General Council of the International Working Men's Association on the Franco-Prussian War (present edition, Vol. 22)
— Second Address of the General Council of the International Working-Men's Association on the war. To the members of the International Working Men's Association in Europe and the United States. London, September 9th, 1870. [London,] 1870.—137, 145
— Zweite Adresse des Generalraths über der deutsch-französischen Krieg. In: Marx, K. *Der Bürgerkrieg in Frankreich*. Dritte deutsche Auflage. Berlin, 1891.—137, 145

Speech on the Question of Free Trade (present edition, Vol. 6)
— Rede über die Frage des Freihandels, gehalten in dem demokratischen Verein zu Brüssel in der öffentlichen Sitzung vom 9. Januar 1848. In: Marx, K. *Zwei Reden*

Marx and Rodbertus. Preface to the First German Edition of 'The Poverty of Philosophy' by Karl Marx (present edition, Vol. 26)
— Vorwort. In: Marx, K. *Das Elend der Philosophie. Antwort auf Proudhon's 'Philosophie des Elends'*. Deutsch von E. Bernstein und K. Kautsky. Mit Vorwort und Noten von Friedrich Engels. Zweite Auflage. Stuttgart, 1892.— 335, 389

May 4 in London (present edition, Vol. 27)
— Der 4. Mai in London. In: *Arbeiter-Zeitung*, Nr. 21, 23. Mai 1890.— 12

On the History of Early Christianity (present edition, Vol. 27)
— Zur Geschichte des Urchristenthums. In: *Die Neue Zeit*, 13. Jg. 1894/1895, 1. Band, Nr. 1-2.— 5

The Origin of the Family, Private Property and the State. In the Light of the Researches of Lewis H. Morgan (present edition, Vol. 26)
— Der Ursprung der Familie, des Privateigenthums und des Staats. Im Anschluß an Lewis H. Morgan's Forschungen. Hottingen-Zürich, 1884.— 199, 202

— L'origine della famiglia, della proprietà privata e dello Stato, in relazione alla ricerche di Luigi H. Morgan. Benevento, 1885.— 161

— Der Ursprung der Familie, des Privateigenthums und des Staats. Im Anschluß an Lewis H. Morgan's Forschungen. Dritte Auflage. Stuttgart, 1889.— 33

— Der Ursprung der Familie, des Privateigenthums und des Staats. Im Anschluß an Lewis H. Morgan's Forschungen. Vierte Auflage. Stuttgart, 1892.— 4, 23, 95, 136, 142, 144-45, 148, 161, 164, 173, 184, 192, 193, 196, 198, 199, 204, 205, 209, 211, 214, 215, 218, 221, 222, 232-33, 250, 251, 273, 311, 385, 427

— L'Origine de la famille, de la propriété privée et de l'État. (Pour faire suite aux travaux de Lewis H. Morgan.) Traduction française par Henri Ravé. Paris, 1893.— 142, 145, 154, 164, 165, 172, 199, 201, 202, 204, 215, 251, 399, 427

— Происхожденіе семьи, частной собственности и государства. (Переводъ съ 4-го нѣмецкаго изданія.) С.-Петербургъ, 1894.— 390

Outlines of a Critique of Political Economy (present edition, Vol. 3)
— Umrisse zu einer Kritik der Nationalökonomie. In: *Die Neue Zeit*, 9. Jg. 1890/91, 1. Band, Nr. 8.— 91

The Peasant War in Germany (present edition, Vol. 10)
— Der deutsche Bauernkrieg. In: *Neue Rheinische Zeitung. Politisch-ökonomische Revue*, redigirt von Karl Marx. London-Hamburg-New York, 1850, H. 5/6, Mai-Okt.— 184

Preface to the Fourth German Edition of Volume I of 'Capital' (present edition, Vol. 35)
— Zur vierten Auflage. In: Marx, K. *Das Kapital. Kritik der politischen Oekonomie*. Erster Band. Buch I: Der Produktionsprocess des Kapitals. Vierte, durchgesehene Auflage. Herausgegeben von Friedrich Engels. Hamburg, 1890.— 48, 93, 146

Preface to Volume II of 'Capital' (present edition, Vol. 36)
— Vorwort. In: Marx, K. *Das Kapital. Kritik der politischen Oekonomie*. Zweiter Band. Buch II: Der Cirkulationsprocess des Kapitals. Herausgegeben von Friedrich Engels. Hamburg, 1885.— 141, 159

Preface to Volume III of 'Capital' (present edition, Vol. 37)

— Manifest der Kommunistischen Partei. Veröffentlicht im Februar 1848. London, 1848.— 160

— Manifesto of the Communist Party. Authorised English translation. Edited and annotated by Frederick Engels. London, 1888.— 159

— Das Kommunistische Manifest. Vierte autorisierte deutsche Ausgabe. Mit einem neuen Vorwort von Friedrich Engels. London, 1890.— 12

— Il Manifesto del Partito Comunista 1847. Con prefazione di Pietro Gori. Milano, 1891.— 148

— Il Manifesto del Partito Comunista (1848). Traduzione del tedesco di Pompeo Bettini. In: *Lotta di Classe*, Num. 8, 10, 12, 13, 15-17, 19-22; 17-18 Settembre, 1-2, 15-16, 22-23 Ottobre, 5-6, 12-13, 19-20 Novembre; 3-4, 10-11, 17-18, 24-25 Dicembre 1892.— 143-44

WORKS BY DIFFERENT AUTHORS

Adler, V. *Die Verkehrsanlagen von Groß-Wien und die Wiener Arbeiter.* In: *Arbeiter-Zeitung*, IV. Jg., Nr. 2, 8. Jänner 1892.— 359

Aeschylus. *Oresteia.*— 201

Ahlwardt, H. *Neue Enthüllungen. Judenflinten.* Dresden, 1892.— 448

Anzengruber, L. *Der G 'Wissenswurm.*— 450

A[rendt], O. *Mittheilung.* Signed: *O. A.* In: *Deutsches Wochenblatt*, III. Jg., Nr. 49, 4. Dezember 1890.— 85

Audorf, J. *Lied der deutschen Arbeiter.*— 180

— (anon.) *Zwanglose Wochenplanderei. Zum Parteikongresse.* In: *Hamburger Echo*, Nr. 245, 18. Oktober 1891 (Erste Beilage).— 316

Auer, I. [Speeches at the Erfurt Congress of the Social-Democratic Party of Germany.] In: *Protokoll über die Verhandlungen des Parteitages der Sozialdemokratischen Partei Deutschlands. Abgehalten zu Erfurt vom 14. bis 20. Oktober 1891.* Berlin, 1891.— 266, 273

August Bebel der Arbeiter-Bismarck. Von einem Socialisten. Berlin [1890].— 310

Aveling, E. *The Cholera and the Hamburg Socialists.* In: *The Pall Mall Gazette*, No. 8577, September 16, 1892.— 531

— *Discord in 'The International'. Continental Opinion on the British Trades Unionists.* In: *The Pall Mall Gazette*, No. 8598, October 11, 1892.— 546

— (anon). *Germany Flooded with Papers from Kentish Town.— A Talk with the Editor.* In: *The Star*, No. 832, September 29, 1890.— 28

— [Statements on Gilles.] In: *Vorwärts*, Nr. 211, 212; 10., 11. September 1891.— 238, 241

— 'In der *Rheinisch-Westfälischen Zeitung* vom 22. Aug. findet sich ein Artikel...' In: *Vorwärts*, Nr. 211, 10 September 1891.— 238

— (anon.) *The New Era in German Socialism.* In: *The Daily Chronicle and Clerkenwell News*, No. 8903, September 25, 1890.— 28

— *The Students' Marx. An Introduction to the Study of Karl Marx' 'Capital'.* London, 1892.— 483

— 'Der Urheber der über mich in der Deutschen Presse...' In: *Vorwärts*, Nr. 212, 11. September 1891.— 238

Aveling, E., Marx-Aveling, E. *Die Wahlen in Großbritannien.* In: *Die Neue Zeit*, 10. Jg. 1891/92, 2. Band, Nr. 45.— 476, 482, 493, 497, 508, 515, 516

Bachofen, J. J. *Das Mutterrecht. Eine Untersuchung über die Gynaikokratie der alten Welt nach ihrer religiösen und rechtlichen Natur.* Stuttgart, 1861.— 201, 202

Barth, P. *Die Geschichtsphilosophie Hegel's und der Hegelianer bis auf Marx und Hartmann. Ein kritischer Versuch.* Leipzig, 1890.— 7, 63, 213

Bax, E. B. *The German Party—Its Misfortunes and Its Faults.* In: *Justice*, No. 389, June 27, 1891.— 211

— *Internecine Divisions in the Socialist Party.* In: *Justice*, No. 440, June 18, 1892.— 448, 475

Bebel, A. [Speech in the Reichstag on 28 November 1891.] In: *Vorwärts*, 8. Jg., Nr. 280, 29. November 1891 (1. Beilage) and in: *Stenographische Berichte über die Verhandlungen des Reichstags. VIII. Legislaturperiode. I. Session 1890/92.* Band V. Berlin, 1892.— 308, 312

— [Speech in the Reichstag on 12 February 1892.] In: *Vorwärts*, 9. Jg., Nr. 37, 13. Februar 1892 (1. Beilage) and in: *Stenographische Berichte über die Verhandlungen des Reichstags. VIII. Legislaturperiode. I. Session 1890/92.* Band VI. Berlin, 1892.— 364

— [Speech in the Reichstag on 15 February 1892.] In: *Vorwärts*, 9. Jg., Nr. 39, 16. Februar 1892 (1. Beilage) and in: *Stenographische Berichte über die Verhandlungen des Reichstags. VIII. Legislaturperiode. I. Session 1890/92.* Band VI. Berlin, 1892.— 364

— (anon.) *Berlin, 7. Oktober. Der 30. September bezeichnete den glorreichen Abschluß einer geschichtlichen Epoche...* in the section: *Ausland. Deutschland.* In: *Arbeiter-Zeitung*, II. Jg., Nr. 41. 10. Oktober 1890.— 64

— *Erklärung.* In: *Berliner Volksblatt*, 7. Jg., Nr. 173, 29. Juli 1890.— 11

— *Die europäische Lage und der Sozialismus.* In: *Vorwärts*, Nr. 235, 8. Oktober 1891 (Beilage).— 267

— *La Femme dans le passé, le présent & l'avenir.* Traduction française par Henri Ravé. Paris, 1891.— 142, 145, 164, 201

— *Die Frau in der Vergangenheit, Gegenwart und Zukunft.* Zürich, 1883.— 142, 145, 164, 201

— *Ein internationaler Kongreß für den Achtstundentag.* In: *Die Neue Zeit*. 11. Jg. 1892/93, 1. Band, Nr. 2.— 553

— (anon.) *Die Reichstags-Wahl in Stolp-Lauenburg.* In: *Vorwärts*, Nr. 256, 1. November 1891.— 294

— (anon.) *Die russische Anleihe.* Signed: *A. B.* In: *Vorwärts*, Nr. 226, 27. September 1891.— 242

— [Speeches at the Erfurt Congress of the Social-Democratic Party of Germany.] In: *Protokoll über die Verhandlungen des Parteitages der Sozialdemokratischen Partei Deutschlands. Abgehalten zu Erfurt vom 14. bis 20. Oktober 1891.* Berlin, 1891.— 265

E[rnst], P. *Jedem der volle Ertrag seiner Arbeit!* *(Erwiederung.)* In: *Berliner Volks-Tribüne*, IV. Jg., Nr. 26, 28. Juni 1890.— 7

Field, A. *The International Labour Congress.* In: *The Star*, June 23, 1891.— 207, 208
— *The International Labour Congress.* In: *The Star*, June 27, 1891.— 219

Fireman, P. *Kritik der Marx'schen Werttheorie.* In: *Jahrbücher für Nationalökonomie und Statistik.* Dritte Folge. Dritter Band. Jena, 1892.— 322, 525

Fischer, R. *Nochmals das 'Recht auf den vollen Arbeitsertrag'.* In: *Berliner Volks-Tribüne*, IV. Jg., Nr. 27, 5. Juli 1890.— 7
— [Speeches at the Erfurt Congress of the Social-Democratic Party of Germany.] In: *Protokoll über die Verhandlungen des Parteitages der Sozialdemokratischen Partei Deutschlands. Abgehalten zu Erfurt vom 14. bis 20. Oktober 1891.* Berlin, 1891.— 266, 273

Fleischmann, A. *Rechtszustände in Ost-Afrika. Eine juristisch-ethnologische Studie.* In: *Das Ausland*, 63. Jg., Nr. 42-43, 20., 27. Oktober 1890.— 198

F[rankel], L. *Zur französischen Arbeiterbewegung.* In: *Sächsische Arbeiter-Zeitung*, Nr. 170, 178; 3., 12. Dezember 1890.— 97

Friedrich II. *Instruction für die General-Majors von der Cavallerie.* (14. August 1748). Signed: *Fch.* In: *Friedrich der Große. Militärische Schriften erläutert und mit Anmerkungen versehen durch v. Taysen, Oberstlieutenant und Abtheilungschef im Neben-Etat des Großen Generalstabes.* Berlin, 1882. In: *Militärische Klassiker des In- und Auslandes. Mit Einleitungen und Erklärungen.*— 182

Fullarton, J. *On the Regulation of Currencies; being an examination of the principles, on which it is proposed to restrict, within certain fixed limits, the future issues on credit of the Bank of England, and of the other banking establishments throughout the country.* Second Edition, with corrections and additions. London, 1845.— 526

Georg von Sachsen [Order of the Day. 8 June 1891.] In: *Vorwärts*, 9. Jg., Nr. 26, 31. Januar 1892.— 346, 348

Gilles, F. *The Independent Socialists in Germany.* In: *Justice*, No. 415, December 26, 1891.— 324

Giraud-Teulon, A. *Les Origines de la famille.* Questions sur les antécédents des sociétés patriarcales. Genève, Paris, 1874.— 193, 194, 202
— *Les Origines du mariage et de la famille.* Genève, Paris, 1884.— 193, 194, 202

[Grunzig, J.] *Die Vorgänge im Lager der deutschen Socialdemokratie.* In: *New Yorker Volkszeitung*, 13. Jg., Nr. 217, 10. September 1890.— 45

Guesde, J. *Briefe aus Frankreich.* In: *Vorwärts*, Nr. 23, 25; 28., 30. Januar 1891.— 117, 130
— *Une interpellation nécessaire.* In: *Le Socialiste*, 2ᵉ année, No. 17, 14 janvier 1891.— 110

Guesde, J., Lafargue, P. *Paris, le 12 mai 1892. Le Conseil national est heureux de porter à la connaissance des Fédérations,...* In: *Le Socialiste*, 3ᵉ année, No. 86, 15 mai 1892.— 423

Haller, K. L. v. *Restauration der Staats-Wissenschaft oder Theorie des natürlich-geselligen Zustands; der Chimäre des künstlich-bürgerlichen entgegengesezt*, Bd. 1-6, Winterthur, 1816-34.— 549

Headingley, A. S. *French and German Possibilists.* In: *Justice*, No. 354, October 25, 1890.— 56

Hegel, G. W. F. *Encyklopädie der philosophischen Wissenschaften im Grundrisse.* Zum Gebrauch seiner Vorlesungen von Georg Wilhelm Friedrich Hegel. Vierte unveränderte Auflage mit einem Vorwort von Karl Rosenkranz. Berlin, 1845.— 286
— *Encyclopädie der philosophischen Wissenschaften im Grundrisse.* Erster Theil. *Die Logik.* In: G. W. F. Hegel. *Werke.* Zweite Auflage, Bd. VI, Berlin, 1843.— 286, 351
— *Vorlesungen über Aesthetik.* Erster Theil. In: G. W. F. Hegel. *Werke.* Zweite Auflage, Bd. X, Berlin, 1842.— 287
— *Vorlesungen über die Geschichte der Philosophie.* Erster Theil. In: G. W. F. Hegel. *Werke.* Zweite Auflage, Bd. XIII, Berlin, 1840.— 286, 287
— *Wissenschaft der Logik.* In: G. W. F. Hegel. *Werke.* Zweite Auflage, Bd. IV, Berlin, 1841.— 213

Herkner, H. *Die oberelsässische Baumwollindustrie und ihre Arbeiter. Auf Grund der Thatsachen dargestellt.* In: *Abhandlungen aus dem staatswissenschaftlichen Seminar zu Strassburg.* Herausgegeben von G. F. Knapp und L. Brentano. Heft IV, Strassburg, 1887.— 344

Horace (Quintus Horatius Flaccus). *Ars Poetica.*— 212
— *Epistolae.*— 328

Hyndman, H. M. *An den Redakteur des 'Vorwärts'.* Under the general heading: *Die Sozialdemokratische Föderation und Mr. Hyndman.* In: *Vorwärts*, Nr. 220, 20. September 1892.— 540, 545
— *The English Correspondence of the 'Vorwärts'. To the Editor of 'Justice'.* In: *Justice*, No. 454, September 24, 1892.— 540, 545

Ibsen, H. *Fruen fra Havet.*— 27

[Kablukov] Каблуковъ, Н. [А.] *Вопросъ о рабочихъ въ сельскомъ хозяйствѣ.* Москва, 1884.— 443

[Karyshev] Карышевъ, Н. [А.] *Крестьянскія вньнадьльныя аренды.* Дерптъ, 1892.— 443

[Kautsky, K.] *Der Entwurf des neuen Parteiprogramms.* In: *Die Neue Zeit*, 9. Jg. 1890/91, 2. Band, Nr. 49.— 209, 239, 240, 246, 266, 273, 316
— *Das Erfurter Programm in seinem grundsätzlichen Theil erläutert.* Stuttgart, 1892.— 322, 367, 389, 492
— (anon.) *Friedrich Engels. Zu seinem siebzigsten Geburtstag.* In: *Die Neue Zeit*, 9. Jg. 1890/91, 1. Band, Nr. 8.— 90
— *Thomas More und seine Utopie. Mit einer historischen Einleitung.* Stuttgart, 1888.— 163, 172-73, 343
— *Vollmar und der Staatssozialismus.* In: *Die Neue Zeit*, 10.Jg. 1891/92, 2. Band, Nr. 49.— 516

Kautsky, K., Eichhoff, W. *Wie Brentano Marx vernichtet.* In: *Die Neue Zeit*, 9. Jg. 1890/91, 2. Band, Nr. 32.—163

[Kautsky, L.] *London den 4. Mai. Die Arbeit von zwölf langen Monaten fand gestern eine Belohnung,...* Signed: *L. K.* In the section: *Ausland. England.* In: *Arbeiter-Zeitung*, III. Jg., Nr. 20, 15. Mai 1891.—192

— *Die englische Wahlschlacht ist beendet;...* Signed: *L. K.* In: *Arbeiter-Zeitung*, IV. Jg., Nr. 32, 5. August 1892.—434

— *Aus England. London, 5. Dez. Wir leben im Zeitalter der Kongresse...* Signed: *L. K.* In: *Arbeiterinnen-Zeitung*, I. Jg., Nr. 1, 1. Jänner 1892.—252

Knapp, G. F. *Die Bauern-Befreiung und der Ursprung der Landarbeiter in den älteren Theilen Preußens.* Theile 1-2. Leipzig, 1887.—6

Knies, C. *Geld und Credit.* Erste Abtheilung. *Das Geld. Darlegung der Grundlehren von dem Gelde, mit einer Vorerörterung über das Kapital und die Uebertragung der Nutzungen.* Berlin, 1873.—526

Kovalevsky, M. *Modern Customs and Ancient Laws of Russia Being the Ilchester Lectures for 1889-90.* London, 1891.—124

— *Tableau des origines et de l'évolution de la famille et de la propriété.* Stockholm, 1890.—22

Lafargue, L. *Ein Gruß aus Frankreich.* In: *Arbeiterinnen-Zeitung*, I. Jg., Nr. 1, 1. Jänner 1892.—293, 331

— *Nachtarbeit für die Frauen in Frankreich.* In: *Arbeiterinnen-Zeitung*, I. Jg., Nr. 8, 15. April 1892.—401

Lafargue, P.
— *Le citoyen Lafargue a adressé ... Monsieur le Directeur, Dans le Temps du 14 Mai...* In: *Le Socialiste*, 2ᵉ année, No. 36, 27 mai 1891.—191
— *Le Droit à la Paresse. Réfutation du 'Droit au Travail' de 1848.* Paris [1883].—24
— (anon.) *Le Gil-Blas interviewer.* In: *Le Socialiste*, 1ᵉʳ année, No. 6, 26 octobre 1890.—54
— *Karl Marx. Persönliche Erinnerungen.* In: *Die Neue Zeit*, 9. Jg. 1890/91, 1. Band, Nr. 1.-2.—55
— [Letter to the Editors of *The Daily Chronicle and Clerkenwell News*.] In: *The Daily Chronicle and Clerkenwell News*, April 20, 1892.—561
— *Der Mythus von Adam und Eva. Ein Beitrag zur vergleichenden Mythologie.* In: *Die Neue Zeit*, 9. Jg. 1890/91, 2. Band, Nr. 34, 35.—174, 194, 200
— *Proposition de loi tendant à la séparation des Églises et de l'État.* In: *Le Socialiste*, 2ᵉ année, No. 66, 26 décembre 1891.—320, 328, 330, 348
— (anon.) *La propriété féodale.* Signed: *Fergus.* In: *La Nouvelle Revue.* Douzième année. Tome soixante-huitième. Janvier-février 1891.—123
— (anon.) *Der Schuß Padlewsky's.* Signed: *X.* In: *Die Neue Zeit*, 9. Jg. 1890/91, 1. Band, Nr. 19.—123, 129
— *Die sozialistische Bewegung in Frankreich von 1876-1890.* In: *Die Neue Zeit*, 8. Jg., Nr. 8, August 1890.—12
— *La théorie de la Valeur et de la plus-value de Marx et les économistes bourgeois.* In:

La Revue Socialiste, Tome XVI (juillet-décembre 1892) [No. 93, septembre 1892].— 129, 141, 159, 174

Lassalle, F. *Reden und Schriften*. Neue Gesammt-Ausgabe. Mit einer biographischen Einleitung herausgegeben von Ed. Bernstein, London. Bände 1-3. Berlin, 1892-1893.— 138, 204, 210, 248, 253, 316, 331
— *Das System der erworbenen Rechte. Eine Versöhnung des positiven Rechts und der Rechtsphilosophie*. In zwei Theilen. Leipzig, 1861.— 129, 331

Lavergne-Peguilhen, M. *Grundzüge der Gesellschaftswissenschaft*. Erster Theil. *Die Bewegungs- und Productionsgesetze. Ein staatswirthschaftlicher Versuch*. Königsberg, 1838.— 549-551

[Lavrov] [Лавровъ, П. Л.] *Задачи исторіи мысли*. Женева, 1888-1891.— 528

Letourneau, Ch. *L'évolution du mariage et de la famille*. In: *Bibliothèque anthropologique*. Tome VI. Paris, 1888.— 202-03

Liebknecht, W. [Speech at the Halle Congress of the Social-Democratic Party of Germany on 15 October 1890.] In: *Berliner Volksblatt*. 7. Jg., Nr. 241, 16. Oktober 1890 (Beilage) and *Protokoll über die Verhandlungen des Parteitages der Sozialdemokratischen Partei Deutschlands. Abgehalten zu Halle a. S. vom 12. bis 18. Oktober 1890*. Berlin, 1890.— 107, 134, 176
— [Speech at the Erfurt Congress of the Social-Democratic Party of Germany on 21 October 1891.] In: *Vorwärts*, Nr. 247, 22. Oktober 1891 (Beilage 1).— 266, 267
— *To the Editor of 'The People's Press'*. In: *The People's Press*, No. 22, 2 August 1890.— 3

McLennan, J. F. *Primitive Marriage. An Inquiry into the Origin of the Form of Capture in Marriage Ceremonies*. Edinburgh, 1865.— 194

Marseillaise (French revolutionary song).— 228, 244

Marwitz, F. A. L. von der. *Aus dem Nachlasse*. Bände 1-2. Berlin, 1852.— 549

Marx-Aveling, E. *Friedrich Engels*. In: *Sozialdemokratische Monatsschrift*, 2. Jg., Nr. 10-11, 30. November 1890.— 88
— *Wie sollen wir organisieren?* In: *Arbeiterinnen-Zeitung*, 1. Jg., Nr. 3, 5. Februar 1892.— 252, 331

Mehring, F. *Die Deutsche Socialdemokratie. Ihre Geschichte und ihre Lehre. Eine historisch-kritische Darstellung*. Dritte durchgesehene und vermehrte Auflage. Bremen, 1879.— 376
— (anon.) *Hängen und Würgen*. In: *Züricher Post*, Nr. 34, 10. Februar 1891.— 133
— *Herrn Eugen Richters Bilder aus der Gegenwart. Eine Entgegnung von Franz Mehring*. Nürnberg, 1892.— 375
— *Kapital und Presse. Ein Nachspiel zum Falle Lindau*. Berlin, 1891.— 195, 375
— *Die Lessing-Legende*. In: *Die Neue Zeit*, 10. Jg., 1891/92. 1. Band, Nr. 17-26; 2. Band, Nr. 30-40.— 387, 553

— [Mendeleyev] Менделѣевъ, Д. *Толковый тарифъ или изслѣдованіе о развитіи промышленности Россіи въ связи съ ея общимъ таможеннымъ тарифомъ 1891 года*. Вып. 1-3. С.-Петербургъ, 1891-1892.— 385

Mendelson, S. *A Warning*. In: *Justice*, No. 367, January 24, 1891.—110

Menger, A. *Das bürgerliche Recht und die besitzlosen Volksklassen. Eine Kritik des Entwurfs eines bürgerlichen Gesetzbuches für das deutsche Reich*. Tübingen, 1890.—368

[Mermeix.] *Les Coulisses du boulangisme*. In: *Le Figaro*, 20 août-20 octobre 1890.—22, 30

Morgan, L. H. *Ancient Society or Researches in the Lines of Human Progress from Savagery, Through Barbarism to Civilization*. London, 1877.—194
— *Houses and House-Life of the American Aborigines*. Washington, 1881.—10
— *Systems of Consanguinity and Affinity of the Human Family*. Washington, 1871.—194

The New American Cyclopaedia: A Popular Dictionary of General Knowledge. Edited by George Ripley and Charles Dana. Volumes I-XVI. New York and London, 1858-63.—113

Nieuwenhuis, F. D. *Jedem der volle Ertrag seiner Arbeit*. In: *Berliner Volks-Tribune*, IV. Jg., Nr. 24, 14. Juni 1890 (Beiblatt.).—7

Peschel, O. *The Races of Man, and Their Geographical Distribution*. New York, 1876.—146

Plechanow, G. *Die sozialpolitischen Zustände Rußlands im Jahre 1890*. In: *Die Neue Zeit*, 9. Jg. 1890/91, 2. Band, Nr. 47-51.—235
— *Zu Hegel's sechzigstem Todestag*. In: *Die Neue Zeit*, 10. Jg. 1891/92, I. Band, Nr. 7-9.—317

[Pushkin] Пушкин, А. *Евгений Онегин*.—280

Ranc, A. M. *Paul Lafargue*. In: *Paris*, 17 novembre 1891.—307, 311, 318

Renan, E. *Histoire des origines du christianisme*. Sixième édition. Livre 1-8. Paris, 1863-1883.—501

Rogers, J. E. Th. *The Economic Interpretation of History (Lectures delivered in Worcester College Hall, Oxford, 1887-88)*. London, New York, 1888.—337, 526
— *Six Centuries of Work and Wages. The History of English Labour*. Leipzig, London, 1884.—337, 343

Roscoe, H. E. und Schorlemmer, C. *Ausführliches Lehrbuch der Chemie*. Bände I-V, Braunschweig, 1877-1896.—470
— *A Treatise on Chemistry*. Volumes I-III, London and New York, 1877-1892.—470

Schiller, F. *Die Verschwörung des Fiesco zu Genua*.—309

[Schlüter, H.] *Marx' Kritik des Parteiprogramms*. In: *New Yorker Volkszeitung*, 14. Jg., No. 51, 28. Februar 1891.—146-47

Schmidt, C. *Die Durchschnittsprofitrate auf Grundlage des Marx'schen Werthgesetzes*. Stuttgart, 1889.—241
— *Die Durchschnittsprofitrate und das Marx'sche Werthgesetz*. In: *Die Neue Zeit*, 11. Jg. 1892/93, 1. Band, Nr. 3, 4.—553

— *Noch einmal das Rätsel der Durchschnittsprofitrate.* In: *Jahrbücher für Nationalökonomie und Statistik.* Dritte Folge, Zweiter Band, Jena, 1891.— 349
— *Die psychologische Richtung in der neueren National-Oekonomie.* In: *Die Neue Zeit,* 10. Jg. 1891/92, 2. Band, Nr. 40, 41.— 469, 526, 553

Schoemann, G. F. *Griechische Alterthümer.* Bände I-II, Berlin, 1855-1859.— 36

Schorlemmer, C. *The Rise and Development of Organic Chemistry.* Revised Edition. Edited by Arthur Smithells. London, 1894.— 470

[Schuster] *Dr. Carl Schorlemmer.* In: *The Manchester Guardian,* No. 14314, June 28, 1892.— 455

Shakespeare, W. *The Comedy of Errors.*— 417
— *Julius Caesar.*— 348

Singer, P. [Speech at the Erfurt Congress of the Social-Democratic Party of Germany.] In: *Protokoll über die Verhandlungen des Parteitages der Sozialdemokratischen Partei Deutschlands. Abgehalten zu Erfurt vom 14. bis 20. Oktober 1891.* Berlin, 1891.— 266

Smith, A. [Letter to Paul Lafargue.] In: *The Daily Chronicle,* April 22, 1892.— 561, 562
— [Letter to George Shipton.] In: *The Daily Chronicle,* April 11, 1892.— 402, 560-62

Soetbeer, A. *Edelmetall-Produktion und Werthverhältniss zwischen Gold und Silber seit der Entdeckung Amerika's bis zur Gegenwart.* Gotha, 1879.— 58

Sorge, F. A. *Briefe aus Nordamerika.* In: *Die Neue Zeit,* 9. Jg. 1890/91, l. Band, Nr. 8.— 74
— *Homestead und Coeur d'Alêne.* In: *Die Neue Zeit,* 10. Jg. 1891/92, 2. Band, Nr. 50, 51.— 514
— *Das Programm der Geldreformer in den Vereinigten Staaten.* In: *Die Neue Zeit,* 10. Jg. 1891/92, l. Band, Nr. 21.— 370
— [Articles on the labour movement in America.] In: *Die Neue Zeit,* 1890-1895.— 299, 329, 447, 453, 463

Stepnyak [Kravchinsky, S.] *The Russian Peasantry. Their Agrarian Condition, Social Life, and Religion.* Volumes I-II, London, 1888.— 539
— *Der Russische Bauer.* Autorisirte Uebersetzung von Dr. Viktor Adler. Stuttgart, 1893.— 539

Stirner, Max, [Schmidt, J. C.] *Der Einzige und sein Eigenthum.* Leipzig, 1845.— 136

Strabo. *Geographica.*— 34

Stumm, [C.] v. [Speech in the Reichstag on 12 February 1892.] In: *Vorwärts,* 9. Jg., Nr. 37, 13. Februar 1892 (l. Beilage).— 364, 371

Sybel, H. von. *Die Begründung des Deutschen Reiches durch Wilhelm I. Vornehmlich nach den preußischen Staatsacten.* Bände I-V, München und Leipzig, 1889-1890.— 94

Tölcke, K. [Speech at the Erfurt Congress of the Social-Democratic Party of Germany on 17 October 1891.] In: *Vorwärts,* 8. Jg., Nr. 244, 18. Oktober 1891 (l. Beilage).— 316

Tooke, Th. *An Inquiry into the Currency Principle; the Connection of the Currency with Prices, and the Expediency of a Separation of Issue from Banking*, 2nd ed., London, 1844.— 526

Vauban, S. *Projet d'une dîme royale.* In: *Économistes financiers du XVIIIᵉ siècle. Précédés de notices historiques sur chaque auteur, et accompagnés de commentaires et de notes explicatives, par M. Eugène Daire.* Paris, 1843.— 383

Veber, A. *Le socialisme intégral.* In: *L'Action*, 11 octobre 1891.— 260

Vollmar, G. von. *In eigener Sache.* In: *Münicher Post*, 19. Juli 1891.— 480

— *Rede, gehalten in der öffentlichen Parteiversammlung vom 1. Juni 1891 im Eldorado zu München.* In: Vollmar, G. *Ueber die nächsten Aufgaben der deutschen Sozialdemokratie. Zwei Reden, gehalten am 1. Juni und 6. Juli 1891 im 'Eldorado' zu München.* München, 1891.— 211, 219, 246, 282

— *Rede, gehalten in der Rechenschaftsversammlung des Wahlvereins am 6. Juli 1891 im Eldorado zu München.* In: Vollmar, G. *Ueber die nächsten Aufgaben der deutschen Sozialdemokratie. Zwei Reden, gehalten am 1. Juni und 6. Juli 1891 im 'Eldorado' zu München.* München, 1891.— 282

— [Speech at the Erfurt Congress of the Social-Democratic Party of Germany.] In: *Protokoll über die Verhandlungen des Parteitages der Sozialdemokratischen Partei Deutschlands. Abgehalten zu Erfurt vom 14. bis 20. Oktober 1891.* Berlin, 1891.— 273, 282, 298

[Vorontzov] В[оронцовъ], В. [П.] *Крестьянская община.* In: *Итоги экономическаго изслѣдованія Россіи по даннымъ земской статистики.* Signed: *В. В.* Т. I, Москва, 1892.— 443

Wachsmuth, W. *Hellenische Alterthumskunde aus dem Geschichtspunkte des Staates.* Halle, 1826-1830.— 34

Wirth, M. *Hegelunfug und Hegelaustreibung im modernen Deutschland.* In: *Deutsche Worte*, X. Jg., Nr. 5, 1890.— 7

Wolf, J. *Das Rätsel der Durchschnittsprofitrate bei Marx.* In: *Jahrbücher für Nationalökonomie und Statistik.* Dritte Folge. Zweiter Band. Jena, 1891.— 241, 287, 349-50

DOCUMENTS

Le congrès international de 1893. In: *Le Socialiste*, 3ᵉ année, No. 107, 10 octobre 1892.— 523

Congrès international ouvrier socialiste de 1891. Bruxelles, le 17 juin 1891. Aux groupes ouvriers de tous les pays. Signed: Pour le conseil général du Parti ouvrier belge le Secrétaire, Jean Volders. In: *Le Socialiste*, 2ᵉ année, No. 41, 1ᵉʳ juillet 1891.— 219, 221

Department of the Interior, Census Office. Compendium of the Tenth Census (June 1, 1880), Compiled Pursuant to an Act of Congress Approved August 7, 1882. Parts I-II. Washington, 1883.— 149

Department of the Interior, Census Office. Compendium of the Eleventh Census: 1890. Parts I-III. Washington, D. C., 1892-1897.— 149-50

Gesetz gegen die gemeingefährlichen Bestrebungen der Sozialdemokratie. Vom 21. Oktober 1878. In: *Reichs-Gesetzblatt,* Nr. 34, 22. Oktober 1878.—8, 11, 14, 19, 47, 87

Programm. In: *Vorwärts,* 8. Jg., Nr. 233, 6. Oktober 1891 (l. Beilage).—261-63

Programm der deutschen Arbeiterpartei. In: *Protokoll des Vereinigungs-Congresses der Sozialdemokraten Deutschlands abgehalten zu Gotha, vom 22. bis 27. Mai 1875.* Leipzig, 1875.—25, 97, 123, 126, 129, 130, 176, 180, 182

Programm der Sozialdemokratischen Partei Deutschlands, beschlossen auf dem Parteitag zu Erfurt 1891. In: *Protokoll über die Verhandlungen des Parteitages der Sozialdemokratischen Partei Deutschlands. Abgehalten zu Erfurt vom 14. bis 20. Oktober 1891.* Berlin, 1891.—265, 267, 273, 316, 368

Protokoll des Internationalen Arbeiter-Congresses zu Paris. Abgehalten vom 14. bis 20 Juli 1889. Deutsche Uebersetzung. Mit einem Vorwort von Wilhelm Liebknecht. Nürnberg, 1890.—23, 26, 28, 40

Protokoll über die Verhandlungen des Parteitages der Sozialdemokratischen Partei Deutschlands. Abgehalten zu Erfurt vom 14. bis 20. Oktober 1891. Berlin, 1891.—265

Protokoll über die Verhandlungen des Parteitages der Sozialdemokratischen Partei Deutschlands. Abgehalten zu Halle a. S. vom 12. bis 18. Oktober 1890. Berlin, 1890.—107, 134, 176, 234

Report from Great Britain and Ireland to the Delegates of the Brussels International Congress, 1891. Presented by the Gas Workers and General Labourers' Union; the Legal Eight Hours and International Labour League; the Bloomsbury Socialist Society; and the Battersea Labour League. London, 1891.—226

Resolutions. Congrès international de Zurich. In: *Le Socialiste,* 3ᵉ année, No. 107, 10 octobre 1892.—524

ANONYMOUS ARTICLES AND REPORTS PUBLISHED IN PERIODIC EDITIONS

Arbeiter-Zeitung, Nr. 39, Wien, 26. September 1890: The article from *Kreuz-Zeitung,* reprinted in the section: *Ausland. Deutschland,* in the correspondence marked: Berlin, den 23. September.—42
— Nr. 6, 6. Februar 1891: *Berlin, 3. Februar. Im Gegensatz zu der stürmischen Bewegung...* In the section: *Ausland. Deutschland.*—126, 129, 133

Berliner Volksblatt, Nr. 239, 14. Oktober 1890: *Der Partei-Kongreß.*—56

Berliner Volks-Tribüne, Nr. 28, 12. Juli 1890 (Beiblatt): *Jedem der volle Erfrag seiner Arbeit. Von einem Arbeiter; Schlußwort zur Debatte.*—7
— Nr. 34, 22. August 1891 (Beiblatt); Nr. 35, 29. August 1891 (1.-2. Beiblatt): *Internationaler sozialistischer Arbeiter-Kongreß.*—232

Critica Sociale, Anno I, No. 3, 20 febbraio 1891: *Pubblicazioni Socialiste.*—142

The Daily Chronicle and Clerkenwell News, No. 9092, May 4, 1891: *Eight Hours Day.—Demonstration in Hyde Park.—Enormous Gathering.*—189

The Daily News, February 10, 1891: *Election News. Nomination at Northampton. Enthusiastic Liberal Meeting.*— 124
— November 9, 1891: *A socialist elected deputy at Lille.*— 288
— February 2, 1892.— 346

The Evening Standard, No. 21023, November 23, 1891: *The Lille Election.*— 301, 304-05, 311, 318

Frankfurter Zeitung und Handelsblatt, Nr. 68, 9. März 1875 (Morgenblatt): *Frankfurt, 8. März.*— 176

Freiheit, Nr. 1-10, 12-16; 3., 10., 17., 24., 31. Januar, 7., 14., 21., 28. Februar, 7., 21., 28. März, 4., 11., 18. April 1891: *Zur Biographie Bakunin's.* Signed: **.— 265, 300

Gil Blas, 17 octobre 1890.— 54

Hamburger Echo, Nr. 33, 8. Februar 1891: *Zur Kritik des sozialdemokratischen Programms.*— 129

L'Intransigeant, No. 4154, 25 novembre 1891: *Le citoyen Lafargue à Bordeaux.*— 304-05, 318

Justice, No. 337, June 28, 1890: *Why, by the way, should Bebel and Liebknecht...* In the section: *Tell Tale Straws.*— 11
— No. 349, September 20, 1890: *The Death of a Hero.*— 30
— No. 353, October 18, 1890: *The Split in France.*— 52, 53, 74
— No. 370, February 15, 1891: *The Northampton Election.*— 138, 140
— No. 371, February 21, 1891: *Dr. Aveling?*— 138, 140
— No. 372, February 28, 1891: *Dr. Aveling Again.*— 138, 140
— No. 381, May 2, 1891: *Eight Hours' Demonstration, Sunday May 3ʳᵈ, 1891.*— 186
— No. 438, June 4, 1892: *We are pleased to hear that a new socialist 'Daily' has just appeared in Paris...* In the section: *Tell Tale Straws.*— 434
— No. 440, June 18, 1892: *Socialism in Aberdeen.*— 448
— No. 443, July 9, 1892: *Stanley goes under; Stanley must be kept under.*— 475
— No. 445, July 23, 1892: *A Socialist F. R. S.*— 484-85

Die Neue Zeit, 9. Jg. 1890/91. I. Band, Nr. 1.— 49
— Nr. 21: *Der Marx'sche Programm-Brief.*— 132, 133, 146
— 10. Jg. 1891/92, I. Band, Nr. 10: *Literarische Rundschau.*— 274

L'Oeuvre Socialiste. Revue politique et littéraire. Paris [1890]. [Advertisement].— 31

The Pall Mall Gazette, No. 8482, May 28, 1892: *The Prospects of Socialism. An Interview with Messrs Bebel and Singer.*— 436

Paterson Labor Standard, Paterson, October 11, 1890.— 75

Le Prolétariat, Paris, 3 mai 1890.— 47

The Review of Reviews, Vol. IV, No. 22, October, 1891: *Character Sketch: Mrs. Annie Besant:*— *Portraits of the leading officials of the Theosophical Society.*— 274

Le Socialiste, No. 17, 14 janvier 1891: *L'Avortement.* Signed: *Docteur Z...*— 117

— No. 45, 29 juillet 1891: *Enfin!* — 224
— 3ᵉ année, No. 76, 6 mars 1892: *A Auguste Bebel.*— 372
— No. 87, 15 mai 1892: *Le Parti Ouvrier.*— 423
Le Soleil, Paris, 16 mai 1892: *Le Parti Ouvrier.*— 420, 321
Der Sozialdemokrat, Nr. 39, 27. September 1890.— 26, 30, 41, 47
The Standard, London, August 17, 1891: *Socialist Congress in Brussels.*— 229

Le Temps, Paris, 14 mai 1891: [Excerpts from speeches by Lafargue and Culine.] — 191
— No. 11118, 27 octobre 1891: *Il y avait trois élections hier...*— 281

Vorwärts. Berliner Volksblatt, Nr. 31, 6. Februar 1891: *Parteigenossen!* Signed by the members of the Social-Democratic parliamentary group.— 127
— Nr. 37, 13. Februar 1891: *Der Marx'sche Programm-Brief.*— 126, 130, 132, 135, 137, 146, 176
— Nr. 48, 26. Februar 1891: *Politische Uebersicht.*— 176
— Nr. 96, 26. April 1891: *Sie haben's erreicht!* — 174, 182
— Nr. 97, 28. April 1891: *Der Streik der Bergarbeiter.*— 174, 182
— Nr. 259, 5. November 1891: *Korrespondenzen und Parteinachrichten.*— 294
— Nr. 25, 30. Januar 1892: *Aus London.*— 345; (Beilage): *Ueber den Rückkauf Elsaß-Lothringens.*— 344
— Nr. 152, 2. Juli 1892: *Die englischen Wahlen.*— 459
— Nr. 154, 5. Juli 1892: *Die englischen Wahlen.*— 464
— Nr. 216, 15. September 1892: *Aus England.*— 541, 544
— Nr. 233, 6. Oktober 1891 (1. Beilage): *Programm.*— 261, 262, 423

Weekly Dispatch, No. 4690, August 30, 1891: *France. (From Our Own Correspondent.) Paris, Thursday Night. 'Herr Liebknecht, the well-known socialist member of the Reichstag, is here...'*— 232

INDEX OF PERIODICALS

Jahrbücher für Nationalökonomie und Statistik — a German economic magazine published in Jena from 1863, as a rule twice a year.— 241

Journal of the Knights of Labor — a newspaper of the American Order of the Knights of Labor; published under this title in Philadelphia in 1890-92.— 224

Justice — a weekly published in London from January 1884, a newspaper of the Social Democratic Federation; appeared under this title from 1884 to 1925.— 3, 12, 30, 52, 53, 56, 74, 140, 186, 211, 232, 324, 367, 434, 448, 475, 484, 493, 541, 544, 545

La Justice — a daily newspaper of the Radical Party; published in Paris from 1880 to 1930; the organ of the Radical Party's left wing in 1880-96.— 155, 281, 290, 292, 547

Kalender — see *Pionier. Illustrierter Volks-Kalender*

Kölnische Zeitung — a German daily published under this title in Cologne from 1802 to 1945; an organ of the liberal bourgeoisie; it was connected with the National-Liberal Party in the last third of the 19th century.— 369, 371

The Labour Elector — a socialist weekly published in London from June 1888 to July 1894.— 552

The Labour World — a weekly published in London from 21 September 1890 to 30 May 1891.— 203

Lotta di Classe — an Italian socialist weekly, the central organ of the Italian Workers' Party; published in Milan from 1892 to 1898.— 391

The Manchester Guardian — an English daily founded in 1821, organ of the Free Traders and from the mid-19th century of the Liberal Party.— 455

Le Matin — a daily published in Paris from 1884 to 1944.— 547

Nationalist — an American magazine of the nationalist clubs; published in Boston in 1889-91.— 113, 125

Neue Freie Presse — an Austrian liberal daily having evening issues; published in Vienna in 1864-1939.— 349

Neue Preussische Zeitung — a daily newspaper of the Prussian Junkers and court circles, published in Berlin from June 1848 to 1939; also known as *Kreuz-Zeitung*, because the heading contained a cross bearing the motto, 'Forward with God for King and Fatherland!' — 42

Neue Rheinische Zeitung. Organ der Demokratie — a daily newspaper of the German revolutionary proletarian democrats during the German revolution of 1848-49; it was published in Cologne under Marx's editorship from 1 June 1848 to 19 May 1849, with an interval between 27 September and 12 October 1848; Engels was also one of the editors.— 41

Die Neue Zeit — a theoretical journal of the German Social-Democrats; published in Stuttgart monthly from 1883 to October 1890 and then weekly till autumn 1923. It was edited by Karl Kautsky from 1883 to October 1917 and by Heinrich Cunow from October 1917 to autumn 1923.— 5, 12, 21, 25, 30, 47, 49, 50, 55, 64, 74, 75, 90, 91,

La Revue Socialiste — a French monthly founded by Benoît Malon, a socialist, who later became a Possibilist; initially a republican socialist and then syndicalist and co-operative organ; published in Lyons and Paris in 1880, and in Paris from 1885 to 1914.— 92

Sächsische Arbeiter-Zeitung — a German Social-Democratic daily; organ of the 'Jungen' oppositional group in the summer and the early autumn of 1890; published in Dresden from 1890 to 1908.— 11, 13, 22, 27, 97, 133

Schwäbische Tagwacht. Organ der Sozialdemokraten Württembergs — a German daily published in Stuttgart from 1881.— 25

Le Siècle — a daily published in Paris from 1836 to 1939; mouthpiece of the opposition demanding moderate constitutional reforms in the 1840s; moderate republican in the 1850s-60s.— 202

Der Social-Demokrat — a newspaper of the Lassallean General Association of German Workers; published under this title in Berlin from 15 December 1864 to 1871; edited by Johann Baptist von Schweitzer in 1864-67.— 389

Social-Demokraten — central organ of the Danish Social-Democratic Party; published daily under this title in Copenhagen from 1872 to 1959.— 409

Le Socialiste — a weekly, founded by Jules Guesde in Paris in 1885; published with intervals till September 1890; organ of the Workers' Party till 1902.— 43, 49, 92, 109, 110, 123, 163, 164, 224, 247, 251, 260, 265, 270, 276, 282, 311, 367, 370, 372, 379, 411, 423, 424, 426, 428, 432, 434, 505, 517-18, 519, 532

Le Soleil — an Orleanist daily published in Paris in 1873-1914.— 420, 423

Der Sozialdemokrat — a weekly central organ of the Social-Democratic Workers' Party of Germany; during the operation of the Anti-Socialist Law it was published in Zurich (September 1879 to September 1888) and in London (October 1888 to 27 September 1890). It was edited dy Georg Vollmar (1879-80) and Eduard Bernstein (1881-90).— 7, 13, 17, 26, 30, 41, 44, 45, 47, 48, 115, 266, 313

Die Sozialdemokratische Monatsschrift — an Austrian magazine published in Vienna in 1889-90.— 88

Der Sozialist — a German-language weekly of the Socialist Labor Party of North America published in New York in 1885-92.— 75, 113

Der Sozialist — a weekly of the Union of Independent Socialists, published in Berlin in 1891-99.— 300, 351, 527

Sozialpolitisches Centralblatt — a Social-Democratic weekly, published under this title in Berlin in 1892-95; its editor was Heinrich Braun.— 552

The Standard — a conservative daily, founded in London in 1827.— 229, 374

St. Johann-Saarbrücker Volkszeitung — a daily published from 1876 to 1902 in Saarbrücken (1881) and St Johann.— 51

The Star — a daily of the Liberal Party, published in London from 1888; initially it was close to the Social Democratic Federation.— 44, 203, 207, 208, 219

The Sun — a daily published in New York from 1833.— 355

SUBJECT INDEX

A

Heterick Memorial Library
Ohio Northern University

DUE	RETURNED		DUE	RETURNED
1.			13.	
2.			14.	
3.			15.	
4.			16.	
5.			17.	
6.			18.	
7.			19.	
8.			20.	
9.			21.	
10.			22.	
11.			23.	
12.			24.	

WITHDRAWN FROM
OHIO NORTHERN
UNIVERSITY LIBRARY

Ohio Northern University

3 5111 00516 3682

HETERICK MEMORIAL LIBRARY
OHIO NORTHERN UNIVERSITY
ADA, OHIO 45810